Popular Catholicism in 20th-Century Ireland

Popular Catholicism in 20th-Century Ireland

Locality, Identity and Culture

Síle de Cléir

BLOOMSBURY ACADEMIC
LONDON • NEW YORK • OXFORD • NEW DELHI • SYDNEY

BLOOMSBURY ACADEMIC
Bloomsbury Publishing Plc
50 Bedford Square, London, WC1B 3DP, UK
1385 Broadway, New York, NY 10018, USA

BLOOMSBURY, BLOOMSBURY ACADEMIC and the Diana logo
are trademarks of Bloomsbury Publishing Plc

First published in Great Britain 2017
Paperback edition published 2019

ISBN: HB: 978-1-3500-2059-7
PB: 978-1-3501-0918-6
ePDF: 978-1-3500-2058-0
eBook: 978-1-3500-2060-3

Names: De Cláeir, Sáile, author.
Title: Popular Catholicism in 20th-century Ireland : locality, identity and
culture / Sáile de Cláeir.
Description: New York : Bloomsbury Academic, 2017. | Includes bibliographical
references.
Identifiers: LCCN 2017018016| ISBN 9781350020597 (hb) | ISBN 9781350020603 (epub)
Subjects: LCSH: Catholic Church–Ireland–Limerick (Limerick)–Customs and
practices. | Catholic Church–Ireland–Limerick (Limerick)–History–20th
century. | Limerick (Limerick, Ireland)–Church history–20th century.
Classification: LCC BX1508.L56 D4 2017 | DDC 282/.419450904–dc23 LC record available
at https://lccn.loc.gov/2017018016

Typeset by Fakenham Prepress Solutions, Fakenham, Norfolk NR21 8NN

To find out more about our authors and books visit
www.bloomsbury.com and sign up for our newsletters.

Contents

List of Illustrations

List of Maps

Acknowledgements

It has taken several years to research and write this book, but the final, crucial phase of the research was guided and supervised by Dr Stiofán Ó Cadhla in University College Cork (UCC), Ireland. My heartfelt thanks are, first and foremost, due to him for his interest in the work, his ideas and his inspiration, his enthusiasm and energy, as well as his kindness and patience at all times. The first phase of the work was supervised by Professor Gearóid Ó Crualaoich, who unerringly guided my early forays into the topic, and helped me to explore many aspects of the area at that stage; while Professor Diarmuid Ó Giolláin read drafts of chapters and provided interesting insights and significant support in the middle phase of the research. I am grateful to these three scholars for their inspiration, support and friendship throughout my academic career. The Irish Research Council for the Humanities and Social Sciences gave me a grant in 2003–4 and this enabled me to carry out some of the field research in the project: my thanks is due to them for this, and to the County Librarian, Mr Damien Brady, and the staff of Limerick County Library, my employers at the time, for their assistance and co-operation in this matter. An Arts Faculty grant from UCC was very helpful in finishing the research, as was the Book Completion Award I received from the Faculty of Arts, Humanities and Social Sciences in the University of Limerick, Ireland, for the Autumn semester of 2015/16. Further thanks is due to Henry Glassie for his permission to quote material, and also to the editors and staff at Bloomsbury and Fakenham Prepress, especially Beatriz Lopez and Kim Storry, for their patience and help in bringing the book to completion.

Libraries and their collections and librarians and their expertise have contributed much to this study. Thus, thanks is also due to Humanities Librarian Pattie Punch and the library staff at the Glucksman Library, University of Limerick, Mary Immaculate College and University College, Cork. The help of Local Studies librarians has been particularly important, with Liam Dunne, Margaret Franklin and Tony Storan of Limerick County Library and Mike Maguire of Limerick City Library providing very welcome support and bringing their own expertise to bear on the project over the period. I am also very grateful to Brian Hodkinson in Limerick Museum for his help with illustrations in the final phase of preparing the work, and to Críostóir MacCárthaigh of the National Folklore Collection for his help and permission to quote material. The help and co-operation of the Redemptorist order has been crucial to this book, and for this I thank Fr Séamus Enright, Fr Joe McLaughlin, Fr Tony Flannery and Fr Paddy Corbett, all of Mount Saint Alphonsus, as well as John Cronin and Marie Jennings in the Redemptorist Provincial Archive in Dublin.

I owe a special debt of gratitude to my colleagues and students in the School of Culture and Communication in the University of Limerick, and especially to everyone at *Léann na Gaeilge* and *Aonad na Gaeilge* for their support and friendship, as well as to many colleagues in Mary Immaculate College, also in Limerick. Special thanks is due to the Head of the School of Culture and Communication, Tadhg Ó hIfearnáin, for his help at all times, and to Roibeard Ó Cathasaigh and Deirdre Ní Loingsigh for their insights and expertise. I am deeply indebted to Maura Cronin for reading and providing advice on drafts of the work, as well as to former colleague Tríona Ní Shíocháin for all the thought-provoking and interesting discussions which kept interrupting our more routine tasks! *Mo bhuíochas ó chroí libh go léir!*

My thanks is also due to the editors of *Béascna* and to the organizers of the Kevin Danaher Lecture in University College, Cork, for the opportunity to air the research and to publish some of it afterwards. Cumann Merriman invited me to speak on this research topic in August 2010, and, again, I am grateful for the experience, while the Kate O'Brien Committee in Limerick, the Department of Irish Folklore in University College, Dublin, the Rathkeale Historical Society and the History Department in NUI Galway all gave me opportunities to speak about the research in stimulating and interesting contexts.

Help, in the form of information and discussion about the topic, the permission to use various resources or in contacting people to interview was given by many people throughout the project. These include Fr Brendan Clifford of the Dominican community in Limerick, John Logan, James P. Mackey, Joan McKernan, Éamonn Ó Carragáin, Mai McKiernan, Patrick J. O'Connor, Lillis Ó Laoire, Matthew Potter and Sheila Quealey. Their kindness and co-operation is gratefully acknowledged, as is the generosity and encouragement given by Críostóir O'Flynn and Maureen Sparling. I also appreciate Seán Curtin's help with photographs and his interest in the project. The ongoing support of friends and their faith in me during the time I have been working on the research has been of immense importance: I offer my thanks especially to Chris Canty, Ann Creed, Elaine Leahy, Kathleen Lysaght, Margaret McCarthy, Paul McNamara, Máire de Paor, Margaret Purtill and Monica Quealey, as well as to all my ex-colleagues in Limerick Libraries for their help, their humour and their long-term friendship.

The study could not have been done without the energy and generosity of the interviewees, on whose testimony most of the writing is based. Some of them are no longer of this world and this makes their words all the more precious. Others have continued to assist me through the provision of additional information and the granting of permission to publish and speak publicly about the work and their contribution to it. I am deeply indebted to them for this, and for their kindness and patience at every stage of the project, and I hope this book is worthy of their efforts.

In this endeavour, as in many others undertaken by me, the help of my family has been crucial. My sister, Eileen, with the generous gift of her time and help on both practical and intellectual levels, deserves a special note of thanks. I am also grateful to my brother, Larry, and my sister-in-law, Elma, for their support and interest in the project, while the gentle, but constant, encouragement provided by my sister, Máire Flannery, and her husband, Liam (from afar!) served as a great comfort in moments of panic. My sister, Caitriona, has also encouraged me in every endeavour I have undertaken: her expertise and professionalism, but also her kindness and sense of humour have been invaluable to me. The interest and support of her husband, Pádraig Lenihan, are also deserving of my thanks. I am deeply indebted to my father, Paddy Clear, and to my late mother, Kathleen Clear, for their enormous help and encouragement in this, and in many other areas of my life, but also for the great stories, discussions and debates which were a constant feature of our lives at home.

My children, Jonathan, Fionnbarra and Sebastian, have each brought their own special gifts into my life: for this, and for their patience and practical help while this work was ongoing, I will always be grateful. And lastly, my deepest gratitiude is owed to my husband, John Fitzpatrick, not just for his interest in the project and his many contributions to it, but even moreso for being there for me through thick and thin, and for his steadfast loyalty and support over the last two decades.

Notes on the Text

(a) This study is an ethnographic portrait of Limerick city between 1925 and 1960. Because it is centred on religious practices, both official and popular, it is the case in many instances that some of these activities are still part of religious and popular culture today. However, in describing the culture of the period studied, I have used the past tense for two reasons: the first is that despite the fact that some customs and practices mentioned are still carried out today, in almost every instance the social and cultural context has changed so much as to render them almost unrecognizable; the second is that frequent allusions to contemporary practices in the text would inevitably raise the distracting question of change and comparison between the two eras, something which is beyond the scope of the current study. Some brief comparisons have been made, however, where relevant to the overall aims of the work.

(b) The 'Archconfraternity of the Holy Family' was the official name for the devotional organization for men operating out of the Redemptorist Church in Limerick city. For the sake of brevity, and as a reflection of how the organization was and is still referred to by Limerick people, I have variously referred to it in the text as 'The Confraternity', 'The Fathers' Confraternity' and 'The Redemptorist Confraternity', as well as giving it its full name. Other confraternities, such as the 'Archconfraternity of the Sacred Cincture' and the women's confraternities/sodalities of various parishes/in various churches, where mentioned, are specified by their own names.

(c) To protect interviewees' privacy, their names, and most of the names of the people mentioned by them, have been changed. However, certain names already in the public domain have been left unchanged because of their historical relevance: these include the names of bishops and of people active in the public life of the city through their musical or other cultural activities.

Preface

The relationship between Irish people and the Catholic religion is a crucial part of how we study the history of post-independence Ireland. Whether the historical focus is political – the organization and operation of government and other administration; or social – how people lived and managed to sustain the following generations; or cultural – the everyday philosophies and metaphysical concepts which provided the answers to life's difficult questions, the influence of both the Catholic Church as an organization and the Catholic religion as a set of beliefs is an inescapable aspect of our understanding of the period. The ever-present religious aspect in people's lives is palpable in the following piece from Frank McCourt's celebrated memoir of his childhood in Limerick city in the 1930s:

> Bridey drags on her Woodbine, drinks her tea and declares that God is good. Mam says she's sure God is good for someone somewhere but He hasn't been seen lately in the lanes of Limerick. Bridey laughs. Oh Angela, you could go to hell for that, and Mam says, Aren't I there already Bridey?[1]

Críostóir O'Flynn's lesser-known, but more measured autobiography of his childhood in the same Irish city, during the same period, portrays a different attitude to misfortune in the following extract:

> The services of Lily Connolly were dispensed with on the spot and she arrived home in tears to her mother, who, no doubt said, 'Well, bad cess to them and may the divil make a ladder of their backbone! Sit in there, *a stór*, the kettle is singing and we'll have a nice cup o' tay – and thanks be to God an' his blessed mother, we never died o' winter yet!'[2]

Although, of course, we must allow that both accounts were written many years after the time they describe, they still represent two very different positions with regard to religious belief. As will become clear in this book, the city of Limerick between the 1920s and the 1960s was, for the Catholic population, a highly controlled intensely ritualistic environment, in which religion informed almost every activity. Did people really feel that they were 'in hell', as demonstrated in McCourt's account of his mother's life, when trying to make the dole money of nineteen shillings a week stretch to cover rent, food and fuel? Or did they have the sense of faith, hope and cheerful practicality which O'Flynn attributes to his maternal grandmother, when her daughter, Lily, was dismissed from her job as a nanny with a rich Catholic family because she brought her charges to dinner in her own home? The fact that this family home was located in one of the worst tenements in Limerick, Arthur's Quay, may have contributed in some way to Lily's dismissal, but it also indicates the material and physical challenges faced by thousands of people in Limerick on a daily basis in dwellings such as these – or that of the McCourts, a small, damp house in a laneway. Some people undoubtedly felt themselves to be 'in hell': others seemed more happy and content, despite the constant material struggle endured by them. Although standards of housing improved in the city over the period, the financial and material struggle was central to many people's lives right up to the 1960s, as the evidence given by people interviewed for this book shows. McCourt remembers religion as a hindrance, promising much and delivering nothing but prejudice and injustice; to others, however, it was, as one interviewee put it, 'the rock on which our lives were built'.[3] While it must be allowed that people's attitude to religion may combine both positive and negative elements, and that they may also hold different opinions about religion at different times and on different occasions, the phenomenal popularity of Catholic rituals in Limerick – and, indeed, in other Irish cities – during the period, shows that for many the engagement with religion was a constant feature of their daily and weekly round, and that the opinion quoted by the interviewee above, which sees religion as foundational to people's lives, was not just widely held, but also acted upon, frequently and intensely.

This situation was to change significantly between the 1960s and the beginning of the twenty-first century. The change was attributable to many factors: from the point of view of the practice of Catholicism itself, the Second Vatican Council and its relevance to a changing Ireland was the most obvious one, as is amply demonstrated by Louise Fuller's comprehensive study.[4] However, the changes in attitudes to religion and in religious practice which began to take place slowly from the 1960s onwards were also connected to major social, economic and political changes in Ireland generally in the second half of the twentieth century. Using sociological sources, including an interim study from the early 1970s, Tom Inglis has discussed the growth of individualization and secularization in Ireland, along with the decline in the value of being a good Catholic – what he calls 'religious capital' – in Irish society.[5] This book examines the place of religion in the overall experience of Catholics in an Irish city before these changes took place, when Catholicism still played a major role in people's lives, in terms of both belief and behaviour. The influence of religion continued to be important after the beginning of the 1960s, and as with any ethnographic study of cultural and social aspects of life, some of the evidence collected may concern a period later than that covered in this study. However, as the overall cultural context of religion and of life in general began to change significantly from the mid-1960s, this work concentrates mainly on Catholicism in Limerick in the first four decades after the foundation of the Irish state in 1922. The book sets Catholicism against the background of an expanding and modernizing urban area, while also exploring the connections between this experience and understandings of culture and identity among people in Limerick during that period.

1

Historical Background

The years between the early 1920s and the beginning of the 1960s were characterized by dramatic political changes in Ireland, following the turbulence of the first two decades of the twentieth century. The Irish War of Independence, sometimes referred to as the Anglo–Irish War, and more colloquially as the 'Tan War' and 'the Troubles', came to an end on 21 July 1921. Thomas Bartlett has made the point that even though this conflict was not on the scale of later wars of independence such as those which took place in Vietnam and Algeria, it was still the case that hundreds of people died, and thousands were injured, in what he terms 'this grim, dour and unglamorous struggle'.[1] In terms of the experience of Irish people born in the late nineteenth and early twentieth centuries, it is perhaps more enlightening to see the War of Independence as part of a suite of significant events. This began with contentious discussions regarding Home Rule, early in the second decade of the twentieth century, and continued with the drama of the 1916 Rising. This, in turn, led on to the Sinn Féin victory in the election of 1918 and the setting-up of the first *Dáil* (the legislative governing assembly), followed by the War of Independence, and the subsequent Anglo–Irish Treaty of December 1921 in which Ireland was partitioned. This was followed by another bloody conflict between those who were prepared to accept this treaty and the partition of the island and those who were not.[2] While the subsequent history of the state of Northern Ireland was to intersect with and influence the history of the rest of Ireland with varying degrees of intensity as the twentieth century progressed, it could also be said that the two differing administrations were to give more formal shape and, indeed, legitimacy to strong cultural differences which had been centuries in the making, and which in both cases were based on the confessional position of the majority of the population. The distastrous consequences of this for the area which became known as Northern Ireland have been well-documented and discussed.[3] After the period of the Civil War (1921–3), events seemed to run more smoothly in the remaining twenty-six counties, perhaps because, during the 1920s, Catholics comprised 92.6 per cent or some 2.7 million of the 2.9 million population of *Saorstát Éireann* (the Irish Free State).[4] Yet this fact was also to shape the ensuing decades in Ireland in profound and far-reaching ways, even if they were not as dramatic. Much of Ireland's development in the post-independence period – policital, economic, educational and social – can be seen to have been underpinned by its relationship with the Catholic religion, both organizationally and culturally. The fact that the Catholic population of the state – or from 1948, the Republic of Ireland – had increased to 94.9 per cent of the population by 1961 shows the position of the religion of the majority strengthening, from a demographic point of view, in the intervening decades.[5] This had a profound impact on many aspects of the lives of Irish people, one that is perhaps most clearly reflected in the education sector. Donald Harman Akenson, in his history of Irish education in the early decades of independence points out that 'education was one of the chief concerns of the church' and comments on the role of the clergy as managers of the state primary schools by saying that 'next to his liturgical and confessional duties it was the parish priest's most pressing responsibility'.[6] The clergy were also proactive in the post-primary sector, with many religious orders providing free secondary education prior to its introduction by the state in the late 1960s. The predominance of the Catholic religion in this sector is clear: out of the 569 secondary schools in the country in 1964, 526 of these were run by Catholics, with 466 of the latter schools run by priests and nuns.[7] Akenson also notes that the technical schools – an earlier state-funded form of post-primary education – were, though 'in theory lay-controlled institutions, in the usual case, were supervised by a priest as chairman of the local vocational committee'.[8] The Catholic Church also played a central role in other aspects of public life: important events such as the opening of the *Dáil* term[9] or that of a new factory were usually preceded by the celebration of Mass.[10] Given its centrality in the lives of Irish people, it would be natural to assume that Catholicism was the religion of state in Ireland. However, Diarmaid Ferriter notes that despite the recognition of the 'special position' of the Catholic Church in Article 40 of the Irish Constitution, which was introduced by Éamon de Valera in 1937, and ratified by the Irish people in that same year, the constitution actually stopped short of making Catholicism an official state religion, 'to the disappointment of many zealous Catholic activists'.[11]

Catholic discourse in post-independence Ireland

Catholicism was certainly central to the social and cultural life of Ireland in many important ways. The role of the Catholic Church in the production, publication and distribution of popular religious reading material was one of these. The Irish branch of the Catholic Truth Society, which had been founded in England in 1884, was set up in 1899, and was to play a major part in the publishing and distribution of books, pamphlets and magazines from then until well into the second half of the twentieth century.[12] The numbers of these – as detailed in the Catholic Truth Society of Ireland (CTSI) Annual Reports – gives some idea of the penetration of this material among the Irish population during the period. In the year 1938/9, for instance, the Society distributed a total of 1,242,650 items across all its categories.[13] Elizabeth Russell's survey of popular reading during the 1930s shows that Irish people were keen readers of many types of books and magazines, including religious ones, and the CTSI record supports this.[14] The Society's distribution level increased steadily in the following years – even despite wartime restrictions on the supply of paper – to a high of 2,978,673 in 1945/6. The figure then fell slightly, but hovered around the 2 million mark for the remainder of the 1940s and reached its highest at 2,989,464 in 1956/7.[15] A survey of the Society's own publications gives some idea of the range of topics covered by its publishing activity, and also of some of the groups of people for whom the pamphlets were intended. Among the titles listed as being in print in the Annual Report of the Society for 1958/9 were, for instance, *That Wonderful Sunday Mass*; *An Unmarried Woman's Hour with Jesus*; *St. Anne: Patroness and Model of Christian Families* (and many other accounts of different saints' lives); *What to Do on a Date*; *What is the Society of Saint Vincent de Paul?*; and *There's Money in Gambling*, to name but a few of the eighty-nine titles (twenty of them newly published and sixty-nine reprints) given in the report.[16] The distribution network for material such as this was closely tied in to the physical location of the church building, whether this was a diocesan parish church or one of the many churches provided by the various monastic congregations in the towns and cities. The bookstand at the back of the church was the main location for the display, and often the purchase, of pamphlets and magazines, though the latter were often distributed through schools and individual promoters covering different neighbourhoods as well.[17]

One of the most popular of these magazines was the *Irish Messenger of the Sacred Heart*: its history – and that of its publisher, the Irish Messsenger Office – provides an interesting example of the scope of popular religious publishing in Ireland in the nineteenth and twentieth centuries. The *Messenger* arose from the devotional organization known as the 'Apostleship of Prayer' or the 'League of the Heart of Jesus', which had been set up in France in 1844 and had been given Papal approval in 1849.[18] Both the magazine and the organization were (and are) associated with devotion to the Sacred Heart of Jesus, which is popularly attributed to St Margaret Mary Alacoque (1647–90) and the revelations experienced by her at Paray-Le-Monial.[19] By the mid-nineteenth century, the cult of the Sacred Heart in Europe was being actively organized and promoted by the Jesuit order. Part of this promotion included the publication of a devotional magazine: the first *Messenger of the Sacred Heart* was published in France in 1861. According to one source, by 1924, the magazine was published in fifty-three editions, including thirty-three different languages.[20]

The Apostleship of Prayer in Ireland was first established in Waterford by Fr John Curtis, S.J., in 1863. The *Irish Messenger of the Sacred Heart* was founded by Fr James A. Cullen, S.J., in 1888, and had achieved a circulation figure of 9,000 by the end of its first year, reaching 13,000 a year later. In 1890, some 25,000 magazines were circulated; in 1892, this figure had reached 42,000. By 1904, when Cullen handed the editorship of the *Messenger* over to his successor, circulation was in the region of 73,000.[21] This magazine was not the only item published by the Dublin-based Irish Messenger Office (IMO). A 1905 advertisement for the 'Messenger Penny Library' states:

> We have now published considerably over one hundred penny booklets. There are included in the list Lives of Saints, histories of famous pilgrimages, biographies of illustrious Founders and Foundresses of many of the great religious orders, booklets dealing in an attractive manner with social problems of the day, and tales – historical, religious and domestic.[22]

By 1914, the IMO was able to advertise 'over 200 very attractive Penny Publications' along with new magazines, *Madonna* and the 'Gaelic Messenger', *Timire an Chroí Ró-Naofa*, a quarterly magazine which had first appeared in 1911.[23] By 1924, a forty-two page publisher's catalogue had become available,[24] and, in 1935, the Irish Messenger advised its promoters to distribute copies of the IMO catalogue, which at this stage contained 'a list of 500 books covering a wide range of subjects'.[25] A further catalogue, published in 1955, lists 451 pamphlets in seventeen categories selling at three pence each, the two main magazines of the house – the *Messenger* and *Madonna*, the *Irish Jesuit Year Book* and a variety of prayer books, pictures, plaques, medals and greeting cards.[26]

The CTSI and the IMO were not the only players in the popular religious publishing market; the Irish Rosary Office, based in Dublin and run by the Dominican Order, was another.[27] It is also important to remember initiatives such as the London-based 'Catholic Book Club', founded by Christina Foyle in 1937, along with F. J. Sheed's 'Catholic Book-a-Month Club' which had been in existence for some years at that stage.[28] A Catholic Book Club book published in the 1950s gave W. A. Foyle as its President: it was during that decade publishing the work of contemplative writers such as Thomas Merton and Ronald Knox, as well as novels by more popular authors such as Frances Parkinson Keyes and Ethel Mannin.[29] Catholic Book Club books were to be found in bookshops and public libraries as well as Catholic libraries such as those to be found in Dublin and Cork.[30] The situation with regard to popular religious publishing in Ireland could be seen as similar to that in Britain during the same period, both in a Catholic context as described by Alana Harris, and in a more general Christian context, as discussed by Callum Brown.[31]

Popular religious publishing was just one of the ways in which the Catholic Church maintained a very high level of visiblity during the first few decades of independence. This visibility was particularly important on occasions such as the Centenary of Catholic Emancipation in 1929, which could be seen as a forerunner of the Eucharistic Congress in 1932.[32] The latter event, though staged in Dublin, was important for those in other areas too: people travelled to Dublin for it, they decorated their own cities, towns and houses for the occasion and many also listened to the Congress proceedings on the radio. The Dublin Eucharistic Congress was made all the more memorable by the use of photographs, and even film, to record the event. In an age of huge political rallies, amplified speeches and much-photographed crowds of loyal supporters, the Congress appeared to connect Ireland and Irish Catholicism with the modern era, and even now, looking at those reels of slowly moving massed ranks of clergy and people carrying banners, it seems to say much about Irish Catholicism in the period: a mass movement in a decade of mass movements, where the conformity of the faithful and the strength of their numbers, along with the dissemination of photographs such as these, were crucial to its image and its success. This is a valid view, and it follows a strong historical tradition of seeing Irish Catholicism as connected on the one hand to political and socio-economic factors, and on the other, to the organizational role and ecclesiastical history of the Catholic Church itself. Assessments of popular religion have also used this framework, viewing official church-centred activity as opposed to and in conflict with traditional popular religious practices.

Catholicism and vernacular religion

In this regard, the work of Emmet Larkin has dominated the discourse of Irish religious history since its publication in the 1970s. His idea of a 'devotional revolution' initiated by Cardinal Paul Cullen in 1850 seemed to fit very well with other aspects of Irish history of the period,[33] and, when viewed along with Sean Connolly's research on pre-Famine popular culture[34] formed a neat and pleasing continuum: a new post-Famine Ireland with an increasingly powerful, English-speaking middle class, assimilating imported, Italianate forms of devotion and rejecting older, native religious practices. Thomas McGrath has, however, argued that the religious practices of late nineteenth century and early twentieth century Ireland can be seen as part of what he calls a 'Tridentine evolution' which had been initiated by the Council of Trent in 1563 but which had been impeded and inhibited by the Penal Laws.[35] He shows that many of the devotions regarded as new by Larkin had been part of both official and popular Catholic culture in Ireland long before the middle of the nineteenth century. He goes on to describe the period from 1875 to 1962 as witnessing 'the triumphant expression of the Tridentine ideal in Ireland'. The complexity of popular religious culture, however, can be sensed in his next observation:

> In this process the practices of popular religion – pilgrimages, patterns, holy wells, stations and native traditions of spirituality which had helped to keep Catholicism alive over two centuries when the Church was not allowed full institutional expression now gave way, sometimes rapidly ... but more usually slowly and occasionally not at all, before the new ... patterns of modernising religious cultural expression that were being developed in conformity with Trent and Tridentine forms.[36]

McGrath's work is important because it helps us to see the conventional historical opposition of pre-famine vernacular traditions and post-famine clerical control, as described by Connolly and Larkin, respectively, in a different way. He shows how vernacular religion and more official devotional forms complemented each other at certain periods of Irish history, thus helping to soften the perceived opposition between them.

One example which illustrates this is that of James Aloysius Cullen S.J. who was, from 1887, the Director of the Apostleship of Prayer in Ireland. He was also, from 1888, the founder and for many years the editor of the *Irish Messenger of the Sacred Heart*.[37] Lambert McKenna's 1924 biography of Cullen, who started his career as a diocesan priest, shows his intense, lifelong involvement with the promotion of official devotional organizations which would now be closely associated with McGrath's 'triumphant expression of the Tridentine ideal in Ireland'. McKenna's account also shows Cullen's lifelong attachment to spiritual reading and reflection and, as one would expect, a strong commitment to Ignatian spirituality: that his religious sensibility was somewhat more wide-ranging than this, however, is illustrated by the following anecdote. Cullen visited Lourdes in 1876 – the apparition had occurred in 1858 – in the hope of a cure for a painful ankle. McKenna says:

Before going, he asked the Blessed Virgin to cure him – or at least, to send him to someone who would cure him. At Lourdes, in spite of his prayers, he felt no relief, but did not give up hope, even when on his return the pain continued as severe as ever. One day, when limping along the road in the outskirts of Enniscorthy, a poor man – a cow-doctor – whom he met, expressed some sympathy with him for his lameness. Feeling sure his prayer was about to be answered, he asked this man for a cure. The man gave him some stuff to put on his ankle, and told him to go to bed for a week, at the end of which time he would be cured. Father Cullen took the stuff, used it as he was directed and went to bed. At the end of a week he rose up, perfectly cured. He used to tell the story afterwards, giving it for what it was worth, but declaring that, for his part, he believed firmly that the Blessed Virgin had heard his prayer and had cured him.[38]

What is interesting here is that Cullen, who could be seen to be central to official devotional culture, doesn't see any opposition between the work of the traditional 'cow-doctor' and that of the Blessed Virgin: rather he felt that the cow-doctor was actually sent by the Blessed Virgin to cure him. Here we see Cullen, in the social and historical context of Enniscorthy in the 1870s, using symbols provided by both official religion,[39] and popular tradition in a creative process that serves to unite these two sources of belief rather than set them in opposition to one another. Sarah Williams has argued that 'orthodox and folk religion cannot be crudely juxtaposed as two separate spheres'.[40] In her work in Southwark in the late nineteenth and early twentieth centuries, she has demonstrated the persistence of folk belief and its coexistence with Christianity in a modern urban community.[41] An approach to research which puts lived, everyday religion at its centre shows that both church-centred activity and what Williams calls 'the more amorphous elements of religious culture' are crucial to our understanding of the history of religion.[42] In the above story, the priest's positive view of traditional healing illustrates the complexity and creativity of religious belief, and indeed, its hybridity, in its interplay with popular culture in late nineteenth-century Ireland.

Catholicism and the Irish revival

The interplay between religion and popular culture took on a new aspect in the closing decades of the nineteenth century as many aspects of Irish culture – including Gaelic games, traditional music and the Irish language – were promoted and celebrated.[43] In the long term, it would emerge that some aspects of Irish heritage had been far more successfully revived than others, but during the period of the Irish revival itself it can at least be said that the awareness of Ireland's history and its Gaelic heritage became much more widespread. This new popular consciousness of the importance of Irish heritage lasted well into the early decades of the post-independence period. There is also the crucial fact that in some areas of the country, some of these elements of popular culture were still extant, or had only recently died out. The collection and publication of traditional prayers, devotional songs and religious legends in the

Irish language was an important feature of the activity of revivalists, from Douglas Hyde's work in the late nineteenth and early twentieth centuries, to the collection and archiving carried out by the government-funded Irish Folklore Commission, which began formally in 1935 and continued until 1970.[44]

Because of this, any assessment of religion in Ireland in the second quarter of the twentieth century must also take account of these cultural factors underpinning the development of Catholicism and its increasingly strong connections to Irish identity in the period, while not forgetting the socio-economic and ecclesiastical developments which have been identified in historical discourse up to now. In this way, while the publication of a booklet, such as the Irish Messenger Office's *Footsteps of St. Patrick Near the River Liffey* in 1922, indicates a modern, educated Catholic reading public, on the one hand, and a highly organized and hugely successful Jesuit-run publishing house, on the other, the cultural significance of an event such as this must also be recognized. It is important to note in the first place that St Patrick was the subject of much discourse in the period of the Irish revival from the late nineteenth century and that his cult continued to be important, in various forms, right through the post-independence period.[45] But it is also crucial to understand that St Patrick had been continually present in Irish popular religion in various ways since his feast day had first been celebrated by Irish monks in the eighth century,[46] and that there were many areas of the country in the nineteenth and twentieth centuries where Patrick featured prominently in placenames, in holy well devotion, and in the oral repertoire of traditional storytellers in both Irish and English.[47]

Similarly, while Louise Fuller's account of mid-twentieth century Catholicism puts the numbers taking part in the Croagh Patrick pilgrimage in July 1950 at 100,000, illustrative of modern large-scale religious practice,[48] Máire MacNeill's assessment of the role of the Croagh Patrick pilgrimage in her 1972 study of vernacular harvest custom, *The Festival of Lughnasa*, gives some idea of the embeddedness of this event, and of the national saint, in Irish popular religion, despite – or perhaps because of – the pre-Christian antecedents of many aspects of his cult.[49] Thus, for many Irish people, reading about St Patrick in a newly published booklet in the first year of Irish independence represented not so much a revival of a long-forgotten entity as a joyful re-imagining of a longstanding cultural phenomenon that seemed particularly appropriate to Ireland's new status. The fact that this booklet centred on the Dublin area may, perhaps, indicate a perception that St Patrick needed more revival in this urban area than in more rural ones – yet it was still possible to collect a St Patrick legend in Limerick city as late as the 1970s.[50]

The same point regarding longstanding cultural embeddedness could be made about the rosary prayer, which had maintained a strong vernacular presence in twentieth-century Ireland, as Patricia Lysaght's research, based on work of the folklore collector Seán Ó hEochaidh in the Irish-speaking area of Teelin, Co. Donegal in the 1940s, shows.[51] This presence and significance had been acquired over the period since the rosary's introduction to Ireland by the Dominican Order in the thirteenth century and predated not only Fr Peyton's 1950s Family Rosary Crusade,[52] but also Larkin's nineteenth-century 'devotional revolution', and the sixteenth-century Council of Trent. This is not to discount the importance of revivals such as these, but to point out that they were underpinned by longstanding cultural continuities which made the re-embrace of a prayer such as the rosary, most especially in the decades (so to speak) before and after independence, seem highly attractive and appropriate.

The involvement of the Catholic clergy in the Irish cultural revival of the late nineteenth and early-to-mid twentieth centuries has to be seen as contributing in large measure to the harmonization of Catholic devotion, popular culture and national identity during the period covered by this book. To attribute this involvement to purely strategic reasons – i.e. to attract more people to the fold – would be to disregard the genuine passion and dedication brought to their work by people such as the lexicographer Pádraig Ó Duinnín (1860–1934) and the early folklore collector P. T. Ó Riain (1896–1959) to name but two.[53] That the content of the *The Irish Messenger of the Sacred Heart* magazine frequently included material on Irish history and heritage shows how the somewhat obscure academic endeavours of some of the clergy were matched by efforts on the part of their colleagues to simplify this material for a more general reading public.[54] The clergy's interest in the Irish language, along with Irish history and popular culture has up to now been obscured by the perceived opposition between 'official' and 'unofficial' religion which has dominated the historical discourse around Irish popular Catholicism in the nineteenth and twentieth centuries. While this opposition was undoubtedly a feature of life and had a strong influence in some cases and in certain areas, understanding the harmonization of clergy and people, to some extent, is also important.[55]

It could be said that Irish people's enthusiasm for Catholic devotion in the second quarter of the twentieth century is at least partly explained by the cultural developments outlined above. In the midst of a changing political landscape which included the ideological challenge of new nationhood, a popular religion partly based on Ireland's Christian heritage, but also incorporating international aspects of devotion may have seemed appropriate and even exciting to many Irish Catholics. The notebook of instructions for the operation of the church used by the Redemptorist clergy of Mount Saint Alphonsus Church in Limerick city – where a 10,000-strong Archconfraternity of the Holy Family was holding meetings five nights a week for men and boys – includes 'St. Patrick', along with 'St. Alphonsus' and 'St. Clement', in the list of 'Novenas said in Pulpit but without Mass'. St Brigid's feast was also honoured: clergy were instructed to move the picture of St Brigid from the parlour of the priests' residence to 'Our Lady's Chapel', one of the most important shrines in the church, on the first day of February. St Patrick and St Brigid – the two most important saints in Irish popular religion – also featured in the banners carried by members of the confraternity in processions, as did St Ita and St Columba, and the Irish seventeenth-century martyr, Blessed Oliver Plunkett.[56] Other saints represented on banners included figures from the scriptures such as St Peter and St Joseph, and later European figures like the Italian eighteenth-century St Gerard Majella, the French nineteenth-century St Thérèse of Lisieux (St Teresa of the Child Jesus / 'the Little Flower'), while devotion to Our Lady of Perpetual Succour was (and is) of course a major aspect, perhaps the main aspect, of the Redemptorists' version of popular Catholic practice.

As is clear from the above, Limerick city in the early decades of Irish independence provides an interesting illustration of the cultural complexity of popular Catholicism in the first four decades of Irish independence. The following section sets out the ethnographic scene which forms the basis for further examination of Limerick people's experience of life – including the Catholic religion – during the period.

Limerick 1922–60: Population, housing and employment

The population of Limerick city was 39,448 in the Census of 1926:[57] it rose by 28.7 per cent between 1926 and 1961, when it stood at 50,786.[58] This rise in population during the second quarter of the twentieth century and the decade following it could be considered modest, especially when compared to statistics for the period between 1961 and 1971. The situation with regard to population in Limerick reflects the situation in Ireland generally at the time, when protectionist economic policies pursued by successive governments led to a lack of expansion and development on the part of Irish industries.[59] However, it is important to note that Limerick's population grew more than those of other Irish provincial cities during the period: the population of the County Borough of Galway grew by 17 per cent and that of Waterford by just 5.8 per cent, while numbers in Cork city actually fell by 0.6 per cent between the Censuses of 1926 and 1961.[60] Limerick's growth figure of 28.7 per cent over thirty-five years is high in comparison with other Irish cities, and it could be seen to reflect stable economic conditions in these decades. The dramatic changes in the economy and, consequently, in the population, in Limerick in the 1960s have been highlighted by Des McCafferty, who contrasts the earlier period of stable, but limited, growth with the decade following 1961 when, as a result of in-migration from rural areas, due to increased employment opportunities in manufacturing, the population of the city and its environs grew by 22 per cent in the space of a decade.[61]

The most dramatic change in people's lives in the city during the second quarter of the twentieth century and the decade following it was the increase in public housing provision which came about as a result of the Housing Acts of 1931 and 1932.[62] The overcrowded areas in the inner city – the lanes and alleyways – were cleared and people were housed in new estates, starting with St Mary's Park, which had 454 houses and was opened in late summer 1935.[63] This estate was built on a field on the island formed by the Shannon and Abbey rivers adjacent to the old 'Englishtown' area, the site of the original settlement of Limerick by the Vikings and later of the Norman administration of the city. St Mary's Park is often called 'the Island Field' by inhabitants of the city. Many other estates, most of which were somewhat smaller in size, were built in ensuing decades.[64] John Logan lists the housing schemes of the late 1930s and early 1940s: ninety houses at Killalee completed in 1937 were followed by: 'ninety-four at Brown's Quay, Thomondgate in 1938; 274 at Janesboro in 1940–1 and 368 at Kileely in 1942 … Approval for a scheme of 336 houses at Prospect in 1942 – which would be completed in early 1944 – was the last before the full impact of wartime restrictions took effect'.[65]

In her study of the townscape of Limerick, Fionnuala Synnott estimates that in the 1950s, over 2,000 local authority houses were built in Ballynanty Beg, Ballinacurra Weston, Rathbane, Garryowen and Assumpta Park.[66] She has also estimated that

3,689 houses of all types were built in Limerick between 1941 and 1960, and that over 78 per cent of these (2,877) were built by Limerick Corporation. The houses built in these years made up 30 per cent of the total number of houses in the city in 1971. It is clear that Limerick changed substantially and significantly between 1935 and 1960: in terms of the physical city and in terms of people's living spaces, their neighbourhoods and the larger general environment in which they lived and worked. These changes, which can be seen in Map 1, made for big practical differences from what went before, but they also affected how people viewed themselves and their city, and themselves in relation to that city. The adaptation of popular culture, including religious culture, to a changed and expanded city is a notable aspect of the practice of popular devotion in Limerick, and it informs many areas of this study.

Employment in the city in the decades from the 1920s to the early 1960s took many different forms: factory work and retailing were central, though it is important to note that factories or shops could vary greatly in size and type of activity. Ranks (Ireland) Ltd, an English-owned flour-milling company, set up in Limerick in 1929, in order to 'get inside the wall of tariffs', employed 700 people at its peak.[67] According to Frank Prendergast, this company's wage bill was a significant factor in Limerick's prosperity at the time. With its own company choir and an annual sports day, the involvement of Ranks in the cultural life of the city was notable. Bacon curing and canning were crucial to the economy as well: Matterson's, O'Mara's and Shaw's bacon factories were the biggest employers in this sector during the period.[68] Hundreds of people – many of them women – were also employed in clothing manufacturing in large industrial environments such as the Limerick Clothing Factory (whose workers

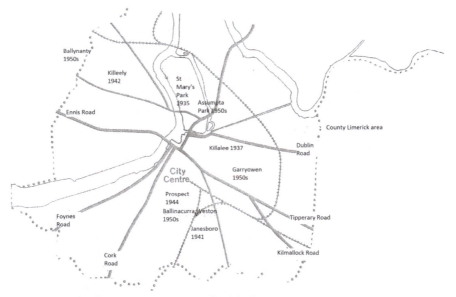

Map 1   Limerick city with locations of public housing estates built between 1935 and 1960.

numbered around 500 in the 1950s), Danus and Crescent Clothing.[69] Other products manufactured in Limerick during the period, in factories of varying sizes, included tobacco, shoes, umbrellas, condensed milk and confectionery.[70] Department stores, such as Cannocks and Todd & Co. also provided significant employment.[71] Smaller businesses were also important: in his account of Limerick's traditional industries, Prendergast lists eleven bakeries in the city in this period;[72] *MacDonald's Irish Directory and Gazeteer* for 1957/8 lists thirty-one drapery shops (besides Cannocks and Todd & Co.), while six shops selling 'Gowns' are listed separately. Services such as garages, laundries, hairdressers and watchmakers/jewellers gave some employment too.[73] Transport workers, whether employed in rail/bus services or in Limerick Docks, also comprised a significant group, while those transporting goods by horse and cart (known as 'carters' or 'carmen'), were also a feature of the working landscape especially in the earlier part of the period.[74] Drivers of vans and lorries began to take over this function as the period progressed.[75] Of the 16,608 'gainfully occupied' people listed in the Census of 1926, 5,975 of these were categorized as 'Producers'. This figure includes 327 'Agricultural Producers', many of whom are likely to have been the growers of cabbage and potatoes living in the Park area of the city. The remainder, 5,648 people working in productive or factory settings of all types, made up 34 per cent of the total workforce. Transport workers, as described above, at 2,253 comprised 13.5 per cent of the total; those working in 'Commerce' (including retail workers), numbering 2,171, represented 13 per cent.[76] At the end of the period studied the Census of 1961 showed that 'Producers, makers and repairers' (not including Agricultural Producers) had experienced a drop in numbers, but still comprised 26.6 per cent of the workforce: transport workers had fallen to 9.9 per cent, while those in 'Finance/Commerce' had risen to 14.6 per cent.[77] These figures provide an interesting profile of the variety of employment in the city during the period, with factories (particularly clothing and food processing) the most important, closely followed by transport, whether this was in bus or rail transport or in shipping at Limerick docks; almost as many employees worked in retailing or business settings. The significance of these large groupings of workers for this study can be seen in a few different ways. In the first place, for many people, their work was one of the elements of a sense of identity which also included being from Limerick and being a Catholic. This is particularly noticeable where a large union, such as the meat factories' Limerick Pork Butchers' Society, had a strong allegiance to the Catholic church,[78] but it can also be seen in the devotional activities of railway workers and drapery workers on specific occasions.[79] In the second place, it is important to understand that the workplace itself was a locus for devotion: activities such as fasting and praying took place in both larger factory settings and in small businesses.[80] This study aims to examine the connections between neighbourhood, work and religion that were crucial elements in the creation of culture in Limerick in this period: understanding the everyday contexts in which people lived and worked is part of this.

Limerick 1922–60: Religion

The population of Limerick County Borough (i.e. Limerick city), as noted above, was 39,448 in 1926. Of this number, 37,640, or 95.4 per cent, were Catholics.[81] The proportion of Catholics to other religions experienced a slight but steady rise during these years in line with the situation nationally as described above: in 1936 it was at 96.8 per cent,[82] in 1946 it had risen slightly again to 97.5 per cent[83] and by 1961 Catholics comprised 97.9 per cent of the population.[84] The relative consistency of this statistic over the period studied is important, as it helps to explain the role of Catholicism as almost a 'given' aspect of mainstream culture in the city – as it was throughout Ireland – at the time.

There were five parishes in Limerick in the years between the mid-1920s and 1960. St Mary's, which occupies the original Viking, and later Norman settlement of the city on King's Island, is the oldest parish in Limerick city, founded in 1111. During the period studied, in 1932, a new parish church for St Mary's was built in Athlunkard Street.[85] St John's, in which the Cathedral of the diocese of Limerick had been built in the late 1850s, covered the population of the old Irishtown, outside the medieval walls of the city.[86] St Michael's in Denmark Steet, its original 1844 chapel rebuilt complete with Italianate bell tower in 1881, covered the Newtown Pery area and the South Liberties.[87] St Munchin's, situated on the North bank of the Shannon in Thomondgate covered the 'Clare side' or north city area generally,[88] and St Patrick's, its church on the Dublin road, covered the east city area.[89]

Limerick was also served by five groups of regular, or monastic clergy, four of whom had a longstanding historical relationship with the city. The Augustinian, the Franciscan, the Dominican and the Jesuit orders had all had medieval foundations in the Englishtown/King's Island area.[90] By the twentieth century, they had built new churches and monasteries in Newtown Pery, which had been established in the late eighteenth century. The Dominicans were situated in Baker Place, near the railway station, in a church originally built in 1816 and renovated in 1863.[91] The Augustinian order moved to the new town in 1823, buying an old theatre in the centre of O'Connell Street: this was converted for use as a church, and approached through an arch from the street: the Priory was located across the street. In 1942, a new church was opened on this site, with the order buying the adjoining premises of the former 'County Club' for use as a monastery. With the new church facade, the Augustinians now had what architectural historian Judith Hill calls a 'full street presence' on the busiest thoroughfare in the city.[92] The Franciscan order acquired a plot of ground in the Henry Street area in 1824, dedicating a church there two years later. In 1873 a new, bigger church was proposed and by 1886 the first stage, complete with friary building had been completed. The interior was decorated in 1909, and the portico and apse were constructed between 1929 and 1931.[93] The Jesuit order, following the effects of the worldwide suppression of the order in the eighteenth century, inaugurated a new foundation in Limerick in 1859, building a church in the Georgian-style Crescent at the top of O'Connell Street.[94] The church, the first in Ireland to be named in honour of the Sacred Heart, was dedicated in January 1869.[95] The building and its decoration were gradually completed over the following seventy years: the high altar being installed in 1876, the facade in 1900, the

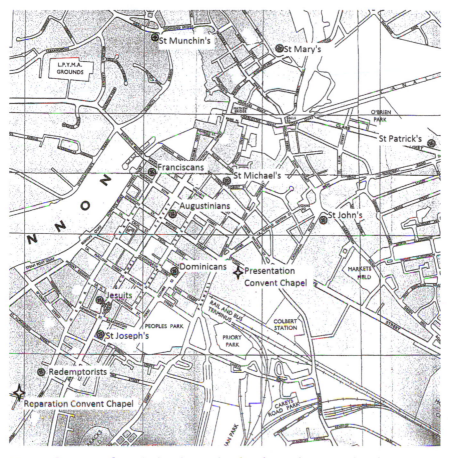

Map 2 Location of parish churches, order churches and convent chapels, 1920–60.

Sacred Heart shrine in 1920, the marble altar rails in 1929 and the Italian mosaic in the sanctuary in 1939.[96] The Redemptorist missionaries came to Limerick city in 1853, and occupied various temporary premises before building their landmark church near O'Connell Avenue in 1858.[97] The Jesuit and Franciscan churches described above both closed in the first decade of the twenty-first century, while the Dominican order, situated in Baker Place since 1816, announced their intention to withdraw from Limerick in 2014.[98] Location of parish churches, order churches and convent chapels during the period studied can be seen in Map 2.

In her study of the architecure of Limerick, Judith Hill makes some interesting points about the design of Catholic churches in the streetscape of the city: the relationship between this and their use in devotion is discussed in Chapter 6 of this book. However, Hill's study also highlights the relationship between the people of the city and the churches, both diocesan and order, as they were initiated, built and decorated during the nineteenth and twentieth centuries. According to Hill, the funding of churches was carried out in roughly the same manner from the mid-nineteenth century until the 1950s:

> St John's Cathedral ... is, in essence, typical. In the early 1850s, when the clergy were contemplating building a cathedral in Limerick, but were unsure whether it could be realised it was decided that the high altar of St John's Chapel should be replaced. The enthusiastic response to this suggested that there was sufficient support to finance a new church building ... and in March 1859 the first mass was said in the cathedral. In three years the inital ambition to replace the high altar of the old penal chapel had not only been transformed into the ambition to build a cathedral but that ambition had been substantially realised. [99]

Hill also points out that many churches were built gradually and only completed and decorated fully after many years had passed, the Jesuit church being the most extreme example. She makes the point that: 'This gradual realisation of the churches, supported continuously by public donation, meant that the catholic churches, more than other buildings perhaps, expressed a popular will and fulfilled a commonly articulated need'.[100] The sense of financial responsibility described here by Hill was not the only way in which people were involved in the decoration of church buildings: the existence of Altar Societies attached to parish or order churches and the large amounts of needlework and/or other crafts done by individual women on an ongoing basis attests to a lively interest in the church as a devotional space along with a strong dedication to its aesthetic aspects, a subject of further discussion in Chapter 7 of this book.[101] This interest and involvement was complemented by the amount of time people spent in the church: as subsequent chapters will demonstrate, church-based devotion in this period, whether organized or informal, was a constant feature of people's lives in the city. The schedule of the Augustinian Church in O'Connell Street in 1959 gives some flavour of this: there were six morning Masses on Sundays, from 8.00 a.m. to noon; four Masses on each weekday morning, from 7.30 a.m. to 10.00 a.m. Devotions took place every evening at 7.00 p.m. or 7.30 p.m.; Confessions every day during some of the morning Masses and all day Saturday, from 10.00 a.m. until 9.30 p.m.[102] Within this framework, the devotional focus varied, including many saints or other spiritual entities over the course of a week, a month or a year: these included the specifically Augustinian cults of Our Mother of Good Counsel, St Rita and St Jude. The meetings of the Augustinian confraternity, the Archconfraternity of the Sacred Cincture, with different nights for men and women, were also held within this general framework.[103] Most of the city churches in Limerick during this period offered a similar number of services and devotional opportunities, though the nature of these varied according to the location of the church. Weekday Masses, for instance, may not have held the same importance in other churches as they did in the commercial heart of the city where people were working nearby; however, the evidence shows that churches could be crowded at different times for different activities. The Redemptorist Archconfraternity, held on weekday evenings, drew big crowds, while the Dominican church was sought out for Marian devotion (more specifically to Our Lady of Limerick) during the month of May and the Novena to Blessed Martin de Porres in October: the Third Order of Saint Dominic, involving a monthly meeting, was also based in this church. Some churches were situated in places where people would pass them, walking or cycling to work or school, and the evidence shows that this also had a bearing on their use.

Any assessment of official Catholicism in Limerick during this period must also take account of the school environment, which was intensely religious. Religious orders involved in education included the Christian Brothers, the Jesuits and the Redemptorists, but also orders of nuns who had been in Limerick since the nineteenth century: the Presentation order, who had schools in Sexton Street in St Michael's Parish;[104] the Mercy order who had schools in St Mary's Parish[105] and the Faithful Companions of Jesus whose school, Laurel Hill, was located on the South Circular Road.[106] In addition to their work in St Mary's Parish, the Mercy order were in charge of the only third-level institution in Limerick at the time, Mary Immaculate College, also located on the South Circular Road, which had been training primary teachers since 1902.[107] Interviewees' accounts show that schools, the activities organized by them and the discourse of Catholicism in which they were constantly engaged, played an important role in both the practice of devotion and the development of belief.

It is clear from the above that Catholicism during this period permeated the physical, the social and the educational environment of the city. Given the extensive infrastructure described above, the extent of Limerick people's involvement with religious ritual is not surprising. The nature of the experience arising out of this involvement in ritual as well as the spiritual and supernatural aspects of belief during the period studied will become clearer as the study progresses: examining the influence of the urban environment on this experience is one of the key aims of this work.

2

Approaches and Perspectives

Locality, identity and culture

The study of religion in modern, urban environments is one which has developed significantly over the last number of decades. J. N. Morris's book on Croydon discusses the changing infrastructure of organized religion and its interaction with local government in one city in the period up to 1914.[1] Hugh McLeod's *Class and Religion in the Late Victorian City* covers London as a whole,[2] while Sarah Williams's book *Religion and Belief in Southwark c.1880–1939* is focused on just one area of the same city.[3] Religion in the context of locality is also a central focus of this book. As noted in the previous chapter, changes in both the physical city and in the social and religious infrastructure of Limerick in the decades after 1922 had a significant effect, not just on religious practice and experience, but on people's lives as a whole in Limerick during the period. The city setting offers its own distinct opportunities for phsyical inter- action between devotion and locality, with the religious procession the most eloquent example of this. Charlotte Wildman's work in Manchester[4] has shown the impor- tance of the procession as an expression of Catholic identity, and that importance is echoed in this work, though the cultural context is somewhat different. The location of churches and their integration with the street life of the city, as discussed in the previous chapter, was also significant in its effect on the day-to-day lives of Limerick people during the period. Thus the framework of locality is, in a practical and physical sense, central to this study.

Locality as a more abstract concept is also important, however. The ethnographic evidence shows a sense of locality as a crucial aspect of the popular culture of Limerick city in the decades between the 1920s and the 1960s. The different dimensions of this consciousness of place can be seen in the way in which senses of locality and identity are articulated in the history and in the lore of the area: Críostóir O'Flynn's autobiography shows how the people of St Mary's Parish on King's Island would have seen themselves as different, for example, from the 'Soda Cakes' found north of Thomond Bridge, in Thomondgate,[5] while Patsy Harrold has explored the distinc- tiveness of the members of the horticultural community of Park in the east of the city, who were referred to as 'the Park Danes' by people from other areas.[6] These different senses of locality as well as the larger sense of simply being 'from Limerick' can also be found in the practice of religion in the city in the period studied. Chapter 3 shows how popular religious ritual was strongly connected to place on more than one level. The Archconfraternity of the Holy Family, the largest religious organization in Limerick at the time, aimed at the men and boys of the city, was organized according to place, not just in terms of the nights identified for various areas of the city, but to the extent that the seating in the church itself reflected the streets of the neighbourhoods present on the night. Women's confraternities were held in their own parishes, again, with neighbours, relations and friends in close proximity. The articulation and discussion of concepts of locality in the community itself is also relevant: accounts from the men's archconfraternity mentioned above show that this was a significant element of the discourse around the devotion. The connection between this discourse and the development of local identity is one of the most interesting and important aspects of the research as a whole. In this way, the study of religion can be seen as closely connected to one of the central concepts in the study of folklore and ethnology, that of locality, with a sense of identity closely allied to this.

The emphasis on concepts and ideas such as place and identity is one example of the ways in which the scope of religious history has broadened in recent decades. From a more broadly cultural perspective, many studies, including those of both Williams and McLeod, take a 'lived religion' approach to the topic, seeing people's beliefs and behaviour outside of the physical church setting as being as relevant to the topic as their purely church-centred activities. Alana Harris uses the same cultural framework for her research into Catholicism in Britain in a later period.[7] In his large-scale discussion of secularization in Britain over the last two centuries, Callum G. Brown justifies this approach, questioning the use of church attendance statistics alone as a measure of religiosity. He argues that aspects such as people's sense of identity and/or a religiously based framework in the discursive environment are equally important in assessing the presence or absence of religion – Christianity in this case – in people's lives.[8] This attention to the overall culture of communities where religion is one element among many shows that religion 'happens' in every aspect of life, and is highly relevant to this research, even with the higher attendance figures for Limerick during the period studied. Looked at this way, the researcher sees people's own practices, perspectives and preferences, even within a rigidly controlled religious framework where church attendance was high, as an important aspect of the history of their communities. In his discussion of Irish folklore and mythology, Gearóid Ó Crualaoich has developed a helpful concept in the interpretation of culturally complex worlds such as nineteenth and twentieth-century cities. Building on Ulf Hannerz's concept of cultural complexity, Ó Crualaoich likens culture to 'a sea or ocean of knowledge' and describes how individuals, groups or communities form 'provisional and dynamic islands of identity, cultural creativity and meaningfulness' from this constantly flowing 'universe of cultural discourse'.[9] Thus it is important to take account of other perspectives besides the purely historical in the interpretation of this research: ethnological perspectives such as that of Ó Crualaoich help us to assess not just everyday experience, but the dynamics of popular creativity arising out of that experience. Williams makes reference to something of this dynamic in Southwark when she says that: 'Folk beliefs continued to combine with more official dimensions of religiosity and overlapped to form a distinct pattern of religious expression'.[10] As shown above in the discussion of locality, creative vernacular culture informed the lives of Limerick city people in significant ways during the period studied. Others, which will be dealt with in various parts of the book, include the way in which official religion, at the popular level, acquired communal aspects in practice, which in turn led to various forms of creativity where religion was concerned. As can be seen later, in Chapter 7, these could either enrich the official discourse or challenge it. It is also important to note the connection between religious discourse and popular custom. The sense of vernacular religion including 'survivals' – people's adherence to older official rituals or customs despite the fact that the Catholic Church had moved on to newer ones – can also be found in Limerick city at this time: evidence of this can be seen in the area of fasting discussed in Chapter 5. An approach which takes account of these phenomena, like that of Ó Crualaoich, puts cultural creativity and meaning-making at the centre of interpretation. The creation of meaningful 'islands of identity' in urban Limerick can be easily seen in the cultural processes described in this book – with the May Eve fires, described in Chapter 4,[11] as perhaps the clearest example of this.

The study of religions is a crucial one, and can provide useful ways of thinking about the topic in hand. Ann Taves has noted the need for religious studies to rise above the binary opposition of reductionist approaches – which attempt to explain away religious phenomena and religious culture through the perspectives of other disciplines – on the one hand, and *sui generis* or essentialist scholarly attitudes – which maintain that religion's uniqueness means that it can only be studied in relation to itself – on the other.[12] She suggests using a 'building-block' approach to the study of religious experience: concentrating on how religious meaning is attributed to events, objects or feelings, and, on another level, how these become more complex formations which can be labelled 'religions' or 'spiritualities'.[13] This situates religious meaning-making within larger cultural processes, where meaning is created and recreated by individuals and groups, rather than looking at religious meanings as static phenomena which are independent of, and separate from, other aspects of life. This dynamic of meaning-making can be seen in many aspects of the material in this book: one of the best examples would be that of the significance attached to breaking the Lenten fast on Easter Saturday or on Easter Sunday morning, described in Chapter 5. Taves's 'building-block' approach works very well in a study which aims to unpack the processes of meaning-making in the study of religious experience. It also allows all kinds of experience to be assessed, and not just the dramatic, revelatory events in individuals' lives which have dominated the study of religious experience since its origins in the early twentieth century. In this way ordinary, everyday experiences are also important, as are the experiences of people in groups or communities.[14] As this book progresses, it will become clear that religious activity for most Limerick city people in the decades concerned was a constant, everyday feature of their lives; it was also integrated with most other aspects of their lives, at home, at work or in school. This integration chimes very well with Taves's notion that the study of religious experience needs to be situated within the larger field of the study of experience in a more general sense.[15] In this way, religion can be assessed as part of the overall culture in an Irish urban environment in the decades studied.

The experiential approach to the study of religion, whether by historians, folklorists/ ethnologists or religious studies' scholars, is that which focuses on the everyday lived experiences of the people practising the religion being studied. Harris, in her study of English Catholicism in the decades after the Second World War, demonstrates how the work of the historians of religion mentioned above, including their attention to the areas of supernatural belief and everyday experience, has played a crucial part in loosening what could be termed the sociological stranglehold on the study of religion. Williams has argued that the 'search for religion in social phenomena means that belief itself continues to elude us'.[16] Harris makes a useful observation about this approach to studying religion: according to her it

> breaks down the dichotomous structural oppositions, often drawn in studies of 'popular religion', between high and low culture, between clerisy and laity, between the public and the private. It is, rather, an approach which seeks to chart, through the difficult and imprecise process of searching for new sources, and re-reading old ones with fresh eyes, the ambivalence and contradictions in the beliefs and practices of the ordinary 'person in the pew'.[17]

This methodology has particular value in the study of Irish Catholicism. As already demonstrated in the historical discussion in the previous chapter, dichotomous approaches to the history of the subject – and especially to the oppositions between official and popular religion – have sometimes obscured the complexity of religious culture and the interplay of elements of this in people's lives. Close examination of the experiences of ordinary people helps us to disentangle these experiences from the large and complex body of official information regarding the Catholic religion in Ireland in the years up to 1960: however, we must also be prepared to see how popular aspects of religion were integrating with official ones, and sometimes even contributing to them. In this sense, dynamism, creativity and meaning-making in everyday life are at the heart of the discussion of culture in this book.

Methodology: Sources and choices

Much of the research on which this study is based has been carried out by means of the ethnographic interview: this information has been supplemented by the use of autobiographies of Limerick people. Local newspapers in circulation during the period studied have been used extensively to document the organization of religion in the city, while local publications, such as parish histories, historical journals and booklets commemorating anniversaries of churches or religious organizations have all been useful for the insight they give into everyday life and culture in the city.

In her useful essay on oral history and the study of communities, Linda Shopes suggests that rather than focusing simply on the general history of the community, it is best to conceptualize this kind of study around a historical problem or issue, thereby asking the question: 'What historical problem defines the community?'[18] In the case of Limerick city and its history, there is no shortage of 'historical problems' affecting the community and its view of itself. In a city which once revelled in 'Limerick's good name as a Catholic city' and in having, in the Redemptorist Archconfraternity, 'the largest body of Catholic laymen in the world'[19] the gradual, but widespread and strongly felt change in Irish people's view of Catholicism over the decades since the 1960s has meant that these qualities, originally perceived as positive and a considerable source of pride to some Limerick people, are now viewed with mixed feelings in that they associate Limerick people's erstwhile religious fervour with the negative aspects of Irish Catholicism in the early to mid-twentieth century.[20] Because of this, the research did not suffer from what Shopes calls 'the celebratory impulse' which sometimes affects oral history projects centred around a local area: neither was the view of the past, also noted by Shopes, 'as a benign refuge from the unsettling present' – while certainly held in some degree by some interviewees – a guiding principle of the overall project.[21]

I carried out a series of interviews with twelve main interviewees, including seven women and five men.[22] The oldest interviewee was born in 1912; five more were born between 1923 and 1928; three were born in the 1930s and a further two in the early 1940s. Two of the people interviewed grew up in the old King's Island/St Mary's – known locally as 'The Parish' – area of the city, with a third moving there when the first large public housing development in the city, St Mary's Park, was built in the mid-1930s. Three more interviewees were born in the city centre and moved to the Killalee estate when it was built by the local authority in St John's parish in the late 1930s. Two interviewees' families had retail businesses in the city centre, with one of these a drapery and the other a greengrocer. The south city was home to two more interviewees while another suburban interviewee lived in the North Circular Road, part of St Munchin's parish during this period. One rural-dweller who was from the nearby County Clare village of Parteen but who worked in the city and later moved there, was also interviewed.

Because the cohort of interviewees is small, this cannot be regarded in any way as a survey of Catholicism in Limerick in the decades after Irish independence. However, it was possible, through a small number of in-depth interviews, to explore the life-experience of Limerick city people, especially its religious aspects, during the period studied. I found that the better I got to know the interviewee, the more we were able to address the somewhat abstract aspects of the study, such as the relationship between religious practice and group identity, or the sensory aspects of certain ritual occasions. These rather more reflective pieces of evidence emanated from deep trust and long conversations in a way that they would not have done in a more widely based study where the relationship between researcher and informants would have been necessarily more formal. It is interesting to note that even among this small cohort, drawn from different areas of the city and with differing socio-economic backgrounds and life histories, some similar patterns emerged in their experience of life and religion in Limerick during the period studied.

The relationship between informant and researcher has been the subject of discussion in the field of oral history for some thirty years, while in the study of anthropology – a discipline which has used fieldwork methodologies to study religion for a much longer period – an awareness of the importance of this relationship to the research process goes back to the 1960s.[23] My own background in folklore and ethnology has informed my approach to these relationships too, in various ways. The collection of folklore in Ireland and its emergence as a subject of study in the early twentieth century was strongly connected to the revival of the Irish language, and one of the leading folklore scholars in twentieth-century Ireland, James H. Delargy, came to the subject – and to the storytellers and their narratives – through the language-learning process in an Irish-speaking area of County Kerry in the 1920s, as did many other folklore collectors during the same period.[24] Because of this, it was the norm to see the storyteller or informant as the expert in their own language/culture, while the collector/researcher was someone who was there to learn, and this was the stance that underpinned my work with the interviewees for this book. The interviewees are the people who walked the streets of Limerick in the 1930s, 1940s and 1950s (who walked everywhere!), visiting a shrine to say a prayer in between visits to the bank and the butcher; the people who walked with their children (or with their parents) to all the city churches to see the Christmas cribs on St Stephen's Day; the people who got up at six in the morning to go to the seven o'clock Mass for the week of the annual retreat, who went to dances and walked home after them, who sang on the bus to Knock; the people who carried their rosary beads everywhere, who prayed in the church, at home, in school, in the factory.[25] I was not there, they were. This gave them an expertise in the subject of the study, and I was always aware of this. In discussing the researcher's expectations of the interview process, Valerie Yow commented with regard to one informant, that: 'He did not say what I thought was important – he said what in his view was important.'[26] My own approach was to establish the topic in general, and certainly begin by asking the questions I had decided upon, but to avoid constantly bringing the interviewee back to the topic in hand if they then decided to talk about something else. The 'something else' had been prompted by the topic in any case, and often turned out to be relevant to the study. For instance, one of the interviewees talked a lot about his work as a pork butcher in one of Limerick's bacon factories, a topic not obviously related to popular religion. But this turned out to be very important in two ways: one was in a straightforward historical sense, in that the connections between the pork butchers' union and Catholicism were significant and indicative of the frequent interaction between work and religion in the city during the period;[27] the other was that his descriptions of life in the bacon factory set a very vivid ethnographic scene, which later helped me to assess aspects of the way life was lived by Limerick city people at the time, and the connections between this way of life and popular religion.[28]

I also see interviewees as having an ongoing stake in how the information they have given is later used in the public sphere. Ruth Finnegan's ethical guidelines are invaluable in this regard, summed up by the statement that: 'The older model, by which one "left the field", typically a far-away colonial country, is now being replaced by continuing interaction rendering these obligations more evident.'[29] The 'obliga-tions' referred to by Finnegan include the need for checking drafts with informants before publication 'not just for factual details but also for interpretations (these may be genuinely contentious)':[30] this approach sees the informants not just as partici-pants, but as collaborators to some extent, maintaining an interest in how their own contribution to the research develops and is narrated in various contexts. Keeping the number of interviewees small has made this approach possible.

The historical nature of the project precluded the use of certain research methods which can be very valuable in the study of religion. Participant observation, a field research method long used by anthropologists and ethnologists, where the researcher takes part in religious rituals and records their own experience of these to add to their knowledge of the culture, was not an option in this case. However, the survival of some of the ritual spaces, such as the Jesuit Church in the Crescent in Limerick, the Franciscan Church in Henry Street and the Dominican Church in Baker Place, and the continuation of some of the devotions current in the period studied into the 1990s, meant that I did carry out some participant observation in novenas and associated shrine devotion at an earlier time, before the closure of two of these churches in the first decade of the twenty-first century. I am only too aware that this is very different from being present in the devotional world as it was in the 1920s and ensuing decades. One of ways in which this historical aspect has affected the project is that in the discussion of belief in Chapter 6, some of the interviewees' evidence concerning certain supernatural phenomena, whether these are from the official belief repertoire, such as hell, or from vernacular belief, such as the *Bean Sí* (or Banshee), was given from the perspective of looking back, rather than being strongly held at the time of the interview. Thus, the evidence concerning belief is not as strong or as dramatic as it would be in a project based in a contemporary religious context: however, the passage of time does allow some points of comparison between the two periods where concepts of the supernatural are concerned, and this is also attempted where appropriate.

My own experience of, and participation in, the religious world of the 1960s and 1970s has been both useful and challenging. Although I was not born until after the end of the period of this study, and therefore could not be said to have been immersed in the culture, I was, as a child and a teenager, surrounded by people who had been immersed in the pre-Vatican II devotional world and who were still, at that time, immersed in aspects of it. This awareness of my own background underpins the reflexive approach used in both the research itself and in its interpretation. Yow has stated that this awareness is now on the 'main stage' of oral history and 'not the side show it used to be'.[31] She states that 'we should not ignore evidence because it does not fit our prior assumptions – we have to be conscious of what our prior assumptions are'.[32] In my case, it might have been tempting to assume that my own relatively sunny post-Vatican II experience of religion in Limerick in the 1960s and 1970s would also emerge from interviews with the older generation: however, this idea was turned upside down in my very first interview, when the interviewee narrated many religion-related incidents in her life in which she was frightened and afraid, and summed up her assessment of religion during the period by describing 'fear' as 'part and parcel of the environment of the time'.[33] This fearful aspect, though not as marked in other interviews, turned out to be an important aspect of the research and its interpretation.[34] During the course of the project I became conscious that although some people's experience was similar in some respects to my own, there were other aspects of life in Limerick that I had never experienced and that I could not and would not experience, and that had no parallel in my experience. On the other hand, my background was helpful in other ways. Being aware of many beliefs already helped me to frame appropriate questions or approach the nuances of topics that might otherwise not have been explored – people's interpretations of the precept (or religious law) of fasting, for instance.[35] My extensive experience of the residual aspects of popular devotion during the 1960s and 1970s also led me to topics that have not often been discussed in the study of popular religious practice or official Catholic ritual in Ireland – such as the feeling of walking, praying and singing in the city streets on a warm summer's evening with thousands of other people. The recognition and exploration of these feelings is an important aspect of this book.

As stated above, consultation of local newspapers for the period between 1920 and 1960 was a crucial part of the research for this project: the most useful publications were the *Limerick Leader* and the *Limerick Echo*. They were of value in a few ways, primarily in assessing the number and scope of ritual activities, not just because they were often advertised in the papers, but because they were frequently reported in great detail as well. The papers were also useful in setting the general 'ethnographic scene' and complex cultural atmosphere within which Catholicism was operating in the period: advertisements for face cream mingling with notices about cinema closures for Ash Wednesday in March; bank holiday cruise advertisements, Croagh Patrick pilgrimage bus details and notices regarding university courses all appearing at the end of July.[36] The opinions and general reportage presented in newspapers was relevant too: the 'Town Topics' column in the *Limerick Leader* could be seen as the official, respectable voice of the city,[37] while reverent accounts of visiting clergy or news from the missions demonstrates the high status of the Catholic Church and its personnel in Limerick and in Ireland generally.[38] However, the slightly gleeful tone in which bishops' pronouncements on fashion or the cinema were sometimes given show that on some religious and cultural topics, a lighter approach, which allowed for various shades of opinion on some topics, was also enjoyed.[39] In the overall, and perhaps most significantly, the newspapers also provide us with a powerful illustration of how the community, at one level, narrated its own culture and fashioned its self-image during this period.

Autobiographies and memoirs of Limerick people are important in this study, too, although these raise some interesting questions about the interpretation of material centred on a particular place. It is worth looking, in the first place, at the relationship between Limerick people and the general history of their city. The image of Limerick, both local and national, has, for almost as long as I can remember, and certainly since the 1970s, been the subject of passionate and heated debate in Limerick: the problems with crime in the city during the early years of the twenty-first century have fuelled this. What is interesting for this study is that historical events concerning the politics of religion in the city (apart altogether from the more general issues regarding Irish Catholicism which are discussed above) have been frequently addressed in this discourse of identity: the need for Limerick city to make amends for the Jewish boycott of 1904 in its centenary year is a good example.[40] Eoin Devereux's study of a community group in the city in the late 1980s illustrates the struggle involving questions of identity at local level in Limerick, and how religion, politics and history are embodied in this.[41] A more widespread and long-running controversy regarding the history of the city in the twentieth century, with religion as one of its central themes, was initiated by the publication of the Pulitzer prize-winning memoir *Angela's Ashes* in 1996.[42] Frank McCourt's eloquent, sad but also very humorous account of his boyhood in Limerick in the 1930s prompted lively and sometimes bitter debate on poverty and living conditions at that time, on education and cultural life, and on religion and the role of the Catholic Church in people's lives, not just in Limerick, but in Ireland in general. Críostóir O'Flynn's *There is an Isle: A Limerick Boyhood* published in 1998 closely parallels the period covered by Frank McCourt, but gives a fuller portrayal of life in the city, with topics such as language, customs, music and education covered in great detail: here the life described is much happier and more fulfilling in spite of the poverty and oppression of the era.[43] The heated and controversial discussions of *Angela's Ashes* – carried on not just in the local newspapers, radio stations and occasionally on national television,[44] show an intense concern with historical truth on the part of the people of Limerick city in the late 1990s with both groups insisting that their version of 'what it was like' in Limerick in the early twentieth century was the 'real' one. Hannerz's idea of culture as 'an organization of diversity' is useful in understanding this debate on the history of Limerick, especially when we consider how he explains this concept as 'not just the nit-picking reminder that individuals are not all alike, but that people must deal with other people's meanings; that is, there are meanings, and meaningful forms, on which other individuals, categories or groups in one's environment somehow have a prior claim, but to which one is somehow yet called to make a response'.[45] Hannerz's distributive model of a complex culture is well illustrated by the publication and reception of Limerick autobiographies in the 1990s. However, close readings of the works themselves, especially those of McCourt and O'Flynn, strongly suggest that Hannerz's distributive model, where the organization of diversity is seen as part of the fabric of complex culture, can also be applied to the culture of Limerick during the period covered by them. Most importantly for this study, the authors' experiences of the Catholic religion are interpreted very differently: it may be that these varying interpretations are applicable not just to the retrospective view, but also to the religious culture of Limerick as experienced, in different ways, by the authors in the second quarter of the twentieth century. Certainly, along with their similar experiences as noted above, interviewees for this research project also had differing experiences, and also varying views of religion. This would suggest that this was also the case at the time.

Ritual and City Life

Definitions of ritual have been many and varied in anthropological and ethnological studies of religion. One of the most useful is that proposed by Lauri Honko in 1973: this definition, because of its relative simplicity, may be applied to many different communities. As will become clear, Honko's definition, despite its simplicity, also has multidimensional aspects which are relevant to this study. According to Honko, 'A ritual is ... traditional, prescribed communication with the sacred'.[1] He explained this by saying that 'in studies of religion it is most economical to restrict the use of the term 'ritual' to situations in which the density of symbolic behaviour is high and correlates in some way with dependence on the 'trans-human' or 'sacred'.[2] It is interesting to find, however, that Honko did not exclude behaviour which is simply ceremonial, i.e. that which doesn't include mystical elements, from the study of ritual. Honko highlighted the connections between ritual and every other aspect of life when he said that 'The real object of study is the relevant total behavior'.[3] This approach has also been used by historians of religion such as Sarah Williams, who has argued that religion shouldn't just be assessed at the points at which it touches the institutional church.[4] There are significant aspects of ritual behaviour which are not church-based, and which may involve belief, just as there are important connections between some rituals and non-religious aspects of life. These can be seen in many environments and contexts in the community studied, something which will become clearer as the chapters of this book unfold. However, in starting to look at the ritual behaviour of Catholics in Limerick city in the period between 1925 and 1960, we do not, in the first instance, have to go beyond Honko's most economical definition. During this period 'traditional, prescribed communication with the sacred' was constant and intense, with what he would call a 'high density of symbolic behaviour'.

The organization of ritual

Catholics were obliged by their religion to attend Mass on Sundays and on religious Holy Days such as the Feasts of the Epiphany (6 January) and of the Assumption of Our Lady (15 August). The Church authorities also recommended that people receive the Sacrament of Penance (i.e. go to Confession) so that they could receive Holy Communion once a month: they were, however, obliged to go to Confession once a year, at Easter. Most Catholics did follow this schedule of obligatory participation in religious ritual: as one interviewee put it 'I'd say that virtually ninety-nine per cent of Catholics practised their religion in those days … it was … so much a part of your life'.[5]

The liturgical calendar of the Catholic Church was the basis for the ritual timetable followed by all Catholics. This was underpinned by the obligatory participation in ritual described above: it was also shaped by life-cycle rites and family customs. As is clear from Kevin Danaher's account, it was also closely related to traditional calendar customs, both historically and, as this study demonstrates, at the level of popular practice.[6] The ritual year began with fasting and abstinence during Advent, followed by the celebration of Christmas: fasting and abstinence during Lent, culminating in the commemoration of the Last Supper on Holy Thursday and the Passion of Christ on Good Friday: the celebration of the Resurrection began at noon on Easter Saturday.[7] The most significant feast of early summer was that of Corpus Christi, when thousands of people formed a procession through the streets of the city and open-air Mass was held in honour of the Blessed Sacrament.[8] Open-air devotions were sometimes a feature of the Feast of the Assumption on or around 15 August,[9] something which, at least in its atmosphere and context, closely parallels the pre-Christian festival of *Lughnasa* described by Máire MacNeill.[10] All Saints' Day on the first day of November marked the beginning of the final phase of the Catholic year. Prayer during the month of November was centred on remembering the dead and praying for their souls. Devotional practice in this area demonstrates an interesting combination of official teaching and unofficial, and perhaps more ancestral, beliefs, operating in an intensely urban environment. The ritual of 'doing the Rounds' for the Poor Souls, which involved praying for the release of specific souls from Purgatory while making as many church visits as possible (people usually simply left and re-entered the same church), was carried out by hundreds of people in each church on All Souls' Day. However, prayer for the dead was said throughout the month of November in any case, with churches drawing up a 'dead list' of people to be included in prayers.[11] The progress of the ritual year was marked by other devotional cults which intersected with the liturgical calendar at various times: novenas or special Masses were held in honour of some fifteen different saints or other religious figures during the year (see Figure 1). There were five different Marian cults and five varying cults of devotion to Jesus. Cults of remembrance, some of these specifically local, though not without connections to national politics and history (such as the two mayors of Limerick who had been murdered during the War of Independence, deceased members of trade unions etc.) were also a feature of the devotional calendar.[12] This overview of the ritual year is perhaps the best illustration of the high density of symbolic behaviour which characterized the religious life of urban Catholics in Limerick during the first half of the twentieth century. The numerous designations applied to the different times of the year demonstrate a highly ordered and codified symbolic system with what Mary Douglas has called a high level of symbolic classification or a strong 'grid'.[13] In other words, everything means something, just as every time is allocated to a particular belief: the ritual behaviour may be similar (e.g. rosary, sermon and Benediction as the form taken by 'devotions') but the significance and the accompanying symbolism at the time, and on the occasion, are very specific.

Figure 1   The Novena to Saint Anthony, Franciscan Church, 1955.

The ritual obligations outlined above, however, do not on their own give a complete picture of the ritual life of Limerick city Catholics in the second quarter of the twentieth century. The activities of religious organizations formed another layer of religious behaviour and these often, though not always, included the mystical element. There were many organizations, aimed at different groups within the Catholic population.[14] One of the most significant divisions was by gender: because of this it is worth outlining the experiences of men and women separately.

Ritual in men's lives

The major weekly ritual event for many men was the meeting of the Archconfraternity of the Holy Family, held in the Redemptorist Church on the Monday, Tuesday and Wednesday nights of every week. The 'Confraternity', to use its popular name, was founded in Limerick by the Redemptorist order in 1868 'to attract the faithful to the pulpit, the confessional and the altar rails'.[15] The organization of different divisions with meetings on different nights of the week was originally designed to cover various areas of the city and surrounding districts. The Tuesday night meeting – 'St Michael's Division' – was the first one to be organized, and was aimed at the men of St Michael's Parish, a city centre parish in which the Redemptorist Church was situated: the Monday night meeting, 'St John's Division', was to cover the King's Island parish of St Mary, and the Irishtown and Liberties parishes of St John, St Patrick and St Munchin.

The Wednesday night meeting, St Clement's was introduced in 1926 without a desig-nated geographical area.[16] Thursday and Friday night sessions were held for teenagers and younger boys respectively.[17]

Neighbourhood participation in the Confraternity was of great importance in the lives of its members. Tommy C, who was a member in the 1950s, described the geographical aspect, stressing the strong connections between the organization and the public housing schemes that had been appearing in the city since the mid-1930s: 'They would have come from St Mary's Park, Ballynanty, Killeely, Killalee … Garryowen was only after coming on the scene, Weston … Janesboro … they would have their different sections then. St John's Parish was on Monday nights.'[18] Joseph L, who was a member in the 1940s and 1950s, described what he felt was the popular perception of the various meetings rather differently, saying that:

> The Monday division I think was largely the rural division, from Parteen and outside it … the Tuesday division was – at least we who – I was in the Monday division – the Tuesday division was known as the 'collar-and-tie' division … and the Wednesday division was the – *definitely* – 'the salt of the earth': Young Munsters and St Mary's Parish and all these places … so … you had these kind of things circling around … but the organization was absolutely fantastic.[19]

The resonance of place in the practice of Confraternity membership, as well as the creativity around ritual in a local context is clear in this account from the Park area of the city:

> The Park people were great to practice their religion. They had a Section in the Confraternity known as 'The Three Wise Kings'. The boundary of the Section was from the corner of St Patrick's, to Lisnagry and Ballysimon. They attended their meeting diligently coming by horse and car, trap, float, side-car, bicycle and on foot in all kinds of weather. When a Confraternity member died, who belonged to 'The Three Wise Kings' his fellow section members formed a guard of honour and wore their ribbons and medals at the funeral. They were the first Section to adopt such a practice and the last to relinquish it.[20]

The number of men participating in the devotional rituals of the Confraternity was of great significance, and not just in the minds of the clergy who organized it: 'Of course the biggest religious operation in Limerick in those days was the Holy Family Confraternity, which … was the biggest Confraternity in the world – supposed to be – there were about ten thousand members.'[21] This same interviewee described the Confraternity as having,

> a certain kind of a very organized business element to it as well, which didn't take, now, from the religious aspect of the devotions … on the morning of the General Communion – which was a big retreat once a year, a big mission … that lasted for a week – you had fellows inside the altar rails, secretaries, and they were noting the amount of people and at the end of the Monday division, there was an announcement that 'Two thousand two hundred and fifty-four people received Holy Communion': and the following week then … was the Tuesday division and

the director ... urging them all to come, he'd say: 'Now last week, the Monday division had two thousand two hundred and fifty-four; is the Tuesday division able to beat that?'[22]

Another man, a member of the Confraternity in the 1950s, said that there was a kind of 'team spirit' involved in being a member of the Confraternity: 'it was like playing for Ireland, or Shannon!'[23] According to him 'You *daren't* ... God, if 'twas a thing that you missed out at all ... the boys in the street wouldn't talk to you. There was that kind of commitment to your section ... And they'd be marking them all off ... and next thing they'd call out "Section of the Week" ... they'd be walking on air ... they'd be about ten foot tall'.[24] An even greater level of commitment was needed during the Confraternity's semi-annual retreat when,

> it was; up at five o'clock in the morning, six o'clock Mass, come back at seven, you didn't go to work until eight so you'd be around playing soccer ... if you were out dancing or anything ... and that time you had to fast, from twelve o'clock at night! ... and they'd be saying to you that night at the dance 'you'd better make sure now – make sure you're there'[25]

Another interviewee, remembering the Confraternity retreats, also mentioned the importance of the effort to be up for early Mass:

> If they kept up the Mass for the week, and if they broke one morning, oh they'd be raging ... they would ... Twelve o'clock the night before, you were fasting from then ... Every evening they'd have eight o'clock devotions and Benediction and sermon, but they'd be up that morning to six o'clock Mass, and I'd say to John 'You'll never be able to get up!' 'I will, the Holy Souls will wake me' he'd say.[26]

The experience of the weekly meeting along with that of the annual retreat is to be felt in the following account:

> I mean it was great, I loved it there ... Tuesday night was our night, you know. But then they used to have a retreat, we'll say, once a year ... and there'd be an awful lot at that. You'd have to go up eight o'clock on Sunday morning for the General Communion and ... the Bishop would say Mass ... and to see the crowds of people there! Then we'd have to go up that night at eight o'clock to finish it off.[27]

The importance of the Confraternity as a social occasion is stressed in some accounts: 'You'd meet everyone on a Monday night'[28] Sometimes, during fine weather, the younger men might go on a walk after the meeting, where they'd meet up with groups of girls. Another interviewee mentioned that the men 'wouldn't miss it! ... it was a routine – the lads would meet and have a chat and maybe a jar'.[29] Timmy G, who used to attend Confraternity meetings with his father and his brother, described this practice:

> Well we'd ... often go into Kennedy O'Brien's for a drink before we'd go home, you know ... the three of us ... and you'd meet people in there and you'd have an oul' crack and that kind of thing.[30]

The public house mentioned here, Kennedy O'Brien's, described by this interviewee as 'a great oul' pub, sawdust on the floor and that kind of thing' was situated near Mount St Alphonsus Church, and Timmy G and his family lived in the same area. He says that 'a lot of the locals around there' would go to Kennedy O'Brien's as well, after their Confraternity meeting. This interviewee also stressed the role played by the Confraternity in the social lives of people who were quiet or shy:

> I'd say going to the weekly meetings, you knew a lot of the people, you know? Even just salute one another, have an oul' chat … anyone now who … kind of, wouldn't have that many friends, we got talking to one another … coming down the road, even.[31]

The large numbers of men walking to and from the meeting together is an important aspect of how the meeting was experienced: 'we always went up in a group – in a gang!'[32] and 'there'd be no room on the footpaths, we'd have to go out on the road'.[33]

Street processions were also an important feature of the activities of the Archconfraternity of the Holy Family from the time of its foundation in 1868 until the late 1930s: the first one had been held on the streets of Limerick in 1877 with 4,000 men taking part, bands playing and banners flying: its purpose was to celebrate the Episcopal Jubilee of Pope Pius IX.[34] One interviewee, who was a child in the 1930s, remembers the Confraternity processions:

> You had the procession around the town, the Fathers' Confraternity, and that was wonderful because all the branches, you see you'd Monday night, Tuesday night and Wednesday night divisions and they'd all come together for the procession and the Blessed Sacrament start around the whole city, and each section would have its own banner, beautiful banners, and they'd have altars set in different little openings into laneways, beautiful altars with a statue and flowers and night lights … a lot of the windows then might have a large picture of the Sacred Heart … I'm telling you, it was very important … 'Twould have been Sunday, it would; I always remember we'd have the dinner early and we'd be all up to my grandmother's to the bay window and the window would be up … and the next thing you'd hear, you'd hear the thump of the drum … and that would be kind of … coming in through John's Square … you'd say 'Oh 'tis coming!' Well, the excitement! … But we'd be looking out for my father or my Uncle Jack and the next thing … we might say 'Oh there's Dadda' the men would hear it and they'd kind of smile and my grandmother would say 'Sssh! Be quiet!' she'd say, you know … but that was a wonderful procession: everyone looked forward to it because it was a great day … they were highlights in your religion that meant a lot and … the men themselves took great pride in that.[35]

This account of a Confraternity procession illustrates the central place that the organization held in Limerick city life in the 1930s (see Figures 2, 3 and 4).

Figure 2 Archconfraternity of the Holy Family Diamond Jubilee 1928. Procession, shown coming from the railway station through Baker Place.

Figure 3 Procession with band and banners near St John's Cathedral, c. 1929.

Figure 4   Archconfraternity of the Holy Family procession, 1938.

However, the point must also be made that the Archconfraternity of the Holy Family was by no means the only devotional organization in which men were involved. Other, smaller, but still popular, organizations open to men included the Archconfraternity of the Sacred Cincture, held monthly in the Augustinian Church and devoted to St Monica and Our Lady of Consolation; and the Third Orders of St Francis and St Dominic, whose meetings were also held monthly, in the Franciscan and Dominican Churches respectively. The Men's Association of the Blessed Sacrament was attached to the Reparation Convent chapel: its purpose was to accumulate Holy Hours of adoration, reparation and prayer on Sundays and on the Eves of First Fridays throughout the year (2,300 hours were accumulated in 1959, for instance) and a Solemn Novena of Reparation was held in January of each year.[36] Some men would undertake membership of organizations such as these as well as their Confraternity membership; others chose not to join the Confraternity, perhaps preferring a quieter ritual scene. One woman described how, when she was a little girl, her father, who had never been in the Confraternity and was not outwardly religious, would bring her up on the bar of the bicycle to the Reparation Convent chapel for Exposition of the Blessed Sacrament on a Sunday afternoon.[37] It is interesting to note the existence of devotional alternatives to the Confraternity: it is also important to realize that, despite its size, membership of the Confraternity was not actually universal amongst Catholic men.

Nonetheless, it is undoubtedly the case that the Confraternity was the most important devotional organization in men's lives in the first half of the twentieth century. The strong perceptions of 'place', both geographical and social, regarding the groupings within the organization demonstrate its role in the formation of a sense of identity in a city that was growing and changing in significant ways from the 1930s: it may also have been used by younger men to strengthen their own group, while both fostering and limiting relationships with women among the group.[38]

For some men, religious ritual also played a role in their working lives. In at least one case, the union representing the labour force had a strong allegiance both to the Catholic Church itself and to devotional rituals: this was the Limerick Pork Butchers' Society, which, from 1890, represented hundreds of workers in Limerick's three bacon factories, Matterson's, O'Mara's and Shaw's. The close relationship between the Catholic Church and the LPBS began when a seven week strike by pork butchers in 1891 was progressed by the intervention of the then Bishop of Limerick, Edward O'Dwyer, who conducted the ballot on the settlement proposals astride his horse in Mulgrave Street where one of the biggest bacon factories was located. As a result of this, Bishop O'Dwyer, a dynamic and somewhat controversial figure in the diocese, was made Honorary President of the Limerick Pork Butchers' Society, a position held by his successors for many years afterwards. The incident inspired the members of the Society to pay for a new shrine to Our Lady to be erected in St John's Cathedral, and to sponsor the maintenance of the shrine in subsequent years. Around this time, the Society decided on 15 August, the Feast of the Assumption, as the date of their annual holiday: the celebration took the form of Mass in the Cathedral, followed by refreshments in a nearby public house: both the Cathedral and the public house were near Shaw's bacon factory in Mulgrave Street.[39] The large attendance at the Mass, described by Tommy C as a 'full house' in the 1940s and 1950s, along with the subvention imposed by the union to sponsor the day, and the fact that the holiday itself was unpaid demonstrates the butchers' commitment to 'Lady's Day' as it was commonly known. Despite the necessity of some butchers reporting for work for a short time on the morning of 15 August in order to load the delivery vans, the general custom was that, Tommy C put it 'they would *never* work a Lady's Day'.[40]

This apparent continuity between devotional rituals and loyalty to the Church is attested to by the participation of the Pork Butchers' Society in other religious events: an undated photograph, possibly taken in 1928, when the Diamond Jubilee of the Archconfraternity of the Holy Family was celebrated with a major procession, shows an altar to the Blessed Sacrament mounted in front of an upstairs window in the union hall of the Pork Butchers' Society in Bank Place, with a banner reading 'Christ, King of Kings'.[41]

From the middle of the twentieth century, changes in working environments began to stimulate a different approach to devotion associated with the workplace: the setting-up of the Our Lady of Perpetual Succour Retreat House on the North Circular Road by the Redemptorist Fathers in the 1950s led to retreat weekends for occupational and other interest groups being organized from then on.[42] In March 1960 for instance, the groups included Shannon Airport workers, Limerick Gaelic Athletic Association, builders and drapers.[43] The inclusion of airport workers is significant: in one interviewee's opinion, the change in employment patterns, especially working hours, brought about by the airport and its adjacent industrial estate 'killed' the Confraternity.[44]

Ritual in women's lives

The overall character of women's ritual behaviour was similar to men's: the observance of weekly obligations overlaid by life-cycle rituals and the calendar of the liturgical year. With regard to other activities, however, women in Limerick city were not part of one large devotional organization in the way that men were: instead their confraternities (or sodalities) tended to be based in their local parishes, or, in the case of younger women, their schools. Máirín M remembers the Sodality as part of her schooldays as a child: 'you automatically joined the Sodality. Actually, even when we were very young in the Presentation ... Sunday school we used to have to go to – we called that Sodality'.[45] Máirín's mother resented the Sodality because she had a business in the city and,

> Sunday was her special day for family ... the shop was closed and her idea of heaven was always to have a picnic: she would cook pork steaks and things on the Saturday night and we'd all head off to Kilkee or Lahinch or somewhere on the Sunday which was lovely, all through the summer. But once you were in the Sodality, you *had* to attend Sunday school ... Until July, so you were missing May and June which would have been the times that she would love to be going, and oh she really resented us having to go over to this Sodality because 'twouldn't finish until – I think it was 12.30 and by the time you'd Mass over and gone to that, the day was gone ... You had to go and that was it if you were going to school.[46]

Thus, in Máirín's experience, not going to the Sodality 'would not be allowed – you had to! You had to go'.[47]

A primary school sodality was also held by the Mercy Order, who were in charge of the girls' school in St Mary's Parish: two interviewees recall their membership of this.[48] Another interviewee remembers the women's confraternity in St Mary's Parish: it was held every Tuesday night. According to her 'the older women would haul us in as soon as we had our Confirmation made'.[49] This confraternity was described as 'very vibrant' in the 1950s: another interviewee remembers joining it at eleven or twelve years of age in the 1930s.[50]

Religious organizations for women were not, however, confined to school or parish. Eileen L, who lived in St Munchin's Parish, remembers joining the Archconfraternity of the Sacred Cincture held in the Augustinian Church (women's section) at the age of around fourteen: her mother had been a member of the Third Order of St Francis.[51] The Ladies' Sodality held in the Jesuit Church, which, like many Jesuit sodalities, was sometimes called the 'Children of Mary' or *Enfants de Marie,* was also a well-known devotional organization in the city. One informant described her sodality membership as follows: 'I was in the Children of Mary in school and I was in the Sodality as an adult, for a while. You had your cloak and your medal. It was enjoyable ... sociable. Benediction, rosary and sermon. One woman there, she was a prefect – very strict: "Where were you last week?" We had a joke about it afterwards'.[52] Kathleen B, who was a member in her early twenties, remembers the Jesuit Ladies' Sodality as having the same format as others, but with 'brilliant preaching!'[53] Grace K's account stresses the element of choice in women's devotional activities. Her parents owned a drapery shop in the city centre and she described how the the various options would be discussed in the shop:

> You'd get a lot of the locals coming in saying 'Oh Mrs Ward, you know, there's a great novena going on here ... and a great novena going on there ... the Augustinians was a great place now, on a Tuesday, I think they had devotions to Our Lady of Good Counsel. And then sometime, I think 'twas in October, St Jude. They'd be flocking to that (laughter) because he's the patron of ... hopeless cases![54]

The social aspect of confraternity/sodality membership was also important,

> ah you might like an altar boy or two as well! ... they used to wear the soutane and the surplice and some had the beautiful lace at the bottom of the surplice, some would have lovely, lovely lace, I think it was a personal thing, their parents gave them. But the altar boys ... there was one or two regular altar boys in St Mary's ... some of the other girls even more so than myself, they would have their eye on them ... and you might be going for that as well![55]

The same point is made in another account:

> And there was a social occasion attached to it as well, going out to Benediction: in the more strict households it would be a great excuse to go out to Benediction, and even in Cooleen, where I used to spend my summer holidays, it was a great chance to get off for the evening, to Benediction, and have a bit of fun around afterwards you know; fun and crack and all the rest you know.[56]

For women, the connections between rituals of devotion and the workplace were also in evidence: in one large clothing factory, in which the majority of workers would have been women, it was customary to stop work at noon while workers recited the Angelus.[57] One interviewee, speaking about workers in general, stated that it was not unusual for people to say the Angelus, albeit in a discreet manner, while continuing to work.[58] A photograph taken in the Danus clothing factory around 1955 shows workers, some men but mostly women, kneeling on the floor between cutting tables and sewing machines while a priest says Mass at an altar at one end of the factory floor (see Figure 5).

While this photograph was taken to show a special Mass held in Danus on the occasion of the opening of the new factory in 1955, and therefore indicates that this was not a regular occurence in the factory, the temporary transformation of the factory floor into a sacred space is a striking in its demonstration of the connections between religion and working life in settings such as this.[59] The combination of official Catholic ritual with modern urban life in this image represents one of the most interesting aspects of this study, and it will be discussed later in the book. However, women differed from men in the fact that the patterns of their working lives were more various and changed more over time, depending on their marital status and family circumstances. This may have inhibited the formation of large work-based devotional groups and may also have influenced their participation in devotional organizations in general. An advertisement by the Reparation Convent for a retreat 'for engaged girls' to be held in April 1960, demonstrates how the emphasis

Figure 5   Mass for the opening of the new Danus clothing factory, 1955.

in discretionary devotional activities for women was different to that in activities organized for men.[60]

Rituals connected to childbirth may have increased the integration of women's religious lives with that of their homes and families, though this was not always in a positive way. It was often the case that mothers were not present at the baptism of their babies, because of the very short interval allowed between birth and baptism – this would be a matter of a couple of days in normal circumstances, or in situations where the baby was ill, it could be a matter of hours.[61] Another ritual, this time centred on the mother who had given birth, was known as 'churching', and was carried out in the weeks after the baby was born,

> after a new baby, the mother was 'churched', they called it. And people say today 'That was a disgrace!' and all that. Actually no, it was more … a blessing, I think … you went to be churched after so many weeks after having a baby. And … I think they'd light a candle. The priest would say a few prayers. You know it was nice in one way … I suppose it kind of gave thanks to God for the baby.[62]

However, other views of the churching ritual were not as positive. Peggy D, born in 1912, who had a large family, described it as follows:

> You were regarded as dirty after having a child … and they encouraging you to have them all the time! There would be a notice in the church 'Churching … on a certain day and you'd go along. There'd always be a few with you. The priest would put his alb over your shoulder and bring you up the church – like you had to be accepted back in. I hated it! But you felt you had to do it.[63]

Grace K, a mother of eleven children, put it like this:

> You'd have to go. 'Twould be on a special day ... as if [having a child] was a mortal sin! He'd just pray over you, bless you. I think he'd put his hand on your shoulder.[64]

The sense that the churching ritual was connected to the post-childbirth transition period in a wider social sense is strong in these two accounts, although this is sometimes associated with previous generations: 'Long ago, my mother told me, no-one would want you into their house unless you were churched ... your own mother would, but anyone else (wouldn't)'.[65] It is interesting that Peggy D, the oldest person interviewed for this research, felt a strong obligation to be churched for this reason, although she also mentions how the practice had died out in her later child-bearing years:

> I had a next door neighbour one time and I couldn't bring the baby in to see her – I hadn't been 'done'. She was very offended ... and she said to me 'Peggy, how is it you never came to see me with the baby?' I said ... 'I was waiting to be churched'. She said 'Peggy, you're the only one doing that now!'[66]

One interviewee's negative view of churching is in contrast to her experience of the more private ritual of the maternity blessing, which she would undergo at the Redemptorist Church at Mount Saint Alphonsus,

> then, when I became pregnant of course it was up there you'd go for the ... you'd have the maternity blessing ... you'd knock at the door or the office ... and she'd get a priest and he'd take you into a room and he'd bless you ... for your pregnancy, that you'd have a safe pregnancy.[67]

The sense here is that the maternity blessing was a choice, and a more private matter, whereas the much more public churching ritual had more of a sense of obligation about it, though this seems to have changed somewhat over the period studied.

The amount of time women had to spend on organized ritual activities was strongly influenced by their family circumstances: Eileen L, one of nine children, spoke about her mother's membership of the Third Order of St Francis in the 1930s and 1940s: 'well in those days too it meant it was a sort of a social occasion as well, to go out at night, once a month, now, the Third Order was once a month'.[68]

Máirín M's account shows the much greater availability and freedom of single women as far as intense devotional activity was concerned: she remembers attending devotions in honour of Our Lady every night during the month of May 'it was lovely because you had all these lovely May hymns and d'you know, you never resented going'.[69] Máirín's evidence also reflects the cultural scene evolving in Limerick city in the 1950s: her membership of *An Réalt*, the Irish language branch of the Legion of Mary, featured significantly in her social life, as it did for another interviewee, Pádraig R. Máirín describes it as follows:

> It was great to be a teenager really – brilliant at that time: there was so much ... it was simple when you look back on it ... but yet like as I said you had ... Monday night was the actual *Réalt*, Tuesday night you'd usually go on your

visitation, or wherever, whatever you had to do ... and then the Friday night was the *Praesidium*, and then you could have a *céilí* maybe on a Saturday night, and ... there was always something happening.[70]

Ritual activities and social organization

Perhaps the most striking aspect of interviewees' evidence concerning ritual is the idea that everybody was participating in devotional rituals: descriptions of the Archconfraternity, for instance, stress the numbers and geographical spread of the membership along with the huge attendance at the actual meetings. Allied to the idea that 'everybody' was involved is the sense of social obligation felt by Catholics regarding their own participation in ritual activities. The sense of 'having to' attend the school sodality, described above, came about because of pressure from the nuns in charge of the school: however, a sense of obligation could also be imposed by people other than clergy or members of religious orders. The feeling that the individual practice of religion was everybody's business was strong: as one interviewee said 'there weren't any ... if you were a defector you were sort of very well known and it was mentioned about you, you know'.[71] This aspect of ritual practice is reiterated in another account: 'We weren't a deeply religious family, although it was the norm, naturally, everybody went to Mass on Sunday, and it would have been known in the house, if not on the street, if you did not go to Mass ... oh it would be noticed, yes'.[72]

As the account of ritual in men's and women's lives above illustrates, the pressure to participate extended well beyond the obligatory ritual of Sunday Mass: Noreen P mentioned that the older women in the neighbourhood would 'haul us in' to the local women's Confraternity: Tommy C described the peer pressure involved in Archconfraternity attendance: Peggy D mentioned the sodality Prefect commenting on her attendance, again within an overall context of friendship. Both Grace K and Peggy D described a feeling of pressure to be churched after childbirth.[73] Other discretionary rituals were also subject to the idea that everybody was participating, or if they weren't, they should be: in describing the Good Friday devotions, one interviewee said:

> You would have the devotions at three o'clock and you'd kiss the cross and ... crowded? All the churches would be full, you know, the same for Mass ... the Confraternities ... the whole parishes went to their Confraternity ... well when I say the whole of them, the bulk of them went ... the few that didn't would be kind of nearly – nearly frowned on! But all the churches were full that time ... 'tis kind of sad now to see what's happening.[74]

The annual Corpus Christi procession was described in a similar way: 'People used to line the streets to watch ... you'd be criticizing them, saying "Why aren't they *in* the procession?"'[75] Another account of this occasion stressed the wide participation both in the preparation for the event and in the procession itself:

> You'd see all the ladders coming out, the men up the ladders, the women holding the bunting ... every place was just a riot of colour ... and every single house

would have … either a picture or a statue in their window, be it a shop or a private house, and an altar, usually a little – maybe linen – cloth … and your flowers at either side, every single house, the whole way up and down, preparing for the Corpus Christi … so everyone could partake, it always happened in the evening time … there was very few people, as far as I recall, *looking* at it, because everybody was *in* the parade![76]

The comment expressed here that everybody in the city was participating in devotional rituals is in striking contrast to Catholic processional culture in other places. Charlotte Wildman characterizes the Whit Walks in inter-war Manchester, for instance, as 'the performance of public, yet episodic, forms of Catholic identity' following the dispersal of Catholic communities throughout the city's new suburbs from 1918.[77] In a more contemporary context, Joseph Sciorra describes the religious processions held by the Italian-American residents of Brooklyn as 'territorial markers that map out geographic boundaries *vis-à-vis* the larger multi-ethnic neighbourhood'.[78] In these two contexts, Catholic processions could be seen as an effort to assert a Catholic identity within an environment where other groups and identities were also to be found. In this sense, Limerick presents a strikingly different ethnographic picture to those portrayed by Wildman and Sciorra, and is also different to other urban communities where religion and religious culture have been studied. In Hugh McLeod's London, in particular,[79] but also, to a lesser extent, in Jeremy Morris's Croydon, the multipicity of denominations and the greater complexity of the religious landscape allied to this meant that people did not have such an intense sense of obligation regarding their own and others' participation in religious rituals.[80] In contrast, Limerick's very high proportion of Catholics along with its relatively small population could be seen to have given rise to what Mary Douglas has called a strong 'group', where the individual is controlled by social relationships to a very high degree.[81] The combination of a highly classified and codified symbolic system or grid, combined with the strong group described above would lead us to characterize Catholicism in early to mid-twentieth century Limerick as a 'religion of control' where, according to Douglas, one would expect 'routinized piety' along with a high value on control of consciousness, and where ritualism is itself a very important element in religious and social control.[82] This is certainly an accurate characterization of Catholicism in Limerick during the period. However, it is also important, as Lauri Honko has said, to look at the 'relevant total behavior', and the place and role of ritual in a wider social context. The strength of religious authority in Douglas's 'religion of control' is undoubtedly an important factor in Limerick city life as it is described by interviewees: however it must be noted that other forms of authority were also very strong in the lives of ordinary people at the time. The founding of the Limerick Pork Butchers' Society and the place of religion in its activities demonstrates how religious ritual can be used to build a strong identity in a factory environment: the negotiation of time off for Mass on Holy Days, and for funerals of little-known acquaintances on a regular basis[83] shows how the 'control' aspect of religious ritual could be worked by people themselves to their own advantage in a situation where control by a different type of authority, such as that of the employer, was also a factor. In the same way, the accounts quoted above show that for young men and women, the sense of obligation regarding confraternities or other types of evening devotion was tempered, if not actually influenced, by the prospect of escape from the authority of the home and the probability of social interaction with other young people: again we see how ritual and its place in a 'religion of control' could be used by young people themselves to negotiate another form of authority and control, that of strict parents.[84] The social aspect of sodality/Third Order membership was also mentioned in the context of married women rearing families, for whom evening devotions could constitute a relief from their hardworking role at the centre of the home and family. This may have been especially the case for women in the highly respectable artisan class, such as Eileen L's mother, for whom the idea of going out with friends on any other kind of social occasion would have been unthinkable.[85] Evidence from the *Corca Dhuibhne* area of west Kerry concurs with this, showing that for women of this same generation (born before 1910 or so), marriage constituted the end of their contact with the world outside the home.[86] This situation varied from place to place and was to change somewhat with succeeding generations, as shown in Caitriona Clear's *Women of the House* which covers the period from 1922 to 1961. However, the overall decline of women's participation in formal employment in these decades points, in any case, to a high number of women working full-time in the home during the period.[87] Thus the attraction of devotional activities, which provided a social outlet with the added bonus of increased respectability and perceived virtue, is understandable. In this way, people may have managed to make the 'control' aspect of official Catholicism work for them on some levels, and especially on the level of escape from the home or factory: this is an important aspect of the creativity of the popular practice of official religion, though it almost certainly did not coincide with the intentions of the clergy who were organizing the devotional activities.

There are some further points to be made about this. The first is that those who did not want to, or feel themselves able to, fit into this controlled environment, however enjoyable it may have been for many of those participating in it, suffered constant pressure to do so. Frank McCourt's account of the strongly perceived connections between membership of the Redemptorist Confraternity and the relief of poverty in Limerick is one of the most eloquent illustrations of this.[88] The second point relates not just to Limerick but to Ireland in general during the period: this is that people whose actions put them, or their families, strongly at odds with the prevailing culture, most especially in the area of sexual behaviour, suffered severe marginalization by the Church and the State, as the experiences of women and children in Magdalen Laundries and Mother and Baby Homes, and that of children and young adults in industrial schools demonstrate.[89] The third point is that the social and entertainment value of devotional rituals was challenged more and more as the century progressed. This is clear from the coverage of religious topics in local newspapers, which, in the 1920s, constituted a large amount of the feature material in many issues. By the 1960s, however, while religious advertising and notification of religious events had increased significantly and religion still formed part of the editorial content, religious topics, both in advertising and editorial content, were competing strenuously with other material: the cinema and the dancehall were foremost in this, but fashion, sport and lifestyle topics were also important. Thus, even though it is certainly true that official

Catholicism in Limerick in the early to mid-twentieth century was a 'religion of control' in Douglas's terms, and that ritual was a crucial element of this, the growing complexity of Limerick city culture, and especially popular culture, during the period, must also be seen as having had an effect on ritual and on people's participation in it. The evidence from interviewees shows that submitting to the control exercised by religion through the religious and social pressure to participate in ritual was harder when alternative entertainment – such as late-night dances or family picnics – were in conflict with it. The fact that Eileen L says that she 'insisted' on going to her Legion of Mary meeting before her first dinner dance in the late 1940s, shows that there was a perceived conflict, within herself, between these two events.[90]

The role of officially organized devotional rituals in Limerick city during the period studied can, therefore, be summed up as follows. It is certainly the case that ritual was an instrument of social control and that the Catholic Church and the State, with the complicity of the community at large, dealt severely with those who didn't submit to this control. On the other hand, ritual events themselves could be seen as attractive when compared to a strict home environment or the (closely supervised) daily grind of factory work: the obligation to participate, thus escaping these forms of control, could be seen in these cases as a positive advantage. Religious ritual also played an important part in identity-building in the modern city which was taking shape from the mid-1930s: this is one of its most important aspects, and it will be discussed later in the book. However, it could also be said that the part played by Catholic ritual changed as other forms of entertainment in the city became more accessible (and acceptable) towards the middle of the century. Because of this, official Catholic ritual during the period must also be viewed as a cultural element positioned among, and competing with, other cultural elements in a twentieth-century urban environment.

Funerals

In her discussion of the genres of ritual action, Catherine Bell has the following to say regarding anthropological study of the rites of passage:

> Some scholars have theorized that there is a deep human impulse to take the raw changes of the natural world and 'cook' them, in the words of Lévi-Strauss, thereby transforming physical inevitabilities into cultural regularities. This impulse may be an attempt to exert some control over nature or to naturalize the cultural order by making physical events into elements of an embracing conceptual order of cognition and experience.[91]

The rituals surrounding death among Catholics in Limerick in the second quarter of the twentieth century fully demonstrate how this 'physical inevitability' was culturally ordered and made experientially coherent through the ritual process. The highly public nature of funerary rituals served to heighten the visibility, and thus the importance, of the symbols used and of the symbolic behaviour engaged in during this time: the urban context must also be taken into account in assessing the expressive function of the rituals of death.

Laying out the corpse

It was customary, in the period studied, for the dead person to be washed and laid out in his or her own home by neighbouring women,[92] and to be waked there before being brought to the parish church for Requiem Mass, followed by burial.[93] This basic structure is indicative of the dual character of funerary ritual in Limerick city, in which strong vernacular aspects were combined with emphatically official ones in the period up to 1960.

The presentation, both of the corpse, and of the room in which he or she was laid out, was of great importance. Kathleen B, whose grandmother owned a shop in King's Island in which habits and other ritual accoutrements were sold, recalls much about the business in the 1930s. The habits were made for the shop by local women, in different designs and using different types and colours of cloth according to the type of habit being made. The dead person's membership of a certain devotional organization, and thus their devotional identity, was reflected in the type of habit worn. Timmy G described his mother's laying out as follows: 'Now, you could pick out any colour, my mother was a member of Our Lady's Confraternity attached to the Sacred Heart Church at that time, so she was laid out in that'.[94] Kathleen B elaborates on the stock in her grandmother's shop:

> She had Cincture habits … if you were in the Cincture you were laid out in the Cincture habit … it was black I know and they had a gamp, like what the nuns wore … then if you were in the Third Order it was plain, simple brown, like the habit they'd wear with the cord, … then if you've the Child of Mary you wore a white habit trimmed with blue satin ribbon … They didn't have the [Child of Mary] cloak on a corpse, just the blue and white habits … And maybe they'd put the Child of Mary medal on as well.[95]

The medals worn by members of the Redemptorist Archconfraternity, which, as Lisa Godson has shown, were an important part of the material culture of the organization, may also have been used in this way,[96] as would other devotional objects associated with different religious organizations, such as the Cincture (or thin leather belt) worn by members of the Augustinian Sacred Cincture Confraternity,[97] or blessed medals or scapulars worn as more personal devotional objects.

Grace K describes being sent from her parents' drapery shop, to the larger Cannock's department store to obtain 'a habit, for a man or a woman, if you hadn't it', when a death was anticipated in her own neighbourhood.[98] As Cannock's was only a ten-minute walk away (at most), this may show the importance of smaller shops in the culture of local areas – not only did the smaller local draper know that a habit would be needed, but also that the family would come to their shop to buy it.

Habits also reflected the economic status of their wearers to some extent, though not, perhaps, as obviously as the way in which ordinary clothing did: 'She'd different prices, if you weren't … if you were poor … and the difference was – God! – the material was different and the trimming was less, and the better one then was the heavier material, more heavily trimmed with brown satin and a red satin heart in the centre'.[99] Habit stockings and gloves were sold in the shop as well, to complete the dressing of the corpse: 'Then she'd have a box with habit gloves, imagine – it's all so morbid – and a box with brown habit stockings. They had to be kept in stock all the time, because they went with the habit!'[100] Certain other items, however, were not kept in stock on a continuous basis: 'She'd do a shroud for a baby … white, and that would have to be made especially because she wouldn't keep those … you know, few babies would die'.[101]

The handling of the habit, even as it was being sold, reflected its importance as a ritual garment: Kathleen B's account demonstrates the impact of this respect and reverence on a child:

> Then, when the habit – I was behind that counter so many times as a small little one, taking it all in – then 'twould be folded very carefully and brown paper and she'd never put twine on it, because you'd think 'twould be wrong to wrinkle it like – there was great respect for the habit – and two little plain pins at each end when she'd turn up and then 'twould be handed like that and they'd take it down to be blessed.[102]

The appropriate dressing of the dead person was important for many reasons: not least of these was the notion of the dead person's change in status requiring a specific approach to the presentation of the self in these new circumstances. In this sense, the habit for the dead performed a function that no other mode of dress could: 'The first time we heard of people being laid out in a suit – that was an American idea – 'twas nearly pagan: you could not believe that 'twould have happened here in Ireland, and it became quite commonplace'.[103] Kathleen's own husband, who died in 1986, had been a member of the Third Order of St Francis, and was laid out in a Third Order habit: both he and Kathleen felt that:

> You should go out of the world in humility, the way you came into it. No matter how you look, you're only a spirit then … and to be dolling up your body to me seemed … well it did come from America … the idea in Ireland long ago of people having the simple habit and that, showed that their faith … all part of their faith. They believed that you were going to God, and God isn't telling you before you go 'You'd better come up with your lipstick on, to me!' Isn't that right?[104]

In his autobiography, Críostóir O'Flynn tells a story which points up the strangeness of 'the way they dicky up the corpse in the fancy funeral parlours today, with cosmetics and other tricks of the trade, and dressed in the best clothes'.[105] The story concerns a Limerick man who went to Kilkee for two weeks' holiday, but died after his first week there:

> When he was laid out in the modern style in the funeral parlour in Limerick, in his best suit and the face touched up, two of his old cronies stood looking down at him and one fellow says to the other: 'Bygor, Michael, d'you know what: he's lookin' the better of the week in Kilkee!'[106]

The humour in this anecdote is centred on the idea of a person who is dead somehow looking more 'alive' than they did before they died: the strangeness of this, and the extreme irony of the situation, is what makes it funny. It is significant that O'Flynn, in describing the customary laying-out of a corpse by neighbouring women, in the person's own home, says that 'a corpse … still looked very dead, with its yellow face and a rosary beads twined in its white fingers'.[107] Inherent in O'Flynn's attitude, and in that of Kathleen B, is the idea that a person who has died should look as if this has happened, and not look as if it has not: the importance of 'looking dead' if you *are* dead, is emphasized. Her comment 'No matter how you look, you're only a spirit then'[108] is a significant one: it shows a discomfort with efforts to deny the physical inevitability of death by pretending that the dead person isn't really any different to the way they were before they died. This effect, brought about by procedures adopted by undertakers from the 1960s, reflects the increasing professionalization of death rituals from that time: however Kathleen B's evidence suggests that not everyone was satisfied with this. Her view, a view which influenced the rituals she adopted for her own husband's funeral as late as 1986, would be that the fact that a person has changed utterly and completely as far as this life is concerned, and has ceased to exist in the everyday material sense would seem to be contradicted by the application of make-up and the wearing of best clothes. Kathleen's evidence suggests that to apply the material values of the living to somebody who is dead is highly inappropriate; another interviewee regarded the wearing of 'best clothes' in the coffin 'a terrible waste'. In this popular interpretation, the value of the habit for the dead can be appreciated.[109] The habit ensured that the dead person looked well in the coffin, but that they did so without subscribing too obviously to the material and aesthetic values of the living: it also acknowledged and expressed the significantly changed status of the person in the new circumstances of their wake and funeral.

The use of the habit for the dead could be seen as an important aspect of the repertoire of symbolic behaviour engaged in by the bereaved on their own behalf and on behalf of the dead person. It shows how, in Catherine Bell's terms, the physical inevitability of death was not denied, but was transformed from a 'raw change of the natural world' into a culturally ordered event, although, as has been seen above and will be further demonstrated below, this culturally ordered event was not without its conflicts and controversies. The devotional designations of the various habits strengthened their symbolic function by stressing the increased importance of spiritual life, and the concepts and categories within it, on the occasion of death. Thus the habit was useful in, on the one hand, helping people to accept the physical inevitability of death by making the person 'look dead'; on the other hand it contributed, along with other ritual elements such as prayers and candles, to the cosmological coherence of the wake and funeral.

Funerals as public events

It is very clear from accounts of religious rituals in Limerick city in the early twentieth century that wakes and funerals were public events, open to anyone who wished to go. O'Flynn tells us that 'When anyone in the neighbourhood, or any relation anywhere, died, even the youngest children were brought along to see the corpse and kneel and pray for the soul of the deceased'.[110]

Tommy C's account shows how this open aspect of the funeral was used by factory workers to get time off work: 'No matter who'd be dead, they always had a funeral to go to, that was a fact of life … you'd be docked … but you had "I had to go to this funeral" … They'd be looking at the paper "Who's dead? Some farmer …" Just to get off, to go up for a few drinks … they didn't mind being docked, that was it'.[111] In cases like this, the workers would go to the pub for a few drinks and wouldn't attend the funeral at all, though 'they might pass up the gate' of the church where the funeral was taking place.[112] This informal arrangement demonstrates the acceptability of the funeral as a reason to be absent from work, even when the worker's relationship to the deceased was questionable, and from the employers' point of view, impossible to ascertain one way or another. A close acquaintance with the deceased was not, in any case, strictly necessary for somebody who wished to attend a wake or funeral, as is clear from Kathleen B's description of wakes in her local area in King's Island in the 1930s:

> The person was waked at home … all the neighbours were in and out all day. As a child, you'd go in for curiosity! Even though you mightn't have the slightest … you'd be kind of afraid but yet you'd be dying to see what 'twas about … with your pal, you might have your skipping-rope even but you'd run in to the house because the people were going in and out … and the candles would be lighting and there'd be chats about it and maybe a drop of wine given.[113]

This account stresses the informality of attendance patterns at the home wake. In an autobiographical account from the Park area of the city, a small child's impression of the home wake stresses, among other things, the crowded aspect of the occasion:

> I was five, she was a hundred, I stood in the hall, my father holding my hand. My dead great grand aunt Maggie, lay in a coffin, which was supported by two chairs, one at each end. My father kissed her on the forehead and encouraged me to kiss her goodbye also. I didn't like the idea and declined. There were magical events occurring. My grandmother's house was more full of people than ever. Women in black shawls, men in dark clothes, all relaxed, talking and tracing. Always someone arriving. There was port wine for the ladies, whiskey and snuff for the men, rich fruit cake in plenty and lemonade and raspberry for us children. In the scullery a half barrel of porter appeared, perched on a wooden butterbox, it was a source of awe. It couldn't be touched. It had to be tapped. Another mystery. A man was awaited to tap the barrel. Paddy (Trap) Doherty was the man and he performed the deft operation. I was shooed out of the way.[114]

The social aspect of the wake described in the accounts above demonstrates the strength of Irish vernacular tradition in the approach to death rituals. The 'chats' and the 'talking and tracing' mentioned, along with the wine, whiskey, porter, lemonade and festive food such as fruit cake are all characteristics of both types of funeral written about by Seán Ó Súilleabháin in the early 1960s: the contemporary wake and the old-fashioned or traditional wake, although the wake games described by him in connection with the earlier tradition are not in evidence here.[115]

Despite this informality, it seems that a coherent ritual pattern, again echoing the popular wake tradition, would usually be followed by the people dropping in, and even by the little girls with skipping-ropes mentioned in Kathleen Browne's account: saying a prayer at the bedside was one element of this: 'Oh you would … anybody that went in, that was the first thing they did, they'd stand in front of the bed and say a prayer and sympathise with the people … they'd come into the room with you, like, and they'd be crying and sad, naturally'.[116]

The wake ensured that the dead person was highly visible, and, as the discussion of habits above demonstrates, there was an acute awareness of this visibility. The ritual also transformed the private house into a public space: during this time the most private area of the house, the bedroom, would be seen by many people, some of whom may never have visited the house before. Kathleen B relates how her grandmother's role in the funerary ritual was not restricted to selling habits for the corpse: she would also take an interest in the preparation of the home for the wake:

> Then she'd say … 'Do you want the candlesticks?' … she'd brass candlesticks … then as well as that she had a very large big linen bedspread that would be given to people that wouldn't … all the people were laid out at home … she'd give the bedspread to them because that would go over the bed for the people that hadn't bedclothes much you know, that would be shabby.[117]

This process is a faint echo of the custom of 'hanging the house' followed by funeral furnishers in England in the nineteenth century, when members of the nobility and landed gentry held 'lyings-in-state' for deceased members of their families.[118] However, Mrs O'Dea's service seems to have been offered in a more neighbourly context: to bring poorer households up to a basic standard of public display, rather than to add to the splendour and ostentation of the rich.

The extent to which the funeral was, perhaps, the most public of family rituals is apparent in Máirín M's evidence regarding the death of her grandmother when she was a child:

> One thing I remember about Christmas when I was six … we had had our Christmas as usual and we were into Little Christmas – *Nollaig na mBan* – and my mother, the Lord have mercy on her, had pneumonia – pleurisy – and she was in bed upstairs. My granny lived with us and she was an invalid, she had been in a wheelchair for a number of years, so she was in bed upstairs and my dad made the breakfast and he said to me would I bring her up her breakfast and when I went up I couldn't wake her and … I put down the little tray I had and I started to shake her and when I put my hand on her she was frozen and of course I ran down to tell my dad and … anyway, she was dead, *go ndéana Dia trócaire uirthi*.[119]

Máirín goes on to relate how she and her two younger sisters were sent out to a neighbour's house while the preparations for her grandmother's funeral were begun,

> and we were out there for quite a number of hours and when we came back I remember the awfulness of 'Christmas is over'– it's funny how the thing just comes back to you – in that we had relatives who had come – obviously heard what had happened, and that time Christmas decorations were … the old-fashioned paper chains and they would be pinned from one corner of a room to another,

criss-crossing one another ... And you'd have your Christmas tree, your crib of course and all the various decorations ... the house would be really decorated, holly everywhere and that ... but my memory of that particular *Nollaig na mBan* was of the relatives coming in and up on chairs, pulling down the decorations and rolling them up – we would have been folding them carefully – and others carrying the Christmas tree between them, all complete with decorations, just lifted out of it and all put out into the shop out on top of the counter I remember. And ... I remember my younger sister saying 'Please, please please give us back our Christmas!'[120]

Máirín's account of these events highlights the contrast between the intimate, finely tuned family rituals of Christmas and the more public and pressurized atmosphere of the family funeral. The family's sense of order and their own procedure for ending the Christmas season, taking the decorations down and putting them carefully away for the following year, is felt to be violated by the haste in which the relatives bring about what is obviously an important change in the appearance and atmosphere of the house: from joyful and colourful Christmas festivity to the bare essentials needed for the funerary ritual. The urgency of this change is apparent from Máirín's evidence and is in itself interesting: the household must convert from Christmas mode to funeral mode, and it must do so quickly. Inherent in this urgency is a palpable sense of expectation. Crowds of people will visit the house in the next few days and the household must, in every sense, including the symbolic, be prepared for them. The absence (through illness) of the interviewee's mother and her ability to negotiate this juxtaposition of ritual events within her own home is also a factor in the pain experienced by the children: as we will see later (Chapters 5 and 6) the part played by mothers and fathers in rituals centred on the family home is of great importance. Máirín's story demonstrates the highly public and visible nature of the funerary ritual, including that part of it which was centred on the home of the dead person. The contrast with Christmas is made more painful by the sense in which a funeral was felt to be 'owned', not just by the extended family, but also by the community as a whole.

Funerals and city life

The public nature of the funerary ritual was increased by the urban setting in which it took place. Perhaps the most visible and dramatic aspect of the funeral was the procession, after requiem Mass, of the hearse, followed by mourners both on foot and in cars or other vehicles, from the church to the graveyard. The funeral procession differed from devotional processions such as the Corpus Christi procession or the Confraternity procession in significant ways: these were held on summer evenings or on Sunday afternoons when shops and other businesses were closed. As accounts of these processions show, people would stand on the footpath or at a well-placed window to watch the spectacle. In contrast, funerals usually took place in the morning or early afternoon, very often on ordinary working days in the midst of the everyday business of the city. It was customary for people to stop and say a prayer while waiting for the procession to pass by: all kinds of oncoming traffic would usually pause and do the same.[121] Thus, this part of the funerary ritual had the power to transform urban life momentarily, and this dramatic visibility heightened its expressive function. Ciarán MacMathúna, in an account of his childhood in the 1930s in St John's Parish in Limerick has the following to say:

> Funerals from the Cathedral were fascinating with horse-drawn hearse and carriages. There is an old Irish saying *an cóngar chun na bainise agus timpeall chun na reilige* [the short cut to the wedding and the long way round to the graveyard, trans. SdeC] ... And, sure enough, funerals instead of coming up Cathedral Place and straight to the cemetery went all around the city through Patrick Street and up William Street. We lived in Mulgrave Street and all the funerals passed that way. We stopped our street hurling or handball to let the funeral pass.[122]

The deliberate lengthening of funeral processions in a parish in which the church, St John's Cathedral, was considered to be too near the cemetery could be seen in two ways. Firstly, it may, both in this context and in that of popular rural tradition, indicate a reluctance to part with the deceased and to prolong the contact with the person, or the entity which represents them, before they are finally buried. Secondly, the longer procession heightened the visibility of the funeral in an urban setting, something which may have been well appreciated by the organizers of the ritual. The route described by MacMathúna would take the procession through the commercial heart of the city where the requisite pause in activity would be all the more dramatic. An account of an incident in St John's Parish in the 1950s shows that not everybody was happy with this kind of procession, however:

> In March, 1955, a well-known parishioner was the first to break with tradition of the long way round for funerals from the Cathedral. Despite the insistence of the Rev Fr Clifford, he refused to have his mother's remains carted by the long circuitous route through the city centre. The priest insisted that the funeral should follow the traditional route but the parishioner was ... demanding that the funeral would not go by the old route but by the shorter and more practical route by Cathedral Place. A compromise was eventually reached and the funeral went by Gerald Griffin Street, Upper William Street ... and Mulgrave Street. In 1958 the funeral of the Bishop, Most Rev Dr Patrick O'Neill, went to Mount St. Laurence by Cathedral Place. Since then all funerals go by that route.[123]

Lawrence J. Taylor's comment is relevant here: 'The contested character of death is rooted in the fact that death is not only a problem, but also an opportunity to reassert a social unit and cultural framework at a particularly potent moment'.[124] The 1950s' controversy described above highlights the centrality of the procession as part of the repertoire of symbolic behaviour in the funeral as a whole: if, as Taylor says, death is a 'potent moment', then the funeral procession is perhaps the most potent moment within the event. The use of this opportunity to 'reassert a social unit' can be seen not just in the coming together of mourners to follow the hearse on foot through the streets of the city, but also in the momentary participation of many others as they watched the funeral go past. The deliberate lengthening of the procession could be seen as an attempt to include as many passing – or rather 'pausing' – participants as possible. The cultural framework mentioned by Taylor is also apparent: the emphasis on the journey of the deceased, which, as MacMathúna points out, is an important element of vernacular Irish tradition, is intensified by the use of the horse-drawn hearse, followed by a group of mourners walking behind it. In Catherine Bell's terms, the 'cultural regularity' of this 'physical inevitability' was to be felt in the symbolic behaviour undertaken by everybody involved. The sight and experience of everyday life stopping for a moment, the reflective demeanour of the mourners and the casual participants' actions in blessing themselves and saying a short prayer gave a spiritual coherence and a strong sense of meaning to the event. Taylor's idea of death as a social and cultural opportunity is amply borne out by this aspect of funerary ritual in Limerick in the second quarter of the twentieth century.

The distribution of power and its effect on the creation of meaning is also of interest in this discussion. The uncontested power of adult relatives in the organization of a family funeral is clear in Máirín M's account of the death of her grandmother: the children, who play a significant role in the rituals of Christmas, are, by contrast, completely powerless. The meaning of the event, however, is still contested, as Máirín's evidence shows. This can be seen as an example of what Lawrence J. Taylor means when he says: 'That is to say, not everyone has the same meaning in mind, and the eventual public character meaning achieves may be negotiated – or may remain in conflicting versions'.[125]

The negotiation of meaning, on the other hand, can be seen in the dispute concerning the funeral procession. In this instance it is significant that the distribution of power is somewhat different, involving a disagreement between the parish priest of St John's and a 'well-known parishioner', who felt himself able to object to the circuitous route which was customary for funeral processions in St John's Parish at the time. The narrator of this story, writing in a parish history published in 1991, gives a clue to the issues at stake when he tells us that the 'well-known parishioner' was unhappy with the idea of his mother's remains being 'carted' around the city centre unnecessarily, as he saw it. This implies a rather more personal, intimate view of the ritual than is allowed for in the very public, but perhaps rather clinical, expressiveness of the procession as it had evolved by this period in the 1950s. In terms of meaning, Fr Clifford's priority could be seen to be the symbolism of the journey of the deceased in which the Church played a crucial and very visible role: the compromise eventually reached allowed this some expression, but shortened the journey undertaken by a considerable distance.

The changing character of funerary ritual

The organization of funerals in the earlier part of the period studied, and in the longer-established communities, such as that of the King's Island area, shows a strong emphasis on the concept of 'separation', as outlined by Arnold van Gennep in *The Rites of Passage*, though van Gennep himself does not apply this concept to funerary ritual in the same way.[126] Separation is evident even in the very early stages: O'Flynn tells us that after the corpse had been washed by neighbouring women 'the piece of soap used was never used again in the house; it was thrown after the cortège as it moved away from the house.'[127] Gerry Griffin describes another aspect of the removal, with his own interpretation of its meaning:

> It was usually a lady or ladies in the area who would come to wash the body. You weren't allowed to wash your own relations because it was deemed to be something that your neighbours would do for you. Once the body was washed the water was usually kept in a pail or basin. The horse hearse would come to the house on the night of the removal with the coffin and it would remain outside the house until the last minute … But once the coffin was put into the hearse and the hearse was leaving the house, the old 'piseógary' was that the evil spirits that would have been contained in the corpse would have been washed out with the water. So to kill those evil spirits and send them to everlasting damnation, the water was thrown under the hooves of the horses so they could trample on the evil spirits and get rid of them.[128]

The wearing of habits, discussed above, was another way of emphasizing the separation of the living person from their remains, and was, as the evidence shows, a central aspect of the wake stage of the funeral. The suspension of normal life, this time in the form of the festivities of Christmas, is painfully evident in the stripping of the house of all evidence of celebration in the preparation for a family funeral: again the emphasis on separation is clear. The long funeral procession could be seen as a way of consolidating and finalizing the separation already achieved and, also in van Gennep's terms, beginning the middle period of transition.

However, the evidence also shows a discomfort, towards the later part of the period, with the cut-and-dried finality of the approach to the wake and funeral. The children whose Christmas was so painfully disturbed in Máirín M's account were, of course, a marginal group in the proceedings and, as pointed out already, completely without the power of contestation at that time. However, these children were young adults by the 1950s, and achieved adulthood in the early 1960s: the evidence shows that one of these adults, at least, retained her opinion of the event. By the 1960s, the highly charged symbolic behaviour of washing and laying out the body, in which the community were intensely involved, had started to become the responsibility of undertakers, thus reducing people's physical involvement with the ritual. The change in dressing the body, which took place very gradually over three or so decades, also shows dissatisfaction with the very obvious separation achieved by the wearing of the habit for the dead, and possibly a desire to mitigate the strangeness of the event by making the corpse look more familiar to those who had been close to the dead person. The long funeral procession, which, as well as interrupting the life of the city, also lengthened the period of liminality experienced by the mourners may, by the 1950s, have been felt by some to be uncomfortably elaborate or simply unnecessary. These various 'discomforts' with the structure of the established ritual and the changes within the ritual gradually brought about by them could be seen to cluster in one area: the desire to experience the ritual in a less elaborate way and to reduce, to some extent, the drama and intensely expressive aspects of it. The underlying attitudes shown by the evidence, as well as by the changes in the ritual towards the end of the period studied could be seen to challenge the accepted ritual hierarchy in which, for instance, the highly public ritual of death took precedence over the more private, familial ritual of Christmas, or the idea that the funeral of one member of the community was something for which the whole city should be made to come to a standstill, albeit a temporary one. With regard to the procession, it is also worth considering the possibility that in an urban environment which had grown and changed significantly in the decades from the 1930s, the more crowded city setting had actually served to depersonalize the long ritual, making it less meaningful, and thus more difficult for the bereaved to endure.

Perhaps, to use the Lévi-Straussian analogy mentioned by Catherine Bell in her discussion of the rites of passage, people felt that the 'raw change' of death did not need quite the same amount of elaborate 'cooking' as was provided by the traditional funerary ritual, or that maybe the 'cooking method' should be speeded up a little.[129] This would account for the gradual adjustment of certain details of the ritual to make it less ornate and dramatic, or perhaps, from another point of view, less tedious and long drawn-out in terms of how it was experienced by those who had been bereaved. In this context, moving the wake out of the home, though a later development, as it did not begin to happen until the mid-1960s,[130] was also an important aspect of the change in the format of the ritual and could be said to have consolidated the changes that preceded and accompanied it.

Community, hegemony and the urban context

The involvement of the local community in the organization of death is to be found in the evidence concerning the more traditional approach to the ritual. The washing and laying-out of the dead person by local women, the neighbours taking charge of children for a few hours so that the wake could be organized, and the fact that the proprietor of the habit-shop was concerned with and involved in the presentation of the bedroom in which the person would be laid out, are examples of this. Seán Ó Súilleabháin describes the rural wake tradition in similar terms.[131] It is also clear, however, that the Catholic Church maintained a high degree of visibility and control, both practical and symbolic, over the ritual process, a situation which had prevailed in Ireland generally since the nineteenth century. The devotional designations of the various habits for the dead ensured the visibility of Church organizations at the wake stage of the ritual, while the prayers constantly being recited over the corpse reinforced the spiritual and devotional context of the event: the Church's role increased and intensified with the removal of the body to the local church for requiem Mass followed by the funeral procession and burial. The high visibility of the clergy in the procession is noted by Ciarán MacMathúna, when he describes priests walking ahead on the footpath wearing 'folded lengths of white linen across one shoulder and tied diagonally under the other arm'.[132] These lengths of linen were usually donated by the family of the deceased. MacMathúna also highlights the connection between ritual and social structure when he says that the number of priests present was a measure of status in the community.[133] In this way, certain aspects of funerary rituals in Limerick in the twentieth century could be said to reflect those which had prevailed in many other European countries since the early modern period. Francois Lebrun's description of funerals in Europe during the seventeenth and eighteenth centuries bears this out:

> The pomp of the funeral depended on the social rank of the deceased. The observance included transfer of the body from the mortuary to the church, a religious ceremony, and burial in the church or cemetery. In the lower classes it was all rather simple: the family and a few friends followed the casket, carried by a few pallbearers. Among the wealthy and the nobility, however, funerals were occasionally far grander. Numerous priests from the parish and religious communities preceded the casket, which was carried in a hearse drawn by caparisoned horses ... the laying to rest of the deceased was always, even in the most modest cases, conceived as a spectacle, in which the entire parish was invited to participate as an actor or spectator.[134]

The similarities here are clear, except that the body is brought from a 'mortuary' rather than from the person's home. This might indicate that the home wake aspect, so crucial to the Limerick city funeral, was either absent or not thought important enough to be mentioned. This difference is significant.

The social and material status of the deceased was also a factor in the English funeral tradition. Julian Litten has commented: 'In an age when success was measured by material possessions and monetary wealth, the nineteenth-century funeral was regarded as a public manifestation of one's acumen'.[135] He also characterizes the 1890s as 'the golden age of the Victorian funeral: the horse-drawn cortège, the flower-decked funeral car with its encased burden, and sable mourning coaches containing weeping ladies swathed in crape and black bombazine, supported in their grief by stiff-lipped husbands, brothers and uncles'.[136] This emphasis on display in the Victorian funeral can certainly be seen in the Limerick city tradition, though it is interesting to note that the devotional designations of the habits described earlier in this chapter by Kathleen B and Timmy G give this display a distinctively Catholic flavour. The shrouds featuring in an English advertisement for Dottridges drapers, dating from 1922, though highly decorative, show no religious references in their ornamentation.[137] Perhaps it is not surprising that the public display of the Limerick funeral included a testament to the devotional allegiance of the dead: as has been seen, this had been a central element of their lives as well.

Again, however, it must be stressed that the funeral in Limerick incorporated an important vernacular element, that of the home wake. This gives the ritual a dual aspect: family and friends managing the wake stage of the funeral at home and then adopting a more public and Church-directed approach, for the Mass, procession and burial. It is also important to remember that even in this earlier period, professional undertakers took over the ritual as soon as the body left the home for the church on the day of the burial, and that from then on it was their responsibility, and that of the clergy, to manage the ritual.

It is interesting to compare this scenario with that conveyed in an incident recounted in the folklore of County Cork – told originally by Amhlaoibh Ó Luínse, and later fictionalized by Donncha Ó Céileachair – in which two sides of a family of a deceased woman cannot agree on her place of burial and her funeral procession is disrupted accordingly. The title of the story 'Siar leí, a Bhuachaillí!' ('Bring her back, lads!') is strongly evocative of the action and energy of the story, in which the clergy do not play a central part.[138] The incident is, of course, a remarkable one, which is why it entered the folk narrative repertoire in the first place. However the fact that it was told as *seanchas* (local lore) would also imply that, at some level, it was thought to give an account of a true event which could – and did – actually happen in the community. An incident similar in both character and atmosphere, if not in its detail, concerns the treatment of the remains of the notorious hangman James 'Stretcher' Ryan, in Limerick, in 1839: his body was twice disinterred from St Patrick's graveyard and thrown into a ditch. He eventually had to be buried within the walls of the County Gaol. The Limerick historian Kevin Hannan comments: 'the people of Park had no intention of allowing the sacred dust of their kindred to be compounded with that of the hated hangman'.[139] This incident is interesting for two reasons: firstly because it is, like Ó Luínse's story, in stark contrast to the orderly, church-centred and controlled death rituals of the early twentieth century; secondly because the Park people – or 'Park Danes' – a distinct community of market gardeners situated in a semi-rural area adjacent to the urban districts of both St John and St Mary's parishes – are mentioned by Hannan in connection with this chaotic and disorderly conduct. This firmly places the incident on the margins of the Limerick city community, even at this early date, though of course it must be remembered that the Park people's actions may have been welcomed and admired by many Limerick city people, despite the disapproving tone of the contemporary *Limerick Chronicle* report.[140] By the time Ó Luínse's piece of narrative was being collected and written down by the Irish Folklore Commission, the event described in it would have been unlikely to happen in most rural communities. In Limerick city in the 1930s and 1940s, however, it would have been absolutely unthinkable: the idea of people acting as a group to take control of the funeral procession and try to wrest this control not from the clergy (note the clergy is not even considered in Ó Luínse's story), but rather from another group within the community, implies a strength of group identity and localized power that does not, at first glance, appear to be present in the community of ordinary people in early twentieth-century Limerick city. Maybe this is the 'individualization' of death mentioned by Lawrence J. Taylor, which, according to him 'is not at all antithetical to Church hegemony. It is precisely the de-communalized individual that can be most totally integrated into the Church – which becomes his community'.[141]

Yet it is overstating the case to describe Limerick city people in this period as 'de-communalized'. It is, perhaps, more enlightening to think of the Limerick city community at this time as 're-communalized', or 're-communalizing' as they constantly negotiated and renegotiated their approach to the rituals of death. In this regard, it is worth looking at the various factors which combined to create the specific dynamic of funerary rituals in the community: as the description above shows, the vernacular tradition, the Catholic Church, the undertakers and the social and economic status of the dead and their families all had a part to play.

The urban context is also crucial. The situation observed by Kathleen B where the neighbours would be 'in and out all day' is not hard to imagine given the proximity of houses to one another in the King's Island area of the city, and in many other areas as well. O'Flynn's description of the funeral cortège moving away from the house and the piece of soap being thrown after it locates the ritual and the enactment of this part of it very firmly in the 'street scene' of the local neighbourhood,[142] while the drama of the funeral procession which came later in the proceedings was certainly enhanced by the street context in which it took place. From Kathleen B's and O'Flynn's descriptions, the community can be seen to have played an active and energetic role, especially in the earlier stages of the ritual: this was in close co-operation with the clergy whose involvement increased as the ritual progressed. However, the evidence also indicates a sense of diverse interests and values underscoring, and eventually influencing the practice of the ritual as outlined above. The image of little girls with skipping ropes going in to say a prayer at the bedside of a person that they didn't know 'out of curiosity' is one that emerges from the urban setting: another, recounted by O'Flynn, also concerns little girls: they would seize the 'ritual soap' after it had been thrown away, and use it in their games of 'house'.[143] The public nature of funerals, combined with the sheer numbers of people in the urban community facilitated the invention of funeral obligations by factory workers who wanted some time off. Even at the intensely formal funeral procession, for which the urban community was pausing in its daily routine, market gardeners would run to scoop the manure dropped by the horses pulling the hearse in order to fertilize their cabbage crop.[144] The differing degrees of involvement in the funeral, and a discreet sense of choice regarding this, is shown by the use of a men's public toilet near Tannery Lane as a convenient excuse to drop out of the traditional long procession.[145] It is not perhaps surprising when this degree of diversity, fostered by the urban context, is considered, that the dispute concerning the funeral procession in the 1950s took place between an individual parishioner and the parish priest, and that the parishioner could be said to have won some important ground. The fluidity and dynamism of urban life is also demonstrated by the fact that, three years later, a Bishop's funeral procession took the very route proposed by the parishioner in 1955, and that since then all funerals from St John's have taken this route.[146] Thus it may be said that while the community at one level was closely integrated with the Catholic Church in its operation of the ritual, the informality and diversity made possible by the setting in which the ritual took place allowed, at another level, a freer and more individual approach which may, as the period progressed, have fostered an ability to dissent and change aspects of it.

Senses of Place

In this chapter, religion is explored in two very different contexts of place. The first, pilgrimage, is strongly connected to twentieth-century official Catholicism both at the level of organization and in its devotional focus. Yet many officially organized pilgrimages were connected to older, vernacular traditions of belief and their associations with particular places. Travel to a place that is different from one's own homeplace has always been an important aspect of pilgrimage, and one which was central to the experience in the period studied. The methods of transport – road, rail and later air – available to pilgrims in the decades from the 1920s to the 1960s highlight the ways in which modernity and official devotion were influencing each other and coming together in significant ways in Limerick city during these years. The second area looked at is that of the May Eve fire, a strong vernacular tradition in the city which had aspects of unofficial belief and only very tenuous links to official Catholicism. The tradition of the May Eve fire grew stronger as it was re-established and renewed in the new public housing estates that were being built in Limerick from the mid-1930s until the end of the period studied. The combination of modernity and popular tradition in the May Eve fire is a striking example of cultural creativity in the city at the time. With regard to culture and creativity in general, Hervé Varenne offers the following comment:

> What is interesting about human activity is what might be talked about as its 'passionate surplus'. Human beings always do more than what we might expect them to do, and the anthropological task is to emphasize this surplus, what we usually talk about as 'culture'.[1]

Although Varenne is here referring to the way in which culture was created, above and beyond the material necessities of life in a new Dublin suburb of the 1980s, the idea of a 'passionate surplus' is useful in assessing ritual aspects of life, both official and unofficial in Limerick in the early to mid-twentieth century. The ritual obligations of Mass, the widespread participation in church-based devotional organizations and the highly organized public rituals could be regarded as the basic necessities, or the 'bread and butter', of official religious life, especially when looked at in the light of Mary Douglas's idea of a strong group and grid.[2] There were other activities in which it could be said that a type of 'surplus motivation' could be said to be operating; where communities, families or individuals participated in ritual – however this was organized – with much more of a voluntary or discretionary aspect. Although the settings in which these types of rituals took place varied considerably, the element of choice, along with a certain degree of spontaneity in deciding to carry them out, was a crucial common factor. Both pilgrimage and the May Eve fires fall into this category, and they both bear an important relationship to place, although as will become clear, this is played out in two completely different ways.

Pilgrimages

Victor and Edith Turner, in their 1978 monograph *Image and Pilgrimage in Christian Culture*, have classified pilgrimages into four basic types: firstly, those established by the founders of historical religions; secondly, those which are overlaid on older religious systems; thirdly, pilgrimages established in the Middle Ages and fourthly, the Post-Tridentine or modern pilgrimage.[3] In Limerick city in the period between 1920 and 1960, at least two of these types of pilgrimage can be identified among the devotional activities carried out by members of the community. Both Lourdes and Knock fit into the profile of the Post-Tridentine or modern pilgrimage as described by the Turners: the centrality of a vision or apparition in stimulating an interest in the area, along with the subsequent establishment of a miracle discourse; the importance of modern communications and technology in the development of the destination is also evident.

International pilgrimages

The Maria Assumpta pilgrimage to Lourdes – in its fifth year in 1935 – originated in St Mary's Parish and was later organized by the Limerick Diocese.[4] The trip was, in this period, timed so that participants could spend the Feast of the Assumption on 15 August at the grotto. The *Limerick Leader* reported in 1935 that about 400 people travelled with this pilgrimage, 100 of them from Limerick, including one 'stretcher case' and a few 'slightly invalided' people.[5] In the same year, 'the second great Irish Franciscan pilgrimage' to Lourdes was comprised of 2,600 pilgrims 'from all parts of the country' along with 120 priests.[6] In the 1950s, the Maria Assumpta or Limerick Diocesan pilgrimage was still going on, and the numbers may have increased somewhat.[7] The Turners' point about the importance of communications technology in the development of this type of pilgrimage is well demonstrated by the example of Lourdes at this period. The cost of going to Lourdes – £15–10s. in 1930; £39–15s. in 1954[8] – was so high that the pilgrimage had to be widely advertised in order to attract a viable number of participants.[9] Newspaper advertising – not just of local pilgrimages but also of nationally organized ones – was a crucial factor in their success. The technology of transport was also of great importance: 1930s' pilgrims from Limerick went to Lourdes by boat and train. In 1954, the journey was still overland, though forty-five more pilgrims, including the Bishop of Limerick, Dr O'Neill, flew from Dublin Airport and joined the main body of the pilgrimage in Paris,[10] while 'a limited number of invalids' were taken directly by air from Shannon Airport.[11]

The newspaper advertising of Lourdes pilgrimages raises an important point: this is the significance of the overlap between tourism and pilgrimage, although, as Stiofán Ó Cadhla's research on the holy well tradition in Ardmore, Co. Waterford has shown, this overlap can be seen in much earlier traditions and in the vernacular context of the pattern day as well.[12] The advertisements and local promotion of Lourdes pilgrimages in the 1930s stress the comfort and convenience afforded by the latest mode of transport, while managing to avoid the notion of outright enjoyment of the trip. In the 'Town Topics' column of the *Limerick Leader* on 5 May 1930, the writer, while advising interested parties to contact the Honourable Secretary of the (first) Maria Assumpta pilgrimage for full details, assures readers that 'the fare of £15.10s. will cover all expenses. There will be no night travel, and meals will be provided in restaurant cars. The organizers have arranged accommodation at comfortable hotels and the trip will include a night in Paris and London'.[13] In the Saturday 30 March 1935 edition of the *Limerick Leader*, a small item with the heading: 'Lourdes by Liner: Oblate Pilgrimage 1935' states:

> Owing to the number of requests received from their Pilgrims of former years, the Oblate Fathers of Inchicore decided to take the Pilgrims to Lourdes this year by trans-Atlantic Liner. Travel by Liner holds out many advantages over the land route. The Pilgrims are saved an amount of worry and fatigue entailed by the number of changes from boat to train etc. Besides, they avoid the long fatiguing train journey through France.[14]

The same reassuring tone can be felt in a 1936 advertisement headed: 'Lourdes, Paris, Lisieux': 'Mr. M. P. Riordan of Riordan's Travel Agency, Limerick, invites you to join his 10 day personally conducted party – 4 nights in Lourdes, 3 in Paris, 1 in Lisieux. 2nd on French railways, excellent hotels … Travel in comfort with a small party'.[15]

It is interesting to contrast the tone of these advertisements and promotional writing with travel advertising in general: the Cork Steam Packet Company, advertising a 'Bank Holiday Cruise De Luxe' on the mv *Inisfallen* to Glengarriff, the Kenmare river and Parknasilla on 4–5 August 1935 also gives the following details: 'Music and deck games. Whist and Bridge drives arranged on request'.[16] Meanwhile the 'Lourdes by Liner' pilgrims would have 'The Blessed Sacrament … reserved in a beautiful oratory on board, and every morning there will be a succession of Holy Masses with Solemn High Mass on both Sundays. The Eucharistic Holy Hour, with special Lourdes devotions, will be held during the voyage'.[17] The detailing of devotions to be carried out on the trip is one aspect of pilgimage discourse during this period: another, perhaps more important, aspect is the association of the group with spiritual leadership. For example, Mr M. P. Riordan's group mentioned above would be affiliated to the pilgrimage led by Archbishop Downey, while the 1935 Maria Assumpta group were to have Dr Keane, the then bishop of Limerick, as their patron.[18] It is interesting too to see other types of pilgrimages, such as those classified by the Turners as centred on the founders of historical religions, benefitting from the communications environment available by the 1930s. Again, reassurance is crucial as the 1935 headline 'All-Catholic Cruise to the Mediterranean' shows.[19] This cruise would include a 'visit to Rome and audience with the Holy Father', while a Catholic pilgrimage in the same year, described as a 'Unique opportunity of visiting the Holy Land' would be led by 'His Grace, the Archbishop of Cashel'. This tour, aboard the ship *Lancastria* would also be calling at Mediterranean ports.[20]

The attitude to international travel conveyed in this type of communication is interesting: the enjoyable aspects are absent and the adventurous aspects are played down. Instead, the emphasis is on comfort, the familiarity of well-known devotions and appropriate authorization and guidance. Erik Cohen's anthropological perspective on travel, explained here by Catherine Bell, is relevant in this regard:

> In a traditional society, one could journey in either of two directions: towards the sacred center that orders the known cosmos or in the opposite direction, towards the 'other', beyond the periphery of the ordered world, where chaos both threatens and beckons. The first sort of journey was legitimate and laudable; the second was suspect and heretical.[21]

The marked effort to reduce the sense of 'otherness' in the pilgrims' view of a proposed journey may be linked to the values outlined above. For most Limerick people in the 1930s, travel abroad was, by any standards, 'beyond the periphery' of their everyday world. In writing about proposed trips journalists and promoters alike tried to introduce a sense of order and predictability into the imagined experience of international pilgrimages, and to minimize their 'suspect' aspects. Cohen's ideas regarding what Bell calls 'the modern world', of which Limerick city was definitely a part in the early twentieth century, are also relevant here. According to him, this has 'no single compelling sacred center since centers of all sorts have multiplied. This 'geographical denouement of the world' can turn multiple places into 'attractions' whose mere difference from one's own appears to hold out the possibility of experiencing a fresh 'authenticity'".[22] That sense of difference or the anticipation of a 'fresh authenticity' is, perhaps, very slightly hinted at in the discourse concerning pilgimages in the 1930s. One wonders what images would be called up in readers' minds by the idea of 'a night in London' or 'a night in Paris' or 'calling at Mediterranean ports'. However the notion of adventure or excitement is denied rather than celebrated, while enjoyment, as stated above, is simply not in the terms of reference at all.

This cautious approach to international pilgrimage travel is of course rooted in the need to see pilgrimages as devotional exercises rather than as holidays. However, it is also important to remember that in Limerick city in the early to mid-twentieth century, foreign travel of any kind was out of the question for most people. In 1935, on what could be seen as the main Limerick pilgrimage, approximately 100 city people travelled to Lourdes out of a population of approximately 41,000.[23] A farewell photograph for the same Maria Assumpta pilgrimage taken after the departure ceremony in St John's Cathedral in 1954 shows approximately 130–40 people, while about forty invalids (not shown in the photograph) were also to travel. While this photograph may include some country participants, it could also show a small increase in the number going from Limerick city. But the proportion of pilgrims – relative to the then population of approximately 50,000 – is still very small.[24] On this occasion, the *Limerick Leader* described 'Scenes of joy and animation ... at the Limerick Railway Station this afternoon when over 500 pilgrims travelling overland on the Limerick

Maria Assumpta pilgrimage were given a hearty send off'. Adding to these the forty or so invalids going by air, and Dr O'Neill's group (numbered at about forty-five), this gives a total of 585 people. In July 1955, the Limerick Diocesan quarterly, *Our Catholic Life* (started in 1954 and first named *Catholic Life*) gives the population of the Diocese as 117,000.[25] This would indicate 0.5 per cent as the proportion of Catholics in the Limerick Diocese going on the pilgrimage.

In 1956, preparations began for the pilgrimage in 1958, which would be the Centenary of the apparition at Lourdes. *Our Catholic Life* announced that:

> In St. John's Cathedral a special Savings Fund for intended pilgrims has been started. Anyone wishing to join may do so by handing in their names at the Sacristy at the following times: –
> Sundays – after 12 o'clock Mass
> Tuesdays – after Confraternity 8.45 p.m.
> Saturdays – 3.30–4 p.m.
> Minimum weekly subscription is 5/–.
> Members may withdraw money by simply giving notice.[26]

By October of the same year, a similar fund had been started in St Munchin's Parish.[27] However this savings scheme, despite its accessibility and convenience, did not increase the numbers going to Lourdes in 1958, which were reported as 'Upwards of 400' – but this number included the sixty-five invalids going from Shannon Airport.[28] A draw for ten free invalid places, funded by the members of the four divisions of the Archconfraternity of the Holy Family, boosted the number of invalids in this year.[29] Meanwhile an 'Associate Membership' was made available to people staying at home. According to the *Limerick Leader*, this would 'enable those who cannot go to Lourdes to be united in spirit with the pilgrims during their stay in Lourdes'.[30] Associate members were invited to submit petitions which would be deposited at the shrine. They were also asked 'to attend Mass and receive Holy Communion each day if possible during the time of the pilgrimage. They are asked also to recite one decade of the Rosary for the general intentions of the pilgrimage'.[31] The newspaper also gave a list of invocations to be said by Associate Members which included prayers to the Sacred Heart, Our Lady and St Bernadette.[32]

The inaccessibility of international pilgrimages for most Catholics is borne out by the people interviewed for this project, who consistently identified these types of pilgrimage with people who had the money to go on them:

> Some of our neighbours now went to Lourdes but they would be people that would be pretty well-off in our eyes … another pilgrimage that people went on, again they would be people that would be wealthy enough to go, would be to Fatima.[33]

Another interviewee makes the distinction between pilgrimages in general and a trip organized for a special event, such as the Holy Year in Rome in 1950. According to her 'a lot' of people went to Rome at this time,[34] and Louise Fuller's account bears this out:

> On 28 April 1950, the first national pilgrimage to Rome in honour of the Holy Year, was led by the Archbishop of Armagh and Primate of All Ireland, Most

Rev. Dr. D'Alton. It numbered 1,000 people. Similar numbers were recorded at the second national pilgrimage to Rome, led by Archbishop McQuaid on 16 October. A further pilgrimage to Rome on 1 October had recorded over 2,000 pilgrims.[35]

This gives a total of approximately 4,000 pilgrims from all over Ireland during the Holy Year, and it may be the case that for at least some of these, the trip was a once-in-a-lifetime experience.[36] For people who were able to go to Rome more often, the trip was taken in a different context:

> well the Holy Year now 'twould be kind of a pilgrimage alright, but before that it wouldn't be a pilgrimage going to Rome. It would be if you were ... people that were comfortably off ... I had relatives in Garryowen now, my mother's people on her mother's side were pig buyers and they were ... they went to Rome – they weren't married, two sisters – and they went to Rome. They were in Rome about seven or eight times I think.[37]

Going to Rome is clearly seen as a form of holidaying here, though the point is made that these two sisters 'were very religious actually and they'd go to Rome'.[38]

It is interesting to imagine these two sisters, who were both affluent and carefree enough to travel to Rome 'seven or eight times'. The implication is that Rome was their favourite holiday destination, but also a place of pilgrimage because they were 'very religious'. It may also be that a pilgrimage is regarded as something that is carried out again and again: in this way, Rome could only be a pilgrimage destination for those who had the money to go there regularly. The attraction of foreign travel, for people with the means and the freedom to go, is clear here, but it is important to note also the 'cultural anchor' provided by the religious context of the trip. In Cohen's terms, whether we see Limerick at this time as a traditional community for whom the 'suspect and heretical' aspects of travel away from the centre had to be reduced, or as a modern community seeking a 'fresh authenticity' (and perhaps we need to see it in both of these ways) for affluent Catholics in Limerick at this period the pilgrimage context was a significant aspect of international travel.

Knock

The shrine at Knock, County Mayo, was the site of an apparition on 21 August 1879. According to the twenty or so people who saw it, the apparition was comprised of three figures, that of Mary, St Joseph and St John the Evangelist, with an altar and a lamb also in view.[39] By request of the local clergy, the event was not reported in the newspapers until January 1880, but in spite of this, according to one source, in the days and weeks immediately after the apparition,

> pilgrims were coming in greater crowds every day to throng Knock church and its surroundings. Invalids too were brought there, and many miraculous cures were being claimed. As it was said that the cement from the apparition gable had wonderful powers, and as many cures were claimed through its use, the cement itself was eagerly sought by all pilgrims. Soon the gable wall was so stripped that

it was in danger of collapsing, and the parish priest was obliged to put a protective covering of boards on the whole lower portion of the gable to prevent further damage to the building.[40]

From early 1880, the newspapers reported huge crowds converging on Knock, and taking bits of cement out of the wall, as well as standing or kneeling while praying with rosary beads, reading out of prayer books or, in an echo of vernacular devotion, doing 'the rounds' of the chapel, using their rosary beads to pray at the same time.[41] In his history of the shrine at Knock, Eugene Hynes places great emphasis on the connection between the already existing popular tradition in the area regarding holy places and the devotion which grew up around Knock.[42] He also notes the parish priest's strong belief in the powers of the cement from the apparition gable, something Hynes regards as 'close to the older traditions that held as sacred, for example, clay from particular holy sites (such as some priests' graves and 'caves' at specific holy wells such as Ardmore), rather than to a devotionally revolutionised spirituality'.[43] This points up, again, the importance of remembering that some clergy held beliefs very similar if not identical to those held in vernacular tradition.

A sense of the shrine's history during this period is conveyed by Kathleen B who describes a visit to Knock made by her family in the late 1800s. Speaking about her grandmother, she says,

> her father was a pig-buyer and they'd go up to Claremorris ... that time ... doing pig-buying ... And she said that after the apparition her father brought herself and her brother, she was very young, and her mother, up to Claremorris, and that the people were walking from Claremorris out to Knock and that they were lining – they – some of them came the night before and slept in the hedge, in the ditches ... People had great devotion, years ago.[44]

This interviewee was born in 1923, so her grandmother may have been born in the 1870s or at the latest, in the early 1880s. Given that she was 'only about four',[45] this would place the date of this visit in the early to mid-1880s, perhaps sometime in the first few years after the apparition.

Knock may be categorized, in the Turners' terms, as a Post-Tridentine place of pilgrimage. We will see how this sense of modernity is embodied in interviewees' concepts of Knock. Organized excursions to the shrine from other parts of the country began to develop very quickly after the apparition date. Significantly, the first of these, in March 1880, consisted of a pilgrimage of fifty people from the Archconfraternity of the Holy Family (or Redemptorist Confraternity) in Limerick. Later in 1880, the Archconfraternity organized a pilgrimage of 500 of their members.[46] Pilgrimages in this organized form were well-established by the early twentieth century and continued as the twentieth century progressed. In 1940, for instance, about 450 people travelled to Knock from Abbeyfeale and other parts of County Limerick hearing Mass in Limerick city on the way.[47] Many Limerick city interviewees, however, associated their own personal, as well as others', experiences of Knock with the post-War decades. The popularity of Knock during this period is clear from Louise Fuller's account, which tells us that 'A figure of almost 8,000 people from all over Ireland was recorded as having taken part in a pilgrimage to Knock on 6 August, 1950'.[48] The sense of the importance of transporting large crowds, and the modern context that this gives the pilgimage is well conveyed by one interviewee:

> When I think back in history I'm always inclined to think – I think before the war and after the war … It had a massive impact on everyone's lives but … they were the boom years for Knock. I remember seeing – there could be anything from six or seven trains a day passing up by Long Pavement … after the war … Huge big long trains – some of them would originate down in Tralee … or Cork or Caherciveen … or somewhere like that. And they'd all pass through Limerick. And … consequently Claremorris was, probably – on a Sunday – was certainly the busiest railway station in Ireland! … You had trains all over the place up there.[49]

Another interviewee described Claremorris station as 'Teeming!' with pilgrims on a Sunday.[50] The sense of the 1950s as an important decade for Knock is borne out by the fact that interviewees born in the 1920s spoke about going there after marriage: 'I was married, well married when I went to Knock, yea. And then it would have been with the local church. You know, organized by the local church'.[51] Joseph L, born in 1925, said 'We did go a few times. But that was when we were grown up … I'd say we would have been working'.[52] Kathleen B, born in 1923, said that she would go to Knock as part of a group: 'Always! … the Dominicans used run a pilgrimage – I go to Knock once a year. Now, I go with the St. Joseph's Young Priests' (Society) – they get up a bus'.[53] Grace K, born in 1928, used to go to Knock with her parents: her father would drive in earlier years, and later they would go on the train. She describes it as '… a great day out! … because you met all the people from Limerick – with 'Oh hello, how are you?' … and they'd all be asking you 'how's Mary Jane?' and 'How's Tom?' … and you know'.[54] A younger interviewee, Noreen P, who was born in the 1940s, remembers being brought to Knock as a child: 'in our case, on our street where I lived, eight houses, and there was a lot of older people, we were the only large family, we had six'.[55] Noreen's family and neighbours would travel to Knock once a year, as a street. She remembers one aunt, in particular, encouraging the trip: 'My aunt Aggie, she was really great for the Church, moreso than … the rest of us – she was very on to all of us going, and the neighbours would go as well … Mostly women … on that trip, the women from next door and up the road from me … and my aunt, and cousins, the girls, yea. I don't remember lads going at all'.[56] Noreen also describes the day itself:

> So all I remember very well is that, we prepared the day before, it was always on a Sunday we went, once a year … But we prepared the night before because we had to be up at six o'clock. I think the train went at around seven, so we'd to walk up, naturally, to the railway station. And it was a whole day out![57]

Noreen describes how the pilgrims, mostly women, would spend the train journey saying 'rosaries going and rosaries coming back'.[58] Grace K also mentions this aspect: 'three rosaries going and three coming back … that was the rule'.[59] Noreen notes how the shrine has changed over the years:

Of course Knock was very primitive then, there were only little huts and it was a real country, bleak place ... there was no basilica then, it was just the bare semblance ... a very small old church ... Whereas I've been there now, the last time I was there was actually last year – last year or the year before. And it's just so terribly commercialized now. And it's hard to home in on the reason you are there, unless you have it inside of you, in your heart.[60]

For this interviewee, the development of Knock as a pilgrimage destination has made it harder to access the spriritual aspects of the visit there. Both she and Kathleen B, in the account given to her by her grandmother of the early years of the shrine, make the connection between a strong sense of devotion and spirituality and a lack of facilities in and around the shrine itself.

With all pilgrimages, the element of choice mentioned above is of great importance. The choice to go or not to go could be made at the level of the family or at individual level. Máirín M, born in 1942 is talking about her childhood when she says: 'We would go to Knock, not often now, my mother wouldn't ever have been a great fan of Knock'.[61] Máirín is talking here about a family pilgrimage to Knock, which may have been the custom for households with children in the 1940s and early 1950s. Timmy G's account stresses his experience of going up as a family group, and not as part of an organized trip:

I like to go up on my own, and do my own thing ... pay my own respects ... I don't like being forced into doing something that I don't like, you know. I mean, if you're going up on a bus, they're saying rosaries going up on the bus and everything ... no, I like to do my own thing, you know, pray in my own way.[62]

This is a somewhat different perspective to the others, and it shows how pilgrimage is – or can be – public and communal or private and individual. These experiences of Knock seem to relate to a later period than that studied, as the family group included Timmy's niece and her husband, who would drive him and his mother and sister there. This attitude to pilgrimage might seem at odds with this interviewee's attachment to the highly organized Confraternity described in Chapter 3, however it is important to remember that close relatives were a constant, and crucial, part of that experience too.

It is interesting to note that despite the association of Knock with modernity, especially in terms of transport, the information available regarding the shrine's earlier history indicates that the format taken by the Knock pilgrimage was very similar to that used to visit older sites such as holy wells on particular saints' days in popular tradition: this is vividly conveyed in Kathleen B's evidence above regarding her grandmother's experience of seeing people walking long distances to the shrine and in the early accounts, also noted above, of people doing 'the rounds' of the chapel. In the early 1880s, Knock was transformed from a relatively local, traditional site of devotion to an officially recognized modern pilgrimage drawing large crowds on buses and trains: however the continuity of devotion and belief in the power of the physical place itself shown by interviewees demonstrates the way in which unofficial and official devotional concepts merged, almost seamlessly in some cases, during this period in Ireland.

Croagh Patrick

The idea of going on a pilgrimage as a young adult, or with a group of friends, rather than with parents or other older relatives, seems to have been more established in the case of Croagh Patrick. This pilgrimage would be classified by the Turners as a Christian pilgrimage overlaid on an older religious system, and Máire MacNeill's treatment of the site in the context of the festival of *Lughnasa* bears this out.[63] MacNeill's account places the association of the mountain then known as *Cruachán Aigle* with Saint Patrick as far back as the seventh century. She traces the history of the pilgrimage, along with the folklore surrounding it through the centuries following, to the modern period: 'In the travel books and discourses on manners and customs which were much read in the late eighteenth and early nineteenth centuries there are many references to the Croagh Patrick pilgrimage, all testifying to its popularity and specifying that thousands of pilgrims visited the mountain each year.'[64] MacNeill also describes the decline of the pilgrimage towards the end of the nineteenth century when, in 1883, the Archbishop of Tuam, Dr McEvilly, tried to 'transfer the penitential exercises from the mountain-top to a chapel at its base.'[65] Harry Hughes's description of the Church-sponsored revival of the tradition gives an interesting view of the cultural atmosphere in some Catholic quarters at the beginning of the twentieth century:

> Dr. John Healy became Archbishop of Tuam on 17 March 1903. Fr. McDonald, Administrator in Westport, sought permission from Tuam to revive the celebration of Mass on the summit of Croagh Patrick. He could hardly have had a better ally, as Dr. Healy had an intense interest in antiquarian subjects. He wrote 'The Life and Writings of Saint Patrick'. Fr. McDonald having obtained permission set about with great zeal, organising Mass for 16 August 1903. Special trains were organized by the Midland Great Western Railway Company for pilgrims.[66]

During the sermon he gave at that first Mass, Fr McDonald spoke about how Dr Healy (who could not be there himself on that day) was determined to 'make this holy mountain, henceforth a place of national pilgrimage'[67] thus giving official ecclesiastical approval to a tradition that had been in existence for centuries. By August 1904, Dr Healy had sanctioned the building of a church at the summit of Croagh Patrick – the lack of one may have been a factor in Dr McEvilly's attempts to transfer devotions to the foot of the mountain some twenty years earlier. Hughes's account of the occasion of the first Mass in the new church, on Sunday 30 July 1905, is, again, eloquent in its evocation of the particular mixture of cultural forces at work in Ireland during this period:

> The now usual arrangements with the railway companies ensured a huge crowd, estimated at 10,000 pilgrims. Fr. McDonald celebrated the first sacrifice of the Mass at 12 a.m. on the altar presented by the Convent of Mercy, Westport, and positioned at the front door with over 20 priests in attendance ... The Westport brass band played a number of airs before the dedication ceremony.[68]

Máire MacNeill, writing in the 1950s, has the following to say: 'Now in the middle of the twentieth century thousands attend it, special trains are run for it from Dublin and other Irish cities, photographs and descriptions appear each year in the newspapers. Although it draws its main support from Connacht and the hierarchy of the province of Tuam, it is assuming the character of a national devotion.[69] Louise Fuller's account gives an estimate of 100,000 as the number of people who participated in the Croagh Patrick 'Holy Year' pilgrimage on 30 July, 1950: the estimated figure for 1951 was 75,000, and for 1953, 70,000. In 1961, the number of participants was estimated to be around 75,000.[70]

For people in Limerick city who had reached their teens in the 1940s, Croagh Patrick was a popular pilgrimage destination in a way that it hadn't been for their parents' generation, though as with other pilgrimages, money was often a factor in the decision to make the trip. Eileen L says:

> We were a big family and money wouldn't have – money would have been a little bit scarce now, for pilgrimages and journeying to and forth and that … But of course when we came into our late teens we were able to make out for ourselves and Croagh Patrick was our destination or place of pilgrimage. Some people did venture as far as Lough Derg, but Croagh Patrick was really the only place of pilgrimage to which we went, our crowd, our contemporaries I mean.[71]

Noreen P, whose experience of Knock was dominated by a family and neighbourhood context spoke rather differently about Croagh Patrick:

> I was about fourteen, fifteen, we took the trip to – first and only one – Croagh Patrick … 'Twas a great thing to go then. And … we went by train there as well and I vividly remember – we must have been about fourteen because … one or two had cigarettes and all I remember was taking a pull and coughing all over the place![72]

The early morning start was also a feature of the trip to Croagh Patrick: an advertisement for a trip to be held on 28 July 1935, stated that the bus would be leaving Limerick at 4.45 a.m., and arriving in Westport at 9.00 a.m.[73] This would allow time to get to the mountain itself, and time to climb to the summit before Mass at noon. The time given for arriving back in Limerick that evening, 6.00 p.m., seems to allow for a very speedy descent of the mountain, though the arrival time may not have been strictly adhered to. The departure time given for a train trip to Croagh Patrick in 1930 is 5.20 a.m., though this did not necessarily mean an extra half-hour in bed, as a small notice in the *Limerick Leader* informed readers that 'Arrangements have been made to have Mass celebrated at 3.30 a.m. on Sunday morning next in the Augustinian Church Limerick for the convenience of Limerick pilgrims to Croagh Patrick. The train leaves Limerick at 5.20 a.m.'[74] In 1940, the train was still leaving at 5.20 a.m., but the early Mass was now at 3.00 a.m.[75] As the Augustinian Church is less than ten minutes' walk from the railway station, this would imply that the pilgrims who attended early Mass would have breakfast after Mass, as they would have fasted from midnight before going to Mass anyway. The idea that one would go to Mass before leaving for a pilgrimage which itself included the celebration of another Mass on the same day is interesting and is perhaps related to an attitude to travel itself, including pilgrimage. One interviewee says:

> Another part of our family ritual was that we never went anywhere – of impor-
> tance – a journey or a holiday, without going to Mass in the mornings first …
> Saturday was usually the day for taking off on our holidays in the boat and … that
> meant that we were in at seven o'clock Mass that morning, back out again and back
> in to the Shannon Rowing Club to take off for the midlands in the boat.[76]

Another interviewee makes the same observation:

> There'd never be a big thing taking place unless there was Mass beforehand, you
> know. If they were going to a match now, they'd go to Mass … they'd go to Mass
> at six o'clock in the morning, you know the Redemptorists would have it … or if
> they were going to Knock or someplace like that. You see … 'twas all devotion.[77]

Unlike Knock, which for some interviewees became a yearly pilgrimage, Croagh
Patrick seemed to be a trip which might be taken once or just a few times. The fact
that many interviewees seemed to have gone there in their teenage years could be to
do with the physical exertion needed to carry out the pilgrimage, which apart from
a bus or train journey involving around ten hours' travel, also necessitated climbing
the mountain itself, a steep, difficult and potentially dangerous slope, unsuitable for
children and older people. Máire MacNeill, speaking about the *Lughnasa* festival in
general makes the following point:

> It was given a special gaiety by the fact that the situation of many of the assembly-
> places put it outside the power of the weaker members of the community to be
> present, and so the aged, the very young and the feeble in health could not attend.
> The festival was enjoyed most by the young, vigorous and high-spirited, by those
> for whom life seemed about to offer its most fruitful joys.[78]

Something of this sense of exhilaration enjoyed by young people going to Croagh
Patrick, as well as the atmosphere and social context of the trip is eloquently conveyed
in this account from Paddy Mulcahy:

> The annual pilgrimage to Croagh Patrick on the last Sunday of July was something
> that we took part in once we were in our late teens. Young men and women left
> Limerick late Saturday night and travelled by train to Westport, by bus to Murrisk
> by foot (and some barefoot) to the top of the holy mountain and back. We soaked
> our feet in the cool mountain stream at the foot of the mountain after the treach-
> erous descent. We breakfasted in Westport and had great communal singing
> sessions, maintained by the euphoria of sleeplessness, while we waited for the
> train home. We got home in the afternoon. We always promised each other that
> we would go dancing that night. We always slept exhausted through it.[79]

As can be seen from the above, the climb was the main activity carried out in Croagh
Patrick itself, and some pilgrims, though not all, did this in bare feet. Again, the
element of choice is significant here: the people who chose to climb in bare feet did not
do it every time and the feeling seems to have been that once the barefoot climb had
been done once, or a few times, that there was no need to keep doing it every time.[80]

The Dublin Eucharistic Congress, 1932

One of the most significant pilgrimage events in the Irish Catholic church in the post-independence period does not fit exactly into any of the Turners' categories, although it is probably closest to the post-Tridentine or modern pilgrimage in many of its aspects: this was the Eucharistic Congress held in Dublin in June 1932. The Eucharistic Congress was a week-long devotional gathering, dedicated to one of the most central beliefs of the Catholic Church – the doctrine of the Eucharist. This doctrine holds that through the commemoration of Christ's Last Supper, the act of Consecration of the bread and wine performed as part of Mass brings about the actual (and not just the symbolic) presence of Christ to those who receive Communion.[81] The Eucharistic movement had begun in France in 1881, and its aim was to promote more frequent communion along with First Communion for children. Since this time Eucharistic Congresses have been held every four years in various countries and are an important part of the acknowledgment and the celebration of this central mystery of the Catholic religion, although the concept of the Eucharist and of its place in the Catholic faith has now broadened somewhat.[82]

In 1932, the event was held over the week of 21–26 June in various parts of Dublin city and was attended by the Papal Legate, Cardinal Lorenzo Lauri, on behalf of Pope Pius XI. The week opened with a Mass in Dublin's Pro-Cathedral, celebrated by the Archbishop of Dublin, and attended by cardinals and bishops from all over the world. Other activities included Eucharistic processions, devotions such as Benediction and recitation of the rosary. The celebration culminated in an open-air Mass in the Phoenix Park on 26 June, which included a message broadcast from Pope Pius XI in Rome and the singing of César Franck's 'Panis Angelicus' by the well-known tenor John McCormack.[83]

The process by which Dublin was chosen as the host city for this event must have involved some significant lobbying in official ecclesiastical circles in the years leading up to the event. However, it must also be noted that there was a high level of awareness among people in Ireland generally of the efforts to bring the Congress to Dublin. As early as the autumn of 1927 – some five years before the event – the popular religious magazine, *The Irish Messenger of the Sacred Heart*, was able to report that:

> During the last few months we have given the names of some thirty Public Bodies, including City Corporations, Town Commissioners, County Councils and Urban District Councils, who have passed Resolutions of approval of the project and promised their support.[84]

The writer goes on to state that in this particular month, according to 'the Dublin and provincial press' the following bodies had pledged their support: Kerry, Kilkenny and Meath County Councils; the Town Commissioners of Bandon, Edenderry and Newcastle West; and the Urban District Councils of Arklow, Longford, Templemore and Enniscorthy. It is noteworthy that these resolutions were not confined to public bodies in Dublin or its surrounding counties. Many of the resolutions of support cite the religious significance of the year 1932 for Ireland. The statement from New Ross

(County Wexford) UDC, quoted in the August edition of the magazine, is particularly eloquent on this point, stating that 1932 will be,

> the fifteenth centenary of the coming of St. Patrick to our country. In what more fitting manner can the Irish people thank the Giver of all good gifts for the priceless gift of Faith, with all it has meant and means for the Irish people, than by a national act of homage to His Divine Son in the Sacrament of the Most Holy Eucharist? Such a public act of worship is, without doubt, calculated to bring down from Heaven the choicest blessings on our beloved country and its people.[85]

This strongly stated and widespread ambition to host a religious event on a large scale may have underpinned other events occurring between this time and the Congress itself. In 1928, in Limerick, for instance, the popular men's devotional organization, the Archconfraternity of the Holy Family based in the Redemptorist Church, celebrated sixty years in the city, with extensive street decorations, processions, devotions and Masses (see Chapter 7). In the following year in Ireland generally, and especially in the cities of Dublin and Cork, the centenary of Catholic Emancipation was celebrated in much the same way: Gillian McIntosh has characterized this as a useful preparation for the 1932 event.[86]

It should be clear from the above that although the Congress was to be held in Dublin and was thus viewed as an event that people would travel to attend, it was also seen as something which would be celebrated in every other part of the country as well. The custom of decorating houses and streets was one of the ways in which people who didn't travel to Dublin participated in the Congress. In Limerick, in the weeks leading up to the event, the city Development Association was encouraging house-holders to decorate their homes, with the *Limerick Leader* reporting at the beginning of June that the Mayor, Alderman P. J. Donnellan was issuing an appeal,

> to the citizens to display flags and bunting and in other ways to assist in giving Erin's oldest Chartered City a festive appearance … it will be seen that Limerick's good name as a Catholic city will be worthily maintained during Congress Week.[87]

Flags and bunting suitable for this purpose were advertised by large drapery shops such as Cannock's, McBirney's and Todd's, with the latter also offering, as a souvenir of the Congress a 'Lovely Irish linen damask table cloth and napkins' with the design including 'a Celtic crest on which the Ardagh Chalice rests, around which are the words – "Souvenir, Eucharistic Congress Dublin 1932"'.[88] A big display advertisement headed 'The Eucharistic Congress Calling' in the same newspaper on 4 June urges people to ensure perfect reception by having their radios tested, or, if necessary, a new one installed by a company called The Scientific Radio Service based in Shannon Street.[89] The discourse around the event assumes from the start that not everybody would travel to Dublin, and the emphasis, in some instances, on celebrating and participating at home is clear. Prayer, and especially the recitation of the 'Congress Prayer' also played a part in this.[90]

However, it was also assumed that many people from all over the country would travel to Dublin for the Congress or for some of the events of the week-long celebration. For those unable to travel for the full event, a day trip by train was organized for the first day of the Congress, 19 June, to 'afford those who travel a fine opportunity of seeing the Dublin decorations for the Eucharistic Congress'. The train would depart Limerick at 9.15 a.m., and leave Dublin that night at 8.00 p.m. Potential passengers were informed that 'it is sure to be a most agreeable and interesting trip, as nothing is being left undone to provide for the comfort and convenience of all'.[91] As the Congress drew nearer, the drapery houses' advertisements included a note that they would be closing their establishments on Monday 27 June 'to facilitate our assistants attending the Eucharistic Congress'.[92] The question of how people travelled to the event is of interest, not just in terms of the mode of transport, but also the question of whether they went as individuals or in small family groups, or as part of an organized contingent. As with all forms of travel, including pilgrimages, ecomonic circumstances played a part in the decision to travel in the first place, the mode of transport and the experience itself. The day trip undertaken by the Mayor and members of the city council on 26 June, to attend the Pontifical High Mass in the Phoenix Park and outlined beforehand in the *Limerick Leader* reflects their high status in the city community:

> It is expected that all the members of the Municipal Council will travel to the Metropolis for the Eucharistic Congress celebrations. The Mayor (Ald. P.J. Donnellan) has reserved a coach for the Council on the special excursion train leaving the city at 4.50 on Sunday morning, 26th inst. On the arrival of the train at Kingsbridge the Mayor will entertain his colleagues at breakfast and on the return journey supper will be served on the train. For the Pontifical High Mass in the Phoenix Park the Corporation have been allotted seats in section 3, letter C.[93]

For others travelling by public transport, the Irish Omnibus Company was advertising a range of special buses at a return fare of 15s., which would give people the option of travelling to Dublin throughout Saturday and also on Sunday morning, coming home on Sunday night. This, presumably, was designed to faciliate their attendance at the Pontifical High Mass in the Phoenix Park on Sunday 26 June, and was aimed at people who wished to travel individually or in small groups with friends and family.[94] However, many opted to travel as members of religious organizations: in the accounts after the event the *Limerick Leader* noted that four special trains had departed the city in the early hours of Sunday, bringing thousands of men from the Redemptorist Archconfraternity along with women from the parish confraternities of St John's, St Michael's and St Mary's.[95] Six hundred members of the Boys' Confraternity (also based in the Redemptorist Church) had attended a children's Mass at the Congress on Saturday 25 June. According to the *Limerick Leader*, the participants – all boys as far as the Limerick contingent was concerned, though it may have been the case that girls from other areas were included in this event – 'got refreshments after Mass' and were then 'conducted on a sight-seeing trip'. They travelled home that night.[96] One hundred and twenty members of the Catholic Boy Scouts had already travelled from Limerick on Saturday 18 June, as part of a group of 1,000 scouts from all over the country who would be camping in Terenure College and would act as stewards during the ceremonies.[97] Overall, the attendance from Limerick – though it is not clear if this figure includes those travelling from rural areas of County Limerick – was estimated at approximately 8,000 – 5,000 men and 3,000 women. On Wednesday 29 June, in a piece entitled 'Limerick's Noble Part' the *Limerick Leader* stated that: 'It is computed that about 8,000 Limerick men and women were present at the Pontifical High Mass and marched in the procession'.[98] It is probable that people travelling to Dublin as individuals or in small groups joined the rest of the Limerick contingent for the ceremonies, where possible. Most of the people interviewed for this research were too young to have travelled to the Congress, but some remembered hearing about it from older members of their families. Eileen L remembered her father and her older brother going. Despite their membership of the Archconfraternity, they seem to have travelled together to the event in the Phoenix Park, and not with the Archconfraternity, as they would have gone separately in the latter case, her brother, aged about fourteen at the time, going to the children's Mass with the Boys' Confraternity, and her father to the Phoenix Park Mass with the men's division. Eileen remembers it as 'a huge event, with huge crowds'. According to her account, her father held onto her brother constantly 'in case he'd lose him'.[99] Grace K also remembers hearing her parents – who drove to Dublin for the occasion – talking about the Congress while she was growing up.

> My parents went! … They did, yes, and we heard all about it! And … where John McCormack sang … and this was marvellous. They were so proud of this, you know.

According to her, they talked about it for ' Oh *years* afterwards, you know'.[100]

For the many people who couldn't travel to Dublin, the radio played an important role in bringing the Congress proceedings to them. The local press were anxious to assure readers that this did not in any way diminish the faith or fervour of those who were not physically present at the ceremonies:

> Hundreds of citizens who were unable to travel to Dublin listened to the ceremonies over the ether. In many parts of the city touching scenes were witnessed as people 'listening in' fell on their knees during the Consecration of the Mass and later when the Legate gave the Benediction. The people also answered the responses to the Rosary and took part in the singing of hymns.[101]

In the same issue of the paper the festive atmosphere in the city was also described: 'All the streets, lanes and alleyways were festooned with flags, bunting, bannerettes and streamers. At different points altars and grottoes were erected, displaying remarkable taste on the part of the people'.[102] The sense of a general celebration for those at home was reinforced by the closure of businesses on Monday 27 June – this was partly due to a decision by the 'Monster Houses' or big drapery firms in the city to faciliate employees travelling to Dublin in their return from the events. However, with other businesses in the city also closing, along with shops in county towns such as Rathkeale, it was, by the week beforehand, being characterized as 'a general holiday', indicating that the Congress was just as important an occasion for those not travelling as for those who were.[103]

One of the most striking aspects of the Dublin Eucharistic Congress is the extent to which it seemed to permeate every corner of popular culture in Ireland in the weeks before it was held and during the event itself. While this could be said, to some extent, about Catholicism in Ireland generally in the post-independence period, there were still some pockets of life where religion did not, under normal circumstances, intrude in any significant way – the pleasurable river cruises discussed above, for instance, or the culture of the cinema and the dancehall. Although these areas were still present in popular discourse in the summer of 1932, the Congress provided a lot of extra news, with many stories and relevant angles pursued before, during and after the event. The clergy, whether Irish or of other nationalities coming from abroad to attend the Congress is one important thread;[104] the world of shipping is another. The *Limerick Leader* of 18 June describes the arrival of eleven 'liner-hotels' to the river Liffey in Dublin bringing over 8,000 participants to the Congress, while the two Irishmen in America – one of whom was from Limerick – who were running the Emerald Isle Steamship Agency 'which has booked several hundred passengers visiting Ireland for the Eucharistic Congress' were also of interest.[105] Other modes of transport crop up in the coverage as well: the send-off given to the three cyclists from Herbertstown, County Limerick, who 'left on Monday morning in full camping regalia en route for the Congress, making nearly fifty-seven miles on the first day of the journey' was considered newsworthy.[106] For these few weeks in June, the Congress was frequently mentioned by the correspondents from adjacent rural areas in counties Limerick and Clare, in a range of contexts: either because people from the locality were travelling to it, or because the local towns were decorated for the event, or because local devotions were held in honour of it or because the celebrations were broadcast in the area.[107]

The Eucharistic Congress also spilled into other areas of reporting: in a small piece entitled 'Busy Already' on Monday 20 June, the *Limerick Leader* warns its readers about 'criminals who make their money by picking pockets and handbags in shops and crowded places' and says that 'Several ladies had their handbags picked in one of Dublin's largest stores on Friday'. Another piece towards the end of the week on 25 June informs readers that, according to a Press Association message, 5 million pounds will by spent by the pilgrims attending the Congress in Dublin. A small item in the newspaper of 18 June tells the story of Tom Fahey 'a Limerick boy' who stowed away on a passenger ship which had arrived at Cobh from America, and who gave as his reason for stowing away 'that he wanted to get to the Congress. A collection was raised among the passengers for Tom, and he was allowed to land at Cobh to carry out his desire'. Some advertisers took the opportunity to boost their businesses by linking them to the event: the radio company and the drapery shops described above played an obviously important role: the fashion trade hoped to cash in as well, with La Moderne 'French millinery and Gown Specialists' declaring on 25 June that they were 'showing the Last Word in Paris Ensembles' but heading the advertisement: 'For the Congress'.[108]

The Dublin Eucharistic Congress of 1932 was an event of extreme importance in twentieth-century Ireland. Like all pilgrimages it was based on travel for a religious purpose, but unlike other pilgrimages it was a once-off event, and it was not centred on a sacred site or person, nor was it associated with an apparition. Its focus on the Eucharist – rather than on a local saint or shrine – meant that the activities of the Congress were carried out by the highest echelons of the clergy, including the Papal

Legate, Cardinal Lorenzo Lauri, visiting from Rome. The Congress's timing, coming after just ten years of Irish independence, and three years after the centenary of Catholic Emancipation, was an important factor in how its meaning was created and understood by organizers and participants at every level. The sheer size of the Congress was part of its drama, as was the fact that Catholicism – and especially Catholicism in Ireland – was the whole point of it. These two factors taken together made it a powerful assertion of religious identity on a national level, and this permeates the discourse around the event. The assertion of religious identity at a more local level can also be seen in the view of the Congress in Limerick. As noted above, 'Limerick's good name as a Catholic city' was mentioned in connection with the proposed decoration of the city for the event, while the loan of the 'famous Limerick Mitre and Crozier, which date from the time of Cornelius O'Dea, who was Bishop of Limerick in the early fifteenth century' to the National Museum in Dublin for a special exhibition during the Congress was also a source of pride.[109] The participation of Limerick people in the events in Dublin was very important too, as is conveyed by this description of the experience of the men who travelled with the Redemptorist Confraternity to the Phoenix Park for the High Mass on 26 June:

> the position allotted to the Confraternity was one befitting the largest organized body of Catholic lay men in the world. In fact, it may be claimed that Limerick was given a place of honour, for the Papal Legate and all the dignitaries of the Church had to pass through the serried ranks of the Confraternity men to reach the High Altar. It is not an exaggeration or a boast to say that the Limerick Confraternity was very much admired. They presented a striking – a most edifying sight … it was an inspiring manifestation of Limerick's undying loyalty to the Church – of Limerick militant.[110]

The writer also mentioned the participation of the women's parish confraternities, describing the members as 'All that is best in the womanhood of Limerick' and noted that the visit of the six hundred Limerick members of the Boys' Confraternity earlier in the week had gone 'without a hitch'.[111] In his discussion of the Eucharistic Congress in general, Terence Brown has commented that:

> Crowds gathered in such numbers that it is tempting to see in the occasion itself a triumphant demonstration by the Irish Catholic nation in honour of the victories won in the long years of struggle since emancipation had reached a climax in independence.[112]

In a sense, the event could be seen as Irish Catholicism shining a light on itself to demonstrate its power and unity to itself and others – an exercise made all the more eloquent by the increasing availability and use of the contemporary media of print, photography and radio. Looking at the Limerick sources, we can see not just that the Congress experience was a highly memorable, once-in-a lifetime one for those who attended, but also that it served as a way of shining a spotlight on Limerick Catholicism. This was true for everyone who would see the Limerick crowds in their front-row position at the Mass in Dublin, but it was also true for Limerick people themselves – whether they travelled or not. In this sense, the representation and visibility of Limerick Catholicism at the Congress was a crucial part of the overall experience and of the memory-building around the event. This makes it a significantly different kind of pilgrimage from those taken to sites such as Knock and Croagh Patrick.

Pilgrimage travel and the ritual order

Pilgrimages, like other forms of travel, involved some expenditure on fares, food and pilgrimage aids and/or devotional goods bought at the pilgrimage site itself. This meant that pilgrimages were only available to those who had the money to go on them. It also connects pilgrimages with the world of leisure activities, so it is not surprising that a definite sense of choice, regarding where to go and how often, is evident among those who had the resources to go. Leisure travel in general was also developing in Limerick at this period: local newspaper advertisements show that summer day excursions to resorts such as Youghal and Killarney were popular and that, in some cases, leisure outings such as these were organized by religious groups such as the Third Order of St Francis, for their members.[113] These latter outings were not pilgrimages, though they may have had some religious aspects.

In Hervé Varenne's terms, pilgrimages could be seen as part of the 'passionate surplus' of religious life in Limerick in the second quarter of the twentieth century. When we look at how these ritual events were organized and carried out, we can see a cultural creativity similar to that identified by Varenne in Dublin in the 1980s. It is also important, however, to note the specific cultural circumstances in Limerick city during the period studied. As stated above, I think we could regard Limerick at this time as a community with both modern and traditional aspects: indeed much of the cultural 'work' undertaken by Limerick people, in all kinds of capacities, at this time could be seen as an attempt to negotiate these two aspects of life. The effect of modern travel on the traditional community and on concepts of space and continuity within that community has been discussed by Diarmuid Ó Gilláin. He points out that the sense of a continuous and evolving landscape that is experienced when travelling by foot or on horseback is broken by the experience of travelling by train.[114] Thus, the strangeness that Erik Cohen identifies with travel away from the centre is intensified and speeded up by train or bus journeys, while the effect on people of travel on large ships and planes would have been proportionately more dramatic. In Ireland, a relatively small country with an extensive road network and a railway service that had been established in the mid-nineteenth century,[115] it may seem inappropriate to apply these concepts of a traditional community to city-dwellers in the 1940s: yet the emphatic insistence of some interviewees that they had never, or rarely been on pilgrimages, or been able to travel anywhere until they were earning their own money, shows that, for many people, travel was a unusual occurence and was not lightly undertaken. For the more affluent, international pilgrimages were possible: but even then, as we have seen, reassurance and constant mitigation of the strangeness of the experience was a crucial part of the discourse concerning these. This was also true of the 1932 Dublin Eucharistic Congress, perhaps because of the crowds expected and the once-off nature of the event. Almost a month beforehand, in a reassuring piece headed 'The Congress Venue: visit to scene' a 'special representative' of the *Cork Examiner* newspaper reported that:

> To-day I walked from Kingsbridge Station to the Fifteen Acres in the Phoenix Park ... I covered the distance very comfortably in twenty-five minutes, walking at an ordinary brisk pace. This ... should convince everybody who will travel on the special trains ... that there will be the most ample time available for breakfast and for reaching the Park long before the Pontifical High Mass will start.[116]

Pilgrimages to Croagh Patrick were not discussed in such detail, but it is useful, in this context of strangeness, to look at the organization of the Croagh Patrick ritual day in terms of familiarity and strangeness as well. Taking the trip organized in July 1940 as an example, we can see that, in the progress of the day, strange or unusual experiences alternate with familiar and reassuring ones. The strangeness of getting up at 2.00 or 2.30 a.m., which, even in July, can be regarded as the middle of the night, is offset by going to Mass in a familiar city-centre church; getting on the train, the first exciting part of the journey, is followed by social and/or devotional activities on the journey which might include saying the rosary with other pilgrims as the journey progresses, experimenting with cigarettes with one's peers or simply talking and getting to know other pilgrims on the train. Arriving at Croagh Patrick and climbing the Reek, perhaps the most difficult and dangerous part of the day, is followed by the familiar ritual of Mass, a 'fresh authenticity' on the summit; the descent followed by more prayers and possibly singing on the train home.

The Croagh Patrick pilgrimage, despite its extensive ancient credentials, was still a distant, difficult and dangerous trip. Familiar experiences, such as Mass, may have helped to ease the harder aspects of it. Praying and singing on the train is of especial importance given the dramatic break in social and environmental continuity brought about by modern travel.[117] In this case, people who went with friends would reinforce their bonds by this trip, people who travelled on their own would start to build the sense of being part of a congregation from the time of the early Mass in the Augustinian Church, and this would be further built by the train journey and by the subsequent climb and descent.

The feelings that people had after coming home from a pilgrimage are also worth noting. Noreen P, describing how she and her family felt after a trip to Knock, says: 'And ... we loved it really: we had been to Knock and we came back and we had our medals'.[118] The challenging aspects of a pilgrimage could also affect how people felt after it. In speaking about Lough Derg, for instance, Kathleen B describes drinking black tea: 'And 'twas *awful*, now ... Awful. And the hardest part of it though was staying awake all night, for one night ... Up, all night. Praying'.[119] However, she goes on to describe another feeling about it:

> But – I don't know, it did something for you ... You see, you can't ignore those ... practices, you can't say that, you mightn't even think 'What actually did it do for me?' But you could have ... you could be more peaceable in your mind, you could be more ... you ... you wouldn't notice it, but it does something for you.[120]

It might be said that the meanings of pilgrimages seem to cluster in a few different areas. The spiritual sense of achievement described by Kathleen B above may have been important, but harder to articulate for people looking back on their teenage years, some sixty years ago. It is significant that this interviewee, who does describe the spiritual benefits in some detail, is still a regular participant in pilgrimages, to Knock for instance, similar to those she would have made in the mid-twentieth century. However, for most interviewees looking back, the sense of achievement is expressed in more general terms. Pilgrimages were enjoyable days out, with all the usual challenges of travel in general, and maybe some extra ones. However, the ritual order described above shows that on the typical 'day out' to Croagh Patrick, extra meanings were built up around the core pilgrimage experience by bracketing it with activities which reinforced social and congregational relationships already in existence, and which may sometimes have built new relationships on the day itself. This in turn connected the meaning of the event with ordinary life and ongoing social activity, whether this was in a family or a neighbourhood context, or in the context of work. In this sense, pilgrimages, though very much an optional activity connected to travel and the world of leisure, were pursued in a way that knitted them firmly into the social fabric of ordinary life in Limerick city.

It is interesting to look at the ritual order as described above in the context of the Turners' model of pilgrimage which relies heavily on the notion of 'communitas' : in its purest form. This is seen as a cultural phenomenon which is the opposite of social structure, where pilgrims (or participants in other rituals) free themselves from the constraints of the everyday world and move towards a liminal state in which their common humanity can be celebrated.[121] John Eade and Michael J. Sallnow have the following to say regarding the Turners' idea of communitas as a central experience of pilgrimage,

> [it] has been subjected to a number of theoretical critiques ... and has been tested in a variety of field settings ... In none of these cases did the investigator find support for the theory; to the contrary, a recurrent theme throughout the literature is the maintenance and, in many instances, the reinforcement of social boundaries and distinctions in the pilgrimage context, rather than their attenuation or dissolution.[122]

The Turners also described what they saw as a type of 'normative communitas', where the pure, more spontaneous type of communitas is constrained by the organizers of pilgrimage, using rules and specific procedures to capture it and impose structure on it.[123] The most extreme example of this in this study is that of the Eucharistic Congress, perhaps because the scale of the operation demanded it. It certainly seems, for the most part, to have been very successful from the point of view of crowd control.[124] The instructions passed on to the participating Boy Scouts that their membership certificate 'duly stamped for the year 1932 ... must be carried on the person at all times'[125] convey something of this atmosphere, and could be seen to foreshadow the later career of the Garda Commissioner in charge, General Eoin O'Duffy who, after his dismissal by *taoiseach* Éamonn de Valera the following year, was to go on to found the fascist Army Comrades Association or National Guard, also known as the Blueshirts.[126] The pilgrimage practices by Limerick people, perhaps because of their strong connections to official Catholicism, would seem to fit the 'normative communitas' model better than the 'pure communitas' one, though few are as exteme in this regard as the Eucharistic Congress, which was exceptional due to its size and scope. More typical perhaps is the mixture of strangeness (and potential liminality), and structure which can be seen in all of the other pilgrimages described above: it is perhaps most obvious in the context of Croagh Patrick, where an adventurous day away from home much favoured by young adults was given a definite devotional structure through official ritual activities which were regularly spaced, in some cases from as early as 3.00 a.m., throughout the day and the following evening.

Eade and Sallnow themselves suggest that pilgrimage may be seen 'not merely as a field of social relations but also as *a realm of competing discourses* ... it is these varied discourses with their multiple meanings and understandings, brought to the shrine by different categories of pilgrims ... that are constitutive of the cult itself'.[127] This idea could certainly be applied to some of the ethnographic evidence from Limerick as outlined above: the attempts, in the advertising of international pilgrimages, to balance the prospect of luxurious travel with a fitting sense of piety and solemn purpose; the teenagers surreptitiously bringing cigarettes on to the Croagh Patrick train, while others were getting ready to say the rosary and sing hymns.

May Eve

In terms of communal ritual, the custom of building a fire on May Eve is one which was important in the city in the first half of the twentieth century. Críostóir O'Flynn, born in King's Island in 1927, describes in his autobiography how one of his earliest memories is that of seeing 'a huge fire blazing in the middle of the road between our footpath and the opening of the broad lane opposite our house'.[128] O'Flynn gives a very interesting account of the custom, as he experienced it in Limerick in the late 1920s and 1930s, but also discusses it in relation to pre-Christian traditions in Ireland, as described by Geoffrey Keating in the early seventeenth century. He quotes from Douglas Hyde's *A Literary History of Ireland*:

> The Christian priests, apparently unable to abolish these cattle ceremonies, took the harm out of them by transferring them to St. John's Eve, the 24th [*sic*] of June, where they are still observed in most districts of Ireland, and large fires built with bones in them, and occasionally cattle are driven through them or people jump over them ... the bones burnt in the fire are probably a substitute for the bones of the cattle that should have been offered up. Hence the fires are called *tine cnámh* (bone-fire) in Irish, and bone-fire (not bonfire) in English[129]

The connection between the May Eve event in Limerick and the St John's Eve fires elsewhere seems sound, given the early summer/midsummer context and the fact that the activities carried out on these occasions were broadly similar. It is more difficult however to say when and how the changes came about in the date from area to area, in what Hyde describes as a Christianization of the custom. The retention, if this is what it is, of the May Eve date in Limerick city is interesting. Kevin Danaher, in his account of May customs, describes fires held in Dublin on the evening of May Day itself, and though he does not date this, from the description he gives it would appear to have been practised in the eighteenth and early nineteenth centuries. Danaher also mentions 'small fires' being lit 'in the side streets' in Belfast, and says 'In Limerick city May Eve is still "Bonfire night"'.[130] Danaher also notes the survival in some areas of the rural custom of the May fire, particularly in the south-east of the country: 'in County Waterford and in the southern fringes of Counties Kilkenny and Tipperary there are still memories of the cattle being driven through small fires or between pairs of fires, of wisps or coals from the bonfire being used to singe the cows' hair or to bless the fields of growing crops'.[131]

In his discussion of the midsummer fires, held on St John's Eve, however, Danaher notes two differing types of bonfire:

> It is clear that a distinction can be made between two fire traditions. On the one hand a large communal fire lit by the inhabitants of the whole townland or village, or of several townlands or even of the whole parish. Such communal fires were lit, in the past, in places in every county in Ireland. On the other hand there were small fires lit by the members of each household, or on each farm, at which ceremonies … were performed for the benefit of that particular household or farm. These, too, were lit in most parts of Ireland, but were, at least in recent tradition, not as widely known as the large communal fires. There is one small area in the south west … where only the small family fires were lit.[132]

It is interesting that the vestiges of rural tradition mentioned by Danaher concerning the May fire in the south east of the country seem to be composed of the small, ceremonial fires held for protection of the farm and household rather than the communal fire. The city traditions, Limerick included, involved the communal fire, usually organized on a street basis. We shall see, however, that this was not without its protective and/or ceremonial elements.

Preparing and setting the fire

O'Flynn, who lived on King's Island, describes the preparation for the fire as follows:

> For a few weeks before May Eve, the boys of our enclave went from house to house collecting fuel of all kinds for the fire, or money in lieu thereof, singing at every door:
> 'The First of May is a very fine day
> Something for the Bone-fire!
> A piece of stick or a piece of coal,
> A ha'penny will not break your soul.
> Knock at the knocker, ring at the bell –

And give us a penny for singin' so well!'
Every house, even the poorest, contributed something, literally 'a piece of stick or a piece of coal' … From the local shops, and from the fathers who worked in certain factories or other likely sources, timber boxes or other material was collected.[133]

The same process is described by an interviewee from the Killalee area: 'for weeks before, we'd go round the houses and collect pennies and ha'pennies … and we'd collect timber'.[134] O'Flynn suggests that there might have been an 'old superstition' that it was unlucky not to contribute anything to the May fire collection; Danaher confirms this (but in the context of St John's Eve) by saying: 'Often the gatherers went from house to house asking for fuel, and, as it was held to be unlucky as well as mean to refuse, they were given not only inflammable rubbish of which the household was glad to be rid, but also turf and firewood'.[135]

On May Eve itself, accounts from Limerick city show that the fire was lit in the middle of the street: O'Flynn lived in the part of King's Island which was near King John's Castle, and describes it as follows:

Because our bonefire was built in the middle of the street, between the front door of our house and the wide opening of Broad Lane opposite, it was not constructed in the pyramid fashion seen nowadays when … fires are situated on some open space of waste ground. Our bonefire was one of quality rather than quantity but of a goodly size and maintained as the night wore on.[136]

The custom of building the fire in the middle of the street continued in the newer areas of public housing built from the mid-1930s on. Áine R, who lived in St Mary's Park says: 'It would be just outside – in our case 'twas just outside … on the street, the middle of the road, making the point that this was facilitated by the lack of cars on the street at that time'.[137] Anthony F, who lived in the Killalee housing estate also notes that 'on the actual night, we'd have a huge fire in the middle of the road'.[138] He also notes the scarcity of cars, especially during the Second World War, and how this affected the materials collected as well as children's lives in the city: 'There were no tyres, that time, during the War when we grew up. We grew up in a great time – there were no cars, there was no petrol, so we could really roam at will, play football on the streets, play handball up in Mallow Street of a summer's Sunday afternoon'.[139] In discussing the communal midsummer fires, Danaher notes that 'Usually there was a set place in each district for the fire, at a crossroads or street corner, on a commonage, on a limekiln, on a height or in some other "public" place'.[140] It is interesting that O'Flynn, who lived in an older area of the city, describes the fire taking place at a junction of two streets, though this may simply have been a practical measure, given the narrower streets in the older parts of the city.[141]

The bone-fire event

The participation of the adults in the community became important at this stage. O'Flynn's account is the fullest:

> On the night itself the people brought out chairs and stools and placed them in a wide circle round the unlit mound. An elderly woman would then be asked to light the fire. The local musicians, my father with the saxophone, Tom Glynn with the violin, and Granny Duffy with a melodeon, got into gear, and the food and drink, along with our purchased goodies, were distributed generously. Fine individual voices contributed solo songs and other songs were sung in unison by the whole gathering as the fire burned high and bright.[142]

Anthony F says: 'people would have forms and chairs outside and they'd bring out music … and they'd be telling stories and singing songs'.[143]
Áine R says:

> We'd all sit around, bring out our chairs, and as I say if there was a sweet or a drop of lemonade or anything … of course most of the women smoked, so you got a bit of that going on. But always the singing, and maybe the children – the younger children might run around, but of course they'd have to be watched. It was always a good fire somehow. But then the singing – 'twas all the singing. But the minute – maybe half-eleven would come then, you know, the children would be brought in then because 'twas time to – all to go in.[144]

Áine gives the starting time of the fire as around seven in the evening, but also tells how people would come and join the fire at various stages of the night: 'we'd sit around singing and then 'twould get dusk and then later on the boys again coming down from the pubs – there was always a few boys or men coming down from pubs in our area – and they'd come along and they'd come over and join the singsong'.[145]

Anthony F describes the following practice in Killalee where each house had a good-sized garden: 'we'd have gone down and sometimes taken potatoes illicitly from the plots that used to be there. People used to grow their stuff, vegetables and things in the plots. We'd often go down and without their permission take the potatoes. Beautiful potatoes and put them into the fire! And have them … there was great entertainment'.[146] O'Flynn gives an interesting description of the later part of the night:

> When the older people had taken themselves and the small children off to bed, and the chairs and stools were being taken back into the houses, some of the bigger boys would go back down the street, to about the gate of the Protestant churchyard, and then run up to the fire and jump over the now lessening flames. And as the fire went even lower, some of the big girls would dare imitate their brothers.[147]

This was also done in Killalee: 'That was another custom … To jump over the fire, again for luck and to prove, I suppose, that they had a big jump, if 'twas a big fire, and 'twould be a big fire, now, 'twould be a big fire!'[148] O'Flynn, while he goes on to ponder the possible significance in a historical context, describes a similar attitude to the jumping: 'at the time, of course, we thought it was just another dare, and the smaller boys were envious of their big brothers who could do it'.[149] Danaher, describing the practice on St John's Eve, enumerates the beliefs associated with the practice in William Wilde's account, but finishes by saying: 'For the most part, the jumpers were the boys and young men and the jumping merely an exhibition of bravado in which daring leaps drew applause and there was much rivalry among the jumpers'.[150] Danaher also says, however that the beliefs given by Wilde are 'still remembered in tradition'[151] but the 'bravado' aspect is definitely the strongest one in the Limerick May Eve tradition, where it occurred. This is borne out by a St Mary's Park interviewee who, when asked about the practice of jumping said: 'No, no I never saw anyone in any way misbehaving now'.[152]

The *gríosach*

As people left the fire at the end of the night, it was the custom to take a shovelful of cinders, sometimes called by the Irish word *gríosach*, and put it into the fire at home. O'Flynn says:

> When the fire had become a low mound of glowing embers, my mother would say to one of us, 'Go in home and get the shovel'. This was the small fireside shovel for taking out ashes. Like every other mother on the street, my mother took a shovelful of the bonefire's embers and placed them in our own grate, with the comment, 'With the help of God now, we won't be without a fire for the coming year'.[153]

Anthony F describes the custom in Killalee: 'towards the end of the night then they'd take what they would would call was a shovel of *gríosach*, *gríosach* is an Irish word, it's the ashes of the fire and everybody took a shovel of the *gríosach* to bring in and put it in their own fireplace, for luck. That was the tradition'[154] A variation of this custom in the Killalee area is given by Pádraig R: according to him, at the end of the night, young people would bring the *gríosach* around to the various houses, offer it along with a blessing to the people of the house, and get money for it.[155] Danaher mentions this custom, or a version of it, as part of the Midsummer tradition in parts of County Clare, where 'the young people carried charred sticks or dead embers from the fire to the houses of the generous and placed them on the kitchen hearth, while they threw ashes from the fire on the threshold of the house where they had been refused'.[156] In St Mary's Park, the custom was also observed: 'But the last thing the neighbours would do, every one of the neighbours would come out and get a shovel of the old, and bring it in and put it in their hearth'.[157] Áine R explains the reason for the custom: 'That was done to keep away the fairies ... Because they believed that in the month of May that there was somehow a lot of fairy stuff going on. They just believed it, you know'.[158]

It is interesting that neither Áine R nor Críostóir Ó'Flynn, both of whom lived in the King's Island area, use the term *gríosach*. Anthony F and Pádraig R use the term, and the former says 'Oh *gríosach*, we never knew it as anything else only *gríosach*.

"A shovel of the *gríosach*" That was one of the words that has survived'.[159] Frank Prendergast's research has highlighted the large number of Irish words that were still being used in the Killalee area in the 1930s, 1940s and 1950s.[160] Another point worth noting is the fairy belief mentioned in connection with the St Mary's Park estate, most of whose residents had moved out from the Newtown Pery area or other city centre areas in the mid-1930s – and the use of the fire as a protection against the supernatural dangers associated with the time of year. Críostóir O'Flynn, a resident of an older area of the Englishtown doesn't mention this in the context of the May Eve fires, neither do the Killalee interviewees.

The May Eve fires and the changing city

The continuity of the May Eve custom in Limerick city over the centuries is hard to establish, and not, in any case central to this study, though O'Flynn's support of Hyde's insistence on calling the event a 'bone-fire' could be seen as significant in this regard. The term 'bone-fire' was used by one interviewee interviewed for this project, and was also given in quotation marks, as a term used by children, by a writer in the local newspaper in referring to the event in 1935.[161] In the later twentieth century, the May Eve fires in Limerick became strongly associated with the public housing estates, but O'Flynn's evidence clearly demonstrates that the event was a well-established part of life in the older city areas also. The 'Town Topics' columnist in the *Limerick Leader* mentions the custom in passing, while describing the weather in April 1935: 'Now that we are within a few days of May Eve – a fact that we are reminded of by the number of urchins engaged collecting coppers for the "bone-fire" – the sharp "nips" that prevailed for some time past have disappeared'.[162] However, a fatal accident which occurred in the city as a result of the fire gatherings in the same year focused the paper's attention on the fires and provoked a different kind of comment:

> It is to be hoped that the remarks passed by Inspector Lyons at the inquest held in the City on a little child who lost her life following burns received at a bon-fire, will have the desired effect. The Inspector expressed the view – one that is shared generally by the citizens – that parents should not permit children of tender years to congregate about open fires. He also stated that there were too many of these open-air fires in Limerick and in that connection he made an appeal to the citizens to co-operate with the authorities in stamping out that very reprehensible practice.[163]

The writer goes on to describe the custom as it appears to him:

> It cannot be denied that the children of Limerick have a penchant for what they term 'bone-fires'. On May Eve, for instance, there is not a lane or an alleyway in the City that has not got its open-air fire, and the wonder is that burning accidents as a consequence are not more frequent. Now that a responsible official has directed attention to the dangers attendant on these fires, parents and the public in general should discourage them as much as possible.[164]

These two separate comments are interesting in the way in which they associate the fire custom firstly with 'urchins' and later on with the population of 'lanes and alleyways'. This would indicate that it was the city-centre community that, at this stage, were most active in the May Eve fire custom. The city suburbs would at this stage have consisted of large thoroughfares such as the Ennis Road and O'Connell Avenue, or roads regarded as being almost 'out in the country', such as the North and South Circular Roads, and the custom does not appear to have been carried out in these areas, during this period, to the same extent. The comments in the *Limerick Leader* predate the opening of the first public housing estate in Limerick, St Mary's Park, by some months. As new public housing developments were built in the following decades, the custom became firmly established in these, as well as in some of the private estates.[165] By the 1940s, perhaps because of the danger to public safety, and most particularly in the light of the death of a child which had occurred in 1935, the fires had been banned in the city centre. The local authority was vigilant in enforcing this ban as Máirín M's account shows:

> And of course we used have the bonfires as well; May Eve ... and ... that would be
> another kind of event in our lives that you'd be going around to all these bonfires
> because, I lived in the city centre, and we wouldn't be allowed have a bonfire. I
> remember one night we had a bonfire in Gerald Griffin Street, the street behind
> us which was a fine wide street, and the firemen came immediately and put it out,
> because there was too much of a danger. So we'd go off to places like Janesboro and
> that – my parents would bring us around to visit all the different bonfires because
> we couldn't have our own.[166]

The association of the May Eve fires with housing estates, and especially the local authority estates, became stronger in the decades following the mid-century and is still very much in evidence (see Map 1 for the locations of estates in the period studied). The disapproving tone of the *Limerick Leader* writer with regard to the fires in 1935 is understandable given the fatality that occurred that year, but it is also obvious from the writer's more benign attitude to the fires the week beforehand that this accident was an unusual and unexpected one. Máirín M's account from the 1940s shows that despite the ban on city centre fires, the event was still looked forward to and enjoyed by some city centre residents, and Timmy G's evidence bears this out,[167] while accounts from the estates themselves testify to their widespread enjoyment in these areas.

Disapproval of the fires, however, became a feature of the discourse regarding them in the decades following the 1960s, as even the account given to UCD's Department of Irish Folklore in 1973 shows. A questionnaire respondent living in the Rosbrien area on the South side of Limerick city first describes the St John's Eve custom in the Lough Gur area in some detail. His source of information for this is a farmer named Pat Casey, on whose land the famous prehistoric stone circle of Lough Gur is situated, and the information given to him by Pat Casey is not just interesting but exciting in that it characterizes the Lough Gur fire as the first to be lit 'in a chain of fires that extended all the way back to West Cork and possibly Kerry, and all of them lit at the sight of the preceding one'.[168] This respondent didn't interview anyone from the urban community for his evidence on the city fires, and writes about them from the point of view of a city resident, but not a participant in the tradition. Thus, while the Lough Gur fire was lit 'in honour of St. John' the reason for the Limerick fires was 'Not known. Seems almost a reflex'.[169] The main attendees at the Lough Gur fire were described as 'the youngest lads of the locality' while the organizers of the Limerick city fires were 'gangs of children in various localities'. The Lough Gur people used 'Miscellaneous pieces of suitable rotten wood' but in the city: 'Materials include old tyres, waste wood of various kinds – anything that will burn. Much vandalistic appropriation of pieces of garden fence, doors of sheds etc, has become associated with bonfires in Limerick City'.[170] Interestingly, the writer acknowledges 'a diminishing of interest' in the Lough Gur custom, remarking that 'Strangely, there may not have been one this year'. He also observes that 'nothing special' by way of activities took place at the rural fire, and, as noted above, characterizes the attendees as mainly children and young people. In Limerick city however, 'People of all age groups' attend the fires, while, at the event itself 'People sing, dance and cook sausages and such-like on the fires in Limerick'. He goes on to comment that 'There is also, at times, much drinking'.[171]

The association here of the fires with what would now be called anti-social behaviour, vandalism and drinking, is noteworthy, though the recent history of the fires lies outside the scope of this study. However, it is interesting to note that acts which could be regarded as dangerous, daring or simply 'cheeky', such as stealing potatoes and attempting the jumps described above, are also a feature of some accounts of the earlier event: Danaher cites many examples of similar behaviour in his account of the Midsummer fires.[172] The main value of the National Folklore Collection account, however, apart from showing the difference in quality and tone between ethnographic information which comes from within the community and that which comes from outside it, is the way it demonstrates the vibrancy of the tradition in the city at this later date. The Lough Gur tradition, fascinating though it is, seems alive in memory only, while the Limerick city custom, with all its potential for annoyance and irritation along with the perceived dangers emanating from it, is definitely alive and 'kicking' in the early 1970s.

Communal rituals and the mediation of modernity

Pilgrimages and May Eve fires were not the only communal rituals engaged in by the people of Limerick city in the second quarter of the twentieth century. Some elements of communal ritual would be included in the cluster of customs carried out on St Patrick's Day, for instance, where people started the day by going to Mass, later took part in or watched the St Patrick's Day parade through the city centre, and in the afternoon spent a few hours along with a large crowd of neighbours and friends at St Patrick's Well in Singland.[173] St Patrick's Day offers an interesting mixture of official religious ritual combined with civic events: the Holy Well visit, though certainly revived with the involvement of the clergy in the early twentieth century and probably encouraged by them on an ongoing basis, could also be regarded as a communal ritual event.[174]

However, looking in detail at both pilgrimages and May Eve customs helps us to see how the Limerick city community may have used two very different types of communal ritual to mediate aspects of modernity in significant ways in the years between 1925 and 1960. In their discussion of the study of culture, Akhil Gupta and James Ferguson have identified 'the ways in which dominant cultural forms may be picked up and used – and significantly transformed – in the midst of the field of power relations that links localities to a wider world'.[175] Travel, in general, and leisure travel, in particular, could be seen as one of the 'dominant cultural forms' of modernity: however, it brought a slight sense of unease and apprehension, as discussed above, with it. The choice of pilgrimage as a form of leisure travel was one which allowed people to explore the experience of travel away from home while still feeling anchored in a communal and cultural sense. The pilgrimage in this context could be equated to what Gupta and Ferguson call 'the complex and sometimes ironic ... processes through which cultural forms are imposed, invented, reworked and transformed'.[176] The cultural transformations inherent in the pilgrimage process can be seen as working in two directions; firstly the one described above where a travel adventure is mitigated by familiarity: secondly, the way in which a pilgrimage, traditionally viewed as a devotional exercise in which penitential aspects were central, was regarded as an enjoyable day out. These two transformations also illustrate the ironic aspects mentioned above: a trip by luxurious trans-Atlantic liner in which much time is spent in the on-board oratory; the singing, smoking, chatting and buying souvenirs that were part and parcel of a devout day pilgrimage. In this sense, we can see the cultural categories of travel and religious ritual leaking into one another and transforming one another, with the participants themselves central to this process. The role of the clergy as organizers, promoters and also, of course, participants in pilgrimages must also be noted: their role in transforming travel into pilgrimage is significant in this context.

It is perhaps tempting in this regard to see the clergy as the agents of imposition of this dominant cultural form, the pilgrimage, on the community. However, while it is true to say that many forms of religious ritual were imposed by the clergy on Catholics at this time, I don't think that this oppositional concept of 'priests and people' is appropriate in the case of pilgrimages, which functioned more as an enjoyable 'optional extra' aspect of religion than as a ritual obligation. In his discussion of Irish culture between 1930 and 1960, Brian Fallon has argued that to 'distinguish between priests and people seems to me arbitrary and even false'.[177] Although I do not agree completely with Fallon's statement (for many purposes we have to distinguish between priests/ nuns and Catholics, in general), I do believe that his comment is applicable to the pilgrimage context. Thus, in Limerick city at this time we see many agents at work, in various different ways, in the process of transforming both the culture of modern travel and the traditional devout and penitential atmosphere of pilgrimage through communal religious ritual.

The construction of new localities, in the physical sense, was a key part of the development of Limerick city from 1935 to 1960. The custom of the May Eve fire is one which eloquently illustrates some aspects of the cultural construction of locality, or 'place making', which accompanied this building programme. Indeed, Gupta and Ferguson's view that places are conceived 'less as a matter of 'ideas' than of embodied practices that shape identities'[178] is strongly borne out by examination of the culture of Limerick city at this time. The practice of lighting fires on May Eve became strongly established in the new estates mentioned in the accounts above, St Mary's Park, Killalee, and Janesboro, as well as in many other estates: Killeely and Prospect in the 1940s, and Ballinacurra Weston and Ballynanty in the 1950s. Accounts show that the estate fires were organized by street and that the communal atmosphere was an important aspect of their enjoyment. In this sense, the participants could be said to have been building a common identity through the practice of the ritual, or, perhaps, rebuilding an identity in a new context, as it is important to remember that many people in the estates knew each other before moving there, or were related to one another in any case. Gupta and Ferguson's view of the mobility and the instability of identities is illlustrated by this, while their contention that 'the apparently immediate experience of community is in fact inevitably constituted by a wider set of social and spatial relations'[179] can be seen in the relationship between the estates and the rest of the city population, some of whom would tour the fires in the estates in the years after the ban was imposed on city centre fires.

It is important to realize that the May Eve custom was not the only cultural form used in the place-making process in the new areas of Limerick in the years between 1935 and 1960. The neighbourhood orientation of the Archconfraternity run by the Redemptorist Fathers was another aspect of this cultural process, while the building of Marian shrines in the 1950s, organized by local committees with the co-operation of the local authority was another.[180] However, the May Eve custom is different to these, not just because of its older history in the city and the new life given to it by its transfer to the new areas, but also because of its role in the development of how these areas saw themselves and were seen by the rest of the city. The bone-fire was the cultural form in which everybody in the area, regardless of economic status, took part. It's also important to note that women and children, who were largely absent from other place-making activities, were active participants in this custom. These inclusive aspects give the May Eve fires a special significance in terms of communal rituals undertaken by people in Limerick at this time.

In looking at the creation of culture in general, and ordinary people's role in this, the May Eve fire is of major significance. The fire event, because of its long history in the city, can be seen as an ancestral tradition: one aspect of this type of tradition, as pointed out by Stiofán Ó Cadhla in his discussion of the Pattern of St Declan at Ardmore, was 'the regular centring of community life into large assemblies where the social world was re-energised'.[181] The accounts of May Eve given by interviewees above certainly convey this sense of social renewal around the event. In Limerick city, from the 1930s, this ancestral tradition was translated by the people themselves into the modern environment of the housing estate: its ritual element along with its other essential aspect, that of street identity, were drawn from and reinforced by official devotional practices, which co-existed with the unofficial beliefs in luck and protection which were also inherent in the event. Because of these factors, the May Eve fire can be seen as a hybridized tradition in which ancestral and modern practices came together and unofficial beliefs were mixed with official devotional elements. This makes it one of the most culturally creative and communally expressive aspects of Limerick city life during the period studied.

5

Ritual Families: Praying and Fasting Together

Within the repertoire of devotional behaviour of Catholics in Limerick city from the mid-1920s to around 1960, there are some rituals which could be regarded as both public and private; both communal and individual. The rosary was one such multi-faceted devotion. The structure of this prayer, whereby one person led it or 'gave it out' lent itself easily to group and public contexts, making it suitable for use in families as well. The rosary also developed a significant private context, with many people using the prayer as a form of personal, individual devotion at home or in the church. The connection between the rosary and the material culture of devotion is noteworthy: the 'rosary beads' (also known as simply 'the rosary') was an important ritual object and was carried by many people at all times. Fasting and abstinence was – and is – a practice which involved, on the one hand, restrictions on the amount of food eaten by people on a daily basis and on the other, the prohibition of certain foods on appointed days. Complete abstention from food for a number of hours before receiving the sacrament of the Eucharist was an integral part of life for Catholics in the period between 1925 and 1960. Fasting was by its very nature a private ritual carried out on an individual basis, yet it also acquired household and other communal aspects in practice. The rosary and fasting are both rituals which, in their different ways, provide an insight into the informal practice of devotion in the context of the family and, to some extent, the workplace. It is also interesting to look at these two areas of devotional behaviour in terms of how ritual is defined and viewed in the study of religion, and to attempt to answer the theoretical challenges posed by the differences between them.

The rosary

The form of prayer called 'the rosary', a term which means 'a crown of roses' according to catechism texts,[1] is thought to have been brought into Ireland by the Dominican order with the founding of monasteries in Dublin and Drogheda in the early thirteenth century. By the start of the Reformation in the early sixteenth century, the Dominicans were estimated to have around thirty-eight monasteries in Ireland: as they were active promoters of the devotion, this would indicate a reasonable level of knowledge and practice of the rosary in pre-Reformation Ireland.[2] The prayer was given papal approval by Pope Leo X in 1520, thus paving the way for its more widepsread adoption as one of the Tridentine devotions promoted after the Council of Trent in 1563.[3] Patricia Lysaght's comprehensive account of the subject shows how the sufferings of the Dominican order during the Reformation did not prevent the rosary from becoming an important aspect of Counter-Reformation spirituality, promoted by the Jesuit order through their Sodality of the Blessed Virgin Mary, founded in 1563.[4] Lysaght notes the paucity of information on popular devotion in Ireland during the seventeenth and eighteenth centuries: despite this, some sources would indicate that the prayer was being said by ordinary people. The rosary also played a central role in the general revival of Catholic devotion in the nineteenth century: according to Lysaght, Catholic Emancipation in 1829, the introduction of the Sodality of the Living Rosary, which had been founded in France in 1826, into Ireland under the patronage of the Archbishop of Dublin in the early 1840s and 'above all the parish missions which took place in the various parishes throughout Ireland between the middle and the end of the century, all contributed to the spread of the Rosary'.[5] By the early twentieth century, the rosary was central to Catholic devotion in all kinds of contexts. Lysaght's study, based on materials collected by the Irish Folklore Commission and including an essay written by one of the Commission's collectors, Seán Ó hEochaidh, and some of his correspondence regarding the topic in the 1940s, demonstrates its importance in North-West Donegal up to, and during this period.

The commitment to the rosary described above, up to and including the twentieth century, was reinforced by the Family Rosary Crusade which was launched in Tuam in the Marian Year, 1954. Drawing on reports given in the annual *Irish Catholic Directory* Louise Fuller describes the movement:

> Fr. Peyton, the Irish-American 'Rosary Priest' had come to Ireland to appeal for greater devotion to the Rosary. Enormous rallies were held all over the country right through the month of May, a traditional month for Marian devotion. Estimates of people attending these rallies were as follows: Galway, 30,000 people; Knock, 18,000; and Sligo, 20,000. A figure 'close on 25,000' was reported as having participated in the pilgrimage to Knock on 15 August, the Feast of the Assumption, in the Marian Year, 1954.[6]

Father Peyton's new promotion of the rosary, building on what was already a substantial base, was to ensure the devotion's continued popularity for at least another generation – up to the 1970s and 1980s. Patricia Lysaght, writing in 1995, describes the rosary as 'probably the most important communal and family prayer, a status which it has not yet quite lost'.[7]

The rosary in the family and the community

It is not surprising, then, to find that the rosary was an important feature of popular religious culture, at every level and in every devotional context, in Limerick city in the second quarter of the twentieth century. In the public sphere, it was, along with sermons and Benediction, an integral part of the devotions carried out at meetings of religious organizations such as confraternities, sodalities and third orders. The prayer was also used in funerals and processions, and, as described above, said by people on trains and buses on their way to a pilgrimage destination, or on the way home.[8] The rosary was also said at home, usually in the evening after tea, and usually in the kitchen: Noreen P is speaking about the 1950s when she says: 'we did say the rosary every night after tea. We'd kneel up on the chairs. It was the thing to do. Oh very definitely'.[9] Máirín M, born in 1942, says: 'We'd say the rosary at night, always'.[10] It is interesting to find that the sense of obligation regarding saying the rosary was not as strong or as straightforward as that regarding attendance at Mass: this is probably because missing Mass was categorized as a sin, while not saying the rosary was not. Adherence to the rosary was the responsibility of the parents in the household, either the mother or the father, or both. It was taken very seriously by some. Eileen L, whose father led the prayer and who would always make sure it was said before he went out at night, describes the effect of his commitment on herself as a young adult and on her nine brothers and sisters of varying ages: 'my father would go out … for whatever business he had to go out for that night maybe, work or whatever … we said the rosary. The family rosary. Everybody would be there for that. And anything people were doing would have to wait until after that. If they were going out anywhere the rosary was always said before we went out'.[11] Another interviewee is speaking about a younger age group when she says 'if you were out playing you would be called in. And not all of us really liked … as youngsters, having to go through all this rigour, but we did it assiduously and we didn't balk at it'.[12] In one house, the interviewee's mother was the leader of the prayer: 'And then in the evening time, we'd say the rosary, of course, every night. And … my mother would give that out as well.'[13] The woman's role is central in Pádraig R's account as well: he describes his mother standing at the front door and shouting 'Rosary!' to get himself and his siblings to come in for it.[14]

The practice of the rosary, however, varied from household to household. Timmy G remembers his family saying the rosary 'maybe not every night, but most nights you would'.[15] Grace K may be talking about her teenage years in the 1940s when she describes her mother leading the rosary 'more or less every day', and also commenting that 'we thought 'twould never end'.[16] Something of the same situation is outlined in another account:

> I remember the nuns saying to us in school, you know, 'Now try to get the family rosary going!' Of course, I … trying to be a good girl would go home and I'd say 'Now, Mam, you know …' and we might start it. And then when the younger children might be crying or they might get cranky or they might say something funny and we'd all start skitting! I always remember my sister at one stage you know – we had a cat and he was playing … and we were 'Holy Mary mother of God …' 'Poooochie!' she'd say like this you see, and of course the whole lot of us would break up you know … And Mam would say 'That's what ye think of the rosary now … that's what ye …' you know she'd give out to us! But I remember those times alright and we did try.[17]

This interviewee was born in 1936, and her account suggests that she was in one of the senior primary or perhaps one of the junior secondary school classes. The promotion of the rosary by the nuns in schools at this point in the late 1940s is interesting, as the

Family Rosary Crusade did not begin until the Marian Year, 1954. In another account the reaction of the family was similar:

> The rosary was said in every house. My father was a very devout man. He was from Newcastle West … he would start the rosary, we'd all be kneeling down in front of chairs. One night we all started laughing and we couldn't stop – he was raging! He said his own after that … the rosary was very strong out the country. Anytime we visited Newcastle West we said it there … the rosary was strong in the city but moreso in the country – it would never be neglected there.[18]

This interviewee was born in 1912 and was speaking about her family home: this would place her father's efforts to get the family to say the rosary anytime between 1920 (when she would have been eight) and around 1930, when she would have been eighteen. The same interviewee made the point that 'Getting the family together for it – maybe it was harder in the city'. This suggests a family of young adults with their own commitments and schedules, similar to Eileen L's, but in this case the ritual was not as strictly adhered to. The question of the various members of the family paying proper attention as the rosary was being said is illustrated in a story told by another interviewee:

> But actually I remember a funny incident about a rosary in that Irene O'Callaghan, Lord have mercy on her, my friend, a very good friend of mine, and her Dad died when she was quite young, he died very suddenly. And … I went up to her house and when the Angelus rang her mother, automatically, even though she was in a bad way because of the father's death said: 'Oh we have to say the rosary.' So we all went, knelt down anyway, with chairs facing … kneeling up … and I remember Mrs. O'Callaghan pointed at the ground and she said to me 'We can fill that hole now' and I didn't know what she meant, and I didn't dare ask. But when the rosary was over, I said to her: 'What did you mean about fill the hole?' 'Just look at the floor there' she said 'That's where my husband knelt every night and because the others would be falling asleep or daydreaming when it was their turn for the decade, he'd be banging his toe on the floor!' And 'twas lino that time everyone had … and actually made a hole in the floor from constantly hitting his toe into this, and even when they'd put down new lino 'twould go through it every single time, there'd be a hole, and 'twas kind of gone right down into it … but … I said God help us … the memory of him![19]

There are some interesting points to be made regarding this account: the first being that the ringing of the Angelus bell reminded Irene O'Callaghan's mother to say the rosary, or perhaps reminded her of the centrality of this prayer in the rituals of death: it was a useful way to physically and spiritually occupy those bereaved, when 'in a bad way'. The account also shows another approach to keeping everyone's attention on the prayer: the father banging his toe on the linoleum floor. The story also illustrates the custom of visitors to the house joining in, quite naturally, with the prayer: it did not require a death in the family for this to happen.[20]

The rosary might also be said at work, especially if the employer was devout. Anthony F mentions this practice while discussing the existence of statues of Mary in the workplace:

there was one ... in McDonagh's, the motors, they were in Bedford Row ... they had a statue of Our Lady and they would all say the rosary. Every Tuesday morning the rosary was said. The whole company would say it ... Every Tuesday morning Mr McDonagh would say the rosary. And they'd all answer the rosary.[21]

The role of the workplace here as a place of devotion is interesting. The rosary is a communal prayer which must be 'led' or 'given out' by one person, who then passes the responsibility of each decade around to each of the participants in the group before resuming the leadership of the prayers at the concluding stage of the devotion. Among the informants interviewed, the father of the house, or occasionally the mother, would 'give out' the rosary. Mr McDonagh, as the owner of the motor company, would lead his employees in the prayer, possibly distributing decades around the workers as they progressed. This is, to some extent, similar to workers having lunch or tea-break together, but the shared prayers spoken in unison and the spiritual content embodied in them, the devotional gestures and posture involved, along with the (possibly) differing parts played by the participants in the ritual make this a somewhat more dramatic and meaningful occasion. This does not necessarily imply that all the participants experienced the same meaning through the ritual, but it helps us to see how the weekly suspension of work on a Tuesday morning and the creation of a 'ritual family' might have marked out this period of time in an eloquent and emphatic way for everybody involved.

Anthony F also mentions that the clothing factory Danus (see Figure 5) was 'famous' in this regard: 'The rosary was always said there and they had the statues of Our Lady.'[22] It is not clear from this account how often the rosary was said in Danus, which after all would have needed to suspend work on its large factory floor for about fifteen minutes in order to say it. The statue was of course equally relevant for saying the angelus, which was said by factory workers every day and took under two minutes. Given the difficulties involved in keeping even a medium-sized family's attention on the rosary for the amount of time it took to say it, it is unlikely that the rosary, even in its shorter form, was attempted very often in Danus. However, the connection in this interviewee's mind between the statue in the workplace, the devout reputation of the Danus factory owners and this form of Marian prayer is interesting in that it suggests a form of Diana Eck's 'grammar of devotion' where different elements: the devout mindset, the statue, the rosary prayer, and the rosary beads are automatically used together, and acquire more meaning in relation to one another when used thus.[23] The presence of devotional objects in workplaces and in other non-religious locations is also of interest here: the statue in the garage, the blessed turf in the car, the holy water font in the home,[24] the statue in the ballroom.[25] These examples indicate a desire to provide what Mircea Eliade has called a sacred 'centre' in a profane space: something that provides an escape from the human condition and a means to transcend it, however briefly.[26] The recitation of the rosary and the angelus at work demonstrates how this desire was acted upon, with the help of both the 'sacred centre' and the appropriate ritual prayers.

The content and character of the rosary devotion

It is important to consider the actual prayers said during the rosary devotion as well. The basic structure, as outlined by the Church in catechism texts, was one which seemed to be used by participants in the devotion at every level. Patricia Lysaght's description of the content follows this pattern and is both comprehensive and useful:

> a set of devotions consisting in the recitation of fifteen decades of tens of *Aves* preceded by a *Pater* and followed by a *Gloria*. Each decade is associated with a 'mystery' or certain aspect of the life of Christ and the Virgin Mary. The mysteries consist of three major groups –the Joyful, Sorrowful and Glorious Mysteries – each of which is divided into five themes or aspects concerning Christ and His Mother, Mary ... This form of the devotion is known as the Greater Rosary while the Lesser Rosary – the most familiar form of the devotion – consists of five decades and a similar number of mysteries.[27]

In Browne and Nolan's *Catechism Notes*, published in 1919, the following description is given: 'The Rosary is divided into three chaplets or crowns each consisting of five decades'.[28] The three sets of decades (or mysteries) are then given, along with the opening prayers and detailed instructions for carrying out the devotion, including the recitation of the Creed. The assumption that only five decades would be said on any one occasion is clear in the following instruction: 'Then name the next Mystery, and so on, till the five are finished. End by saying the Hail, Holy Queen. It is usual to say the five Joyful Mysteries on Mondays and Thursdays; the five Sorrowful, on Tuesdays and Fridays; and the Glorious on Wednesdays, Saturdays and Sundays'.[29] The rationale for the division of the prayer into mysteries is given in the opening explanation of the devotion: 'The word Rosary means a crown of roses. It consists of meditation on the chief mysteries in the lives of Our Blessed Lord and His Mother, and of prayers to obtain the graces promised to us in these mysteries'.[30]

In discussing the forms of the rosary in North-West Donegal in the mid-twentieth century, Patricia Lysaght comments that the evidence collected by the Irish Folklore Commission indicates that the people in this area and in other areas of the country were 'by and large, unfamiliar with the mysteries'[31] even though they certainly did recite the five decades of the rosary.[32] More significant for this community, perhaps, were the prayers accompanying the decades:

> a variety of traditional prayers were recited to start off and conclude the rosary. The prayers said after the recitation of the decades, were concerned with the physical and spiritual well-being of the family and community, and included prayers for: a happy death, protection from violent or sudden death, and, of particular relevance for a sea-faring community, protection from drowning and the perils of the sea. Prayers were said, on the one hand, for the maintenance of good family and neighbourly relations, and on the other, for the protection of the family and its belongings from the so-called evil eye and the evil intentions of members of the local community. A *Pater* and an *Ave Maria* were also recited for the maintenance of family and community honour, and especially for the

protection of the girls of the townland from the undesirable (and fleeting) attentions of unworthy outsiders. The family and community dead were never far from the thoughts of the living, and thus a variety of prayers were always said after the rosary for the suffering souls in purgatory.[33]

In Limerick city, the evidence suggests that the 'trimmings', the extra items which Lysaght terms 'traditional prayers' in the Donegal context, varied greatly from household to household. For instance, Noreen P says: 'Naturally you'd say the "Hail Holy Queen" at the end and … a few different prayers … you'd be praying for different people'.[34] Grace K's family simply said the rosary, and apart from the usual 'Hail Holy Queen' prayer at the end 'that'd be that, and there'd be no litany after it'.[35] Joseph L notes the difference in the length of the trimmings said in his own family home and those said by his wife's family, which he experienced after marriage.[36] For Eileen L, in whose family the rosary was an important ritual, the trimmings were 'as long again, half, as the rosary … easily'.[37]

She also lists the prayers said:

They include the Litany of the Sacred Heart, the Litany of Our Lady, the long Act of Devotion … the long Act of Reparation to the Sacred Heart of Jesus. It also included … the six … *Paters*, *Aves* and *Glorias* … of the Cincture; and also included prayers to St Jude and St Blaise, and … and then our own intentions would come in after that. It was quite a long rosary, I can tell you![38]

She adds that 'of course we had the *Memorare* and we had a prayer to St Joseph every night'. These prayers, despite their length, were not read from prayer-books: 'my father was the leader, and we just got to know them by repetition. Even the long Act of Reparation to the Sacred Heart of Jesus, which is a beautiful prayer … I still know it – 'twas a beautiful prayer, but 'twas very long!'

This experience might not be typical, but it is worth asking whether, given the variety of approaches and attitudes to the rosary, there was any 'typical' experience? Eileen L's account illustrates one strand of the experience of the devotion in Limerick city. It is clear that her family was a devout one, like the families in Donegal to whom Lysaght refers. The difference in the repertoire of discretional prayers is striking, however: the litanies, acts of reparation, and prayers such as the *Memorare* were, in their language and atmosphere, much more evocative of the spiritual atmosphere of official Catholicism than were the community-based prayers of the Donegal people described by Lysaght above. This need not necessarily be seen as an urban–rural divide: Eileen L's father came from a small village in County Kilkenny and her mother from a rural area of County Offaly, though it might have been the case that her father's slightly more urban background may have influenced his experience and subsequent choice of prayers, and it is certainly the case that living in Limerick city during most of his adult life would have reinforced this. Thomas McGrath has made the point that cities may have absorbed Tridentine devotions more readily than country areas during the Counter-Reformation and in the ensuing centuries, and this would have influenced the repertoire of prayers said to accompany the rosary in significant ways.[39]

It is interesting too to see how long, elaborate prayers such as the Litany of the Sacred Heart and the Litany of the Blessed Virgin were memorized and recited orally, rather than read out of prayer books, while the children of the household learned them 'by repetition'. Though it may be the case that the leader of the prayers, Eileen L's father in this case, used a prayer book as an *aide-memoire* in the process, this could still be seen as a reflection of the overwhelmingly oral nature of popular Catholicism at this time: the strong emphasis on speaking and singing from memory rather than reading was to be found in many contexts, even when the material being recited had been learned from hymn books or catechisms – the latter being the case with the Sacrament of Confirmation when the bishop would ask questions of the children to be confirmed, and expect them to know the answers 'off by heart'.[40] A connection between prayer and performance can also be discerned here, with the participants themselves deciding on the tone, preferred pace and pitch of the recitation. Pádraig R's evidence indicates that a choice of language also existed in houses where Irish was spoken[41]. The orality of official Catholic devotion in Limerick and in Ireland generally may have been an important contributing factor to its popularity: this point is further discussed in the Conclusion.

The centrality of the rosary in devotion of all kinds is clear, along with a strong sense in the culture of the period that it was a desirable feature of family life for Catholics, even before the Family Rosary Crusade of the 1950s. Brian Fallon has argued that the Catholic clergy in Ireland succeeded in doing 'what Communism, for instance, never quite achieved in Eastern Europe, though it tried hard to do so – that is, to create an ideological power-base in the private home, and they achieved it in a country where the family unit counted above and before everything else'.[42] Though this was certainly true in some households (for example, the very serious and elaborated ritual which was firmly established in Eileen L's home) it also seems that a variety of attitudes were adopted to the devotion. The less elaborate but very consistent devotion carried out in Noreen P's and Irene O'Callaghan's families demonstrates another, perhaps less intense approach. In the households where the devotion was not sustained, the varying degrees of frustration experienced by parents and older siblings in trying to engage the devout attention of younger members of the family during an informally organized ritual which could nonetheless last about twenty minutes, is also in evidence. The daydreaming, laughing and giving in to distractions described demonstrates that, in some households, at least, the 'ideological power base' referred to by Brian Fallon was not as strong as in others. But these varying experiences may also indicate the different meanings of the process within the same genre of ritual action: for older people, the means of escape into the metaphysical realm, which brought with it the contemplation of ancestors and the comfort of hope derived from prayer; for children and young adults, the necessary suspension of play or the delay in getting out for the night, along with the humorous aspect of forbidden distractions.

The rosary beads

The *Complete Illustrated Guide to Catholicism* describes the 'rosary' as 'a round of prayers that are centred on the Blessed Virgin Mary' before going on to state that:

> The rosary is also a physical object that enables believers to keep track of their prayers. It consists of a small crucifix on a circular string with a medal and a series of beads of various numbers. The beads are divided into groups of ten beads called decades, each group preceded by an individual bead set apart slightly from the others. It is used to say the prayers that form the rosary.[43]

The practice of referring to the ritual object by the name used for the prayer itself is potentially confusing, and sometimes solved by the use of the term 'a pair of rosary beads' but in Limerick in the twentieth century and in Ireland generally this object was (and still is) known simply as a 'rosary beads'.

Historical sources show that the rosary beads was a popular ritual object at least as far back as the approval of the devotion by Pope Leo X in 1520, and possibly much further. Eamon Duffy demonstrates the established status of the beads as a devotional object in his study of the Reformation in a village in Somerset:

> Rosaries were among the most prized possessions of devout women in Tudor England. Worn at the waist and constantly fingered, they were often the costliest item a woman owned, and an important part of female status and identity. The bequest of one's rosary to an image, to be draped around it on high days and holidays or to hang on its surrounding shrine, or simply to be sold to help finance the cult, was a token of special affection for a saint, and a sign of the donor's desire to be remembered in the saint's powerful intercession.[44]

Irish sources also point to an early use of rosary beads: Peter O'Dwyer mentions a reference to beads as far back as 1487, before going on to say that

> The Anglo-Norman community used little Rosaries of eleven beads (one Pater and ten Aves) to entwine around their fingers. John Hunt suggests that a sculpture dated c. 1400 ar Jerpoint, Co. Kilkenny may be of St. Dominic with a Rosary ... in 1578 Bishop Maurice McBrien of Emly arrived in Waterford from Rome. He had 'seven pairs of beads in his baggage which was searched' The wearing of beads around the neck was quite common.[45]

The rosary beads continued to be a valued object in the lives of the clergy in ensuing centuries, as this statement from Fr James Cullen, the founder of the *Irish Messenger of the Sacred Heart* shows: 'What blessings it has brought me, my Rosary beads! It is my companion by day and night, on land and sea, in joy and sorrow. I expect every blessing to come to me through it, above all at the hour of my death'.[46] The rosary beads was used by ordinary people too, and by the twentieth century was certainly the most popular devotional object in Irish Catholicism, in both a household and a personal sense. The interiors of houses on the Aran and Blasket Islands, in photographs taken by Thomas H. Mason in the early 1930s are striking in their material simplicity, with most of the objects in the kitchens directly related to the provision of food, clothing and shelter: knitted socks hung up to dry in the heat of the fire and bunches of onions hanging from the ceiling. Objects of a purely cultural nature are few, however. In the Aran Islands interior virtually the only object in this category is the rosary beads hanging by the fire. A rosary beads is also hanging in the Blasket Island kitchen, although in this interior a small clock and a religious calendar are to be seen as well.[47] The rosary beads hanging in the kitchen also features in John Healy's account of his childhood: 'The clock would strike ten. Grandma would put her sewing aside. From a nail on the wall she'd take the big Rosary beads … we got up from our seats, knelt down with our backs to the fire and one another … and made the responses'.[48]

Colleen McDannell, in her book on the material culture of Christianity, includes the use of the rosary beads in a list of pious acts called 'Sacramentals' by the Catholic Church: she explains the term as follows:

> Evolving out of the concept of the sacrament is the notion of a 'sacramental', something that is more than a sign or a symbol but less than a sacrament … Eventually, making the sign of the cross with holy water, praying with a rosary, giving alms, eating food blessed for holiday celebration, or even having a car blessed, all became sacramentals.[49]

It may be the case that the idea of a 'Sacramental' was born of the Church's need to accomodate the use of physical elements in official religious ritual: in a religion that was heavy with linguistic content, such as prayers and stories, and with abstract symbolic concepts, the tactile aspects of objects such as rosary beads and substances such as holy water may have brought a sense of balance into popular religious experience.

Catechism texts from the second quarter of the twentieth century also discuss 'Sacramentals', and although the rosary beads is not always referred to in these accounts (it is included in the discussion on prayer instead), it is clear from the mention of religious objects such as scapulars, medals and blessed candles, and from the inclusion of substances like holy oils and holy water that 'Sacramentals' have important material aspects.[50] Moreover, the guidance given on the topic of the rosary demonstrates the centrality of the beads in the prayer and thus the importance of the material aspect of the rosary as a devotion: 'Then on the Crucifix say the Creed; on the large bead, Our Father; on the three small beads, Hail Marys; and on the next large bead, Glory be to the Father, etc.'[51] *Catechism Notes* also states that 'indulgenced beads' should be used in the devotion, which suggests that the beads themselves should have been blessed before use,[52] while the 1959 *Catechism Key* refers to 'blessed rosaries' as 'Sacramentals'.[53]

In Limerick city, as elsewhere, the rosary beads was a popular devotional aid. Because the rosary was said in many different contexts as well as in private, individual prayer, it was customary for people to carry their rosary beads with them at all times. Kathleen B says: 'Yes, the rosary beads was very much part of your life: you would carry it around with you always. You might attach a medal with a relic onto it – someone might bring it back from Lourdes'.[54] Eileen L also said that she would always carry her rosary beads around with her and noted she had been told by her sister-in-law that her late mother-in-law 'always carried her rosary beads with her! ... always ... [she] would go back into the house to bring her rosary beads ... if she was going someplace! So Annie told me, yea.' Eileen L also pointed out that it was usual for men to carry the rosary beads with them too, stating that her brother-in-law still carries one and that her father 'always did. In a withered leather pouch'.[55] The custom of having the rosary beads about one at all times, whether engaged in devotional activities or not is illustrated by the case of Michael Manning, arrested in the early hours of 19 November 1953, for the unlawful killing of Catherine Cooper. He was later found guilty of this crime and was hanged on 20 April 1954. Manning, whose pockets contained a rosary beads on the night of his arrest, had spent the day drinking in various public houses in the city and outlying areas.[56] Máirín M's account makes it clear that children also carried rosary beads:

> people would give you, if they were in Lourdes or that would bring you a rosary bead and yea, you certainly would hold onto the same one all the way through ... you would carry it in a purse always, you'd carry it in a ... little leather purse, you know, and ... you would always have it and you'd never go to Mass without your prayer book and your ... missal and your rosary beads.[57]

Áine R paints a vivid picture of her mother's use of both the rosary prayer and the rosary beads in her description of her mother's faith: 'And I can honestly say it's prayer got her through, you know. Yea. No matter what time you'd wake during the night – I slept on the end of my mother's bed – and every time you wake, she'd have a rosary, and she'd be praying. Aw gee – she never stopped!'[58]

People's attachment to their rosary beads is also evident from the texts of the advertisements in the 'Lost and Found' column of the *Limerick Leader* from the 1930s through the 1950s. It is interesting to see rosary beads appearing as an item of some value among the watches, pens, handbags, money, jewellery, gloves, overcoats and small furs appearing in the Lost category during these decades. The following example, from April 1950, includes a description of the beads: 'Lost on March 30, between St Joseph's Church and Woolworth's, Rosary Beads, purple beads, silver chain and cross. Will finder please leave into this office'.[59] An earlier advertisement from 1930 gives a more detailed account: 'Lost – Mother of Pearl and Silver Dolour Rosary Beads on Christmas morning after 7.30 Mass, either in Dominican Church or between it and 10 Pery Square'.[60] Another item details the medals attached to the rosary beads: 'Lost, Rosary Beads (Lourdes, Sacred Cincture & Child of Prague), in red bag on Saturday, January 7. Will finder please return to this office'.[61]

In one advertisement, it appears that two people have ended up with the wrong beads, through forgetting to take their beads (or the little leather purse in which the beads were generally carried) with them when making a purchase (probably a newspaper) outside the church: 'Lost: will the lady who left Mother o' Pearl Rosary Beads to stallholder outside Jesuits' Church last week please return to This Office, the one which was given back to her, when she will receive her own in exchange'.[62] An item appearing in a few editions in the first week of January 1940 states: 'Lost (this Monday morning) between Glentworth St and Jesuit Church Rosary Beads (two or three beads missing from decade). Will finder please return to Limerick Leader Office'.[63]

The appearance of rosary beads as lost items in the local newspaper testifies to the value placed on them by their owners. This is not surprising: rosary beads were usually bought or given as gifts by those returning from a pilgrimage, and they were sometimes made of valuable and/or aesthetically pleasing materials like mother of pearl or silver. The owners' attachment to their own rosary beads, even when they are missing beads, or they have received another in exchange, is also clear from the texts of the advertisements. In this context it must be remembered that it was the custom to get a rosary beads, or indeed any other object used in devotion, blessed by a priest before using it. This had implications for the disposal of the item later on. It was very important that the rosary beads was not just thrown around or put in the bin: this could lead to its desecration (however inadvertent) by disrespect or improper use. Ideally, a blessed object should be destroyed completely by burning.[64] Thus a lost rosary beads was a cause for concern, because the owner did not know where it was or who was using it. The idea that a rosary beads could be lying on a footpath or in the gutter somewhere was a disturbing one. This sacred or 'blessed' quality is likely to have been a factor in their owners' eagerness to resolve this anxiety by getting them back. The sacredness or 'blessedness' of the rosary beads was reinforced by its constant presence and frequent use in all kinds of devotional and ritual situations. Críostóir O'Flynn mentions the corpse 'with a rosary beads twined in its white fingers', while Máirín M's evidence shows that it was usual to bring the beads to Mass, and indeed, to say one's own private rosary and other private prayers while hearing Mass,[65] the latter a centuries-old practice in official devotion in Europe, as Francois Lebrun's research demonstrates.[66]

Colleen McDannell has made the point that 'Roman Catholicism most clearly delineates how and under what conditions something material can mediate between God and humanity ... Sacramentals can appear in almost every aspect of daily life and, like sacraments, serve as a doorway between the secular and the sacred worlds'.[67] The rosary beads, whether hanging on its hook in the kitchen or carried in a small leather purse, whether given as a gift or brought home from a shrine as a souvenir, whether used to dress a corpse, to pray in bed at night or privately at Mass, illustrates, perhaps more than any other object, the role of 'something material' in spiritual processes. The combination of the sacred and the secular mentioned by McDannell is potently expressed by the rosary beads, a bought commodity which was also blessed; an intensely physical item made of various materials and carried on the person but which enabled communication with sacred beings such as Our Lady, God and the saints.

Fasting and abstinence

The custom of observing a fast and abstaining from meat can be traced back to the early Christians. Catherine Bell points out that fasting, which started as a private act of devotion, later became 'a duty imposed on the whole congregation', and thus, a feature of the calendar of the Christian Church. It had become the custom generally, most especially in a Lenten context, by the twelfth century, when St Bernard of Clairvaux noted that 'kings, and princes, clergy and laity' all fasted during the forty days of Lent. The spiritual principles involved are articulated by Catherine Bell as follows: 'Fasting in the liturgical seasons of Advent and Lent were meant to prepare the Christian for the great holidays of Christmas and Easter, respectively ... Penitence was certainly one of the main reasons for Christian fasting, but fasting was also an emulation of Christ's forty days in the desert without food or water and a method of disciplining one's physical desires'.[68] A contemporary Catholic source puts it like this: 'Participating in fasting and other forms of abstinence are understood to be physical self-control that mirrors spiritual discipline ... Catholics are also encouraged to allow a sort of spiritual plenty to fill the space no longer occupied by temporal delights – Lent is a time of prayer and meditation'.[69] In a catechism text from 1959, 'meant for use in Ireland, Britain, North America and Australia' the subject of fasting is included in the section entitled 'The Six Commandments of the Church'. (These are called 'Precepts' in other texts.) The explanation of the Second Commandment 'To fast and abstain on the days appointed', is quite specific regarding the reasons for the practice. These may be summarized as follows: to punish oneself for sins committed and to practice self-denial which tames desire, which in turn leads to stronger resistance to temptation and sin.[70] The reader is also referred to the section entitled 'How to avoid sin' in a previous chapter of the text.

Regulating the fast

Catherine Bell outlines the details of fasting and abstinence in a historical context, stating that the Advent fast was usually less severe than that carried out in Lent, which originally involved just one meal a day, not to be eaten until after sunset. Bell notes how this parallels later Muslim practices, before going on to say: 'By the ninth century, however, this single meal had been moved to noon, and a light snack was allowed at bedtime; meat was still forbidden and at various times animal products like milk, butter and eggs were also avoided'.[71]

Although the regulation of fasting and abstinence has changed over the centuries, it is also important to realize that practices varied significantly from place to place. This is not surprising, given the strong connections between this type of devotional practice and local material culture. Some twentieth-century catechism texts are careful to distinguish between regulations in different fasting 'zones' such as Australia and New Zealand, the USA and Canada, and Ireland and Great Britain. Even then, the catechism states: 'The days of fast and abstinence are not the same in every country and diocese. Be guided by announcements at Mass'.[72] The regulations themselves in the pre-Vatican II era were based on the *Code of Canon Law* promulgated in 1917. Fuller points out that Catholics were to abstain from meat on every Friday throughout the year, and describes the Lenten fast as follows:

> Those between 21 and 60 years of age were bound by the laws of fast and absti-
> nence. Every day during Lent, except Sundays and St. Patrick's Day, was deemed a
> fast day. Only one full meal was permitted, and a 'light repast' each morning and
> evening. The quantity and type of food allowed in these repasts was regulated by

the approved custom of each diocese. The law of abstinence forbade the use of flesh-meat or soup made from meat or meat extracts. Ash Wednesday and all the Fridays of Lent were days of both fast and abstinence.[73]

A small sample of catechism texts published in the years between 1919 and 1960 show some variation in these regulations and also some significant differences in the way the information is presented. So while in one text, in 1919, everybody is bound 'under pain of mortal sin' to fast, a catechism for children published in 1958, makes no mention of this.[74] It is interesting that the interviewees for this project, when reflecting on the subject of fasting during the period studied, did not mention mortal sin in this context, despite (in some cases) feeling some anxiety around the topic. The complicated nature of the fasting and abstinence regulations along with the variations even in their written description, which was no doubt continued in their verbal presentation by priests and nuns, meant that the regulations were open to interpretation to a significant extent. It could also be said that the degree to which the rules could be enforced was limited because of the personal and familial context of the practice.

Receiving the Sacrament of the Eucharist or Holy Communion was to be preceded by hours of fasting as well. In the 1919 edition of the *Catechism Notes*, the section on how to prepare for the sacrament includes the guideline 'We must be fasting'.[75] It is probably safe to assume, given interviewees' evidence on the subject, that this means fasting from midnight the night before; however the 1944 edition leaves no room for doubt by including 'from midnight' after this.[76] Perhaps this is because change was on the way in this regard: by 1960 *Catechism Notes* was simply stating 'We must observe the Eucharistic Fast'.[77] A clearer explanation is given in the *Catechism for Children* of 1958: 'You must not take anything to eat for three hours before receiving Holy Communion, nor anything to drink for one hour. Alcoholic drink is not to be taken for three hours before receiving. Water never breaks the fast. Sick people, even though they are not in bed, may take non-alcoholic drink and medicine, in solid or liquid form, any time before receiving'.[78]

Fasting from midnight was an obligation which affected not just the times of Masses (early morning Masses were very common) but also the frequency of Communion in people's lives. Canon Law stated that Catholics should receive at least once a year; organizations such as the Archconfraternity of the Holy Family encouraged men to receive on a monthly basis, in the 'General Communion' organized for them according to their different divisions; however the Church had been promoting a more frequent reception of the sacrament since Pope Pius X's Decree on Daily Communion in 1905.[79] For people who liked to receive Communion weekly or even daily, fasting was therefore a regular, or maybe even a constant feature of life.

Perceptions of fasting and abstinence

Interviewees' experience of fasting and abstinence begins with their own understanding of the official regulations. Eileen L's knowledge on this topic is perhaps the most detailed: reciting from memory, she gives a list of days of fast and abstinence throughout the year: 'The Wednesdays and Fridays of Lent; the Wednesdays, Fridays and Saturdays of the four Ember weeks; the vigils of Pentecost and All Saints; the vigil of the Immaculate Conception.[80] The 'four Ember weeks' referred to here are weeks in which, historically, blessed ashes were distributed. They fell in spring, after the first Sunday of Lent, in summer in Whit-week, in autumn after 14 September and in winter after 13 December, which occurred during the season of Advent.[81] The question of who exactly was obliged to fast and abstain was one which was interpreted in various ways. One interviewee, though she expressed some uncertainty about this, said 'I think children under seven and people over sixty-five were exempt, but I could be corrected on that'.[82] Another interviewee also mentions sixty-five as the upper age-limit, though Fuller's account of Canon Law and the catechism texts state it as sixty. Pregnant women were not officially excluded, though one interviewee, a mother of ten, said: 'There was a lot more fasting in Lent than there is now, Wednesday and Friday, fast and abstinence. I was always pregnant so I always had a great excuse – I never fasted! I think you were exempt if you were pregnant – sure you couldn't be fasting then!'[83] Another interviewee, who had eleven children, was of the same opinion, 'well the understanding of that then, pregnant women needn't fast', although she pointed out that people would still give up sweets and sugar in their tea for Lent.[84] This interpretation of the guidelines in the context of pregnancy is understandable, given the flexibility regarding the health of the person in the fasting regulations, although it is equally easy to imagine pregnant women, and indeed, members of the clergy from whom they may have sought guidance, dismissing pregnancy as any kind of health consideration at all: Eileen L's evidence bears this out.[85]

The fast day diet, in the era from 1917 onwards, was supposed to consist of one full meal and two 'collations' – the light repast described in Fuller's account above, which also states that this was to be followed every day in Lent, except St Patrick's Day. Máirín M described it as follows: 'the two collations were very, very simple. It would be kind of tea and two slices of bread, type of thing ... or an alternative of milk and two biscuits, that type of thing ... I remember feeling hungry ... I do yea ... I do, I remember feeling hungry'.[86] The exact proportions of the main meal, however, were not specified anywhere, though Eileen L said 'On the other side, we were allowed two hours for our main meal. Two hours! ... So you could eat all you wanted in those two hours – you could drag it out for the two hours! Which was an awful cheat really!'[87]

It is important to note that many people's experience and knowledge of fast and abstinence encompassed the period before 1925 as well as the period after 1960. Joseph L, for instance, was able to describe his parents' earlier fasting as much stricter than was the case later: 'Of course the fasting in the 1930s was much less rigid than the fasting in the 1910s. Because I remember my father and mother talking about – you could only have black tea and all that kind of thing, on certain days of the week, you know ... this was back in the early century'.[88] A 1964 account given to the Irish Folklore Comission from Cratloe, Co. Clare (about six miles from Limerick city and about three miles from Joseph L's childhood home), described the food in the earlier fast in more detail: 'The usual food was: breakfast, yeast bread with jam instead of butter; dinner, potatoes and fish cooked in water. On Ash Wednesday, Spy Wednesday and Good Friday black tea was used, and for dinner red herrings or ling'.[89] The fact that butter was forbidden while jam, arguably a 'fancier' food, wasn't, is linked to the longstanding historical perception of dairy and animal products in general as luxurious aspects of the diet. Another interviewee's father retained the earlier customs even after the regulations had changed: 'And I remember my father on Good Friday now, he'd work a day … But he still would not have butter on his bread on Good Friday and he would have black tea, you know'.[90] This is an interesting example of the practice of religion at the popular level, where older regulations are adhered to despite the official changes in the regulations of the Church.

The regulations were relaxed again in the decades following the 1960s, and it is clear that Kathleen B is referring to this later period when she describes the abstinence customs: 'That time Spy Wednesday and Good Friday, but then they cut off Spy Wednesdays … Good Friday fast and abstinence. You know, one meal and two collations … The other weeks of Lent was just Friday – well the normal – Friday, no meat was ever eaten on Friday, anyhow'.[91] Both Kathleen B and Eileen L mention exercising restraint when having a snack, something which is likely to pertain to the more relaxed atmosphere of the 1960s and later, rather than to the earlier period. Eileen L says: 'And we would have a cup of tea in the morning – we didn't know coffee in those days – and maybe one biscuit, but we wouldn't go beyond one biscuit'.[92] Kathleen B describes a similar situation at night-time, when she took three biscuits with a cup of cocoa, when only one was allowed.[93]

Fasting with fellow workers and families

Áine R recalled the practice of the fast in the context of the factory where she worked:

> But Lent! I'll never forget Lent … because I was working in the Irish Wire. We started work at eight o'clock … according to the religion you could only take one meal and two collations. Now the collations in our case would be two slices of bread and butter … and if we took that before we went to the factory, then we couldn't have anything at ten o'clock when we had our break. So you can imagine trying to work – I was starving![94]

The sense that everybody was fasting is eloquently conveyed by the factory situation, as this interviewee goes on to say that:

> The only thing we'd talk about the minute we'd all meet in the cloakroom was 'What did you have this morning?' 'I only had one slice of bread and I kept one for my ten o'clock break'. This all went on you know … Then at night we could have our two slices when we went home from work. Great days! We never had a weight problem, which I needn't tell you anyway … That was Lent and it was very strict at the time, and … thank God we did our best.[95]

The communal attention given to fasting and abstinence in a work context was also remembered by Anthony F, who was working in a bakery in Croom from 1950 to 1954. He first described the practice the workers had of making their own breakfast at work in the mornings, we all cooked our own breakfast you see ... they'd all have rashers and eggs or whatever 'twould be. We'd all send out to the shops nearby and get them and cook them and you'd have, might have cold meat and a bit of cress picked up now the previous day from a stream and brought in. Or rasher, or fish and we'd all change a bit around.[96]

The situation on Fridays was different however, when meat couldn't be eaten. The following story illustrates the communal aspect of fasting in this case:

They'd all observe the fast and they'd all be watching each other ... 'twould only be eggs that we'd have that day, or fish. But, Timmy Ryan, I remember it one day, he said to Paudie McNamara, says he, 'Today's a fast day' he said 'you can't have meat' and Paudie was furious at being reminded of it. He got his fried eggs and fried them anyway, and then the next minute Timmy passes him down with rashers and eggs. 'Hey!' he said 'Didn't you tell me that today was a fast day?' 'Ah well' says he 'I'm over sixty-five!'[97]

The sense of an older person in the community, at work, in this case, keeping an eye on the spiritual welfare of younger people echoes the situation described earlier regarding women's membership of the parish sodality. The funny aspect, Timmy Ryan's own exemption, is underscored by his more serious sense of authority and the fact that Paudie McNamara did actually conform, despite being 'furious' at the reminder. In other situations, the matter might be handled rather more delicately. Críostóir O'Flynn tells a story about the time his mother went to Dublin with her sister-in-law,

a girl named Birdie Murphy who proved to be an enterprising business woman, opening a clothes shop in the Irishtown and another later on near the railway. On some occasion when she was going by train on a business trip to Dublin, Birdie kindly invited my mother to go with her. My mother heartily enjoyed this unexpected outing but it was afflicted at an early point by canonical rectitude – the pair of them were just about to tuck into a fine breakfast of rashers, eggs and sausages on the train when my mother suddenly remembered that it was a Friday (I'm sure Birdie momentarily regretted inviting her just then!) and so the fragrant rashers and sausages were left untouched and those two decent Christian women from Limerick had to concentrate on a fried egg with tea and toast to sustain them all the way to Dublin.[98]

This story is interesting in the way that it shows how, just as in the bakery story above, it was quite possible to 'forget' or 'almost forget' the law of abstinence. This lapse could presumably be rectified by telling it in one's next Confession. But it also implies that breaking the fast, though undesireable, was not regarded by people as a mortal sin either, despite the ruling of the Church on this matter. If it had been, the period between breaking the fast and one's next Confession would be a time of discomfort and even fear. This somewhat relaxed attitude on the part of some people (though not all) is borne out by the fact that (bacon) rashers and sausages were available on the train to anyone who wanted them, even on a Friday. It seems that the slight discretion given to people in deciding whether or not they were fit to fast and/or abstain was used to the full.

The situation in families was more complex because of the varying ages of the members: technically, those under the age of twenty-one were not obliged to fast, though as we have seen, not everyone was aware of this exemption. Moreover, it was generally felt that people, including children, should give up some form of pleasure or abstain from something for Lent, whether they were fasting or not. Kathleen B said 'for the rest of the Lent then you did some little spiritual thing yourself, you'd go off sweets or you'd go off something, you know'.[99] Máirín M spoke about this in the context of St Patrick's Day: 'Patrick's Day was your break, and we really looked forward to that because in addition to the whole idea of the one meal and two collations sweets were totally out in our house, and of course 'twas a big thing then Patrick's Day we'd have our little *bailiúchán*[100] of sweets ready for to eat ... and that would be a big thing'.[101] The family context was also described by Anthony F: 'People were very ... I mean we thought of it as children ... you'd go off sweets or something and the rest of the family wouldn't allow you to break it. We'd all be watching one another like and ... my mother and father, so if we went off something we really went off it for Lent'. This same interviewee mentions abstinence during November: 'November was the month of the Holy Souls. And 'twas a very very common custom then ... it still is ... that people would go off drink or something for the Holy Souls. They'd do that ... we all do it ... we go off sweets or something for our ... for our people'.[102]

Noreen P talks about people's attitude to the Eucharistic fast (i.e. fasting before receiving Holy Communion at Mass) in the following piece,

> nowadays as you know, we can eat practically just before you go – well before you go to Mass anyway ... but ... actually we fasted from midnight the night before ... it was the thing to do at that time. We didn't question it ... it was the thing to do and everybody did it ... we were actually very good people ... we were very docile. Even the older people, you know they took it ... it's totally different nowadays.[103]

Catherine Bell's discussion of fasting in the Islamic tradition provides some interesting areas of comparison with Catholics in Limerick in the first half of the twentieth century. Writing in 1997, Bell states that 'fasting sets Muslims off as a distinct community (*umma*) in contrast to their non-Muslim neighbors'.[104] This suggests that fasting is used as an aspect of culture which distinguishes the group from other groups within a larger, perhaps urban, community. This was unlikely to be a significant element of the practice in Limerick in a population which was overwhelmingly Catholic during the period studied. However, cultural practices can also be used expressively within the community itself, as Bell points out: 'the communal aspects of fasting are a powerful assertion and extension of doctrinal conformity in a manner that serves to differentiate the more devout from the more casual believer'.[105] These shades of devotion can be seen in the situations described above where female factory colleagues empathized with each other and encouraged each other in keeping the fast, while the story about Croom bakery demonstrates a more open approach to pressurizing co-workers in this regard. The situation in families would indicate that children too participated in encouraging and correcting those who broke or were in danger of breaking the fast, though this might more often be applied to the unofficial abstention from sweets which was widespread among the younger age group. Thus, though fasting was an individual and familial matter, in some ways and especially in certain situations it became everybody's business to make sure that it was adhered to. Brian Fallon has argued that the Catholic Church in this period managed to extend its 'ideological power base'[106] from the church (and school) to the private home: the evidence above shows how this was evident, at least to some extent, in the workplace as well. It also shows how a high level of ritual conformity was achieved among people in general. This is related to Mary Douglas's idea of the 'religion of control' discussed in Chapter 3, where frequent ritual activity is used by the 'strong group' to make sure that others conform.[107] Catherine Bell explains her view of the process as follows: 'The role of peer pressure in what has been called the quintessential act of individual submission ... points to subtler ways in which a religious community socializes its members in physical practices that reproduce central doctrinal traditions and identities'.[108]

Fasting and material culture

It is important to set the experience of fasting against the changes over time as well as the variations in people's material circumstances that influenced their attitude to and experience of food in general. Timmy G sums up the situation when he says 'in those days you wouldn't have as much food to eat ... as you have now ... so ... it wasn't much to fast. You weren't missing a whole lot, you know!'[109] Críostóir O'Flynn's account of his childhood in King's Island, in the early 1930s is valuable for the ethnographic detail he gives in this regard. Shopping habits, valuable indicators of access to food and fuel, are described as follows: 'In the small provision shops that were a feature of every street, it was a common sight to see customers buying an ounce of tea, which the shopkeeper weighed out from a packet into a paper twisted into a cone, or a quarter pound of butter or sugar. Some local shops also kept coal for sale by the stone'.[110] Children's awareness of food shortage is also made clear:

> We knew from what some of our schoolmates or neighbours told us that there were families where actual hunger was a constant factor in life and where, even in winter, sometimes there was not enough fuel in any form for fire or cooking. And one of the warnings we got from older brothers and sisters was to keep a close eye on the few slices of bread-and-butter we brought to the convent school; otherwise when lunchtime came round we might find that our lunch had disappeared.[111]

The fact that more or less everybody in the area was in a similar situation – O'Flynn states that his own family was 'no exception' – did not mitigate the embarrassment felt by those whose home circumstances were exposed to the community, as the following incident illustrates:

> On a summer's evening a little lad from a house not far from ours came dancing up the street chanting happily at the top of his voice, 'I got two cuts of bread for my sup-per!' His declaration and his happiness were quickly cut short as he was

followed and retrieved by his irate mother, who dragged him home while boxing his ears in the approved fashion.[112]

O'Flynn also describes mothers in working-class families rationing the final slices of loaves of bread, and often having to drink their own tea without any.[113] Accounts such as this make it clear that many would not even have had access to the amount of food actually permitted by the fast. There is also the fact that if a family was lucky enough to acquire meat or another food forbidden by the regulations during the fast, they would have to break the fast, thus committing a sin, to eat it, or, in the absence of home freezers or even fridges, let it go to waste and still go hungry themselves. The irony of the imposition of fasting regulations on people whose normal diet was restricted by poverty in any case was not lost on the people themselves, nor was the contrast between their own circumstances and those of the clergy implementing the regulations, as Críostóir O'Flynn's comment demonstrates:

> The bishops who made the laws about Friday abstinence did not have to dine on a mackerel or a pot of colcannon (I often wonder what the parish priest's housekeeper dished up for his Reverence on Fridays) but they were worse than those Pharisees who were condemned as hypocrites by Christ because they made burdens for others to carry but never raised a finger to help. No priest or bishop ever came around our streets asking the mothers how they were managing to feed their big families, on Friday or any other day.[114]

The difficulties experienced while fasting at work, described by interviewees above, present a somewhat different scenario: they show how young working people in the 1950s, in a situation of relative plenty, found it hard to eat less than they usually did. This was exacerbated by the fact that they had to fast within the structure of the working day, and also by the way their fast was watched by their colleagues, though this was approached by the female workforce in Irish Wire in a way that was significantly different from the male workforce in the bakery in Croom. For Máirín M, whose mother was a greengrocer and a keen cook, a strong sense of hunger felt during Lent in the 1950s is a distinct memory, while her little collection of sweets ready to be eaten on St. Patrick's Day indicates that for her, the period of the fast was a definite contrast to her experience at other times of the year.

Fasting and feasting

The practice of fasting could be seen as an important element of Mary Douglas's model of a 'religion of control' where limitations placed on the body play an important role in a larger ritual framework with a dense symbolic grid and a strong, active social group. However, it is also important to consider how the mental discipline, bodily control and physical hardship of the fast contrasted with the times both before and after it. Looked at in the larger context of European cultural history, Limerick city can be seen as, to some extent, following the patterns of fasting and feasting identitifed by Peter Burke in his study of popular culture in Early Modern Europe, despite the significant differences between the periods and places involved. In describing the phenomenon of Carnival, the street festival which took place in many European countries before the beginning of Lent, Burke points out that:

> Carnival did not have the same importance all over Europe. It was strong in the Mediterranean area, in Italy, Spain and France; fairly strong in Central Europe; and at its weakest in the north, in Britain and Scandinavia, probably because the weather discouraged an elaborate street festival at this time of year.[115]

Here, Ireland could be bracketed with Britain and Scandinavia, where the weather was not suitable for street festivals. The lack of major urban centres in Ireland, certainly as far as the period discussed by Burke was concerned, may also have been a factor.[116] However, Burke also notes that the twelve days of Christmas were 'treated as Carnivalesque'[117] and the evidence from Limerick city in the early to mid-twentieth century supports this. This can be seen most obviously in the area of food, which had a central role to play in the celebration of Christmas, which came immediately after the Advent fast. Interviewees, remembering this time, vividly recall the food eaten on coming home from Midnight Mass on Christmas Eve, when the Advent fast was finally over. Meat figured largely in this meal, which would take place in the early hours of the morning before going to bed. Kathleen B described 'the beautiful big iron pan on the range and the sausages and rashers' and also mentioned the local dish, 'suet packet', made in Treacy's in King's Island: 'And 'twould have thyme … it was made at Treacy's, specially. And there'd be thyme and a little bit of onion, 'twas flavoured … but 'twas beautiful. Done with a mill'.[118] Áine R particularly remembers the sausages bought by her mother for Christmas Eve:

> Oh and she'd always buy sausages, we always had sausages on Christmas Eve. But we'd have to wait till after twelve, because 'twas a fast … And we'd stay up – some of us would go to midnight Mass, and we'd stay up, just to come back. But those sausages! They tasted gorgeous! Nothing today tastes the same you know.[119]

In Eileen L's home, steak and onions were eaten after Midnight Mass, showing, again, the importance of meat after a period of fasting and abstinence.[120] Christmas Day itself also involved special food, although, like the feast after Midnight Mass, this also varied from household to household. Críostóir O'Flynn describes the buying of the Christmas goose as 'the greatest shopping event of the year', going on to say,

> when it was brought home it was hung in the shed, well-protected, until the night when it was to be plucked. The feathers were kept to make a pillow or a cushion and the wings became brushes for the range and the hearth. The goose itself 'died a sudden death' on Christmas Day … but the giblets … and the carcase made great soup.[121]

Kathleen B's and Máirín M's families both had turkey, with the latter explaining how some of their neighbours in the lane nearby would also be given their Christmas dinner from the turkey.[122] In Áine R's home, a half-head (i.e. pig's head) would be bought:

And always my mother would get … a half-head. Now a half-head, most people would know, was a pig's head cut in two halves. And you'd buy that, 'twas cheap. And, at that time, you'd boil cabbage with it. There was a lovely flavour off of it. And there was little bits of meat on it, d'you know. 'Twas the flavour, and the cabbage was lovely. But … my mother loved the half-head. We'd always have it on Christmas. Unless my uncle might send down something because he worked in Shaws. But otherwise 'twould be the half-head anyway.[123]

Sweet food and drinks were also important. Kathleen B mentions the plum pudding as part of the meal eaten after Midnight Mass, while O'Flynn refers to the custom of each member of the family giving a stir to the mixture as it was being made.[124] He also comments on how 'a big stock of lemonade and other minerals was laid in for Christmas', as well as the feelings of discomfort brought about by 'a few days of glorious guzzling'.[125] Áine R describes the dessert on Christmas Day as follows:

Christmas was something in our house. 'Twas the one day in the year we had custard and jelly, for one thing … Yea, I remember my friends next door, one Christmas – I even said it to the girls lately – once, one Christmas we were in their house, and they had so much jelly, that they started pelting it at each other! And of course, God, can you imagine like … I remember that – I mean that means you must have had a lot of jelly, you know, because we didn't do it – we normally loved the jelly.[126]

The strong sense of festivity is in evidence in all the interviewees' accounts above: that Christmas was a time for special food that would not be eaten at any other time of year. Peter Burke might well be describing Christmas in Limerick city in the early to mid-twentieth century when he comments that Carnival 'was opposed to the everyday, a time of waste precisely because the everyday was a time of careful saving'.[127] The idea of eating sausages, and even steak in the early hours of the morning, with all the festivities (and extra food) of the next day still to come was certainly in opposition to everyday life, and was all the more dramatic coming immediately after the Advent fast. According to Burke, this opposition was an important aspect of Carnival, which, in the communities studied by him, because of its timing, was more in opposition to Lent than to Advent. Another aspect of Carnival is also discussed by Burke: 'Carnival was an enactment of "the world turned upside down", a favourite theme in the popular culture of Early Modern Europe; *le monde renversé, il mondo alla rovescia, Die verkehrte Welt*'.[128] There is some feeling of this in Áine R's evidence regarding her friends throwing jelly at one another. It is clear that having jelly was a rare event, yet the instinct here is not to save or hoard it or make it last as long as possible (which may actually have been possible with jelly, unlike some other foods). Instead, in a Carnivalesque reversal of the everyday, the girls start throwing it at one another.

Elements of Carnival can also be seen in the St Stephen's Day custom of the Wren Boys, mentioned by some interviewees and carried out in many city areas on 26 December up to the 1970s, and continuing – albeit in a somewhat different format – up to the present day in some. Anthony F describes his own experience:

St Stephen's Day and we'd go round, we'd blacken our faces and 'The Wran Boys' and we'd go round in groups or clusters. There might be no more than five or six in each but we'd … go back and we'd make a bit of money, I remember making a half-crown now around 1940. A half-crown then, like, was big money today.[129]

In the Park area of the city, the wren was still being killed up to the 1950s. One interviewee, speaking in the late 1980s, remembered fourteen or fifteen birds being killed on St Stephen's Day in Park in the 1940s. According to him, it would then be put on a stick and brought around to the houses: the old people wouldn't give the children money until they saw the dead wren on the stick of holly or ivy.[130] According to Áine R's evidence, the Wren (or 'Wran') Boys were also active in St Mary's Park: they would be gone by noon, and then the people would go out and tour the churches to see the different Christmas cribs.[131] This custom, involving a mixture of walking around the churches, meeting and talking with other families, prayer and aesthetic enjoyment (see Chapter 7) could be seen as bringing the world back to normal after the excesses of Christmas Eve and Christmas Day – the exercise and fresh air playing a large part in this. The element of feasting next appeared on Shrove Tuesday, the day before Ash Wednesday, when Lent began. Máirín M describes Shrove or 'Pancake Tuesday' as 'a big event in our house, making the pancakes, making the batter, leaving it settle etc., and we would have a feed until we were fit to collapse from eating too much and … that was it!'[132] A sense of celebration reappeared on St Patrick's Day, when the Lenten fast was broken for one day and many people went to St Patrick's Well in Singland after Mass and the civic parade were over.[133] As mentioned above, Máirín M also gave an account of children saving their sweets for St Patrick's Day.

Peter Burke has highlighted the suggestion that 'in traditional societies, a man lives in remembrance of one festival and in expectation of the next'.[134] In Limerick city during the period studied, the anticipation of Easter, when the Lenten fast was finally over, could be seen in this light. The experience of breaking the fast is here described by Eileen L: 'You felt good about Easter Sunday morning – and Easter Sunday when you started to eat chocolate and everything … it was a great feeling'.[135] As noted above, Máirín M frames her account of Lenten fasting with descriptions of the occasions of plenty which preceded it, interrupted it and followed it. Her account of ending the fast at Easter is as follows:

I remember on Easter Saturday Lent finished officially I believe – or so it did for us anyway as children in Limerick – at twelve o'clock on the Saturday of Holy Week … in our house anyway and all of the people that lived around me. And I remember as children what we used to do was all the neighbours' children would come to our – we had a yard at the side of our house – and we would have a table set up there which was really just a big timber box with a tablecloth on it! … And everybody would bring their little *bailiúchán* of Easter eggs and chocolates or whatever they could get and we would wait, and the minute the Angelus would ring, all the bells around Limerick the Angelus bell would ring, in every church, at twelve o'clock. It was always a feature, bells everywhere in Limerick … and when the twelve o'clock would ring … we were at the off and we'd all have our Easter eggs! (Laughter) And that was one of the main features as far as I was concerned about Lent and Lent was over, thank God![136]

These accounts are interesting in a few ways. Firstly, they show how interviewees who participated in the strict physical control of the body fully appreciated the value of its opposite: the freedom to eat as much as they liked of whatever foods they liked. The children's appreciation of this is particularly striking. The creativity of children, in a ritual sense, is also noteworthy here. Coming at the end of the ritually intense period of Lent and Holy Week, the children's response is to create a ritual occasion for what *they* saw as significant – beginning to eat their Easter eggs and other sweets. This is an example of meaning-making where, in Ann Taves's terms, religious significance is ascribed to actions and events in a creative process linking prescribed religious behaviour (i.e. fasting) to other aspects of life, thus providing a continuum of experience in which there is no definite dividing-line between religious experience and that which would not normally be termed as such.[137] The urban context is crucial to this: the nearness of neighbouring children that could freely gather and bring their 'goodies' without parental involvement, along with the drama of waiting for the bells to ring in the various city churches at noon contributed to the children's creation of a ritual feast on Holy Saturday. For them, and probably for many others, however they may have marked the occasion, the Lenten fast, and the bodily control it required, may only have attained its full meaning when contrasted with the sense of freedom and plenty which followed it.

The rosary and fasting: From everyday life to ordered cosmos

The rosary and fasting, though occupying a somewhat similar ritual context in people's lives, were very different from each other from the point of view of form and structure. Here, it is useful to review their functions in the culture of Limerick city during the period studied and to link them, in these terms, to the ideas of various writers on ritual.

The rosary not only fulfils basic definitions of ritual, Honko's 'traditional, prescribed communication with the sacred' for instance,[138] but also provides scope for a more detailed exploration of its features in Roy Rappaport's terms. Rappaport has identified a number of what he calls 'logical entailments' of ritual. He explains this approach by saying that as ritual is comprised of 'sets of enduring structural relations among specified but variable features or elements ... [it] can not only claim to be socially and materially consequential, but to possess *logical entailments* as well'.[139] Rappaport provides a list of thirteen elements which go to make up the sets of structural relations, or logical entailments, and it is not difficult to see how some of these may be applied to the rosary prayer. The notion of the 'generation of a concept of the sacred', for instance, can be seen in the thematic arrangement of the fifteen mysteries. The Joyful Mysteries, to take one example, consist of the Annunciation, the Visitation, the Nativity, the Presentation and the Finding of the Child Jesus in the Temple.[140] Three out of the five of these events (or events equivalent to them in meaning, if not in their actual details) happen to ordinary families, four, if the Presentation is seen as equivalent to Baptism, but the meditation upon them in the context of the prayer gives them a sacred aspect which is then expanded upon in the fifth and final mystery in the chaplet when the Child Jesus shows his special qualities in the temple. This generates a concept of the sacred around the events of ordinary life, while Rappaport's related element 'the sanctification of the conventional order' can be seen in the cultural connection between this family-themed prayer and its importance in real families, a connection which was promoted and re-emphasized by the Family Rosary Crusade discussed above. In this sense, the family was not seen as merely a biological accident or a convenient social arrangement: it was also a group of people who prayed together and participated in a sanctified version of life by doing so. The wildepread custom of placing the Sacred Heart picture in the household kitchen (where the rosary was usually said) with its red lamp permanently lighting gave a visual, material and sometimes, through the family-themed text beneath the image, discursive aspect to this sanctification of ordinary life. At least two more of Rappaport's 'logical entailments', his 'establishment of convention' and 'sealing of social contract' can also be seen in the rosary event, whether this took place at work or at home: the custom of one leader with the responsibility for distributing decades to the others, for instance, and the different roles played by strong-minded parents and idealistic or obedient young people.

It's also important to note the inversion in the conventional order brought about by those who rejected the ritual by being continually distracted or by simply not being there. Bell, in her discussion of the actions of anti-religious Jews gathering publicly to eat pork on Yom Kippur, has the following to say: 'Like many inversions, however, such acts of defiance may simply help delineate the normative values of the community'.[141] It might be inaccurate to portray the absence of the rosary, or a failure to say it properly in some homes as 'acts of defiance', but it could be said that lapses such as these made the ritual, when it was carried out consistently and with reasonable success, all the more emphatic and effective in the lives of those who participated. It is also clear that the rosary occupied a central place in the lives of those who were dedicated to it: said every day at home with the family and on many religious occasions; recited privately during Mass and in bed at night; prayed on trains, buses and in cars. This is a good example of an aspect of Mary Douglas's dense symbolic 'grid' and its role in a religion of control. In terms of the meaning of a frequent, almost ever-present, ritual such as this, Rappaport says:

> The frequency of ritual performances may also be related to the extent to which the liturgical order … guides continuing daily behavior … which … may be related to the vulnerability of the order being realised to violation or even dissolution by the pressures and temptations of everday life.[142]

The rosary could be seen as a form of resistance against other cultural forces in Ireland in the twentieth century, particularly from the time of the Family Rosary Crusade in the 1950s, as the 'pressures and temptations' of life, in the area of popular culture, most especially those of the cinema and the dancehall, increased. The question of the various competing discourses is largely outside the scope of this study, but in this context it is sufficient to point out that the frequency of the rosary would have been effective in this regard. Rappaport also discusses the metaphysical aspect: 'Brief but frequent rituals … do not transport participants to a divine world but attempt an opposite movement; they attempt to realize a divine order in mundane time'.[143] If this ritual strategy was to work, the rosary, rather than being rendered ordinary by being said so often, would instead infect everyday life with its own spiritual aspect. It is impossible to know with any certainty whether the rosary did this or not. It must also be said that people's feelings about a particular ritual can be seen only as one level of analysis, while the effect of the ritual in their lives in general can be seen as another. However, some people's intense dedication to the rosary (Eileen L's father and Áine R's mother would be two examples) shows that for them it was a crucial element of the symbolic grid of which it was a part. The rosary was practised very differently by these two people: for Eileen L's father it was an elaborate family ritual adhered to at all times; for Áine R's mother, who did not succeed in establishing the rosary as a family ritual, it was an important personal prayer. These examples illustrate the multi-faceted nature of the ritual along with its complex role in people's lives.

In terms of the analysis of ritual, fasting presents a very different challenge. Despite the extensive guidelines and parameters laid down in catechisms and frequently explained by the clergy, it was, in practice, a ritual without any particular form or liturgical order; it was carried out without prayers or accompanying gestures. However, fasting is of course the counterpoint to ritual feasting, and it is probably true to say that the more formal ritual elements tend to attach themselves to the feasting events in any case as both Catherine Bell's treatment and interviewees' evidence, discussed above, shows.[144] Fasting and abstinence, then, involved a lack of action rather than anything else, though it is important to remember that people had to make the effort to seek out fish to eat on Fridays: advertisements by fish merchants in Limerick show that this was an important aspect of their business.[145]

The social and material contexts of fasting have already been discussed, but its deeper meanings also need to be looked at. The relationship between fasting and concepts of time is one area of meaning; physical effort and bodily involvement is another. It is useful to look at fasting in the context of the overall organization of Lent in Ireland in the early to mid-twentieth century. Rappaport's notion that 'ritual may transform mere extent into ordered cosmos'[146] is relevant here in considering how time was marked and shaped in the most basic way during this period. Rappaport also discusses the organization of time in complex societies, saying that in the absence of the common work-practices prevailing in tribal or peasant communities, ritual can 'mark or establish periodicities in accordance with which non-ritual agencies may conduct and regulate a range of activities within a common temporal regime'.[147] In this way, Lent wasn't just a feature of the local church or the weekly Confraternity meeting, it was also 'on' in the factory, on the shop-floor, on the train and in the home. As we have seen, the breakfast or tea-break in the bakery or in the factory during Lent was markedly different to these occasions at other times. In the same way, Sunday Mass didn't just happen in the church, it 'happened', or began to happen the night before (or three hours before, in the later part of the period), as people marked this time by not eating. The feeling of hunger, or that of missing meat, gave the period a certain character. In the case of the anticipation of Sunday Mass, other preparatory activities, such as polishing shoes and assembling clean clothes to wear could also contribute to the experience. Rappaport says 'The primary purpose of some ritual constituents, like the use of drugs, sensory overload, sensory deprivation and alternation between overload and deprivation, seems to be to disrupt mundane canons of reality'.[148] The drama of fasting can be found not just in the sensory deprivation mentioned by Rappaport, but also in the tensions arising from conformity or lack of it in various social situations.

The ritual power of the rosary and the practice of fasting and abstaining lies partly in their simplicity. Certainly the rosary is spiritually and discursively complex, but it is a simple ritual to carry out, even without a rosary beads (itself a small and convenient object). As long as people knew the basic prayers said in the rosary, for as we have seen the 'trimmings' and even the awareness of the mysteries varied from place to place, it was possible to say it anywhere or at any time. This explains its use in the home, the workplace and on occasions of travel as well as in many devotional contexts. Thus, its ability to sanctify the mundane was considerable, and it may have done this for many people. Similarly, fasting and abstaining required a strong attitude of mind rather than any special equipment or personnel. It could be done anywhere: in fact, it is clear that the achievement of fasting or 'sticking to it' in various tempting situations (the train journey being perhaps the most tempting of those described above!) was part of the challenge. In this sense it did constitute a disruption of mundane life, however uncomfortable this may have been.

The somewhat optional nature of the rosary and the custom of fasting and abstaining also added to their power. Despite the fact that fasting was a precept of the Church for which very specific guidelines were given, the evidence shows that these were open to interpretation and that some people did interpret them for themselves although it is important to note that this depended very much on the situations in which they found themselves. In this sense whatever one's notion of the details of the obligation to fast, managing to do so was the result of a decision at some level, even if this was just the decision to conform. Similary the rosary was a prayer to be said in personal and familial contexts, but it need not necessarily be said at all. The people who established the rosary at home or in the workplace did this because they decided to do so and stuck to it. It is clear that some people were more motivated than others in these areas: those, for instance, who would start the rosary on the train. But for people like this and for those who went along with them, everyday, personal rituals such as these helped to mark time and sanctify life in social and physical contexts: transforming the undifferentiated days, weeks and hours into Rappaport's 'ordered cosmos' in an ongoing and effective way.

Devotion and Belief

In her survey of classic devotional manuals, Margaret Miles notes how Christians from medieval times to the early modern period lived their lives 'in the face of the expectation of an inevitable judgement in which their destiny of everlasting reward or punishment would be decided by an omniscient and unbiased judge'.[1] Writing in the 1980s, Miles comments that the lack of this type of belief among many late twentieth-century historians of Christianity could prevent scholars from realizing its importance as a 'strongly motivating and organizing pressure'[2] in the lives of the people studied. Certainly, this is something to take into account in looking at both official Catholicism and its practice at the popular level in Limerick city in the years between 1925 and 1960, and it is particularly relevant to the area of personal devotion. In looking at devotion carried out by individuals, the intensity of belief underpinning the ritual process must always be taken into account. In this area, too, the extension of religious values into people's everyday lives can be seen: a personal, individually oriented ritual such as Confession, for instance, was closely linked to the penitent's non-ritual activities while their own private prayers, whether at their favourite shrine or at home, were likely to involve thought about the rest of their lives as well. In this sense, personal religious practice could be said to be connected to a deeper level within the person than were the bigger communal rituals in which the social framework loomed so large: however, it must also be said that the wider social aspect is by no means unimportant in the understanding of these rituals.

It could be said that the context for this part of the study is provided by intense personal belief: this was most obviously derived from official Catholic teaching but also, in more subtle ways, from vernacular or more traditional concepts of the super-natural. This belief was strongly held and acted upon in a particular social, physical and metaphysical framework. However, though this is definitely true in a general sense, it will also become clear that there were variations in both the intensity of the various aspects of belief, and in people's approaches to the rituals connected to them.

Sin – consequences and remedies

In looking at everyday life in Limerick during the period studied, it is at the level of the individual person's beliefs and behaviour that concepts of right and wrong can be seen most clearly. However, it is useful, in the first place, to look at how these ideas were presented to Catholics in general in the first half of the twentieth century. Through their religious education, people were taught that human beings were born with original sin on their souls. Original sin is described and discussed in the 1919 text, *Catechism Notes* as follows:

> The sin committed by Adam, who was the origin and head of the human race. It comes to each of us with our human nature ... We naturally lean or tend to what is bad ... God cannot look on us with love so long as original sin is on our souls ... By resisting these bad inclinations we win a higher place in heaven.[3]

As well as original sin, Catholic doctrine, during the period studied, stated that humans had to contend with actual sin, which could be committed by thought, word, deed or omission. In this text, the definition of the various kinds of actual sin is given as follows:

> Actual sin is divided into Venial sin and Mortal sin. Venial sin means lesser sin, so called because it is more easily pardoned than Mortal sin. No number of venial sins will make a mortal sin, or take away sanctifying grace. Mortal sin is the death of the soul – venial sin is the sickness which often leads to death.[4]

The text then lists three conditions which must be fulfilled before the sin is regarded as a mortal sin: (i) 'grave matter' which meant that the action had to be 'very serious and very bad'; (ii) 'full knowledge' which meant that the person knew the action was a mortal sin; (iii) 'full consent' which meant that the action had to be carried out 'on purpose'. Punishments for sin are divided into 'Eternal' and 'Temporal' kinds: the former 'lasts forever in Hell, and is suffered only for unforgiven mortal sins', while the latter 'will end either with this life, or in Purgatory. It is suffered for venial sin and for forgiven mortal sin'.[5]

The question of the exact action necessary to commit a mortal sin is a complex one, however. The *Catechism Notes*, in its various editions implies, albeit somewhat vaguely, that breaking any of the Ten Commandments is a mortal sin when it says: 'If we wilfully break one of the Commandments by mortal sin, to keep all the others will not save our souls'.[6] The 1958 *Catechism for Children*, perhaps because it is aimed at children from fourth to sixth class in primary schools, gives clearer guidance on what may constitute a mortal sin. The implication here is that while it is always wrong to break one of the ten 'Commandments of God', certain serious breaches of these laws are mortal sins. For instance, as part of a long discussion of the 'Fourth Commandment of God: Honour thy father and thy mother', the catechism advises children to do what they are commanded to do by their parents: 'Do it at once and do it cheerfully. Don't delay. Don't grumble. Don't sulk. God loves obedient children and He makes them very happy even in this life'.[7] However, the treatment of this Commandment also includes a section on 'Citizens and Rulers'. Under this heading, the text states that to 'join a society that plots to overthrow by force or other sinful measures the lawful government'[8] is a mortal sin. Under the heading of the Seventh Commandment ('Thou shalt not steal') the following guidance is given: '*To take unjustly*. You commit a mortal sin if you mean to take a large amount, even though you steal it in small sums'.[9] The discussion of the Eighth Commandment, answering the question 'Is a lie always sinful?', states that: 'A lie is always sinful, and nothing can excuse it; it is a mortal sin, when it does serious injury to our neighbour'.[10]

It can be understood from the treatment of the areas of right and wrong in the catechisms, outlined above, that some sins were viewed as so obviously grave or 'mortal' that it wasn't necessary to actually list them: murder, adultery or theft of significant amounts, for instance. Other mortal sins needed clarification however: incremental theft as described above, telling a damaging lie about somebody else, joining a subversive organization. The specific mention of the latter, in a text aimed at Irish schoolchildren in 1958, is interesting. In general, it seemed to be understood that while breaking one of the Ten Commandments (termed 'The Commandments of God' in the catechisms) was always a sin, there were shades of sinfulness within these areas of behaviour and the more severe breaches of these laws were mortal sins. The catechisms also explained another set of laws: these were called 'The Commandments of the Church' or 'The Precepts of the Church'. There were six precepts, concerning, respectively, attendance at Mass on Sundays and holy days of obligation; fasting and abstinence; Confession; Communion as part of the Easter Duty; support of the Church; and laws concerning marriage. The Precepts or Commandments of the Church really read like a practical guide to religious and particularly ritual behaviour: what to do and when to do it. The catechism texts explain that while the Ten Commandments of God cannot be changed, the commandments or precepts of the church can be changed or dispensed with 'by the same authority that made them'.[11] The question of whether their non-fulfilment constituted a sin varies according to the individual precept, and from text to text as well. The *Catechism for Children* tells us that non-attendance at Sunday Mass is a mortal sin, while the *Catechism Notes* emphasizes the mortal sin of breaking the laws of fast and abstinence.[12] Other precepts, those concerning disallowed marriages for instance, are not given in any great detail, presumably because the clergy were involved in the arrangements in any case and could veto any unsuitable union if, according to them, this was necesssary. The long explanations given on fasting and abstinence are understandable in this context – the clergy could not supervise the actual ritual themselves. In the same way, non-attendance at Mass, or being involved in political organizations could remove the faithful from the ambit of the clergy (to some extent).

Heaven and hell

The formal teaching of the Catholic Church detailed above could be seen as an example of the 'motivating and organising pressure' mentioned by Margaret Miles. It is interesting to see how this motivational discourse was reproduced and interpreted by the people who were reading and memorizing the catechism texts in schools. It must also be noted that guidelines such as this were reinforced through sermons at Mass or during missions, and in prayer texts such as those said as part of the rosary, as well as in other media. The evidence, in general, demonstrates that the official teaching of the Church was fully understood and closely followed at the level of popular practice.

Interviewees' comments are testimony to the effect of the catechism texts, and to the way in which they were mediated in church and in school: 'When we were young growing up we firmly believed that if you died in mortal sin you went down to the pit of hell and you would be burning for all eternity'.[13] Noreen P, when asked about heaven, said 'Heaven was the place – the beautiful place to go. And, whereas we had that in our mind, definitely, a beautiful place, with garden, flowers, music, everything … we heard more about the opposite – hell. Which was damnation and fire and … a terrible terrible place to go'. According to this interviewee, hell was spoken about in school and in sermons, especially those given by the Redemptorist Order as part of a parish mission held once every five years: 'And definitely the idea of hell was portrayed in the most unbelievably gruesome way, so that you'd be feeling like you were a terrible terrible sinner for doing the least little thing'.[14] In his evidence, Timmy G encompasses the people's attitude to hell and the Catholic Church's portrayal of it, contrasting it with the situation today:

> I'd say the majority of the youth now, you couldn't frighten them. There'd be no use telling them 'you're going to hell' … they wouldn't give a hoot, you know? I mean, at that time, the innocence of people – they believed in hell fire and all that the souls were burning, kind of. But it's a different type of hell now, it's not being in the presence of God'.[15]

Noreen P also highlighted the sense of fear involved in thinking about sin, especially where some people, and some sins, were concerned:

> And some people took it very seriously, depending on your upbringing or … the environment you were in. Some people took it too strict altogether and probably went a little mental because of … being afraid to do this or afraid to do that or afraid to – in the case of men – go out with a girl, and Oh God – there were such guidelines there! God help us! If they went by what the brothers in school said and the priests preached on the mission in particular … there would have been no procreation at all!

In the convent school attended by Máirín M in the 1950s, religious films were shown: she remembers one in particular about the Children of Fatima, in which Our Lady allows them to see the fires of hell. Máirín describes the film and the ensuing discussion as follows:

> all the people burning and the way it was done … at the time it was the most terrifying sight that you'd end up in Hell someday you know and they had these bodies down with their hands up, trying to plead with – to be taken up out of it, you know … the following day you'd have a discussion on what had happened … this would be the thing about, you know, that's one place you never want to go, so the thing of committing sin, like, a venial sin or a mortal sin that you'd end up all the days … but if it was a venial sin you could be forgiven when you'd go to Confession … then … you'd want to have your soul clear because if you died and you didn't go to Hell if you hadn't committed a mortal sin, you'd go to Purgatory.[16]

This worldview, put forward in the catechisms and eloquently recounted by interviewees, is interesting in that it connects people's everyday actions, in every sphere of life, to their eventual fate in the afterlife. This takes belief beyond the realm of ritual into everyday actions and their consequences. It also puts the responsibility for a disordered cosmos, in the form of sin, on the individual person, something Catherine Bell associates with European and American approaches to dealing with affliction of various kinds. In her discussion of religions in which possession and exorcism are used, such as the Ndembu tribe studied by Victor Turner, she notes: 'In particular, possession cultures identify powerful forces and influences outside the individual, while Euro-American culture often identifies them within the individual'.[17] While it is true that concepts of the devil and of original sin in the Catholic religion (and in other Christian denominations) would suggest a source of disorder outside, or beyond the control of, the person, the concept of Actual Sin put the responsibility for much that was wrong with the world on its human inhabitants, while the remedies and solutions to the problem of evil were seen as residing almost totally within the individual person.

This approach to dealing with the affliction of sin meant that people were focusing on their own behaviour, in every area, in order to make sure that they didn't die with what they regarded as serious sin on their souls. The ritual of Confession played a crucial role in this process. There were also other ways to keep away from what were regarded as tempting circumstances and situations thought to be sinful: personal prayer was one of the most important of these, and it was important in many different ways. Catholics were advised to use regular morning and night prayer to continually focus and refocus on their faith; short prayers – called 'Aspirations' in the catechism texts and referred to as such by both Church personnel and lay-people – could also be said throughout the day, and particularly in times of temptation.[18] Certain prayers were also regarded as powerful enough to gain indulgences (or forgiveness from sin) for certain periods of time.[19] Some prayers could even be recited in order to compensate for the sins of others; this process, known as 'Reparation' was promoted by certain orders, such as the Jesuits through their Apostleship of Prayer organization, and by the enclosed religious order founded specifically for this purpose, the Marie Reparatrice or Reparation nuns who set up a convent in Limerick in 1884. Reparation was partly the basis of an annual organized devotion in the Marie Reparatrice convent in the South Circular Road during the period studied, but could also be carried out on an individual basis.[20] Prayer was also used to help to free the souls in purgatory, who were waiting to go to heaven.

What is striking about the culture of affliction described above is the extent to which the official teaching of the Catholic Church and the people's concepts of sin, hell and the uses of prayer are practically one and the same. Perhaps this is not surprising, given the extent to which official religion permeated the social, cultural and educational fabric of the modernizing city (as described in Chapter 1). However, it is interesting to note that even among the most devout individuals and communities, this detailed knowledge and understanding of orthodox practice co-existed with older forms of vernacular religion and supernatural belief, a point which will become clearer and more important as this discussion progresses. For now, it is perhaps enough to say that the communication of the discourse of official Catholicism to ordinary Catholics in Limerick city in the period studied was highly effective and successful from the point of view of supernatural belief.

Confession: Guidelines and experiences

According to the Code of Canon Law, promulgated in 1917, Catholics were, and still are, obliged to 'confess their sins carefully at least once a year'.[21] In catechism texts from the early to mid-twentieth century, Confession is discussed in great detail as one of the Sacraments of the Church: the frequency of the ritual is, however, set out in the Precepts or Commandments of the Church, where it is stated that sins must be confessed once a year (usually as part of the preparation for Catholics' Easter Duty: receiving Holy Communion during the Easter season).[22] The catechisms also mention Confession in the context of the 'state of grace' necessary before receiving Holy Communion in any case. The *Catechism Key* of 1959 states that to 'make a good Communion (**to receive worthily**), three things are needed'. The first of these is described below, with the key terms in bold print as is the author's practice in this text:

> **State of grace**. Food is no use to the dead. Communion is no use to man who knows he is dead in mortal sin. If you are in mortal sin, and you make an act of perfect contrition, the mortal sin goes away. Yet, you must not go to Communion until you have first gone to Confession. This is the law of the Church. To go to Communion, when you know you are in mortal sin is a very bad sin of sacrilege. *It can be quite lawful to go to Holy Communion for months without going to Confession. If you are afraid to go to Communion because of doubts about being in the state of grace, ask advice at Confession.*[23]

This put the responsibility of deciding whether Confession was necessary on the individual person: their decision would depend on their concepts of the different kinds of sin. The *Catechism Notes* of 1944 explains the kinds of sin in the context of Confession as follows:

> Confession of mortal sins: We are bound to confess all known mortal sins. If we forget a mortal sin it is forgiven with the others, but we should tell it in our next Confession, if we remember it.
> Confession of venial sins: We are not bound to confess venial sins but it is better to do so. If we want to receive absolution and have no mortal sins, we must tell and be sorry for at least one venial sin.[24]

The fear of sin, and of the consequences of dying in a sinful state, most especially in a state of mortal sin, was one of the main motivating factors in the decision to go to Confession on a weekly basis even though according to the Church guidelines, once a year should have been enough. One interviewee says: 'we all went to Confession, every week of course'.[25] Another says 'We went to Confession regularly, once a fortnight'.[26] The regularity of Confession in a person's life also depended on how often they wanted to receive Communion: 'But we did go … what was very important, that you went … as you went to Mass on Sunday, you went to Confession on Saturday night or Saturday afternoon. And there would be seats and seats of people waiting'.[27]

Contrition and penance were central themes in the devotional discourse during Lent and it is clear that the approach of Easter was a time that was deemed appropriate for this. Even for people who went to Confession more often, the sacrament took on an extra importance during the season of Lent:

> But you'd have to go especially for Lent … between Ash Wednesday and Trinity Sunday, you always went to Confession. But the church used to be *black*, going to Confession. Queues! And what our mothers used to do to us then: your mother would send you down, to sit in the queue, move up in her place, until you came to the box, and there might be three or four of us sitting down for our mothers, together, from Keane Street, and when the mothers would come then – they'd be busy minding the babies or doing something – they'd all come in and … we'd get out of the way and they'd go in to Confession then. Save their time![28]

Given the centrality of penance during Lent, it is not surprising that fasting and abstinence, both during Lent and at other times, were topics in Confession frequently. Breaking a fast was regarded as a sin that needed to be confessed, though whether this lapse was regarded as a mortal sin or not varied somewhat (as is clear in Chapter 5). In her discussion of Lent, Áine R shows some anxiety regarding the matter:

> But the minute … if we broke that in any way, we were all at Confession on Saturday, every one of us, and we were all – we'd the same thing 'Father I broke the fast.' That was the biggest sin! … And he'd say 'Ah well try again now.' Most of them were nice, you know … and they'd say 'Ah continue to try again.[29]

Áine stresses the slight urgency felt by herself and her friends to confess the broken fast as soon as possible, and, in their case, the priests' reactions seemed to be quite comforting and reassuring. The sense of urgency in the following account by Noreen P is much stronger:

> I remember when I was about ten probably, or nine … one day, for some reason or other … I went to Communion as per usual and … I realised after I had got Communion that I had eaten something before I came out. And I was in a panic, in a terrible, terrible panic … I thought the whole world would have known. And I felt – it was very important to confess what I had done. And I went around to the Canon – not sure whether I told anybody or not but I did go around the corner of the church to the sacristy, and Canon Quin was there, and I told him very frighteningly that I had eaten something before I got Holy Communion. So he told me to kneel down on the *prié-dieu*, and he said some prayers, and forgave whatever had to be forgiven. And that was that frightening experience over me![30]

The worry here may be linked to the fact that the broken fast was a Communion fast rather than simply a Lenten one: the age of the interviewee at the time of the incident may also be a factor here. The palpable sense of fear in this account is an accurate indicator of how some people experienced the area of affliction and the Church's methods of dealing with it. This interviewee also said, 'We just didn't question' in her assessment of both the belief or worldview elements and the authoritarian aspects of religion, and she described fear as being 'part and parcel' of religion at the time.[31] Canon Quin's reaction seems quite neutral however, though he does not comfort or reassure this penitent: perhaps absolution – regarded as the appropriate rite of affliction in this case – was felt to be comfort enough, and the interviewee does note a sense of relief after it.

Another incident involving young females, in a slightly less serious vein, shows Canon Quin in a different light, though his composure must have been put to the test in this case:

> I remember the first time that I found out that babies don't get brought by the nurses (Laughter) … and when one of the girls found out … 'No, that's not what happens! Nurses don't bring them … you know … they come another way!' And every one of us went down to Confession and we said – every one of the pals – 'Father, I know how I came into the world' I can still remember what we said! (Laughter) We were only after finding out that they grow in … your mother, you know … Now that's all we knew at that time! And we had to go down to Confession with it! … 'Twas Canon Quin, and he said 'Well yes, yes. You know that now.' We were all twelve, thirteen, fourteen … 'Ah – yes. And it's a little seed – you know it comes from a little …' I can remember every word he said 'It's a little seed, and it grows and … you know, becomes a baby'. And that was … we all came out anyway, delighted 'cause the priest had left us go and he thought we were alright and we were happy. So … we'd a lot to learn![32]

This story is interesting because it shows the uncertainty of young people regarding their interpretation of the doctrine of sin. The idea that simply knowing *something* of reproduction, something that perhaps they felt should not be known by them, or something that somehow belonged to the adult world, was enough to propel them to Confession. The sense of sin, and perhaps shame, here is made stronger by the connection between reproduction and sexuality – a connection felt instinctively rather than consciously understood by the girls. The relief felt by them in finding out that they have done nothing wrong is in large measure due to Canon Quin, who could be said to have risen to the occasion by reassuring each of them in turn that this new knowledge of theirs was both true and legitimate: he even attempted to expand slightly on what they already knew. The age of this interviewee at the time places the incident around 1948 to 1950.

Noreen P also describes a much more serious transgression, and the fear of both the sin itself and the Confession of it, in the following story:

> But one incident that stands out very very much in my mind regarding Confession: my sister was about three years older than me, she palled around with my cousin and other girls who were her age and I was the younger one tagging along. I'd say I was about ten – or nine – and they were a little bit older. And we were … going to the Savoy one Saturday afternoon … to the pictures … and we were going down Bridge Street hill and we kind of could see in by the Cathedral that there was … a funeral going on. And being – one or other of us anyway, it certainly wasn't me because I was the younger of the group that were going to the pictures – but somebody anyway said 'Let's go in and see who's getting buried' … and knowing full well that we shouldn't have been in there but somebody was just a bit nosy, for want of a better word, and in we went anyway and they were filling in the grave,

and we just looked, like, 'gawking' as we used to call it in those days, getting a bit of information, for no reason, other than that's the way we were inclined then. And … oh yes, I think we debated on the fact whether or not it could be a Catholic, it could be a Protestant funeral, we didn't know, because both – sometimes – there's only a very odd one or two Catholic graves in there … But when we heard anyway – which is significant actually in the light of nowadays – we heard at the end, they said the 'Our Father' and we thought 'We're fine' but at the end then the prie – the reverend said 'For thine is the kingdom the power and the glory' and we *flew* like the hammers of hell out of – when we heard it we thought 'twas – oh it was the *worst*; we had been at – or witnesssed – a Protestant burial! And we flew like the hammers of hell out that gate and we didn't stop till we got – I think we stopped at the – which is now the Hunt Museum – the Custom House, and we just wondered 'What are we going to do? What are we going to do?' And we went to the pictures anyway but didn't enjoy the pictures one single bit![33]

Noreen later mentions this incident as part of her explanation of her concept of sin: 'Answering your mother back, not doing your homework; they were venial sins. But mortal sin would have been … a terrible thing like … where we heard – we attended the Protestant funeral. We thought that would have been a mortal sin'.[34] The sin of attending a Protestant burial is covered by the interpretation of the First Commandment, which as well as forbidding idolatry and superstition also obliged Catholics 'under pain of sin to avoid dangers to our faith'. The *Catechism for Children* lists the principal dangers to faith as follows: 'attendance at non-Catholic worship or schools, marriage with non-Catholics, and books and companions hostile to the Church or its teaching'.[35] The interpretation of the First Commandment in this way is interesting in that it attempts to preserve Catholics' faith by limiting their exposure to influences outside of their own religious environment. This sectarian approach to Christianity, rooted in the Reformation and Counter-Reformation, and profoundly affected by the history of Catholicism and Protestantism in Ireland since then, is historically complex and for that reason cannot be assessed here. However it is a useful framework for thinking about some questions central to this study: firstly, it illustrates how elements of belief were enmeshed with social control strategies in very practical ways; secondly, it shows how the fight against competing religious elements was also built into practical devotional strategy. Thirdly, it raises the question of the relationships between Catholics and Protestants in Limerick city during this part of the twentieth century: aspects of this will be further discussed in Chapter 7.

The importance of confessing this sin at the next possible opportunity was uppermost in the girls' minds as the afternoon progressed. Noreen next describes the decision they had to make regarding the choice of confessor:

And since it was Saturday, we … it was the norm, as I said, to go to Confession on Saturday evening, and we debated with ourselves who would we go to, would we go to – one priest – it's alright to mention priests[36] – Fr. McNamara or – God rest their souls, or Canon Quin. So we thought the Canon would be quite harsh maybe – he would not under … he would be strict. And we opted, I think we opted for – we did actually, for Fr. McNamara. And we each concocted a story, there were four of us altogether, and we said 'You say 'We didn't know, we wondered, we didn't know till we heard the words, and then we flew out, and we didn't hear any more, we put our hands up to our ears to stop any – hearing any more, and because we knew it was wrong'. So we told, each of us went in anyway, and there was somebody before me and I could hear the intonation, and we didn't expect this from this particular priest, Fr. McNamara, but he 'You … what?' and we could hear, and oh … so each of us went in anyway and told our little story, and we were told, I forget the penance, naturally, it's fifty years back now or more, and … we certainly were glad to get out of the Confession box safe, because we thought – we had imagined that the nuns would be informed, and our parents would be informed and we'd probably be excommunicated![37]

The confessor's possible or actual reaction to the sins confessed, even in normal circumstances, emerges as an important aspect of the accounts of the ritual in many cases and shows that Confession had significant personal aspects. Noreen describes the experience of waiting for Confession, in general, in these terms: 'And there would be seats and seats of people waiting. And you'd to sit and wait your turn. And you'd sometimes hear whisperings … you shouldn't be hearing … the priest might get a little irate with somebody who had a big sin and you'd hear the intonation of the voice … you may not hear what he was saying'[38]

The personal nature of the ritual of Confession also meant that, at the level of popular practice, even though penitents had a strong belief in Confession and a well-developed sense of the official doctrines of the Church regarding sin, they still held their own views and interpretations of such matters. These might concern the perceived seriousness of a particular sin or might involve a sense of how the ritual should be conducted:

> You were allowed – you could take one biscuit and a cup of tea at night or a cup of cocoa, I suppose, and I took three biscuits and I remember – weren't we very innocent – I told that in confession at the Jesuits, thinking he'd say like 'Ah don't worry, like, you're observing, you're very good to be even thinking …' And do you know he smartly said to me 'I didn't hear three mentioned' he said, 'I heard one' That was the answer I got! Came out, like, with my tail between my legs.[39]

According to Timmy G, some priests, in listening to sins, would react 'if you had done anything kind of wrong' by telling the penitent to leave and refusing to give them absolution. He comments:

> We weren't murderers or adulterers or anything like that, but some men … I don't know whether it was their religious piety or whatever, but for a minor thing, they could give out to you … Which I think was wrong because God said that you're to be forgiven seventy times seven, you know?[40]

According to this interviewee, other priests if hearing of a situation like this would be reassuring, saying 'Aw, take no notice of that man!' Timmy also noted the kindness of the Jesuit priests, describing one in particular:

> There was one man, God rest his soul … in the Jesuits. I used to love him, he was

a lovely man. A lovely man. He was an awful man for soccer matches. He used to go – loved to see Limerick playing up there in the Markets Field. I remember I went to him to Confession … and he loved all sports, boxing and that kind of thing. And I went to Confession to him one day and I was telling him and … no response. And when I looked closely there was the poor man and he fast asleep. And I said 'Did you hear my Confession, Father?' 'No', he says, 'but I'll give you absolution' … He says 'I was up late last night listening to the fight'. He was a lovely man. A lot of the Jesuits were.[41]

The mention of the Jesuit order here is a reminder that city people, especially as adults, had access to a wide variety of confessors, and the evidence shows that they did exercise choice in their approach to the ritual. Eileen L describes her own approach as follows:

And it was … more often than not you got a very sympathetic … more often than not. Now you might meet the one, alright, you might meet the one or two and I think the only thing after that is you – you would pray for that person … Because obviously they weren't *au fait* with what they were supposed to be. They were supposed to be Jesus Christ, listening to you. Not a priest, just Christ, there, listening to you. You forget he's a priest. And you tell him what you're worried about. And you'd be worried about many a thing![42]

The implication here is that even though the penitent would resolve to pray for an unsympathetic confessor, she would thereafter try to find a more understanding one: 'We would … find one that you liked, that, you know, you could talk to. Unfortunately there were some … that would have reacted in a way that wasn't quite Christ-like I suppose really you know'.[43] The ability of the priest in Confession to convey the kind of forgiving attitude that Eileen associated with Jesus Christ himself was the criterion used by her in choosing a confessor. This same interviewee, a native of the city but now living outside it also commented that she now misses having a regular confessor, 'someone that I could relate to, month after month' because of living in the country. The ease of combining ritual with everyday city life is clear here, as well as the constant availability of the order priests in the many churches in the city centre. It is important to remember that the convenience and sense of choice regarding all kinds of ritual, both public and private was much greater in the decades before the 1980s than it subsequently became: there were large numbers of clergy in the city and churches were open all day.

Confession as a rite of affliction

The relief and reassurance that Confession brought is in evidence in some of the above accounts. Eileen L here describes the particular fulfilment that she experienced:

It was a good – it was a good … exercise, Confession. You had someone to ask things of and get little guidelines from … things that would be bothering you … unecessarily, half the time! And they would be put right for you … Oh yes, oh yes, indeed I think it's an awful pity it isn't there now. A lot of people would be more at ease with themselves. Young people especially – young adults and adults – young adults, you know? You'd be surprised the feeling of … lightness, after coming out from Confession … But you always felt … relieved, after it. Relieved, you know, really, I mean that now, I really do. A weight … less down, less down in yourself[44]

The concern for young people expressed here is interesting in that the three experiences of intense relief described above concern a child and young teenagers. Tommy C makes the connection between young people, especially young men, and Confession in his discussion of the subject as well,

my own belief is this now: we have an awful lot of young people today in our society committing suicides, 'cause they've no-one to talk to. They have *nobody* to talk to. Nobody cares about them. Women will talk. Women will be telling you – women will always talk but blokes won't … They have no-one to talk to. You see them there – they go in there, be jeepers, they'd go in to Confession before Saturday night before they'd go off and they'd have a few drinks, d'you know what I mean, and this is it, and then they'd go off, and they'd be grand … 'Twas great. It was someone to guide you as well. It was great, great.[45]

These accounts of Confession illustrate Bell's view of how rites of affliction demonstrate the 'all too human side of religion, namely people's persistent efforts to redress wrongs, alleviate sufferings and ensure well-being'.[46] But, according to Bell, rites of affliction do much more than this and her description of the wider role of these rituals is also relevant here: 'Yet these rites also illustrate complex cultural interpretations of the human condition and its relation to a cosmos of benign and malevolent forces'.[47] In this case, the devil and sin – both original and actual – could be seen, from the Catholic point of view, as malevolent forces which could be fought and controlled, primarily by the ritual of Confession. The 'management' of the various good and evil components of the cosmos is of crucial importance here. Bell goes on to say that 'While human efforts at maintaining this order appear to pale in comparison to the power attributed to gods, ancestors and demons, rituals of affliction hold all these powers to some degree of accountability and service'.[48]

The accountability and responsibility of the 'good' forces in maintaining the right order can be seen both Timmy G's and in Eileen L's attitude to their confessors and to the entities represented by them, God and Jesus Christ. According to Eileen, a response that was 'not quite Christlike' was the wrong one to adopt when faced with a penitent in Confession. This implies a particular interpretation of the ritual of Confession, and more especially a view of how the priest should behave, backgrounded with a firm idea of the reaction Christ would have if confronted with a penitent sinner. Having a view of what Confession should 'deliver' is not unique to this informant, but it does seem to be more connected to adults' lives than to childrens'.[49] However, Noreen P's story about the Protestant burial also demonstrates the young girls' conscious choice of confessor based on his likely reaction to their experience. These examples taken together provide an interesting view of the localized practice of official religion in an urban context: ordinary people's personal knowledge of the confessors and their various characteristics and imagined reactions was used to negotiate the ritual occasion and ultimately influence how the ritual of Confession was experienced by them, something that would have been much more difficult, and maybe impossible, in a rural setting. Bell makes another interesting point about rites of affliction when she says,

> even though this genre of rites may be particularly effective in maintaining the status quo of the traditional social order in a community, they demonstrate that the human realm is not completely subordinate to the realms of spiritual power; these rites open up opportunities for redefining the cosmological order in response to new challenges and new formulations of human needs.[50]

The rite of Confession as practised by ordinary people in Limerick city illustrates this point: informants' views of the ritual show how their own needs and views changed how they participated in the ritual, while the detailed catechism texts and their various interpretations of sin show the ongoing struggle to define and redefine the problem of evil and the official approach to dealing with it, at the level of dissemination of the doctrine among the ordinary people during the period studied. *The Complete Illustrated Guide to Catholicism* dates the 'gentling' of Catholic rhetoric on hell to the time of the Second Vatican Council in the 1960s and goes on to contrast the current catechism definition of hell with the former view:

> The Catholic catechism describes hell as a state of being where the individual chooses to reject God's love, thereby dying in mortal sin. By choosing to exclude him or herself from God, and by not repenting, he or she will be separated from God for eternity – this is hell. [51]

This is in marked contrast to the earlier Catholic – and, indeed, other Christian denominations' official discourse in which ideas and images such as 'the fires of hell', 'wicked spirits wandering around the world for the ruin of souls',[52] the temptations of the devil and humans' 'strong inclination to evil' were much more important.[53] These images and concepts, as we have seen, were also a significant element in interviewees' world view in the period studied. In her discussion of the relationship between ritual and belief, Bell points out that, 'When expressed in ritual, this sociocosmic order is implicitly understood as neither human nor arbitrary in its origins; rather, it is natural and the way things really are and ought to be.'[54] The strength of belief in hell on the part of both the people and the 'agents' of the belief i.e. the clergy, along with the power of Confession to manage the problems associated with it, are among the most important elements of the religious imagination of the period.

Private devotion

As mentioned above, private prayer was regarded by the Catholic Church as an important aspect of the ongoing wellbeing of the individual soul. The *Catechism for Children* puts the point clearly and simply: 'Prayer is a raising up of the mind and heart to God, to adore and praise Him, to thank Him for His favours, to beg His grace and blessings, and to obtain pardon for our sins … We should pray very often but especially on Sundays and holydays, every morning and every night, and in all dangers, temptations and afflictions'.[55] The text also advises its readers to 'Pray with perseverance, that is, keep on praying. Do not easily give up. Get into the habit of prayer, while you are young, and you will be more likely to persevere later'.[56] The *Catechism Key* – aimed at schools, but also at an older age group, explains why prayer is necessary:

> No man can keep from mortal sin for long, unless he gets grace. The best ways to get grace are prayer, the Sacraments and the Mass. Prayer is saying nice things to God, or to God's friends in heaven … Get into the habit of kneeling down to pray every morning and evening. Parents should remind their children about this. To say no prayers for a very long time would be a mortal sin. Neglect of night and morning prayers is often due to late hours.[57]

The process of turning one's mind to God or 'God's friends in heaven' was, in Limerick during the period studied, one which could be carried out in many different ways, as will become clear from the accounts given below. Morning and night prayers for instance could be said privately or as a family; sprinkling holy water while saying a prayer was both a familial and a private ritual; going to daily Mass and Communion, though it involved a public ritual and was strongly encouraged in catechism texts, still involved an element of choice on the part of the participant: choosing to go to Mass at all, and then choosing from the large number of Masses that could be attended in the city churches on any weekday could be seen as individual or private aspects of this practice, along with the fact that many people said their own private prayers while hearing Mass in any case. Visiting a church to pray at a particular shrine, or to say the Stations of the Cross are other examples of private devotion carried out in a public place. Visits to holy wells and pilgrimages fall into this category too, while the very simple, habitual actions of blessing oneself before eating while quickly saying grace or blessing oneself while passing a church or a graveyard should not be forgotten either.

Private prayer and ritual at home

The saying of morning and night prayers varied somewhat from household to household as the various interviewees' childhood experiences show. Eileen L, born in 1926, is speaking about her schooldays and her life as a young adult when she describes the rushed atmosphere in her family in the mornings: 'We always said our morning prayers … we were always asked did we say our morning prayers. In my house anyway … possibly we said them in a very tearaway attitude, you know? Always in a hurry!'[58] Other interviewees mentioned saying morning prayers in their own rooms with Timmy G describing these as 'just a few … the "Morning Offering" and "Angel of God"'.[59] The morning prayer was more communal in Joseph L's home in the 1930s and 1940s: 'Well, … prayer was … very much our family life as well … Funnily enough my mother was the leader of the prayers on our house … She was! But … we used to say morning prayers … my mother used to give out the morning prayers, that's right, yea. And we'd say them … probably after the breakfast … before we went out'.[60]

The custom of saying morning prayers with the family was carried on into the 1960s and 1970s by this interviewee, who used to say them with his children in the car while driving them to school.[61]

The custom of sprinkling holy water while saying a short prayer or simply blessing oneself was carried out in many households. Holy water, listed under the category 'Sacramentals' in the catechisms, is described as follows in the 1919 edition of the *Catechism Notes*:

> HOLY WATER. – Natural water mixed with salt, and blessed by the Priest. It has great power over evil spirits. It is used by the Church in the blessing of persons and things. We should always have it in our homes, and use it often during the day, and when going to bed at night. We should frequently sprinkle the dying with it.[62]

The protective qualities attributed to salt are in evidence here in official Catholic teaching: its parallel in vernacular belief is an example of the common ground between official and unofficial belief in Ireland. Interviewees' evidence shows that these guidelines were taken very seriously by them. According to Máirín M, holy water was used 'all the time' in her childhood home: she also makes the following observation: 'actually nowadays, any houses that have a holy water font, they're usually just inside the main door … I know in our house we had a holy water font outside *every* door – bedroom door. Yea … on the landing on the way up. And you would automatically just bless yourself as you would pass … all the time'.[63] Grace K's evidence supports this.[64] The use of holy water at night was of particular importance, as evidence from a number of interviewees shows: many remember their parents using it on the children of the house at bedtime. Máirín M says: 'she would definitely as we would be going to bed she would certainly sprinkle, or my Dad would always do it, as well, yea. But it was just … it was just part of our family really, this whole thing'.[65] Anthony F describes his childhood home in a similar way:

> And we always kept holy water in the house, and … Easter water as well, was a very common thing, you'd get a bottle of water at Easter, blessing ourselves going out, out of the house and when you'd come in and Dadda at night time – the last thing, we'd all be in bed – but he'd say 'Bless yourselves!' 'In the name of the Father and the Son and the …' Last thing at night … And that was our protection from evils and *púcas* and all sorts of things.[66]

Kathleen B describes the practice in her family: 'and when you were a child, I suppose all houses were the same but my mother when you'd be in bed at night 'In the name of the Father, the Son and the Holy …' and I remember we'd say 'Mamma, you've us drenched!' You know, holy water was very … shake the holy water … yes, around the place'.[67] Áine R's mother would do this as well:

> I remember, the holy water … oh always, we had one neighbour and the minute Easter Saturday morning would come she'd bring us a big bottle of the Easter water. She called it Easter water. My mother'd be delighted to get it … for blessing us. Oh yea … she would … She always did it at night, you know, she did, before we'd all … 'Lord, watch over us all' you know, this was done.[68]

The protection of holy water for people leaving the house is mentioned above in Anthony F's account, while Grace K says 'We'd never go out without using holy water' but also comments that her faith in its power is still strong.[69] Likewise, Máirín M describes how she herself has carried on the tradition with her own family: 'And if you were leaving the house, my mother would always *drown* you with holy water! … And to this day, I do that to my family, if they're going off anywhere on journeys or anything, they laugh at me, but they still accept it you know? … And … just say a little prayer, d'you know, bring them safely. So it's something I suppose they grew up with'.[70] This interviewee's continued use of holy water with her grown-up children demonstrates her belief in its protective power. Timmy G makes an interesting comment about the persistence of the belief in holy water:

> The mother was a great believer in shaking the holy water around at night – she wouldn't go to bed until she had the holy water done. And I still carry on that! You know? Ask God to bless the house … when you grow up in a Catholic home, there's a lot of things stick to you. Although you might change your views, but there are some basics you wouldn't forget.[71]

Kathleen B also elaborates on her own current belief:

> I've a big plastic bottle! I'm never without holy water. And I'm not – 'tisn't that I'm very holy at all, but I'm sensible enough to realise, holy water is a sacramental … I mean, I put holy water now, I'm on – alone at night and I feel secure if I shake holy water and I feel that it does something, you know … I remember when my mother died now, and if I came down, you know you're shocked like when you're younger – well I wasn't that young when she died, just about – I was about forty-one or two – but you'd come downstairs at night and you – kind of after someone has died – you've that kind of a feeling about you. And if you put your hand on the holy water, instead of running back up the stairs, you walked up the stairs. I found that. Yes, it has – holy water has a very – it has – and even people should use it in a car because you're protected, I think.[72]

Here the interviewee is keen to stress that she is not 'very holy', or that she is not using holy water because she wants to be pious. Instead it is a question of belief, not just in the power of holy water to protect, but also to console and calm. Her conviction is highlighted by the example she gives of the consolation she received after her mother's death, when she had 'that kind of a feeling' – a feeling of closeness to death and its mysteries, and a certain sense of fear, exacerbated by being downstairs in the house at night-time. In this context, holy water seems to have dispelled her fears and given her the courage to walk, instead of run, back upstairs. Her mention of protection in the context of car travel is interesting: people did (and do) use holy water in cars whether it is sprinkled around while a short prayer is said or while people bless themselves, or whether it is simply left in the car all the time, as a protective substance. Máirín M has a different perspective on this type of protection:

> I can well remember a particular neighbour, Joan Murphy, and always, she came to our house on Easter Saturday night with a sod of turf and Easter water …

Having had them blessed, now … A sod of turf, yea. And the sod would be broken up into a lot of pieces, she would have them in a bag, and they'd be broken up into little pieces, and she'd give each of the neighbours a few … as far as I remember she used to get them in the Dominican, and … the blessing would happen there. And the symbolism; the holy water was sprinkled around the house and on every member of the household for Easter, and the … the turf, the blessed turf was to prevent the house from burning. And I remember subsequently when we acquired a car, which was a big thing at that time, the first thing that went into our brand new car when we collected it down in Ford's Garage in Cork was a little bit of one of the sods of turf. In case – my mother … in case the car would go on fire.[73]

In her discussion of sacramentals, Colleen McDannell points out that,

While a priest might be needed initially to make the sacramental valid, the point of the sacramental is to allow non-ordained men and women to integrate the sacred into their daily lives. Lay people become 'priests' and decide when and where the sacramentals will be employed. Unlike a sacrament, that guarantees grace *ex opere operato* (independent of the character of the priest), the efficacy of sacramentals depends on the spirituality of the people who use them.[74]

Máirín's account above is a good example of this: the Dominican priests were initally involved in blessing the Easter water and the sods of turf, but from that time on they were the business of neighbours and family – not just in terms of breaking up the turf and distributing it, but also in deciding where and how it was to be used. Thus in Máirín's home, the holy water was put into every font in the house to be used at night or when leaving the house, but also when simply walking from one part of the house to another; the turf was put into the new car, to ease fears about its possible combustion, though it is important to remember that the holy water may have been put into the car as well. In this case the blessed substances were imbued with meaning and significance by the decisions made to use them in this way. This demonstrates McDannell's idea that sacramentals help people to integrate the sacred into their daily lives, but also that these substances become imbued with the spirituality of those who use them. The sacralization of the car was increased by the short prayers sometimes said by travellers for a safe journey. Pádraig R was able to recite one of these, and more examples can be found in the collection of traditional prayers, *Ár bPaidreacha Dúchais*.[75]

It is also important to recognize the process here of introducing sacred elements into the home, whether these have the protective function of holy water described above, or a more symbolic function, such as that of the Sacred Heart picture or of an altar to Our Lady. Mircea Eliade has characterized this transformation of the home from profane to sacred space as a result of the human instinct to create a sacred centre in everyday contexts: a 'longing for transcendent forms' which help people to briefly escape from the mundane world into 'a divine state of affairs'.[76] The recitation of the rosary (discussed in Chapter 5), along with the family and private prayer and the rituals associated with holy water discussed above demonstrate that for many people transcendence, or at least, the attempt to transcend, was at the heart of their lives at home. The quality of sacredness with which the holy water fonts and holy pictures imbued the domestic space was an important part of this process. The fact that these items were among those most frequently left in abandoned houses in the first decade of the twenty-first century is testament to their changed status in Irish domestic life.[77]

Visiting the church

As is clear from the discussion of organized ritual in Chapter 3, the years between 1920 and 1960 could be seen as an intensely devotional period, in so far as the Catholic Church was concerned. In Limerick city, as in many other parts of Ireland, attendance at weekly Mass in their local parish church or in one of the order churches in the city was the norm for most Catholics, while many also attended weekly devotions organized by confraternities and sodalities in their own area or in a city centre church. However, people also visited churches at other times, on a more personal basis. Eileen L remembers going to Mass before school:

> It would be seven o'clock Mass, in the Franciscans. A fine walk in from where we lived near the Salesian school on the North Circular Road, in to the Franciscans at seven o'clock, back out again ... breakfast and make it into school by nine! And Cannock's clock in those times ... in those days was right exactly where we could see it going up the Strand. We knew exactly how much more time we had before getting to the Presentation.[78]

It is interesting that because of the far-flung nature of the suburban parish in which this family lived, it was easier for them to go to Mass in the Franciscan church. This may have influenced their devotion to saints as well: 'St Anthony would be very much invoked. Because we lived near the Franciscans as well. The Augustinians and the Franciscan churches were our two churches, although we were actually parishioners of St Munchin's. It was too far away from us. We came in over the bridge to the two churches that were the nearest to us ... the Augustinians and the Franciscans'.[79] Kathleen B describes how people would say the Stations of the Cross in the church, sometimes staying back after devotions to say them, or sometimes visiting the church especially:

> it was very common to go into the church and find people saying their stations. You know, they meditated on the passion of Christ ... they'd go round ... go round to each station and say a prayer at each station and meditate ... the stations were very much observed then ... oh always. People said their stations ... you know, we'll say they had the confraternity in St Mary's now was every Tuesday night, for the women. Well, after the confraternity you'd find people staying back and saying their stations of the cross.[80]

The evidence also shows that going into the church to say a prayer, or a few prayers was part of the everyday routine for many people. Eileen L mentions that she would never pass a church without going in to say a prayer at the Tabernacle, where the eucharist is kept:

I've never passed a church without going in, and 'twould be straight to the Tabernacle and that's why I'm so sorry the Tabernacle has been moved from the centre of the church to the side. Because the Tabernacle is the essence of the church, really. It's what the church is about, it's the house of God and Jesus is there in the Tabernacle. No matter where we'd be going, in a hurry, even in a hurry, now, you would make a time to run in, and just say something, and come out again. That is true.[81]

Fitting in a visit to the church among other city-based tasks is what is meant by this, rather than literally going into every church every time one would pass it: this point is made clear from other evidence given by this interviewee.[82] The 'Lost and Found' advertisements in the *Limerick Leader* in the 1940s and 1950s may also demonstrate this point: one, from 1940 states 'Lost: Lady's gold wristlet watch, on 23rd January, between St. Joseph's Church and Lr. Mallow St., or vicinity: sentimental value'.[83]

This may imply that the church had been visited and the watch consulted in the church before leaving it: the day in question was a Tuesday. Other advertisements concerning the loss of rosary beads have been examined in Chapter 5, but again in some of these the church is used as a point of departure or arrival: 'between Dominican Church and Dominic Street' for instance; 'between Glentworth St. and Jesuit Church'; 'between St. Joseph's Church and Woolworth's'.[84] In some cases, a clue is given as to the activities carried out: the lady who placed the following advertisement in May 1950 may have needed her reading glasses in both locations: 'Lost this morning, Lady's spectacles pink rims in a black silk case between National Bank William St. and the Friary. Reward offered. Return to National Bank'.[85] It is easy to imagine the distress felt by the person who placed this advertisement later in the same month: 'Lost: on Saturday morning 27/5/1950 £1 Note, between Messrs. Todd and the Redemptorist Church. Reward if returned'.[86] These pieces of information, though small, present a vivid ethnographic picture of Limerick life in the middle decades of the twentieth century: a time when people walked or cycled around the streets of the city centre, in some cases perhaps living there also, in others, having come from some other part of the city to shop or visit the bank. The use of churches as landmarks in these advertisements indicates that a visit to the church, for a weekday Mass, to say the stations or, perhaps, to visit a particular shrine, was an integral part of their city itinerary for many people. It also demonstrates the churches' role as well-known locations in the city centre. The fact that they are mentioned in conjunction with bigger shops and banks, rather than smaller businesses could indicate a deliberate use, in the advertisements, of places that the largest possible number of people would know – and it is clear that churches were definitely in this category.

In her book *The Building of Limerick*, the architectural historian Judith Hill discusses the city churches in some detail, noting the large amount of building and renovation of Catholic churches that took place from 1850 to 1940. During this period, nine city centre churches (including St John's Cathedral) were built or renovated/rebuilt. Hill assesses the architectural impact of the churches built on the streets in the following passage:

> The city churches were truly urban, fitting as they did into the line of the street and using the established pattern of entrance, steps and door. However, they did

break some rules and, in the process, transform the streets. At ground level their wide entrances punctuated the general uniformity of the railings and regular flight of narrow steps. O'Connell Street possessed a succession of such openings by the end of the period; the Augustinians at the bottom, followed by the Jesuits in the Crescent and St. Joseph's at the top. The limestone in which they were built contrasted with the brick of the terraces in which they were set. And their height, projections and towers gave them city-wide significance.[87]

This is an interesting assessment in that it shows that the churches, and, in particular, those in the main thoroughfare, O'Connell Street, were integrated into the streetscape but still visually distinct from the businesses or dwellings that flanked them. In her discussion of the Jesuit church in the Crescent, Hill uses its features to make a more general point regarding Catholic churches:

> There are no railings and no gates. The high doors are open all day. This encouragement to enter is a common feature of these churches and is in conspicuous contrast to the protestant tradition where railings, a gate, a garden and a path are used to define and separate the church from the street. Not only were the catholic churches to be visible and prominent, they were to be accessible.[88]

This description is helpful in understanding the role played by churches in city centre life in the late nineteenth and early to mid-twentieth centuries. There were many churches with many different shrines and devotions, all open all day for informal, individual visits. In this provision of choice and variety, churches could be seen to play a part in the lively, modern life of the city during this period. This aspect of Catholicism is in contrast to the feelings discussed by interviewees in Chapter 3, where they felt 'everyone' was going to Mass on Sunday, or where they felt pressure to join religious organizations: for young people and adults, personal visits to churches were chosen on the basis on preference, enjoyment or convenience. Máirín M, while speaking about her preference for the Dominican church during May devotions, makes a more general point regarding the choice of churches:

> we would go ... 'tis strange, we seemed to go to different churches for different things – the Dominican now was the one we would go for (May devotions) ... but you see ... they were all within a very short distance, for us, you know ... Bells, oh Limerick was a city of bells! Every Mass – there was Masses all – on the hour and on the half-hour but there was hardly a time when you wouldn't hear bells ringing somewhere, about five minutes before Mass would begin it tended to be, as far as I remember, they would ring the bell as a kind of a warning that the priest was getting ready. So if you were doubtful about the time, and you'd recognise the bells – you'd recognise the Augustinians, you'd recognise the Presentation, from our house, now, all these ones, and you'd say 'Oh that's it' if you weren't sure there was a quarter-past eleven in the Augustinians, now I remember.[89]

This interviewee's mention of bells evokes the urban scene in an eloquent and powerful way, just as Eileen L's mention of the importance of Cannock's clock does in her account of going to early morning Mass above. Máirín's mention of the

Presentation bell is also noteworthy: the role played by convent chapels – also available for Mass or personal visits – in the devotional life of the city is significant. Noreen P's explanation of her father's religious sensibilities is also relevant here: she describes him as 'non-parochial' and notes that he wasn't a member of a confraternity, before saying:

> But he did have religion … but … not to be known to be having it – he wasn't outward … But he certainly had it because he used to bring me very often on the bicycle, on the bar of the bicycle up to the Reparation Convent Chapel and … actually they still have, in this year 2004, they still have … Exposition of the Blessed Sacrament every – I think it's Sunday from two to four, or some … hours at a time anyway. And lay-people can go in there. But my father God rest him, I remember him vividly for that, he used to bring me up there, to the Reparation Convent Chapel and it was very quiet, as it is nowadays. Very very quiet remote place. And … not remote so much as quiet, where you could … 'twas different than the other churches, that it was … there was silence, *total* silence observed.[90]

She also recounts how her father, who worked in the Glentworth Street area 'would go into the Dominican to light a candle or whatever'. A sense of this man's devotional preferences is palpable here: the choice of the quiet atmosphere of the convent chapel or the intimate and deeply personal experience of lighting a candle over the highly organized and regimented, albeit convivial, atmosphere of the Redemptorist Confraternity is a significant one. The role of devotion in his close relationship with his daughter is also clear from Noreen's discussion of Christmas customs: 'I was very very close to my father and he brought me – I was the baby in the family – he would bring me everywhere, places like that. And it was very regular, on, as you said, St Stephen's Day. We went to every crib in the city'.[91]

The substance of devotion and belief

The discussion above concerns the forms of devotion undertaken by people and the integration of these forms into their everyday lives. However, it is also important to consider the metaphysical dimension of personal prayer, and, in particular, the super-natural entities on whom these devotions were centred. The dead were perhaps the most important group to which, and for whom people prayed, especially at the end of October or beginning of November. It is important to highlight, before discussing the church-based devotion, the way in which the practice of official Catholic devotion to the dead was underscored by vernacular belief in this area in both city and country areas in Ireland in the twentieth century.[92] Hallowe'en customs were described by some interviewees,[93] while Críostóir O'Flynn gives the following description of the customs that his father, a native of Watergate in the Irishtown, carried out every night before going to bed:

> My mother's own story was that, on their first night in their cosy one-room home, when it came time to go to bed, they knelt and said the Rosary, as most people did in those days; then 'himself' carefully swept the hearth, poked up the dying

embers of the fire, carefully arranged the only two chairs in position at the fireside, and placed two cups of water on the table. When his puzzled young bride asked him why he was going through this ceremony, he told her that the ritual was always observed in his family home in Watergate, and that it was to ensure that if any of Them came to visit during the night they would find a welcome and rest by the family fireside. When she asked who he meant by 'Them', he explained that any of their dead relatives might be spending some of their Purgatory revisiting the scenes of their life … My mother assured us that she couldn't sleep that night with the terror of peeping at the glowing embers in the fireplace and the two empty waiting chairs. She tolerated her new husband's practice … for a few nights, but eventually issued the ultimatum – she would not get into bed unless he desisted; which, being more in love with his lovely living young wife than with his dead ancestors, he promptly did.[94]

O'Flynn's parents married in 1918, and the above anecdote shows the strength of the belief in the presence of the dead at that time. It is also important to note that it was not through lack of belief that his wife insisted that he abandon the custom, but because she really did think that the practice might encourage the spirits of the dead to visit the house – and, given the layout of the dwelling, that they would actually be in the same room with them.

The time leading up to death and the actual moment of death were areas of great importance in traditional belief as well. Áine R, from the St Mary's Park estate, also on King's Island, describes the belief in the *Bean Sí* (usually anglicized as 'Banshee') as follows:

The boy across the road was dying and … myself and my sister woke up, Mamma was over because they were having a kind of a wake – he was dying you know – and God help us, we heard what I believe is the *Bean Sí*. And I mean it's different than a dog howling, you know, it really is, you know. It's a very very sorrowful, mournful … female cry. It's – you'll never ever hear the likes of it until you hear it. And I have a friend – I had a friend at the time, well Mamma knew him, and he was up in Plassey – and we used to talk about this as well. And he was after going to play cards, he was in his late teens, and he was up, wherever he was, up Plassey, some house up there. And he was coming back down, and 'twas well after twelve, and he heard the *Bean Sí*. So of course, getting a fright, he ducked in under one of the bridges, and he stayed there now shivering, really shivering and … this shadow passed. A woman's shadow, and the hair was very long, flowing behind, and … you know, he saw that. So, whatever you could make of that. But the *Bean Sí* existed in those days![95]

Anthony F, who lived in the Killalee estate, noted the importance of the *Bean Sí* in the area when he was growing up in the late 1930s and 1940s as well.[96] Evidence from the Park area of the city, concerning the earlier part of the century also shows strong traditional belief in the same phenomenon.[97]

The moment of death is at the centre of the following story told by Áine R:

My uncle was drowned down in, near Baals Bridge, and Mamma's mother – 'twas Mamma's brother you see – so her mother was sitting down knitting. Now the uncle had gone out just to go for a walk or something ... and ... he had sat on the wall and whatever happened he fell off the wall – he might have been drunk, I mean he might have had a drink. But ... that was at about ten past eleven. And at the same time, the mother looked up – she was knitting – and he was standing at the door! He was standing there, and he just had his hand against the door just looking at her. And she said ... 'My God what are you doing back early?' or something. But he was gone as quick as he stood there. And they came up then half an hour later and told her. He was after being pulled out of the river. I mean, anyone that can explain that! ... at the time he would – that his spirit would have left his body ... he visited his mother. So, if anyone doesn't believe in life after ... I can tell you there's plenty of evidence to the ... you know ... because we've a thousand stories like that.[98]

These stories show the intensity of popular belief around death and dying in various areas of Limerick city in the early to mid-twentieth century. It is not surprising to find, then, that praying for the dead was a major aspect of official devotion also: again, this is an area which points up the syncretism between official Catholicism and vernacular belief which was discussed earlier in the book. The month of November which came at the end of the Church year was the time allocated to praying for the suffering souls in Purgatory – people who had died but who hadn't yet achieved the happiness of heaven. Máirín M here explains the custom of 'rounds' on All Souls' Night (2 November) for this purpose:

That was the 'rounds' we used to call it – I don't know if it's the same everywhere. But everybody did rounds for the holy souls. And ... oh this was a big thing here, because the more rounds you did, the more people you helped and the holy souls couldn't help themselves, this was what we were always taught. So they were dependent on you, so you see, you were going to do the best you could.[99]

Doing the 'rounds' involved making as many separate visits to the church as possible, while saying certain prayers on each visit. Máirín explains how this worked in practice:

You would head off, after tea I remember, down – now we tended to do the rounds in the Augustinian Church in O'Connell Street and the Augustinian has two main doors, side by side, facing out onto O'Connell Street. So the way we cheated really, was that you would [have] queues of people and [what] you'd do is you would go in one door and it was six Our Fathers, six Hail Marys and six Glories – now the thing is, you had to have gone, from my memory, to Confession and Communion beforehand or ... your prayers were null and void, and they wouldn't get indulgences, yea ... So, you did that. You went and you said your six of each prayer, and you went out the other.[100]

It was the custom to pray for specific people that had died, rather than just the holy souls in general:

Six Our Fathers, six Hail Marys and six Glory, for each person you wanted to get an indulgence for ... oh yea. People were doing them for people they would have known who had died, and people they wouldn't have known – maybe their grandmothers who had died before them or – oh yes people were praying for their own dead really, that was my memory of it now, maybe other people had a wider view, but that was what we did in our … family. And I think that anyone I knew that's what would be in mind. But as I said you'd go in one door, you'd say your prayers, and you'd go out the other door. And you'd go down the steps, and come back up the other steps and in again, and you kept doing these rounds, in and out and in and out. Because 'twas every visit to a church during that time – and as far as I remember, it was All Souls' night was the night that that happened, and you only had that night to do it, and once the church would close, the churches would close that time, from my memory, was around nine, so you were doing it I suppose maybe from six to nine, that type of thing. Now I think other people visited a number of churches, but as I said, this was our way of doing it – go in one way and out the other way![101]

Going in and coming out of the church and saying prayers for as many souls as possible on each visit lent a certain atmosphere to the occasion. According to Máirín there would be 'hundreds and hundreds' of people there: 'I mean you were literally moving as part of a big group in and a big group out all the time – it was just like a constant flow of people … 'twas like doing the rounds, I suppose that was the whole idea'.[102] But this was not a procession, either,

> because everyone was doing their own thing. I might decide to do my … to say for so many people, you know maybe I'd say six Our Fathers for my grandmother, six for my grandfather, and try and do a few at the one time. And go out and come back in and do them again … As far as I remember now that was the way it went. But the more you got done the more people you could include![103]

Máirín also emphasizes the sense of individual purpose on this occasion,

> it was quiet, it was strange because there was quietness and you know you didn't have this thing of … people when they'd go out they'd stop and meet someone and have a chat and come in – that usen't to happen to my memory. There was no ceremony, nothing like that. 'Twas just something you did anyway, 'twas just out and in and this was what you were doing … yourself to gain indulgences for the dead.[104]

The firm belief that prayers said by people on earth could get the suffering souls in Purgatory into heaven is the basis of this devotion: the sense of urgency in Máirín M's account above illustrates this. This belief is also the basis for a humorous story 'Raghadsa go Flaithis Dé!' ['I'm going to heaven!'] told by the Muskerry storyteller, Amhlaoibh Ó Luínse, in which people praying during a wake are reminded by the corpse lying in the kitchen how their prayers can help the souls in Purgatory. In this case, the 'suffering soul' is the corpse himself: he sits up and tells the assembled company that he is being refused entry to heaven because when he was alive he had predicted that, if justice was done, he would get in. He eventually manages to attain heaven, however, through the prayers of an old woman in the corner of the kitchen, who has asked a dead relative of her own to intercede for this man, and he sits up and informs the assembled supplicants of this before lying down again, for good this time.[105] Ó Luínse's gentle humour is at its best in this light, funny account of belief in life after death though it is important to remember that his tongue-in-cheek treatment of the topic does not necessarily imply disbelief in the spiritual principles involved: belief in the story itself is another matter. The story is of interest here for a few reasons: firstly it illustrates the importance of the ongoing connection between the living and the dead which is also evident in Máirín M's account above. Secondly, it provides a striking contrast in terms of the ritual context: gathering in the kitchen of the wake-house to pray for a departed soul was a common practice and could have just as easily happened in the city during the period up to the 1960s. However, Máirín's image of a surging crowd of 'hundreds and hundreds' of people going from the church to the street and back again while everybody prayed for 'their own dead' is an emphatically urban one, and illustrates the development and growth, in a modern urban context, of an older ritual. Thirdly, the story illustrates one of the most important principles of belief in the holy souls, also stated by Máirín above: they could not pray for themselves, but they could help others, both living and dead, while people on earth could help them. It also shows that the power of dead ancestors was not confined to the holy souls: people who had reached heaven could also help the living, or in this case, the newly dead.

One of the ways that the holy souls could help people was to wake them if they needed to get up early in the morning. This belief is interesting in the way it extends the relevance of the holy souls from the annual devotion into an everyday context and from the physical church itself into the home. Kathleen B recounts a conversation with her husband regarding the annual retreat he was attending at the Redemptorist church: 'Oh if there was a retreat then, every evening they'd have eight o'clock devotions and Benediction and sermon. But they'd be up that morning at the six o'clock Mass, and I'd say to John "You'll never be able to get up!" "I will – the Holy Souls will wake me!" he'd say. Now there was more devotion to the Holy Souls!'[106] Áine R remembers the same idea: 'And the devotion to the Souls ... oh my God that was very real. If we wanted to get up early in the morning we'd pray to the Holy Souls, to Purgatory. Wasn't that a funny thing? We always did it! ... It worked! Well, we never slept it out, you know. If there was something important going on ... we had no alarm clock – too poor! (Laughter)'.[107] Anthony R explains how this devotion worked for him:

> But a very very common belief then – and I used it myself, absolutely – to pray to the Holy Souls to call you in time in the morning. That was a great custom altogether, it never failed. Never failed! And afterwards when I ... well maybe this is a ... somebody ... a cynic might suggest that this was auto-suggestion, but when I'd be finished work we'd say around half-two, sometimes half-one in the day I'd go home, and I'd go – lie down for a half an hour and I'd ask the Holy Souls to call me, say at five o'clock or whatever it was. Bang! Sharp on time! That's incredible, but true. 'Tis true. Maybe 'tis auto-suggestion, I don't know. But anyway, they were the customs we had.[108]

The power of the holy souls to wake people early in the morning or at any time of the day that the person needed to be woken is interesting, and may be connected to the idea that the holy souls themselves could not rest because of their state: thus they would be awake and suffering while everybody else slept. Also, their chief role in Purgatory was now to atone for their own sins here on earth by helping others:

> Well, we were told that they can no longer do anything for themselves, but they can help you. And I firmly believe it … as regards when somebody goes … I definitely think because when John died a lot of things went right, you know. I firmly believe that they do help. I know 'tis a mystery, but we don't know but I … believe anyhow. Some people had great devotion to the Poor Souls and got many requests, like, granted, you know, through prayers to the Poor Souls.[109]

Kathleen B's reflection on the holy souls, and on the way she felt her husband was helping her after he died illustrates an important aspect of the concept of sin and the afterlife: this is that almost nobody went straight to heaven after death. The *Catechism for Children* explains this point as follows:

> *Heaven.* If we die in the state of grace, we are sure of heaven, though we may not go there at once. We may be sent to purgatory to be punished for our sins … *Purgatory.* We will be sent to purgatory is we die in venial sin or if we have not made up for our sins before death.[110]

The implication here is that most people, unless perhaps they had been lucky enough to die straight after coming out of Confession, were destined to spend at least some time in Purgatory. The custom of doing the rounds for the holy souls described above, and especially that of praying for grandparents or long-dead family members that one had never met, would suggest that people believed that the ordinary person could spend many years there. One of the reasons why Amhlaoibh Ó Luínse's story is funny is that it describes people finding out that a soul has actually managed to reach heaven – something that was impossible for anyone to know. The idea that one might actually come to know one's destiny had a more serious side too, as the following story told by Tommy C shows,

> so the story was, there was this chap who was very fond of drink … and he'd do anything for money. And the bloke said to him, 'If you do this' he said – he was living at home, he said 'Just' – 'cause every house had a set, had the candles and the things – 'Just light two candles' he said, 'Go into bed at twelve o'clock, light the two candles, and just put your hands like that across your chest and say 'If I die tonight, where will I go?' What you have to do, he said, and then wait five minutes and say it again' and he said 'If you do that' and lo and behold, yer man was beating down the priest's door at half-twelve, stone grey. Young man … after doing that … He got such a fright … this was the whole thing. He got such a fright.[111]

The implication here is that people were better off not knowing for certain where they or anybody else was destined to go after death. This uncertainty made people pray harder for the poor souls, but it also meant that they were available, in the long-term, to help the living in various ways. Kathleen B's evidence, in showing the feelings she had after the death of her mother and her husband, illustrates the strong sense of the supernatural that people felt in the period after a loved one had died. It is not surprising therefore that devotion to the holy souls was a meaningful part of many people's spiritual lives. The sense in which the dead were still somehow present in the environment of the living, rather than off in some faraway place, is another interesting point about this: it is not too far from the idea in traditional belief that supernatural entities such as *na daoine maithe* or 'the good people' (also known as the fairies) were present in the immediate physical area. Amhlaoibh Ó Luínse's belief legends are noteworthy in the way the stories show that *na daoine maithe* and the dead are described in a similar way as inhabiting the local landscape.[112] In Limerick city, the sense that the dead were somehow present in the immediate environment could be seen as an aspect of the syncretism between official Catholic teaching, which placed the dead very definitely in heaven, hell, purgatory or limbo, and the traditional ancestral belief that the dead could still be perceived among the living. This type of 'blended', but nonetheless very firmly held belief, is one of the most striking aspects of religion in Limerick city during the period studied.

The holy souls were not the only spiritual entities to which people were devoted, however. The 'Thanksgivings' column in the *Limerick Leader* in the 1930s and subsequent decades show that people asked for special favours from Jesus and Mary, though the exact form of the devotions to these central figures varied: those asking for favours from Jesus might ask the Sacred Heart or Christ the King, for instance, while devotees of Mary could ask Our Lady of Good Counsel or Our Lady of Perpetual Succour, whose shrines were to be found in the Augustinian and Redemptorist churches respectively. The fluency of supplicants regarding the supernatural entities and their various forms is illustrated by the following entry from 1930: 'Grateful thanks to Sacred Heart and Adorable Heart of Jesus, His Blessed Mother, invoked under many titles, Saints Joseph, Anthony, Holy Souls, Saints Francis, Philomena, Blessed Oliver Plunkett for recovery from serious illness. A Sinner'.[113] Other saints referred to in published thanksgivings include St Anne and St Gerard (both of whom had shrines in their honour in the Redemptorist church): St Jude and St Rita (to whom shrines had been erected in the Augustinian Church). The combinations of saints and spiritual entities in some advertisements is interesting, especially when a hierarchy of power is indicated: 'Heartfelt thanks to Sacred Heart for several favours obtained through his Blessed Mother, the Little Flower and neglected poor souls in purgatory – a believer in prayer'.[114] The 'Little Flower' referred to here is St Thérèse of Liseiux, and she is ranked between Our Lady and the 'neglected poor souls', those who had no-one to pray for them. The belief illustrated here is that Our Lady had interceded with the Sacred Heart to obtain favours for this supplicant, who did not feel he or she could go 'straight' to God himself (in the form of the Sacred Heart). The area of published thanksgivings is complex and deserving of separate treatment, but it does give some indication of the repertoire of saints and other supernatural forces regarded as important and effective in Limerick during this period.

Interviewees' evidence in this area points to many of the same saints or entities while also including some others: St Martha or the Blessed Sacrament, for instance. The choice of a certain saint for a specific purpose was sometimes a factor: St Anthony was known to be helpful in finding lost things; St Gerard Majella was the patron saint of motherhood; Blessed Martin de Porres (whose shrine was in the Dominican church, and who was canonized in 1962) was helpful in cases of sickness while St Jude was known to be the patron saint of 'hopeless cases'. The Sacred Heart was often chosen for big, almost impossible favours, though the thanksgiving included above for 'many favours' implies that this was not always the case. Sometimes the choice of saint was based on a previous experience, when the devotee felt that their prayers had been answered. Grace K's evidence regarding St Gerard Majella highlights this aspect. She points out that St Gerard's shrine is 'down a step' in the Redemptorist Church from that of Our Lady of Perpetual Succour, the latter the centre of a novena that she and her husband would do each year. She describes praying to St Gerard for a safe pregnancy for each of her eleven children – 'and they were all perfect. Thank God'. This interviewee's devotion has continued since then, with St Gerard the saint she would go to if she 'wanted anything, seriously'.[115] Máirín M's childhood experience also illustrates this point, though her devotion is to Our Lady of Perpetual Succour (now usually referred to as Our Lady of Perpetual Help):

> Our Lady of Perpetual Succour is my lady! Up in the Redemptorist Church, from the time I was very young. And that originated I remember from the time when my youngest sister was – oh she must have been only about two, I'd say – and on a Saturday morning she swallowed the key of the car! Of all things! (Laughter) … she did! How she put it … and that time it was a little Baby Ford car, our first car, and it was about the size of a Yale key now that you'd have for a door. How she ever swallowed it nobody could ever figure out but she had it in her mouth, and chewing on it – I think she was teething or something, at the time – and the next thing she coughed and it was gone back.[116]

Máirín, who was seven or eight years of age at this time, had great difficulty convincing the adults that her sister had actually swallowed the key:

> And I was there and I saw what happened and the – everybody tried to persuade me that she couldn't have swallowed it but I *knew* she had! But anyway of course because of the fact that I had seen it happen, nobody believed me first and then she was brought down for X-rays and they could see it quite clearly on the X-ray! (Laughter.) So I was blamed then that I hadn't … so … but I remember, somebody came, my mother, they were praying hard because it seems if it kept going down a certain way, she might pass it, naturally … of course … how we got on to this now! (Laughter.) But … otherwise she'd have to have an operation so my mother was really upset … But a friend of hers came in and said to her "Do you know Our Lady of Perpetual Succour is marvellous if you're in trouble, she'd never let me down" so she said "I'll go up and pray for you" and my mother said 'No, I'll go up and pray for myself'. So she brought me with her I remember, and I can remember that was the first time I really felt pleading with Our Lady, please please please. Because I felt – I thought she was going to die, and that if she died it was my fault, you know. And … I remember praying and praying and she did pass the key … It was as green as green could be but anyway … she did, she did, and it went through her, but anyway she passed it and … I was so grateful to Our Lady.[117]

Máirín felt 'convinced ... absolutely' that her prayers had been answered on this occasion, and this had a long-term effect on her faith in Our Lady of Perpetual Succour,

> to this day, every time I've trouble, it's strange ... often I was in Dublin – living in Dublin for seven years – and if I had a big problem, if something was really going wrong in my life I would make an effort to come to Limerick and ... whatever it is ... about Our Lady ... it *had* to be Our Lady's shrine. I know there's no logic in it. But it's the place where I get most ... a feeling of 'somebody is helping' – that I'm able to leave it there and know that it'll be dealt with. I just have this thing of ... even at the present time I go up there in the morning to eight o'clock Mass, I'd go, and go to Our Lady's shrine ... Always. Oh yea. I don't go every day needless to say but any time I have a problem I will always ... Our Lady of Perpetual Succour would be my lady.[118]

Place, performance and meaning

The belief underlying the enactment of personal and private devotion, whether this was carried out at home or in the church, is of crucial importance in understanding this area. At its heart this belief, to some extent, echoes that found by Margaret Miles in her study of classic devotional manuals: the assumption that the normative human condition is to imagine oneself at the point of death.[119] This may seem somewhat extreme in a discussion of Limerick city in the first half of the twentieth century: the texts studied by Miles were written in the fifteenth century, and earlier. But understanding a state of mind in which the contemplation of death was a regular occurrence is basic to the analysis of personal devotion: the experience of crisis or the fear of death – as shown by Máirín's story above – is another state of mind in which belief and its relationship to personal devotion are highlighted. Concepts of sin, heaven and hell, discussed above, show how people dealt with their own personal salvation by regular attendance at Confession, while the sense of nearness to the dead, and especially to the holy souls, is illustrated by their centrality among the supernatural entities in the substance of devotion. The sense of supernatural forces somehow being 'held accountable' is also important, while the way in which official teaching and vernacular belief are seamlessly blended with each other, especially where the dead are concerned, indicates the syncretic nature of religious belief in the community. It is clear from all of the above that in the area of personal prayer the sense of the supernatural, and its connection to meaning, was strong, and constant.

However, the material aspects of people's lives, and of devotion itself must also be noted. The application of a sense of the supernatural to the everyday is striking in this context. The sprinkling of holy water in the home is an example of this. Roy Rappaport has some interesting thoughts on the topic:

> it may be suggested that physical display is 'performatively stronger' or 'performatively more complete' than utterances. Whereas a performative utterance achieves a purely conventional or institutional effect through a conventional informative

procedure, posture and movement, in adding physical dimension to the procedure, may seem to add physical dimension to the effect as well.[120]

This would suggest that the performance of the ritual as well as the sensual experience of the holy water on one's skin, whether one was sprinkling it or being sprinkled, gave a stronger sense of protection than the utterance of a prayer would have on its own. In the same way, visiting the Confession box and kneeling down in the dark to tell one's sins gave a powerful physical and sensual context to the ritual. The formulaic nature of the sins being told in some cases was immaterial to this: it may even be said that this kind of formulaic behaviour may have strengthened the belief in the power of the ritual to cleanse and purify the soul. Visiting the church to pray privately was another area where the physical, and spatial, aspects were a crucial element in the enactment of meaning. Hill's work shows how churches were integrated into the Limerick streetscape, while still remaining distinct from adjoining buildings. The location of city churches – including some important shrines – can be seen in Map 3.

Rappaport's discussion of holy places includes the following comment: 'As such they are separated from the daily world, but even when the separation from the daily world is not great there is likely to be a boundary between them, the crossing of which is a marked act ... often requiring some sort of formal gesture or posture'.[121] In this sense, personal visits to churches, though sometimes integrated with shopping or visiting the bank, were acts that were physically marked out from other activities, dipping one's fingers into the holy water font and blessing oneself could be seen as Rappaport's 'formal gesture or posture' above, and were thus imbued with specific meaning. Meaning lay in the prayers said in the church, whether these were formal devotions such as the Stations of the Cross, specific prayers recited before a shrine, short aspirations repeated over and over again or the person's own personal prayers, but the physical act of entering the sacred space was a crucial factor in creating and enacting this meaning. This might be more intense when a special trip was made to the church, as Eileen L's vivid memories of going to Mass before school demonstrate. Máirín M's story of her sister swallowing the key of the car is perhaps the most striking example of the importance of practical, physical engagement in the enactment of belief. Her mother's decision to 'go up and pray for myself' shows that her own physical presence at Our Lady of Perpetual Succour's shrine was regarded by Máirín's mother as more powerful than her neighbour's. Likewise, Máirín's own trips from Dublin to the shrine in Limerick in later years were an important element in her belief in Our Lady's powers to help her. In this process, even the problem itself, whatever it may be, takes on a material aspect, as Mairín feels she is 'able to leave it there and know that it'll be dealt with'. The power of practical action and that of devotional materials is also demonstrated in Tommy C's story of the man who had a frightening vision of his own afterlife: in this story the physical trappings of death, the anointing set, of which there was one in every house according to the interviewee, along with the penitent posture of crossing the arms over the chest, provide the context for the supernatural experience.

Bell concludes her account of the genres of ritual action by discussing how practical engagement strengthens belief. She is referring to Hindu ritual in the following

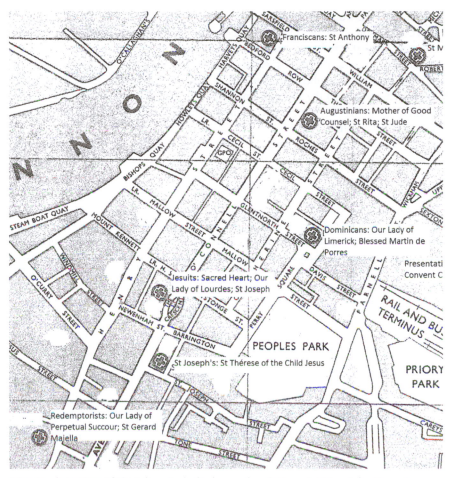

Franciscans: St Anthony

St M

Augustinians: Mother of Good Counsel; St Rita; St Jude

Dominicans: Our Lady of Limerick; Blessed Martin de Porres

Presentati Convent C

Jesuits: Sacred Heart; Our Lady of Lourdes; St Joseph

PEOPLES PARK

St Joseph's: St Thérese of the Child Jesus

PRIORY PARK

Redemptorists: Our Lady of Perpetual Succour; St Gerard Majella

Map 3 Location of churches, including popular shrines, in Limerick city centre, 1920–60.

passage: 'A lecture about the power of ancestors will not inculcate the type of assumptions about ancestral presence that the simple routine of offering incense at an altar can inculcate. Activities that are so physical, aesthetic and established appear to play a particularly powerful role in shaping human sensibility and imagination'.[122] While physical action and spatial context is a part of every type of ritual, it is in the area of personal devotion that the connections between these elements and supernatural belief can be most clearly seen. Bell's mention of the 'established' activities is also important: the integration of devotion into everyday life at home, in the car or around the streets of the city was a significant aspect of its power to make the supernatural present in people's lives, though of course this sense was more pronounced at certain times. The positioning of holy water fonts in the home, the shrines in some housing estates and the churches in the streets of the city add up to what Lawrence Taylor, in his study of Catholicism in rural Donegal, has called 'sacred geography'.[123] The role of the clergy, who would certainly have encouraged this, shows how they also appreciated the importance of the physical and the tactile in creating and maintaining belief. In the city context, the larger number of points of contact with the sacred did not necessarily mean a more intense spiritual experience, though this might have been the case with some people. It did mean however that people had a wide choice in terms of how they chose to enact the supernatural in their lives whether they were at home or out and about in the city: the evidence gathered from interviewees and from the local newspapers reflects this.

It is, however, crucial to remember that the supernatural belief underpinning people's devotional activities was the most important factor in how they encountered the sacred in their lives in the city: this is why a man who was 'mad for money' ended up at the priest's door after midnight; and it's also why the silver screen, with all its drama and glamour, was powerless to assuage the fear felt by four young girls who had attended a Protestant burial. It was through the strength of this belief that the physical aspects, visiting a shrine, kneeling in the Confession box, sprinkling oneself with holy water, acquired such meaning and power.

Creativity: Senses and Speech

This chapter is concerned with aesthetics and creativity in two areas: firstly, that which is connected to the visual, the aural and other sensory experiences of popular devotion or other religious activities; secondly that which is to be found in popular discourse around religion and other aspects of city life in the period studied. The uses of devotion as a path to goodness and happiness, along with its power to protect or to help in difficult situations, or in a crisis, were made clear in Chapter 6. But the evidence shows that devotion also had an aesthetic function, and that this was an important part of the experience of religion for many people. In this discussion, I will look at the occasions and contexts in which the sensual aspects of religion were experienced most strongly, while also looking at how these were connected to meaning. People's own contribution to religious sense-experiences are very important too, in that they reflect an active, conscious creativity in devotional contexts. The larger effect of aesthetically rich devotional experiences and their relation to belief will also be discussed. In the second half of the discussion, the creativity of popular discourse will be explored through an examination of jokes and humorous anecdotes current in Limerick city in the period studied. The discussion will focus on how these items of folklore, apart from their obvious entertainment value, may have functioned as a means of negotiation of various areas of life, including religion. The difference between the type of creativity involved in the telling and retelling of jokes and anecdotes, and that involved in the aesthetic aspects of devotion is significant: this difference will be addressed in the final part of the chapter.

Senses

Christmas and Easter

One of the most important features of the Catholic religion in Ireland for much of the twentieth century was its power to provide a spectacle, in visual terms, for those participating in various devotional activities. The decoration of the interiors of churches with pictures, shrines, statues and other types of ornament was one important aspect of this and was frequently discussed in detail in the popular press, when new churches were opened or when new decorative features were introduced into an existing church.[1] There were also certain times of the year when the sense of spectacle in churches was much greater. Christmas is an example of this, when it was the custom, on Christmas Day or (more usually) on the day after, St Stephen's Day, to tour the city churches in order to see the various cribs:

> On St Stephen's Day you'd bring the children on a tour of all the churches in the city to see the cribs – I brought mine from top to bottom! They laugh now about it! We lived in the city centre area that time. The best one was in the Redemptorists – the figures were lifelike. They were lovely customs. There wasn't much more to do with children that time.[2]

Peggy D's evidence, above, shows how the tour of the cribs was seen as a form of entertainment for children: judging the best crib is part of this. Grace K's evidence supports this.[3] Máirín M's family toured the cribs on Christmas Day. She describes the custom from the children's point of view: 'Christmas Day … And you just want to kind of play with your toys, and do everything … no! They always had to get dressed up and off and around we'd … walk … walked everywhere. Every one of the cribs! Out even to St Munchin's Church I remember … Visiting baby Jesus and say a prayer in every one of them'. Meeting other children at the cribs was an important aspect for Máirín:

> But when you were going around, to do the rounds you'd meet up with other families and 'twould be kind of swapping 'What did you get?' and 'What did I get from Santa …?' do you know this kind of thing? … at the churches or walking to them … Oh all children would be there, the mothers and – usually if you were after getting a scooter or a doll or – whatever you had – they would come along as well, you know.[4]

The question of which crib was the best is also a feature of this account: 'The Redemptorists were the "Fathers" we used to call them and they would be very much into Christmas and all … they had the best crib in Limerick … Oh fantastic … their Wise Kings were something to see! (laughter) … they had lovely lovely statues'[5]

Noreen P, who was the youngest of her family, had a particularly close relationship with her father. He used to bring her to 'every crib in the city' on St Stephen's Day.[6] Kathleen B makes the point that in her family, they didn't have a crib at home, but that 'the crib was in the church'. She and her family used to visit the churches on St Stephen's Day: 'you'd go into each church and you'd see lots of people all coming in and out all to see the crib'.[7]

Holy Thursday, the Thursday of Holy Week which brought Lent to a close and was followed by the celebration of Easter was another time when people toured the churches: this time it was to see the displays of flowers that were a feature of the Exposition of the Blessed Sacrament that took place on that day on the Altar of Repose. Speaking about life at that time in general, Peggy D said: 'They had lovely customs alright. On Holy Thursday the churches would all be decorated with flowers – it'd be beautiful. People would go around to all the churches: there'd be Exposition all day. They'd get a new outfit especially for that!'[8] Grace K remembers 'Flowers! Oceans of flowers!'; she also emphasizes the social aspect 'Holy Thursday was a big night … because everyone would be wearing their best … going around, and you'd meet them.

The people you met, maybe coming out of the Augustinians, you'd meet them coming down from the Redemptorists, because they'd Saint Joseph's to go into going up'.[9] Áine R remembers touring the churches with her friends on Holy Thursday:

> Holy Week was always lovely, especially Holy Thursday … Because Holy Thursday, in those days, Pádraig remembers it as well now … all the altars, on Holy Thursday were done up with candles and flowers. Now, I don't know how many people would remember it but our job was, because we were on our Easter holidays, we'd go round – myself and maybe five or six of the girls – would go round, each church, every one of the churches and Limerick is full of churches, but we got them all in, that's the way our afternoon would go and some of our morning as well. That's what we did, we went round to see … And we'd be judging which was the nicest and we'd be talking about it afterwards, you know … that's what we did. That was Holy Thursday.[10]

One of the main aims of touring churches at Christmas, as pointed out by Máirín M above, and also mentioned by Kathleen B was to say prayers to baby Jesus in the crib. Exposition of the Blessed Sacrament, the devotional context in which the churches were decorated with flowers and candles on Holy Thursday, also involved devout behaviour, prayer and total silence. It is interesting to find, however, that the visual and material pleasure involved in looking at cribs and at other children's toys, in showing one's own toys, in seeing arrangements of flowers and candles and perhaps dressing up, or dressing in new clothes, that is to say the material and aesthetic aspects, were also regarded as important on these occasions. The fact that city people had access to such a large number of churches (around ten, not including convent chapels, all within walking distance of each other) lent a sense of choice and variety to these occasions: the slight competitive aspect added to this. The urban context is a crucial part of this custom, which involved walking from church to church and meeting other people doing the same: this could not have been done in the same way in far-flung parishes in rural areas. This is an example of a devotional practice which, although it was centred on official Catholic spaces, developed its own momentum and atmosphere as a popular activity carried out by hundreds of people on St Stephen's Day. The clerical involvement, in this case, seems to have been limited to making the best possible effort with the decoration of the crib in the days before Christmas, though it must be remembered that lay-people may have helped with these too. There is no evidence that people were strongly urged by the clergy to visit all the cribs, as they were, say, to attend confraternities, sodalities or annual retreats. Visiting the cribs could, perhaps, be seen as an example of the creativity of the city population during the period in terms of how they brought official devotion and popular practice together in a kind of 'hybrid' religion, where the sociable and sensual aspects of devotion were combined in a family occasion particularly suited to a modern, urban environment.

The sense of spectacle in the church is also to be felt in a more serious context: Timmy G describes the ceremony on the Feast of Christ the King, held on the Sunday before the beginning of Advent, when 'you'd have army officers there … with their drawn swords and they'd a guard of honour alongside the monstrance going around the church … it was something nice, you know?' A different sense of drama, with a somewhat more menacing aspect is to the fore in the following account of the *Tenebrae* ceremony held on Holy Thursday (the Thursday of the week before Easter, known as Holy Week) in St John's Cathedral. The purpose of the ritual was to commemorate Christ's death. Máirín M describes it as follows:

> I remember there were lots and lots of priests involved in this – and they would come ... there was a lot of chanting went on. And they had a type of candle-holder which ... to my memory, symbolised the twelve apostles. It was slanted in a v-shape, with the candle on top representing Christ, and six at either side. They were lighted at the start of the ceremony, and at the end of each session, an altar boy would come and quench a candle until eventually the church was in darkness because that was the only source of light during the *Tenebrae*. And at that point this dreadful, dreadful sound would suddenly start into a crescendo of like crashing noise, and as a child it would terrify you. But I think it just symbolised the death of Christ and the thunder – the noise – and that the sound was being made, to my knowledge, with what they called 'clappers' – which were like two big wooden bats ... a number of people would have two each and just bang them together. But the sound ... that was quite frightening ... It was night-time ... Because the church would be total darkness and it was very eerie, I can remember that.[11]

The Latin word *tenebrae* means 'shadows or darkness' and the ritual, which dates from the fifth century, was originally designed to help Christians experience Christ's death as if they were there.[12] The combination of sound and light described here was certainly very effective in achieving this, some 1,500 years later. A sense of light and dark is also a factor in this interviewee's description of Good Friday:

> Always at three o'clock on Good Friday we would have the Stations of the Cross, in all the various churches ... and as a child and even when I grew into adulthood, I *always* was of the impression – because we were told and it just seemed to happen – maybe 'twas imagination, but that the earth used to darken at three o'clock every Good Friday ... And for some reason, it always seemed to happen, even if there was a nice day.[13]

A sense of nature being in sympathy with the religious mood here is significant, because it extends the religious atmosphere beyond the confines of the church building to the city environment in general. The transformation of the city into a ritual space on Good Friday can be seen in Figures 6 and 7, where the congregation is gathered outside St Munchin's Church in Thomondgate – with some sitting on the historic Limerick Treaty Stone for a better view – on Good Friday in 1929.

A sense of the sacredness of a particular time is also in evidence here, something discussed by Mircea Eliade in this context when he says:

> Every ritual has the character of happening *now*, at this very moment. The time of the event that the ritual commemorates or re-enacts is made *present*, "re-presented" so to speak, however far back it may have been in ordinary reckoning. Christ's passion, death and resurrection are not simply *remembered*

Figure 6 Congregation outside St Munchin's Church, Thomondgate, Good Friday 1929.

Figure 7 Congregation in the grounds of St Munchin's Church, and in the vicinity, Good Friday 1929.

during the services of Holy Week; they really happen *then* before the eyes of the faithful. And a convinced Christian must feel that he is *contemporary* with these transhistoric events.[14]

With regard to Limerick city during the period studied, it's also important to realize that the sense of religious uniformity at the time contributed to this shaping of the environment. Kathleen B's description of the absence of sound, or sense of 'silence' around Good Friday below demonstrates that this atmosphere was deliberately created: 'And the Good Friday then ... everything was ... very strictly observed, very ... Shut down, yes. And there were no dances in Lent. That's another thing now that I'm remembering. No dances, and ... 'twas very sombre, sad'[15]

This sense of silence can also be found in customs relating to death, both within and outside the church. Máirín M's account of the custom of doing the rounds for the Holy Souls in the Augustinian Church on All Souls' Night (discussed in the previous chapter) states that despite the crowds and crowds of people present, the ritual was carried out in total silence. Anthony F who lived in the Killalee area recounts how, if someone in the neighbourhood died, all the radios would be put off on the street and the blinds would be drawn.[16] The idea of manipulating the environment to echo the occasion of death is also a feature of the rituals of death inside the home, as was clear from the discussion earlier in the book.

Decoration of the city

The sense of celebration on certain occasions described in the church setting above can also be seen in contexts outside of the church. In these outside contexts, people were actively involved in the decoration of streets and other public spaces, rather than simply participating and enjoying church-based decoration, as they did at Christmas and Easter. The decoration of the streets for the annual Corpus Christi procession, an evening event which took place in June, is one example: judging by the ages of the interviewees involved, these descriptions could be said to apply to the late 1930s, the 1940s and the 1950s.[17] Other evidence indicates that the custom of decoration of public spaces on special occasions may have been even stronger in the earlier part of the period. An account of the decoration of the streets of Limerick for the Diamond Jubilee (or sixtieth anniversary) of the founding of the Redemptorist Archconfraternity of the Holy Family in 1928, the highlight of which was a procession involving a visiting Cardinal, describes elaborately constructed and decorated altars, arches, banners and streamers in every part of the city, while flags and small altars were a feature of almost every house. The connections between these religious decorations and a sense of locality, and the symbolic representation of this, is striking. The visit of Cardinal van Rossum to Limerick for the occasion was marked with a procession to welcome him and other visitors to the city. An arch spanning the breadth of Davis St, just outside the railway station is written in Irish, with the inscription *Fáilte go Luimneach in ainm Íosa, Muire agus Íóseph* translating as 'Welcome to Limerick in the name of Jesus, Mary and Joseph' – a reference to the Holy Family to which the Confraternity was dedicated (see Figure 8).

Figure 8   An arch constructed outside Limerick railway station to welcome Cardinal van Rossum and other visitors to Limerick for the ACHF Diamond Jubilee in 1928.

Figure 9   A replica of the Arms of Limerick, erected at the entrance to Wolfe Tone Street for the Diamond Jubilee of the Archconfraternity of the Holy Family, 1928.

Figure 10   A replica of the walls of Limerick at St John's Gate, built for the
Diamond Jubilee of the Archconfraternity of the Holy Family, 1928.

The entrance to Wolfe Tone Street was spanned by a 'gate, representing the old
Castle of Limerick with coat of arms and motto'[18] (see Figure 9).

The entrance to John's Street (in St John's parish) was described as follows:

> A committee which had charge of the decorations in that locality showed origi-
> nality beyond the ordinary by erecting a most faithful replica of the old historic
> St. John's Gate very close to the ancient site. With elaborate care the committee,
> working on an ingenious design of Mr. J. Savage, of John St., erected a skeleton
> frame of the gate which they afterwards covered with canvas, which had been
> skilfully painted to represent the stone-work.[19]

The committee also positioned 'two ancient guns of the city' at either side of the gate
(see Figure 10).

At Baal's Bridge, the entrance to St Mary's Parish (known in Limerick as simply
'The Parish'), an arch was erected over the bridge with 'a splendid painting of the
Treaty Stone on canvas' (see Figure 11).

The *Limerick Leader* writer also commends the committee in charge of the nearby
Sandmall for the bunting, banners and 'beautiful altars of the Blessed Virgin ... set up
and charmingly decorated with flowers and pictures'. The traditional fishing-boats of
this area, the sand cots moored on the Abbey river, and owned by the Abbey fishermen
(known as 'Sandmen'), were draped in bunting and multi-coloured lanterns for the
occasion.[20]

Religious imagery and religious themes were a central feature of the decorations.
The following description of the altar at the junction of Upper Gerald Griffin Street
and Parnell Street is a good example:

Figure 11 Arch erected on Baal's Bridge for the Diamond Jubilee of the Archconfraternity of the Holy Family, 1928.

The altar, which had been first erected on a timber frame to a height of about 14 feet, was covered on the outside with canvas, which had been artistically painted to represent stone and masonry work, while the inside was draped with blue and white – the colours of the Virgin Mother. The actual altar was a most realistic imitation of marble work, being made from timber which had been specially prepared and painted, and for the clever designing of which great credit is due to Mr. John Henry, Parnell St., who was ably assisted by a most energetic band of workers from the locality in which the structure stood.[21]

A life-size statue of the Blessed Virgin stood on the altar, and 'surmounting the entire altar and shrine was a plain cross made of glass and electrically illuminated in a very clever manner'. Another altar erected in Ellen Street, with statues, candles, flowers and foliage, can be seen in Figure 12.

The representation of church architecture and interiors, through the painted imitation of stonework and marble in this temporary structure is interesting. Another local group went so far as to build a miniature chapel, with an altar inside, which had both an entrance and an exit, and was 'freely used by throngs of people', at the Patrick Street end of Matthew Bridge.[22]

Limerick's religious history is to be felt in the re-erection, by a Mrs O'Donoghue, of the 'altar at which the first Mass [was] ever celebrated by a Redemptorist priest in the city', on its original site, while a Lourdes grotto 'erected unaided by Miss M. Collins, 4 John St., on a disused building site' had large stones covered with moss, a bower of evergreens and 'by an arrangement worked from the rere a continuous flow of water percolated through the crevices of stones and moss while in the foreground was a

Figure 12   Altar constructed in Ellen Street for the Diamond Jubilee of the Archconfraternity of the Holy Family, 1928.

figure respresenting the little peasant girl, Bernadette, in a posture of worship with real shoes beside her and a bundle of firewood'.[23]

The above is a small sample of the descriptions of the decoration of the city for this occasion: it is important to note that many places of employment, such as McMahon's Timber Yard in Upper William Street, the Civic Guards Barracks, the 'Standard Stores' in Patrick Street and the Railway Hotel were decorated too.[24] The photographic evidence suggests, however, that it was in the residential streets and areas of the city, rather than in the mainly commercial areas such as O'Connell Street and William Street, that the most elaborate and interesting decorations were created.

In these areas, the general pattern seemed to be that everybody made an effort to decorate their own house or property (including boats!), and that street or area committees, sometimes led by talented individuals, were responsible for the larger structures. Sometimes individuals, such as Mrs O'Donoghue and Miss Collins mentioned above, worked alone to create something unusual. While the connection between the decorations and popular religious discourse, such as the story of the apparition at Lourdes, is interesting, the desire to create replicas of church buildings, altars and features of church interiors in neighbourhood streets may show a signif-icant attachment to these sacred spaces, something identified by Judith Hill in her discussion of the building of the city churches themselves during the nineteenth and early twentieth centuries.[25] The historical aspects of the decorations are important too: the replicas of King John's Castle and the old city entrance, John's Gate and the painting of the Treaty Stone show a strong sense of local history at work in the process of development of Limerick's Catholic identity at this point in the late 1920s. It is noteworthy too that it was an occasion associated with the Redemptorist Confraternity that was the motivation for this celebration: the people's response speaks eloquently about the role of that organization in their lives at the time.

The decoration of the city environment described above presents an opportunity to add another dimension to the understanding of religion in Limerick city at that time. Looked at from the conventional historical point of view, this occasion could be seen as strongly representative of the high point of official Catholicism in Ireland as it existed in the late nineteenth and early twentieth centuries. However, it also demonstrates the people's creativity in their use of stories, symbols and spaces to transform their immediate environment and to celebrate their identity and their belief in visual and material ways. It is important to remember that this form of expression was not confined to Limerick, but was also to be found in other Irish cities on certain occasions, with the centenary of Catholic Emancipation and the 1932 Eucharistic Congress the best known of these.[26] It is also interesting to note that creativity such as this was a feature of popular Catholicism in New York and other American cities during the same period.[27] In all these cases, including Limerick city, this can be characterized as a version of popular, urban religion which has, through the creative use of stories, symbols and physical materials, become locally vibrant, meaningful and enjoyable on many different levels.

Textiles

For some people, the ongoing process of decoration for devotional purposes formed a significant part of their lives. Many women were involved in the decoration of church interiors, particularly textiles and flowers, through altar societies such as the one in St Mary's Parish, or that attached to the Jesuit Church.[28] The Mount Saint Alphonsus archive in the Redemptorist Monastery contains a book with a list of gifts and donations given to that church from around 1890 to the 1940s. The votive offerings of jewellery and other items given in petition to the shrine of Our Lady of Perpetual Succour constitute one noteworthy aspect of this: the contributions, in many different forms, to the decoration and embellishment of the church interior constitute another.[29] These contributions include gifts of flowers, both real and artificial; gifts of bought items such as flower pots; and payment for the painting of the interior of the church, or part of it. By far the biggest category of donations, however, is in the area of decorative textiles. It can be seen from the listing of these items that certain women had an ongoing, intense involvement with devotional textile work centred on the Redemptorist church. A Miss Purtill of St Alphonsus Avenue, for instance, whose name first appears in 1923, created a wide variety of items from then until 1941.[30] The fact that some of these items were exquisite examples of contemporary Irish craft at that period is discernible from the way the donations are recorded: in April 1930, for instance, Miss Purtill donated '1 Red Tabernacle Veil, Irish Poplin, embroidered gold'; in October 1932 'A beautiful Limerick Lace alb'.[31] The references to the distinctive Irish poplin, a mixture of silk and wool woven in Dublin since the eighteenth century, and Limerick lace, by then an internationally known local craft, show an awareness on the part of the recording scribe of the value and cultural significance of items such as these.[32] Sometimes Miss

Purtill worked on larger projects, with the co-operation of the monastery and the help of others: the list for August 1935 records: '1 altar cloth made and embroidered for each altar by Miss Purtill and Miss McGann. Material provided by the House'. The sense of group involvement is again evident in 1938, when an embroidered altar cloth and two lace albs are listed as having been donated by 'Miss Purtill & Co'.[33]

It is clear that not everybody was interested in this kind of activity, but for those who were, it was an important creative aspect of their religious lives. Grace K, a former member of an altar society based around Dominic Street recounts the enjoyment involved in evenings spent handsewing and embroidering devotional textiles and talking with the other women there. An appreciation of beautiful textiles was not confined to those who created them, as the Redemptorist listing above shows. Máirín M's description of the process of creation of her Communion veil shows the same kind of appreciation: she refers to this item as,

> an heirloom that I cherish now at this stage, it's an heirloom to me. But it was actually a neighbour of ours, May Spillane, who was brilliant at making Limerick lace, and about, I think, a year before I started – before I made my First Communion, she … started to make my veil. And it's very very big … I actually at times give it as a loan as an altar cloth if there's any special event going on. And it's beautifully done with the chalices in the four corners and the host and that type of thing. But she put months and months of work because what she had was a whitewashed wall, I remember in her yard of her house, at the back, and the whitewashed wall was so that the sun would reflect because it was very difficult on the eyes, and she had it on a big frame, and every day when I'd come home from school I used to go out to see the progress, and you'd hardly see it because the stitches were so tiny. But it was fabulous and I still have that, I treasure that.[34]

Other interviewees' vivid memories of items worn on the occasion of their First Holy Communion also testify to the sensual power of textiles and other aspects of dress on that ritual occasion. Noreen P, whose dress came from her aunt in Dublin, also remembers the 'lovely white socks – frilly socks – and the shoes'.[35] Áine R, who had, with her family, decided to carry flowers and a purse despite the nuns' disapproval of these accessories recalls the occasion as follows:

> It was a lovely day. And of course, the veil was borrowed. The dress was bought and 'twas lovely. White shoes, buckskin, aaw! (Laughter) But yes, we were lovely and … I remember being down there and of course the nuns had told us not to have flowers or a purse. Like, they were after telling us before that now, 'That's immoral' or not immoral – or 'disrespectful' or something, and I was ashamed of my life because some of the nuns appeared at the church, St Mary's and here was I, well somebody was minding my flowers, and the purse, but afterwards when they were at the door, and we coming out, I was saying 'Oh Jesus they'll kill me now when I get to the school on Monday!' because I had flowers and a purse.[36]

Áine remembers her mother being able to buy her a cotton summer dress with the money she collected on her First Communion Day (around £1); she also gives a vivid description of her Confirmation outfit:

But … Confirmation of course, I still remember that. And the year I made it, it was Pentecost Sunday, it was, again, my aunt – my mother had an old coat, my aunt turned it, and made it look new and made a tam to match. She did. And … 'twas lovely. And she made my dress out of a bit of cotton 'twas pique, with white flowers. So there, I was lovely.[37]

The involvement of mothers, and female friends and relatives in the material processes involved in dressing children for ritual occasions is a notable element in the accounts above. Charlotte Wildman stresses the same aspect of female creativity in her discussion of the Whit Walks in Manchester[38] and evidence from France shows that a similar situation prevailed there during the same period.[39]

Máirín M later became active in devotional textile work herself, through the sodality for past pupils of the Presentation school. Some of the work involved converting wedding dresses donated by women who had married, into priests' vestments to be sent to the missions. Máirín, who later donated her own wedding dress for the same purpose, describes the work:

We did that every Monday night … some of the nuns were very good at cutting-out. They obviously had their patterns and the vestments were for the priests on the missions. They would be sent off. But one of my specialities at the time was … these tiny tiny little crosses that had to be put on the altar cloths, they were tiny little red crosses, there was a name on them … tiny tiny little red crosses and they had to be done in a certain way … 'twas like tapestry nearly, very tiny and … I loved embroidery anyway but I used to spend a lot of my Monday nights doing these because other people found they couldn't do them – they were tiny – they were hardly … the cross itself, completed, was I suppose, maybe a half an inch … and done in red on the white. And they would be used for, you know, the cloth on the chalice and all that type of thing, as well, and they'd be somewhere on the altar cloths as well.[40]

The enjoyment and satisfaction of doing the work itself is obvious from the above, but Máirín also mentions other aspects:

I can't remember a time when it started. It was just something that we seemed to get involved … but it was lovely. There was a lovely sense of being part of something, again, I remember … 'twas over in the Presentation School and 'twas in an upper room there now … I can't recall exactly … and there'd be a few nuns and we'd sit and chat around and, you know, you were sewing and … great camaraderie there. It was lovely.[41]

It is important to understand all the different aspects of culture involved here: the creativity and aesthetic fulfillment of craft is one aspect, but the sense that this is for a higher spiritual purpose is also present: the donation of wedding dresses shows that it was regarded as appropriate to use clothing worn for one sacramental occasion to enhance, in a more long-term sense, similar ritual occasions in different contexts. The ritual element is enhanced, albeit unconsciously, by the interviewee's use of the phrase 'upper room', which echoes the phrase used to describe the last supper in two of the Gospels.[42] The recycling of wedding dresses, however, belongs to the later part of the period studied, as, for most people, the choice of a white wedding dress that would not be worn again didn't become the norm in Ireland until the mid-1950s.[43] The positive sense of group activity described by Máirín is also noteworthy: the continued involvement of past pupils with their convents, whether in an ongoing way such as that described above, or on an occasional basis, perhaps returning for the annual May procession, was an important feature of many women's lives, both single and married, during the period.[44] A longer-term sense of positive involvement in the life of the wider city is also a factor in this case: according to Máirín, these past pupils were the same group with whom she later started the 'Meals on Wheels' service in co-operation with Limerick Social Service Centre.[45]

Singing in devotional activities

It is important to note, in the first place, that singing was a central part of Catholic devotion in general and is mentioned by many interviewees as a memorable aspect of many different types of devotional occasions. Anthony F, for instance, mentions the 'lovely, beautiful hymns' sung at the Archconfraternity of the Sacred Cincture in the Augustinian Church.[46] O'Flynn asks his readers to 'imagine about two thousand men' singing hymns such as 'Faith of Our Fathers' in unison, to convey a sense of the atmosphere of the weekly meeting of the Redemptorist Confraternity. [47] The way in which singing combined with other aesthetic elements to create the sense-experience of devotion in the month of May is explained here by Máirín M. Describing the May procession held in the grounds of the Presentation Convent as something that 'will live in my memory forever', she goes on to say:

> But May was a very special month, and on the first of May – I always associate it with Fr Sidney McKeun singing ... 'Queen of the May': 'Oh Mary we crown thee ...' absolutely beautiful. But ... in every home, there would be an altar, first of all, with a statue of Our Lady and two little vases and a blue lamp – night light, lighting from the first of May until the last day of May and bluebells were the thing, I always remember, wild bluebells ... we always went out to Curragh Chase or out where Bunratty Castle is now, at the back of that, they'd grow wild, and we'd always get them there. But at school the country children – as we used to say – would bring in the flowers, and every week there was always ... they'd be kept fresh all through the month of May. But the May procession then was one of the main events ... and it was held in the – the nuns had lovely grounds – in the lawns and the grounds of the convent, and everybody would assemble. There'd be a couple of hundred because all past pupils and everything would be there.[48]

Another memory of Máirín's in which singing played a part concerns the celebration in the Redemptorist Church on the evening of Christmas Day:

> And then we would have ... to be back to the Redemptorists for six o'clock, on ... Christmas Day for the blessing of the thousand candles. That went on. And they ... would light a thousand candles ... that still goes on to this day. But, funny, the

thing I remember most about that was, once – I don't know what age I was – but Tommy Drennan ... he was a boy soprano that time and – oh he was fantastic. But all the little altar boys they had a special type of vestment they used to wear like, it was cream, a cord around their waist, and they'd all be of a size, all be much the same. And they'd be lined up there inside the altar rails, facing down to the crowd and Tommy Drennan would sing 'O Holy Night' and – aw! – it was just fantastic.[49]

According to Máirín, this service would be 'Absolutely packed. If you weren't there in time you wouldn't get inside the door of the Redemptorists!'[50]

Accounts of Benediction also stress the way in which the singing of the Latin hymns, *Tantum Ergo* and *O Salutaris*, contributed to the overall experience. Benediction, as its name implies, involved (and still does) Exposition of the Blessed Sacrament while Latin hymns were sung, followed by the blessing of the congregation with the Blessed Sacrament and finally the recitation of the Divine Praises. In describing this experience Peggy D said 'I used to love Benediction ... *Tantum Ergo, O Salutaris.* You'd be off at seven o'clock in the evening to Benediction.'[51] Noreen P here describes the women's confraternity in St Mary's Parish: 'And we went down duly every Tuesday night and there would have been rosary, I'm sure, a sermon, and followed by Benediction ... Benediction was really really lovely, there was a lovely warm feeling ... the priest would bless us with the monstrance, that was the whole idea of Benediction, and ... the smell of the incense ... would warm you to the whole thing.'[52] Anthony F explained that as Mass was on Sunday morning, Benediction would be held in the evening. He describes it as follows:

> Every Sunday without fail the Benediction was held in the evening. We all had to go to Benediction, the whole parish was there, like, children were all sent down. But I suppose 'twas the nearest thing to a drug – I never used these drugs in my whole life, thank God, but that was a drug. The incense rising, coupled with the magnificent Plain Chant, the Gregorian chant, the combination of that. The *O Salutaris,* and the *Tantum Ergo,* and the Plain Chant and the ... the responses, in Latin, of course, that was that time. All the music that we ever did was all in Latin.[53]

These accounts show how Benediction appealed to the senses, especially sound and scent, as the singing and the incense are important aspects of them. In his discussion of a more body-centred approach to the human sciences, Paul Stoller has pointed out that 'it is especially important to incorporate into ethnographic works the sensuous body – its smells, tastes, textures and sensations' and has argued that 'disembodied approaches to the anthropology of religion present only partial pictures of religious practices'.[54] Benediction is perhaps the most obvious example of a ritual experience which cannot be fully understood without due consideration of its bodily and sensuous aspects.

Liturgical singing

However, singing was also regarded as an activity in its own right, and was pursued as such, in a few different contexts. Anthony F's considerable singing talent was useful in the choir of St John's Cathedral which was also his parish church. He was a boy soprano who had won three gold medals for singing in the first *Féile Luimní*[55] competition in 1946:

> And because we were handy singers, Fr. O'Grady, afterwards Canon O'Grady ...
> he recruited us then, for the choir. And – in the Cathedral choir, and Professor
> Charles Michael King Griffin from Miltown Malbay was the music teacher and
> part of the job of being organist in the Cathedral, you also had to be the music
> teacher for the priests or the would-be priests outside in St Munchin's. So we knew
> all the liturgy in Latin.[56]

It is clear from this that the role played by the choirmaster in the education of diocesan seminarians also influenced the repertoire learned and sung by the members of the parish choir. The Cathedral choir was an important one, and Anthony, whose family could not afford to go on pilgrimages, made memorable trips to Knock and Drogheda for different devotional occasions when a member of it.[57]

Another way in which devotional singing was promoted was through the annual liturgical festival which took place in St John's Cathedral. This singing festival, which took place once a year, over a weekend for much of the period studied, was centred on the type of singing referred to by interviewees as 'Plain Chant', also sometimes called 'Plainsong' or 'Gregorian Chant', the latter name referring to the sixth-century Pope who is said to have introduced it.[58] Plain Chant involves singing in unison, without any different parts or harmonies: the text is usually in Latin, and the repertoire includes not just specific pieces such as those mentioned above in connection with Benediction, but also, as implied by Anthony F, the complete text of the Mass itself. The beginnings of an active interest in this type of music in Limerick city seems to date from around 1935, when an elementary course in Plain Chant, conducted by a 'Rev. John Burke, B. A., U.C.D.' was held in Limerick.[59] This course, which took place over a ten-day period, was aimed at clergy, nuns and teachers. In this same year, adult and juvenile prizes were offered by the Bishop of Limerick, Dr Keane, for Plain Chant singing in the Thomond *Feis*.[60] Within a few years this interest had evolved into an annual festival for pupils of secondary schools, held in St John's Cathedral every May.[61]

Interviewees' memories of this event are remarkably vivid. In Máirín M's school, the Presentation Convent in Sexton Street, the preparation took place over a number of Saturday mornings:

> Every Saturday morning you had to go to school, there was school on Saturday as
> well ... and the main feature of Saturday school was the choirs. And each teacher
> would teach their own class a certain amount during the week and then Saturday
> morning we would have Sister Alphonsus ... she was an aunt of Billy Whelan
> now who composed the music for 'Riverdance' ... She was brilliant! Absolutely
> brilliant! She was so vivacious, she was a tiny little woman ... And ... she would

take the school as a whole, she would put all these separate classes together and we would have these huge choirs on Saturday morning.[62]

Kathleen B, also a Presentation pupil, but at an earlier time, remembers that 'we'd march from the Presentation over': she remembers the Laurel Hill pupils, who would have had a much longer walk from the South Circular Road, being there as well.[63] Eileen L and Noreen P also remember going to the festival, the former from the Presentation, the latter from St Mary's (Mercy) Convent in King's Island. Máirín M states that boys' schools participated as well.[64]

All the interviewees who remember this event have positive memories of the experience of participation in it. Eileen L says 'Oh I loved it! I – I lived for it, every year ... We all paraded through the town to ... St. John's Cathedral, and a Reverend Dom Winoc ... a Benedictine from Belgium but living in Glenstal, he was up there in the pulpit, and he was conducting us. And did we love it! Oh that beautiful Plain Chant!'[65] Grace K, who attended a convent boarding school in County Limerick remembers this as well 'We had ... a priest from Glenstal, Dom Winoc, coming out teaching us the Plain Chant, you know. It was lovely.'[66] Noreen P is emphatic in her description of it:

> But what I do remember is a thing that I *loved* in secondary school in particular: the schools would converge, I think it was once a year, and the schools like CBS would come, Presentation, St. Mary's ... well there was no secondary in St John's, they came down to us to go to school, but there was the Plain Chant ... And the *Kyrie* and the *Gloria* and – it was – I can still hear in my mind's ear ... the *Kyrie* and the *Gloria* and it was just *beautiful.* We would fill the Cathedral! ... Oh Plain Chant was really lovely, Síle, it was really, it just – the voices lifted, it was *beautiful!* ... And anytime I hear the Gregorian chant now on – the monks from the Abbey on a CD, it brings it right back to me. It was beautiful altogether.[67]

Máirín M says 'there would be a time when we would all come together, all the schools of Limerick in St John's Cathedral ... and you would have all this Plain Chant, everybody singing together, the *Credo* ... *in Unum Deum*, I could sing it for you today ... the various things, the Plain Chant, it was absolutely brilliant!'[68] Kathleen B discusses specific groups in the Cathedral in the late 1930s, when there were fewer secondary schools in the city: 'And we were always on the top, Laurel Hill first, then ourselves. I think we were the only secondary schools you see that time. And then the boarders of Laurel Hill were in the organ gallery. And they were like angels singing! Beautiful!'[69]

Evaluations of singing

It is interesting here that interviewees' memories of this are not confined to the event in general, but, in many cases, include perfect recall of the some of the repertoire also. Anthony F, who was still active in liturgical singing at the time of this research, describes his own approach to remembering:

And my God ... how I lament the passing of the Latin thing – I could sing it – when I'm sitting in a car, if I'm coming down from Dublin, I start at the beginning of the Mass; just to keep myself alive maybe or occupied, and I start with the *Kyrie,* and the *Gloria* and the *Credo* and the *Sanctus* and I go through the whole lot of them. And I can still sing the liturgy that we sang on Good Friday and Holy Thursday, all through Holy Week.[70]

This interviewee's experience of singing is to be felt in his assessment of the aesthetic aspect of religious music as it has developed since the 1960s. He appears to be speaking about musical decisions made mainly by the Catholic Church, but also possibly including some lay choir-conductors and choirs themselves when he says 'I think that we made some mistakes. One of them was we abandoned our ancient hymnology and all the hymns that we used to sing and they tried all these new, bloody rubbish things that nobody ever remembered the following week!'[71] His preference for the church music of the pre-Vatican II era is clear in the following:

Latin is the most beautiful language in the world, and the easiest language in which to sing. And very expressive, and Italian, and I – I'm singing all my life ... But I was in operas and music societies and all my family ... it isn't an exagger-ation to say Síle that within the last century now, up to a few years ago all the major musical events and societies in Limerick city, there was a [member of my family], some of the extended family, cousins and uncles and aunts they were all involved in it. So music was a very big thing. But sacred music equally, and 'twas magnificent. And especially the Plain Chant. And then Dom Winoc Mertens came over from Belgium out to Glenstal and there was a great rejuvenation of the Plain Chant ... I love it and I love the hymns and I sing them myself. And I still go to the Latin Mass outside in St Patrick's once a month.[72]

The musician's perspective, an aesthetic one, is the main point here, although Anthony's remarks also indicate an important connection between musical activity in the city generally and that associated with religion. Kathleen B's evalu-ation of the singing, and more specifically the Plain Chant, takes a slightly different angle:

The Plain Chant was lovely ... I think they should bring it back, because ... Do you know why? I mean if you like music and you listen to the monks, the Plain Chant, it does something for you. It – it touches your soul, kind of. And if you were in the church and the Plain Chant, it made everything more solemn. And it made you realise more where you were ... and of course the Mass was in Latin that time, you know.[73]

Eileen L connects the feelings brought about by devotional singing with belief, in the context of Benediction:

Benediction was just ... such a lovely lovely expression of ... of reverence and awe. It was really ... the Blessed Sacrament wouldn't be normally out on show on the altar, except for Benediction. And I think maybe we were reared that way, with reverence and awe, you know, for – for the Blessed Sacrament, the Eucharist. And 'twas only out for a very short time and we got the blessing. Then the … the Plain Chant. The Gregorian Chant and the prayers … lent themselves to just that feeling of … ah, 'twas lovely, it's a pity it's gone, it really is.[74]

The musical city

The Plain Chant festival and its promotion by the clergy and by the Benedictine Order in particular, could be seen as related to the early music revival which had been under way in Britain since the late nineteenth century.[75] However Anthony F's evidence above indicates that interest in music in Limerick city, through opera and musical societies, was strong in any case in the 1940s and 1950s. Tom Hayes has discusssed the prevalence of music-making through marching bands in the nineteenth century, and O'Flynn's account shows a continued interest in this area in the twentieth.[76] O'Flynn, whose father was a coalman by day, also worked as a musician in a dance band, testifies to the interest in music among people in general when he says: 'sometimes on a summer evening when my father was practising the saxophone, with the window opened as far as it would go, some of the boys and girls used to come and sit on the pavement under the window enjoying the music'.[77] It is clear that an interest in music-making was not confined to those who played instruments, nor to those who belonged to marching bands, choirs or musical societies. Singing informally with family, friends and neighbours was quite usual. The accounts of May Eve in Chapter 4 show that singing was a central feature of special occasions such as this, but other evidence shows that singing was normal in many other contexts as well. According to one source, the singing, both communal and individual (including much material from the repertoire of opera and light opera) to be heard in Limerick during this period while passing public houses on the way home at night was memorable.[78] Áine R, speaking about her childhood in the St Mary's Park area of King's Island in the late 1930s and early 1940s has the following to say:

> And singing, well we all – everybody on our street sang. I mean, we'd go round singing! … I don't know what it was, but even at night we'd be all in bed you know and my mother would say 'Shh! Listen now!' And all the lads – the other lads – would be coming up from somewhere – all singing, at the tops of their voices, and we knew them all by name you see. They had lovely voices! I mean everybody did.[79]

Áine also describes the repertoire of local singers:

> In general you'd get 'Heart of my Heart', that was a very funny one, I remember the Murphys would come up singing that, and … 'Jealous Heart' was another one, you know, and there was a lot on the radios at the times like, and of course 'When I grow too old to dream' … my grandfather taught me that one, and a few others like that you know. "Rose Marie I love you, I'll always …" you know that one!' (Laughter) … there was always something going on, my grandfather was great though, and he was a lovely singer![80]

O'Flynn's account also mentions the singers in the Island Field: when he and his family moved from King's Island across the Shannon to a new house in O'Dwyer Villas in Thomondgate, they could see St Mary's Park from their bedroom windows on the other side of the river, and,

> when we lay in bed in our new house on a summer's night we could hear, coming across the water from the new estate over there, songs from light opera and musical films sung by the finest of voices as some fellows made their way home from the cinema or the pub or a dance. One fellow we loved to hear singing 'You Are My Heart's Delight', and some other fellow who fancied himself as Nelson Eddy used to give a powerful rendering of 'The Indian Love Call'.[81]

Listening to neighbours singing was also a feature of Anthony F's youth:

> Declan O'Brien's mother next door to St. John the Baptist School – she was a Keating herself, and her brother was the greatest boy soprano … Jim Keating, he was a beautiful boy soprano, but she had the same voice and she could be heard all over the garden when she'd be hanging out the washing and the people would hear her six houses or gardens away![82]

The custom of singing during bus and train journeys, usually where a special excursion with a group was being undertaken, was also widespread, as the evidence concerning pilgrimages, shows.

This attachment to spontaneous, informal singing could be seen as part of the strong residual orality of a culture in which recorded sound played a limited part, although it is also interesting to note that recorded sound could be said to have fuelled and stimulated communal singing or informal individual singing, as Áine R's and O'Flynn's evidence above shows. Looked at in this way, the enthusiasm for Plain Chant, which was learned off by heart and sung without hymn books, is understandable.[83] In a world in which singing was an everyday activity, teenagers didn't need much persuasion to translate this into a devotional context. As practised singers, which almost everybody was, and as regular attendees at Mass, the airs and the Latin texts were easily learned by them: as Catholics with strong supernatural beliefs, the sense of a higher world attained by this art was, as their evidence shows, both palpable and highly memorable.

Art, sense and meaning

The sensual and aesthetic aspects of devotion are of crucial importance in assessing the nature of religous experience in Limerick city in the decades from the 1920s to the 1950s. Here, it is worth returning to Clifford Geertz's classic definition of religion as, first of all, 'a system of symbols which acts to … establish powerful, pervasive, and long-lasting moods and motivations …'.[84] In this era, the festive decoration of the churches, the transformation of the city streets, the delicate and intricate work involved in decorative textiles and the practice of religious singing are all ways in which 'powerful, pervasive and long-lasting moods and motivations' were established and sustained, by both the clergy and the people themselves. The range of activities discussed above demonstrates how this creative process worked not just on an annual or occasional basis, but on a regular devotional and even, in the case of textiles, a constant, everyday basis as well. It is interesting too, to look at how these sensual aspects of devotion, and the 'moods and motivations' brought about by them, may have affected belief. Roy Rappaport discusses this point by highlighting the connections between art and religion in the work of Rudolph Otto:

> Whether or not the roots of art are set in the soil of religion, or whether its roots and those of religion are together set in a yet deeper stratum of the human condition, many students have remarked not only upon their association in practice but on similarities in their evocative qualities and effects. Otto recognized an association between art and religion ... he suggested that religious experience may flow out of aesthetic experience. 'In our experience of the sublime and the beautiful we dimly see the eternal and the true world of Spirit and Freedom' ... He also claimed that the ways in which we experience art and religion are similar.[85]

Rappaport also draws on Susanne K. Langer's work concerning aesthetic experience: 'For Langer, art is "significant form" and its significance is "that of a symbol, a highly articulated sensuous object, which by virtue of its structure can express the forms of vital experience which language is peculiarly unfit to convey'.[86] Rappaport uses Langer's ideas, along with those of Otto and William James to show how religious art, through its evocation of emotional responses, plays an important part in unifying 'the reasons of the heart' with 'the reasons of reason':[87] in other words, that the sensual experience provides the essential counterpoint to the structured discourse, or 'story' of ritual, by engaging the feelings and emotions brought about by the contemplation of beauty. In looking at Benediction, for instance, it could be said that the basic understanding of the Blessed Sacrament contained in the monstrance which is used to bless the congregation is brought about by the background information – or 'reasoned discourse' – about the Eucharist known to all the participants: the story of the Last Supper and the consecration. The Divine Praises also outline, through the use of language, the basic tenets of Catholic belief, in an overall context of blessing. But, as informants stated, it was the aesthetic element, the incense and, perhaps moreso, the singing, that brought about the feeling which completed the occasion. Rappaport also states that these feelings can mean different things to different people, and informants bear this out: to Anthony F, it was 'like a drug'; to Noreen P 'a lovely warm feeling'; to Eileen L it was 'reverence and awe'.

The power of the aesthetic, however, can be seen to work on many levels, and thus goes well beyond the example of Benediction outlined above. Rappaport has also stated that 'the significance of works of art in ritual could lie either in the objects produced and then contemplated or manipulated, or in the act of making them, or both'.[88] In this way we can see how, for example, the painstaking work of making a replica of King John's Castle involved not just an appreciation of the visual, but also of the communal and the historic: the emotions aroused by the finished work were not confined to a sense of wonder at the skill and artistry involved, but would have extended to a sense of pride in both the communal effort and a satisfying sense of history in the 'Limerick-ness' of the image: the admiration of the rest of the city population and of visitors to the city for the occasion, palpable in accounts by the local press, must have 'loaded' these emotions, though spiritual in origin, with strong social and cultural significance. Something of the same social and cultural context, though in a much quieter, less dramatic, and more long-term setting, can be seen in the creative textile gatherings described by Máirín M and Grace K. The Plain Chant festival embodies many of these levels too: the long preparation and the anticipation of the event; the excitement of walking through the streets of the city to the Cathedral; the sheer beauty of the singing of the massed choirs and the feelings of ecstasy brought about by this had a powerful emotional effect on the teenage participants.

It is in this area that religion can be most clearly seen as what Lawrence J. Taylor has called 'a sensibility':[89] where the sense-experience serves to unify not just the reasoned belief discourse with its emotional aspects, but also the agents of the Church with the ordinary believers: in all the examples discussed above, the enjoyment of aesthetic experience was the common denominator, and it was a powerful one. However, religion was not all about unity: many of its aspects needed to be reconciled to other aspects of the life of the community in general. The creative negotiation of these areas, through language, is the subject of the next section.

Speech

Ritual humour

It should be clear from previous discussions in this study that ritual language was a central part of the experience of popular religion in Limerick city in the second quarter of the twentieth century. The description of the rosary in Chapter 5, for instance, shows that the recitation of prayers, both the official texts of the rosary itself and the discretionary prayers added by individuals and families, was an integral part of people's lives, whether they were at home or partaking in church-based or other public devotion. That both Latin and English were universally used in prayer and devotional singing adds to the complexity of the role of language in ritual. It is not surprising therefore that language was also the instrument used to negotiate the interface between ritual and ordinary life, and that language was also used humorously to negotiate the difference between ritual language and ordinary language.

The Redemptorist Archconfraternity was an organization which had a high profile and a dynamic role in men's lives, and indirectly, in people's lives in general, in the city throughout the period. The importance of street decoration in the public rituals held by this confraternity is clear from the discussion above. The interface between this activity and the commercial life of the city can be felt in the following anecdote from Kathleen B:

> The Confraternity – they'd have their own processions: the Monday, Tuesday and Wednesday night divisions. You'd hear the bands away in the distance. You know the two pubs on the corner of Broad Street? Quilligan's and Clohessy's … one time

there was a banner stretching between them 'Happy We Who Thus United' – we thought it was very funny![90]

Here, the formal, idealistic text of the hymn is applied to the rivalry between two local public houses: it would be interesting to know whether the people hanging up the banner saw this same irony in it, or whether the humorous juxtaposition of happy Christian unity with everyday commercial rivalry was accidental.

The manipulation of hymn texts, this time deliberate, was also a feature of the boys' Confraternity, according to O'Flynn's account:

> But I must confess that when we sang those hymns in the Boys' Confraternity, we sometimes amused ourselves by altering a word here and there. Thus in ... ('Faith of Our Fathers'), we sang the final line as 'And faith*less* until death' And instead of being 'lost in wond'ring contemplation' we were 'lost in wandering constipation.[91]

O'Flynn also describes the children's creativity where the catechism was concerned. He makes no secret of his contempt for the pompous language used in the catechism text in the following piece:

> We had also acquired, from our big brothers as usual, the unorthodox answers which Sister Felicitas and the other nuns never heard ... we even adapted the Catechism's final ridiculous item, 'What means Amen? Amen means 'So be it'. We said: 'Amen means so-be-it, a little dog with four feet, runnin' down O' Connell Street, cryin' out: Pigs toes tuppence each'![92]

People's names and nicknames were also used to alter religious texts. One of O'Flynn's companions, Seán Daly, was in this category. O'Flynn tells us that:

> In our section, we relished the singing of the hymn 'Daily, daily, sing to Mary', because of the presence among us of Seán Daly, who lived in the house opposite ours, and whose father and older brothers were house-painters. (Seán joined them later.) He was very popular with all of us, and a reliable fighter if we clashed with hostiles from another street, but as all house-painters were colloquially known as *dabbers*, we could not resist taking a rise out of our own comrade whenever the organist struck up that hymn. We all roared 'Dabber Daly, sing to Mary' and were threatened by fist and grimace with meela murder by Seán.[93]

O'Flynn also relates the following anecdote: 'a poor *amadán* named Jim Mack was rushing along late to the church when he heard the massed voices inside singing 'Jim Mack, you're late, Jim Mack, you're late.' (What they were actually singing was 'Immaculate, Im-ma-cu-late'.)[94] Again, this item involves wordplay based around a person's surname. A nickname, and its connection to religion, is the basis of this story told by Tommy C:

> There was Eddie Power – they used to call him 'The Devil' ... Eddie 'The Devil' Power, and one Sunday evening he was at devotions, very tired, very hungover because the pubs were open from four to seven on Sundays. He was holding a candle for the renewal of vows and he lit the hair of the man in front of him by accident. Just then the priest said 'Renounce the Devil' and Eddie said 'Ye're all down on me!'[95]

Though the humour in the above incident centres on language, it also hinges on the disruption of the ritual order through inattention caused by tiredness and, in this case, inebriation. The following anecdote concerns a similar situation with regard to fatigue:

> And 'twas at the evening devotions of about a Thursday night that I was really burning the candle at both ends myself. I was really – and I fell asleep up in the Redemptorists. And next thing all of a sudden – they were all singing 'Ave, Ave, Maria …' and just as the – I jumped up and they all sat down and I went 'Ave!' And oh good jeepers above, everyone was looking around and I had to dive on to the ground and hide! Shure … you were overtired![96]

The sense of having to 'sit through' the devotions also comes through in this story told by Joseph L:

> We were all sitting there one night and there was a fellow in front of us who had a flea on him and was trying to catch it. He was making all kinds of *geáitsé*-s, twisting and turning in the seat. Eventually someone leaned forward and said to him 'Why don't you drive him out into the open and let us all have a go at him?'[97]

Misunderstanding of ritual language and the language of devotion is another source of amusement in the folklore of religion. The gentle humour in the following anecdote results from an innocent mistake made by the speaker:

> They had the one-hundredth anniversary celebrations and for that they had a big procession through the streets. It was pouring out of the heavens and by the time they got back to the Redemptorists they were all soaked to the skin. There was a fellow said 'That's the last centenary celebrations I'm ever taking part in!'[98]

A story told by Máirín M also concerns misunderstanding of terminology, this time in the context of the Plain Chant Festival:

> But a thing I remember about Sister Alphonsus one time anyway, she had the whole choir, the whole school there assembled and 'twas coming to a crescendo and we were all there and she was saying 'Will ye look happy! Will ye look happy – ye all look so morbid!' And when we were leaving anyway she says 'Oh your facial expression is also important!' you know because obviously this is part of … the … whole aspect of it … and anyway I remember just as we were leaving that day she turned and she said 'Girls, girls! Will ye please all pray to St Jude …' and what she said was '… Help of Hopeless Cases'. But it's funny, years later Josie, who was my best friend always growing up, and we were – ah it was a good few years later – we were at a dance and we were passing some comment about you know all the goodlooking girls were being asked to dance and we were kind of sitting there, we're the wallflowers, and the next thing Josie says to me 'D'you know we should start praying to St Jude!' This was when we first started going dancing now. 'We should start praying to St Jude …' and … I said 'Why?' and she says 'Don't you remember Sister Alphonsus telling us he's the help of hopeless faces?' All through the years she thought that's what … (laughter). That's what she thought … that's always what she thought (laughter) she'd said at the time

so every time I think of St Jude I think of the help of hopeless faces ... the help of hopeless faces![99]

The stories and anecdotes outlined above represent an important aspect of the creation of meaning in popular Catholic ritual in Limerick city in the early to mid-twentieth century. The meaning is achieved in a few different ways: in the first place the manipulation of ritual language, which attempts to change some of the more esoteric concepts into more practical and down-to-earth (or earthy) ones. Thus the high-flown notion of being lost in 'wond'ring contemplation' is, with typical schoolboy humour, deflated to 'wandering constipation'; 'Jim Mack you're late' makes four simple words out of 'immaculate' – a long word used a lot in religious discourse, but rarely in other contexts, while conjuring up a funny image of its subject hearing his name sung by the singers in the church. The fact that this item was also collected by the Irish Folklore Commission in County Limerick might indicate its more widespread use in anecdotal humour outside of the city.[100] The humour in the unthinking use of 'centenary celebrations' is centred on the sense of the contrast between the ordinary person, soaking wet, disgruntled and planning the avoidance of that fate in the future, but momentarily forgetting that his presence at the next centenary of the Confraternity – which would be celebrated in 2068 – was well-nigh impossible. The 'hopeless faces' joke is also a gentle humorous play on an innocent mistake, but it is a funny mistake because it juxtaposes the idea of St Jude and his 'Hopeless Cases' (normally assumed to be reserved for people in desperate need of medical or, perhaps, educational help) with the predicament of teenage girls at a dance hoping to be 'asked up'. It's important to note also that Sister Alphonsus's invocation of St. Jude regarding the girls' expressions when singing involved a certain amount of humour on her part as well.

Inherent in many of these anecdotes is the humorous combination of the somewhat intellectualized world of official religion with people's lives outside of the devotional world: the pub, the dance, and even bowel movements (or lack of them). Some of the narratives above combine these worlds even more strongly by bringing the world of the street and the neighbourhood into the devotional setting: 'Dabber Daly' is one example; Eddie 'The Devil' Power is another. The story about the flea again contrasts the formal, reverent setting of the Confraternity meeting with one of the common physical discomforts of life at the time. Fleas may have been an important theme in the humour of this era in Ireland, though the further investigation of this area is beyond the scope of this study. However, these jokes also highlight another side to popular devotion as it was practised in Limerick during these years: the undercurrents of humour, irony and informality which were a feature of that highly organized and ritualized world. These undercurrents provide an interesting counterpoint to the superlatives used by the local press in reporting devotional events throughout the period studied. In 1926, for instance, the description of the closing of the Annual Retreat for St Michael's Division of the Archconfraternity, where as many as 2,781 men received Communion, included phrases such as 'fervent congregation', 'greatly impressive scenes' and 'that wondrous picture of piety and faith so pre-eminent in all ceremonies connected with the great Arch-Confraternity'.[101] The tone of the reports towards the end of the period studied in 1960 were equally effusive, if the account of the 1960 Corpus Christi procession is anything to go by: according to the *Limerick Leader* it was 'a striking manifestation of faith'; there were 'devout scenes' and 'edifying scenes' among the 7,000 partici-pants in the procession and the closing prayers in St John's Square, while thousands looked on.[102] The ritual humour discussed above shows that people were well able to diffuse the formality, the reverence and the tense atmosphere required to sustain the ritual proceedings by humorous use of their own localized names and nicknames, by disruption of the ritual order, whether accidental or deliberate, and the enjoyment of this disruption. This is particularly true of the Redemptorist Confraternity, where thousands of men sat with their own families, friends and neighbours at a night-time meeting for nearly an hour every week. The ability to bring the localized culture of the street into the church setting is a striking aspect of this discourse. To say that many of these people were also devout and prayerful at other times is not a contradiction, but merely demonstrates the multi-layered, multi-functional nature of religion and religious culture and meanings in a given community. However, the glimpses of popular culture afforded by these small devotional narratives indicate the presence of a social scene in Limerick city at the time which is perhaps most accurately characterized by Tommy C's description of the atmosphere in the bacon factory where he worked:

> And there'd be always joking going on, d'you know, they were a terror for – there was – they were the wittiest people I've ever worked with in my whole life. They were funny! They were the most devious divil – always up to tricks. Up to tricks the whole time, no matter what would be going on, they were always tricking, and that's how they worked all the day long.[103]

Negotiating authority

The talk, the jokes and the tricks mentioned above show informal culture functioning in a practical way in the mid-twentieth century setting of the large urban factory. The negotiation of authority is an important aspect of this, and it is also connected to religion: Tommy C's evidence is valuable in the insight it provides into this area. Tommy, a former official of the Limerick Pork Butchers' Society, characterizes the relationship between the bacon factory bosses and their workers as one of 'us and them'. According to him, they would dump the leftover meat before a long weekend rather than give it to the workers; if people took it and were caught taking it, they'd be reprimanded.[104] The custom of giving time off for funerals and the fact that the boss could give a worker £50 to pay for a family funeral, 'but the next morning he'd make a kick for you', may, perhaps, be more of an indication of the view of death in the community than a sign of concern for workers' welfare in general. It is interesting to see that despite a very well-organized union structure, workers still used many unofficial and personal channels of communication with the factory, along with well-developed resistance strategies, in order to improve their situation. A humorous note is to be felt in Tommy's description of the latecomers' method of waiting until the supervisor, who would be walking up and down the factory floor, was up at the other end before they'd slip in.[105] Other issues were more serious: teenage boys going as a group to look for men's wages, for instance, or the situation arising when the factory called people in for casual work on a daily basis:

> Then they had very skilled workers, d'you know what I mean, the blokes, and if they hadn't enough to cover for those, they'd have to send for those, so you could be in the house, and they might send for your brother, and your brother'd say 'I'm not going in unless my other brother's going.' (laughter) So they'd have to bring the two of them.[106]

On one occasion the factory needed a set of keys held by one of the casual workers who wasn't actually working on that day:

> And then there was one man there now, he used to be going around with the keys of the – and they said to him, they came down to the door one day and they beeped the van, and he said 'I'll be down in a minute.' 'No we don't want you at all, just send down the keys'. Of course there was war then over it, they'd be all saying 'Aw the *keys*! Get down the *keys*!' Aw there used be war.[107]

These examples are interesting for two reasons: firstly they show the continued importance of oral, informal and unofficial relationships in the twentieth-century urban environment both in the factory itself and in the neighbourhood: as has been seen in previous chapters this was a significant factor in many aspects of religious culture too, and in popular culture in general. Secondly, they raise the question of people's relationships with different kinds of authority in the city at the time. This is a complex area, and impossible to deal with comprehensively in this context. The general situation in Ireland at the time was that, in practice, the Catholic Church was regarded as the ultimate authority and took precedence over employers and family members in people's lives. That this was a cause of much wrongdoing and distress in many cases is clear, and the experience of some interviewees bears this out. Examples from this research would include the experiences of the ritual of 'churching' and the distress caused by the very negative reactions of some priests in Confession to being told relatively minor sins.[108] The example of the triangular relationship between the pork butchers, the bacon factory bosses and the Catholic Church is an interesting one, however, because, as recounted in Chapter 3, it shows how the historic intervention by the Church in a labour dispute inspired the long-term loyalty of the union, which translated into a particular form of devotion carried out on the Feast of the Assumption every year. Added to this, in the context of the wider city, was the relationship between the directors of the Redemptorist Confraternity and its members, both bacon factory workers and men in general: the evidence shows that the loyalty and affection in which the organization itself was held sometimes extended to its personnel as well.[109] Tommy C's anecdotes show how this relationship, and that between friends, was sometimes negotiated in a humorous manner. The following anecdote relates to the later part of the period studied, when the Redemptorist Retreat House had been set up on the North Circular Road:

> There'd be blokes that would be ballhopping the priest you see, they'd tell the priest 'Such a bloke here now he has an awful problem with the drink, Oh Jesus his

poor wife's heart is broken'. This chap would be quietest bloke in the world! And the priest would come up then … 'Ah I heard you have a bit of a problem d'you know what I mean, with your drinking' and they would have no problem at all!! … and the priest would say 'Would you like to come up for some weekend?' And they hadn't the courage to say … and … 'I will of course Father' 'I know you've a bit of a problem with drink.' Your man would only – mightn't drink two pints in a week! (Laughter.)[110]

Tommy describes the retreats themselves as 'a howl' and 'a pantomime'.[111] Every retreat would start on Friday night, and some of the participants would go for a few drinks before going to the retreat house. As the night progressed, a rule of silence came into play, which people evidently found difficult to keep. Tommy here describes the sustained muttering which was the method of communication over the weekend:

And then, once you got up then, you could talk, but you couldn't talk *after* a certain time. To get you into it, and that was the whole thing. And then you were going around – of course then blokes were saying 'What won such-a-race?' … (laughter). They'd be waiting for the … 'What won such-a-race?', 'Did Man United win?' 'Did Arsenal win?' Oh Jesus above in heaven … the kids, I wonder who won such-a-thing, I heard such-a-person died, Oh Jesus I should – I'll go up and tell the priest, I should be going to that funeral.[112]

It is important to note that the situation described above belongs the the later part of the period studied when the relationship between clergy and people may have been becoming more relaxed and less authoritative. The Redemptorists' desire and, indeed, their considerable ability to move with the times is evident in the founding of the Retreat House in an era when the growth of shift work in the new-style factories in the Shannon Industrial Estate meant that the structure of the traditional Confraternity was not compatible with people's lives.[113] It is interesting to see how, in this new setting, the talking, joking and 'tricking' so integral to the culture described by Tommy C was still a crucial part of the men's relationships, even in the supposedly 'silent' setting of the weekend retreat.

In discussing the negotiation of authority, it is important to distinguish not just between the different atmospheres prevailing at various times, but also between different kinds of relationships between priests and people. Timmy G comments that,

years ago when I was growing up priests were put on a pedestal, by the older generation … if a priest came along and I was with the parents I'd have to go out on the road and let the priest walk along, you know. You … showed that much respect … you have outstanding priests who really believe in what they're doing, very helpful and that. But you have others that were kind of aloof … they weren't down to earth with the people … they were a different level altogether.[114]

One point worth considering is that the regular clergy operating in the city centre churches may have had a more positive, flexible relationship with people than the 'secular' or diocesan priests, though this would vary over time and with changes of personnel as well. However, it was the diocesan clergy in the parishes who administered the sacraments in the parishes and made the hard decisions about baptisms, marriages and funerals. The stories in Chapter 6 regarding Confession show the fear of parish clergy experienced by some people in this context, while Noreen P's evidence, pertaining to an even later period, shows her difficulties with the authoritarian attitude of the parish clergy towards her marriage to a member of the Church of Ireland.[115] It is important to note that for many people, a positive, active attitude to devotion and belief did not preclude disapproval of and extreme distaste for this authoritarian position on the part of the clergy, even when they felt they had to submit to it. The following joke, which dates from the earlier part of the period, is an interesting example of this distaste. It concerns a well-known Limerick character called Thomas 'Gurky' McMahon, one of the first people to take up residence in the 'Island Field' or St Mary's Park, opened in 1935.

> Gurky McMahon was passing Cruise's Hotel one day when a priest called him and ordered him to hold his horse while he went into the hotel. Gurky told him he could hold his own horse and started to walk on, but the priest said to him 'I could stick you to the ground for that kind of insolence, my man!' Gurky said 'Why don't you stick the horse to the ground so, Father?' and went on his way.[116]

This story, told by Joseph L, was part of the repertoire of his father-in-law, P. J. Larkin. Another story told by Larkin also concerns the diocesan clergy:

> The Bishop was walking along O'Connell Street one day when he saw a well-known 'character' on the other side, a bit the worse for wear. He called out 'Drunk again Packie?' The reply came 'So am I, Father!'[117]

These stories show strong disapproval of both the arrogance and high-handedness of the priest, and the patronizing attitude of the bishop: they are set firmly in the people's domain, the main street of Limerick city, O' Connell Street, where the well-known and long-established Cruise's Hotel was situated until the urban renewal programme of the early 1990s. In the first story, the priest's supernatural power, referred to by himself, is mocked. Gurky McMahon's role indicates that the joke may have been widespread in Limerick, as Gurky was a popular character in the city's folklore during this period. In the 'Packie' story, the implication is that the Bishop might easily be as intoxicated as the drunkard he sees across the street. The fact that these jokes were told by P. J. Larkin is interesting: according to his daughter, Eileen L's evidence regarding the rosary, Lenten fasting and daily Mass, this man was very devout. But he also relished jokes like these, which demonstrates, again, the multi-faceted nature of religion and the ability of people themselves to separate the feelings and the beliefs experienced in devotion from the larger questions of power and control associated with the way in which religion functions in the community.

Community and identity: Margins and centres

As has been seen already, a sense of place was one of the most important cultural elements in Limerick city in the period between the 1920s and the 1960s. Local identity was to be felt at many levels: that of the street, the parish and the city as a

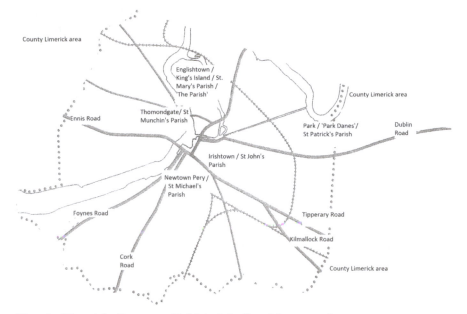

Map 4   Limerick city areas with historic/colloquial names of areas.

whole. The various areas of the city, along with the more general and/ or informal names used to refer to them, can be seen in Map 4.

The building of the first public housing estate in St Mary's Parish in 1935 brought over 300 new households into the old Island Field area, a change which O'Flynn, one of the original King's Island community, describes as 'Paradise Lost'.[118] However, one of the most striking aspects of this new, modern estate is the extent to which traditional culture, that of the May Eve bonefire, for instance, informal singing and belief in fairies and ghosts, was a feature of life there in the 1940s and 1950s.[119] It is also interesting that one of the most famous figures in Limerick folklore, Thomas 'Gurky' MacMahon was living in St Mary's Park during this period until his death in the early 1970s, though he may have spent some time in England too. The feelings of strangeness and marginality attaching to the new estate in its early days can be felt in the following story:

> On his first day in the new house, Gurky had to go up to the shop for milk. When he came back, he couldn't find his house, he didn't know which one it was – all the houses were the same. He asked the children playing in the street 'Excuse me, did ye see a man coming out of a house with a jug in his hand?[120]

The way the main character of this joke refers to himself as 'a man' rather than 'me', which he does in at least three extant versions, is central to its humour: not only are the houses new, but the people living in them are somehow 'new' too, and almost strangers to themselves.[121] The St Mary's Park houses were clean and comparatively modern, and a far cry from the tiny lane cottages and dilapidated tenements of the old city centre areas. The following anecdote is centred on conditions in the older type of dwelling:

> When Gurky MacMahon was moving from his old place to the new house in St. Mary's Park, he brought all his stuff down with him, but he never brought his mattress. They said to him 'Why didn't you bring down your mattress, Gurky?' 'That's all right', he said 'Sure 'twill follow me down!'[122]

The humour in this story hinges on the tension between the new, cleaner environment and the older, flea-ridden one: maybe, in the end, Gurky did actually leave his mattress after him to go to the new house. Again, the comic value of the irritation and slight sense of shame caused by the presence of fleas in the household is exploited here, while Gurky's insouciance in the matter is celebrated.

The ability to change and adapt to new circumstances is only one aspect of the creation of culture: the view of other groups is another important way in which people define themselves and their own community. The well-documented Jewish Boycott which took place in Limerick in 1904 is one example of the treatment of a marginal group in the city by the Catholic majority.[123] Relationships between Catholics and Protestants – a tiny, and decreasing minority in the city in the period between the mid-1920s and 1960 – were complex. On the one hand, Catholics were not allowed to attend Protestant services, under pain of mortal sin (see Chapter 6), and mixed marriages were discouraged. This defensive attitude was reflected in the combative language used in hymns such as 'Faith of Our Fathers', sung regularly at the Redemptorist Archconfraternity and at other devotions. On the other hand, sectarianism in the form in which it was carried out during the Jewish Boycott was discouraged by the mid-1930s, as is illustrated by the official reactions of both Catholic Church leaders and the local authority when property owned by Protestants was deliberately damaged during street disturbances in Limerick in 1935.[124] The fact that these disturbances occurred at all shows that sectarianism at street level was alive and well, however. This is also demonstrated by O'Flynn's description of the exchanges between the schoolboys at the Protestant Villiers School in King's Island and himself and his friends:

> 'Proddy-woddy ring the bell!
> All the soupers down to hell!'
> … the young lads from Villiers School were no daws when it came to vituperation. When they were safely at the corner of our street and Castle Street, before turning down towards Thomond Bridge (many of them seemed to live in the Ennis Road area) they would shout back at us:
> 'Hail Mary full of grace,
> The cat fell down and broke his face'.[125]

O'Flynn also records his shock and that of his friends when a Protestant boy of about twelve one day shouted what 'we reported … euphemistically to our parents as "Eff the Pope"'. Another incident involving a turnip seized from one of the O'Flynns by the Villiers schoolboys and then used as a rugby ball before being thrown into the Shannon prompted Mrs O'Flynn to chase the Protestant boys, and to complain to the school next day: '[She] was sympathetically received, but she was subsequently told that none of the Villiers pupils remembered anything about such an incident. She noticed, however, that from then on the older Villiers lads, like those Wise Men from the East who were warned by an angel, went home by a different route'.[126]

O'Flynn's account of this relationship is interesting in that it shows the two religions encountering each other at the robust and honest level of children's culture. There is no suggestion at any point that the two groups of children might play together, and the sense that they inhabit separate worlds is strong. O'Flynn and his friends didn't normally play with children from the Ennis Road area anyway, whether they were Catholic or Protestant: geography and social class are factors here too, and it is difficult to know to what extent Catholic Ennis Road children and Catholic King's Island children might have played together if they had been meeting each other more. The Villiers pupils would have been regarded as exotic, in any case, because of their religion. In the 1960s and 1970s, and even later in some, although not all Limerick communities, it was usual to discreetly mention to close friends and family who didn't already know, that a particular person was a Protestant, perhaps to save potential embarrassment or tactless behaviour.[127] The two rhymes quoted above are of interest in different ways. The 'Souper' rhyme refers to Catholics who 'took the soup' from Protestant benefactors during the Great Famine of the 1840s, and by this process were converted to the Protestant religion.[128] The 'Hail Mary' rhyme, which ridicules a Catholic prayer by juxtaposing its opening lines with the image of a small domestic animal, is similar to the rhyme used above by O'Flynn and his friends to ridicule the text of the Catechism by introducing the image of the 'little dog' and the 'pigs' toes' selling for tuppence. These items of folklore demonstrate the cultural divide between Protestants and Catholics. However, a story told by Joseph L about his father-in-law (a factory owner in the city who dealt with some of the large department stores) gives a somewhat different perspective:

> He was friendly with George Miller, and George Miller was a Protestant … he was working in Cannock's. Cannock's was always known as a Catholic house – I think a nun in Belgium owned it … well they were out on the boat one day and George told him there was a woman in, buying sheets in Cannock's. She was humming and haw-ing over the price of them … she said 'They're a bit dear … I think I'll go over to Todd's – I might get a better bargain over there'. And George whispered to her 'Ah but they're Protestants over there you know!' … she ended up buying the sheets from him![129]

This anecdote is very interesting for a few reasons. First, it shows a Catholic and a Protestant enjoying their leisure time together – and there surely must have been many cases of this in the various interest groups, sporting clubs, and other associations throughout the city. The story itself shows the ability to treat these religious categories – taken so seriously at ecclesiastical levels – with irreverence and humour, and furthermore to exploit the prejudice they inspired in some, for commercial gain. The ability to share the humorous irony of the situation with a Catholic friend afterwards extends the irony even further, and also demonstrates the way in which cultural categories were not as fixed or as immutable as they would appear to be, in both official religious regulations and unofficial popular culture.

It is also interesting to examine relationships between different groups of Catholics in the city. Again, this is a cultural element strongly linked to place. Jokes or humorous comments about areas and particular communities, whether they have a religious theme or not, illustrate some of the meanings attached to place in the Limerick city community at the time. St Mary's Parish in King's Island, the oldest in Limerick, was noted for its sense of tradition and pride in its heritage. The following comment, originally from P. J. Larkin (quoting an acquaintance of his, Jimmy Power) and relayed here by Joseph L illustrates one view of 'The Parish': 'One time they had a banner up "God Bless the Pope and St Mary's Parish" – (and, as Jimmy Power said, to hell with the rest of the world!!)'.[130]

One of the most strikingly distinct groups in Limerick at the time was that of Park, a horticultural community located in St Patrick's Parish, to the east of the city centre. The 'Park Danes' as they were called by some people, grew cabbage and potatoes which they sold in the markets in Limerick. They were noted in the city for their attachment to a more rural, traditional way of life than the rest of Limerick people. As seen in Chapter 3, they were also involved in organized devotional activities and most particularly in the Redemptorist Confraternity. Two jokes collected in Limerick city in the late 1980s illustrate a certain view of Park people with regard to religion:

> When they all went over on a Diocesan Pilgrimage to Rome, there were Park people there. Well there was this fella, a big old innocent Parkman, I'd say he was about six foot four. When they went in for an audience with the Pope, well you know now, it's a big hall, very formal, like. Well this fella broke out from the crowd and ran up to the Pope 'Oh your Holiness' sez he 'We'd die for you in Park!'[131]

This story, like many humorous ones, involves a juxtaposition of two contradictory domains: the intimate, rural world of Park with its small gardening plots, its lanes and cottages on the one hand, and the palatial grandeur of the headquarters of a global religion, where thousands of people are blessed by one very remote and elevated figure. The irony is that the Park people were known to be very devout and loyal to the Church – it's just that (according to this joke) they didn't understand the wider Catholic world: it is supposed that more travelled and worldly-wise Catholics i.e. the rest of the city population, would know how to behave in the Vatican. It is interesting to contrast this with the account of the banner over St Mary's Parish, from P. J. Larkin above: in this it is implied that the 'Parish' people are bit too clever and self-interested, whereas the Park people are portrayed as devout, but innocent. The fact that the man from Park is 'big' perhaps serves to accentuate his innocence. The Parkman in the following story is also tall:

> There was this priest in the Confraternity and one night he gave a sermon about the way the Jews murdered Christ. Well this big oul' innocent Parkman went out after it, and he went up to Collooney Street (that's what Wolfe Tone Street used to be called). Well there was this big Jewman coming up the street and didn't yer man knock him down. 'What's up with you?' sez the Jewman to him 'Sure didn't ye kill Christ' the Parkman sez back to him. 'But that was 2,000 years ago' sez the Jewman 'I know' sez the Parkman 'but I didn't hear it till tonight!'[132]

The humour here is to be found in the sense of the Parkman being so bowled over by the sermon that he assaults a Jew, despite the fact that, as the rest of the population no doubt understands, the Crucifixion is so far back in time as to be irrelevant to contemporary Christian–Jewish relations. But this joke also merits further examination. Considering that the story of the Jewish Boycott in Limerick in 1904 also involved a Confraternity sermon and disturbances on Collooney Street, it could be said that the joke unconsciously promotes a certain perspective on this historical event. Evaluations of the history of 1904 in Limerick city differ somewhat,[133] but it is true to say that the attacks on Jewish property and the assaults on people themselves in that year were inspired by a Redemptorist sermon condemning the moneylending practices of the Jewish community in the city at that time. The joke attempts to manipulate historical reality in multiple ways: firstly it universalizes the grievance by associating it with the Crucifixion, thus distancing it from the specific history of Limerick; secondly, it takes the harm out of the attacks on the Jews by describing a mild assault followed by a conversation; thirdly, it disassociates the attack from the population of Limerick city in general and locates it in the marginal community of Park; fourthly, it attributes the attack to innocence and devotional loyalty to Jesus, on the part of the 'big oul' innocent Parkman', rather than to knowing evil intent, which a less innocent (city) person might have had.

The myriad uses of speech and its role in local culture should be clear from the above, whether this involves the manipulation of ritual language, the negotiation of various kinds of authority (including the Catholic Church) or relationships with the 'other' in both contemporary and historical contexts. The nature of the relationships between various groups of people in the city is also noteworthy, as it illustrates the extent of unofficial and informal contacts between people as well as the importance of orality in these kinds of relationships. The various contexts of the jokes and anecdotes shows how these folkloric elements found their way into ritual situations, and indeed, constituted a significant aspect of some people's experience of ritual. The self-definition involved in categorizing the 'other' is also a significant process in the creation of the 'islands of identity' mentioned by Gearóid Ó Crualaoich:[134] while the various uses of language to manipulate official or 'given' religious concepts and categories shows both the elaboration of meaning-making and its creative refinement at the popular level.

Senses and speech in popular devotion

It is useful here to assess the different kinds of creativity which have been surveyed in this chapter and to look at how these acted upon each other in a popular religious context. It is clear that the material, sensual and artistic instinct in many people was stimulated and used to the full in popular devotional contexts for much of the period under study: from the sensual enjoyment of decorative church interiors during festive seasons to the active, communal transformation of city streets; from the creation of beautiful textiles at home or in groups, to learning and singing Plain Chant in school, at Benediction or in the Cathedral. It also seems that the aesthetic aspect helped to 'complete' the belief aspect in ritual situations, and also that, for some people, the belief aspect enhanced the aesthetic process: in other words, the enjoyment of creating something, be it a flower-laden May altar or a beautiful sound, was increased by the sense of the spiritual meaning inherent in both the process and the finished product. It could be said, therefore, that the sensual and the spiritual aspects of popular religion enjoyed a reciprocal, mutually beneficial relationship: each acted upon the other to enhance and reinforce their significance in the world of popular devotion and in the ritual events in which they were used.

The creative role of language, or more correctly, informal speech, was quite different, however. Of course language, in general, played an enormous part in both religious education and ritual processes, whether at home, in school or in the church. It is also important to remember just how much formal religious language was learned off by heart by children and young adults, and remembered and used by everybody on the very frequent ritual or other religious occasions in which they were involved. This repertoire included the formal rosary prayers, the litanies or other rosary trimmings, answers to catechism questions, answers to Confirmation questions, the (Latin) responses to the Mass, popular hymns, Latin hymns for Benediction, short exclamatory prayers (known as 'ejaculations' or 'aspirations'), as well as prayers for specific occasions such as the Act of Contrition, Grace before Meals and the Morning Offering.

The centrality of language in human civilization and culture, and consequently in religion, has been eloquently demonstrated by Roy A. Rappaport. Language is the system of symbols used to name, categorize and describe cultural phenomena: without this, no meaning is possible.[135] On a more concrete level, it is clear from the above that the way in which the Catholic religion was embodied in language in Limerick during the early to mid-twentieth century, through naming, categorizing, explaining, repeating, singing and answering, was constant and intense. But Rappaport has something else to say about language: this is that with language, including the arbitrary relationship between the sign and the signified, comes the possibility of the lie.[136] Rappaport's main argument, that 'religion is as old as language, which is to say precisely as old as humanity' is not at issue here.[137] But the concept of the 'lie' and the fact that it is regarded as intrinsic to language highlights the potential of language as a critical tool which may be used to deconstruct accepted meanings and explore alternative ones. It is perhaps natural then that the creativity of informal speech was used to challenge, rather than to reinforce, the highly charged devotional atmosphere and intensely controlled ritual world of Catholic Limerick in the period under study. As can be seen above, this was done in a few ways, and was regarded as acceptable when carried out in a humorous context. The role of language, and the creativity around language, is in striking contrast to the more sensual, material and aesthetic forms of creativity in popular devotion, which elevated and celebrated belief and its meaning at both an individual and a communal level. Language and folklore, in the form of alternative texts, jokes and anecdotes, introduced laughter, irony and even ridicule to the ritual world, while helping to define and reinforce local and devotional identities in the process.

Conclusion

I want to see people as they are: free and stuck in the world. My interest is in the constant interplay of will and circumstance ... I ask not how people fit into the plots of others, but how they form their own lives, not what people do once in a while, but what they do all the time.

Henry Glassie, *Passing the Time: Folklore and History of an Ulster Community* (1982): 14–15[1]

It is interesting to compare this study of Catholicism in Limerick in the post-independence period with studies of religion centred on other urban areas in the nineteenth and twentieth centuries. There are, of course, always differences between people's lives and cultures in different places and time periods, as can be seen, for instance, from Williams's study of Southwark[2] in the nineteenth and twentieth centuries and Wildman's account of Manchester between the two world wars,[3] as well as from McLeod's and Harris's more broadly based research, the former on religion in general in the London area in the Victorian period[4] and the latter on Catholicism in the north of England up to the 1980s.[5] Taken together with this research, these studies of religion demonstrate how Ireland fitted into the wider history of religion in urban areas in the nineteenth and twentieth centuries. Callum Brown's term 'discursive Christianity' which he applies to British culture in the period up to the early 1960s is a very useful one for reflecting on Irish culture as well, as many aspects of this book have shown.[6] Brown's discussion of what he calls 'the salvation industry' is also highly relevant: his description of the role of voluntary organizations (of many denominations) in religious culture in Britain in the nineteenth and early twentieth centuries, including their penetration of 'home and office, school and hospital, street and pub, parliament and town hall' bears a striking similarity to the ethnographic scene portrayed in this study.[7] It can also be said that Irish people were participants in the same religious movements and practices as Catholics in other countries – Father Peyton's Family Rosary Crusade in the 1950s, for instance, discussed in an English context by Alana Harris, and in the context of popular creativity, the early twentieth-century street decorations described by Joseph Sciorra in New York and the devotional processions studied by Charlotte Wildman in Manchester. We know, too, from Sarah Williams's study of Southwark, that vernacular culture can play a significant role in religion in urban contexts, and again this can be seen in Limerick city in the middle decades of the twentieth century.

However, the situation in Limerick – and perhaps in Ireland generally – during the period would seem at first glance to be considerably simpler to assess. With the vast majority of the population Catholic, and a strong sense of religious authority to be felt at all levels of society, along with very high church attendance, it would appear that the story of the Catholic Church in Ireland and its central position in education and society in general provides the answer to every question about religion and life in Ireland: this has been the basis for many important studies of Irish society in the decades after independence.[8] However, it is also important to try to unpack the culture of Irish Catholics during this period of seemingly homogeneous adherence to the practices and precepts of official Catholicism: what were their experiences and their understandings of religion? What did religion mean to them? How did it relate to other parts of their lives? What this study has shown is that vernacular culture – including, crucially, a strong sense of locality – was one of the most important elements in the meaning of religion among Limerick people at the time. A sense of identity – both Limerick and Irish – was also important. The concepts central to the study of folklore, the characteristics of ritual and the aspect of religious experience all provide valuable perspectives for deeper understandings of these aspects of culture.

Orality in the city context

As has been seen throughout the book, but especially in Chapter 7, the Limerick city community in the first decades of the twentieth century was one in which informal culture had an important place. Talk, chatting, singing, 'tricking', nicknames and jokes were important aspects of life, as the examples drawn from street and factory life demonstrate. This was perfectly complementary to an official religion which, even as late as the early 1960s, gave priority to oral communication of its message, in contrast to the Protestant faiths 'whose members sought to seek guidance from the Scriptures … which it was the duty of every man and woman to read'.[9] Orally delivered sermons were a crucial part of the weekly devotions of the various Catholic confraternities and sodalities in Limerick, their themes varying according to the seasons of the Church year, the scriptures used on the day or other devotional contexts such as the feast day of a saint or other religious figure. Singing of hymns, whether in the church or in other settings, did not involve the use of hymn books or sheets: instead the hymns were absorbed from others in the ritual setting and sung from memory; the Plain Chant liturgies used in the secondary schools' festival, described in Chapter 7, were learned off by heart by the singers and also sung from memory. The basic rosary prayers, discussed in Chapter 5, again involving a lot of repetition, were always recited from memory, while the accompanying prayers or trimmings, which varied from household to household, were known by the members of the households in which they were said, even though a prayerbook may have been used as an *aide-memoire* in some cases. Even in the case of the catechism, in which the book played an important role, the final aim of the religious education process was to be able to recite the text from memory, and the written layout of the catechism texts themselves reflected this, with the slightly ritualized 'question–and–answer' format the most prominent one. The emphasis on the spoken word in Catholicism, and most particularly in Catholic ritual settings, during this period fitted in very well with what could be seen as the significant residual oral aspects of a culture in which most people were literate when they needed to be, but where talk, jokes and anecdotes were valued, where informal singing was enjoyed and where face-to-face communication was still the most important kind.

It is important too, to understand the creative processes involved in the culture of devotion as outlined above. In the first, the enthusiasm for singing and the enjoyment of the beauty of language is noteworthy, while the ability to judge a good sermon engages another set of values as far as the spoken word is concerned. However, the creative manipulation of the spoken language is also to be found – in the jokes, the wordplay and the funny anecdotes which balanced the overwhelmingly devout atmosphere of the time with humour, irony and even critical or cynical commentary on religious topics. Writing is also a creative act, and the published Thanksgivings discussed in Chapter 6 demonstrate this, while the co-ordination of devotion with travel and even with international tourism described in Chapter 4 shows the ritual-ization of modernity at work in another context. These areas taken together give some idea of Honko's 'milieu … (and) … context ' as it applied to Limerick city during the period studied: a literate, urban community in which oral culture was central; a world of printed mass-communication in which ritual had found a small but significant place; the excitement of modern transport tempered with devotional practices.[10] A process of creative engagement with what Gearóid Ó Crualaoich calls the 'universe of cultural discourse' is in evidence in all these areas.[11] Ó Crualaoich has likened this engagement to the creation of 'provisional and dynamic islands of identity, cultural creativity and meaningfulness',[12] and nowhere is this more striking than in the context of locality.

Locality, identity and meaning

The co-ordination of a sense of locality, or place, with the practice of religion and with religious culture may be looked at on many levels: it is one of the most complex and multi-faceted aspects of this study, but it is also one of the most important. The levels which must be examined include engagement with physical places and the connec-tions between this and devotion; the creative use of city space and the enactment of meaning in this context; and finally the discourse around places in popular religion and the connections between this discourse and the building of meaningful identities both within the various communities and for the city as a whole. It is also important to consider the various people and groups of people who were active in the creation of culture in the city. As far as official devotion was concerned, the clergy had an obviously proactive role in building up and maintaining their congregations, with the various groups of regular clergy particularly to the fore in this regard, while Limerick Corporation's activities in the years from 1935 provided new living spaces and settings for the creation of renewed communities. As has been seen in the various chapters of this study, the ordinary people of Limerick were also active in creating culture, in both their responses and resistance to official versions of religion and city life. Limerick people, as groups and as individuals, can be seen to have worked both with, and independently of, the various forms of authority in the effort to create a meaningful environment in the city in these decades. The most striking examples of this creativity, in so far as it pertains to place, are outlined in the following discussions.

The May Eve fires

One of the most interesting examples of engagement with place can be seen at work in the public housing estates that were being built in Limerick city from the mid-1930s. As recounted in earlier in the book, the May Eve fire was one of the most important ways in which communities celebrated their culture on a street-by-street basis in these new areas. On the one hand, the process of collection of materials and money, the activities at the event itself and the custom and belief aspect of the *gríosach* indicate a strong connection to the older vernacular traditions of both city and country areas, while the blessings given distributing the *gríosach* at the end of the night show the influence of popular devotion. The fact that May Eve is still a notable event in the yearly calendar of both old and new public housing estates in the city indicates the tenacity of this custom, although many of its aspects have changed dramatically since the 1960s. In the period studied, May Eve could be seen as a crucial process in re-imagining and sacralizing the environment of older communities which had been uprooted from their city centre areas. It is interesting, and somewhat ironic, that the wider streets and green areas of the new estates lent themselves to this custom much more readily and safely than the more confined and cluttered lanes and alleyways of the older city centre neighbourhoods. This was almost certainly a factor in its success in the new areas. The inclusive nature of the event, in which everybody participated, and children, young adults and women were particularly to the fore, is another of its essential aspects. This strong sense of local, communal agency in the May fire is noteworthy.

The May Eve event is also distinctive because of the way in which ancestral beliefs and practices are used with prayers to enact meaning in the new public housing estates in the city: this all contributes to what could be seen as a hybrid popular culture involving both belief and practice in a modern urban setting, one which, as noted above, has proved itself, in essence, more longlasting than many of the other practices discussed in this study, despite the changes which have been wrought on it by the intervening decades.

The streets of the city

The city centre area of Limerick must be considered in rather a different light as it was longer-established and included both business and residential areas in the period studied. The centre of Limerick in the twentieth century was, and still is, located in the Newtown Pery area of the city which been built by extending the southern axis of the original island settlement in the eighteenth and early nineteenth centuries.[13] The introduction of churches into this new area during the nineteenth century by the Dominicans, the Augustinians, the Franciscans and later the Jesuits, all of whom had had foundations in the older city, represents a significant step in the transformation of the new city space into one in which religious devotion played a part. This could be seen as the sacralization of profane space: a manifestation of what Mircea Eliade calls 'nostalgia for paradise'. He describes this further as 'the desire to be always, effort-lessly, at the heart of the world, of reality, of the sacred, and, briefly, to transcend, by natural means, the human condition and regain a divine state of affairs'.[14] By the early twentieth century, the new city was no longer merely a collection of shops with people working and shopping in them, and a collection of houses with people living in them: it now, gradually, acquired its own sacred centres: its own means of escape from normal everyday life into another world. The importance of these spaces in personal devotion has been discussed in Chapter 6. But the transformation of the city went beyond the siting of sacred spaces in buildings on city streets: as has been seen in Chapter 7, on certain occasions the streets themselves were not just transformed, but transfigured by devotional decorations created by people themselves to celebrate important religious events. Instances of communal street-creativity in a religious context such as this has also been found in other parts of the world during the same historical period, as Joseph Sciorra's work has shown,[15] while the expressiveness of street processions in Manchester has been well-documented by Charlotte Wildman in her work on the Whit walks.[16] Perspectives from Irish medieval studies are also useful here: Tomás Ó Carragáin has noted how renowned sacred centres such as Rome and Jerusalem inhabited the imaginations of early Irish scholars and monks;[17] the account of the decoration of the Limerick streets for the Diamond Jubilee of the Archconfraternity of the Holy Family in 1928 in Chapter 7 shows how other sacred and significant places and times inspired the creativity of city residents on that occasion. The Lourdes grotto is one example; the history and built heritage of Limerick itself another. Most striking for this study perhaps is the way in which a miniature church and imitation church interiors were reproduced at various points along the route of the Jubilee procession, thus bringing these sacred centres on to the very streets themselves. The way in which the streets were used in popular devotion on a more regular basis is of interest too. Ó Carragáin has shown how medieval church settlements may have influenced the curvilinear layout of certain towns in Ireland, where the church is seen to be surrounded by the streets of the town.[18] While the rectilinear streets of Newtown Pery could never be seen as curving, nor as centred on one place, it is interesting to find the connection between religion and roughly circular or oval shapes reflected in the routes of city processions in the twentieth century. The processions did not stick to the rectangular streets of the new town, even when they originated there, but originally took in parts of King's Island and also the Irishtown on the eastern side of the city before ending up at St John's Cathedral: if they had started at the Redemptorist Church near O'Connell Avenue, this would be more of an oval-shaped route. Later proces-sions also took an oval route from the top of O'Connell Street to St John's Cathedral via Broad Street in the Irishtown. The need to go through a variety of streets and to be seen by as many people as possible would also have influenced this choice of route, as

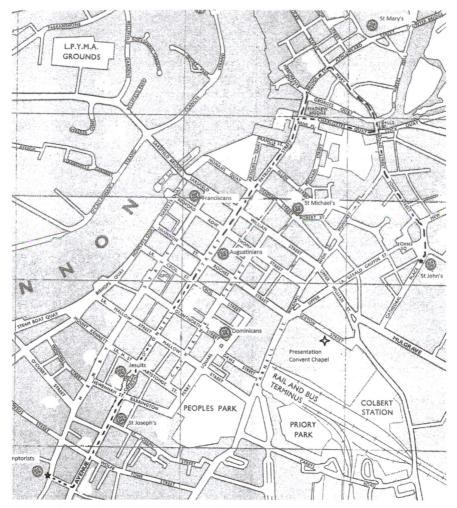

Map 5   Procession routes.

it would have in the case of the funeral processions discussed in Chapter 3. The processions also had to reach certain points on the religious compass of the city: starting and/or finishing at the Redemptorist Church for the Confraternity processions, and finishing at St John's Cathedral for the Corpus Christi procession (see Map 5).

It would, of course, be overstating the case to say that these 'ritual routes' were chosen in order to reflect the curvilinear shapes of the foundations of the medieval Church in Ireland. However, it is true to say that whatever the practical and social reasons for the choice of routes, the experience of the participants in devotional processions was that of walking in a curve or an oval rather than in straight lines. This echoes the vernacular tradition of doing the rounds at a holy well or walking around a graveyard on the occasion of a burial.[19] In a round which was repeated over and over again, the May procession in the grounds of the Presentation convent also followed an oval route.[20] The status of convent grounds in the city, as holy places where ordinary people did not go except on special occasions or with special permission, also reflects the early Christian idea discussed by Ó Carragáin of 'a hierarchy of sanctity': that certain areas were only open to the clergy or other religious personnel.[21] Interviewees' evidence shows that a similar idea prevailed in the convent chapels, where the nuns' area was separated from and sometimes unseen by ordinary worshippers.[22]

All of the above points, taken together, illustrate the importance of the physical city in popular devotion in Limerick in the first half of the twentieth century. The concept of the holy and the forbidden attached to convent grounds and parts of convent chapels provided a sense of mystique regarding certain locations in the city, and was an important expression of the hierarchy of sanctity as it applied to a modern city. The 'popular will' mentioned by Judith Hill in relation to the construction of new sacred spaces in the nineteenth and twentieth century expressed itself not just in the subscriptions and the ongoing practical participation in the decoration of churches, but in the way the religious imagination was applied to reproducing these sacred spaces in the streets themselves on special occasions. It may be significant that some churches in the city were in a ongoing state of development in the 1920s and ensuing decades. The role played by the church buildings in the cityscape, and the value placed on them in popular devotion, both in practical and symbolic terms, is clear. The use of the streets themselves in devotion is also important: the unifying roundabout processions imposed on the varied plans of the different areas of the city gave a traditional ritual feel to what was a disparate, multi-functional space, while the transformation of the streets for religious occasions demonstrates the importance of the street as a site of creative representation, not just of religion, but of history and identity as well.

The Redemptorist Confraternity and concepts of place

The question of local identity was also a very important aspect of people's practice of devotion in the Archconfraternity of the Holy Family, also known as the Redemptorist Confraternity, or the 'Fathers' Confraternity'. The element of locality, as both an idea and a practical reality was central to the people's experience of many religious rituals, but especially that of the Confraternity. In an account written in 1918 to commemorate the Golden Jubilee of the organization, the writer explains as follows the designation of the members by neighbourhoods: 'the purpose being that the attendance might be registered and that the members living in the same locality might come to know each other, and assist each other when sick, dying or dead, the principle of division being, in general, that of the locality'.[23] The difficulty in locating people and clarifying addresses in the lanes and back streets of the city in the late 1860s is also described in this account. However, this method of dividing the membership was retained, and became far easier as the city grew and new housing estates were built. The Redemptorists' choice of 'locality' as the principle of division turned out to be an inspired one, and may show how the Redemptorists were able to use their awareness of the traditional concept of place, and the strong sense of identity around this in Limerick at the time to promote official devotion. This could be seen as another example of the interplay of vernacular culture with officially organized religion and the subsequent history of the Confraternity shows how these concepts of place were creatively combined by both people and clergy over a number of years. Having members from the same street going on the same night bolstered the attendance figures: the enjoyment of walking up to the 'Fathers' with friends, and the various social activities following the devotions is also clear. In his discussion of the features of ritual, Roy Rappaport discusses members of congregations, saying that 'they can make certain assumptions about each other from the mere fact that they are participating together in a liturgical order with which … they are usually thoroughly familiar. They can assume that they stand on common ground and as such are members of a common community'.[24] This means that members of congregations have a special relationship with one another by virtue of their participation in a ritual. However, the relationships of those attending the Confraternity were far more than congregational: people didn't just walk up to the church together, and meet up afterwards; they also stood and sat and prayed and sang and listened to sermons in close physical proximity to brothers, neighbours, friends and possibly workmates (see Figure 13).

Chapter 3 shows how the various localities played a part in the official discourse of the Confraternity, but also, and this is particularly true of the Park community, that the Confraternity Section membership was an element of the culture of the local place itself. On the other hand, the vernacular culture of local areas also played a part in the unofficial aspects of the devotion as discussed in Chapter 7. Understanding these close connections between devotion and local identity is crucial to understanding the possible meanings of the Confraternity and its various rituals to members of the various communities participating in it.

One of the ways in which this might be understood is in terms of Akhil Gupta and James Ferguson call 'place-making'.[25] This has already been discussed in Chapter 4 in relation to the May Eve fires. It is also relevant to the Marian shrines erected in many public housing estates in 1954, though this initiative is beyond the scope of this book.[26] One important aspect of place-making is the question of how the community sees itself in relation to others. It is clear that the Confraternity played an important part in developing and maintaining identity through its geographically organized Divisions and Sections: these were adapted and expanded to take account of new areas as these were built from the mid-1930s. The sense of local identity developed by people through their membership of the Confraternity was operating in Gupta and Ferguson's 'wider set of social and spatial relations' where residents of various areas saw themselves as groups within the larger city context.[27] The sense of a group identity fostered through the Confraternity was strengthened further by its links to larger worlds. The first of these links is found in the popular idea that the Limerick Archconfraternity was the largest organization of its kind in the world.[28] This added a potent layer of local ('Limerick') identity, seen as operating within international Catholicism, to the strong localized identities already in place. But the most effective link to a larger world was the metaphysical one: a link to heaven and the means to get there; a link to hell and the means to avoid it; a link to right and wrong and good and bad; a means to answer difficult questions and to accept the unanswerable ones.

Figure 13   Archconfraternity of the Holy Family, Redemptorist Church, candlelit ceremony.

In this context, the intellectual stimulation and enjoyment derived from sermons at the Confraternity or other devotions was a significant element of some interviewees' experience of ritual.[29] Factors like these, in addition to the social aspects, help to explain interviewees' comments that they 'loved' devotions or that they 'wouldn't miss' the Confraternity.[30] Thus it is important to understand the qualitative difference between devotional rituals as discussed here and, say, a general meeting of the residents of all the different areas in Limerick for some practical purpose. The social process involved in coming together for the devotional ritual along with people's experience of the ritual itself all contributed to the way in which these devotions were able to copperfasten local identities while at the same time fitting those identities into larger contexts – not just national and international contexts, but metaphysical and cosmological ones as well. This is particularly noticeable in the case of the Confraternity: in leaving their neighbourhoods and walking up to the Fathers, people represented themselves and their areas to the wider city, while the Confraternity represented Limerick to the Catholic world, and to God. The power and coherence of this cultural process for those who participated fully in it should not be underestimated. This may be what is meant by the comment made by one interviewee that "We had a great life growing up ... bonded and rooted and founded in our religion. It was our whole life, it was like breathing in the air ... that was the backbone and the rock on which our lives were built".[31]

Experience

Watching and watching over: The community as family

The experience of living a life which was, as stated above 'bonded and rooted and founded in our religion' must be examined too. Limerick city in the period between the 1920s and the 1960s was a modernizing urban area, but as Sarah Williams's research in Southwark has shown, vernacular belief – even in a city such as London – can form a vital part of the worldview of urban communities.[32] Limerick, like other urban areas in Ireland in the early twentieth century, also had many characteristics associated with orthogenetic cities, where the culture of the city is influenced by the surrounding countryside:[33] the fairy belief in the St Mary's Park area could be seen as an example of this. Kazimierz Dobrowolksi's work on Polish communities stresses the inclination towards a uniform culture in the peasant world.[34] It is interesting that aspects of developing modernity in Limerick in the twentieth century, such as the housing estates and the mass devotional movements, may have served to reinforce this tendency rather than to challenge it. In his history of myth and ritual in family life, John R. Gillis has contrasted the lives of pre-modern families with those of today by saying that they 'found their homeplaces elsewhere than their own dwellings and felt much more at home in the world than we ever can'. He describes the visiting customs of eighteenth-century North America as follows: 'People entered without knocking, even without acknowledgement, and seated themselves at the hearth or the table with an air of familiarity that we would find quite astonishing and disturbing'.[35] Glassie's discussion of the storytelling tradition in Fermanagh in the late 1970s conveys something of the same atmosphere: 'Ceilis are not planned. They happen. At night you sit to rest and perhaps a neighbour or two will lift the latch and join you at the hearth'[36] Anthony F's description of life in Killalee in the 1930s and 1940s is reminiscent of this: his father was a baker, and was often asked to call other men early in the morning for the annual retreat, when the men would be attending Mass at 6.00 a.m.:

> And I remember Mam Quirke now from Pennywell below, originally a Park family – *very* devout family, Bridie Quirke and Peggy Quirke and all them – she'd walk into our house at night-time above in Killalee and my father'd be in his drawers, his underwear getting ready to go to bed, and of course the custom, they'd never knock at the door, they'd just walk in – he could have been in any state of undress! But she'd say 'Tom, don't forget to give us a shout in the morning' for the boys, to call them. And that was a common thing.[37]

This kind of familiarity, and sense of being, in Gillis's terms, 'at home in the world' can be discerned in many kinds of Limerick communities in the period studied: Noreen P's street pilgrimages to Knock and Críostóir O'Flynn's account of his neighbourhood in King's Island are two other examples.[38] The various cultural agents' ability to build actively on this, whether through the May Eve fires, the neighbourhood shrine committees or the clergy's devotional movements, may demonstrate an overall attachment to the social value of community which was common to all, and a self-conscious effort to perpetuate and foster this while safeguarding against the possibility of isolation in new neighbourhoods. In some cases, large centres of employment such as factories, particularly when the workers were also neighbours, also reinforced the sense that everybody was familiar with everybody else's movements and knew each other's worlds as intimately as they knew their own.[39] The way in which this was a factor in ritual participation and the contribution of this social scene to the highly ritualized environment of Mary Douglas's 'religion of control' has already been discussed. Joseph L's humorously ironic account of the General Communion in the men's Confraternity gives an interesting example of the attitude: 'On the day of the General Communion, people would be going up to receive Communion aisle by aisle. Then, (laughter), the priest would say: 'If there is any man here who for any reason may not receive Holy Communion, he may remain in his seat and *no-one will take the slightest notice of him*' (laughter) – well, that definitely wouldn't be true anyway!'[40] The implication here is that the main reason that somebody would stay in their seat and not receive Communion was that they had committed a serious sin and hadn't confessed it. To the interviewee, the priest's idea that nobody would take 'the slightest notice' of this was ridiculous – they would be intrigued, maybe even horrified. In circumstances such as these, it may have been easier to go to Communion, thus compounding the sin already committed and, from a liturgical point of view, take the risk of dying with even more serious sin on one's soul than to face the disapproving gaze of neighbours, friends, relatives and clergy, along with hundreds of other men.

John R. Gillis's idea, discussed above, that people were 'at home in the world' implies that the world outside the private house was seen as an extension of home, rather than as a completely different place. In the complex culture of Limerick city in the first half of the twentieth century, this could not be said to apply to everyone, or even to all the people interviewed, but it definitely did apply to some people and to some communities more than others. This might be what is meant by Tommy C when he says:

> I grew up in a working-class area, Gerald Griffin Street ... moved to Killalee when I was fifteen. While I was in Gerald Griffin Street, all the people I palled around with – there was a lot of unemployment ... I started off as a messenger boy myself. *Nobody* was ever in trouble with the law ... There was a watchful ... everyone watched over everyone. And there was an honesty about them. Even when they found money, they handed it up. There was that honesty about them.[41]

The sense of supernatural belief and the idea of an all-seeing God added another dimension to this, and not always a positive one. Noreen P has stressed the sense of fear she felt in relation to religion in general, and the correct enactment of ritual in particular. It is interesting that in three separate traumatic experiences of unwitting or accidental wrongdoing on her part, she identifies a feeling that 'everyone' would know as being one of the most frightening aspects. On her First Communion day, when the host stuck to the roof of her mouth – despite warnings from the nuns that this should not happen, she says 'I got a terrible, terrible fright altogether because ... nobody knew but myself, but I thought everybody knew'. A few years later, at the age of nine or ten, Noreen realized one Sunday morning that she had broken the Eucharistic fast: 'I went to Communion as per usual, and ... I realised after I had got Communion that I had eaten something before I came out. And I was in a panic, in a terrible terrible panic ... I thought the whole world would have known'. When she and her friends attended a Protestant burial, they felt a great pressure to confess this sin because 'we had imagined that the nuns would be informed, and our parents would be informed and we'd probably be excommunicated!'[42] Here the sense of 'knowing' or omniscience associated with supernatural beings is somehow extended to the whole community, whom Noreen imagined standing in judgement over her for her sins. The sense of aloneness and isolation from the main group is an important factor in the trauma she describes, even though in two of the examples it is later remedied by Confession. But Noreen P's feelings on these occasions may be important indicators of how people who did not find themselves able to participate fully in the culture of Limerick city at this time may have experienced that world.

'... that was your world ...' – experiencing devotion in the city

The complex culture of Limerick city in the decades from the 1920s to the 1960s must also be kept in mind in any assessment of religion and life in general, as it was experienced at the time. A sampling of *Limerick Echo* advertising from March and April 1926, for instance, includes many religious items: a series of Lenten lectures was being held at the Jesuit Sacred Heart church in the Crescent, with titles such as 'Christ and His Friends'; 'Christ and the Sinner'; 'Christ and the Poor' and 'Christ and His Mother':[43] other notices include one for the Retreat of the St John's Division of the Archconfraternity of the Holy Family, another for a Triduum to Our Lady of Good Counsel in the Augustinian Church, yet another for a High Mass to celebrate the patronage of the Feast of St Joseph.[44] Other areas of culture are also represented however: a notice of an 'Irish Ireland Concert in St. Ita's Hall, Thomas Street'[45] on St Patrick's Night appears on 9 March and this is flanked by a small advertisement encouraging readers to 'Finish the evening at Mullaney's, Bedford Row. Chips, Coffee, Bovril etc.'[46] Towards the end of March, as Easter drew nearer, the newspaper also carried advertisements for Michael Egan, Wine Merchant in Patrick Street, who lists the many 'Light White Wines' available in his shop before assuring readers that 'These Wines are guaranteed Perfectly Pure. The French wines are shipped from Bordeaux, and the German Wines from Coblenz'.[47] Newspaper advertising in the later part of the period shows the growing importance of popular entertainment and of shops and shopping in the lives of city people: from the mid-1930s, display advertising is dominated by cinema notices and, depending on the season, advertisements for dances and day trips.[48] By the 1950s, 'Fashion Parades' are being advertised, while department stores and other shops are, in the texts of their advertising, also engaging in the discourse of national and international fashion.[49] The fact that O'Flynn's father, who worked as a coalman by day, was able to make a second income from playing the saxophone in a dance band from the the late 1920s shows the importance of popular music even at this early date. O'Flynn is understandably bitter regarding the suspension of dances during Lent, which caused a serious drop in income for musicians for this period every year.[50] An unsuccessful judicial appeal to the authorities in the 1930s, in which they were asked to reconsider this policy for the sake of the musicians involved, shows the supreme power of the Church at this time in matters concerning entertainment and leisure. The presiding judge, District Justice Flood's comment that 'It will inflict no undue hardship' shows, first and foremost, the obeisance of the civil authorities to the Church, but it is also, in the ignorance of the judge's comment regarding the lives of ordinary people, indicative of the class divide in the city at the time.[51]

The relationship between popular culture and devotion also had other aspects, some of these directly related to the urban environment. The idea that devotion was in conflict with other more enjoyable activites in people's lives has already been discussed in Chapter 3. Two interviewees' views of the rosary are also relevant here: Peggy D's comment that it may have been harder to get people together for the prayer in the city implies that the younger members of the family were out with their friends, while Eileen L's memory of everybody, regardless of what their plans were, having to assemble for the rosary before going out, implies that young people *had* plans of one sort or another on a regular basis.[52] Tommy C's evidence shows how late-night dances conflicted with Confraternity retreats and Máirín M recounts her mother's resentment of the school sodality because it interfered with summer picnics.[53] Thus, devotion was challenged, and possibly more and more as the period progressed, by the increasing variety of other entertainments available to people. One way in which the Catholic church, or its more zealous members, may have responded to this was to introduce sacred elements into the environments of popular culture: the statue of Our Lady in the Stella Ballroom in the 1950s is the most obvious example of this.[54]

However, devotion also functioned as a form of enjoyment in itself, and again, the urban environment had a part to play here. Eileen L's eldest sister, presumably one of those who was impatient to get out to a dance or a date, but had to say the rosary first, married a County Offaly farmer in the late 1940s: according to Eileen's evidence, one of the aspects she missed most about Limerick after marriage was the wide variety of religious activities available in the city, especially during Holy Week and Easter.[55] The customs of visiting the Altars of Repose on Holy Thursday and the cribs at Christmas were also seen as forms of entertainment, the latter especially suited to children. Kathleen B stresses the thrill of watching the Confraternity processions during her childhood in the 1920s, while music, whether that of the boy sopranos in the Redemptorists on Christmas night, or the sound of 2,000 men singing a rousing hymn, was another important aspect of the entertainment value of devotion. Máirín M's membership of *An Réalt*, described in Chapter 3, demonstrates how religious devotion, language activism, charitable involvement and entertainment were combined to fill at least four nights of her week as a teenager in the 1950s. The cultural complexity of the city at the time, along with the scale and variety of activities made possible by this, must have made a significant contribution to the continued success of devotional activities of all kinds up to the 1960s, while the counterpoint provided by other elements of popular culture may have helped to provide some much-needed relief from religious activities as well.

It is also important to identify the core experience lying at the heart of all this activity and to explore the deeper feelings underlying the social processes which made up the practice of religion and of life in general in Limerick during this period. The sense of security arising from living in this world is palpable in some interviewees' comments: Eileen L says 'it wasn't a bad life, really … it wasn't a bad way to be! You got a lot of guidelines and – we had parameters on everything, you know, and they helped … you know. They really helped'.[56] Kathleen B is speaking about singing at the liturgical festival when she says: 'I mean that was your world, you know? … and that was your world … you were very happy! You know … that was a great day, the day at school that you were marching over to the Cathedral'.[57] Máirín M's description of the Corpus Christi procession is also useful here,

> it must be so hard for somebody in this day and age to contemplate exactly what it was like to have everyone that you knew, walking, in the same direction, singing the same hymns, saying the same prayers, you just felt … it just made you feel part of where you were … 'twas something, you know, you didn't question at the time … I suppose it just felt very much … part … you were part of a community … part of something bigger.[58]

The 'something bigger' mentioned here by could refer to many things: the sense of a smaller community or street or parish taking part in a larger event has already been discussed. But the comment could also indicate the feeling of many elements of life coming together in a deeper way: the feeling of being totally in 'your world' identified by Kathleen B above, the sense in which religion was like 'breathing in the the air', mentioned by Anthony F[59] (see Figure 14).

These feelings could be seen as what Clifford Geertz describes as the 'powerful, pervasive and longlasting moods' established by the 'system of symbols' that is religion: according to Geertz, the formulation of a 'general order of existence' that seems 'uniquely realistic' is the method by which this is achieved.[60] It is interesting to look more closely at how this was done in Limerick city in the period up to 1960, and for some years after this date as well. As has been discussed extensively above, the symbolic power of the concept of place was one of the most basic ways in which cultural agents of all kinds engaged creatively with popular devotion. Related to this was the development of sacred spaces, both permanent and occasional ones, in the city environment. The churches' physical presence in the midst of shops and offices was a powerful reminder of the more spiritual presences to be accessed within, while the church bells were a frequent aural stimulus to devotion for those who could not see the church itself. In the same way, the holy water fonts inside the front door or outside other rooms, the May altars, the Sacred Heart or other holy pictures provided physical reminders of devotion in the home.

It is also important to look at the substance of belief engaged by these material objects and the actions associated with them. The power of story can be felt in people's year-round dedication to doing the Stations of the Cross in the church, as described by Kathleen B.[61] The mysteries of the rosary also involved a series of stories, while the discourse around Christmas and the tour of cribs reinforced one of the most central of these, the Nativity. The significance of Easter was further strengthened by people's physical involvement in marking the season: the practice of fasting during Lent and feasting when Easter arrived was a powerful method of enacting the meaning of the feast. Fasting during Lent was also effective in the sanctification of time, as shown in Chapter 5, but it must be remembered that the relationship between time and the

Figure 14 The Corpus Christi procession reaches its conclusion outside St John's Cathedral, 1959.

sacred was constantly highlighted in other, more frequent ways as well: the holy water before bedtime, the morning prayers, the evening rosary, the early Masses on Sunday, the Sunday evening Benediction, the weekly confraternity meetings, the summer processions, the annual novenas. The devotion to the Holy Souls in November, but also, more informally, on a year-round basis, indicates the central place held by people's relationships with the dead in their beliefs. The idea among people, in general, that the dead were still present, both needing help and able to give it, appears to be stronger in the period under study than almost any other belief in supernatural beings. Of course, people still prayed to the Blessed Sacrament, and to Jesus, in the form of the Sacred Heart, and to Our Lady in one form or another, depending on their own allegiance to a particular version of Our Lady or to a certain shrine in the city.[62] Some interviewees, for various reasons, identified or were dedicated to particular saints as well: St Anthony, St Gerard Majella, St Rita, St Margaret of Cortona, St Anne and St Thérèse of Lisieux, were all mentioned as having some devotional importance,[63] but few of these entities gave the sense of being present in people's lives in the way that their own dead relatives did.[64] Related to this is the belief in the afterlife, and it is not surprising, given the interest and belief in the dead, to find that this was one of the most intensely felt 'moods and motivations' of official Catholic religion in Limerick at this time. Furthermore, although interviewees did have some general idea of heaven, their main images of the afterlife were those of hell and purgatory. The fear of sin, especially serious sin and its consequence, hell, was a strong motivator, perhaps one of the main motivators, in devotion and in life in general. In terms of experience, this provides an interesting counterpoint to the sense of familiarity and security engendered by the atmosphere of popular religion in the city at the time: it could be said that the other side of this feeling of being 'at home in the world' was the fear of falling out of step and, literally – in many people's minds – into the flames of hell. However, it is also crucial to remember the more abstract moments of beauty and transcendence experienced by people, the most striking of these being the liturgical singing, with May processions and Corpus Christi processions also notable in this regard. It would be wrong to characterize these as simply enjoyable sensual experiences: the evidence shows that the sensual enjoyment was underscored by belief, which was after all the *raison d'être* of these events in any case, while the sense of community was, as we have continuously seen, also an important contributor to many of these events.

The experience of popular religion in Limerick city up to 1960 or thereabouts is one which amply demonstrates what Glassie calls 'the interplay of will and circumstance' and the way in which people are both 'free and stuck in the world'. The evidence shows how interviewees used the choices they had – of devotions, of confessors, of pilgrimages, of churches, saints and shrines – to balance the sense of obligation and the feeling of being controlled and watched. The combination of will and circumstance can also be seen in how the fear engendered by supernatural concepts such as sin, hell and purgatory did not deter them from communing with their own dead; nor did it prevent their creativity in areas of religious devotion where beauty and sensuality, as well as irony and humour could be used and enjoyed to the full. It can be said, therefore, that although Limerick city people in the decades between the 1920s and 1960 spent much of their time fitting into 'the plots of others', they were also able to 'form their own lives': the teenage boys' summer evening walks after devotions; the women chatting around the May fires; the young people smoking on the train to Croagh Patrick; the intense discussions of fasting in factories and bakeries; the children called in from the street for the rosary; the grandparents remembered and prayed for in the rounds for the Holy Souls; the urgent trips made to shrines; the Christmas tours of cribs; the beauty of embroidery and lace, and the pride in their making; the jokes, anecdotes and wordplay and the stifled laughter at the boys' Confraternity. All of these images are indicative of the creativity of Limerick people within the overall context of a highly ritualized and controlled religious environment: perhaps the most striking aspect of this creativity is its variety and complexity. People, including children, and communities used their creativity to establish and re-establish rituals of their own, parallel to official religious ones; they also worked creatively to challenge the authoritarian or tedious aspects of religion, while using other creative abilities to support and enhance the aspects of devotion most loved by themselves, as individuals or as communities. This study shows that it is not just in scholarly circles that the multi-functional nature of religion, as described by Lawrence J. Taylor, is understood,[65] but that in real communities, and certainly in Limerick city in the first half of the twentieth century, this principle was not just understood, but acted upon in a constant and creative way.

Notes

Preface

1 Frank McCourt, *Angela's Ashes: A Memoir of a Childhood* (London: Harper Collins, 1996), 162.
2 Críostóir O'Flynn, *There is an Isle: A Limerick Boyhood*. (Cork: Mercier, 1998), 204.
3 Anthony F, interview, Limerick city, August 2009 (AF).
4 Louise Fuller, *Irish Catholicism since 1950: The Undoing of a Culture* (Dublin: Gill & Macmillan, 2002).
5 Tom Inglis, 'Individualisation and Secularisation in Catholic Ireland', in Sara O'Sullivan (ed.), *Contemporary Ireland: A Sociological Map* (Dublin: University College Dublin Press, 2007), 67–82.

Chapter 1: Historical Background

1 Thomas Bartlett, *Ireland: A History* (Cambridge: Cambridge University Press, 2010), 403.
2 See J. J. Lee, 'Rebellion: 1912–1922', in *Ireland 1912–1985: Politics and Society* (Cambridge: Cambridge University Press, 1989), 1–55.
3 See, for instance, David Harkness, *Northern Ireland since 1920*. (Dublin: Helicon, 1983); Eamon Phoenix, *Northern Nationalism: Nationalist Politics, Partition and the Catholic Minority in Northern Ireland, 1890–1940* (Belfast: Ulster Historical Foundation, 1994); Nicholas Mansergh, *The Unresolved Question: The Anglo-Irish Agreement and its Undoing, 1912–1972* (New Haven: Yale University Press, 1991).
4 Census of Ireland, 1961, 'Catholics 1926–1961', in Vol. 7, *Religion and Birthplaces*, 1.
5 Ibid.
6 Donald Harman Akenson, *A Mirror to Kathleen's Face: Education in Independent Ireland 1922–1960* (Montreal: McGill-Queen's University Press, 1975), 107.
7 Timothy Patrick Coogan, *Ireland Since the Rising* (Connecticut: Greenwood Press 1976 [1966]), 213–14.
8 Akenson, *A Mirror to Kathleen's Face*, 107.
9 The *Dáil* refers to the legislative governing body in Ireland, equivalent to the British House of Commons.
10 Coogan, *Ireland Since the Rising*, 213–14.
11 Diarmaid Ferriter, *The Transformation of Ireland 1900–2000* (London: Profile, 2005 [2004]), 369–70.
12 Terence Brown, *Ireland: A Social and Cultural History 1922–1979* (London: Harper Perennial 2004 [1981]), 69.
13 *Catholic Truth Society of Ireland Annual Report for Year Ending 28th February, 1959* (Dublin: Catholic Truth Society of Ireland [CTSI], 1959).

14 Elizabeth Russell, 'Holy Crosses, Guns and Roses: Themes in Popular Reading Material', in Joost Augusteijn (ed.), *Ireland in the 1930s: New Perspectives* (Dublin: Four Courts, 1999), 11–28.
15 CTSI, *Annual Report February 1959*.
16 Ibid., 4–5.
17 See Mrs John Boland, *How to Run a CTS Case* (London: Catholic Truth Society, n.d. c. 1927).
18 Lambert McKenna, *Life and Work of James Aloysius Cullen, S.J.* (London: Longman's, Green & Co., 1924), 261.
19 Mary Francis Budzik, Michael Kerrigan and Charles Phillips, *The Complete Illustrated Guide to Catholicism* (London: Hermes, 2009), 222–3.
20 McKenna, *Life and Works of James Aloysius Cullen*, 261.
21 Ibid., 267–9.
22 *Irish Messenger of the Sacred Heart*, January 1905, 24 (henceforth *IMSH*).
23 *Irish Catholic Directory and Almanac 1914* (Dublin: James Duffy & Co., 1914), 149.
24 *Irish Catholic Directory and Almanac 1924* (Dublin: James Duffy & Co., 1924), 98.
25 *IMSH*, January 1935, 46.
26 *Classified List of Publications* (Dublin: Irish Messenger Office, n.d., c. 1955).
27 See www.dominicanpublications.com (accessed 23 September 2016).
28 For an interesting insight into the relationship between various players in the English Catholic publishing market at this time, see 'Letters to the Editor', *The Tablet*, 4 December 1937, www.archive.thetablet.co.uk (accessed 17 November 2015).
29 George Ineson, *Community Journey* (London: Catholic Book Club., n.d., library date label showing it was borrowed from Cork Catholic Library and stamped with return dates between January 1960 and April 1963).
30 'About the Library', www.catholiclibrary.ie (accessed 17 November 2015).
31 Alana Harris, *Faith in the Family: A Lived Religious History of English Catholicism 1945–82* (Manchester: Manchester University Press, 2013), 17–19; Callum G. Brown, *The Death of Christian Britain: Understanding Secularisation 1800–2000*, 2nd edn (London: Routledge, 2009), Chapters 4, 5.
32 Gillian McIntosh, 'Act of "National Communion": The Centenary Celebrations for Catholic Emancipation, the Forerunner of the Eucharistic Congress', in Joost Augusteijn (ed.), *Ireland in the 1930s* (Dublin: Four Courts, 1999), 83–95.
33 Emmet Larkin, *The Historical Dimensions of Irish Catholicism* (New York: Arno, 1976).
34 S. J. Connolly, *Priests and People in Pre-famine Ireland 1780–1845* (Dublin: Gill & Macmillan, 1982).
35 Thomas G. McGrath, 'The Tridentine Evolution of Modern Irish Catholicism 1563–1962: A Re-examination of the "Devotional Revolution" thesis', in *Recusant History* 20 (1990–1): 512–23.
36 Ibid., 521.
37 McKenna, *Life and Works of James Aloysius Cullen* (London, 1924).
38 Ibid., 162–3.
39 Ruth Harris, *Lourdes: Body and Spirit in the Secular Age* (London: Viking, 1999), 169.
40 S. C. Williams, *Religious Belief and Popular Culture in Southwark c.1880–1939* (Oxford: Oxford University Press, 1999), 10.
41 Ibid., 54–86.

42   Ibid., 5.

43   Diarmuid Ó Giolláin, 'Folklore and Nation-Building', *Locating Irish Folklore: Tradition, Modernity, Identity* (Cork: Cork University Press, 2000).

44   Mícheál Briody, *The Irish Folklore Commission: History, Ideology, Methodology* (Helsinki: Finnish Literature Society, 2007).

45   See for instance *Féile Pádraig Annual Souvenir Brochure from Limerick* (Limerick: Coisde Lá Le Pádraig Executive Committee, 1956).

46   Bartlett, *Ireland: A History*, 10–11.

47   See, for instance 'Saint Patrick on Inishmore' (told by Hugh Nolan, collected in 1972), Henry Glassie, *The Penguin Book of Irish Folktales* (London: Penguin, 1985), 52–3; 'Cromm Dubh agus Naomh Pádaraig' (told by Peig Sayers, collected in mid-1930s) in Kenneth Jackson, *Scéalta Ón mBlascaod* (Baile Átha Cliath: An Cumann le Béaloideas Éireann, 1938), 61–2.

48   Fuller, *Irish Catholicism since 1950*, 23.

49   Máire MacNéill, 'The Mountain Pilgrimages', *The Festival of Lughnasa: A Study of the Survival of the Celtic Festival of the Beginning of the Harvest* (Oxford: Oxford University Press, 1962), 71–105.

50   Patsy Harrold, 'Park and its People: Origin and Folklore', in Kevin Hannan and Patrick J. O'Donnell, *Patrick's People: Historical Perspectives on an Ancient and Developing Community* (Limerick: n.p., 1994), 67–70.

51   Patricia Lysaght, 'An Choróin Mhuire in Iar-Thuaisceart Thír Chonaill sa bhFichiú hAois' ('The Rosary in North-West Donegal in the Twentieth Century'), *Sinsear: The Folklore Journal* 8 (1995): 13–54.

52   Fuller, *Irish Catholicism since 1950*, 25.

53   For accounts of the Irish-language activities of some Jesuit clergy see F. MacBrádaigh S.J. (ed.) *An Chuallacht Léannta: ceiliúradh ar Íosánaigh agus léann na Gaeilge* (Baile Átha Cliath: FÁS, 2013); for Christian Brothers' activity see Mícheál Ó Cearúil, *Gníomhartha na mBráithre: aistí comórtha ar Ghaelachas na mBráithre Críostaí* (Baile Átha Cliath: Coiscéim, 1996).

54   Síle de Cléir, 'Reading, Writing and Religion: The Messenger in Ireland, 1888–1960', MLIS diss., University College Dublin: Dublin, 1998, 50–3.

55   The complexity of the relationship between priests and popular religion / popular culture can be sensed in the repertoire of folklore collected by Augusta Gregory about the wise woman Biddy Early and priests' varying views of her, in the north Clare / south Galway area in the early twentieth century. Lady Augusta Gregory, *Visions and Beliefs in the West of Ireland* (Gerrards Cross: Colin Smythe, 1970 [1920]), Chapter II.

56   Mount St Alphonsus Archives, Limerick. Church Services (notebook), 1940.

57   Saorstát Éireann, *Census of Population 1926*, Vol. 1, 13.

58   *Census of Population of Ireland, 1961*, Vol. 1, 12.

59   Jonathan Haughton, 'The Historical Background', in J. W. O'Hagan (ed.), *The Economy of Ireland: Policy and Performance of a European Region* (Dublin: Gill & Macmillan, 2000), 26–37.

60   Saorsát Éireann, *Census of Population 1926*, Vol. 1, 10–13; *Census of Population of Ireland*, 1961, Vol. 1, 9–12.

61   Des McCafferty, 'Aspects of Socio-Economic Development in Limerick City since 1970: A Geographer's Perspective', in Liam Irwin, William Nolan, Gearóid Ó Tuathaigh and Matthew Potter (eds), *Limerick: History and Society* (Dublin: Geography Publications, 2009), 593–614.

62   Matthew Potter, *The Government and the People of Limerick* (Limerick: Limerick City Council, 2006), 415.

63   Ibid., 416–17.

64   Ibid., 433.

65   John Logan, 'Frugal Comfort: Housing Limerick's Labourers and Artisans, 1841–1946', in Liam Irwin, William Nolan, Gearóid Ó Tuathaigh and Matthew Potter (eds), *Limerick: History and Society* (Dublin: Geography Publications, 2009), 557–82; 575. For a survey of housing and social conditions in Limerick up to 1930, see Ruth Guiry, *Public Health and Housing in Limerick City 1850–1935: A Geographical Analysis* (2013), dspace.mic.ul.ie (accessed 10 August 2015).

66   Fionnuala Synnott, 'A Study of the Townscape of Limerick', MA diss., University College Galway, 1979, 201.

67   Frank Prendergast, 'The Decline of Traditional Limerick Industries', in David Lee and Debbie Jacobs (eds), *Made in Limerick: History of Industries, Trade and Commerce, Vol. 1* (Limerick: Limerick Civic Trust, 2003), 1–22, 15.

68   Ibid., 6–11.

69   Ibid., 16–19.

70   Ibid., 4–5.

71   Debbie Jacobs, 'Limerick Clothing Manufacturers and Retailers', in D. Lee and D. Jacobs (eds), *Made in Limerick, Volume 1* (Limerick: Limerick Civic Trust, 2003), 23–36.

72   Prendergast 'The Decline of Traditional Limerick Industries', 4–5.

73   *MacDonald's Irish Directory and Gazetteer, 1957–58* (Edinburgh, 1958), 165–70.

74   Síle de Cléir, 'An Pháirc', Field Research Project in Folklore and Ethnology, University College Cork, 1988, 34.

75   For a visual record of this trend, see the extensive photographic collection in Sean Curtin, *Limerick: A Stroll Down Memory Lane, Volumes 1–16* (Limerick: Sean Curtin Publications, 2004–16).

76   Saorstát Éireann, *Census of Population, 1926*, Vol. 2, Table 6 (A).

77   *Census of Population of Ireland, 1961*, Vol. 3, 16–17.

78   See Chapter 3: 'Ritual and City Life'.

79   See, for example, 'The Arch-Confraternity: Limerick's Proud Boast' *Limerick Echo*, 11 May 1926; 'Letter from J. O'Dwyer, Loco Dept., G. S. Railways, Limerick', *Limerick Leader*, 16 February 1935.

80   See Chapter 5: 'Ritual Families'.

81   Saorstát Éireann, *Census of Population, 1926*, Vol. 1, 13.

82   Saorstát Éireann, *Census of Population, 1936*, Vol. 3, 12.

83   *Census of Population of Ireland, 1946*, Vol. 3, 10.

84   *Census of Population of Ireland, 1961*, Vol. 7, 12.

85   Brendan Connellan, *Light on the Past: Story of St. Mary's Parish, Limerick* (Limerick: Brendan Connellan 2001), 1–37.

86   Kevin Hannan and W. Fitzmaurice, *In the Shadow of the Spire: A Profile of St. John's Parish* (Limerick: The Parish, 1991), 7–22.

87   Frank Prendergast, *St Michael's Parish: Its Life and Times* (Manchester: Gabriel Communications, 2000), 3–5.

88   http://www.limerickdioceseheritage.org/StMunchins.htm (accessed 21 February 2011).

89   Michael Moloney, 'The Parish of St. Patrick's', in K. Hannan and P. J. O'Donnell, *Patrick's People: Historical Perspectives of an Ancient and Developing Community* (Limerick: n.p., 1994), 7–14.

90   Connellan, *Light on the Past*, 41–56.

91   Myles Nolan O.P., *Saint Saviour's Priory Limerick 1227–1977* (Limerick: n.p., 1977), 27–31.

92   Thomas C. Butler O.S.A., *The Augustinians in Limerick* (Limerick: St. Augustine's Priory, 1988), 31–42; see also Judith Hill, *The Building of Limerick* (Cork: Mercier, 1991), 157.

93   Bartholemew Egan O.F.M., *Franciscan Limerick: The Order of St. Francis in the City of Limerick* (Limerick: Franciscan Fathers, 1971), 39–63.

94   Connellan, *Light on the Past*, 55–6.

95   Francis Finegan S.J., *Limerick Jesuit Centenary Record 1859–1959* (Limerick: Sacred Heart College, 1959), 12–13.

96   Hill, *Building of Limerick*, 163.

97   *The Church of Saint Alphonsus, Limerick* (leaflet available in church itself, 2010): see also Patrick J. O'Connor, *Exploring Limerick's Past* (Newcastle West: Oireacht na Mumhan Books, 1987), 157.

98   The Jesuit Sacred Heart church closed in 2006 and was taken over by the Order of Christ the King in 2012; the Franciscan church closed in 2008 and has been used for exhibitions and other community events since then. See 'Old Jesuit church continues restoration work' *Limerick Leader*, 26 April, 2014; 'Franciscan Friars to donate items to Sacred Heart', *Limerick Leader*, 3 August, 2013; 'No fixed timeline for Dominican retreat: Order announce intention to 'withdraw' from Limerick', *Limerick Leader*, 27 September 2014.

99   Hill, *Building of Limerick*, 154.

100 Ibid.

101 'List of donations and gifts to the church by members of the public 1889–1960', Box D 7, MSA Archives, Mount Saint Alphonsus, Limerick; see also Kathleen B, conversation, 5 March 2004 (KB).

102 *Augustinian Church, Limerick: Year Book, 1959* (Limerick: Augustinian Fathers, 1959), 3.

103 Ibid.

104 *Presentation Convent Limerick Centenary 1837–1937* (Limerick: Presentation Order, 1937), 11–16.

105 Connellan, *Light on the Past*, 75.

106 Caitriona Clear, *Nuns in Nineteenth-Century Ireland* (Dublin: Gill & Macmillan, 1987), 43.

107 Sr Loreto O'Connor, *Passing on the Torch: A History of Mary Immaculate College, 1898–1998* (Limerick: Mary Immaculate College, 1998).

Chapter 2: Approaches and Perspectives

1   J. N. Morris, *Religion and Urban Change: Croydon 1840–1914* (Suffolk: Boydell Press, 1992).

2   Hugh McLeod, *Class and Religion in the Late Victorian City* (London: Croom Helm, 1974).

3   Williams, *Religious Belief and Popular Culture in Southwark*.

4   Charlotte Wildman, 'Religious Selfhoods and the City in Inter-War Manchester', *Urban History* 38 (1) (April 2011): 103–23.

5   O'Flynn, *There is an Isle*, 12–13.
6   Patsy Harrold, 'Park and its People', 67–70.
7   Alana Harris, *Faith in the Family*.
8   Callum G. Brown, *The Death of Christian Britain: Understanding Secularisation 1800–2000*, 2nd edn (London: Routledge, 2009), 1–15.
9   Gearóid Ó Crualaoich, *The Book of the Cailleach: Stories of the Wise-Woman Healer* (Cork: Cork University Press, 2003), 6.
10   Williams, *Religious Belief and Popular Culture in Southwark*, 6.
11   May Eve was (and still is, in some areas) bonfire, or 'bone-fire' night in Limerick city.
12   Ann Taves, *Religious Experience Reconsidered: A Building-Block Approach to the Study of Religion and Other Special Things* (Oxford: Princeton University Press, 2009), 7.
13   Ibid., 16–55.
14   Ibid., 5.
15   Ibid., 56–7.
16   Williams, *Religious Belief and Popular Culture in Southwark*, 5.
17   Harris, *Faith in the Family*, 15.
18   Linda Shopes, 'Oral History and the Study of Communities: Problems, Paradoxes and Possibilities', in Robert Perks and Alistair Thomson (eds), *The Oral History Reader*, 2nd edn (London: Routledge, 2006), 268.
19   *Limerick Leader*, 4 June 1932, 8.
20   For instance, in the late 1990s, when it was decided to locate Ireland's new classical radio station, to be called 'Lyric FM', in Limerick, this was satirized on radio as 'Cleric FM'. Author's experience, 1998–9.
21   Shopes, 'Oral History and the Study of Communities', 263.
22   These are: Áine R, Anthony F, Grace K, Joseph L, Kathleen B, Máirín M, Eileen L, Noreen P, Pádraig R, Peggy D, Timmy P and Tommy C (to protect their privacy, all interviewees' names, and most names mentioned by them have been changed. See 'Notes on the Text').
23   Valerie Yow, 'Do I Like Them Too Much?': Effects of the Oral History Interview on the Interviewer and Vice-Versa', *Oral History Review* 24 (1) (Summer 1997): 55–79.
24   Mícheál Briody, *The Irish Folklore Commission*, 79–85.
25   For shrine visits, see Chapter 6; for Christmas customs see Chapter 7; for annual retreats see Chapter 3; for pilgrimages see Chapter 4; for the rosary beads, see Chapter 5.
26   Yow, 'Do I Like Them Too Much?', 73.
27   See Chapter 3, 'Ritual in Men's Lives' (Tommy C's evidence).
28   See Conclusion, 'Watching and Watching Over: The Community as Family'.
29   Ruth Finnegan, *Oral Traditions and the Verbal Arts: A Guide to Research Practices* (London: Routledge, 1992), 224.
30   Ibid., 225.
31   Yow, 'Do I Like Them Too Much?', 79.
32   Ibid., 71.
33   See Noreen P's evidence in Chapter 6, 'Sin: Consequences and Remedies'.
34   See Conclusion: 'Watching and Watching Over: The Community as Family'.
35   See Chapter 5.
36   See, for instance, *Limerick Leader*, 2 February 1960; *Limerick Leader*, 20 July 1935.
37   See Chapter 4, 'May Eve', for examples of this discourse.

38 See, for instance, 'Award to Irish Nun', *Limerick Echo*, 7 January 1936; 'Bishop Heelan in County Limerick', *Limerick Leader*, 22 July 1935; see also Mary Kenny, *Goodbye to Catholic Ireland* (London: Sinclair-Stevenson, 1997), 131–2.

39 See, for instance: 'The Silk Stocking Vogue: Bishop of Non-Payment of Debt', *Limerick Echo*, 11 May 1926; 'Its Growing Influence: Speech by Most Rev. Dr. Keane to St. Michael's Temperance Society' in *Limerick Echo*, 4 February 1936.

40 Editorial article: 'Embarrassment?' *Limerick Leader*, 7 February 2004.

41 Eoin Devereux, 'Negotiating Community: The Case of a Limerick Community Development Group' in Chris Curtin, Hastings Donnan, Thomas M. Wilson (eds), *Irish Urban Cultures* (Belfast: Institute of Irish Studies, 1993), 63–77.

42 McCourt, *Angela's Ashes*.

43 O'Flynn, *There is an Isle*.

44 For instance, 'The Late Late Show', a popular Friday night television chat show on RTÉ 1 featured a heated argument between Gerry Hannan and Frank McCourt in April 1999.

45 Ulf Hannerz, *Cultural Complexity: Studies in the Social Organization of Meaning* (New York: Columbia University Press, 1992), 14.

Chapter 3: Ritual and City Life

1   Lauri Honko 'Theories Concerning the Ritual Process: An Orientation', in Lauri Honko (ed.), *Science of Religion: Studies in Methodology* (The Hague: Mouton, 1979), 373.

2   Ibid.

3   Ibid.

4   Williams, *Religious Belief and Popular Culture in Southwark*, 5.

5   Joseph L, County Clare, interview, 30 March 2004 (JL).

6   Kevin Danaher, *The Year in Ireland* (Cork: Mercier, 1972).

7   Eileen L, County Clare, telephone conversation, 19 May 2004 (ELa); Kathleen B, Limerick city, interview, 2 April 2004 (KB); Máirín M, County Limerick; interview, 5 April 2004 (MM).

8   Eileen L, County Clare, interview, 30 March 2004 (EL); KB; MM; for a detailed plan of the proposed procession in 1960, and an account of the event see *Limerick Leader*, 15 June 1960; 18 June 1960 and 20 June 1960.

9   See for example *Limerick Leader*, 22 August 1960.

10 Máire MacNeill, *The Festival of Lughnasa*. 'Lughnasa' is also the Irish term for the month of August.

11 MM.

12 *Limerick Leader*, 1926, 1930, 1940, 1950, 1960; Mount Saint Alphonsus Archives: Box D: *Church Services 1940 Augustinian Church, Limerick: Yearbook, 1959*; Finegan, *Limerick Jesuit Centenary Record 1859–1959*.

13 Brian Morris, 'Religion: Meaning and Function', in Brian Morris, *Anthropological Studies of Religion: An Introductory Text* (Cambridge: Cambridge University Press, 1987), 227–8.

14 For an overview of the activities and organization of Confraternities and Sodalities in Ireland in this period see Colm Lennon and Robin Kavanagh, 'The Flowering of the Confraternties and Sodalities in Ireland c.1860-1960', in Colm Lennon (ed.),

Confraternities and Sodalities in Ireland: Charity, Devotion and Sociability (Dublin: The Columba Press, 2012), 76–96.

15   *Souvenir of the Diamond Jubilee: Arch-Confraternity of the Holy Family, Mount Saint Alphonsus, Limerick* (Limerick: Limerick Leader, 1928), 15.

16   *Souvenir of the Diamond Jubilee*, 5.

17   MSA Archives: Archconfraternity registers 1926–60.

18   Tommy C, Limerick city, interview, 16 June 2004 (TC).

19   JL; according to Fr. Paddy Corbett CSSR, the membership of the Archconfraternity of the Holy Family reached 10,000 in 1960 (telephone conversation, June 2010).

20   Ann Noonan, 'St. Patrick's Parish: 19th and 20th Centuries', in K. Hannan and P. J. O'Donnell, *Patrick's People: Historical Perspectives of Ancient and Developing Community* (Limerick: n.p., 1994), 139–77; 142.

21   JL.

22   JL.

23   Tommy C. Limerick city, pre-interview conversation, 14 June 2004 (TCa). 'Shannon' refers to a high-profile rugby club in the north of the city.

24   TC.

25   TC.

26   KB.

27   Timmy G, interview, 9 September 2015 (TG).

28   TC.

29   Peggy D, Limerick city, interview, 10 March 2004 (PD).

30   TG.

31   TG.

32   AF.

33   TG.

34   *Souvenir of the Diamond Jubilee*, 16.

35   KB.

36   *Limerick Leader*, 9 January 1960.

37   Noreen P, Limerick city, interview, 29 March 2004 (NP).

38   TC.

39   Prendergast, 'The Decline of Traditional Limerick Industries', 8–9.

40   TCa: TC.

41   Tommy C, private collection of photographs and LPBS memorabilia.

42   'Gerardus' and 'Limerick's Memorial to Our Lady', in *Féile Pádraig Annual Souvenir Brochure from Limerick*, 111–13.

43   *Limerick Leader*, 12 March 1960.

44   TC.

45   MM.

46   MM.

47   MM.

48   KB, pre-interview session, 5 March 2004 (KBa); MM.

49   NP.

50   NP; MM.

51   EL.

52   MM.

53   KBa.

54   Grace K, interview, 10 September 2015 (GK).

55   NP.

56 EL.
57 Elaine Leahy, conversation, 20 May 2004.
58 MM.
59 Curtin, *Limerick: A Stroll Down Memory Lane, Volume 5*, 39. I am grateful to Sean Curtin for his information regarding this image.
60 *Limerick Leader*, 16 April 1960.
61 KB.
62 KB.
63 PD.
64 GK.
65 GK.
66 PD.
67 GK.
68 EL.
69 MM.
70 MM; PR. 'The *Praesidium*' is the term used to refer to the local organization of the Legion of Mary; Máirín is here referring to a meeting of her local *Praesidium*. The Irish term *An Réalt* was used to designate the Irish-language branch of the Legion of Mary in Limerick and the name translates as 'The Star'; the *céilí* mentioned here by Máirín is an organized public dance with Irish music and dances.
71 JL.
72 NP.
73 GK; PD.
74 KB.
75 KB.
76 MM.
77 Wildman, 'Religious Selfhoods', 104.
78 Joseph Sciorra, 'We Go Where the Italians Live: Religious Processions as Ethnic and Territorial Markers in a Multi-ethnic Brooklyn Neighborhood', in Robert A. Orsi (ed.), *Gods of the City: Religion and the American Urban Landscape* (Bloomington: Indiana University Press, 1999), 310–40; 311.
79 McLeod, *Class and Religion*, see especially Chapter 2: 'Who Went To Church'.
80 Morris, *Religion and Urban Change*, see especially Chapter 3: 'The Churches in Victorian Croydon'.
81 Morris, *Anthropological Studies of Religion*, 228.
82 Ibid., 228–30.
83 TC.
84 See also Paddy Mulcahy 'Growing up in St. Patrick's', in K. Hannan and P. J. O'Donnell, *Patrick's People: Historical Perspectives of Ancient and Developing Community* (Limerick: n.p., 1994), 277–8.
85 Eileen L, various conversations, 1975–2016.
86 One interviewee had the following to say 'Chloíodar leis an dtigh agus leis an gclann. Ceapaimse ná raibh aon rud eile ach cúram an tí. Sníomh. Níochán. Bácáil. Ag beiriú. Tindeáil ar mhuca agus – mar sin' ('They kept to the home and the family. I think they had nothing else but the care of the house. Spinning, laundry, baking, boiling, tending to pigs, that kind of thing'), Síle de Cléir, 'Éadach, Feisteas agus Maisiú i Saol Traidisiúnta Oileáin Árann agus Chorca Dhuibhne', MA diss, University College, Cork, 1992, 283.

87   Caitriona Clear, *Women of the House: Women's Household Work in Ireland 1922-1961* (Dublin: Irish Academic Press, 2000), 25-6.

88   McCourt, *Angela's Ashes*, 162-5.

89   See 'Justice for Magdalenes' website: www.magdalenelaundries.com (accessed 30 September 2011); for access to information about life in industrial schools, see www.childabusecommission.ie (accessed 30 September 2011). See also Mary Raftery, *Suffer the Little Children: The Inside Story of Ireland's Industrial Schools* (Dublin: New Island Books, 1999); Frances Finnegan, *Do Penance or Perish: A Study of Magdalen Asylums in Ireland* (Kilkenny: Congrave Press, 2001). See also 'Mother and Baby Homes Commission of Investigation', www.mbhcoi.ie (accessed 4 March, 2017).

90   EL.

91   Catherine Bell, 'The Genres of Ritual Action' in *Ritual: Perspectives and Dimensions* (Oxford: Oxford University Press, 1996), 94.

92   AF; Críostóir O'Flynn, *There is an Isle*, 206-8.

93   Interviewees' evidence varied as to whether Requiem Mass was always held.

94   TG.

95   KB.

96   Lisa Godson, 'Display, Sacramentalism and Devotion: The Medals of the Archconfraternity of the Holy Family, 1922-39', in Colm Lennon (ed.), *Confraternities and Sodalities in Ireland: Charity, Devotion and Sociability* (Dublin: Columba Press, 2012), 110-25.

97   AF.

98   GK.

99   KB.

100   KB.

101   KB.

102   KB.

103   KB.

104   KB.

105   O'Flynn, *There is an Isle*, 206.

106   Ibid., 206-7.

107   Ibid, 206. An interview given by the Limerick funeral director Gerry Griffin, published in 2006, shows that the dilemmas presented by the funerals of victims of traffic accidents, along with the sophistication of current embalming techniques, have led to a similar approach to the presentation of the corpse in contemporary funeral practice: 'You don't want to sanitise it and make it so that the family don't even realise the person has died. I think that would be wrong ... So there's a very fine balance between making things bearable and making things invisible.' Eoin Shinners 'Gerry Griffin: Funeral Director', in D. Lee and D. Jacobs (eds), *Made in Limerick, Volume 2: A History of trades, Industries and Commerce* (Limerick: Limerick Civic Trust, 2006), 255-6.

108   KB.

109   PD.

110   O'Flynn, *There is an Isle*, 207.

111   TC.

112   TC.

113   KB.

114   Paddy Mulcahy, 'Growing up in St Patrick's', 277.

115   Seán Ó Súilleabháin, *Caitheamh Aimsire ar Thórraimh* (Baile Átha Cliath: an

Clóchomhar, 1960) 1–4; 13–20. Published in English as *Irish Wake Amusements* (Dublin: Mercier, 1979).

116 KB; Ó Súilleabháin, *Caitheamh Aimsire*, 3–4.

117 KB.

118 Julian Litten, *The English Way of Death: The Common Funeral since 1450* (London: Robert Hale, 2002 [1991]), 168.

119 MM. *Nollaig na mBan* (Women's Christmas) is the Irish term for the Feast of the Epiphany. *Go ndéana Dia trócaire uirthi* translates as 'May the Lord have mercy on her'.

120 MM.

121 This custom was followed at least until the late 1990s in the Thomondgate, Killeely, King's Island, and Irishtown (St John's) areas of Limerick (author's personal experience during this period in the city); also interviews: Áine R, 6 August 2009 (AR); AF; TG; GK.

122 Ciarán Mac Mathúna, 'Memories of St John's Parish Limerick', in K. Hannan and W. Fitzmaurice, *In the Shadow of the Spire* (Limerick: n.p., 1991), 47.

123 Hannan and Fitzmaurice, *In the Shadow of the Spire*, 129.

124 Lawrence J. Taylor, 'Bás in Éirinn: The Cultural Construction of Death in Ireland', *Anthropological Quarterly* 62 (4) (1989): 175–87; 179.

125 Ibid., 176.

126 Arnold van Gennep, *The Rites of Passage* (Chicago: University of Chicago Press, 1960), 11.

127 O'Flynn, *There is an Isle.*, 206.

128 Shinners, 'Gerry Griffin: Funeral Director', 251–2. 'Piseógary' (sometimes spelt 'pisheoguery'or 'pishroguery') is an anglicization of the Irish words *piseog/pisreog* – meaning superstition.

129 Bell, 'The Genres of Ritual Action', 94.

130 Shinners, 'Gerry Griffin: Funeral Director', 249.

131 Ó Súilleabháin, *Caitheamh Aimsire*, 2.

132 Hannan and Ftizmaurice, *In the Shadow of the Spire*, 47.

133 Ibid. 47.

134 Francois Lebrun, 'The Two Reformations: Communal Devotion and Personal Piety', in Philippe Ariés and Georges Dubuy, *A History of Private Life: Vol. 3: Passions of the Renaissance* (Harvard: Belknap Press, 1989), 69–109; 85-86.

135 Litten, *English Way of Death*, 165.

136 Ibid., 170.

137 Ibid., 84.

138 Donncha Ó Cróinín and Seán Ó Cróinín, *Seanachas Amhlaoibh Í Luínse* (Baile Átha Cliath: Comhairle Bhéaloideas Éireann, 1980), 253–4; Donncha Ó Céileachair 'Sochraid Neil Chonchubhair Dhuibh', in Síle Ní Chéileachair agus Donncha Ó Céileachair, *Bullaí Mhártain* (Baile Átha Cliath: Sáirséal agus Dill, 1955), 36–44.

139 Hannan and Fitzmaurice, *In the Shadow of the Spire*, 44.

140 *Limerick Chronicle*, 9 May 1839.

141 Taylor, 'Bás in Eirinn', 185.

142 O'Flynn, *There is an Isle*, 206.

143 Ibid.

144 MM, conversation, April 2003 (MMa).

145 AF.

146 Hannan and Fitzmaurice, *In the Shadow of the Spire*, 129.

Chapter 4: Senses of Place

1 Hervé Varenne, 'Dublin 16: Accounts of Suburban Lives', in C. Curtin, H. Donnan and T. M. Wilson (eds), *Irish Urban Cultures* (Belfast: Institute of Irish Studies, 1993), 99–121; 99.
2 See Chapter 3, 'Ritual and City Life'.
3 Victor Turner and Edith Turner, *Image and Pilgrimage in Christian Culture* (New York: Columbia University Press, 1978), xvi.
4 *Limerick Leader*, 14 August 1935.
5 Ibid.
6 *Limerick Leader*, 21 August 1935.
7 *Catholic Life: Quarterly Magazine of the Limerick Diocese*, Vol. 1, No. 3, October 1954, 19.
8 The cost of these pilgrimages in 2015, when measured against the average wage in the years 1930 and 1954 would be £2,559 and £2,459, respectively, www.measuringworth.com (accessed 23 September 2016).
9 *Limerick Leader*, 5 May 1930; *Catholic Life: The Quarterly Magazine of the Limerick Diocese*, Vol. 1, No. 1, April 1954, 13.
10 *Limerick Leader*, 14 August 1954.
11 *Catholic Life*, April 1954, 13.
12 Stiofán Ó Cadhla, *The Holy Well Tradition: The Pattern of St. Declan, Ardmore, County Waterford, 1800-2000* (Dublin: Four Courts, 2002), 36–8.
13 *Limerick Leader*, 5 May 1930.
14 *Limerick Leader*, 30 March 1935.
15 *Limerick Leader*, 25 April 1936.
16 *Limerick Leader*, 20 July 1935.
17 *Limerick Leader*, 29 July 1935.
18 *Limerick Leader*, 25 April 1936; *Limerick Leader*, 25 March 1935.
19 *Limerick Leader*, 23 February 1935.
20 *Limerick Leader*, 26 January 1935.
21 Bell, 'The Genres of Ritual Action', 249.
22 Ibid., 249.
23 Saorstát Éireann *Census of Population 1936*, Vol. 3, 72. The population of Limerick in 1936 was enumerated as 41,006.
24 *Census of Population of Ireland, 1956*, 28. The population of Limerick in 1951 was 50,820.
25 *Our Catholic Life: The Quarterly Magazine of the Limerick Diocese*, July 1955, 16.
26 *Our Catholic Life*, Easter 1956, 24.
27 *Our Catholic Life*, October 1956, 31.
28 *Limerick Leader*, 13 August 1958.
29 *Limerick Leader*, 13 September 1958.
30 *Limerick Leader*, 13 August 1958.
31 *Limerick Leader*, 13 September 1958.
32 Ibid.
33 MM.
34 KB.
35 Louise Fuller, *Irish Catholicism since 1950*, 23.
36 ELa.

37   KB.
38   KB.
39   Michael Walsh, *The Apparition at Knock: A Critical Analysis of Facts and Evidence* (Dublin: Veritas, 2008 [1955]), 15–19.
40   Ibid., 100.
41   Ibid., 103.
42   Eugene Hynes, *Knock: The Virgin's Apparition in Nineteenth-Century Ireland* (Cork: Cork University Press, 2008), 21–5. The phrase 'devotionally revolutionised' refers to the characterization of Irish Catholicism during this period in Emmet Larkin's *The Historical Dimensions of Irish Catholicism*. See 'Historical Background'.
43   Ibid., 121.
44   KB.
45   KB.
46   Walsh, *The Apparition at Knock*, 103.
47   *Limerick Leader*, 27 July 1940.
48   Fuller, *Irish Catholicism since 1950*, 23.
49   JL.
50   EL.
51   EL.
52   JL.
53   KB.
54   GK.
55   NP.
56   NP.
57   NP.
58   NP.
59   GK.
60   NP.
61   MM.
62   TG.
63   Máire MacNeill, *The Festival of Lughnasa*, 71–105.
64   Ibid, 79.
65   Ibid.
66   Harry Hughes, *Croagh Patrick (Cruach Phádraig – The Reek): An Ancient Mountain Pilgrimage* (Westport: Harry Hughes, 1991), 24.
67   Ibid.
68   Ibid.
69   MacNeill, *Festival of Lughnasa*, 80.
70   Fuller, *Irish Catholicism since 1950*, 23.
71   EL.
72   NP.
73   *Limerick Leader*, 20 July 1935.
74   *Limerick Leader*, 26 July 1930; 23 July 1930.
75   *Limerick Leader*, 27 July 1940.
76   EL.
77   GK.
78   MacNeill, *Festival of Lughnasa*, 70.
79   Paddy Mulcahy, 'Growing up in St. Patrick's', 278.

80   NP; KB; EL.
81   Budzik, Kerrigan and Phillips, *The Complete Illustrated Guide to Catholicism*, 122–3.
82   'The 1932 Congress (Archive)', www.iec2012.ie (accessed 17 August 2016).
83   Ibid.
84   *Irish Messenger of the Sacred Heart*, September 1927, 388.
85   *Irish Messenger of the Sacred Heart*, August 1927, 342.
86   Gillian McIntosh, 'Act of "National Communion"', 83–95.
87   *Limerick Leader*, 4 June 1932.
88   *Limerick Leader*, 11 June 1932.
89   *Limerick Leader*, 4 June 1932.
90   Ibid.
91   *Limerick Leader*, 11 June 1932.
92   Ibid.
93   *Limerick Leader*, 15 June 1932.
94   *Limerick Leader*, 18 June 1932.
95   *Limerick Leader*, 29 June 1932.
96   Ibid.
97   *Limerick Leader*, 20 June 1932.
98   *Limerick Leader*, 29 June 1932.
99   ELa.
100 GK.
101 *Limerick Leader*, 29 June 1932.
102 Ibid.
103 *Limerick Leader*, 11 June and 18 June 1932.
104 See, for instance, 'Home for Congress: Limerick Man Back from Australia', in *Limerick Leader*, 18 June 1932; 'Cardinal Bourne: Limerick Visit Ends', *Limerick Leader*, 20 June 1932.
105 'Liner-Hotels for Congress', in *Limerick Leader*, 18 June 1932, and 'Native of Glin gets important post in America' *Limerick Leader*, 11 June 1932.
106 See 'Herbertstown Notes: Cycling to Congress', in *Limerick Leader*, 25 June 1932.
107 See, for instance, 'Kilbehenny Sparks', *Limerick Leader*, 11 June 1932; 'Clare Searchlights', *Limerick Leader*, 18 June 1932.
108 *Limerick Leader*, 18 June, 20 June and 25 June, 1932.
109 *Limerick Leader*, 4 June 1932 and see also 'Lent from Limerick: Priceless Treasures for Congress', *Limerick Leader*, 20 June 1932.
110 *Limerick Leader*, 29 June 1932.
111 Ibid.
112 Brown, *Ireland: A Social and Cultural History*, 28.
113 See, for example, the Third Order (of St Francis) Excursion to Killarney, advertised in *Limerick Leader*, 25 July 1925; the trip to Mellary by bus for members of the St John's Ambulance Brigade which would include a visit to Lismore Castle and St. Carthage's Cathedral, *Limerick Leader*, 27 May 1935.
114 Diarmuid Ó Giolláin, *An Dúchas agus an Domhan* (Cork: Cork University Press, 2005), 63.
115 See Kevin O'Connor, *Ironing the Land: the Coming of the Railways to Ireland* (Dublin: Gill & Macmillan, 1999).
116 *Cork Examiner*, 30 May 1932.
117 Ó Giolláin, *An Dúchas agus an Domhan*, 63.

118 NP.
119 KB.
120 KB.
121 Turner and Turner, *Image and Pilgrimage in Christian Culture*, 32–4.
122 John Eade and Michael Sallnow (eds), *Contesting the Sacred: The Anthropology of Christian Pilgrimage* (Urbana: University of Illinois Press, 2000 [1991]), 4–5.
123 Turner and Turner, *Image and Pilgrimage in Christian Culture*, 252.
124 Although see account of 'terrible crush and confusion' at Kingsbridge Station, *Munster Express*, 1 July 1932.
125 *Limerick Leader*, 4 June 1932.
126 Brown, Terence. *Ireland: A Social and Cultural History*, 150–1.
127 John Eade and Michael Sallnow, *Contesting the Sacred*, 5 (emphasis in original).
128 O'Flynn, *There is an Isle*, 32.
129 Ibid., 217.
130 Danaher, *Year in Ireland*, 95–6.
131 Ibid.
132 Ibid., 137–8.
133 O'Flynn, *There is an Isle*, 218.
134 AF.
135 Danaher, *Year in Ireland*, 138.
136 O'Flynn, *There is an Isle*, 218.
137 AR.
138 AF.
139 AF.
140 Danaher, *Year in Ireland*, 139.
141 O'Flynn, *There is an Isle*, 218.
142 Ibid., 219.
143 AF.
144 AR.
145 AR.
146 AF.
147 O'Flynn, *There is an Isle*, 219.
148 AF.
149 O'Flynn, *There is an Isle*, 219.
150 Danaher, *Year in Ireland*, 144.
151 Ibid.
152 AR.
153 O'Flynn, *There is an Isle*, 220.
154 AF.
155 Pádraig R, Limerick city, conversations, May 2004 and May 2007 (PRa).
156 Danaher, *Year in Ireland*, 138.
157 AR.
158 AR.
159 AF.
160 Frank Prendergast, 'Irish Idiom in Limerick City's Vernacular English', *North Munster Antiquarian Journal* 40 (2000): 73–88.
161 AR; *Limerick Leader*, 27 April 1935.
162 Ibid.
163 *Limerick Leader*, 22 May 1935.

164 Ibid.
165 The May Eve 'bonfire' was a regular feature of children's lives in the writer's homeplace, Clareview Estate in the Ennis Road area, in the 1960s and 1970s.
166 MM.
167 TG.
168 National Folklore Collection, Vol. 1855, 99.
169 Ibid., 98–100.
170 Ibid.
171 Ibid.
172 AF; Danaher, *Year in Ireland*, 138–44.
173 AR; PR; AF.
174 Hannan and O'Donnell, *Patrick's People*, 5.
175 Akhil Gupta and James Ferguson (eds), *Culture, Power, Place: Explorations in Critical Anthropology* (London: Duke University Press, 1997), 5.
176 Ibid.
177 Brian Fallon, *An Age of Innocence: Irish Culture 1930–1960* (Dublin: Gill & Macmillan, 1998), 30.
178 Gupta and Ferguson, *Culture, Power, Place*, 6.
179 Ibid., 7.
180 See Sean Curtin, *The Marian Year Jubilee 1954–2004: Limerick's Contribution to a Celebration of Faith* (Limerick: L&S Publications, 2004).
181 Ó Cadhla, *The Holy Well Tradition*, 32.

Chapter 5: Ritual Families: Praying and Fasting Together

1   *Catechism Notes* rev. edn (Dublin: Anthonian Press, 1960), 103.
2   Patricia Lysaght, 'An Choróin Mhuire', 13–54 (includes English summary).
3   Budzik, Kerrigan and Phillips, *Complete Illustrated Guide to Catholicism*, 227; 70–1.
4   Lysaght, 'An Choróin Mhuire', 19.
5   Ibid., 53.
6   Louise Fuller, *Irish Catholicism since 1950*, 25.
7   Lysaght, 'An Choróin Mhuire', 53.
8   See Chapter 4, 'Senses of Place'.
9   NP.
10   MM.
11   EL.
12   NP.
13   JL.
14   PR.
15   TG.
16   GK.
17   AR.
18   PD.
19   MM.
20   In my own experience of growing up in Limerick in the 1960s and 1970s, it was normal for visiting family members and close friends to join in the rosary, especially if it was being said when they arrived. However, this would not always apply to the

younger generation, though it would apply more to cousins than to friends. In the case of a bereavement, it would have applied to everybody, however.

21 AF.

22 AF.

23 Discussed in Bell, 'The Genres of Ritual Action', 110.

24 See Chapter 6, 'Devotion and Belief'.

25 A photograph, in Sean Curtin, *Limerick: A Stroll Down Memory Lane, Volume 3*, shows the Stella Ballroom on Shannon Street, with a statue of Our Lady over the stage area. The photograph is undated, but Curtin suggests that the statue may have been erected in the Marian Year 1954, but also says: 'It remained there for several years, though' (14).

26 Mircea Eliade, *Patterns in Comparative Religion* (London: Sheed and Ward, 1983 [1958]), 383.

27 Lysaght, 'An Choróin Mhuire', 50.

28 *Catechism Notes* 2nd edn (Dublin: Browne & Nolan, 1919), 100.

29 Ibid., 101.

30 Ibid., 100. The literal translation for the Irish term for the rosary, *An Choróin Mhuire* is 'Mary's Crown'.

31 Lysaght, 'An Choróin Mhuire', 53.

32 Autobiographical evidence from the late nineteenth century suggests that in some households at least, fifteen decades were said. See Mící Mac Gabhann, *Rotha Mór an tSaoil* (Indreabhán: Cló Iar-Chonnachta, 2009), 34.

33 Ibid., 53–4.

34 NP.

35 GK.

36 JL.

37 EL.

38 EL.

39 Thomas G. McGrath, 'Tridentine Evolution', 512–13.

40 NP.

41 PR.

42 Fallon, *An Age of Innocence*, 186.

43 Budzik, Kerrigan and Phillips, *Complete Illustrated Guide to Catholicism*, 226.

44 Eamon Duffy, *The Voices of Morebath: Reformation and Rebellion in an English Village* (London: Yale University Press, 2001), 75.

45 Peter O'Dwyer, *Mary: A History of Devotion in Ireland* (Dublin: Four Courts, 1988), 186–7.

46 McKenna, *Life and Works of James Aloysius Cullen*, 163–4.

47 T. H. Mason, *The Islands of Ireland* (London: Batsford, 1935).

48 John Healy, *Nineteen Acres* (Galway: House of Healy, 1978), 9.

49 Colleen McDannell, *Material Christianity: Religion and Popular Culture in America* (London: Yale University Press, 1995), 19.

50 *Catechism Notes* (1919), 108; *Catechism Notes*, 29th edn (Dublin: Anthonian Press, 1944), 111.

51 *Catechism Notes* (1919), 101.

52 Ibid., 102.

53 Rev. James Abbott, *Catechism Key for Primary and Continuation Schools and for Converts* (Dublin: Gill, 1959), 70.

54 KB.

55 EL.

56 Dermot Walsh, *Beneath Cannock's Clock: The Last Man Hanged in Ireland* (Cork: Mercier, 2009), 54.

57 MB.

58 AR.

59 *Limerick Leader*, 3 April 1950.

60 *Limerick Leader*, 8 January 1930.

61 Limerick Leader, 28 January 1950.

62 *Limerick Leader*, 24 February 1940.

63 *Limerick Leader*, 1 January, 3 January and 6 January 1940.

64 As a child/teenager in Limerick in the 1960s and 1970s, I was strongly aware of this. That this belief is no longer widespread is demonstrated by David Creedon's photographs of abandoned houses, where holy pictures, statues and missals are frequently among the least-valued items left for estate agents to deal with as they see fit. See Siún Hanrahan, 'Ghosts of the Faithful Departed', *Irish Arts Review*, Spring 2008.

65 O'Flynn, *There is an Isle*, 206; MM.

66 Francois Lebrun, 'The Two Reformations: Communal Devotion and Personal Piety', 69–109.

67 McDannell, *Material Christianity*, 19.

68 Bell, 'The Genres of Ritual Action', 123–4.

69 Budzik, Kerrigan and Phillips, *Complete Illustrated Guide to Catholicism*, 241.

70 Abbott, *Catechism Key*, 43.

71 Bell, 'The Genres of Ritual Action', 123.

72 Abbott, *Catechism Key*, 42.

73 Fuller, *Irish Catholicism since 1950*, 20.

74 *Catechism Notes* (1919), 36–7; *Catechism for Children* (Dublin: Browne & Nolan, 1958), 92.

75 *Catechism Notes* (1919), 59.

76 *Catechism Notes* (1944), 60.

77 *Catechism Notes* (1960), 60.

78 *Catechism for Children* (1958), 92.

79 Fuller, *Irish Catholicism since 1950*, 98.

80 EL.

81 *Catechism Notes* (1919), 104.

82 MM.

83 PD.

84 GK.

85 ELa.

86 MM.

87 EL.

88 JL.

89 National Folklore Collection, Vol. 1720, 109.

90 EL.

91 KB.

92 EL.

93 KB.

94 AR.

95 AR.

96 AF.
97 AF.
98 O'Flynn, *There is an Isle*, 202.
99 KB.
100 Irish word for 'collection'.
101 MM.
102 AF.
103 NP.
104 Bell, 'The Genres of Ritual Action', 124.
105 Ibid., 125.
106 Brian Fallon, *An Age of Innocence*, 186.
107 Mary Douglas, *Natural Symbols* (London: Barrie and Rockcliff, 1970), 103–4.
108 Ibid., 125.
109 TG.
110 O'Flynn, *There is an Isle*, 29.
111 Ibid., 29.
112 Ibid., 28.
113 Ibid., 28.
114 Ibid., 201–2.
115 Peter Burke, *Popular Culture in Early Modern Europe* (London: Temple Smith, 1978), 191.
116 L. M. Ó Cuileáin, *An Saol in Éirinn* (Baile Átha Cliath: Oifig an tSoláthair, 1976), 23–55.
117 Burke, op. cit., 193.
118 KB.
119 AR.
120 MMa.
121 O'Flynn, *There is an Isle*, 193.
122 KB; MM.
123 AR.
124 KB; O'Flynn, *There is an Isle*, 193.
125 Ibid., 194.
126 AR.
127 Burke, *Popular Culture*, 178.
128 Ibid., 188.
129 AF.
130 Mike D, conversation, 29 January 1988. Síle de Cléir, 'An Pháirc'.
131 AR.
132 MM.
133 AR; AF.
134 Burke, *Popular Culture*, 179.
135 EL.
136 MM. *Bailiúchán* is the Irish word for 'collection'.
137 Taves, *Religious Experience Reconsidered*, 14.
138 Honko, *Science of Religion*, 373.
139 Roy A. Rappaport, *Ritual and Religion in the Making of Humanity* (Cambridge: Cambridge University Press, 1999), 27.
140 For a list of the fifteen Mysteries, see *Catechism Notes* rev. edn (1960), 103–4.
141 Bell, 'The Genres of Ritual Action', 128.

142 Rappaport, *Ritual and Religion*, 209.
143 Ibid.
144 Bell, 'The Genres of Ritual Action', 120–3.
145 See for example, *Limerick Leader*, 2 March 1960.
146 Rappaport, *Ritual and Religion*, 210.
147 Ibid., 208.
148 Ibid., 257.

Chapter 6: Devotion and Belief

1   Margaret R. Miles, *The Image and Practice of Holiness: A Critique of the Classic Manuals of Devotion* (London: SCM Press, 1988), 5.
2   Ibid.
3   *Catechism Notes* (1919), 7.
4   Ibid., 20.
5   Ibid.
6   Ibid., 26; *Catechism Notes* (1944), 26; *Catechism Notes* (1960), 26.
7   *Catechism for Children* (1958), 60.
8   Ibid., 62.
9   Ibid., 65 (italics in original).
10   Ibid., 66.
11   *Catechism Notes* (1944), 37.
12   *Catechism for Children* (1958) 69; *Catechism Notes* (1944), 37.
13   JL.
14   NP.
15   TG.
16   MM.
17   Bell, 'The Genres of Ritual Action', 117.
18   See, for instance, Abbott, Catechism Key (1959), 47.
19   See, for instance *Catechism for Children* (1958), 94.
20   The Apostleship of Prayer was founded in France in 1844 and was set up in Ireland in 1863 (de Cléir, 'Reading, Writing and Religion', 33); Caitriona Clear, *Nuns in Nineteenth-Century Ireland*, 110; *Limerick Leader*, 9 January 1960.
21   Louise Fuller, *Irish Catholicism since 1950*, 20.
22   *Catechism for Children* (1958), 69–72.
23   Abbot, *Catechism Key* (1959), 57. Italics in original.
24   *Catechism Notes* (1944), 69.
25   AF.
26   GK.
27   NP.
28   AF.
29   AR.
30   NP.
31   NP.
32   AR.
33   NP.
34   NP.

Notes   221

35   *Catechism for Children* (1958), 54.
36   To protect informants' privacy and the privacy of others mentioned, all names (including those of the clergy) have been changed. See 'Notes on the Text'.
37   NP.
38   NP.
39   KB.
40   TG. Timmy is referring here to Matthew 18.21-22.
41   TG.
42   EL.
43   EL.
44   EL.
45   TC.
46   Bell, 'The Genres of Ritual Action', 119.
47   Ibid.
48   Ibid., 120.
49   See Kathleen B's comment above on her Confession regarding eating three biscuits.
50   Bell, 'The Genres of Ritual Action', 120.
51   Budzik, Kerrigan and Phillips, *Complete Illustrated Guide to Catholicism*, 153.
52   Phrases from 'Prayer for the Conversion of Russia' and 'Prayer to Saint Michael the Archangel': in the author's experience the former was (and sometimes still is) said between the decades of the rosary; the latter was a 'trimming' said after the rosary in the author's family in the 1970s.
53   *Catechism Notes* (1960), 6–7; *Catechism for Children* (1958), 18–19.
54   Bell, 'The Genres of Ritual Action', 137.
55   *Catechism for Children* (1958), 74.
56   Ibid.
57   Abbot, *Catechism Key* (1959), 47.
58   EL.
59   GK; TG. 'Angel of God' refers to the prayer invoking the protection of the guardian angel during the day to come.
60   JL.
61   JL.
62   *Catechism Notes* (1919), 109.
63   MM.
64   GK.
65   MM.
66   AF. The *púca* [usually anglicized as 'Pooka'] is a mischievous supernatural being associated with fairy belief.
67   KB.
68   AR.
69   GK.
70   MM.
71   TG.
72   KB.
73   MM.
74   McDannell, *Material Christianity*, 20.
75   PR; Diarmuid Ó Laoghaire, *Ár bPaidreacha Dúchais* (Baile Átha Cliath: FÁS, 1975), 171–86.
76   Eliade, *Patterns in Comparative Religion*, 383–5.

77 Hanrahan, 'Ghosts of the Faithful Departed'.
78 EL.
79 EL.
80 KB.
81 EL.
82 ELa. In this conversation Eileen indicated to me that she thought an elderly acquaintance was strange because he used to go 'from church to church'.
83 *Limerick Leader*, Saturday, 17 February 1940.
84 *Limerick Leader*, 4 May 1940; *Limerick Leader*, 6 January 1940; *Limerick Leader*, 3 April 1950.
85 *Limerick Leader*, 8 May 1950.
86 *Limerick Leader*, 31 May 1950.
87 Hill, *Building of Limerick*, 157.
88 Ibid.
89 MM.
90 NP.
91 NP.
92 See 'The Return of the Dead', in Seán Ó Súilleabháin, *A Handbook of Irish Folklore* (Dublin: Folklore of Ireland Society, 1963 [1942]), 244–50.
93 AF; AR.
94 O' Flynn, *There is an Isle*, 24–5.
95 AR.
96 AF.
97 De Cléir, 'An Pháirc'; for a fuller account of the *Bean Sí* tradition see Patricia Lysaght, *The Banshee: the Irish Supernatural Death-Messenger* (Dublin: O'Brien, 1996 [1986]).
98 AR.
99 MM.
100 MM.
101 MM.
102 MM.
103 MM.
104 MM.
105 Ó Cróinín and Ó Cróinín, *Seanachas Amhlaoibh Í Luínse*, 143.
106 KB.
107 AR.
108 AF.
109 KB.
110 *Catechism for Children* (1958), 48. Italics in original.
111 TC.
112 Ó Cróinín and Ó Cróinín, *Seanachas Amhlaoibh Í Luínse*; see, for instance 'Na daoine maithe ag iomáint' ('The good people playing hurling'), 167–8; 'Slua daoine ón saol eile' ('A crowd of people from the otherworld'), 142.
113 *Limerick Leader*, 3 May 1930.
114 *Limerick Leader*, 10 May 1930.
115 GK.
116 MM.
117 MM.
118 MM.

119 Miles, *Image and Practice of Holiness*, 9.
120 Rappaport, *Ritual and Religion*, 143.
121 Ibid., 257.
122 Bell, 'The Genres of Ritual Action', 137.
123 Lawrence J. Taylor, *Occasions of Faith: An Anthropology of Irish Catholics* (Dublin: Lilliput, 1995), 35–76.

Chapter 7: Creativity: Senses and Speech

1   See, for instance, 'Beautiful Craftsmanship: Improvements in Jesuit Church', *Limerick Echo*, 18 July 1926.
2   PD.
3   GK.
4   MM.
5   MM.
6   NP.
7   KB.
8   PD.
9   GK.
10 AR.
11 MM.
12 Budzik, Kerrigan and Phillips, *Complete Illustrated Guide to Catholicism*, 243.
13 MM.
14 Eliade, *Patterns in Comparative Religion*, 392–3. Italics in original.
15 KB.
16 AF.
17 EL, born 1926; AF, born 1933; MM, born 1944.
18 *Souvenir of the Diamond Jubilee: Archconfraternity of the Holy Family, Mount Saint Alphonsus, Limerick* (Limerick: Limerick Leader, 1928), 11.
19 Ibid., 13.
20 Ibid.
21 Ibid.
22 Ibid.
23 Ibid.
24 Ibid., 13–14.
25 Hill, *Building of Limerick*, 154.
26 Gillian McIntosh, 'Act of "National Communion"'.
27 Joseph Sciorra, 'The Strange Artistic Genius of This People: Ephemeral art and architecture of the Italian immigrant Catholic feste, 1890–1960'. Paper given at the joint AFS/ISFNR Annual Meeting, Miami, October 2016.
28 KB; 'Crescent Altar Society' (advertisement for a Gift and Jumble Sale), *Limerick Leader*, 7 May 1960.
29 'Votive Offerings to Our Lady of Perpetual Succour' September 1925, MSA Archives, Church Services, Box D; 'List of Donations and Gifts to the Church from Members of the Public', 1889–1960, MSA Archives, Church Services, Box D (D7).
30 'List of Donations and Gifts to the Church from Members of the Public', 1889–1960, MSA Archives, Church Services, Box D (D7).

31   Ibid.
32   Mairead Dunlevy, *Dress in Ireland: A History* (London: Batsford, 1989), 115, 172, 177; Matthew Potter, *Amazing Lace: The Limerick Lace Industry* (Limerick: Limerick City Council, 2014).
33   'List of Donations and Gifts to the Church from Members of the Public', 1889–1960, MSA Archives, Church Services, Box D (D7).
34   MM.
35   NP.
36   AR.
37   AR.
38   Wildman, 'Religious Selfhoods', 118.
39   Marie Guinard-Eliès and Catherine Bertrand-Gannerie, *La Communion Solennelle: Histoire, traditions et témoignages* (Rennes: Editions Ouest-France, 2010), 69–73.
40   MM.
41   MM.
42   Mark 14.15; Luke 22.12.
43   Caitriona Clear, '"The Minimum Rights of Every Woman?": Women's Changing Appearance in Ireland, 1940–1966', *Irish Economic and Social History* XXXV (2008): 68–80.
44   MM; see also 'Address and Presentation of Church Bell from Past Pupils', *Presentation Convent Limerick Centenary 1837–1937* (Limerick: Presentation Order, 1937), 69.
45   MM.
46   AF.
47   O'Flynn, *There is an Isle*, 280.
48   MM.
49   MM.
50   MM.
51   PD.
52   NP.
53   AF.
54   Paul Stoller, *Sensuous Scholarship* (Philadelphia: University of Pennsylvania Press, 1997), xv–xvi.
55   Publicly sponsored talent competition held in Limerick every year with the co-operation of schools and music/drama teachers.
56   AF.
57   AF.
58   Budzik, Kerrigan and Phillips, *Complete Illustrated Guide to Catholicism*, 64.
59   *Limerick Leader*, 7 September 1935.
60   'Town Topics', *Limerick Leader*, 1 May 1935. The Thomond *Feis* may have been the forerunner of the *Féile Luimní*.
61   Kathleen B, born in 1923, would have been fifteen in 1938 and has clear memories of this event; Eileen L, born in 1926, remembers the festival in the early 1940s. The festival lapsed for three years in the early 1950s but was reinstated in 1954: Noreen P, born in 1941 and Máirín M, born in 1942, both remember participating in the mid-1950s; see also Dom Winoc Mertens O.S.B., 'Liturgical Festival', in *Catholic Life*, July 1954, 17.
62   MM.
63   KB.

64 EL; NP; MM.
65 EL; 'Glenstal' refers to the Benedictine Abbey in Glenstal, Murroe, Co. Limerick.
66 GK.
67 NP; 'the monks from the Abbey' refers to the Benedictine monks in Glenstal Abbey.
68 MM.
69 KB.
70 AF.
71 AF.
72 AF.
73 KB.
74 EL.
75 Harry Haskell, *The Early Music Revival: A History* (London: Thames and Hudson, 1988), 37–8.
76 Tom Hayes, 'A Virtuous Alliance: Muscular and Musical Christianity in Late Nineteenth-century Limerick', in Liam Irwin, William Nolan, Gearóid Ó Tuathaigh and Matthew Potter (eds), *Limerick: History and Society* (Dublin: Geography Publications, 2009), 515–31; O'Flynn, *There is an Isle*, 125–34.
77 Ibid., 73.
78 Michael Synnott (author's grandfather), Limerick city, conversations, early 1970s.
79 AR.
80 AR.
81 Críostóir O'Flynn, *There is an Isle*, 335.
82 AF.
83 ELa.
84 Clifford Geertz, 'Religion as a Cultural System', in Michael Banton (ed.), *Anthropological Approaches to the Study of Religion* (London: Tavistock, 1968), 1–46, 4.
85 Rappaport, *Ritual and Religion*, 385.
86 Ibid.
87 Ibid., 386.
88 Rappaport, *Ritual and Religion*, 385.
89 Taylor, *Occasions of Faith*, 32.
90 KBa.
91 O'Flynn, *There is an Isle*, 280–1.
92 Ibid., 182–3.
93 Ibid., 281; 'meela' is an anglicization of the Irish word *míle* meaning 'a thousand' or 'a great many'. 'Meela murder' is a common expression in Hiberno–English.
94 Ibid., 280: *amadán* is the Irish word for 'fool'.
95 TCa.
96 TC.
97 JL. *Geáitsé* is an Irish word meaning 'antics', in this context.
98 JL, post-interview conversation, 30 March 2004 (JLa).
99 MM.
100 See National Folklore Collection (Schools' Collection), Vol. 10, 24–5 (Tineteriffe School, Co. Limerick.) I am grateful to Máire D. Uí Riain, Doon, Co. Limerick for bringing this to my attention.
101 *Limerick Echo*, 27 April 1926.
102 *Limerick Leader*, 20 June 1960.

103 TC.
104 TC.
105 TC.
106 TC.
107 TC.
108 PD; GK; KB; EL; TG.
109 See, for instance, *Limerick Leader*, 26 January 1935.
110 TC.
111 TC.
112 TC.
113 J. J. W. Murphy, 'Our Lady of Perpetual Succour Retreat House', in *Our Catholic Life*, Easter 1956, 9–10, 23.
114 TG.
115 NP.
116 JL.
117 JL.
118 O'Flynn, *There is an Isle*, 290–8.
119 AR.
120 As told to the author by her father, Patrick Clear, in the 1970s.
121 The other two versions can be found in: Seán Bourke, 'Gurky McMahon was buried today', in *Old Limerick Journal* 1 (December 1979): 10–11; O'Flynn, *There is an Isle*, 293. A similar joke was part of the oral repertoire in the town of Newcastle West, County Limerick in the 1950s. Patrick J. O'Connor, personal communication, August 2011. See also Patrick J. O'Connor, *The New Houses: A Memoir* (Newcastle West: Oireacht na Mumhan Books, 2009).
122 Told to the author by John Fitzpatrick, County Limerick (a resident of the Killeely estate, Limerick city, in the 1960s and 1970s), March 2011.
123 Dermot Keogh and Andrew McCarthy, *Limerick Boycott 1904: Anti-Semitism in Ireland* (Cork: Mercier, 2005).
124 See *Limerick Leader*, 22 July 1935.
125 O'Flynn, *There is an Isle*, 83–4.
126 Ibid., 84.
127 Author's own experience of Limerick city from the 1960s to the 1990s.
128 D. J. Hickey and J. E. Doherty, *A Dictionary of Irish History since 1800* (Dublin: Gill & Macmillan, 1980), 544.
129 JLa.
130 JL.
131 Told to author by Limerick city taxi-driver, name unknown, January 1988.
132 Ibid.
133 See Keogh and McCarthy, *Limerick Boycott 1904* and O'Flynn 'Was there a Pogrom in Limerick?', in O'Flynn, *Remember Limerick* (Dublin: Original Writing, 2014), 1–78.
134 Ó Crualaoich, *The Book of the Cailleach*, 6.
135 Rappaport, *Ritual and Religion*, 7.
136 Ibid., 11–17.
137 Ibid., 16.

Chapter 8: Conclusion

1   Henry Glassie, *Passing the Time: The Folklore and History of an Ulster Community* (Dublin: O'Brien Press, 1982), 14–15.
2   Williams, *Religion and Popular Culture in Southwark*.
3   Wildman, 'Religious Selfhoods'.
4   McLeod, *Class and Religion*.
5   Harris, *Faith in the Family*.
6   Callum Brown, *The Death of Christian Britain*, 12–13.
7   Ibid., 57.
8   See Chapter 1, 'Historical Background'.
9   Budzik, Kerrigan and Phillips, *The Complete Illustrated Guide to Catholicism*, 79.
10   Lauri Honko, *The Folklore Process* (Turku: Nordic Institute of Folklore, 1991), 28.
11   Ó Crualaoich, *The Book of the Cailleach*, 6.
12   Ibid.
13   Hill, *Building of Limerick*, 90–142.
14   Eliade, *Patterns in Comparative Religion*, 383.
15   Joseph Sciorra, '"We Go Where The Italians Live": Religious Processions as Ethnic and Territorial Markers in a Multi-ethnic Brooklyn Neighborhood', in Robert A. Orsi (ed.), *Gods of the City: Religion and the American Urban Landscape* (Bloomington: Indiana University Press, 1999), 310–40.
16   Wildman, 'Religious Selfhoods'.
17   Tomás Ó Carragáin, *Churches in Early Medieval Ireland: Architecture, Ritual and Memory* (New, Haven: Yale University Press, 2010), 58.
18   Ibid., 57–9.
19   Anne Ridge, *Death Customs in Rural Ireland: Traditional Funerary Rites in the Irish Midlands* (Galway: Arlen House, 2009), 130–1.
20   MM; author's personal experience of same procession in the 1960s and 1970s.
21   Ó Carragáin, *Churches in Early Medieval Ireland*, 58–9.
22   NP.
23   Jim Kemmy, *The Limerick Anthology* (Dublin: Gill & Macmillan, 1996), 11.
24   Rappaport, *Ritual and Religion*, 41.
25   Gupta and Ferguson, *Culture, Power, Place*, 6.
26   See Sean Curtin, *The Marian Year Jubilee 1954–2004*.
27   Gupta and Ferguson, *Culture, Power, Place*, 7.
28   JL; TG; see also O'Flynn, *There is an Isle*, 279; *Limerick Echo*, 27 July 1926.
29   AF; KB.
30   NP; PD; TG; KB.
31   AF.
32   Williams, *Religious Belief and Popular Culture in Southwark*, 6.
33   Ulf Hannerz, *Cultural Complexity: Studies in the Social Organisation of Meaning* (New York: Columbia University Press, 1992), 198.
34   Kazimierz Dobrowolksi, 'Peasant Traditional Culture', in Teodor Shanin, *Peasants and Peasant Societies: Selected Readings* (London, 1988 [1971]), 261–77.
35   John R. Gillis, *A World of Their Own Making: A History of Myth and Ritual in Family Life* (Oxford: Oxford University Press, 1997), 17.
36   Glassie, *Passing the Time*, 71.
37   AF.

38 Críostóir O'Flynn, *There is an Isle* (this theme is to be found throughout the book).
39 TC.
40 JL.
41 TC.
42 NP.
43 *Limerick Echo*, 9 March 1926.
44 *Limerick Echo*, 30 March 1926; 20 April 1926; 9 March 1926.
45 *Halla Íde* 'St Ita's Hall' is the headquarters of *Conradh na Gaeilge*/The Gaelic League in the city.
46 *Limerick Echo*, 9 March 1926.
47 *Limerick Echo*, 30 March 1926.
48 See, for instance, *Limerick Leader*, 7 September 1935; *Limerick Leader*, 28 July 1945.
49 See Síle de Cléir, 'Ireland', in *Berg Encyclopedia of World Dress and Fashion, Volume 8: West Europe* (Oxford: Berg, 2010), 314–20.
50 O'Flynn, *There is an Isle*, 203.
51 *Limerick Echo*, 25 February 1936.
52 PD; EL.
53 TC; MM.
54 Curtin, *Limerick: A Stroll Down Memory Lane, Volume 3*, 14.
55 EL.
56 EL.
57 KB.
58 MM.
59 AF.
60 Geertz, 'Religion as a Cultural System', in Banton (ed.), *Anthropological Approaches*, 4.
61 KB.
62 EL; MM.
63 EL; GK; PD; AR; NP.
64 KB; AR; AF.
65 Taylor, *Occasions of Faith*, 32.

Sources and Bibliography

Interviewees

(NB – all interviewees' names and surname initials have been changed. See 'Notes on the text')

Áine R, Limerick city.
b. 1936. Limerick city centre, then lived in St Mary's Park, now Killalee.
Interview, Limerick city, 6 August 2009
+ other conversations 2004–11.

Anthony F, Limerick city.
1933–2015. Limerick city centre, then Killalee estate.
Pre-interview telephone discussion: 1 August 2009
Interview: Limerick city, 5 August 2009

Grace K, Limerick city.
b. 1928, Limerick city centre, now living in Dooradoyle area.
Interview: Limerick city, 10 September 2015.

Joseph L, County Clare.
b. 1925, County Clare (three miles from Limerick city), went to school and worked in
    city. Lived in Ennis Road area 1966–89, and in County Clare 1989–date.
Interview: County Clare, 30 March 2004
Post-interview session: County Clare, 30 March 2004
+ many other conversations.

Kathleen B, Limerick city.
b. 1923, grew up in King's Island, Limerick city, now living in Ennis Road area.
Pre-interview session: Limerick city, 5 March 2004
Interview: Limerick city, 2 April 2004

Máirín M, County Limerick.
b. 1942, Limerick city centre, lived in Dublin and Limerick, now living in rural area
    approx. six miles from city.
Pre-interview: Limerick city, 9 March 2004
Interview: Limerick city, 5 April 2004
+ handwritten notes, and many other conversations and telephone calls.

Eileen L, County Clare.
1926–2016. Born in Limerick city centre, lived in North Circular Road area until married
    (1950); lived in Co. Clare and Limerick (as Joseph L above)
Interview: County Clare, 30 March 2004.
+ many other conversations in person and on the telephone.

Noreen P, Limerick city.
b. 1941. King's Island, Limerick city.
Pre-interview session: Limerick city, 15 March 2004.
Interview: Limerick city, 29 March 2004.

Pádraig R, Limerick city.
b. 1926. Limerick city centre. Living in Killalee now.
Conversations about May Eve: Limerick city, May 2004 and May 2007.
Interview: Limerick city, 6 August 2009.

Peggy D Limerick city.
1912–2004. Born and lived in Limerick city.
Interview: Limerick city, 10 March 2004.

Timmy G, Limerick city.
b. 1935. St Joseph's Street area, Limerick city.
Interview: Limerick city, 9 September 2015

Tommy C, Limerick city.
b. 1938. Limerick city centre, then Killalee estate. Worked in bacon factories, spent some
    years working in England also.
Pre-interview telephone discussion: 14 June 2004
Interview: Limerick city, 16 June 2004
Post-interview session: Limerick city, 16 June 2004.

Note: The interviewees' evidence in this book was gathered mainly by recorded interview, but also by shorter conversations and casual chats. The letter 'a' following the interviewee's pseudonym in the Endnotes indicates that the evidence was gathered other than by formal interview.

Newspapers and archive sources

Census of Population of Ireland of 1946.
Census of Population of Ireland, 1961.
Saorstát Éireann, *Census of Population 1926.*
Saorstát Éireann *Census of Population 1936.*
Cork Examiner, May–June, 1932.
Limerick Echo, 1925–35.
Limerick Leader, 1925–60.
*Munster Express,*May–July 1932.
MacDonald's Irish Directory and Gazetteer, 1957–58 (Edinburgh, 1958).
Mount Saint Alphonsus Archives, Limerick.
Archconfraternity of the Holy Family Registers, 1916–60.
Box D: Church Services.
National Folklore Collection, Vols 1720, 1855.
National Folklore (Schools') Collection, Vol. 10.

Unpublished material

Cléir, Síle de, 'An Pháirc', ['Park'] Field Research Project, University College Cork: Cork, 1988.

Cléir, Síle de, 'Éadach, Feisteas agus Maisiú i Saol Traidisiúnta Oileáin Árann agus Chorca Dhuibhne' ['Cloth, dress and adornment in the Aran Islands and West Kerry'], MA diss., University College, Cork: Cork, 1992.

Cléir, Síle de, 'Reading, Writing and Religion: the Messenger in Ireland, 1888–1960', MLIS diss., University College Dublin: Dublin, 1998.

Synnott, Fionnuala, 'A Study of the Townscape of Limerick', MA diss., University College Galway: Galway, 1979.

Catechisms, prayer books, booklets, magazines and ephemera

Abbott, James. *Catechism Key for Primary and Continuation Schools and for Converts.* Dublin: M. H. Gill and Son Ltd, 1959.

Augustinian Church, Limerick: Year Book, 1959. Limerick, 1959.

Boland, Mrs John, *How to Run a CTS Case.* London: Catholic Truth Society, n.d.

Catechism for Children. Dublin: Browne and Nolan, 1958.

Catechism Notes, 2nd edn. Dublin: Browne and Nolan, 1919.

Catechism Notes, 29th edn. Dublin: Anthonian Press, 1944.

Catechism Notes, rev. edn. Dublin: Anthonian Press, 1960.

Catholic Life: The Quarterly Magazine of the Limerick Diocese, Vol. 1, No. 1, April 1954.

Catholic Life: the Quarterly Magazine of the Limerick Diocese, Vol. 1, No. 3, October 1954.

Church of Saint Alphonsus, Limerick (leaflet available in church itself, 2010).

Classified List of Publications. Dublin: Irish Messenger Office, n.d., c. 1955.

Féile Pádraig Annual Souvenir Brochure from Limerick. Limerick: Coisde Lá Le Pádraig Executive Committee, 1956.

Irish Catholic Directory and Almanac 1914. Dublin: James Duffy & Co., 1914.

Irish Catholic Directory and Almanac 1924. Dublin: James Duffy & Co., 1924.

Irish Messenger of the Sacred Heart. Dublin: Irish Messenger Office, various volumes from 1888–1960.

Our Catholic Life: The Quarterly Magazine of the Limerick Diocese, July 1955 (formerly *Catholic Life,* see above).

Our Catholic Life: The Quarterly Magazine of the Limerick Diocese, Easter 1956.

Our Catholic Life, the Quarterly Magazine of the Limerick Diocese, October 1956.

Presentation Convent Limerick Centenary 1837–1937. Limerick: Presentation Order, 1937.

A Short Catechism of Catholic Doctrine. Cork: Diocese of Cork, 1953.

Souvenir of the Diamond Jubilee: Arch-Confraternity of the Holy Family, Mount Saint Alphonsus, Limerick. Limerick: Limerick Leader, 1928.

Books and articles

Akenson, Donald Harman. *A Mirror to Kathleen's Face: Education in Independent Ireland 1922–1960*. Montreal: McGill-Queen's University Press, 1975.

Bartlett, Thomas. *Ireland: A History*. Cambridge: Cambridge University Press, 2010.

Bell, Catherine. 'The Genres of Ritual Action', in *Ritual: Perspectives and Dimensions*. Oxford: Oxford University Press, 1996.

Bourke, Seán. 'Gurky McMahon Was Buried Today', *Old Limerick Journal* 1 (December 1979): 10–11

Briody, Mícheál. *The Irish Folklore Commission: History, Ideology, Methodology*. Helsinki: Finnish Literature Society, 2007.

Brown, Callum G. *The Death of Christian Britain: Understanding Secularisation 1800–2000*, 2nd edn. London: Routledge, 2009.

Brown, Terence. *Ireland: A Social and Cultural History 1922–1979*. London: Harper Perennial, 2004 [1981], 69.

Budzik, Mary Frances, Michael Kerrigan and Charles Phillips. *The Complete Illustrated Guide to Catholicism*. London: Hermes, 2009.

Burke, Peter. *Popular Culture in Early Modern Europe*. London: Temple Smith, 1978.

Butler, Thomas C. *The Augustinians in Limerick*. Limerick: St. Augustine's Priory, 1988.

Catholic Truth Society of Ireland (CTSI). *Catholic Truth Society of Ireland Annual Report for year ending 28th February, 1959*. Dublin: Catholic Truth Society of Ireland [CTSI], 1959.

Clear, Caitriona. *Nuns in Nineteenth-Century Ireland*. Dublin: Gill and Macmillan, 1987.

Clear, Caitriona. *Women of the House: Women's Household Work in Ireland 1922–1961*. Dublin: Irish Academic Press, 2000.

Clear, Caitriona. '"The Minimum Rights of Every Woman?": Women's Changing Appearance in Ireland, 1940–1966', *Irish Social and Economic History* XXXV (2008): 68–80.

Cléir, Síle de. 'Ireland', in *Berg Encyclopedia of World Dress and Fashion, Volume 8: West Europe*. Oxford: Berg, 2010, 314–20.

Connellan, Brendan. *Light on the Past: Story of St. Mary's Parish, Limerick*. Limerick: Brendan Connellan, 2001.

Connolly, S. J. *Priests and People in Pre-famine Ireland 1780–1845*. Dublin: Gill & Macmillan, 1982.

Coogan, Timothy Patrick. *Ireland Since the Rising*. Connecticut: Greenwood Press, 1976 [1966].

Curtin, Chris, Hastings Donnan and Thomas Wilson (eds). *Irish Urban Cultures*. Belfast: Institute of Irish Studies, 1993.

Curtin, Sean. *The Marian Year Jubilee 1954–2004: Limerick's Contribution to a Celebration of Faith*. Limerick: L&S Publishing, 2004.

Curtin, Sean. *Limerick: A Stroll Down Memory Lane, Volumes 1–16*. Limerick: L&S publications/Sean Curtin Publications, 2004–16.

Danaher, Kevin. *The Year in Ireland*. Cork: Mercier, 1972.

Devereux, Eoin. 'Negotiating Community: The Case of a Limerick Community Development Group', in *Irish Urban Cultures*, Chris Curtin, Hastings Donnan and Thomas M. Wilson (eds). Belfast: Institute of Irish Studies, 1993, 63–77.

Dobrowolski, Kazimierz. 'Peasant Traditional Culture', in *Peasants and Peasant Societies: Selected Readings*, Teodor Shanin (ed.). Harmondsworth: Penguin 1988 [1971], 261–77.

Douglas, Mary. *Natural Symbols*. London: Barrie and Rockcliff, 1970.

Duffy, Eamon. *The Voices of Morebath: Reformation and Rebellion in an English Village*. London: Yale University Press, 2001.

Dunlevy, Mairead. *Dress in Ireland: A History*. London: Batsford, 1989.

Eade, John and Michael Sallnow (eds). *Contesting the Sacred: The Anthropology of Christian Pilgrimage*. Urbana: University of Illinois Press, 2000 [1991].

Egan, Bartholemew. *Franciscan Limerick: The Order of St. Francis in the City of Limerick*. Limerick: Franciscan Fathers, 1971.

Eliade, Mircea. *Patterns in Comparative Religion*. London: Sheed and Ward, 1983 [1958].

Fallon, Brian. *An Age of Innocence: Irish Culture 1930–1960*. Dublin, 1998.

Ferriter, Diarmaid. *The Transformation of Ireland 1900–2000*. London: Profile, 2005 [2004], 369–70.

Finegan, Francis. *Limerick Jesuit Centenary Record 1859–1959*. Limerick: Sacred Heart College, 1959.

Finnegan, Frances. *Do Penance or Perish: A Study of Magdalen Asylums in Ireland*. Kilkenny: Congrave Press, 2001.

Finnegan, Ruth. *Oral Traditions and the Verbal Arts: A Guide to Research Practices*. London: Routledge, 1992.

Fuller, Louise. *Irish Catholicism since 1950: The Undoing of a Culture*. Dublin: Gill & Macmillan, 2002.

Geertz, Clifford. 'Religion as a Cultural System', in *Anthropological Approaches to the Study of Religion*, Michael Banton (ed.). London: Tavistock, 1968.

Gennep, Arnold van. *The Rites of Passage*. Chicago: University of Chicago Press, 1960.

Gillis, John R. *A World of Their Own Making: A History of Myth and Ritual in Family Life*. Oxford: Oxford University Press, 1997.

Glassie, Henry. *Passing the Time: Folklore and History of an Ulster Community*. Dublin: O'Brien Press, 1982.

Glassie, Henry. *The Penguin Book of Irish Folktales*. London: Penguin, 1985.

Godson, Lisa. 'Display, Sacramentalism and Devotion: The Medals of the Archconfraternity of the Holy Family, 1922–39', in *Confraternities and Sodalities in Ireland: Charity, Devotion and Sociability*, Colm Lennon (ed.). Dublin: Columba Press, 2012, 110–25.

Gregory, Augusta (Lady). *Visions and Beliefs in the West of Ireland*. Gerrards Cross: Colin Smythe, 1970 [1920].

Guinard-Eliés and Catherine Bertrand-Gannerie. *La Communion Solennelle: Histoire, traditions et témoignages*. Rennes: Editions Ouest-France, 2010.

Gupta, Akhil and James Ferguson (eds). *Culture, Power, Place: Explorations in Critical Anthropology*. London: Duke University Press, 1997.

Hannan, Gerard. *Ashes: The Real Story of Two Boys from the Limerick Lanes*. Limerick: Treaty Stone Publishing, 1997.

Hannan, Kevin and W. Fitzmaurice. *In the Shadow of the Spire: A Profile of St. John's Parish*. Limerick: The Parish, 1991.

Hannan, Kevin and Patrick J. O'Donnell. *Patrick's People: Historical Perspectives on an Ancient and Developing Community*. Limerick: n.p., 1994.

Hannerz, Ulf. *Cultural Complexity: Studies in the Social Organization of Meaning*. New York: Columbia University Press, 1992.

Hanrahan, Siún. 'Ghosts of the Faithful Departed', *Irish Arts Review*, Spring 2008.

Harkness, David. *Northern Ireland Since 1920*. Dublin: Helicon, 1983.

Harris, Alana. *Faith in the Family: A Lived Religious History of English Catholicism 1945–82*. Manchester: Manchester University Press, 2013.

Harris, Ruth. *Lourdes: Body and Spirit in the Secular Age*. London: Viking, 1999.

Harrold, Patsy. 'Park and its People: Origin and Folklore', in *Patrick's People: Historical Perspectives on an Ancient and Developing Community*, Kevin Hannan and Patrick J. O'Donnell (eds). Limerick: n.p., 1994, 67–70.

Haskell, Harry. *The Early Music Revival: A History*. London: Thames and Hudson, 1988.

Haughton, Jonathan. 'The Historical Background', in *The Economy of Ireland: Policy and Performance of a European Region*, J. W. O'Hagan (ed.). Dublin: Gill & Macmillan, 2000, 26–37.

Hayes, Tom. 'A Virtuous Alliance: Muscular and Musical Christianity in Late Nineteenth-century Limerick', in *Limerick: History and Society*, Liam Irwin, William Nolan, Gearóid Ó Tuathaigh and Matthew Potter (eds). Dublin: Geography Publications, 2009, 125–34.

Healy, John. *Nineteen Acres*. Galway: House of Healy, 1978.

Hickey, D. J. and J. E. Doherty. *A Dictionary of Irish History since 1800*. Dublin: Gill & Macmillan, 1980.

Hill, Judith. *The Building of Limerick*. Cork: Mercier, 1991.

Honko, Lauri. 'Theories Concerning the Ritual Process: An Orientation', in *Science of Religion: Studies in Methodology*, Lauri Honko (ed.). The Hague: Mouton, 1979.

Honko, Lauri. *The Folklore Process*. Turku: Nordic Institute of Folklore, 1991.

Hughes, Harry. *Croagh Patrick (Cruach Phádraig – The Reek): An Ancient Mountain Pilgrimage*. Westport: Harry Hughes, 1991.

Hynes, Eugene. *Knock: The Virgin's Apparition in Nineteenth-century Ireland*. Cork: Cork University Press, 2008.

Ineson, George. *Community Journey*. London: Catholic Book Club, n.d.

Inglis, Tom. 'Individualisation and Secularisation in Catholic Ireland', in *Contemporary Ireland: A Sociological Map*, Sara O'Sullivan (ed.). Dublin: University College Dublin Press, 2007, 67–82.

Jackson, Kenneth. *Scéalta Ón mBlascaod*. Baile Átha Cliath: An Cumann le Béaloideas Éireann, 1938.

Jacobs, Debbie. 'Limerick Clothing Manufacturers and Retailers', in *Made in Limerick: History of Industries, Trade and Commerce, Vol. 1*, David Lee and Debbie Jacob (eds). Limerick: Limerick Civic Trust, 2003, 23–36.

Kemmy, Jim. *The Limerick Anthology*. Dublin: Gill & Macmillan, 1996.

Kenny, Mary. *Goodbye to Catholic Ireland*. London: Sinclair-Stevenson, 1997.

Keogh, Dermot and Andrew McCarthy. *Limerick Boycott 1904: Anti-Semitism in Ireland*. Cork: Mercier, 2005.

Larkin, Emmet. *The Historical Dimensions of Irish Catholicism*. New York: Arno, 1976.

Lebrun, Francois. 'The Two Reformations: Communal Devotion and Personal Piety', in *A History of Private Life: Vol. 3: Passions of the Renaissance*, Philippe Ariés and Georges Dubuy (eds). Harvard: Belknap Press, 1989, 69–109.

Lee, J. J. 'Rebellion: 1912-1922', in *Ireland 1912-1985: Politics and Society*. Cambridge: Cambridge University Press, 1989.

Lennon, Colm and Robin Kavanagh. 'The Flowering of the Confraternities and Sodalities in Ireland c.1860–1960', in *Confraternities and Sodalities in Ireland: Charity, Devotion and Sociability*, Colm Lennon (ed.). Dublin: The Columba Press, 2012, 76–96.

Litten, Julian. *The English Way of Death: The Common Funeral since 1450*. London: Robert Hale, 2002 [1991].

Logan, John. 'Frugal Comfort: Housing Limerick's Labourers and Artisans, 1841-1946', in

Limerick: History and Society, Liam Irwin, William Nolan, Gearóid Ó Tuathaigh and Matthew Potter (eds). Dublin: Geography Publications, 2009, 557–82.

Lysaght, Patricia. 'An Choróin Mhuire in Iar-Thuaisceart Thír Chonaill sa bhFichiú hAois: suíomh do dheabhóid mheánaoiseach Eorpach i gcráifeacht agus saol traidisiúnta na ndaoine', *Sinsear: The Folklore Journal* 8 (1995): 13–54

MacBrádaigh, F. S.J. (ed.). *An Chuallacht Léannta: ceiliúradh ar Íosánaigh agus léann na Gaeilge*. Baile Átha Cliath: FÁS, 2013.

Mac Mathúna, Ciarán. 'Memories of St. John' s Parish Limerick', in *In the Shadow of the Spire: A Profile of St. John's Parish*, Kevin Hannan, and W. Fitzmaurice. Limerick: n.p., 1991, 47.

MacNeill, Máire. 'The Mountain Pilgrimages', in *The Festival of Lughnasa: A Study of the Survival of the Celtic Festival of the Beginning of the Harvest*. Oxford: Oxford University Press, 1962.

Mansergh, Nicholas. *The Unresolved Question: The Anglo-Irish Agreement and its Undoing, 1912–1972*. New Haven: Yale University Press, 1991.

Mason, Thomas H. *The Islands of Ireland*. London: Batsford, 1935.

McCafferty, Des. 'Aspects of Socio-Economic Development in Limerick City since 1970: A Geographer's Perspective', in *Limerick: History and Society*, Liam Irwin, William Nolan, Gearóid Ó Tuathaigh and Matthew Potter (eds). Dublin: Geography Publications, 2009, 593–614.

McCourt, Frank. *Angela's Ashes: A Memoir*. London: HarperCollins, 1996.

McDannell, Colleen. *Material Christianity: Religion and Popular Culture in America*. London: Yale University Press, 1995.

McGrath, Thomas G. 'The Tridentine Evolution of Modern Irish Catholicism 1563–1962: A Re-examination of the "Devotional Revolution" thesis', *Recusant History* 20 (1990–1): 512–23.

McIntosh, Gillian. 'Act of "National Communion": The Centenary Celebrations for Catholic Emancipation, the Forerunner of the Eucharistic Congress', in *Ireland in the 1930s: New Perspectives*, Joost Augusteijn (ed.). Dublin: Four Courts, 1999, 83–95.

McKenna, Lambert. *The Life and Work of James Aloysius Cullen, S.J.* London: Longman's, Green and Company, 1924.

McLeod, Hugh. *Class and Religion in the Late Victorian City*. London: Croom Helm, 1974.

Miles, Margaret R. *The Image and Practice of Holiness: A Critique of the Classic Manuals of Devotion*. London: SCM Press, 1988.

Moloney, Michael. 'The Parish of St. Patrick's', in *Patrick's People: Historical Perspectives of an Ancient and Developing Community*, Kevin Hannan and Patrick J. O'Donnell (eds). Limerick: n.p., 1994, 7–14.

Morris, Brian. 'Religion: Meaning and Function', in *Anthropological Studies of Religion: An Introductory Text*, Brian Morris. Cambridge: Cambridge University Press, 1987.

Morris, J. N. *Religion and Urban Change: Croydon 1840–1914*. Suffolk: Boydell Press, 1992.

Mulcahy, Paddy. 'Growing up in St. Patrick's', in *Patrick's People: Historical Perspectives of an Ancient and Developing Community*, Kevin Hannan and Patrick J. O'Donnell (eds). Limerick: n.p., 1994, 277–8.

Nolan, Myles. *Saint Saviour's Priory Limerick 1227–1977*. Limerick: n.p., 1977.

Noonan, Ann. 'St. Patrick's Parish: 19th and 20th Centuries', in *Patrick's People: Historical Perspectives of an Ancient and Developing Community*, Kevin Hannan and Patrick J. O'Donnell (eds). Limerick: n.p., 1994, 139–77.

Ó Cadhla, Stiofán. *The Holy Well Tradition: the pattern of St. Declan, Ardmore, County Waterford, 1800–2000*. Dublin: Four Courts, 2002.

Ó Carragáin, Tomás. *Churches in Early Medieval Ireland: Architecture, Ritual and Memory*. New Haven: Yale University Press, 2010.

Ó Céileachair, Donncha. 'Sochraid Neil Chonchubhair Dhuibh', in *Bullaí Mhártain*, Síle Ní Chéileachair agus Donncha Ó Céileachair. Baile Átha Cliath: Sáirséal agus Dill, 1955, 36–44.

O'Connor, Kevin. *Ironing the Land: The Coming of the Railways to Ireland*. Dublin: Gill & Macmillan, 1999.

O'Connor, Loreto. *Passing on the Torch: A History of Mary Immaculate College, 1898–1998*. Limerick: Mary Immaculate College, 1998.

O'Connor, Patrick J. *Exploring Limerick's Past*. Newcastle West: Oireacht na Mumhan Books, 1987.

O'Connor, Patrick J. *The New Houses: A Memoir*. Newcastle West: Oireacht na Mumhan Books, 2009.

Ó Cróinín, Donncha and Seán Ó Cróinín. *Seanachas Amhlaoibh Í Luínse*, Baile Átha Cliath: Comhairle Bhéaloideas Éireann, 1980.

Ó Crualaoich, Gearóid. *The Book of the Cailleach: Stories of the Wise-Woman Healer*. Cork: Cork University Press, 2003.

Ó Cuileáin, L. M. *An Saol in Éirinn*. Baile Átha Cliath: Oifig an tSoláthair, 1976.

O'Dwyer, Peter. *Mary: A History of Devotion in Ireland*. Dublin: Four Courts, 1988.

O'Flynn, Críostóir. *There is an Isle: A Limerick Boyhood*. Cork: Mercier, 1998.

O'Flynn, Críostóir. 'Was there a Pogrom in Limerick?', in *Remember Limerick*, Críostóir O'Flynn. Dublin: Original Writing, 2014, 1–78.

Ó Giolláin, Diarmuid. 'Folklore and Nation Building', in *Locating Irish Folklore: Tradition, Modernity, Identity*. Cork: Cork University Press, 2000.

Ó Giolláin, Diarmuid. *An Dúchas agus an Domhan*. Cork: Cork University Press, 2005.

Ó Laoghaire, Diarmuid. *Ár bPaidreacha Dúchais*. Baile Átha Cliath: FÁS, 1975.

Ó Súilleabháin, Seán. *Caitheamh Aimsire ar Thórraimh*. Baile Átha Cliath, 1960.

Ó Súilleabháin, Seán. *A Handbook of Irish Folklore*. Dublin: Folklore of Ireland Society, 1963 [1942].

Ó Súilleabháin, Seán. *Irish Wake Amusements*. Dublin: Mercier, 1979.

Phoenix, Eamon. *Northern Nationalism: Nationalist Politics, Partition and the Catholic Minority in Northern Ireland, 1890–1940*. Belfast: Ulster Historical Foundation, 1994.

Potter, Matthew. *The Government and the People of Limerick*. Limerick: Limerick City Council, 2006.

Potter, Matthew. *Amazing Lace: A History of the Limerick Lace Industry*. Limerick: Limerick City Council, 2014.

Prendergast, Frank. 'Irish Idiom in Limerick City's Vernacular English', *North Munster Antiquarian Journal* 40 (2000): 73–88.

Prendergast, Frank. *St. Michael's Parish: Its Life and Times*. Manchester: Gabriel Communications, 2000.

Prendergast, Frank. 'The Decline of Traditional Limerick Industries', in *Made in Limerick: History of Industries, Trade and Commerce, Vol. 1*, David Lee and Debbie Jacobs (eds). Limerick: Limerick Civic Trust, 2003, 1–22.

Presentation Convent Limerick Centenary 1837–1937. Limerick: Presentation Order, 1937.

Raftery, Mary. *Suffer the Little Children: The Inside Story of Ireland's Industrial Schools*. Dublin: New Island Books, 1999.

Rappaport, Roy A. *Ritual and Religion in the Making of Humanity*. Cambridge: Cambridge University Press, 1999.

Ridge, Anne. *Death Customs in Rural Ireland: Traditional Funerary Rites in the Irish Midlands*. Galway: Arlen House, 2009.

Russell, Elizabeth. 'Holy Crosses, Guns and Roses: Themes in Popular Reading Material', in *Ireland in the 1930s: New Perspectives*, Joost Augusteijn (ed.). Dublin: Four Courts, 1999, 11–28.

Sciorra, Joseph. 'We Go Where the Italians Live: Religious Processions as Ethnic and Territorial Markers in a Multi-ethnic Brooklyn Neighborhood', in *Gods of the City: Religion and the American Urban Landscape*, Robert A. Orsi (ed). Bloomington: Indiana University Press, 1999, 310–40.

Shinners, Eoin. 'Gerry Griffin: Funeral Director', in *Made in Limerick Volume 2: A History of Trades, Industries and Commerce*, David Lee and Debbie Jacobs (eds). Limerick: Limerick Civic Trust, 2006, 255–6.

Shopes, Linda. 'Oral History and the Study of Communities: Problems, Paradoxes and Possibilities', in, *The Oral History Reader*, Robert Perks and Alistair Thomson (eds), 2nd edn. London: Routledge, 2006, 261–70.

Stoller, Paul. *Sensuous Scholarship*. Philadelphia: University of Pennsylvania Press, 1997.

Taves, Ann. *Religious Experience Reconsidered: A Building-Block Approach to the Study of Religion and Other Special Things*. Oxford: Princeton University Press, 2009.

Taylor, Lawrence J. 'Bás in Éirinn: The Cultural Construction of Death in Ireland', *Anthropological Quarterly* 62 (4) (1989): 175–87.

Taylor, Lawrence J. *Occasions of Faith: An Anthropology of Irish Catholics*. Dublin: Lilliput, 1995.

Turner, Victor and Edith Turner. *Image and Pilgrimage in Christian Culture*. New York: Columbia University Press, 1978.

Varenne, Hervé. 'Dublin 16: Accounts of Suburban Lives', in *Irish Urban Cultures*, Chris Curtin, Hastings Donnan and Thomas M. Wilson (eds). Belfast: Institute of Irish Studies, 1993, 99–121.

Walsh, Dermot. *Beneath Cannock's Clock: The Last Man Hanged in Ireland*. Cork: Mercier, 2009.

Walsh, Michael. *The Apparition at Knock: A Critical Analysis of Facts and Evidence*. Dublin: Veritas, 2008 [1955].

Wildman, Charlotte. 'Religious Selfhoods and the City in Inter-War Manchester', in *Urban History* 38 (1) (April 2011): 103–23.

Williams, S. C. *Religious Belief and Popular Culture in Southwark c.1880–1939*. Oxford: Oxford University Press, 1999.

Yow, Valerie. 'Do I Like Them Too Much?: Effects of the Oral History Interview on the Interviewer and Vice-Versa', *Oral History Review* 24 (1) (Summer 1997): 55–79.

Electronic resources

www.archive.thetablet.co.uk (accessed 17 November 2015).

www.catholiclibrary.ie 'About the Library' (accessed 17 November 2015).

www.childabusecommission.ie (accessed 30 September 2011).

www.dominicanpublications.com (accessed 23 September 2016).

www.dspace.mic.ul.ie. Guiry, Ruth. 'Public Health and Housing in Limerick City

1850–1935: A Geographical Analysis' MA diss, Mary Immaculate College, Limerick, 2013 (accessed 10 August 2015).

www.iec2012.ie 'The 1932 Congress (Archive)' (accessed 17 August 2016).

www.justice.ie/en/JELR/Pages/PB09000504 *Report by Commission of Investigation into Catholic Archdiocese of Dublin* (Murphy Report on Church's handling of allegations of child abuse by clerics) (accessed 26 July 2011).

http://www.limerickdioceseheritage.org/StMunchins.htm (accessed 21 February 2011).

http://www.limerickdioceseheritage.org/StJosephs/textStJosephs.htm (accessed 4 August 2011).

www.magdalenelaundries.com (accessed 30 September 2011).

www.mbhcoi.ie (accessed 4 March 2017).

www.memorylanelimerick.com for more historical photographs of Limerick. (accessed September 2016).

www.measuringworth.com (accessed 23 September 2016).

Illustrations and maps

Figure 1: Sean Curtin Collection
Figure 2: Limerick Museum: 1998.0522
Figure 3: Redemptorist Provincial Archives, no. 1091
Figure 4: Sean Curtin Collection
Figure 5: Sean Curtin Collection
Figure 6: Redemptorist Provincial Archives, no. 1079
Figure 7: Redemptorist Provincial Archives, no. 1087
Figure 8: Redemptorist Provincial Archives, no. 1066
Figure 9: Redemptorist Provincial Archives, no. 1061
Figure 10: Redemptorist Provincial Archives, no. 1062
Figure 11: Redemptorist Provincial Archives, no. 1048
Figure 12: Redemptorist Provincial Archives, no. 1040
Figure 13: Limerick Museum: 1998.1699
Figure 14: Sean Curtin Collection.

Maps 2, 3 and 5: based on Limerick Corporation, *Limerick Official Guide and Street Map* (1976)
Maps 1 and 4: based on maps from Limerick County Council, *Limerick Environs Development Plan* (1974)

Index

Page references in *italic* denote an image.

Theory of Technology

David Clarke, *editor*

Transaction Publishers
New Brunswick (U.S.A.) and London (U.K.)

New material copyright © 2005 by Transaction Publishers, New Brunswick, New Jersey. Originally published in *Knowledge, Technology, & Policy,* Fall 2002, Vol. 15, No. 3, copyright © 2002 Transaction Publishers and Fall 2003, Vol. 16, No. 3, copyright © 2003 Transaction Publishers.
www.transactionpub.com

This book is printed on acid-free paper that meets the American National Standard for Permanence of Paper for Printed Library Materials.

Library of Congress Catalog Number: 2004047954
ISBN: 0-7658-0844-7
Printed in the United States of America

Library of Congress Cataloging-in-Publication Data

Theory of technology / David Clarke, editor.
    p. cm.
    Papers originally published in Knowledge, technology, & policy, Fall 2002, Vol. 15, No. 3 and Fall 2003, Vol. 16, No. 3.
    Includes bibliographical references and index.
    ISBN 0-7658-0844-7 (pbk.)
    1. Technology—Management. 2. Technology—History. I. Clarke, David, 1942- II. Knowledge, technology, & policy.

T49.5.T53 2004
600—dc22

                      2004047954

Contents

Foreword

Jared Diamond, in *Guns, Germs, and Steel* (Norton, 1997), often draws attention to troubling hiccups in the history of technology. His favorite is the Phaistos Disk of 1700 B.C., a still-undeciphered document with characters stamped (not scratched) into soft clay. It is clearly "printed" yet it took another 2,500 years for printing to "take off" despite its obvious benefits. A more popular example is Leonardo da Vinci's drawing of a helicopter that lay fallow until Igor Sikorsky designed a successful model in the twentieth century. But sometimes technology gets stuck or even reverses itself. The Chinese just up and quit the merchant marine business one day. After the fall of the Roman Empire "we" forgot how to make glass and concrete for a while. And we have been stuck with the QWERTY keyboard, despite its disadvantages, for fifty years more than necessary.

In contrast, science seems to proceed reasonably and calmly, progressing at the same rate whether there is government support or not (as Terence Kealey has shown). Popular imagination has it that the change from Classical Mechanics to the Theory of Relativity was revolutionary in the earlier part of the last century. But the hullabaloo was really concentrated in circles of artists, architects, and literary types. Classical Mechanics still explained 99 percent of phenomena and worked perfectly well for most applications of physics. Of course, relativity changed the field and opened new areas of research, but it didn't set off a causal chain leading to Political Correctness among physicists. *That* came from the science-challenged side of the campus.

In short, the orderliness of science doesn't make it better or classier—but it *does* make it easier to theorize about. But there is a more menacing side to technology, too. In science one can see things coming to a certain extent and, within limits, invoke policies, for better or worse, that direct or stymie science's progress—especially if science has adapted to government funding. Thus has stem-cell research and cloning been proscribed in certain ways. But the Internet came upon us like a summer storm. It even took Microsoft by surprise. DDT unexpectedly made birds' eggshells thinner. Technology is currently unpredictable and therefore scary. A better fundamental understanding, if possible, might make it less scary.

Our first chapter comes from Rias van Wyk and is a good whack at parsing "technology," the *thing*, from several different angles. Rias' continued stimulating discussion of the Innovation Management Network Listerv, moderated by Christopher Bart of the Technology & Innovation Management SIG of the Academy of Management, has been instrumental in bringing this volume to life.

Next comes Karol Pelc's effort at mapping the discipline—but now we are moving away from technology considered purely on its own towards *management* of technology. This hybrid, usually of business and engineering, has been a fast-growing academic field for fifteen years now. Next Jon Beard pursues a similar mapping endeavor but limits himself to looking after patterns of the *literature* of management of technology. Next Tom Clarke takes us on a tour, based on long-term empirical experience, of how the *people* of technology present unique challenges to not just management but whole organizations (hint: they don't want to be managed).

Then Richard Howey, a student of Rias van Wyk's, tries to place enterprise software—of which he is a reflective practitioner—into a meaningful pattern of technology management.

Turning the lens around are authors Fred Foldvary and Daniel Klein (Dan serves on *Knowledge, Technology & Policy's* Editorial Board, by the way). They take a rather more teleological view, not really caring what technology *is* but rather what it *does*—and, better yet, what it makes *possible*. Is this not another route to definition? And what they claim it is capable of is eliminating mountains of meddlesome, noisome, expensive mediators, in the forms of regulations, regulators, and *dirigisme* in general.

Then queen-of-the-arts parade-rainer John Cogan maintains that our Aristotelian search for the *essence* of technology is doomed. And all because of some clever tennis shoe marketing.

Peter Bond looks at technology from a biological angle. There's been a school trying to do this to the whole universe since the writings of Köhler, Bertalanffy, Lewin, and Hempel. New to this thread are concepts such as "autopoiesis," "radical constructivism," and "actor-network theory."

Finally, late arrival Kelvin Willoughby drags us through the semantics morass, and a funky fen it is indeed.

I only hope that you enjoy reading this as much as we did writing it.

David Clarke
Sarzeau, France

1

Technology: A Fundamental Structure?

Rias J. van Wyk

Because technology plays such an important part in our daily lives, in our businesses, and in government policy, we need to understand it better. But technology has not undergone the elegant simplification that marks the development of most fields of knowledge as they grow to maturity. To achieve simplification we need first to discover the fundamental structure that underpins all technologies. Such a structure may well turn out to be one of the more significant conceptual foundations of the new century. What is the state of knowledge in this area? Beginning with Babbage early in the nineteenth century, many attempts have been made to create such a structure. The history of these attempts is poorly recorded with no well-documented central theme. One approach, called Strategic Technology Analysis (STA), seems to have advanced a little further than most others. It focuses on the intrinsic characteristics of technologies. Based on these characteristics, the field offers a set of frameworks for analyzing individual technological entities as well as entire technological landscapes. These frameworks cover the (1) anatomy, (2) taxonomy, (3) evolution, and (4) ecology of technology. This chapter traces the development of these frameworks. It recommends that they be scrutinized anew and evaluated as part of a revitalized search for fundamental structure.

Background

A fascinating quest of the past few years has been the search for a fundamental theoretical structure that underpins all of technology. This search could possibly yield one of the most significant conceptual foundations for the

Rias J. van Wyk is director of the Technoscan Centre in Edina, Minnesota. He may be reached at <vanwyk@technoscan.com>.

twenty-first century. Such a fundamental structure would materially improve our understanding of technology, enhance our ability to manage it better, and increase our effectiveness in formulating public policy in this area.

It is not hard to find evidence of the need for fundamental structure. In scholarly debate the terminology of technology is not used in a consistent manner. The very word has vastly different meanings—ranging all the way from computers and software to the totality of all tools devised by humankind. When describing individual technologies we do not refer to consistent distinguishing characteristics. Concepts like nano-technology, space technology, nuclear technology, and information technology exist side by side. And yet each relies on a different descriptor. This draws attention to a related issue. In technology we do not have a commonly accepted formal taxonomy, a way of classifying all technologies. Different organizations use different versions, mostly custom-made. All in all the theory of technology does not seem to have a satisfactory overall paradigm. The status of the field can best be described as being in the "unstructured," "pragmatic," or "pre-paradigmatic" phase.

In the practice of technology management, there is also evidence of the need for better structure. Most corporate managers will admit to being blindsided by new technology. Rare indeed is the CEO who systematically maps the global technological landscape and who knows where to expect definitive developments. In the case of technology policy, very few policymakers have a coherent view of the technological frontier and understand the intricate interplay of specialization and fusion in technological evolution. In the world of investments, monies flow in and out of technology-based companies more on the basis of fashion than on the basis of rational technology analysis. Is it not ironic that in the international stock markets, technology has become synonymous with disruptive and impoverishing volatility?

Why does such an unstructured state of affairs exist? The answer is that for most people it does not appear extraordinary; it reflects the inherent nature of technology. The popular view of technology is that it consists of a large number of separate fields, each with its own special characteristics and terminology. There is no big picture and there is no unifying concept. And, some would argue, there is no need for them. Most people would say that we understand technology well enough as it is. In fact things are going very well. More and more is costing less and less. We now advance further in a shorter space of time than ever before. Also, we are not doing this blindly. We can make roadmaps for individual technologies and we can plot their progress into the future. Problems do exist, but they are of a detailed nature and can probably be cured with a little better science and engineering.

It is against this backdrop that we hear the voice of those in favor of fundamental structure. This voice asserts that in spite of a general level of satisfaction with technology, we still lack comprehensive understanding. We do not yet have the "big picture." We cannot show where our roadmaps lie on a global technological atlas. In fact, we do not even *have* such an atlas. Much tidying-up needs to be done. No wonder then that in the seventies Friedrich Rapp, a technology philosopher, exclaimed, "But it is an astonishing fact that the commonly accepted and carefully investigated philosophy of science has not yet found its counterpart in a philosophy of technology" (Rapp, 1974: vii). No wonder too that in the nineties Chris Farrell, a technology manager, started a groundbreaking article with the assertion "Technology is in need of a unifying concept to aid in its comprehension" (Farrell, 1993: 161). And no wonder that, at the close of the millennium, a study group sponsored by the National Science Foundation in the United States stressed the need for a "framework and a book of knowledge of the Management of Technology" (Khalil, 2000: 20).

The Search for Fundamental Structure

What do we mean by fundamental structure? Every field of knowledge seems to undergo a deep and elegant simplification at some stage of its development. So, in the eighteenth century, biology was raised to a new level of elegance by the Linnean taxonomy. In the nineteenth century physics benefited from the electromagnetic spectrum, while chemistry was irrevocably simplified by the periodic table of the elements. Then, in the twentieth century, macroeconomics was given structure through the elements of final demand and the Keynesian equation. These fundamental structures help us form a simplified big picture against which to map all the individual details that constitute a field of knowledge.

Frequently these fundamental structures receive only scant attention from contemporary professionals. Sometimes they are pointedly ignored. Sometimes they are met with skepticism and derision. This seems to be inherent in the process of diffusion. However, in the end, elegance and economy of thought do prevail. The structures enter daily use, everybody forgets the turbulence associated with their creation, and we all are the better off.

What is the position with respect to technology? Interestingly enough, technology was one field that early on attracted the attention of a universal thinker, Charles Babbage (Mazlish, 1993: 137.) In the early nineteenth century, and even before the creation of the periodic table and the electromagnetic spectrum, Babbage advocated a general understanding of what he called "the processes of manufacture"—today we may call them manufacturing technologies. To support this general understanding he offered a classification (discussed later). More important at this stage is Babbage's approach. "The difficulties of understanding the processes of manufacture have unfortunately been greatly overstated. To examine them with an eye of a manufacturer, so as to be able to direct others to repeat them, does undoubtedly require much skill and previous acquaintance with the subject; but merely to apprehend their general principles and mutual relations is within the power of every person possessing a tolerable education" (Babbage, 1835: iv). He then proceeded to outline his taxonomy of processes of manufacture. Unfortunately, and in spite of its appeal to people with a "tolerable education," Babbage's pioneering effort in this field remained largely unexplored. It never grew into a general system for understanding. The flurry of universal thinking that characterized the eighteenth and nineteenth centuries did not succeed in endowing technology with a profound simplification that would make it more comprehensible.

For over a century-and-a-half, the question of fundamental structure seems to have lapsed into relative obscurity. Nevertheless, a continuous but thin stream of authors addressed this issue. But these efforts did not follow a consistent line of investigation and seemed to be isolated from each other. We cannot offer a complete review here but can illustrate the type of initiatives with some examples from the late twentieth century.

In the United States the early sixties saw a concern with understanding the phenomenon of "automaticity" (Amber and Amber, 1962). Here we should recall that automation was a prevailing concern at the time and that "data automation" was an early term for what is now known as *IT*. The sixties also saw the work of James Bright and his classic analysis of the basic trends in technology development (Bright, 1963).

The seventies saw further advances. On the continent a publication in German of a "systems theory of technology" had a defining influence on the development of fundamental structure (Ropohl, 1979). In the United States, Miller published a monumental work, *Living Systems*. This book provided a most useful set of templates for comprehending technology (Miller, 1978). These two approaches augment each other admirably.

In the eighties the initiatives seemed to proliferate—a development that may have been associated with a revival of the field of management of technology (MOT). At MIT, the Management of Technology Group led by Ed Roberts lent considerable weight to emphasizing the importance of fundamental structure and encouraging scholars in this area. Elsewhere, writings appeared on the "functional approach to technology" (Majer, 1985), "technometrics" (Sahal, 1985; Grupp and Hohmeyer, 1986), and "metatechnology" (le Duff and Maïsseu, 1988). The eighties also saw the appearance of a comprehensive text on *A Theory of Technology* (De Gregori, 1985).

The nineties saw further creative ideas on unifying concepts. Examples included "theoretical technology" (Farrell, 1993) and "technocology" (Badawy, 1996).

Where do we stand today as we enter the new millennium? Is technology still in its pre-paradigmatic or uncodified phase in terms of its overall theory? Quite rightly we may ask: Is there no candidate to offer us a fundamental structure? Is it not time to take stock of what we have, to refocus our efforts, and to move forward towards a generally accepted set of frameworks?

In this spirit of reexamination we wish to focus on one initiative that seems to have progressed a little further than most others towards a comprehensive theory—an initiative that has become known as "strategic technology analysis" (STA). In the following sections we explore this initiative a little more fully.

Strategic Technology Analysis (STA)

Strategic technology analysis (STA) may be defined as an approach to evaluating technologies on the basis of their intrinsic characteristics. It offers frameworks that provide structure to technology analysis. These frameworks help us analyze individual technological entities as well as entire technological landscapes. This may sound like a simple and unremarkable statement, but it contains two powerful notions.

The first is the emphasis on inherent characteristics. This draws attention to the role of the intrinsic potency of technologies as opposed to their external features.

The second is the concept of the technological entity. This is not a commonly-used expression. Technology analysts chose it, and only after much soul-searching, because they needed a unit of analysis on which they could focus. They needed an object of inquiry that they could dissect and classify, and for which they could track evolutionary trends. In the end it provided the key to a whole new field of knowledge.

An analogy to biology helps illustrate the significance of the concept. The theory of biology is concerned with understanding individual living species like tulips, daisies, cats, and dogs. In seeking common structure across different species, biologists conceive of levels of generalization. They would, for instance, arrive at the categories *plants* and *animals*. To find yet deeper persistent structure, biologists conceive of yet higher levels of generalization at which the objects of their inquiry are called *organisms*. Organisms are the formal units of analysis in biology.

In the case of technology, engineers have a deep understanding of individual *technological species*, e.g., jigs, dies, processors, and lathes. At a higher level of generalization these may be grouped into tools and machines. The analogy to biology holds up quite well. But at the highest level of generalization a problem arises. There is no word in common English usage that is the technological equivalent of *organism*. There is no set of structured thoughts to deal with technology at this level.

While at first blush this appears to be a trivial observation, it was a significant signal for the technology analysts. The absence of such a word reflected a rather primitive state of affairs intellectually. Being unnamed, technological phenomena at his level were unidentified and, amazing to say, virtually unknown to the vast majority of people.

In recognizing the existence of technological entities, the analysts there-fore took a major philosophical step. A commonly occurring but hardly no-ticed phenomenon was brought into view. Henceforth, technological entities could be discussed, observed, and classified and their evolutionary trends tracked.

Having identified what it is that they were going to analyze, the analysts then asked themselves four fundamental questions:

1. Is there a common framework for analyzing individual technological enti-ties—a possible *anatomy* for technology?
2. Can these entities be grouped into a number of logical and distinct catego-ries—is there a *taxonomy* of technologies?
3. Is there a simple set of trends that describe the long-term trajectories along which these entities develop—are there patterns of *evolution* in technol-ogy?
4. Are there criteria for the social acceptance of technology—are there guide-lines for understanding the *ecology* of technology?

The pursuit of these questions started roughly in the seventies and contin-ues to this day. It is involving individuals in various centers around the world. It has seen many false starts and much reworking. At this stage it has yielded a set of five frameworks that constitute its core theory—one framework each in response to question 1, 2 and 4, and two frameworks in response to question 3. These have been published, refined, and experimented with in practice. They are reviewed below. This review takes the approach of "work in progress." The frameworks are not offered as *faites accompli.*

The Anatomy of Technology

Definition

The first step in creating the theory of STA was to define technology. The question of definition is complex, as is to be expected due to the relatively primitive state of affairs in technological theory. We will not retrace the debate here. The suggested definition is: *Technology is created competence. It is expressed in technological entities consisting of devices, procedures, and acquired human skills.*

Four points about this definition are important:

*   The term *created* describes the artificial nature of technology. It is made; it does not occur spontaneously in nature.
*   The term *competence* emphasizes that technology is concerned with *ways and means* for taking action; it is not concerned with the ultimate *ends* of doing so.

- The term *technological entity* has already been referred to. It may be visualized as a repository of competencies.
- Finally the expression *devices, procedures, and acquired human skills.* This expression reflects the constituent elements of a technological entity. The hardware and software components are clear. *Skill* requires a qualification. While a certain type of human skill is included, humans as a whole are not. Humans are not technological entities and not part of the definition of technology.

Clearly this definition gives rise to a number of questions. But dealing with all of them would involve theorizing beyond the scope of the article. We will have to do it elsewhere. The next question to be addressed here is, how do we dissect a technological entity and discern its unique features?

Framework of Basic Features

A framework of basic features is suggested below. In this framework *function* refers to the role that the technological entity plays within a given system. To simplify the description of function, it starts off with a single sentence using one verb and one noun. As it turns out, it is possible to reduce the many possible verbs to three major activities: *process, transport,* and *store.*

- *Processing* involves receiving inputs of one kind and transforming them into outputs of another kind.
- *Transporting* involves receiving inputs and moving them a certain distance before releasing them.
- *Storing* involves receiving inputs and holding them for a period before releasing them.

Framework 1
Basic features

Characteristic	Question
Function	What does the entity do?
Principle of operation	How does it do it?
Performance	How well does it do it?
Structure	How is the entity composed?
Fit	What is the hierarchial position?
Material	What is the entity made of?
Size	How large is the entity?

The many possible nouns, reflecting the objects to which the above actions apply, can also be reduced to three categories; matter, energy, and information.

- *Matter* is that which has substance—symbolized by *M*,
- *Energy* is that which performs work—symbolized by *E*,
- *Information* is that which conveys meaning—symbolized by *I*.

Using the simplifying structures outlined above, it is possible to describe the function of any technological entity in terms of one of nine sentences (Ropohl, 1979.) The entity acts on M, E, or I to either process, transport, or store them.

Principle of operation refers to the way in which the technological entity performs its function. Unfortunately, this is an area in which no vast simplification seems possible at this stage. Examples have to suffice. So the handling of M and E could involve mechanical, chemical, or biological processing. The handling of I could involve electronics or optics. And there are many more examples.

Performance describes how well the technological entity executes its function. There are various measures of performance, many of them uniquely associated with a particular entity. However, four measures occur repeatedly and are useful starting points for individual analyses. The four performance measures are:

- *Efficiency*: measured as the ratio of output to input. As mentioned, the predominant output is M, E, or I depending on the function that the entity performs. For each entity, inputs can be M, E, or I depending on which aspect of efficiency is being expressed.
- *Throughput*: a measure of capacity expressed as output in relation to time. The expression depends on whether a *processing, transporting,* or *storing* entity is being observed. For a *processing* entity the ratio is simply M/T, E/T, or I/T. For a *transporting* entity output has to be adjusted to include distance, e.g., for a matter transporting entity the output would be; M x distance. (A similar adjustment would be made for E and I handling entities.) The final expression would then be M x distance/T. For a *storing* entity the output includes a measure of time, e.g., M x T for a matter store, with a similar structure for E and I stores.
- *Density*: i.e., functional density reflecting the output of the entity in relation to the physical space required by it. M/S, E/S, and I/S are the major expressions.
- *Precision*: i.e., a measure of accuracy, clarity, fineness, or tolerance.

Structure refers to the appearance and fundamental design of a technological entity. As in the case of principle of operation, there is no simple format to call on to describe structure. Analysts normally look at three aspects: *shape, configuration,* and *complexity.*

- *Shape* is a very obvious feature. To say that an entity is round, square, or box-like helps us picture its overall appearance. Technological innovations are frequently based on the use of new shapes. For instance, the recent attempt at using tiny balls as the basis for semiconductor circuits could introduce a whole new approach to the way in which electronic devices are built.
- *Configuration* refers to the way in which the technological entity is assembled. Again there is no simple systematic key for describing configuration. It is useful to look for the most obvious features first to see whether these contain an element of uniqueness. In the case of an aircraft, are the wings above or below the fuselage? In the case of an automobile, is the engine in the front or in the back?
- *Complexity* is usually associated with the number of subsystems that make up the system, and the links between these. The more the links the greater the complexity.

Fit refers to the compatibility between an entity and the greater system in which it is imbedded. In discussing fit it is useful to refer to the appropriate level in the technological hierarchy. The concept of the technological hierarchy is one of the most useful tools in technology analysis. It reminds us that no technological entity exists by itself. It usually is part of a larger agglomeration, and is itself an agglomeration of more basic units. The technological hierarchy may be thought of as consisting of a number of levels. Again there is no international standard categorization of these levels. The following key can serve a guide.

- Multi-system system
- Multi-product system
- Product
- Component
- Part
- Material

Entities at a higher level in the hierarchy are typically more complex than entities at the lower levels.

There are many *materials*. We may simply think of the periodic table of the elements and of all the possible combinations of these. However, in practice we can usually work quite comfortably with five or six categories (Ashby, 1987).

- Metal
- Plastic
- Ceramic
- Glass
- Pure carbon
- Composites

In addition, it is useful to distinguish in our minds what the role is that the material plays. These can be:

• Functional
• Structural

These roles have also been referred to as *primary* and *secondary* roles. The former relates to special attributes of the material, such as photovoltaic, magnetic, conductive, and the like, and is usually associated with the principle of operation. The latter refers to the provision of structure and containment.

Size is one of the most obvious yet frequently overlooked features. Is the entity on the "human scale" which is about one yard or meter, i.e., 10^0 meters, on the macro scale, i.e., 10^3 meters, or on the micro scale, i.e., 10^{-3} meters down to 10^{-9} meters?

Use of the Basic Framework

In practice this framework has been used to structure technological presentations. Non-specialists use it to understand descriptions of technologies offered by specialists. Specialists use it to structure their presentations in terms of a "common grammar." In addition to its utility value the framework also provides the key to four further frameworks. The characteristics identified are used over and over again throughout the field of technology analysis.

The Taxonomy of Technology

Background

The next step in the quest for fundamental structure was to find an appropriate system of classification. It turned out that this was one of the unresolved issues in the philosophy of technology. It reappears each decade in the list of unfinished business (De Meyer, 1988; Farrell, 1993).

In a review of approaches to technological classification, Horner distinguishes between two major categories (1992):

• A bibliographic or linguistic approach
• A taxonomic approach

The first approach looks at what has been created and then sorts individual creations into meaningful categories. When many creations of a like kind are available, the relevant category becomes large and is appropriately subdivided. When creations of a certain kind are not seen, the category simply does not come into existence. The second approach relies on an underlying theoretical system. Examples include those classifications referred to in the section *The Search for Fundamental Structure.*

The task of technological classification was a daunting one. To achieve simplicity while being comprehensive is almost a contradiction in terms.

Early History

One of the earliest attempts at classification is the one by Charles Babbage, referred to earlier. He suggests the following categories (xiv-xv):

- Accumulating power
- Regulating power
- Increase and diminution of velocity
- Extending the time of action of forces
- Saving time in natural operations
- Exerting forces too great for human power, and executing operations too delicate for human touch
- Registering operations

As mentioned before, this classification did not gain widespread acceptance and the need for an adequate system remains to this day.

Recent History

In the sixties Teichmann offered a particularly perceptive review of various approaches to technological classification. He suggested five approaches:

- Characteristics of historical development
- Natural laws or scientific concepts embodied in the technology
- Branch of production
- Function within a branch or process of production
- Principles of construction

Originally published in German, these views were translated into English in the mid-seventies. Teichmann himself was not very satisfied with the state of knowledge on technological classification. "A cement mixer and a machine for kneading dough have, as far as I know, a similar structure, but I have never known the two of them assigned to the same category of technical appliances" (Teichmann, 1974). More work was needed.

The Functional Classification

How did the technology analysts proceed? In addition to reviewing the history of classification, they reviewed Framework 1 as described above. They then tried to identify which technological characteristic would offer a suitable basis for classification. It turned out that technological function has long been a basis advocated by a group of German philosophers, notably Ropohl (1979.) This approach has four advantages.

- It starts with a simple three-fold classification and then expands into a nine-fold one.
- It can be expanded further—it is compatible with more comprehensive systems.
- It is intuitively appealing.
- It is possible to condense the entire array of technological entities into a one-page format.

The essence of the nine-cell classification of technological functions is given in Framework 2. The functional classification provides a cell for any technological entity, whether large or small, simple or complex, modern or ancient. It applies to each level of the technological hierarchy from multi-system systems down to individual parts.

The functional classification is not a strict taxonomy. Technological entities do not belong in only one cell or another. Certain entities can be put to different uses. Classification is very much in the eye of the beholder.

When we use the classification we have to obtain clarity on:

- The predominant *output* that best describes the technology observed.
- The level of the *technological hierarchy* that we are focusing on.

Framework 2
Nine-cell functional classification

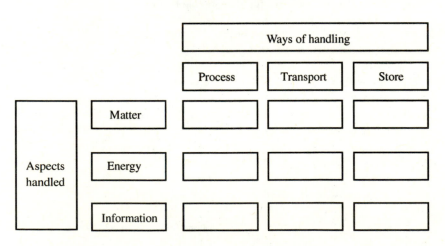

- The *role* of the entity being observed. Is it to be observed independently, i.e., in terms of its immediate task; or is it to be observed in conjunction with others, i.e., within a larger system?

Use of the functional classification

In practice the nine-cell classification has been used in a number of applications:

- To structure a technology scan—to identify landmark technologies and to place these within a comprehensive map of the technological landscape.
- To structure a technology audit—to place core competencies in an appropriate setting.
- To provide an overview of technology projects within a research program.
- To observe interaction between various technologies.

The nine-cell classification of technological functions is offered here as a useful approach to structure thinking on technology. It is not the final word. It is not a strict taxonomy and it is open to flexible interpretation. But it does help us reduce the whole array of technologies into a simple viewable format and it does help us understand where our own technological initiatives fit into an overall framework.

The Evolution of Technology

We cannot think of technology without being aware of continuous change. The technological landscape evolves all the time. This thrust is fed by the enormous amount of resources that humankind devotes each year to creating new technology. To view this change, technology analysts sought a simple model.

History

Over the years many authors have addressed this question and have identified different kinds of trends. These include:

- Envelope curves (Ayres, 1968)
- Technological trajectories (Dosi, 1982)
- S-curves (Foster, 1986)
- Substitution curves (Mansfield, 1961; Linstone and Sahal, 1976)
- Learning curves (Abernathy and Wayne, 1974)
- Curves of performance parameters (Bright, 1978), and many more.

This is one area well served by theory. The question for us is whether it is possible to combine these various manifestations of technological change into one comprehensive model.

Earlier Approaches

The best known approach to understanding technological change at the macro level came from Bright—more than three decades ago (1963). He suggested that the whole of technological evolution could be captured in seven trends:

- Increased capability in transportation.
- Increased mastery of energy.
- Increased control over the life of animate and inanimate things.
- Increased mastery of materials.
- Extension of human sensory capabilities.
- Increasing mechanization of physical activities.
- Increasing mechanization of intellectual activities.

For many years this was the most frequently used approach to analyze technological change at the macro level. It was extremely powerful, comprehensive, and intuitively appealing.

However, for the purpose of technology analysis, it needed refining. It would have to be compatible with the first and second frameworks described above. It would have to use the unit of analysis already agreed to.

The Cascade Model

The technology analysts proposed a view of technological evolution as a cascade of trends. Five levels may be distinguished as technological change "cascades" through the technological landscape. The model is illustrated in Framework 3.

At *level one*, technological change is viewed in terms of changing material characteristics. Materials are becoming progressively better both *functionally* and *structurally*. Examples of functional improvements include increased conductivity, increased magnetic strength, increased surface to weight ratio, and increased tolerance of heat; to name a few. Examples of improvements in the structural sense include greater strength and greater rigidity.

At level *two*, technological change is viewed as improvements in *size*, improvements in *principle of operation,* and improvements in *structure*.

- *Size*: Some entities are becoming larger, some smaller, and some both larger and smaller. Ships, aircraft, and containers are increasing in size.

Framework 3
Cascade of technological trends

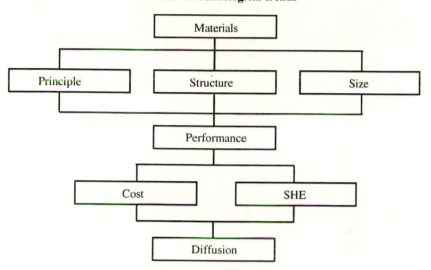

Electronic components are getting smaller. Motors and batteries are exhibiting both size trends.

- *Principle of operation*: In each technological field new principles of operation emerge to challenge existing ways of doing things. In information handling, for instance, the simplest signal can be given manually, mechanically, electro-mechanically, electronically, and optically.

- *Structure*: Some entities change shape and configuration; most become more complex. The configuration of integrated circuits is changing as the architecture requires a structure capable of containing more transistor elements in a given space. Advanced aircraft are highly complex when compared to their predecessors—they have many more components and many more links between these. Increasing complexity is usually expressed in terms of the M, E, I accumulation. Many technological entities start their evolutionary path as passive devices in which humans or animals provide energy and in which humans inspect and guide. They are merely M in structure. When a motor is added, the structure becomes M+E. Finally, when monitoring, control, and instrumentation are added the structure becomes M+E+I.

At level *three* technological change is viewed as improved performance. As mentioned earlier, the most frequently encountered measures of performance are: *efficiency, throughput, density,* and *precision.* These concepts have already been defined.

- Examples of *efficiency* improvement include metal processing (M_o/E_i), power stations (E_o/E_i), and low power sensors (I_o/E_i). In this expression the subscript "o" refers to output, and the subscript "i" to input.
- Examples of *throughput* improvement include cement manufacture (M_o/T), electric motors (E_o/T), and data transmission (I_o/T),
- Examples of *density* improvement are found in bridges (M_o/S), electric storage batteries (E_o/S), and computing (I_o/S).
- Examples of improvements of *precision* are metal processing, control over energy flow, and instrumentation.

At level *four* technological change is viewed as two phenomena:

- A *decrease in real cost per unit of output* when employing the technological entity.
- An improvement in *safety, health,* and *environmental impact.* This trend, frequently referred to as SHE, is one of the most compelling in modern technological evolution.

At level *five* technological change is viewed as a change in the composition of the landscape. Two ways of viewing this are: the way in which a new technology *substitutes* for an old one, or the patterns according to which a new technology *diffuses* through the landscape.

Pursuing the topic of technological evolution, the analysts addressed the question of a metric. This brought them face-to-face with the well-researched area of graphing technological trends. A full discussion of this area would reach beyond the intention of this article. One aspect only is dealt with, namely the well-known S-curve as it applies to the performance parameters in technology.

The Chart of Constraints

An S-curve depicts an empirically observed curve type reflecting an often-repeated pattern in technological evolution. Successive generations of technological entities exhibit an increase in performance. This starts slowly, is followed by an escalation, and eventually ends in slowdown. The question is, why is the S-curve such a persistent pattern?

The answer is that the entity reaches a constraint which then has to be overcome before the entity can evolve to higher levels of performance. Much is learned of technological evolution by examining the constraints (Ayres, 1988). Two classes are distinguished:

- Constraints of the first order—temporary barriers that are overcome by technological evolution.
- Constraints of the second order—fundamental theoretical limits as imposed by the laws of physics.

Examples of these constraints are given in Framework 4.

Framework 4
Chart of technological constraints

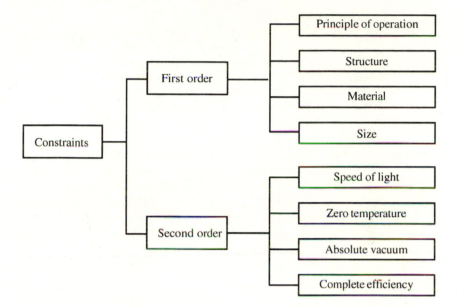

To chart a breakthrough zone, analysts have to determine whether a slow-ing down in the progress of performance is due to a temporary barrier or theo-retical limit. If it is due to a temporary barrier and the theoretical limit lies far away, then the conditions are there for a breakthrough zone—a domain of unconquered territory into which technological evolution can proceed.

The Ecology of Technology

From the outset it was clear that STA could not deal with technology as an isolated phenomenon. Technologies interact with nature and society—influ-encing and being influenced by—these systems. The question that the ana-lysts had to deal with was how to depict and evaluate these interactions. They considered a number of approaches among which are: (i) General systems theory, and particularly that part devoted to living systems, and (ii) environ-mental impact analysis, and its related field, industrial ecology. All of these approaches provided rich insights, but required quite complex depictions. The analysts had to turn elsewhere.

They noted the work of De Vulpian and his efforts to chart the interaction between social and technological trends. He identified four classes (1984).

- *Synergy*—denoting the enthusiastic social acceptance of a given tech-nology. The music CD is an early example, the Internet, a more recent one.

- *Deviation*—denoting the initial rejection of a technology and its subsequent acceptance. PCs provide a good example. The machines themselves did not sell well initially. Exciting software, like the spreadsheet, provided the impetus.
- *Enforced acceptance*—denoting the mandated introduction of a given technology by an authority such as a monopoly or government enterprise. State-run telephone systems and state-run nuclear power plants are examples.
- *Allergy*—denoting the social rejection of a particular technology. Nuclear power in the eighties would be a case in point.

The question that the analysts then asked is whether there is a simple structured way of examining a technological entity to enable people to form some opinion as to its social acceptability. The short answer is that it is extremely difficult to do so. People react to technology in both a rational and an irrational manner. We may be able to offer some views on rational behavior; the irrational remains elusive. The analysts then developed a profile of social preferences in technology, based on rational considerations. This is the *fifth framework of strategic technology analysis.*

Clusters of Social Values

"The new word in the marketplace is values—and what consumers want are companies making socially responsible products or providing socially responsible services" (Rodick, 1990). The key word is *values*. How can we relate values to technology? One approach is to identify a number of themes related to technology and then to find clusters of values around these themes. Six themes may be identified. These are summarized in Framework 5.

Framework 5
Profile of social preferences

Safety	Ensure safety to manufacture and use
Health	Promote health during manufacture and use
Environment	Strive for habitability, sustainablility, and diversity
Energisitcs	Pursue energy efficiency
Entropy	Minimize loss of natural order
Economics	Respect social values in economics

- *Safety*—technology should not threaten human safety; it should be neither toxic nor hazardous.
- *Health*—should contribute to healthy living.
- *Environment*—technology should contribute to a habitable environment, emphasizing diversity and sustainability.
- *Energy*—technology should strive for efficient energy ratios. This may be explained in terms of the energy equation $E_1 + E_2 = E_3 + E_4$, where E_1 represents energy sources that are free, such as wind and sun. E_2 represents energy inputs that have a cost, e.g., fuel. E_3 represents useful outputs of energy. And E_4 represents waste such as friction. Society favors technologies with a good energy ratio E_3/E_2.
- *Entropy*—technology should contribute minimally to entropy, i.e., it should be restrained in the extent to which it uses up ordered resources and leaves disorder. The movement towards entropy is a persistent and inescapable trend at the level of society at large; technological entities should not exacerbate the situation.
- *Economics*—technology should be economically justifiable. It should not cost more than the value it produces. However, we should remember that economics does not constitute a single simple criterion; it is itself intertwined with a complex system of social values. There are at least eight individual economic objectives, many of which reflect social values: (1) Economic efficiency. (2) Contribution to economic growth as measured in GDP/capita. (3) Stable money. (4) Stable international monetary ratios. (5) Non-cyclical economic development. (6) Equitable distribution of means. (7) Balanced geographic development. (8) Differential social empowerment.

The Special Role of Environmentalism

During the past few years, environmentalism has achieved high prominence. Environmental criteria are being written into national legislation and international regulation. This has created a whole new system of environmental requirements. These apply to:

- Locally produced *products*
- Locally employed *processes*
- Imported *products* (i.e., local standards are made to apply to imported products)
- Foreign *processes* (i.e., local standards are made to apply in the plants of foreign producers who wish to export their goods to the regulating country)

A further tendency is for countries to use environmental criteria not only to safeguard the environment, but also to act as trade barriers to protect local producers.

Ultimate Environmental Criteria

There is a strong tendency for environmental criteria and standards to be-come increasingly stricter. Historically this has grown from a situation where there were no regulations whatsoever to the point where "conserve, re-use, re-cycle" became a general guideline. Many environmental regulations at present aim at making the producer responsible for the ultimate disposal of all prod-ucts with which that producer has been involved. Pursuing this trend to its theoretical extremity, we wonder about the ultimate environmental criterion. Could a notion like "molecular accountability," i.e., making the producer responsible for "each molecule taken from, and returned to, the environment," offer us a glimpse of the future (Simmonds 1991: 93)?

While the issues of environmental criteria are being debated, the frame-work for analyzing the ecology of technology does offer us a view of technol-ogy in relation to other systems. This view may be characterized by the notion of "technological harmony." This involves the successful harnessing of high potency technologies while respecting the valid aspirations of people and the sovereignty of nature.

Status of Strategic Technology Analysis

At this stage STA exists as a set of frameworks providing a common ap-proach to analyzing all technologies. These frameworks serve mainly as mind-tools for technology managers. And while they go a long way towards creating structure and a common language, they do not have the precision of the funda-mental structures of the natural sciences. At best they parallel some of the fundamental structures of the social sciences. It remains an open question whether the precision of the natural sciences will ever be achieved. More work needs to be done. As a basis for this endeavor, it is appropriate to ask what the present status of the knowledge is and how widely it is understood.

While the field is well known and understood within a narrow circle of adherents it has not, at this stage, attained high visibility in the community at large. There is no informed single audience waiting in anticipation for knowl-edge of this kind. If the pattern of diffusion of other fundamental structures is anything to go by, this knowledge will disseminate slowly, radiating out circle by circle, appealing to one limited audience at a time. Acceptance will be neither rapid nor automatic. As in the case of other fundamental structures its utility is not immediately apparent. For the majority of engineers, who think about technology in very specific terms, the frameworks of STA may appear "too general." For physicists, chemists and other serious professionals STA is not rocket science. And for management theorists and policy analysts the frameworks may appear as "too technical." In fact, like so many innovations, STA simply does not fit nicely into any existing box.

But in spite of these sources of inertia, STA has had an impact. Four areas may be distinguished:

- First, it has helped individual adherents achieve greater insight into technology and a more coherent grasp of the technological landscape.
- Second, it has shaped academic courses and professional programs in the area of MOT.
- Third, it has provided a base for corporate procedures to map, track and anticipate technological change, to grow technology foresight and align it with overall strategy.
- Fourth, it has had an impact on other fields of knowledge.

Many *individuals* who have studied STA and have acquired the associated mental skills, change their habits when thinking about technology. Instead of absorbing and manipulating information in terms of the specifics associated with a particular technology, observers channel the information through the new frameworks. This helps these observers to see the big picture and to discover useful connections to families of technologies. It is quite remarkable how rapidly minds can switch from a pre-paradigmatic state to a highly structured one without being objectively aware of the process of transition. Reality in the new guise appears obvious and unremarkable.

As far as the development of *academic courses and professional programs* are concerned, these have benefited from the upsurge of interest in MOT in the late eighties. This field had lain dormant for a decade and a half. In 1987, and following the publication of a rallying text *Management of Technology: The Hidden Competitive Advantage*, MOT again became a focus of much attention. In the United States a number of initiatives were launched by academic and commercial enterprises. One example was the establishment of the Center for the Development of Technological Leadership (CDTL) at the University of Minnesota, created with a grant from the Honeywell Foundation.

The Center was created to champion the concept of MOT and introduced a new academic degree, the Master of Science in the Management of Technology (MS-MOT). In developing this program, CDTL sought to incorporate a unique approach to MOT—an approach that could be termed "technology-centered." STA offered the necessary frameworks for such a technology-centered approach and, in the early nineties, a course based on STA was introduced into the MS-MOT program. The University of Minnesota thus became the first university in the United States to use STA to structure academic course-work. At present STA provides the template for three courses in the MS-MOT program, as well as for professional offerings to executives in the area of technology foresight.

Today, STA is taught in academic programs at a number of universities throughout the world. In Asia this initiative is spearheaded by Nanyang Technological University (Singapore), in Europe by the Rotterdam School of Management, and in Africa by the University of Cape Town. It is also taught in a number of corporate universities. It forms the basis for professional seminars hosted by various Associations, such as the International Association for the Management of Technology (IAMOT).

As far as *corporate procedures* are concerned it is a little difficult to give a detailed review of these in an article of this nature. Companies that have adopted STA are typically companies that are innovative and that have highly explorative management cultures. Some of them sense a commercial advantage in being pioneering technological thinkers and prefer to maintain confidentiality. Companies that have adopted STA typically navigate the future by drawing maps of the technological universe. They divide this universe into three major domains, nine regions, and a list of landmark technologies that they can observe and track. These landmark technologies provide the first suggestion of disruptive or enabling technologies that companies need to incorporate into their strategic thinking.

STA has extended its influence into *other fields*—although on a very limited scale. In the mid-nineties a specialized activity arose called the Management of Medical Technology (MMT). From the outset the protagonists of this activity sought a basic discipline that could provide a unifying focus for their efforts. They identified STA as one possible candidate and invited contributions from this field. See "A macro map of medical technologies: Some introductory thoughts" that appeared in *The International Journal of Healthcare Technology and Management* (Van Wyk, 2000).

However, generally speaking, STA is still largely undiscovered. It has yet to enter the mainstream of thought of the science and engineering fraternities. It has yet to be explored in the literature on science and technology policy. It has yet to enter the literature on economics. It has only marginally influenced the literature on corporate strategy. And it has not yet influenced the theory of investment analysis. All of these are areas of possible application of STA.

Recommendations

How should we proceed? While this article has focused specifically on the development of STA, the underlying question should be seen in its broader perspective. STA is one candidate to provide fundamental structure to technological thinking. The important question remains the overall quest for such a fundamental structure. This paper suggests that the search for such a structure be revitalized as a matter of high priority. While doing so STA should be evaluated together with all the other candidates.

We can begin by asking ourselves four questions:

• Which candidate theories provide frameworks that can be used to describe the fundamental structure of technology?

- Does STA merit consideration as one of them?
- How robust are the frameworks of STA and how can they be refined?
- Can they be used to enhance our procedures in; (i) MOT education and practice, (ii) corporate governance and strategy, (iii) S&T policy, (iv) economic analysis, (v) investment decisions?

In addressing these questions we should gain a clearer picture of the merits of STA. We can also decide whether it is appropriate to promote the field beyond its present circle of adherents in MOT and how we should go about doing so. In this decision we should be mindful of the potential impact of fundamental structure in technology and the possibility of it becoming "one of the most significant conceptual foundations of the 21st century."

Acknowledgments

I wish to express my appreciation to Dr. Stephen Japp and Ms. Patsey Kahmann, who read through and commented on the manuscript. This expression of appreciation does not imply any delegation of responsibility.

References

Abernathy, W.J. and Wayne, K. "Limits to the learning curve" in Tushman, M.L. and Moore, W.L. 1984. *Readings in the Management of Innovation*, London, Pitman, pp. 109-121 (reprinted from the *Harvard Business Review*, September/October 1974.)

Amber, G.H. and Amber, P.S. 1962. *Anatomy of Automation*, Englewood Cliffs, N.J. Prentice Hall.

Ashby, M.F. 1987. "Technology in the 1990s: Advanced materials and predictive design. *Proceedings of the Royal Society, Discussion Meeting*, 4-5 June 1986, London, The Royal Society.

Ayres, Robert U. 1988. "Barriers and breakthroughs: An 'expanding frontiers' model of the technology-industry life cycle," *Technovation*, Vol. 7, Issue 2, May, pp. 87–115.

Ayres, Robert U. 1968. "Envelope curve forecasting," in Bright, James R (ed): *Technological Forecasting for Industry and Government*, Englewood Cliffs, New Jersey (Prentice Hall), pp. 77–94.

Badawy, M.K. 1996. "A new paradigm for understanding management technology: A research agenda for 'technocologists'," *International Journal of Technology Management*, Vol. 12, No. 5/6, Special Issue, pp. 717–732.

Bright, J. R. 1963. "Opportunity and threat in technological change," *Harvard Business Review*, Vol. 41, No. 6, November/December pp. 76–86.

De Gregori, Thomas R. 1985. *A Theory of Technology*, Ames, Iowa (The Iowa State University Press).

De Meyer, 1988. "The way forward in the strategic management of technology," *R&D Management*, Vol. 18, No. 2, pp. 107–109.

De Vulpian, A. 1984. *New Directions for Innovations in Products and Services*, Congress d'Esomar, Rome and Paris, COFREMCA., p. 32.

Dosi, Giovanni. 1982. "Technological paradigms and technological trajectories," *Research Policy*, Vol. 11, pp. 147–162.

Farrell, C.J. 1993. "A theory of technological progress," *Technological Forecasting and Social Change*, Vol. 44, pp. 161–178.

Fisher, J.C. and Pry, R.H. 1971. "A simple substitution model of technological change," *Technological Forecasting and Social Change,* Vol. 3, pp. 75–88.

Foster, Richard. 1986. *Innovation: The Attackers Advantage*, New York (Summit Books).

Gaynor, G. 1996. *Handbook of Technology Management*, McGraw Hill, New York, pp. 5.9- 5.24.

Grupp, H. and Hohmeyer O., 1986. "A technometric model for the assessment of technological standards and their application to selected technology intensive products," *Technological Forecasting and Social Change*, Vol. 30, pp. 123-137.

Horner, D.S. 1992. "Frameworks for technology analysis and classification," *Journal of Information Science*, Vol. 12, No. 1, pp. 57-68.

Khalil, T.M. 2000 *Management of Technology: The Drivers of Technological Changes in the Twenty First Century*, University of Miami.

Le Duff, R. and Maïsseu, A. 1988. *L'Anti-declin, ou les mutations technologiques maitrisées*, Paris, E.S.F.

Linstone, H.A. and Sahal, D. 1976. *Technological substitution*, Elsevier, New York.

Majer, H. 1985. "Technology measurement: The functional approach," *Technological Forecasting and Social Change*, Vol. 27, pp. 335-351.

Mansfield, E. 1961. "Technical change and the rate of imitation," *Economica*, Vol. 29, No. 4, pp. 741-766.

Mazlish, B. 1993. *The Fourth Discontinuity*, Vail Ballou Press, Binghamton, New York.

Rapp, F. 1974. *Contributions to the Philosophy of Technology*, Dordrecht, Holland, D. Reidel Publishing Company.

Rodick, A. 1990. "Macmillan educational lecture" Conference of the Geographical Association. Referred to in Ledgerwood, G, Street, E, and Therivel, R., 1994, *The Environmental Audit and Business Strategy*, Pitman Publishing, London, p. vii.

Ropohl, Gunter. 1979. *Eine Systhemteorie der Technik*, Munich and Vienna Carl Hanser Verlag.

Sahal, D. 1985. "Foundations of technometrics," *Technological Forecasting and Social Change,* Vol. 27, pp 1-38.

Shurig, R. 1984. "Morphology: A tool for exploring new technology," *Long Range Planning*, Vol. 17, No. 3, pp. 129-140.

Simmonds, W.H.C. 1991. "Is sustainability the key to professionalism in futures?" *Futures Research Quarterly*, Vol. 7, No. 1, Spring, pp. 85-95.

Steyn, H. de V. and de Wet, G. 1994. "Technological limits and the hierarchies of product systems," *Technological Forecasting and Social Change*, Vol. 46, No. 1, pp. 11-15.

Teichmann, D. 1974. "On the classification of the technological sciences" in Rapp, F. (ed) *Contributions to a Philosophy of Technology*, Dordrecht, Holland, D. Reidel Publishing Company, pp. 134-139.

Van Wyk, R.J. 1979. "Technological forecasting: A macro-perspective." *Technological Forecasting and Social Change,* Vol. 15, pp. 281-296.

Van Wyk, R.J. 1988. "Management of technology: New frameworks." *Technovation*, Vol. 7, pp. 341-351.

Van Wyk, R.J. 2000. "A macro map of medical technologies: Introductory thoughts." *International Journal of Health Care Technology and Management*, Vol. 2, Nos. 1/2/3/4, pp. 206-217.

2

Knowledge Mapping: The Consolidation of the Technology Management Discipline

Karol I. Pelc

This chapter presents a method of conceptual mapping of knowledge during the consolidation process of an interdisciplinary domain into an emerging discipline. This approach allows tracking the evolution of an emerging discipline of technology management. Knowledge consolidation is the result of colliding source disciplines and the simultaneous influence of changing paradigms. Three paradigms have played major role in recent development of the emerging discipline: (1) engineering management paradigm, (2) management of technology paradigm, and (3) technological entrepreneurship paradigm. The changing needs of practice drive the process. Knowledge mapping approach identifies elements of that process. Those elements (concepts) are identified and used for building a map of knowledge. The impact of different source disciplines (such as economics, management science, psychology, engineering sciences, systems science, and sociology) is characterized by affinities they have with concepts developed and applied in the emerging discipline. Linkages among those concepts are graphically interpreted in the map of knowledge.

Introduction

In recent decades, advances in new technologies and their growing impact on economies accelerated the evolution of technology management as a discipline. This acceleration has been stimulated by the needs of managerial and engineering practice. A historical perspective on various components of the

Karol I. Pelc is a professor at Michigan Technological University, Houghton, Michigan, where he is also the director of the Center for Technological Innovation Leadership and Entrepreneurship (CenTILE). He may be reached at <kipelc@mtu.edu>.

emerging discipline, their origin and interaction, may provide the basis for understanding of the current state of the discipline and its potential directions of development. On one hand, the new discipline is pulling knowledge from more traditional source disciplines; on the other, it is driven by practice-based interaction of different paradigms. Terminology, concepts, methods, and techniques used for managing different aspects of technological change are gradually consolidated into a set of closely related elements of the new discipline. In recent decades, knowledge of the technology management discipline has been continuously expanding. At the same time the discipline has been restructuring under the influence of new paradigms and consolidating into a well organized set of basic concepts. This process fits well with a more general model of knowledge transformations in scientific disciplines that was presented by A. Reisman (1987). He views "knowledge consolidation as a means of more efficient and more effective teaching and learning of new or of existing knowledge."

The purpose of this paper is to present a knowledge consolidation process as a result of two factors, which contributed to the present scope and conceptual map of technology management discipline: impact of complementary paradigms and contributions of the source disciplines.

Complementary Paradigms of an Emerging Discipline

Technology management is emerging as a discipline from a broad pool of interdisciplinary knowledge addressing specific needs of managerial practice. Those needs are evolving in close relation to dynamics of technology both as an object of management and due to its remarkable impact on economy and society. These are reflected in a sequence of three paradigms, which are complementary to each other, and lead to expansion of the scope of new discipline.

Engineering Management Paradigm (EM)

The evolution of knowledge base for technology management may be viewed as a process that started in the 1940s when initial courses and educational programs of engineering administration and/or engineering management were established. In 1969, the results of a national survey indicated that over 64 percent of engineers had managerial responsibilities for projects, teams, sections or major departments, programs, and divisions (Babcock, 1991). The engineering management paradigm was: *Many engineers become managers of projects, technical organizations or functional areas of company hence they should be educated how to manage operations, projects and organizations.* The emphasis of that education was on management of technical functions, such as production, quality assurance, design, product development, and R&D. Later, in the 1970s and 1980s, engineering management became an active area of research and experienced rapid institutional growth in the universities (Kocaoglu,1990). It still plays an essential role within the framework of technology (and engineering) management discipline.

Management of Technology Paradigm (MOT)

Parallel to the process described above, and partly as a result of it, the technological change has been accelerated and amplified. Impact of new technologies on success of many companies, and on the national economy as a whole, indicated that *managing technology is essential for competitive advantage, hence it should be integral part of business processes, organizations and strategies.* This view became a new paradigm of the 1980s (NRC Task Force, 1987). This recognition of business needs stimulated growth of new educational programs in "management of technology" (MOT), which sometimes developed in addition to former engineering management programs (for example in the National Technological University), or were based on expansion of engineering management or compilation of both in many schools. The focus of the programs is on integration of technology and business strategy, with all conditions and consequences of that integration.

Technological Entrepreneurship Paradigm (TE)

In the 1990s, technological innovation became an engine for start-ups and new projects. The success of a new technology-based company depends on its ability to match technology with customer needs, to develop markets, to attract venture capital, and to apply sound business practices. Hence *technological entrepreneurship becomes a critical area of expertise that supports commercialization of new technology through new business start-ups. It combines engineering creativity with business initiative.* Expertise is needed in the area of starting and developing a new technology-based company, in addition to technology management education, which, until recently, emphasized the capability to manage technology within an established organization,. The new paradigm of *technological entrepreneurship* is still in its formation stage. At the same time, both the needs of practice and academic interest are growing. E. Roberts (1991) contributed greatly to the advancement of this new subfield of technology management discipline.

The evolution of technology management discipline may be viewed as a gradual expansion and simultaneous integration of knowledge in the context of three paradigms presented above. This process is illustrated in Figure 1.

Elements of Conceptual Map of Knowledge

The goal of developing a conceptual map of knowledge in technology management is to represent a *knowledge landscape* of the discipline by iden-

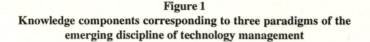

Figure 1
Knowledge components corresponding to three paradigms of the
emerging discipline of technology management

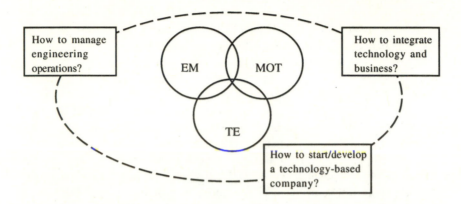

tifying its basic elements, their interconnections and linkages with *knowledge environment* external to the discipline. That environment may be viewed as a set of more traditional disciplines, which contribute to the technology management discipline by sharing the following three categories of knowledge:

- Terms, concepts, dictionary
- Empirical statements and observations; descriptive and prescriptive information on facts and events
- Models, theories, and methodological tools.

In this way the *source disciplines* provide a frame of reference for development and evaluation of concepts, trends, and interactions in the emerging discipline. That interaction is shown in Figure 2.

A map of a discipline consists of graphical elements representing basic concepts (knowledge elements) and connections among those concepts (Pelc, 1996). The map represents two types of linkages/impacts:

- Affinities of selected concepts with the source disciplines
- Associations and linkages among concepts within the emerging discipline.

Selection of concepts for knowledge map may be based on expert opinions, bibliometric studies, or may be derived from the content analysis of representative publications. The latter approach is used in this paper for illustrative purposes. A set of basic commonly applied concepts has been identified in selected major textbooks that are being used in technology management

Figure 2
Interaction between source disciplines and a new emerging discipline

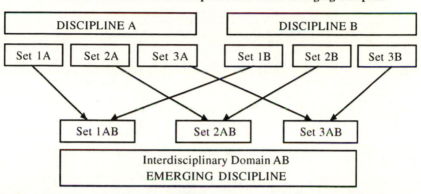

Sets 1A and 1B: Terms, concepts, dictionary (of source disciplines A and B respectively)

Sets 2A and 2B: Statements, descriptive and prescriptive information, reports, observations, facts, events (of source disciplines)

Sets 3A and 3B: Methodological tools, models, and theories (of source disciplines)

Sets 1AB, 2AB, 3AB: Elements of interdisciplinary knowledge domain AB for an emerging discipline

courses. Even though terminology and exact titles of respective chapters/ sections of those texts differ from each other, their aggregation is possible and their correspondence established. A review of such texts selecting for eighteen concepts from the current map of technology management is shown in Table 1.

Genetic Analogy and Affinities with Source Disciplines

Analogy to genetic process may be used to explain linkages and interactions between the emerging and source disciplines. The source disciplines provide "genes" (concepts) which are combined to create a "genetic mix" of knowledge in an interdisciplinary domain. Consolidation of that knowledge leads to emergence of a new discipline, elements of which maintain "inherited" affinities with the source discipline.

Elements (concepts) of the emerging discipline of technology management may be classified according to their affinities with source disciplines, as suggested by the model presented in Figure 2. An affinity may be either with a single source discipline (single affinity) or with two source disciplines (dual affinity), or with multiple source disciplines (multiple affinity). Examples of those three levels of affinities are presented in Table 2.

This table suggests that the concepts (knowledge elements) of technology management may be grouped into seven clusters based on similarity of affini-

Table 1
Basic concepts of technology management presented in selected textbooks

	Burgelman, R. A., Maidique, M. A., Wheelwright, S. C., *Strategic Management of Technology and Innovation*, McGraw-Hill Irwin, 3rd ed., 2001	Khalil, T. M., *Management of Technology*, McGraw-Hill, 2000	Narayan, V. K., *Managing Technology and Innovation for Competitive Advantage*, Prentice Hall, 2001	Tushman, M. L., Anderson, P., *Managing Strategic Innovation and Change*, Oxford University Press, 1997
Technology evolution	Technological evolution	Technology life-cycles	Levels of technology development	Technology cycles Technological discontinuities
Technological innovation	Architectural innovation	Process of technological innovation & model	Process of technology change: innovation	
Creativity and innovation concepts	Patterns of industrial innovation	Creativity factors, types of innovation	Drivers of innovation Types of innovation outputs	Developing new product concepts
Technology strategy	Design and implementation of technology strategy	Technology strategy Linking technology and business strategy	Technology strategy Technology-business connection Technology in a value chain	Technology strategy: evolutionary perspective
Core and distinctive competencies	Distinctive technological competencies; core competencies	Core competencies		Core competencies, core capabilities and core rigidities
Technological forecasting and planning	Technology in corporate planning	Technology planning Forecasting technology	Technology intelligence Mapping the technology environment Tools for forecasting	
Technology portfolio	Technology portfolio matching to business portfolio	Technology portfolio	Portfolio of technology appropriation projects	
R&D management and globalization	Effective R&D capabilities	R&D management; global management of R&D	Productivity of in-house R&D; Globalization of R&D	Managing R&D Global innovation Innovation in transnational corporation Stimulating global R&D communication

ties with their source disciplines. It can be used for graphic interpretation of linkages among those concepts in a knowledge map of the discipline.

Knowledge Map of Technology Management

A conceptual map of knowledge in the technology management discipline may be designed on the basis of the following rules of representation:

Table 1 (cont.)

Product and process innovation	Technological innovation; limits of the technology S-curve	Evolution of production technology and product technology	Technology evolution Innovation dynamics Product development Process innovation and value chain	Technology-product relationship
New product development	New product development learning cycle Project plans Design-built-test cycle		Product development: principles and process	Managing new product development (a paradox)
Dominant design	Dominant design paradigm			Managing product families Dominant design
Technology/market and competitiveness	Ecology of competition; competing technologies	Technology/market interaction Global competitiveness	Technology-market matrix Competitive consequences of techn. change	Marketing and discontinuous innovation Logic of global business
Technology sourcing	Technology sourcing; absorptive capacity	Acquisition of technology	External sourcing of technology capability	Alliances in implementing technology strategies
Technology transfer	Technology transfer from R&D Communication between engineering and production	Technology transfer	Marketing of technology Collaborative arrangement for technology strategy implementation	
Diffusion of technology		Diffusion of technology	Process of technology change: Diffusion Dynamics of diffusion	Technological substitution
Organizations/teams	Development teams; ambidextrous organizations; learning organization	Design of organizations (structures)	Organizing for innovation	Product development teams, managing technological change through organizational structure
Technological entrepreneurship	Managing the internal corporate venturing process	Entrepreneurship	Project valuation and financing	Entrepreneurial vehicles in established co. Entering new business
Intellectual property and knowledge management			Intellectual property strategy	Managing intellect Information creation

- List of concepts to be represented (as illustrated in Table 1)
- List of source disciplines
- List of affinity clusters related to source disciplines (as in Table 2)
- Circle as a symbol of each concept (diameter represents amount of information, publications, documents, databases, etc.)
- Connections between concepts represented by arrows of impact/association, e.g,. reflected by citations
- Location of each element on the map according to the affinity clusters.

Table 2
Affinities of technology management knowledge with source disciplines (examples)

Technology management concepts	Source disciplines	Type of affinity
Technology strategy Technological forecasting Core/distinctive competencies Technological entrepreneurship	Economics Engineering Systems science	Triple affinity
Product and process innovation New product development Dominant design Technology sourcing R&D management and globalization	Economics Engineering Management science	Triple affinity
Technological innovation Technology portfolio Technology planning	Economics Management science	Dual affinity
Creativity and innovation concepts	Engineering Cognitive psychology	Dual affinity
Intellectual property and knowledge management	Economics Law/ethics	Dual affinity
Organizations/teams	Management science Sociology	Dual affinity
Technology evolution Technology/market and competitiveness Diffusion of technology Technology transfer	Economics	Single affinity

An example of knowledge map based on these rules is presented in Figure 3.

Conclusion

Expansion of knowledge in the domain of technology management was accompanied by simultaneous consolidation. A number of concepts have been coherently used in research publications, textbooks, and educational programs. The new discipline integrates three complementary paradigms reflecting the dynamic evolution of technology management practice. Several other disciplines contribute to the pool of knowledge needed for problem solving in technology management. Analysis of affinities between basic conceptual elements of new discipline and the source disciplines may be used for creating a typology of those concepts and for mapping of knowledge in technology management. The map also presents linkages among the basic concepts. The approach presented in this paper may also be applied in the future studies of dynamics of knowledge base for technology management.

Figure 3
Knowledge map of technology management (an example)

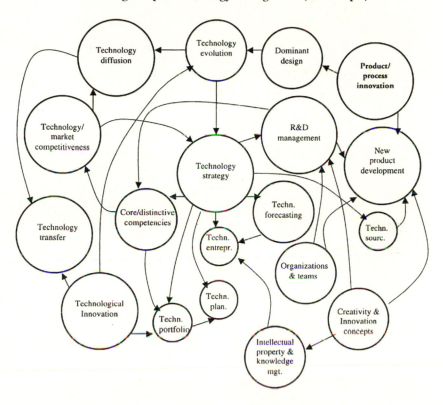

Acknowledgment

Research presented in this chapter was partly sponsored by the National Science Foundation through the Action Agenda Initiative for Systemic Engineering Education Reform, Grant No. EEC-9872533 (in the framework of the Enterprise Program at Michigan Technological University). An earlier version of this paper was presented at the annual conference of the International Association for Management of Technology, March 2002.

References

Babcock, D. L. (1991). *Managing Engineering and Technology*, Prentice Hall, Englewood Cliffs, N.J., pp.14–17.

Kocaoglu, D. F. (1990). Research and educational characteristics of the engineering/ technology management discipline, *IEEE Transactions on Engineering Management*, 37, 171–176.

NRC Task Force (1987). *Management of Technology: The Hidden Competitive Advantage*, National Academy Press, Washington, D.C.

Pelc, K. I. (1996). Knowledge mapping: A tool for management of technology. In: *Handbook of Technology Management* (G. H. Gaynor, ed.), pp. 13.1–13.19, McGraw-Hill, New York.

Reisman, A. (1987). Expansion of knowledge via consolidation of knowledge, *Proceedings of ISMIS 87*, the Second International Symposium/Colloquium on Methodologies for Intelligent Systems, ORNL-6417, Oak Ridge National Laboratories, p. 13.

Roberts, E. (1991). *Entrepreneurs in High Technology*, Oxford University Press, New York.

3

Management of Technology:
A Three-Dimensional Framework with
Propositions for Future Research

Jon W. Beard

Profound change in organizational technology, including office, manufacturing, and transaction technology; the rapid pace of technology change; and
the increasingly global and competitive marketplace have stimulated organizations to rethink how they do business, leading to a nascent discipline on the
management of technology (MoT). Yet, the literature that exists is fragmented
and dispersed through the traditional technology and functional-business-
discipline literatures, creating difficulty for those interested in the management of technology to locate and integrate the available knowledge. This
inquiry proposes and develops a three-dimensional framework of the management of technology literature. Its purpose is to visually and spatially represent
the relationships among the various components of the MoT literature along the
three proposed dimensions relevant to MoT. Propositions for future development
and research on the management of technology are derived from the model.

Introduction

The management of technology (MoT) is a conceptual domain of the organizational sciences and practices that recently have been recognized as being

Jon W. Beard is the editor of *Impression Management and Information Technology*
(Quorum, 1996) and *Managing Impressions with Information Technology* (Quorum,
forthcoming). He may be reached at <jonwbeard@sbcglobal.net>. An earlier version of
this chapter was presented at the Fifth International Conference on Management of
Technology (IAMOT), 1996, Miami, Florida.

economically crucial. Trends such as the globalization of the marketplace, ever-shorter product lifecycles, and increasing collaboration among even competing organizations have led to increasing stress on organizations. Profound changes in organizational technology, including office, manufacturing, and transaction technology, have stimulated organizations to rethink how they do business. Organization downsizing, the popularity of concepts such as business process reengineering, and the emergence of the Internet and e-business are obvious testimony to the changing environment. Recent materials in the popular business press magazines, such as *Business Week* (c.f., *Business Week*, 1994, "Now Comes the Corporate Triathlete") and *Fortune* (c.f., *Fortune*, 1993) and in the academic press (c.f., Aldridge, 1990; Burgelman, Maidique, & Wheelwright, 2001; Collins, Gardiner, Heaton, Macrosson, & Tait, 1991; Johnson & Rice, 1987; Khalil, 1993) also provide evidence for this argument. Yet, the literature that exists on the management of technology is fragmented and dispersed throughout the traditional technology and functional-business-discipline literatures. The lack of a unifying model creates difficulty in locating and using the available knowledge for those interested in the management of technology (cf. Khalil, 1998; National Research Council, 1987). This inquiry develops a three-dimensional framework that is intended to function as a means of orienting the MoT literature.

The discussion following is divided into three sections. First, a definition of management of technology is presented as the cornerstone for the rest of this paper. Using the components from the definition, the next section presents the proposed dimensions and develops the integrated framework. One sample application of the framework is presented. Building on that framework, the final section suggests and explores avenues for future development and research on the management of technology. These research suggestions include issues related to the further refinement of the proposed framework, as well as suggestions for future research on specific areas of MoT that may be deficient.

Management of Technology: A Definition

The concept of technology is both expansive and illusive. According to the *American Heritage Dictionary* (1985), technology is "the application of science, especially to industrial or commercial objectives," or "the entire body of methods and materials used to achieve such objectives" (p. 1248). Christensen and Bower (1996) describe technology as "the process by which an organization transforms labor, capital, materials, and information into products and services" (p. 198). In describing technology, Burgelman, Maidique, and Wheelwright (2001) indicate that they are referring "to the theoretical and practical knowledge, skills, and artifacts that can be used to develop products and services as well as their production and delivery systems" (p. 4). Burgelman, et al. (2001) go further noting that a technology may be tacit or remain unarticulated, as represented in experience and craftsmanship. By extension, therefore, technology can be rooted in a variety of organizational artifacts, including people, equipment, tools, materials, as well as cognitive and physical processes. Narayanan (2001) notes that technology embeds the notion of "knowledge," and that the development and application of technology is a social process.

Therefore, the successful development, implementation, and management of technology require attention to a multifaceted, multidisciplinary array of issues. Narayanan (2001) suggests that MoT "focuses on the principles of strategy and organization involved in technology choices, guided by the purpose of creating value for investors" (p. 8). Yet, the embedded nature of technology makes its management even more complex than suggested above. Due to the increasingly integrated nature of people, technology, and organizations, not only are we concerned with the capabilities resulting from advances in science and engineering (i.e., technology), but we are also required to pay attention to the people involved, the raw materials required, the financial constraints, and the competitive and environmental circumstances (National Research Council, 1987). This complexity requires the consideration of and appropriate balance among sometimes-conflicting objectives.

To further the discussion and to add precision to the evolving MoT domain, the National Research Council (1987) developed the following definition to organize, guide, and stimulate research efforts on the management of technology:

> Management of technology links engineering, science, and management disciplines to address the planning, development, and implementation of technological capabilities to shape and accomplish the strategic and operational objectives of an organization (National Research Council, 1987, p. 2).

Building from this definition, the next section distills and briefly explores the three dimensions of the integrative framework. Several examples of different types of and purposes for frameworks are also presented.

A Three-Dimensional Framework

The purpose of a framework is to provide organization and structure to a body of information or knowledge. It can be very general and broad, or can be much more specific or detailed. The organization can be based on objective or subjective criteria, yet should have a systematic or logical structure. Several examples may be useful.

Sample Frameworks

Until the mid-1880s, no useful organizational structure had been developed in chemistry that could function in explaining and accounting for the similarities and differences in the elements known at that time (Wilbraham, Staley, Matta, & Waterman, 2000). Dmitri Mendeleev discerned a way to organize the elements. Mendeleev arranged the elements in order of increasing mass, and then arranged the columns so that those with similar properties would be next to one another. Blank spots were left in the structure where Mendeleev and others were able to predict that missing elements would ultimately be identified. The known elements were arranged in columns and rows based upon the similarities of their atomic properties, yielding a table format called the Periodic Table of Elements.

The Periodic Table was further revised in the early twentieth century by Moseley (1887-1915), who organized the elements based on their atomic number instead of their mass (Wilbraham, Staley, Matta, & Waterman, 2000). In this arrangement, which is still in use today, there are seven rows in the table, called periods, with repeating patterns of physical and chemical properties in the elements across the row. The elements in each column of the table, called groups, have very similar physical and chemical properties. Knowledge of the relative location of a particular element within the table can yield a great deal of predictive information about how the element will interact with other specific elements based on the physical and chemical properties consistent with that location in the table. Therefore, objective data about an element —its atomic number, mass, and atomic structure—provide a useful organizing framework, specifically the Periodic Table of Elements, for working with the elements.

Another example comes from the field of biology. Dating back to the time of Aristotle, and even further back to Plato, scientists had worked to devise a logical categorization or classification scheme for living things (Mayr, 1982). In the mid-eighteenth century, Carolus Linnaeus devised an approach that would allow every living organism to be assigned to a category based on common structural traits shared by similar living organisms (Postlethwait & Hopson, 1989). A series of increasingly specific groups are identified by these common traits or characteristics, which has come to be known as the Linnaean Hierarchy (Mayr, 1982). The hierarchy consists of seven levels, specifically kingdom, phylum, class, order, family, genus, species.

But this can be a somewhat subjective arrangement. For example, there is some disagreement on the number of kingdom, the top-most level of the hierarchy, which should be used for the initial categorization. According to Mayr (1982), four, five, or six kingdoms exist depending on how some types of living things are grouped. The classification of a living thing into its genus and species, the two most specific levels of categorization, is also subject to some debate in delineating the important criteria that should, or should not, be used for making the classification. Living things in the same genus are very similar based on certain characteristics, with the potential for many different species from the same genus. The species level is the categorization that uniquely identifies a living creature from all other living things. It is relatively common for the classification of a species to be adjusted based on different characteristics or new details about the organism (Mayr, 1982; Postlethwait & Hopson, 1989). This is particularly true for extinct creatures or plants for which there is little available data and for recently discovered creatures for which there are few samples. Therefore, the classification process is rigorous, but subjective, leaving room for some disagreement and future revision as new information on a living thing is forthcoming. According to Mayr (1982), taxonomists have classified well over 2 million species, both those currently alive and extinct. Yet, as many as 8 million unnamed and undiscovered species still remain to be classified.

In physics the search for the Grand Unified Theory has been underway for about a century. Empirical tests of the predictions of the Standard Model of physics, the framework currently used, show that the model provides a good general structure and explanation of the relationships of the multitude of subatomic particles (Particleadventure, 2002). But, it is not able to adequately explain all of the known particles and their known and theoretically predicted interactions. The Grand Unified Theory, however, once successfully derived, is believed to be able to successfully integrate the four basic forces in the universe—strong, weak, gravitation, and electromagnetism—and explain the interactions among all of the subatomic particles.

Other classification schemes exist beyond the examples above, such as the key word or topic classification approaches used in various disciplines. For example, in the information systems field, a classification structure has been developed and continues to evolve to "provide a description of the discipline, introduce a common language, and enable research of the field's development" (Barki, Rivard, & Talbot, 1993, p. 209). The common language, or vocabulary, is particularly important in an evolving field, for it allows similar concepts that may be called different things to be linked over time.

The examples above provide evidence of the usefulness of both an objectively designed and a subjectively designed frameworks or taxonomy. Whether objective or subjective, if agreement can be reached on the method of structuring or classifying a body of knowledge, it can lead to useful outcomes.

A Framework for Management of Technology

As the organizational environment escalates in complexity, it is increasingly important to be able to manage technology because of its impact on the economic well-being of the firm and, therefore, individuals. However, to properly manage technology will also require the consideration and implementation of appropriate structural and behavioral changes within organizations (National Research Council, 1987). Unfortunately, the literature on MoT has been described as being largely "limited, fragmented, and uncoordinated across the various subfields" with "partial theories" and "diffused" research (National Research Council, 1987, p. 15). While MoT research is largely problem-driven, these shortcomings in the MoT literature may be hindering needed research progress and represent potentially missed opportunities to build on the work of others. The proposed three-dimensional structure is an attempt to provide a framework to deal with the dispersed literature.

The axes of this model create a structure, shown in Figure 1, which was derived from the definition of MoT above. It is intended to show the relationships among the various components of the literature along the three fundamental variables relevant to MoT as suggested by the definition. These variables, or axes, are: macro (organization-level of analysis) vs. micro (individual-level of analysis), objective (actual measures of the "object" under scrutiny) vs. subjective (measures of perception), and human (person-focused) vs. technology (technology-focused). For the sake of brevity, certain generalizations have been made in this discussion. Each of these dimensions is discussed in more detail below.

Macro/Micro Dimension

The goal of MoT is to "shape and accomplish the strategic and operational objectives of an organization" (National Research Council, 1987). This as-

Figure 1
A three-dimensional framework on management of technology

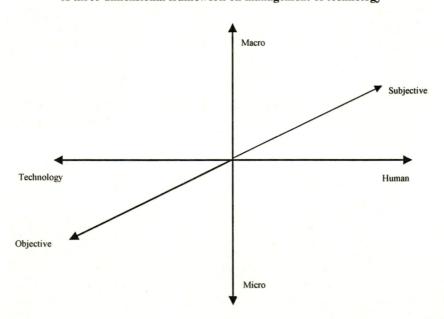

pect of the definition suggests a breadth of focus toward MoT that has not always been obvious in the literature.

The origin and, perhaps, the heart of the MoT literature has typically been focused on the macro, or strategic, dimension (c.f., Burgelman, et al., 2001) of organizations. The goal has been the alignment of the technology capabilities with the organization's needs. MoT is "concerned with the identification, acquisition, development, and application of relevant technological knowledge and expertise in achieving the organization's goals and objectives" (Jones, Green, & Coombs, 1994, p. 157). This orientation is appropriate at first glance, for the majority of the decisions regarding technology and its ultimate uses originate at the top levels of the organization. Of course, technology often enters the organization through the individual efforts of just a few innovative individuals (Rogers, 1995) and then, when successful, is taken up by the rest of the organization. While the alignment of the technology with the strategic direction of the organization is necessary, the implementation and operation of the technology ultimately takes place at the group and individual level. Unfortunately, this group- or individual-level aspect seems to have been overlooked, or at least discounted, in much of the MoT research.

For example, in the introduction to a special journal issue on computer-aided design, Majchrzak and Salzman (1989) noted that although the capability of technological resources to vastly improve organizational "flexibility, innovation, efficiency, and customer responsiveness" exists, as many as 75 percent of the advanced manufacturing technologies have not realized their expected benefits (p. 174). Inadequate planning for the necessary organizational change to adapt to and take advantage of the technological change is one of the primary reasons for these failures in expectations (Majchrzak & Salzman, 1989). Zuboff (1998) has presented another powerful description of the impact of the dynamics of changing technology:

> The material alterations...were manifested in transformations at intimate levels of experience—assumptions about knowledge and power, their beliefs about work and the meaning they derived from it, the content and rhythm of their social exchanges, and the ordinary mental and physical disciplines to which they accommodated in their daily lives...a world of sensibilities and expectations was being irretrievably displaced by a new world (p. xiii).

Although not exhaustive, these views suggest the need for a broader approach, to include both a macro- and micro-focus.

As another example, business process reengineering was one of the 'hottest' topics in business and the business press in the early 1990s. Hammer and Champy's (1993) *Reengineering the Corporation,* one of the best-selling business books of the early 1990s, championed this concept. Yet, in spite of its promise, many reengineering efforts fell well short of their projected goals. It was soon recognized that the reengineering process would shrink the organization, which ultimately means a reduction in jobs. Many of those lost jobs came from the ranks of middle management, the same people who were responsible for undertaking and implementing the changes needed for reengineering to succeed. Needless to say, there was often some resistance from these same people. The recognition of reengineering failures led to a new book, entitled *Reengineering Management* (Champy, 1995), to address the managerial issues. The largely macro focus of the first book led to an oversight—it was the micro dimension, consisting of the individuals involved, where the change was necessary.

Various discipline-based approaches from across the management domain can address the heterogeneous perspectives related to MoT. To generalize, issues can range from the macro-organizational focus of strategic/policy management and organization theory, to the applied orientation of industrial engineering, to the more micro-organizational approaches of organizational behavior and industrial-organizational psychology. The concern is that the typical MoT approach, while recognizing their existence, tends to discount the more micro-focused disciplines since they are addressed elsewhere in the organization sciences. Unfortunately, many of these micro-focused disciplines do not adequately address technology-related concerns. Therefore, one dimension, or axis, of this framework is proposed to acknowledge the breadth of perspectives, where the unit of interest may range from an organization, or even an industry, to an individual. Each of these levels of attention is important to the management of technology and may stimulate consideration of MoT-related issues across the organizational continuum.

Objective/Subjective Dimension

According to the National Research Council (1987), the "management of technology links [the] engineering, science, and management disciplines." A common point for contention between the perspectives of business/management and engineering/science is understanding the sometimes discordant approaches of subjective perceptions and human decision making versus precise, objective measurement. This is not to suggest that the organization sciences do not have objective research, nor that engineering and science are without subjectivity, as noted in the discussion of the Linnaean Hierarchy above. Instead, it is directed at the nature of the primary object of attention (i.e., people and organization versus generally inanimate objects/technology). This is similar to the quarrels and discussion on the uses of quantitiative versus qualitiative research that have occurred throughout the history of science (Van Fleet & Beard, 1988). Faulkner (1982) has noted that "quantitative data permit the research to discover and represent something that is happening," a way to describe with precision, "but they do not explain the 'meaning' of that happening to those experiencing it" (p. 85). In considering the management of technology, similar concerns arise, for not all issues are measurable with precision.

Therefore, it is recognized that both objective and subjective approaches are potentially worthwhile means of assessing MoT issues. Some problems lend themselves to solution through the analysis and inspection of precise, objective data; others are better addressed with more qualitative methods of assessment and understanding. Subjective approaches, in particular, may be necessary given the socially constructed nature of technology (Narayanan, 2001). Both, however, can contribute to the larger comprehension of MoT. This dimension, or axis, is proposed as a means of building this range of approaches into the MoT framework.

Human/Technology Dimension

The final dimension, or axis, is one where we take a human, or person-focused, approach at one extreme, to a technology-focused approach at the other. The MoT definition specifies "the planning, development, and implementation of technological capabilities" (National Research Council, 1987). This, too, is where the dichotomy between business/management and engineering/science may appear. The function of the management perspective is typically to address people- or organizational-oriented issues, which may range from organization design and structure to leadership, group dynamics, job design, and personality and individual differences, among many others. The technology-oriented issues are directed more at discovering the best ways to optimize and tune the technology to do its job. It is possible for the capabilities of a technology to exceed the operational capabilities of the human operators. The midpoint of this dimension, or the point where the two extremes intersect, would be where the attention is directed at the joint optimization of the two, focusing on topics such as the design of machine controls or user-interface issues. Unfortunately, depending on our perspectives we often tend to favor one end of this dimension or the other. This favoritism can affect the planning for and development of new technologies, will impact the implementation process, and will ultimately affect the success or failure of the technology.

A General Application of the Framework

For example, traditional work in organizational behavior might focus on issues related to job design, such as the Job Characteristics Model (c.f., Hackman & Oldham, 1980). This approach is directed at an individual's perceptions of the objective properties of their job. Using the proposed model of MoT, this would be placed on the framework along the macro/micro dimension and the objective/subjective dimension. If it were being used more specifically to gain understanding of a particular type of technology environ-ment, then the third axis (i.e., the human/technology dimension) would also be used. The model, therefore, is designed to be flexible and versatile enough to allow for the placement of and connection to research concepts from other disciplines in relation to the three defined axes. This resiliency is intended to stimulate and encourage investigations of and integration with currently dis-connected, yet related, literatures.

As a visual example, suppose twenty separate pieces of literature were placed on the framework as shown in Figure 2. After placement based upon the three dimensions, three separate clusters become more obvious. These are labeled Cluster 1, Cluster 2, and Cluster 3 in the figure. As portrayed in this framework, the items in Cluster 1 are similar based on objective measures, a macro emphasis, and a human-oriented focus. Cluster 2 has a similar general location, only the strength of each of the dimensions is lower than for Cluster 1. Perhaps Cluster 1 contains research at the organizational level, while Clus-ter 2 is more focused on division- or team-based organization. Therefore, the framework can also represent the strength of the presence or absence along a particular dimension. Cluster 3 is on the subjective side of the framework, with a slight macro orientation and an emphasis on technology.

Comprehensive Framework of Management of Technology

The outcome of combining these three dimensions is a comprehensive framework of MoT, shown in Figure 1. MoT is at the center of the three-dimensional structure. With this model it is possible to take the MoT literature and "map" it onto the framework based on the three dimensions described above. The three axes allow for the literature to be mapped based on one, two, or all three dimensions. Depending on the strength or emphasis of the particu-lar dimension, the literature may be represented as being closer to or further from the relevant axes. As parts of the MoT literature are placed in this frame-work, the mapping illustrates the relationship among the various parts of the literature, or sub-literatures, and how they can be integrated into a more coher-ent body of knowledge on the management of technology.

Directions for Future Development and Research

There are several opportunities for use of the proposed integrative frame-work. The framework allows for the "mapping" of the management of technol-ogy literature in relation to the proposed dimensions along and within the axes, as shown in Figure 2. This mapping process might be in relation to one, two, or all three axes. The location of each item of research on or within the framework suggests its relationship to the proposed dimensions as well as to the other literature that is also mapped. The mapping process should yield a

Figure 2
Positioning research within the framework

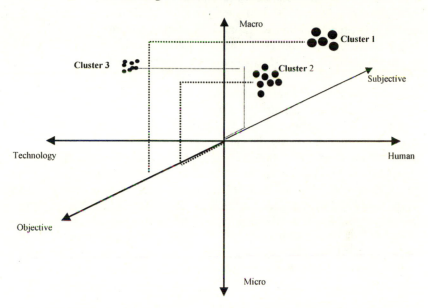

three-dimensional perspective of the MoT literature, which is now graphically and spatially arranged. If clusters develop, as they probably will, it will be due to a common relationship of the research within that cluster along one or more of the axes. Where common ground exists and is identified, opportunities are created for synergy from what may have been disconnected research and experience.

A second outcome from the mapping process will be the identification of a lack of research mapped into various areas. Since MoT is largely problem-driven, this paucity of research may be due to the lack of importance of the relationships suggested in the framework or may be due to a lack of recognition of the types of questions that need to be investigated. In either case, it may be just as important to recognize not only the wealth of research in certain areas or along certain dimensions, but also the poverty of research on specific issues and from certain perspectives. This recognition may stimulate discussion and lead to the identification of unanticipated avenues of investigation. In addition, too much clustering may suggest an overabundance of work along various axes, indicating a lack of communication within the MoT domain and a potential misallocation of resources toward issues that have already been heavily scrutinized.

This is reminiscent of the debate within the management information system (MIS) discipline in the early 1980s as it struggled to identify and codify the literature (c.f., Bariff & Ginzberg, 1980; Keen, 1980; Mason & Swanson, 1980). Out of this discussion grew recognition of the interdisciplinary roots of MIS and a broadening of the questions asked, and investigated. Interestingly, and largely separate from MIS research, it is about this time that business and industry began to recognize the need to better manage its information resources, leading to the rapid growth in the position of chief information officer (CIO).

Other avenues of investigation may be directed at the proposed model itself. The framework is intended to stimulate discussion of the MoT literature as a whole and to address the concerns about the lack of a unifying model and the often-fragmented literature. The question exists, however, on whether the proposed framework is sufficient or appropriate for this task. For example, the proposed dimensions may not be the best or most appropriate. Other potential dimensions might be to contrast research on the creative process of innovation versus the process of diffusion of an innovation. Perhaps an axis might have the five different levels of adoption defined by Rogers (1995), specifically "innovators," "early adopters," "early majority," "late majority," and "laggards." Categorizing this research might yield some interesting insights in how the literature clusters. Additional potential dimensions might also exist. The dimensions used in the proposed framework were derived from the MoT definition developed by the National Research Council (1987).

A more recent path of research within the MIS literature, somewhat parallel to the one mentioned above, may also be instructive. Beginning in the early-to-mid-1980s and progressing well into the 1990s, there has been a debate about the "key issues" in MIS research. The discussion was joined when several projects were directed at determining what were the key issues in MIS research and practice (c.f., Ball & Harris, 1982; Brancheau, Janz, & Wetherbe, 1996; Brancheau & Wetherbe, 1987; Niederman, Brancheau, & Wetherbe, 1991). The issues were largely determined through Delphi surveys of practicing senior executive managers and chief information officers. The most interesting outcome of this research has been the evolution from obviously technical concerns in the mid-1980s, to predominately management-related concerns in the late-1980s, and finally to integrative concerns (ones which focus on leveraging and taking best advantage of the technology's capabilities through proper alignment with the organization and workers) in the early-1990s. Given the growing importance of MoT, and its relative youth as a codified discipline, it may be instructive to examine other recently-developing, technology-related disciplines as our research framework evolves.

Finally, MoT is a problem-driven discipline, with most problems being organizationally and situationally specific. Yet, there are opportunities to learn from the mistakes and successes of others. The difficulty has been, however, that the literature is so fragmented, with little structural guidance to orient the research, that communication and transmission of knowledge have been problematic. The integrative framework proposed above is an effort to provide some structure to the MoT literature with enough breadth and depth to allow for and encourage connections to related literature beyond the scope of typically MoT efforts and, perhaps, outside the sphere of knowledge of the MoT managers and researchers.

Conclusion

The model described above is proposed and offered as a parsimonious way of classifying or categorizing the literature on the management of technology. It suggests that the MoT literature may be organized based on a three-dimensional framework. These dimensions are macro/micro, objective/subjective, and human/technology. The framework is intended to stimulate discussion, not to be the final, cumulative model of MoT. The dimensions that have been delineated were derived from the initial perspectives on and definition of MoT as presented in the report by the National Research Council (1987). While alternative dimensions undoubtedly exist, this model is intended to capture the breadth and depth of the MoT domain and topics as well as to provide opportunities to connect with and integrate appropriate literatures from other disciplines. It is recognized that refinements to the model may be desired after discussion of the merits of the proposed framework. With these dimensions in place, however, it may be possible to more easily speculate on, test, and integrate disparate literatures, showing where and how they may overlap with the evolving discipline we call management of technology. Applying a structure, such as the one propose above, provides opportunities to discern unforeseen connections with other domains of the business, science, and engineering practice and literatures. These connections will only increase in importance as the consequences of advances in science and technology continue to propagate throughout the business and organizational environment.

References

Aldridge, M. D. (1990). Technology management: Fundamental issues for engineering education? *Journal of Engineering and Technology Management*, 6, 303-312.

The American Heritage Dictionary, Second College Edition (1985). Boston, MA: Houghton Mifflin.

Ball, L. & Harris, R. (1982). SMIS members: A membership analysis. *MIS Quarterly*, 6(1), 19-38.

Bariff, M. L. & Ginzberg, M. J. (1980). MIS and the behavioral sciences: Research patterns and prescriptions. In E. R. McLean (Ed.), *Proceedings of the First International Conference on Information Systems*, pp. 49-58, The Society for Management Information Systems.

Barki, H., Rivard, S. & Talbot, J. (1993). A keyword classification scheme of IS research literature: An Update. *MIS Quarterly*, 17(3), 209-226.

Brancheau, J. C., Janz, B. D., & Wetherbe, J. C. (1996). Key issues in information systems management: 1994-1995 SIM Delphi Results. *MIS Quarterly*, 20(2), 225-242

Brancheau, J. C. & Wetherbe, J. C. (1987). Key issues in information systems management, *MIS Quarterly*, 11(1), 23-45.

Burgelman, R. A., Maidique, M. A., & Wheelwright, S. C. (2001). *Strategic Management of Technology and Innovation, 3rd Edition*. Boston, MA: McGraw-Hill Irwin.

Business Week (1994). Here comes the corporate triathlete, January 31, 71-72.

Chammpy, J. 1995. *Reengineering Management: The Mandate for New Leadership*. New York: HarperBusiness.

Christensen, C. M. & Bower, J. L. (1996). Customer power, strategic investment, and the failure of leading firms. *Strategic Management Journal*, 17, 197-218.

Collins, G, Gardiner, P., Heaton, A., Macrosson, K. & Tait, J. (1991). The management of technology: An essential part of training for engineers and scientists. *International Journal of Technology Management*, 6(5/6), 568-593.

Faulkner, R. R. (1982). Improvising on a triad. In J. Van Maanen, J. M. Dabbs, Jr., & R. R. Faulkner (Eds.) *Varieties of Qualitative Research*, pp. 65-101. Beverly Hills, CA: Sage.

Fortune (1993). Making high tech work for you. Special Issue, Autumn.

Gattiker, U. E. (1990). *Technology management in organizations*. Newbury Park, CA: Sage.

Hackman, J. R. & Oldham, G. R. (1980). *Work Redesign*. Reading, MA: Addison-Wesley.

Hammer, M. & Champy, J. (1993). *Reengineering the Corporation: A Manifesto for Business Revolution*. New York: HarperBusiness.

Johnson, B. M. & Rice, R. E. (1987). *Managing Organizational Innovation: The Evolution From Work Processing to Office Information Systems*. New York: Columbia University Press.

Jones, O., Green, K., & Coombs, R. (1994) Technology management: Developing a critical perspective. *International Journal of Technology Management*, 9(2), 156-171.

Keen, P. G. W. (1980). MIS research: Reference disciplines and a cumulative tradition. In E. R. McLean (Ed.), *Proceedings of the First International Conference on Information Systems*, pp. 9-18, The Society for Management Information Systems.

Khalil, T. M. (1998). Management of technology: Future directions and needs for the new century. National Science Foundation, NSF Grant No: DMI-9725914.

Khalil, T. M. (1993). Management of technology education for the 21st Century. *Industrial Engineering*, 25(10), 64-65.

Majchrzak, A. & Salzman, H. (1989). Introduction to the special issue: Social and Organizational dimensions of computer-aided design. *IEEE Transactions on Engineering Management*, 36(3), 174-179.

Mason, R. O. & Swanson, E. B. (1980). Measurement of an MIS foundation. In E. R. McLean (Ed.), *Proceedings of the First International Conference on Information Systems*, pp. 65-68, The Society for Management Information Systems.

Mayr, E. (1982). The Growth of Biological thought: Diversity, Evolution, and Inheritance. Cambridge, MA: Belknap Press.

Narayanan, V. K. (2001). *Managing Technology and Innovation for Competitive Advantage*. Upper Saddle River, NJ: Prentice Hall.

National Research Council (1987). Management of Technology: The Hidden Competitive Advantage. Washington, D.C.: National Academy Press.

Niederman, F., Brancheau, J. C., & Wetherbe, J. C. (1991). Information systems management issues for the 1990s. MIS Quarterly, 15(4), 475-500.

Particleadventure, 2002. As found at www.particleadventure.org/particleadventure/ , October 10.

Postlethwait, J. H. & Hopson, J. L. (1989). *The Nature of Life*. New York: McGraw-Hill.

Rogers, E. M. (1995). *Diffusion of Innovations, Fourth Edition*. New York: The Free Press.

Van Fleet, D. D. & Beard, J. W. (1988). Lessons for management research from a history of science. Annual Meeting of the Academy of Management, Los Angeles, CA.

Wilbraham, A. C., Staley, D. D., Matta, M. S., & Waterman, E. L. (2000). *Chemistry, 5th Edition*. Menlo Park, CA: Addison-Wesley.

Zuboff, S. (1988). *In the Age of the Smart Machine: The Future of Work and Power*. New York: Basic Books.

4

Unique Features of an R&D Work Environment and Research Scientists and Engineers

Thomas E. Clarke

Not only is good management of research the critical difference between a thriving research organization and an average one, but research is the most difficult to manage of all functional activities. (Lamontagne Report, 1972, Vol. 2, referenced in Vol. 6, Ch. 10, p. 8 of the 1994 Report of the Auditor General of Canada)

Senator Maurice Lamontagne, during his extensive review of science policy in Canada, identified three reasons or factors why managing research is different from managing other human activities:

- the uncertainty of outcome of research;
- the difficulty of measuring the results or impacts of research when each research task is unique; and
- the differences in the expectations, values, attitudes, and motivation of scientists and engineers from those of other employees (i.e., the people element).

Thomas E. Clarke graduated from the University of British Columbia with a Master's in Physics in 1967. During his employment at Atomic Energy of Canada Ltd., he became interested in the effective management of scientists and engineers and returned to U.B.C. to obtain an MBA in organizational behavior. Subsequently, he held numerous positions in the Canadian government relating to R&D. During this time he designed Canada's Industrial Innovation Center Program to support the training of future technical entrepreneurs and to provide advice to small high-tech businesses. In 1980, he started his own consulting firm, Stargate Consultants Limited, <www.stargate-consultants.ca>, which specializes in science policy/program studies and R&D management training. He may be reached at <stargate@island.net>.

To this list can be added at least two more major factors: the rapid rate of change of the scientific knowledge base, and the unique organizational characteristics of a creative and productive R&D-based institution which differs from the more traditional characteristics seen in most non science-based government departments.

This review of the uniqueness of the R&D work environment and R&D personnel will elaborate on these five factors and show why managing R&D projects and personnel is generally more difficult than managing other organizational functions.

Uncertainty Associated with Scientific Activities

R&D, by its very nature, is an activity that is aimed at generating new knowledge, testing hypotheses about how matters in the physical or social world act and react, and in general, providing know-how which can be used to create or improve activities or systems in that part of our life to which they pertain. (Salasin and Hattery, 1977, p. 5)

A major distinguishing feature of R&D that differentiates it from other functions in an organization is the level of uncertainty associated with it. R&D is characterized not only by uncertainty in terms of project duration, or budget, but also by the nature of the results. This is especially so at the research end of the R&D spectrum, which is usually regarded as the stage from basic scientific research through to experimental development.

A fully competent scientist may tackle a research project, and conduct it in a totally acceptable manner, and still not obtain the output required to answer the scientific question or solve the problem being addressed. In most organizations this would be considered a failure, and reflect badly on the worker. In a well managed R&D organization, the results would be viewed as valuable in that a line of research has been shown to be unproductive, and another approach must be made. The researcher would not be blamed for this "failure."

In another situation, totally unexpected results might be obtained which may lead to even greater benefits. Is it a failure that the original objectives were not met? Technically, yes, but only a bureaucratic mind or "bean counter" would insist on calling it a failure. 3M's glue that would not permanently stick to anything was clearly a technical failure at one level, but a huge success at another given the widespread use of "Post-It" notes in all their many manifestations.

Uncertainty associated with scientific activities can also take the form of "by-products" of the research process that the observant scientist must recognize. As we all know, penicillin was not a planned discovery, but the result of Alexander Fleming noting something unusual in a petri dish.

As noted above, the uncertainty associated with R&D projects makes it much more difficult for managers to plan and budget. Research activities may take longer to produce results, and may need more resources that originally planned. This does not allow for the traditional annual budget cycles found in most government departments. Multi-year funding must be in place so that the research momentum is kept constant.

Most other professionals, such as medical doctors and lawyers, usually deal with an existing knowledge base (e.g., well understood diseases or prior case law) or known technology; this is not the case for research scientists or engineers. They are either developing a new understanding of a natural phenomenon, developing new analytical techniques, or solving a problem for which there is no known solution. In some cases, they must throw out what they think they know and work in totally unknown territory. No other professional occupation faces the situation of pushing back the frontiers of science or engineering *to go where no one has gone before*.

Difficulty of Assessing the Contribution or Impact of the Research Results

The output of research is knowledge and it is difficult to predict in advance, with any accuracy, the quality, quantity or usefulness of the knowledge that will be generated from any given research project. Yet accountants, finance officers, bureaucrats, and politicians like to be able to show quantitative evidence that the resources invested in research have tangible results or impacts, usually within the time frame of their budget or evaluation period or their term of office.

Senator Lamontagne stated in his review of Canadian science policy that "even when the results can be measured, the delay between the successful conclusion of a research project and the impact may be so great, that it is hard to use the knowledge of the results as a basis for planning for the future."

In many instances, the impact of one line of research must await developments in other areas of science or technology before their impact or application can be seen. The impact or applications of laser technology, for example, languished for years before practical applications were developed. No one could have predicted such widespread uses from a substitution for record player needles to optical surgery. On more than one occasion Nobel Prizes in science have been awarded years after the initial scientific discovery, because at the time the value or importance of the discovery to the field was underestimated.

When trying to measure R&D productivity and output, stronger emphasis should be placed on non-financial performance indicators such as value creation, utility to the customer, market share changes, ability to maintain technological leadership in core business categories, and ability to implement new technology when needed to meet competition (Wolff, 1991).

Another difficulty facing R&D managers is to conduct the annual performance appraisal of scientific staff in a fair and accurate manner. Assessing the contribution of a scientist's output to a field, or the eventual impact that contribution will have in the future can be especially challenging. In some cases, a scientist's manager may be ill-equipped to evaluate the scientist's performance because of a lack of an in-depth knowledge of the scientific field of the scientist being evaluated.

Rapid Advancement of Scientific or Technical Knowledge

In no other area of human endeavour is change more dominant than in the areas of science and technology. In almost no other profession is the pace of change as rapid. Medical procedures change relatively slowly; changes in management practices and theory can be measured in years; changes in law can take decades. In contrast, it has been estimated that the half-life of initial engineering education is less than five years.

Technological obsolescence is a constant fear of scientists and engineers because it is very easy to fall behind. An assignment that takes a scientist away from his or her work for six months, may, depending on the field, force the scientist to have to study the field anew for a year just to catch up with colleagues. Continuous learning throughout the lifetime of working scientists and engineers is a must if they are to stay at the forefront of their discipline and contribute to it.

Technological obsolescence also applies to equipment and analytical procedures. Out-of-date equipment or techniques limit the ability of the researchers to be involved in "cutting edge" research and also the services a laboratory can offer to its internal or external clients.

Thus R&D managers and scientific organizations must operate in a way that assists their scientific and engineering staff to avoid obsolescence. Actions such as assignment of projects that demand the acquisition of new skills and knowledge, and liberal policies on attendance at professional meetings and conferences to meet with their national and international colleagues to learn about the latest advances, are extremely important if the organization wants an R&D laboratory with vitality. Conference attendance cannot be considered a luxury. Some organizations such as Exxon in the United States go as far as having joint degree programs with local universities and encourage their staff to obtain advanced degrees.

Failure to avoid technological obsolescence in either people or equipment will result in inadequate or overly expensive solutions to problems, problems avoided and not solved, and a general reduction in the organization's ability to fulfill its mandate or to survive. Thus avoiding technological obsolescence in the face of rapidly evolving science and technology is another unique characteristic of the R&D work environment.

Research Cannot Be Stopped and Restarted Easily

One of the important consequences of the rapid change in the scientific knowledge base is that research projects that are of an inherently long-term nature cannot be stopped and then quickly restarted like a production line. Scientists and engineers will not sit around waiting for a green light to restart a project. In order to maintain their scientific expertise, they will go on to other projects or employers, thus making them unavailable for the original project.

An additional problem is that it takes time to build an effective research team. Once a team is split up, it may take six months to a year to bring it back to the functioning level it was at before the breakup. The passage of time may force the members of the team to play catch-up, if their field of activity has moved ahead in areas that they have not been working in, but are of importance to the team activity. The original objectives of the team might have to be modified in the light of advancements that have taken place since the team's breakup.

Differences in Expectations, Values, Attitudes, and Motivation of Scientists and Engineers

Research scientists and engineers, while sharing many attributes with highly trained people in other professions, have some characteristics that are more associated with them, than with other professionals.

Orientation Toward Things, Not People

In general, people who go in for science or engineering are oriented more towards things or natural phenomena than people. Many are characterized as having a poor grasp of social skills and do not make friends easily. They are more comfortable working with things that they can objectively measure and control (Badawy, 1983). In addition, many scientists, more than engineers, are introverts who prefer the company of a few friends or acquaintances rather than being surrounded by strangers at a party.

One result of this orientation is the reluctance among many research scientists and engineers to take on managerial responsibility. Unlike many other professionals, scientists and engineers do not seek out promotion to the ranks of management as this would force them to interact with people to a greater degree and detract from their focus on their scientific profession. They simply would not derive any satisfaction from a management position. In a survey of scientists and engineers in the Canadian federal government conducted several years ago, to determine their views on becoming a supervisor, one respondent when asked whether he would like to be a supervisor said, "*Hell no, I would rather drive a cab.*" This author has also noted the difficulties some government laboratories have in encouraging competent scientific staff to move into managerial positions.

Orientation Toward Profession, Not Employer

Research scientists and, to a lesser extent, engineers care more about how their colleagues around the world think about their work than their immediate supervisor. Scientists or engineers with what is called a "cosmopolitan" orientation:

- are low on loyalty to their employing organization;
- are high on commitment to advancing knowledge in their professional field; and
- look for rewards from their peers in their professional community.

Badawy (1971), in a study of role orientations of scientists, concluded that the goal orientation of scientists was towards:

- advancement of knowledge for its own sake;
- establishing a reputation through publishing;
- having research achievements that will bring professional recognition; and
- advancing and moving ahead as specialists in their field.

This orientation may be the result of the socialization process that research scientists and engineers are subject to while attending university and obtaining advance degrees.

Other professionals, including some scientists and engineers, are more likely to have a more "local" orientation to their work that is described as:

- being very loyal to their employing organization;
- having a low commitment to advancing knowledge in their professional field; and
- looking for rewards from their employer.

Other Expectations and Values

Because professionals invest more time and energy in educational preparation for their work than do most other employees, they bring unique, higher and more specific expectations to work. (Miller, 1988)

Miller (1988) outlines some generalized organizational and work-values usually held by professionals:

- professionals feel that they have a moral and ethical right not to follow the direction of management when it goes against their principles and values;
- being critical of management is a professional responsibility—and often fun;
- individualism is desirable, perhaps even one of the rights of the professional;
- the goal of good science for the scientist—or of a powerful effective program for the programmer—is often more important than and transcends organizational goals in the eyes of the professional; and
- when professionals apply personal knowledge and expertise in a creative way, this usually builds a strong emotional bond (ownership) with the work output. This can be good because it supports a drive for excellence, and/or bad because it often means the professional resents the organization's need for a project end and the passing of the output to another phase.

Bench Researchers Insist that Their Immediate Managers Have a Scientific or Technical Background

There is a strong expectation among scientists and engineers "at the bench" that their immediate R&D managers will, themselves, have a scientific or engineering background. The myth of "a manager is a manager is a manager" falls apart very quickly in an R&D environment. The manager is expected to be able to provide substantive advice and act as a sounding board for technical ideas or proposals. This cannot be done by someone who does not have scientific or technical training in the scientific or technical field under study.

Many studies have noted that an R&D manager's initial credibility comes from their credibility as a contributing scientist or engineer, and then later, hopefully, as an effective manager.

Motivating and Rewarding Scientists and Engineers Is Different

Managers motivate their scientists and engineers by the work environment they create. (Koning, Jr., 1993)

Scientists and engineers, perhaps more than other professionals, are highly motivated when they are allowed to satisfy their psychological needs for achievement, recognition, professional growth, and working on challenging, interesting projects. Even in times of economic and job uncertainty, the opportunity to do challenging, interesting work and to gain recognition are the most powerful motivators of scientists (Bucher and Reece, 1972).

In a review of the R&D management literature on reward and recognition systems for creative scientists and engineers, Clarke (1996) found that the literature tends to emphasize intrinsic rewards over direct financial incentives.

Research scientists and engineers generally respond more positively to intrinsic forms of reward and recognition such as:

- praise and feedback from colleagues, both within and outside their organization;
- freedom to develop their own ideas (autonomy);
- being assigned work of significance and importance;
- having the freedom to select, within broad parameters, their research projects;
- being assigned challenging, interesting projects; and
- allowing the scientists and engineers to participate in decision-making that affects them and their work.

More traditional forms of reward and recognition such as salary increases, stock options, financial bonuses, or promotion into management are not as effective with scientists and engineers, as long as they consider their base pay to be fair and satisfactory.

In summary, scientists and engineers with a more cosmopolitan orientation want the opportunity to work on challenging projects that are adequately funded and that will result in some meaningful output that will be recognized and praised by their peers.

Characteristics Associated with Science-based Organizations

Organizations that rely on the output of creative research scientists or engineers for their survival have different characteristics than those organizations who rely on other attributes to meet their organizational objectives or mandate.

Participative Managerial Style Encouraged

R&D should not be treated in the same manner as on-going repetitive operations... Procedures that are applicable to production or widespread application are not ordinarily properly applicable to R&D. (Salasin and Hattery, 1977, p. 5)

In reviews of the literature concerned with the management of R&D personnel, the need for a science-based organization to promote a participative style of management is a dominant theme. An autocratic approach to management is just not effective when an organization requires both creativity and productivity. Martell and Carroll (1995) point out that traditional human resources management practices (HRM) may not work in environments that stress technological innovation and managers face a special challenge in identifying the HRM practices that most effectively support innovation.

Protestations to the contrary, most organizations are not looking for creative output from their employees. They want employees that can follow instructions and operate within a very narrow band of decision-making authority.

Sharing of decision-making authority is a key element of the participative style. In more traditional organizations, people at the senior levels of the management hierarchy have both the power and knowledge to make effective decisions. In knowledge-based organizations, the power to make decisions may still be at the top, but the ability to make effective decisions concerned with the knowledge base of the organization lies at the bottom of the hierarchy, with the bench scientists and engineers. Thus in order to make effective decisions, those with the power must consult with and get input from those with the knowledge to ensure that the decision is the right one.

Another factor that contributes to the unique characteristics of an R&D-based organization is the inability of R&D managers to stay current and at the leading edge in many scientific or technical fields at once. An R&D manager may be supervising a group of scientists or engineers who operate in different fields than the one in which the manager trained. They are the experts. In addition, time pressures on R&D managers may limit their ability to even stay current in their own field. The net effect is that the R&D managers do not know as much as their employees about what should be done in the progress of a research project and how best to do it. They must consult with their staff if the organization is to meet its objectives. Even in the case of work conducted by a technologist, the technologist may be the best person to decide on the physical layout of an experiment.

Long-term vs. Short-term Planning Horizons

A distinguishing feature of an effectively managed R&D organization is their taking a long-term view of their research activities. Unfortunately, many private sector firms in the United States and Canada have succumbed to the disease of "short-termitus."

In industrial organizations, managers, especially those with no technical background, often fail to appreciate that in R&D there can be a long time between investment of resources, including human resources, and tangible results in the form of products or processes that contribute to the company's bottom line. This time frame, especially on the research end of the R&D spectrum, is often well beyond the typical five-year planning cycle of most organizations and usually beyond the "annual budget" time frame. Research managers in government laboratories with mandates to support sustainable growth creation and economic growth or improved quality of life, probably have greater problems in measuring the impacts of research.

One of the major problems in the decline of U.S. businesses in the late 1970s has been attributed to the failure of American managers to keep their companies technologically competitive over the long term (Hayes and Abernathy, 1980). Management that measures both company and managerial performance using only short-term financial measurements create an environment "in which no one feels he or she can afford a failure or even a momentary dip in the bottom line." Yet research, by its very nature, means that some projects will "fail" or may take a long time to produce the hoped-for results. Managers who rely on objective, quantifiable criteria to measure performance cannot relate to the uncertainties of research. The preponderance of financial analysts and accountants in company boardrooms resulted in a reduction in funding for long-term research and a concentration on short-term work that was less risky, less innovative, and that would produce results quickly. A similar emphasis on the short-term is still seen today; an emphasis not adopted by our competitor, Japan.

Other studies (including Baldwin 1991, NSB Committee 1991, Heininger 1988, Steele 1988) have pointed out that financial considerations, such as the use of discounted cash flow techniques and cost-benefit analyses to select projects, and demands for short-term return on investment have contributed to the decline in technology leadership in the United States.

R&D managers have to be aggressive in trying to get corporate management to look at R&D as a long-term investment in the viability of the organization and encourage the CEO to establish the research budget outside the time frame of the regular budget control process (Leet 1991).

Delayed Age of Joining the Work Force Shortens the "Window of Creativity"

Unlike many professional disciplines, research scientists usually require training up to the Ph.D. level, and research engineers to at least the Master's level. This results in them joining the work force at a much later age than most employees. In general, scientists reach their creative peak between twenty-eight and forty years of age. After that, they may remain very productive, but not have the same creative spark that they had earlier. Thus scientific organizations have a "ten to twelve year window" within which to encourage and elicit creative work from their scientists and research engineers. In most organizations, creativity is not called for, and experience over the years is of more importance to their success.

Retention of the Best and Brightest Researchers is More Critical

Retention of professional employees is of vital importance to science-based organizations. It may have taken years for a scientist or engineer to acquire sufficient understanding of his or her specialty to be of creative and productive value to their employer. If they leave, the productive, creative capacity of the firm will be lowered immediately. It may not be possible to replace that person in a timely manner to avoid a whole research program being closed down. Even if a replacement can be quickly found, it may take months before the person is able to achieve the same level of performance as the person they are replacing.

While few people are irreplaceable in the long term, an organization may pay a high price if a key, well-respected, knowledgeable researcher suddenly resigns. The price can be measured in terms of lost research momentum, considerable financial costs of finding a suitable replacement that may involve searching the worldwide scientific community, and the cost in terms of lowered organizational reputation if it is seen as not being able to retain its best and brightest. This last cost could prevent the organization from being able to hire the needed replacement even when identified.

Lower Level R&D Managers are Still Scientific Contributors

Another feature of the R&D environment which is different from many other professional activities is the fact that at the lower levels of R&D management, the managers work side-by-side with their subordinates on research projects in their field of expertise. They not only manage the R&D project but also actively take part in the execution of the project.

In most other professional occupations, a move into management means dropping their professional activities and supervising the work of others. They do not "get their hands dirty" with the actual day-to-day work, except in emergencies.

Dual Promotion Ladders

Another unique feature of science or engineering based organizations is the existence of the "dual promotion" ladder. (In some organizations there are more that two promotion paths.)

As noted earlier, scientists are not generally anxious to climb the traditional corporate management ladder. This poses a problem for organizations wanting to reward scientists for excellent performance. To overcome this difficulty, many progressive R&D based organizations have established a second promotional ladder (some have a third ladder specifically for engineers) so that scientists or research engineers can be "promoted" and rewarded or recognized by movement up this technical or scientific ladder. These scientific ladders have rungs comparable to the rungs on the management ladder but do not involve the person having to take on additional managerial duties. Each step or rung on the technical ladder has its own title such senior research scientist, principal research scientist, etc., and the salary and perquisites associated with the step are the same or comparable to the equivalent step on the managerial ladder. It is common for scientists at the higher levels of the technical ladder to also wield considerable influence over the research direction of the organization.

The existence of a dual or multi-path promotion ladder also avoids putting pressure on productive scientists or engineers to leave research in order to "get ahead" in the organization in terms of higher salaries or organizational power. In many cases, when scientists move to the managerial ladder just to get more financial compensation, the organization loses a productive, highly motivated scientist and gains an unfulfilled, mediocre manager.

In almost no other organizational structure does dual promotion ladders play such an vital role in maintaining the creativity and productivity of the organization. There are, in fact, several possible alternate career paths for scientists or engineers besides staying at the "bench" or going into R&D management: there is S&T policy development, health, safety or environmental regulatory/standards activities or R&D business development.

Conclusion

The dedication of research scientists and engineers in pushing back the frontiers of science and converting knowledge into practical applications is a hallmark of this professional community.

R&D personnel and the R&D work environment have many features that are either unique, or although shared with other professionals and their work environments, are of greater importance to the effective operation of an organization.

Among these features or characteristics are:

- the rapid pace of change of the R&D knowledge base;
- the considerable uncertainty associated with the outcome of R&D activities;
- the orientation of many scientific professionals towards working with things rather than people;
- reluctance by many researchers to take on managerial responsibilities;
- orientation of many researchers toward their profession not their present employer;
- researchers having a value system which emphasizes independence, freedom, and autonomy to make decisions concerning their work;
- a strong need to experience achievement, gain recognition from their peers, have opportunities for professional growth, and to work on challenging, interesting projects;
- an insistence that their immediate supervisors have credibility as scientists or engineers;
- a lack of interest in traditional avenues of managerial promotion and reward;

- the difficulty in evaluating and recognizing valuable outputs of research when they occur;
- the need for long-term planning horizons;
- the relatively older age of the scientists and engineers when they enter the work force and the short window of opportunity in which they are creative;
- the damaging effect that prematurely losing a highly creative researcher can have on the organization's ability to meet its objectives;
- the requirement of a working environment in which bench research personnel must be consulted on the direction and conduct of research projects in order to arrive at effective decision; and
- the need for a "dual promotion" ladder to reward scientists and engineers in a manner designed to increase their motivation to be creative and productive and to avoid losing them to a career path which does not use their abilities to the fullest or provide them with adequate job satisfaction.

The management of the technological innovation process and R&D personnel has been the subject of study for the past fifty years (Clarke and Reavley, 2001). In all this work, no one has argued that R&D can be managed or supported in exactly the same manner as any other organizational activity. The special features of R&D management and the R&D work environment are clearly recognized. Only those science-based organizations that acknowledge these differences and modify their management approach accordingly have any long-term future.

References

Badawy, M.K., "Managing Career Transitions," *Research Management*, Vol. 26, No. 4, July-August, 1983, pp. 28-31

Badawy, M.K., "Understanding the Role Orientations of Scientists and Engineers," *Personnel Journal*, Vol. 50, No. 6, June, 1971, pp. 449-454, 485

Baldwin, Carliss Y., "How Capital Budgeting Deters Innovation - And What to Do About It," *Research-Technology Management*, November-December, 1991, Vol. 34, No. 6, pp. 39-45

Bucher, G.C. and Reece, J.E., "What Motivates Researchers in Times of Economic Uncertainty," *Research Management*, Vol. 15, No. 1, January, 1972, pp. 19-32

Clarke, Thomas E., "Review of Literature on Rewards and Recognition for R&D Personnel," Nanaimo, B.C.: Stargate Consultants Limited, February, 1996

Clarke, Thomas E. and Reavley, Jean, "Science and Technology Management Bibliography 2001," Nanaimo, B.C. Stargate Consultants Limited, 2001

Government of Canada, "Science and Technology for the New Century: A Federal Strategy," Ottawa, Minister of Supply and Services Canada, March 1996

Hayes, Robert H. and Abernathy, William J., "Managing Our Way to Economic Decline," *Harvard Business Review*, July-August, 1980, pp. 67-77

Heininger, S. Allen, "R&D and Competitiveness - What Leaders Must Do," *Research-Technology Management*, November-December, 1988, Vol.31, No 6, pp. 6-7

Koning Jr., John W., "Three Other R's: Recognition, Reward and Resentment," *Research-Technology Management*, Vol. 36, No. 4, July-August, 1993, pp. 19-29

Lamontagne, Maurice, "A Science Policy for Canada," Ottawa, Ontario, 1972

Leet, Richard H. "How Top Management Sees R&D," *Research-Technology Management*, January-February 1991, Vol. 34, No. 1, pp. 15-17

Martell, Kathryn D. and Carroll, Jr., Stephen J. "The Role of HRM in Innovation Strategies," *R&D Management*, January, 1995, Vol. 25, No. 1, pp. 91-104

Miller, Donald B., "Challenges in Leading Professionals," *Research-Technology Management*, January-February, 1988, Vol. 31, No. 1, pp. 42-46

National Science Board Committee on Industrial Support for R&D, "Why U.S. Technology Leadership Is Eroding," *Research-Technology Management*, March-April, 1991, Vol. 34, No. 2, pp. 36-48

Salasin, John and Hattery, Lowell, in "The Management of Federal Research and Development: An Analysis of Major Issues and Processes," McLean, VA, The Mitre Corporation, 1977, pp. 3-16

Steele, Lowell, W., "Selecting R&D Programs and Objectives," *Research-Technology Management*, March-April, 1988, Vol. 31, No. 2, pp. 17-36

Wolff, Michael, "What Does the CEO Want?," *Research-Technology Management*, July-August, 1991, Vol. 34, No. 4, pp. 10-12

5

Understanding Software Technology

Richard A. Howey

Software is a difficult technology to understand strategically. Many frameworks developed for strategic technology analysis are specific to physical technologies. This chapter analyzes two frameworks, the cascade model of technology evolution and the concept of technology potency. Modifications to the cascade model are proposed that make it more compatible with software. Difficulties with the concept of technology potency when applied to software are illustrated and directions for further research are pointed out.

Understanding Software Technology

Software is a troublesome technology. It just does not seem to fit the same mold as other, more physical, technologies. Its existence is abstract. You cannot pick it up and hold it in your hand. (You can pick up a diskette or CD-ROM on which a copy of the software is stored, but that is not the same as picking up the software itself.) You cannot measure it using physical units like kilograms, centimeters, megawatts, or microvolts.

Yet software is an extremely important technology to modern business and to society at large. Enterprise Resource Planning (ERP) software packages such as PeopleSoft and SAP are critical to many businesses. Software technologies such as relational databases and operating systems are vital components of numerous business systems. Software helps implement important new

Richard A. Howey is a senior consultant at Watson Wyatt Worldwide where he applies data warehousing and other advanced analytical software technologies to satisfy the information needs of human resources management professionals. He has over twenty-six years of experience in information systems as a software developer, project manager, and consultant. He may be reached at <rich_howey@yahoo.com>.

business processes such as knowledge management. The World Wide Web is largely a software phenomenon. Indeed, software was the primary technology in the recent dot-com (or dot-bomb) debacle. The failure of so many dot-com ventures is a testament to the disaster that can occur when software technology and its business implications are misunderstood. On the other hand, the success of software giants such as Microsoft, Oracle, SAP, and PeopleSoft is a testament to the rewards that can be reaped when software technology and its business implications are properly understood.

It is important for technology management professionals to get a better handle on software technology. This paper examines some of the issues involved in understanding software. Specific issues addressed include defining software technology and developing frameworks for the strategic analysis of software technology.

Defining Software Technology

Before proceeding too far, we need a definition of software technology. Such a definition should be compatible with a definition of technology overall. Dr. Rias van Wyk of the University of Minnesota has developed a working definition of technology:

> Technology is created competence as manifested in devices, procedures, and acquired human skills.[1]

This definition can easily be shown to encompass software as well as other technologies. Software is certainly a created competence. It is manifested in many devices. Procedures are used to implement its development, maintenance, and operation. Its development, maintenance, and use are acquired human skills.

This definition is quite interesting for certain things that it does not say. For example, it does not say that technology is an application of science. Indeed, we can implement technologies where we do not truly understand the underlying science. The first primitive man that made a bow and arrow and used it to hunt certainly did not understand the science behind his invention. Yet, he was using technology. Thus, it is reasonable to exclude an understanding of the underlying science as a necessary condition for something being a technology.

One interesting term in this definition is the word "device." Usually, we think of a device as a specific physical entity. Software is the set of instructions that tell a general purpose device, a computer, what to do to perform some specific function such as computing a payroll. It conceptually turns the general purpose computer into a special purpose device. We can think of the software as encapsulating the major properties of this conceptual special purpose device. In other words, we can think of the software as a "virtual device."

In addition, some software packages can operate on many different hardware/computer devices. That is part of software's attractiveness. The ability to operate software on different hardware platforms with different costs and performance characteristics is one of the reasons we implement a capability in software rather than hardware. For example, the Oracle data base management system is available on large parallel servers, mid-range servers, small servers, and personal computers. Software is scalable by changing the hardware platform on which it is executed. The performance characteristics of the software can vary dramatically depending on the hardware platform where it is executed. Yet many other properties of the software will remain the same no matter what hardware platform it is executed on.

Thus, it is useful to think of software as a virtual device that is independent of the hardware platform on which it is going to be executed. Given this concept, Dr. van Wyk's definition can be clarified to explicitly include software virtual devices:

> Technology is created competence as manifested in devices (including both physical devices and software virtual devices), procedures, and acquired human skills.

Now we will turn to specifically defining software technology. The Software Engineering Institute (SEI) at Carnegie Mellon University is one of the foremost authorities on software technology. The SEI defines software technology as follows:

> Technology is the practical application of scientific knowledge in a particular domain or in a particular manner to accomplish a task. ... Software technology is defined as: the theory and practice of various sciences (to include computer, cognitive, statistical sciences, and others) applied to software development, operation, understanding, and maintenance.
>
> More specifically, we view software technology as any concept, process, method, algorithm, or tool, whose primary purpose is the development, operation, and maintenance of software or software-intensive systems. Technology is not just the technical artifacts, but the knowledge embedded in those artifacts and the knowledge required for their effective use.[2]

Some contrasts between the two definitions are striking. First, the SEI definition makes scientific knowledge the basis for technology while Dr. van Wyk's definition did not. This is probably not a major issue since software must be implemented in programming languages and all programming languages are human creations that have a mathematical basis. Thus, while not all technology must have an understood scientific basis, software technology must—at least in the programming languages that are used to construct the software if nothing else.

In addition, the SEI definition only includes acquired abilities that are applied in the development, operation, and maintenance of software. It does not appear to include the end-product software application itself within the scope of its definition. While it may include components that are used to build software applications such as data base management systems and object request brokers, it appears to exclude the software applications themselves. This can be verified by examining the SEI web site that lists technologies. None of the software technologies listed are end-user applications.[3] Dr. van Wyk's definition, as clarified, can certainly include software applications under the category of software virtual devices.

This is a more serious issue since an understanding of the application of software to solve business problems and to enable new business processes is a critical issue for modern business. This is not a major concern for the SEI since its primary focus is software development for the U.S. Department of Defense. But, software applications that can implement important business functions must be a major concern of technology management professionals.

In addition, much of the focus of software implementation can be expected to switch from professional software engineers to end-users of software that will be enabled to develop much of their own application capabilities. Dr. Barry Boehm estimates that by the year 2005, there will be:

- 55 million end-user "programmers" who will assume much of the role of application developers
- 750,000 professional infrastructure implementers
- 2 million professionals that will implement application generators and composition aids, develop systems using application composition, and integrate large-scale systems.[4]

Understanding the end-user application capabilities that will allow so many non-professional programmers to act as application developers is important to business and therefore to technology management professionals.

On the other hand, Dr. van Wyk's definition (as clarified) includes everything implied by the SEI definition. "Created competence as expressed in devices (including both physical devices and virtual software devices), procedures, and acquired human skills" is a superset of "any concept, process, method, algorithm, or tool, whose primary purpose is the development, operation, and maintenance of software or software-intensive systems."

Given these issues, it is desirable for technology management professionals to define software technology based on Dr. van Wyk's definition of technology rather than to simply use the SEI definition. Some elements of the SEI definition are useful, however, primarily for adding clarity. Therefore, the following definition of software technology is proposed:

Technology is created competence as manifested in devices (including both physical devices and software virtual devices), procedures, and acquired human skills. Software technology is any technology that is implemented as computer software or that supports the development, operation, understanding, and/or maintenance of software.

Frameworks for Strategic Analysis of Software Technology

To assist in the strategic analysis of technology, a number of frameworks have been developed. However, these frameworks have been easier to apply to physical technologies than to software. In the following paragraphs, we examine two of these frameworks, the cascade model of technological evolution and the concept of technological potency, in relation to software.

The Cascade Model of Technology Evolution

The cascade model is a framework for understanding how technology evolves. The model defines five levels through which technological changes cascade as illustrated in Figure 1.[5]

At the first level, many technological changes are driven or enabled by changes in materials. At the second level, technological change is viewed as improvements in size, principle of operation, and structure of the technology. At the third level, technological change is viewed as improved performance as the technological entity evolves. At the fourth level, the technological change is viewed as a reduction in real cost per unit of output and an improvement in safety, health, and environmental impact. At the fifth level, the improved technology is viewed as diffusing through the technological landscape.[6]

The model as stated cannot be easily applied to software. It is too specific to physical technologies. For example, software does not depend on materials. However, the model can be generalized so that it can be applied to software as well as other technologies. Figure 2 illustrates a proposed generalized cascade

Figure 1
Cascade model of technological evolution

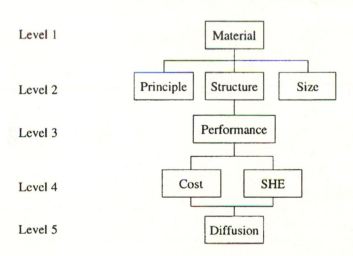

Figure 2
Generalized cascade model

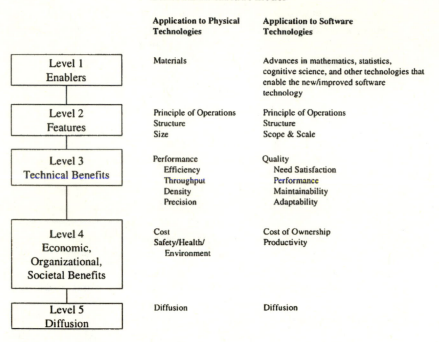

	Application to Physical Technologies	Application to Software Technologies
Level 1 **Enablers**	Materials	Advances in mathematics, statistics, cognitive science, and other technologies that enable the new/improved software technology
Level 2 **Features**	Principle of Operations Structure Size	Principle of Operations Structure Scope & Scale

Level 3
Technical Benefits
	Performance
	   Efficiency
	   Throughput
	   Density
	   Precision
		Quality
		   Need Satisfaction
		   Performance
		   Maintainability
		   Adaptability

Level 4 **Economic, Organizational, Societal Benefits**	Cost Safety/Health/ Environment	Cost of Ownership Productivity
Level 5 **Diffusion**	Diffusion	Diffusion

model and indicates how the generalized model can be applied to physical and software technologies.

The proposed generalized cascade model is discussed in detail in the following paragraphs.

Level 1—Enablers

Many improvements in technology depend on improvements in materials science. However, improvements in software do not depend on materials. On the other hand, improvements in software technology do depend on something. Technologies build on each other. For example, the modern ERP system would not exist were it not for advancements in database management systems and client/server computing. The World Wide Web would not exist were it not for the hypertext markup language (HTML), the hypertext transport protocol (HTTP), and the Internet. Artificial neural network data mining software products would not exist were it not for the development of the mathematical model of the multilayer perceptron (MLP) and back-propagation algorithm that is used to train the MLP to recognize patterns in data. These other technological advances enable the various new or improved software technologies.

Thus, we can generalize the first level of the cascade model to "Enablers." In the case of physical technologies, the enabler is often improved materials. In the case of software technologies, the enablers may be one or more other software technologies, hardware advances, mathematical developments, or other types of technology advances.

Level 2—Features

At the second level, principle of operation and structure apply to software just as well as they do to other technologies. Software certainly has structure. For example, ERP systems are structured as a set of applications built using a common infrastructure that includes a programming language and a centralized database. Principles also govern the operation of software technologies. ERPs, to continue our example, are built on the principle of using a common database to share information between many functional applications. Software also has size that can be measured in such things as source lines of code and function points. But does size measured in such units really have meaning when analyzing software at a strategic level? Probably not.

However, from a strategic standpoint, it could be very important to know whether a software technology applies on a global scale like the World Wide Web, an enterprise scale like an ERP, a departmental scale like a sales and marketing data mart, or on an individual user scale like a spreadsheet or word processing program. It could also be important to understand the scope of a software technology as far as the range of applications it encompasses. For example, an ERP might encompass applications as diverse as human resources, finance, manufacturing, and supply chain management. On the other hand, a word processing application may do only just that one function—word processing.

Thus, we can apply the second level of the cascade model to software pretty much as it is. We note that size for software does not relate to its physical size —that really has no strategic meaning. Size, in a strategic sense, relates to the scale and scope of the software technology. We might label this level of the model as "features" of the new or improved technology.

Level 3—Technical Benefits

Performance at level 3 of the cascade model is a difficult concept to apply to software. As noted earlier, software performance can vary dramatically based on the hardware on which the software is executed. Yet many properties of the software remain constant no matter what hardware platform it is executed on. Thus, it would be desirable to find a concept of "performance" for software that is independent of the hardware platform.

In physical technologies, improvements in performance are typically improvements in:

- Efficiency—e.g., an improvement in material produced vs. energy consumed for a new metal processing technology
- Throughput—e.g., an improvement in material produced vs. time for a new cement manufacturing technology
- Density—e.g., an improvement in bits of data stored per unit of volume for a new data storage technology
- Precision—e.g., an improvement in the accuracy of laser measurement technology[7]

These performance improvements can be physically measured and related to some way in which the new or improved technology is better than older technologies. There is some measurable benefit to the new technology.

Software technology also has its benefits, even when considered separately from the hardware on which it is executed. For example, an ERP has the benefit of a higher level of integration between business applications. Object oriented programming languages have the benefit of making it easier to reuse software components in another application.

We can generalize level 3 of the cascade model to be the technical benefits of the new or improved technology. The SEI has developed a taxonomy of software quality improvements. This taxonomy provides a good starting place for defining the benefits of a software technology[8]:

1. Need Satisfaction Measures
    1.1. Effectiveness
        1.1.1. Necessity of Characteristics
        1.1.2. Sufficiency of Characteristics
    1.2. Responsiveness
    1.3. Correctness
        1.3.1. Completeness/Incompleteness
        1.3.2. Consistency
        1.3.3. Traceability
        1.3.4. Provably Correct
    1.4. Verifiability
        1.4.1. Testability
2. Performance Measures
    2.1. Dependability
        2.1.1. Availability/Robustness
        2.1.2. Reliability
            2.1.2.1. Accuracy
        2.1.3. Safety
        2.1.4. Trustworthiness
            2.1.4.1. Vulnerability

There are several things that should be noted about this list. First, performance does have a somewhat different meaning for software than it does for physical technologies. The closest sub-items on the SEI taxonomy to the items previously listed for physical technology are under category 2.2 Efficiency/Resource Utilization (i.e., 2.2.1 Capacity, 2.2.2 Real-Time Responsiveness/Latency, and 2.2.3 Throughput). However, unlike physical technologies where these things can be directly measured, they can only be relatively measured in software. They can only be directly measured when the software is executed on a specific hardware platform. Thus, in software, we can speak of a new message-oriented middleware technology as being relatively more efficient in terms of its throughput in moving information than older technologies. But we can't specify exactly what the actual improved throughput is unless we do so on a specific hardware platform such as a 100 megabit per second Ethernet network as opposed to a 10 megabit network.

Another thing that should be noted is that category 5, Organizational Measures, refers to the economic benefit of the software technology. Economic benefits do not simply spring into existence by themselves. They are a result of some other benefits of the technology, such as those listed in categories 1-4 of the SEI taxonomy. Thus, we will retain categories 1-4 from the SEI taxonomy as candidates for level 3 of the generalized cascade model and save category 5 for later. We will name this level of our generalized cascade model as "technical benefits" and note that it refers to improvements in performance for physical technologies and in quality, as defined by categories 1-4 in the SEI quality taxonomy, for software.

Level 4—Economic, Organizational, and Societal Benefits

This level currently lists improvements in cost and safety/health/environment. This can be generalized to the economic, organizational, and societal benefits of the technology. We will place category 5 of the SEI quality taxonomy at this level.

Level 5—Diffusion

Diffusion, at level 5 of the cascade model, applies equally well to software as it does to other technologies. Hence, no modifications to this level of the model are required.

Technology Potency

The concept of technology potency relates to understanding the possibility of breakthroughs in a technology. Clearly, there is value to investing in technologies where breakthroughs are imminent.

The likelihood of an imminent technical breakthrough may be present when the following conditions hold:

- A technological trend is approaching a barrier.
- The said barrier is lower than an ultimate limit.
- A large, unconquered territory remains for the technology to advance into.
- The forces promoting technological change are expected to remain strong.[9]

A classic example of a breakthrough is the breaking of the sound barrier. In the early days of jet airplanes, it appeared that nobody could exceed the speed of sound. According to the laws of physics, the speed of light is the ultimate limit that cannot be exceeded. The speed of sound is far lower than the speed of light, so a breakthrough was possible. The desire for speed, in addition, was strong. So experimental aircraft kept pushing the mach 1 barrier. Finally, the Bell X-1 with Chuck Yeager in the cockpit broke the mach 1 barrier and ushered in the era of supersonic flight.

As another example, in 1950, permanent magnets based on alnico could achieve an energy density of about 100 kilojoules per cubic meter. In 1980, they still could only achieve 100 kilojoules per cubic meter. They had reached a barrier. However, permanent magnets using rare earths could theoretically produce energy densities of over 500 kilojoules per cubic meter. Clearly, 100 kilojoules per cubic meter was well below the theoretical limit. By 1970, rare earths could achieve 200 kilojoules per cubic meter. By 1985, they could achieve 350 kilojoules per cubic meter. A breakthrough had been achieved by rare earths.[10]

This framework is relatively easy to apply to a physical technology such as permanent magnets because it is possible to physically measure the performance parameters. These are physical performance parameters and relate to level 3 in the cascade model. One can graph the measured parameters over time and see them leveling off as they approach the barrier. One can also hypothesize ultimate limits based on the laws of physics.

It can be harder to apply this framework to software. We will illustrate this with an example. A goal of knowledge management software is to capture tacit human knowledge, store it, and disseminate it for use. How does one measure the ability of a software technology to do that? The United States Navy has developed some guidance for defining such metrics:

The most important characteristic to consider when choosing or defining a KM [knowledge management] performance measure is whether the metric tells if knowledge is being shared and used. For example, a metric for a best practices database might be the number of times the database was accessed. A large number of accesses or "hits" suggests that people are reading the document, but this does not definitively indicate whether it was useful to anyone or whether it improved operation efficiency or quality. A better metric would be to track database usage and ask a sampling of the users if and how it helped them.[11]

The physical performance measure, database hits, really is not a good measure for this technology. While it is an easily measured physical quantity and relates to level 3 of the cascade model, it just does not capture anything important. We really need to measure the concept of tacit human knowledge – the kinds of knowledge that people ordinarily keep inside their heads and have difficulty articulating to others.

The problem here is that the thing that the software acts upon, human knowledge, is itself an abstract concept and is not easy to measure. With nothing useful to measure at level 3 of the cascade model, we end up having to measure human satisfaction with the KM software/system via some kind of user survey. That measures an organizational or societal benefit of the technology rather than something about the technology itself and therefore it really relates to level 4 of the cascade model rather than to level 3. Since this is one more level removed from the actual technology itself, it makes it that much harder to measure parameters, define theoretical limits, and forecast breakthroughs.

Granted, there are many metrics at level 3 of the cascade model that can be applied to software. Reiner Dumke of Otto von Guericke University of Magdeburg, Germany maintains an impressive bibliography of the software metrics work.[12] Size metrics, complexity metrics, quality metrics, testing metrics, project management metrics, etc. have been defined. These metrics help us manage software projects and may even help forecast some breakthroughs in the development, operation, and maintenance of software. However, these are not necessarily the kind of measurements we need to look at in forecasting breakthroughs in the application of software. In our example, we need a measurement of tacit human knowledge. That is not a measurement of the software itself, but a measurement of the intangible, abstract form of information that the software is designed to manage.

This simple example illustrates how much more difficult it can be to determine the potency of a software technology than it is a physical technology.

Conclusions

We can draw the following conclusions based on the analysis presented in this chapter:

- Software is an important technology to understand on its own, divorced from the hardware on which it is executed. However, it is not easy to do so. For example, it is not easy to define software technology.
- Existing definitions of software technology exclude software applications themselves and focus on the technology of developing, maintaining, and operating software. This may be adequate for some purposes, but it is inadequate for strategic analysis of software for business purposes. It does not include the applications for which software is used to solve business problems. A new definition is proposed to overcome that limitation.
- Some of the concepts of technology analysis can be generalized so that they can be applied to both physical and software technologies. In particular, we have shown how the cascade model of technology evolution can be generalized to apply to software as well as to other technologies. This gives us a common framework that we can use to understand all technology evolution at a strategic level.
- Technology potency is a more difficult concept to apply to software technologies than it is to physical technologies because it is much harder to measure the key performance characteristics and to define theoretical limits. This makes the analysis of potential software breakthroughs particularly challenging. Measurement of software technology potency may be a fruitful area for further research.

Notes

1. Van Wyk, Rias J. (1999). Technology and the Corporate Board. Minneapolis, MN: University of Minnesota. p. 16.
2. Software Engineering Institute. "Defining Software Technology." 2000. http://www.sei.cmu.edu/str/descriptions/defining.html, (14 June 2002).
3. Software Engineering Institute. "STR Technology Descriptions." 2002. http://www.sei.cmu.edu/str/descriptions/index.html, (14 June 2002).
4. Reifer, Donald J. (2002). Making the Software Business Case. Boston MA: Addison-Wesley. p. 7.
5. Van Wyk, Rias J., Technology and the Corporate Board, p.32.
6. Van Wyk, Rias J., Technology and the Corporate Board, pp. 32-34.
7. Van Wyk, Rias J., Technology and the Corporate Board, p. 33.
8. Software Engineering Institute. "View the Quality Measures Taxonomy." 2000. http://www.sei.cmu.edu/str/taxonomies/view_qm_body.html, (22 June 2002).
9. Van Wyk, Rias J., Technology and the Corporate Board, p. 38.
10. Van Wyk, Rias J. (1999). Strategic Technology Analysis Workbook. Minneapolis, MN: University of Minnesota. pp. 12-13.
11. Chief Information Officer Department of the Navy (2001). Metrics Guide for Knowledge Management Initiatives. Washington, DC: Department of the Navy. p. 19.
12. Dumke, Reiner. "Software Metrics – A Subdivided Bibliography." 2002. http://irb.cs.uni-magdeburg.de/sw-eng/us/bibliography/bib_main.shtml. (June 27, 2002).

6

The Half-Life of Policy Rationales:
How New Technology Affects
Old Policy Issues

Fred Foldvary and Daniel Klein

The justifications for many public policies are dissolving as technology advances. New detection and metering technologies are being developed for highways, parking, marine farming, and auto emissions, making property-rights solutions viable. Information becomes more accessible and user-friendly, suggesting that quality and safety are better handled by the private sector, undercutting consumer-protection rationales. As for public utilities, new means of producing and delivering electricity, water, postal, and telephone services dissolve the old natural-monopoly rationales for control and governmental provision.

Most market-failure arguments boil down to claims about market mechanisms being blocked by transaction costs. But technology has trimmed transaction costs and made the old rationales for government intervention increasingly obsolete.

Besides trimming transaction costs, technological advancement accelerates economic change and multiplies the connections between activities. It

Fred E. Foldvary, <ffoldvary@scu.edu>, received his Ph.D. in economics from George Mason University, Virginia. He currently teaches economics at Santa Clara University, California. His areas of research include public finance, public choice, social ethics, and the economics of real estate. Daniel B. Klein received his Ph.D. from NYU and is Associate Professor of Economics at Santa Clara University. He has written in several areas of public policy and in economic and political philosophy more generally. He may be reached at <dklein@scu.edu>. This essay is a variant of the first chapter of a forthcoming (NYU Press/Cato Institute) volume of the same name and edited by the same authors.

brings fundamental upsets to even our best understandings of current arrangements and their shortcomings. Thus, by making the economic system ever more complex, it makes the notion that regulators can meaningfully know and beneficially manipulate the system ever less credible.

Technology sets what may be called an intellectual half-life on policies and their justifications.

Introduction

Writers have occasionally noted that a policy's appropriateness depends on the current state of alternative technologies, and that technological changes make old policies obsolete and new policies worthwhile (Hayek 1979: 47; Rosen 1992: 68). Most market failure arguments boil down to claims about invisible hand mechanisms being obstructed by some kind of transaction costs. If technology trims transaction and production costs—by making it easy to charge users, define and enforce property rights, exit and utilize substitutes, gather information, gain assurance of quality and safety, enter and compete in markets—the invisible hand works better. We argue that *technological advancement tends to enhance the case for free enterprise policy*. It reduces the strength of market failure arguments and the case for intervention.

Our conclusion is bolstered by a second, Smith-Hayek, line of argument. Technology heightens the complexity of the economic system. The more complex a system, the less knowable it is, and the less likely government interventions are to benefit society.

Technological advancement might not enhance the case for free enterprise in every area of policy, but it does in many.

Technology Works to Resolve Market Imperfections

Theories of market failure and governmental remedies are not absolute doctrine but depend on the institutional and technological context. The invisible hand—the nexus of voluntary social mechanisms—may fail, in a significant sense, if transaction costs obstruct gainful exchange. But better technology reduces such costs. Applications of market failure theory may be found to have a technological "half-life," after which their validity dissolves.

Some would challenge the general claim, arguing that, just as technology enhances the knowledge and capabilities of private entrepreneurs, so it enhances that of public-spirited regulators and officials. Government becomes more effective because of technology. No doubt there is much to the challenge. Government agencies too can run highways as toll roads. Or, consider a common argument against regulation: that it introduces noncompliance problems and requires costly enforcement. Insofar as technology facilitates government monitoring and enforcement, the case for government regulation gains strength.

However, if both free enterprise and the government are technically capable of, say, producing tomatoes, the sheer incentive argument recommends free enterprise. Good government itself is a public goods problem (Tullock 1971); government often fails to do the good that it is technically capable of. The free enterprise system, on the other hand, generally creates for its participants incentives to pursue what is good for society. Hence, the incentive advantage recommends free enterprise, given technical and institutional workability.

Technology Enables Metering, Excluding, and Charging

New technology is making it increasingly possible to define and enforce property rights, and to charge for the use of property. The following are examples of this expanding capability.

Highways and Parking

It has traditionally been argued that charging for highway use or parking space would entail significant transaction costs, such as delays and inconvenience for motorists, the handling and securing of bulky cash, and costly or unsightly toll booths or parking meters. Yet these difficulties have been lessened considerably. On highways with electronic tolling, the charge is automatically recorded as the car rolls by, with no need to line up and stop. Highway users can now pay highway tolls as easily as they pay a monthly phone bill, weakening the case for operating highways as "freeways" and strengthening the case for privatization.

Street parking is another service that entrepreneurs can charge for. Modern parking meters no longer require coins for fixed periods of time, but can electronically vary the charge and dispense with time restrictions. New in-vehicle meters with LCD displays operate like pre-paid phone cards; anyone with curb space to rent could do so without even erecting parking meters. One could imagine turning on-street parking space over to private entrepreneurs or adjoining land owners, to rent by the minute using high-tech meters.

Lighthouses

The lighthouse has long served as an example of a public good that cannot be supplied by purely voluntary means. Ronald Coase (1974) explored the history of lighthouse provision in Britain and showed that private entrepreneurs built, owned, and operated lighthouses, and made profits. Payments from ships for lighthouses were mandated at nearby ports, however, so, as

David Van Zandt (1993) has explained, the arrangement depended in such cases, after all, on a form of taxation. Whatever the lessons of the historical experience, technology has dissolved any argument for government financing of lighthouse services. By virtue of radar, sonar, satellite-based electronic guidance, and the feasibility of scrambled or encrypted signals, the lighthouse is becoming largely antiquated as a navigational aid. Thus, technology has turned the canonical public good into a museum piece.

Marine Resources

The foundation for the invisible hand is private property rights. New technologies are enhancing the ability to define, secure, trade, and enforce private property in marine resources. Just as ranchers and cattlemen in the American West secured and built up their property with such innovations as branding and barbed wire, today entrepreneurs can do likewise in oceans with the technologies of livestock herding, "fingerprinting," tagging, sonar, satellite tracking, habitat creation, fencing, gating, and guarding. Technology has strengthened the intellectual case for aquatic farming and ranching.

Air Pollution

Common law traditionally treated air pollution as a nuisance, and that spirit concords with a policy of pollution charges, made feasible by technology. For emissions from cars, the sensor technology developed by Donald Stedman measures pollution levels in the exhaust. When coupled with automatic license plate readers, the technology enables officials to send gross-polluting motorists a pollution bill. A direct polluter-pays approach is much more efficient than command-and-control methods such as smog check programs, alternative-fuel requirements, electric vehicles, and mandates on automakers. Although remote sensing is a program for regional governments to undertake, it is nonetheless a property-rights approach to the problem: It protects the public airshed from violation and leaves nonviolators undisturbed in the use of their own property. It is like protecting public buildings from graffiti by setting up video surveillance, rather than by placing restrictions on who can buy spray-paint and permanent markers at the local hardware stores.

Technology Facilitates Quality and Safety Assurance

Many "consumer protection" interventions suppose that quality and safety assurance cannot be adequately provided by voluntary practices and the tort system. Consumers suffer from "imperfect" or "asymmetric" information, which makes for transaction costs in marketplace decisions. The cost of overcoming ignorance is high or even insurmountable, and, in consequence, consumers are vulnerable in a free market to false representations of quality and safety. Services that are hired infrequently or are especially hard to understand need to be restricted according to government approvals and permissions. This line of thinking justifies the Consumer Product Safety Commission, the Food and Drug Administration, the Securities and Exchange Commission, the National Highway Traffic Safety Administration, the Occupational Safety and Health Administration, and local and state occupational licensing, business licensing, and housing codes.

As consumers demand assurance, however, voluntary market processes find ways of supplying it. Service providers assure quality and safety by building and conveying a good reputation. They obtain certifications and seals of approval, seek affiliations with trusted sources, and develop a brand name. Consumers, for their part, also look to rating or recommending agents to ascertain reputations. All these methods and media depend on the generating, collecting, interpreting, formatting, storing, retrieving, and transmitting of information about service providers.

Medical Services and Products

Information technologies are enhancing quality assurance in medical care. Computer technology coupled with practice review and monitoring have given hospitals, clinics, health organizations, and insurers new means of evaluating practitioner performance. These institutions function as certifiers. Furthermore, because of the Internet and other media, consumers themselves are more able to gain pointed expertise, by learning of available therapies, tapping knowledge of fellow patients, and checking the credentials and affiliations of practitioners. The Internet provides consumers with both technical knowledge and assurances. Also, rating organizations can develop a good reputation for conveying accurate assessments of sellers and manufacturers. Using the Net, consumers may look merely for the "thumb's up" (or seal of approval), read detailed reviews, or click to another vendor who provides better assurance.

Money and Banking

Electronic commerce can be extended to the private issuing of money, revitalizing the case to get rid of banking regulations. Critics of free-market banking suggest that the system would be marred by bank runs and panics, hyperinflation, embezzling, and counterfeiting. These are lapses of quality. Can banks meaningfully assure quality? Would a free banking system prevent such problems? Managing solvency and providing assurances of solvency are especially viable today. Up-to-the-moment financial statements and assessments can be generated and made widely available. Contractual arrangements giving banks options to delay redemption or withdrawal could be more easily posted, managed, and conveyed to worried depositors. Inflation and counterfeiting can be discouraged by rapid feedback mechanisms, such as adverse clearing. In an information age, reputation stays more current and counts for more.

Regulators claim that individuals suffer from an insurmountable ignorance about their own needs and the true quality of available options. Restrictions imposed in the name of quality and safety hamstring many important areas of business and everyday life. Yet in every instance new technology is making claims of information asymmetries and consumer vulnerability less and less credible and proving that the demand for assurance elicits supply.

Technology Dissolves Natural Monopoly Arguments

The so-called public utilities—water, sanitation, electricity, natural gas, telephone, and cable television—have long featured an interconnected network or grid, by which water, gas, or electrons are distributed from central sources to users throughout the community. The construction and operation of the distribution system involve large up-front costs that are irreversible. Adding users to the system entails low marginal cost, and distributing product entails low current cost. Thus, in this standard portrayal, a single distribution system continues to enjoy economies of scale as it adds volume over time. The cost structure, therefore, will, in a free market, give rise to a single provider— a natural monopoly. The single provider may then charge high prices, produce low quantity and quality, and make excessive profits. Would-be competitors do not enter and bid down prices because, once they would have sunk investments into a competing system, the incumbent firm will lower its price and possibly bring losses to both firms. Hence no one would be foolhardy enough to challenge the monopolist. Upon this reasoning, regulators and interventionists have argued that government ought to supervise such utilities and control their prices.

Whatever the historical validity of the natural monopoly argument, it is clear that in many service areas technology has brought alternatives that belie the traditional assumptions about costs and integration requirements. Furthermore, rapid change itself complicates the problem of regulators and planners.

Electricity

The current electricity crisis in California is not the result of "deregulation" but, on the contrary, the restructuring of the industry that left in place restrictions on production, control, and pricing. Modern technology favors true deregulation of electricity. Increasingly viable is small-scale generation, powered by diesel, natural gas, or other fuels. On-site generators provide users— office buildings, factories, housing developments, or even single homes—with the option of creating their own self-contained loop. The costs of creating anew competing loops have also fallen by virtue of computer-controlled drilling and line laying, allowing workers to snake under streets and buildings without above-ground disturbance. Such developments dissolve the assumptions of high fixed and sunk costs. Entry and competition in the market would, in a free market, be very viable. Furthermore, technology has greatly advanced the possibility of combining electricity generation with steam power, heat, and air conditioning, and of combining electricity distribution with telecommunications, vastly complicating the job of any regulator who presumes to know how to improve upon the invisible hand.

Water and Sanitation

Technology has also made more viable the on-site recycling of water. Homes, developments, businesses, and so on could, if permitted, often choose not to hook up to the centralized utility pipes. The substitute for transporting massive amounts of water via the grid, both to and from users (the latter to deal with waste water), is to develop on-site systems. Such systems would inventory raw water, treat water according to a quality hierarchy for local uses, and then recover raw water from the waste for inventory and reuse. On-site water and waste treatment involves refinement, disposal, and replenishment. So-called gray water could be treated and used for landscaping, cooling, fire fighting, and sanitation. The small amount of water for sensitive human uses, such as bathing, cooking, and drinking, would be distilled to a purity and a safety that the current one-quality-fits-all water systems could not hope to match. The "black water" from toilets and kitchen-disposal units would be treated and disposed of via sewage, vacuum truck, or other method. Depending on recovery rates, the system would need replenishment from rainwater catchments, trucked water, or other sources. Combining on-site utilities may yield economies of scope (the heat from an electricity generator could warm and distill water, for example).

Postal Services

Postal service has long been a government monopoly in the United States and most countries, and one could well argue that there was never a good economic reason for this. Modern technology makes a free-market position stronger than ever, since postal communication now competes with alternatives such as faxes, email, and the Internet. Such alternatives make price-gouging fears especially far-fetched. Express mail is already provided by private competitors, and the Internet provides for electronic bill paying and the transmission of documents with electronic signatures. The removal of monopoly protection for the USPS would enable a consolidated contracting of the distribution of goods to rural areas, enabling a company to deliver newspapers, packages, and mail in one delivery.

Telecommunications

Telephone line and television cable networks have been regarded as natural monopolies because laying down multiple grids would duplicate great and uneconomical fixed costs. Long ago, J. Maurice Clark (1923:321) concluded, however, that telephone companies showed no economies of scale, "but rather the opposite." The monopolization of telephony in the United States resulted chiefly from government policy that restricted competition and mandated regulated telephone rates (Thierer 1994). Technology has further weakened any claim of natural monopoly. Fiber optic line and drilling technology make competing lines more viable than ever. Wireless telephones and satellite television transmissions provide expanding dimensions of competition. Technology is blurring the lines of telephony, cable television, and Internet service. Change is rapid, and the hazard of regulatory fossilization is greater than usual.

The Complexity/Unknowability Argument

While admitting some symmetry in the effects of technology, we believe that there is an important asymmetry that goes against government. Any form of government intervention or enterprise depends for its justification on an understanding of what the private enterprise economy would otherwise be lacking or failing to achieve. Justification for occupational licensing depends on consumers being unable, in a regime without licensing, to obtain quality and safety assurance. Utility regulation depends on theories of natural monopoly. Government activism is predicated on a belief that regulators or planners can *know the economy well enough* to restrict, manipulate, or supplement it beneficially.

Yet, after Adam Smith and Friedrich Hayek, the classic argument against government intervention is, aside from incentive problems, that the economy is too complex to know, and therefore too complex to direct or manipulate in a beneficial manner. Like the spontaneous patterns of roller skating in a roller rink, the more complex the system, the more mischievous is the notion of centralized control. In a complex system such as that of 200 skaters in a roller rink, we ought to rely on decentralized decision making. After all, even if the rink is without bound the increased complexity does not pose a comparable problem for the individual skater. He does not interpret the whole; he utilizes pointed knowledge in pursuing opportunities of his particular time and place.

Technology enhances government's ability to gather, collate and convey information, to monitor actions, identify transgressions, and enforce compliance. Technologies expand the informational capability of government. But

technology accelerates economic change and multiplies the connections between activities. It integrates dimensions, connects multitudinous variables,
and, moment-by-moment, alters constraints and opportunities. To know market arrangements—either those current or those that would exist under alternative policy—such fundamentals would have to remain unchanged for the
time being. Yet technology makes the whole economy—that which is to be
known—far more complex. It brings fundamental upsets, now and again, to
even our best understandings of current arrangements and their shortcomings.
After all, society includes the thoughts and potentialities of private individuals and organizations, each of whom has likewise enjoyed vastly expanded
informational capabilities.

In his recent book *The Lexus and the Olive Tree*, Thomas Friedman relates
comments from a friend that illustrates the contest between informational
capability and complexity. He quotes Leon Cooperman, former director of
research for Goldman, Sachs:

> "When I joined Goldman Sachs in 1967 . . . I was the head of research and I hired
> analysts. In those days, a typical analyst covered seventy-five companies . . . I was
> recently talking to one of the analysts I had hired back then and he told me he was
> terribly overworked now because he had to cover twelve companies. I just laughed.
> Only twelve companies? But you have to look into those twelve companies so much
> more deeply now in order to get some edge that it takes up all of his time." (Cooperman
> quoted in Friedman 1999: 101-102)

One might imagine that, because of today's high speed data access, compu-
tation, and so on, the analyst would have enhanced informational capabilities,
enabling him to cover *more*, rather than fewer, companies. But his informational capabilities do not keep up with the complexity of the world to be
analyzed.

In 1879, Cliffe Leslie, an Irish economist and keen expositor of Adam
Smith, wrote: "[T]he movement of the economic world has been one from
simplicity to complexity, from uniformity to diversity, from unbroken custom
to change, and, therefore, from the known to the unknown."[1] In later years
Friedrich Hayek took the point further: the economic world has moved not
merely to the unknown, but to the *unknowable*. The effect of technology is
asymmetric in the epistemic situations in which it leaves, respectively, private
actors versus social planners (such as those at the FDA or the Anti-Trust Division). *Technology's heightening of society's complexity outstrips its heightening of the social planner's informational capabilities.*[2] Hayek, like Smith,
drew a lesson for policy: Except in the most clear-cut cases of systemic harm
like air pollution, the supposition that government officials can figure out
how to improve upon the results of decentralized (i.e., voluntary) decision
making becomes more and more outlandish. In his Nobel lecture, Hayek (1974)
called that supposition the *pretense* of knowledge. As intellectuals who pon-

der the complex workings of the social world, we really know little aside from one hardy fact: If those who participate in an activity do so voluntarily, each is probably bettering his or her own condition. The more complex the system, the more skeptical we ought to be about claims to knowledge that go beyond and against that hardy fact.

There are, then, two ways in which technological advancement enhances the case for free enterprise: (1) It reduces the costs that had obstructed (actually or supposedly) invisible hand mechanisms, and (2) it makes the economic system ever more complex, and makes the notion that interventionists can meaningfully know and beneficially manipulate the system ever less credible.

Policy Areas in Which the Conclusion May be Doubtful

Some cases seem to go against the general tendency. Technology might make it especially difficult to secure and appropriate the value of one's intellectual products, such as basic scientific research, patents, software, music, and writings, because current technology vastly facilitates the replication of "knock-offs" and sharing without authorization. The situation might call for stepped-up government enforcement of patents and copyrights (whether one considers that government intervention or property rights enforcement), or more interventionist measures such as subsidization of knowledge and cultural products—akin to European television subsidies financed by taxes on television ownership (a policy that DeLong and Froomkin 2000 sometimes seem to favor). However, unauthorized replication might, too, have a short technological half-life, as new technologies develop methods to foil unauthorized replication.

It may be argued that technology favors expanded government control of pollution because it enhances the effectiveness of detection, measurement, impact assessment, and enforcement. However, common law traditionally treated air pollution as a nuisance, and direct polluter-payes policies keep to that spirit. If government uses new technologies to define and enforce property rights in water, airs, or animal resources, that might be seen as defensive Nightwatchman functions compatible with the principles of free enterprise.

National security is another area where technology might suggest a larger role for government. Capabilities to create advance quickly, but, alas, not as quickly as capabilities to destroy. New destructive capabilities in arms, biotechnology, and, eventually, nanotechnology might recommend vigorous national security measures. Again, depending on the measures, we might not deem them "government intervention" but rather Nightwatchman functions.

Improved technology, as previously mentioned, might improve regulators' knowledge of particular sets of activities, and recommend more interventions such as anti-trust restrictions. Decades ago, Kenneth Arrow wrote: "Indeed, with the development of mathematical programming and high-speed computers, the centralized alternative no longer appears preposterous. After all, it would appear that one could mimic the workings of a decentralized system by an appropriately chosen centralized algorithm" (Arrow 1974: 5). Even though few today advocate "the centralized alternative," many still feel that by virtue of information technology government can actively manage or guide significant portions of the economy. Again, however, the growth of the complexity of the whole ought to humble even our latest technologies of knowing and intervening. Even at the level of piecemeal intervention such as anti-trust policy, justification relies on a pretense of knowing that such interventions are likely to improve in the whole upon what the un-intervened system would produce.

Finally, it might be argued that technology will make government more transparent and hence more accountable. We may put more trust in government because any abuse or outrage will be more readily exposed and investigated (Brin 1998). This optimistic factor surely has some validity; there has been a profusion of web sites supplying information about candidates, their positions, the voting records, their contributors, and so on. One may argue that technology will facilitate public discourse, public understanding, and participation in direct democracy. Perhaps government can be made more accountable and reliable through "electronic town meetings," in which each citizen may delegate their voting rights to proxies (as in shareholders' meetings). If government were thereby improved, the case for activism would be strengthened.

Our conclusion, therefore, makes no claim to entirety or universality. We do not say that technology favors the case for free enterprise in all areas of policy. We submit a hypothesis that says "tends to," "mostly," "usually," "in general" . . .

Concluding Remarks

The appropriateness of alternate policies depends on the state of technology. As technology advances, the intellectual case for specific policies changes. Thus, technology imposes on policies and their justifications what may be called an expected intellectual half-life. The faster technology advances, the shorter will be the half-life policy rationales.

This paper suggests, more specifically, that technological advancement usually favors the effectiveness of free enterprise over government intervention. If that is the case, interventionists especially need to concern themselves with the intellectual half-life of their positions, lest they promote policies appropriate yesterday but no longer appropriate today or tomorrow.

Just as policy depends on the state of technology, so technology depends on policy. The technological advancements help solve social problems. In doing so, they bring affected parties some kind of profit. Technological advancement is itself a member of the invisible hand, the invisible hand's tending of its current shortcomings. Voluntary social mechanisms and technological advancement enjoy a complex dialectic of mutual improvement.

Notes

1. Cliffe Leslie [(879): 224. He writes also: "And just in proportion . . . as industry and commerce are developed, does the social economy become complex, diversified, changeful, uncertain, unpredictable, and hard to know, even in its existing phase" (p. 223).
2. See Roger Koppl (2000), who writes, "the level of complexity is likely to outstrip our analytical engine" (105).

References

Arrow, Kenneth. 1974. "Limited Knowledge and Economic Analysis." *American Economic Review* 64: 1-10.

Brin, David. 1998. *The Transparent Society: Will Technology Force Us to Choose Between Privacy and Freedom?* Reading, MA: Addison-Wesley.

Coase, Ronald H. 1974. "The Lighthouse in Economics," *Journal of Law and Economics* 17, October: 357-76. Reprinted in Cowen 1988.

DeLong, J. Bradford and A. Michael Froomkin. 2000. "Speculative Microeconomics for Tomorrow's Economy." On DeLong's webpage: http://econ161.berkeley.edu/

Friedman, Thomas L. 1999. *The Lexus and the Olive Tree*. New York: Farrar, Straus and Giroux.

Hayek, Friedrich A. 1979. *Law, Legislation and Liberty: Volume 3, The Political Order of a Free People*. Chicago: University of Chicago Press.

Hayek, Friedrich A. [1974]. "The Pretense of Knowledge" (Nobel lecture). In Hayek's *New Studies in Philosophy, Politics, Economics and the History of Ideas*. Chicago: University of Chicago Press, 1978.

Koppl, Roger. 2000. "Policy Implications of Complexity: An Austrian Perspective," in *The Complexity Vision and the Teaching of Economics*, ed. D. Colander: 97-117. Northampton, MA: Edward Elgar.

Leslie, T.E. Cliffe. 1879. "The Known and the Unknown in the Economic World" (originally published in *Fortnightly Review*, June 1). Reprinted in *Essays in Political Economy*. London: Longmans, Green, & Co., 1888: 221-42.

Rosen, Harvey S. 1992. *Public Finance*. Third edition. Homewood, IL: Irwin.

Tullock, Gordon. 1971. "Public Decisions as Public Goods," *Journal of Political Economy*, 79, no. 4: 913-918.

Van Zandt, David E. 1993. "The Lessons of the Lighthouse: 'Government' or 'Private' Provision of Goods." *Journal of Legal Studies* 22, January: 47-72.

7

Some Philosophical Thoughts on the Nature of Technology

John Cogan

It is a commonplace to note that mankind has a love-hate relationship with technology; and, like all love-hate relationships, it is fashioned out of misunderstanding. In this case I suggest that it is a misunderstanding of exactly *what it is* that *is* technology.

What I will suggest in what follows is that the love-hate relationship we have with technology arises, in part, from the way an answer to the question regarding the nature of technology has been sought. But another part of this misunderstanding is due to the tension between the basic themes of those interrogators trying to answer the question who are split between the arts and the sciences. Taking the classical distinction within the university between the arts and sciences in hand, I will claim that, although these branches of the university define technology in different terms, they nevertheless share a common method to seeking the answer, namely, the method of seeking the *one thing* that all technologies share—the *essence* of technology. Thus, when we are able to compose the differences between the approaches, we will near the time when we have a more adequate understanding of technology. But, given the current formulations, this seems to be something of a circular errand since we need an understanding of technology before we can understand the difference between the approaches. After all, are not the sciences and the arts differentiated precisely on their stand with respect to technology? It would seem, then, that we cannot understand technology until we understand the thematic approach of the arts and the sciences and we cannot understand their respective approaches until we have an adequate understanding of each branch; but

Dr. John M. Cogan has a Ph.D. in Philosophy from Southern Illinois University at Carbondale. He may be reached at <jmcogan@siu.edu>.

we cannot have an adequate understanding of each branch until we know where it stands with respect to technology. How is this conundrum to be solved?

In the process of trying to bring clarification to this problem, I am struck first of all by the fact that our use of the term "technology" has turned it into something of a "buzz" word—a word that aims more to impress than convey meaning. Lately even tennis shoes are drenched with something called "technology." Additionally, there is a continual effort on the part of academics to uncover the "*nature* of technology," that is, an effort that is carried out as if we did not already know what that nature is. I think that this effort expresses a genuine confusion as to the nature of technology and it is a confusion that I believe can be clarified by taking a page from Wittgenstein's work. In the remainder of my article, I will try to survey the broad use of this term, introduce a couple of attempts to define it, and then follow up with the suggestion of a possible remedy.

On a recent news program, film footage of the war in Afghanistan was running while the newscaster's voice was saying something to the effect that this war was being fought on "a different level" owing to the technology that we now have. The implication was that the picture of the Navy Tomcat taking off from an aircraft carrier was a representation of the technology in question. A poster advertising a company's new sport shoes also touts its product as a "new technology." Indeed, there is a sense of the term "technology" that would include the caveman's use of a rock to kill a beast as well as mnemonic devices used to learn lists of things. This breadth of use suggests that the term "technology" is as comfortably applied and at home with respect to things as to methods, even to ideologies. So, what is technology?

A close examination of the "love-hate" aspect of the relationship might help to narrow our analysis. Part of what we love about technology, aside from the many helpful gadgets and devices we get, is that it is easily presented as being independent from human purposes and aims; that is, it presents itself as a tool simpliciter. If bad things result, then it is not the fault of technology but the use to which it was put by humans, e.g., "guns don't kill people; people do." We love this aspect of technology because it reminds us of our own freedom and independence; and its ability to stand aloof in its own objectivity far from human imperfection makes it appear as something of an ideal, a "knight in shining armor." It is this sense of independence that is addressed by Barrett in his *The Illusion of Technique*[1] who shows that, contrary to the promise of freedom suggested by the independence of technology itself, we actually have "mind-forged manacles."

On the other hand, we tend to hate technology, as anyone who has worked with Windows 3.1 can attest. It is true that part of what we hate about technology is the difficult time we have adjusting to it and its own imperfections in the early stages of development, but that is not the thorn in the rose for us. What really irks us about technology is the threat to our feelings and emotions that it seems to pose. We hate machines precisely because they are unfeeling and when we find an individual who is likewise unfeeling we refer to her or him as a machine. Thus, the barriers we have to overcome when we decide to understand the nature of technology derive in part from our love and hatred of technology. Those who are trying to understand technology from a position of love emphasize the ideality of technology and either minimize or fail to see altogether the human component. Similarly, when the nature of technology is approached from the hate side it is often the case that its ideality is eclipsed and its anti-pathos is made prominent. It seems to me, then, that the first step in gaining an understanding of technology consists in seeing that neither of these approaches has returned, as Husserl says, "to the things themselves." Neither of them has taken a *hard* look at all of the things we call technology.

The observation that technology is not an isolated phenomenon may seem obvious but given the fact that it is precisely this observation that often goes unheeded, it bears bringing up. Both those who love technology and those who "hate" it like to think of technology as an island, that is, as not being connected to human aims, purposes, desires and the like, i.e., value free. Nothing could be further from the truth. Technology is not an island and if the bell rings, then it is *we* who ring it and *we* who hear it. It is just as misguided to claim that there is no such thing as a bad technology as it is to claim that there is no such thing as a bad human, and for the same reasons. It is the use to which they are put that makes both bad. Wise people make the distinction that what we hate about others is what they do and not they themselves; likewise, what we hate about technology is the use to which it is put and not it itself. I believe it is crucial to our survival that we make this distinction both with respect to others and with respect to technology. Failing to do so allows for the generation of thoughts of destruction impelled by hateful feelings, which have the effect of producing havoc in our world. There is great need for harmony in our mental and feeling worlds and we will not have harmony in our everyday world until it reigns within—since it is we who are the creators of our everyday world.

But how does noticing that technology is not an isolated phenomenon help us to gain an understanding of the nature of technology? It helps us in this way. Once we understand that what we are calling "technology" is *not* an isolated phenomenon, "entire of itself," then we are in a better position to know what it is we are trying to understand and how we should respond to it. In this regard, let me now turn to Wittgenstein.

Our use of the term "technology" tempts us to think that because we apply it to a great array of things that, therefore, there must be some *one* thing that they all have in common, namely, the *essence* or *nature* of technology. Wittgenstein urges us to resist this temptation and notice instead that what is at work here is not a common essence but merely "family resemblance."[2] It is true that we call both the caveman's use of the rock and the laser guided missile "technology," but that does not mean that they share a common essence. It means only that in the great family of uses of the term "technology," the family resemblance can be seen in each of these cases. But this insight has not prevailed in the many efforts to define technology.

It should come as no surprise that those aligned with technology strive to understand it and define it in technological terms, that is, in instrumental terms —terms of use, method, and tool, while those in the arts strive to understand technology in less invasive and manipulative terms, that is, they strive to understand it in the more philosophical terms of its essence—its being. Thus, we get definitions from the science side of campus like the one Larry Hickman offers us in his *Philosophical Tools for Technological Culture*[3]: "Technology in its most robust sense, then, involves the invention, development, and cognitive deployment of tools and other artifacts, brought to bear on raw materials and intermediate stock parts, with a view to the resolution of perceived problems." Heidegger, on the other hand, in his "The Question Concerning Technology," [4] unabashedly searches for the essence of technology but reminds us that "the essence of technology is by no means anything technological" any more than that which pervades every tree is itself a tree. It seems to me that, given their respective definitions, Hickman has a viewpoint and Barrett and Heidegger share another. Of course, my claim is that, as insightful as each of these efforts is, none of them ultimately succeeds because each fails to give full weight to some element of technology, either pertaining to its ideality or to its pathos. What is this telling us?

On its face, Hickman's definition seems to cover all the bases but there is no reference as to whether the deployment he mentions is constructive or destructive. In this way, the ideality and knight-in-shining-armor aspect of technology is exalted to the exclusion of the more feeling and humanistic aspects; since it is precisely in those aspects that the prospect of destructive use looms largest. The definition is such that it punctuates the view that technology exists in a world apart and should be considered only as it is in itself; and that any question as to use or misuse, i.e., constructive or destructive consequences of technology, has nothing to do with technology itself but must be left up to others to sort out.

It should be noted that Hickman's definition does, however, provide for a kind of token acknowledgement of the human aspect by allowing for application to "perceived problems," but this ignores the question as to *whose* problems these are. The argument could be made that the most odious feature of technology is that it rests in the hands of those to whom the thriving and nurturing of the feeling world of individuals is a problem. This, understandably, only serves to exacerbate the perceived fragmentation in society because, in the same way that use conveys meaning in language, the use of technology conveys the intent of those who brandish it. The net effect of such use of technology is that the community becomes polarized. But it does not become polarized along the lines of support for technology as one might expect, but rather along the lines of feeling. The antipathy for technology that some feel is not the result of technology *qua* technology, but rather the use to which it is put, i.e., to the constructive or destructive use. The housewife likes technology when it takes away hand wringing and hanging out to dry with a washing machine and dryer but not when it takes her children away to war. Wars seem to be fought either when they *have* to be fought or when the state of technology inflates the sense of confidence in winning the war. When wars *have* to be fought, the housewife fights along with her children and technology has nothing to do with it.

But Heidegger's attempt, to my mind, fares no better. Let me summarize his argument to make my point. Heidegger's method in "The Question Concerning Technology" is one whereby he alternates between questioning and unpacking. As each term arises, he questions it and attempts to understand it or unpack it in terms of another, but related, expression. He then starts over by questioning and unpacking the new term, always unpacking it in terms of yet other related expressions. Thus, Heidegger seeks to uncover the essence of technology first by questioning the term "technology," and then by unpacking it in terms of "contrivance." He says: "The manufacture and utilization of equipment, tools, and machines, the manufactured and used things themselves, and the needs and ends that they serve, all belong to what technology is. The whole complex of these contrivances is technology." (p. 288) This produces the statement that "technology itself is a contrivance." In this way he moves from contrivance to instrumentality; from instrumentality he moves to causation and from there to "being responsible for," which idea is included in the original Greek word, αιτια, translated as "causes." The causes in question are the four causes of Aristotle.[5] He illustrates this with the example of a sacrificial vessel and notes that each of these ways of being responsible for the bringing into appearance of the sacrificial vessel act together as a unity in the verb "to occasion." He says that this verb gives "a more inclusive meaning" to "being responsible for" insofar as "to occasion" means to let what is not present arrive. He says, "Occasioning has to do with the presencing of that which at any given time comes to appearance in bringing-forth." (p. 293) He then notes that bringing-forth comes to pass "only insofar as something concealed comes into unconcealment." (p. 293) "Unconcealment" is then understood, or unpacked, in terms of "revealing," which, in turn, is understood as αληθεια, or truth. Here, Heidegger pauses to summarize for us.

We are questioning concerning technology, and we have arrived now at *αληθεια*, at revealing. What has the essence of technology to do with revealing? The answer: everything. For every bringing-forth is grounded in revealing. Bringing-forth, indeed, gathers within itself the four modes of occasioning—causality—and rules them throughout. Within its domain belong end and means as well as instrumentality. Instrumentality is considered to be the fundamental characteristic of technology. If we inquire step by step into what technology, represented as means, actually is, then we shall arrive at revealing. The possibility of all productive manufacturing lies in revealing.

Technology is therefore no mere means. Technology is a way of revealing. If we give heed to this, then another whole realm for the essence of technology will open up to us. It is the realm of revealing, i.e., truth.[6]

Although Heidegger continues his analysis so as to end up with the fact that the essence of technology is art, we can already see the tell-tale one-sidedness of his attempt. Whereas, the previous definition painted a one-sided *technological* picture of the essence of technology, Heidegger's definition paints a one-sided *humanistic* picture—the essence of technology is, as he says, "*nothing* technological"; it is art.

What I see at work here are various aspects of this problem in tension with one another. On the one hand, there is the tension born of the love/hate relationship we have with technology; and, on the other hand, there is the tension born of various attempts to derive or find the essence of technology. In the first case, various attempts at explaining the nature of technology are dominated by either the love or hatred of technology. In the second case, the various attempts at explaining the nature of technology vie for position through emphasizing different aspects—sometimes the more technological aspects, sometimes the more humanistic ones—yet all the while utilizing the same method. In the remainder of my essay I will suggest that once we clear up the second of these cases, the first will clear itself.

The problem I see with the attempts noted above is that they have taken the broad spectrum of experiences that are called by the single name of "technology" and assumed that there was some *one* thing, viz., the *essence* of technology, that unified them all and gathered them together under that rubric. However, this is not always the case. Consider the proceedings that we call "games" and how the great variety of games we play make up a complicated network of similarities overlapping and criss-crossing—sometimes overall similarities, and sometimes similarities of detail. Wittgenstein calls these similarities "family resemblances" owing to the fact that they overlap and criss-cross in the same way as family traits do between members of a family, i.e., the way build, features, color of eyes and hair, gait, temperament, etc. overlap and criss-cross. If we understand all the uses of the term "technology" on the model of family resemblance, then we can see that there does not have to be one single "essence" or "nature" that all the instances of that use share.

What this means to the love/hate relationship is quite straightforward. Once we see that what is at work is family resemblance between uses of the term "technology" and not an individuated essence, then the illusion of a focalized essence that is somehow standing over and against the feeling world evaporates. What was a boogeyman is now seen to be just the coincidental action of the wind in the trees and shadows cast by the streetlamp performing in concert. We can rid ourselves of the boogeyman either by closing the shutters and pulling down the blinds or by simply seeing the connection between what we thought was a boogeyman and the action of the wind, light, and shadows. With respect to technology and the humanities, there is no conspiracy. There is no conspiracy on the part of the friends of technology aimed at squelching the feelings of everyone else and neither is there a conspiracy on the part of the friends of the humanities aimed at turning everyone into "bleeding hearts." There *is* no conspiracy because there *can be no* conspiracy; there can be no conspiracy because there is no common theme around which to build a conspiracy, since each of us likes and dislikes different aspects of both the humanities and the sciences.

I started out with the observation that we tend to have a love-hate relationship with technology and suggested that this relationship was due, in part, to the thematic difference between the arts and sciences and to the *way* that an answer to the question of the nature of technology was sought. I further suggested that the way the answer was sought contributed to the existence of what I have been calling the love-hate relationship with technology. Although the arts and sciences gave us different definitions of the nature of technology, each reflecting the predominance of their respective thematic approaches, my criticism was that they both sought the answer in a common essence. I then suggested that, owing to the widely divergent uses of the term "technology," a more appropriate model for understanding these uses was the model of family resemblance put forward by Wittgenstein. It is only once we get beyond looking for a common essence or nature of technology that we can begin to make decisions based on constructive and destructive uses of technology. When we understand the many uses of the term "technology" on the model of family resemblance, we take less notice of "essences" of technology and more notice of the uses to which technology is put, i.e., whether constructive or destructive. It is here that axiology can take a turn and begin to acquit itself admirably with respect to such features of our experience. In this regard it seems to me that both the arts and the sciences can benefit from a dose of study into what is constructive and what is destructive in our experience.

Notes

1. William Barrett. 1979. *The Illusion of Technique*, New York, Anchor Books.
2. See, for instance, *Wittgenstein's Philosophical Investigations*. 1958. New York, Macmillan Company, trans. G.E.M. Anscombe, especially §§61 ff.
3. Larry Hickman. 2001. *Philosophical Tools for Technological Culture: Putting Pragmatism to Work*, Indianapolis, Indiana University Press, p. 12.
4. Martin Heidegger. 1977. "The Question Concerning Technology" in *Martin Heidegger Basic Writings*. New York, Harper and Row. pp 287-317.
5. Let me note here that, for Aristotle, the **τελοs**, or what has come to be called the "final cause" was not a cause at all in the sense of what we might call an efficient cause. Aristotle only recognized motion as causal and, in this regard, all motion begins with the heavens. Heidegger seems not to be as familiar with his Aristotle as, perhaps, he

should have been. Heidegger is correct, however, in emphasizing that the Greek term αιτια means to "be responsible for" but it was Cicero's unfortunate translation of the term into "causes" that created the confusion. Aristotle held that what we term the "four causes" were really more like "the four conditions" of any process whatsoever that must obtain if we are to understand it. Thus, each is an answer to a question that we might ask of any process: what is it?, out of what is it made?, by what agent?, and for what end? Additionally, the τελος should not be understood as "purpose" or "intention" as is commonly held. For Aristotle, only man has purposes or intentions, so the τελος of natural processes should be understood more on the model of patterns of outcomes that nature reaches repeatedly. Heidegger, himself, notes this as a misinterpretation.

6.   Heidegger, p. 294.

8

The Biology of Technology—
An Exploratory Essay[1]

Peter Bond

The primary objective of this chapter is to establish a basis for the development of a socio-biological approach to understanding the phenomenon of technological society and technical change, one that also serves to bridge the gap that has grown between natural science and social theory. The objective stems from the belief that an ecological crisis is looming that will require a new form of pragmatism from which new instruments for analysis, evaluation, and implementation can emerge and which, of necessity, will be multidisciplinary in character. One possible intellectual framework is proposed, that of a biology of technology, a conceptualization of human organization woven from an unlikely mix of theoretical perspectives. The most consequential of these is structural determinism, a tenet of autopoietic theory (also known as the biology of cognition). Other elements, including actor network theory, a metatheory of technology, and cognitive anthropology are explored before proceeding to consider some implications should the thesis be adopted.

Peter Bond directs Lawton-David Associates, a firm offering specialty consulting and learning facilitation services in business strategy, knowledge, and innovation management. Prior to this he was director of Studies for Technology and Manufacturing Management at Liverpool John Moores University, UK. Originally a materials scientist, he moved from industry to commerce in 1980 becoming an advisor to regional government on new technologies and later business development manager of a venture capital provider. Current interests include the practical application of complexity science to organization development and technical change. He may be reached at <plbond@ polytechnics.fsnet.co.uk>.

Introduction

Technology is a relatively new word; like *scientist,* it was coined in the mid nineteenth century. Originally it did not refer solely to hardware, the meaning that prevails today, but rather to a discourse, a particularly scientific discourse, such that the body of knowledge of the many new techniques of the industrial revolution was rapidly expanded (Gille 1986: 1136–7). Technology, the body of knowledge, was the result of systematic study of a wide spectrum of techniques, not simply of manufacturing, but also of measuring and analytical devices that enabled further development of the scientific method itself. Bertrand Gille says of technology: *"This term should be understood as a knowledge which...is distinguished from science by its subject matter and technical reality but is nevertheless a science by its psychology and by its methodic way in which it poses problems; by the importance of expressing in a 'dissertation' the 'operation' of technique, the precision of its steps, the generality of the concepts to which it gives freedom and the use it makes of mathematics through the precision of its observations and measurements."* (Gille 1986: 965) Following the principles outlined by Max Boisot with regard to epistemological space (Boisot 1995), technology is more properly interpreted as the codified and abstracted knowing about doing; about practices, about means to ends, and technical systems.

The chapter is presented in two parts. Following a brief introduction of technical evolution and a summation of the problems posed by technical progress, the case for the development of a socio-biological theory of technology is made. Some possible candidates for a foundation or theoretical framework are introduced, including a metatheory of technology from philosopher of technology Andrew Feenberg, Charles Laughlin's biogenetic structuralism, and, crucially, Maturana and Varela's theory of "autopoiesis." Feenberg's metatheory of technology is presented as a bridge between the cognitive and the socio-technical dimensions of human systems, and is strengthened by employing a more detailed understanding of the cognitive object from Jean Piaget, Ernst Von Glasersfeld, and the "autopoietic" theory of Maturana and Varela. The universally applicable notion of structural determinism is then introduced as the key element of a human system development concept based on a synthesis of technology, knowledge, and culture.

The Long View of Technology and Culture

For millions of years the hominid species has added continuously to nature's already vast collection of objects. As the product of human workmanship and human intentionality, they are all artifactual, if not entirely artificial (Dipert 1993). They serve to improve the functioning of complex social systems and as such they are social objects. This is, of course, only correct to a point;

improvement is a relative concept and depends on where a boundary is drawn around its effects. Human beings are one of nature's objects and, creationist arguments aside, were not designed. Humankind has emerged from millions of years of natural system evolution. Co-evolving with us is a supporting web of techniques that now constitutes a globe-encompassing technical system harnessed to the imperatives of capitalist production. That web of technical relations began to emerge with the creation of many simple tools that served a social purpose within the limited operational domains of isolated groups of people. Even more significantly, Donald (1999) suggests that our tool using ability was an evolutionary precursor to the development of our capacity for language—tool using came before language (see also Donald 1991 and 1997).

In those days (to distort a well-known phrase of global corporations), we thought locally and we acted locally, and the artifacts that survived enabled historians and archaeologists to distinguish the major and minor civilizations: the Chinese, the Aztecs, the Romans, the indigenous people of North America, and so on. Similarly, anthropologists use artifacts, including stone tools and cave paintings, to delineate hominid species. Thus great civilizations were characterized through the elaborate network of means by which artifacts were produced, the multiplicity of techniques that formed because of the unique and particular way we think.

It is, however, a mistake to see a civilization's technology simply in terms of crafting techniques. Two other categories are significant, first the techniques for regulating collective and individual behaviors, involving ritual practices and associated artifacts supported by pseudo–scientific explanations of the way the world worked. Second are the techniques of communication, or symbolic technologies, of which the written word is one and objects of art another. Taken together, such practices define a civilization and provide a basis for their maintenance and reproduction. In effect, *praxis* is the foundation of societies and thus organizations. From a different starting point, Anthony Giddens has recognized this in his thoughts on the constitution of society (Giddens 1985). His intention was to explain why societies displayed persistent characteristics or features over relatively long periods of time and yet were still able to change. These features he referred to as structural characteristics, which appeared to both shape and facilitate practices. His theory of "structuration" emerged as an attempt to establish the inextricable link between practice and structure and its centrality in the constitution and reproduction of social life. What Giddens has called practice has herein been referred to as technique. Technology, the knowledge of technique, is thus the essence of human systems. It is what philosopher of technology Joseph Pitt refers to as "humanity at work" (Pitt: 2000), but extended to all forms of human activity, even play. An attempt will be made presently, with reference to the idea of structural determinism, to show that technology, the knowledge of the totality of the means by which a social grouping achieves its aims (collectively and individually), is in effect the structure of an organization. From one point of view this is culture, defined by one anthropologist as follows. Culture is essentially an instrumental apparatus by which man is put in a position to better cope with the concrete, specific problems that face him in his environment in the course of the satisfaction of his needs, a system of objects, activities, and attitudes in which every part exists as a means to an end. Such activities, attitudes and objects are organized around important and vital tasks into institutions such as family, the clan, the local community, the tribe, and the organized teams of economic cooperation, political, legal, and educational activity (Malinowsky 1944).

The "Technology" Dilemma

In great measure, capitalist industrial society is geared to the design, production, and diffusion of solutions. By such processes natural objects are simultaneously transformed, destroyed, degraded, decomposed, recomposed, transposed, transferred, and transported—for a profit. At the beginning of the human epoch, Nature was the only raw material and simple tools were used to change it into forms more useful to human kind. Now the artificial, the machines, the cities, and many other manifestations of deconstructed nature, have become a primary source of raw material from which new concepts, new solutions, and even new art, are fashioned. One view, probably the dominant one, is that the more extensively nature is displaced the more society improves, and the more complex in character are the artifacts a society produces the more progressive it is. Although many have challenged this ideal, by the late twentieth century some had concluded that their concerns had come much too late. They would say we are trapped within a viscous circle of invention and innovation in which every technical solution draws forth another, a process of "technicization" that is certain to destroy the society it serves. Technicization is a roller coaster we need to get off, a process that Jacques Ellul (1964) considered to be "indefinitely additive." New techniques bring forth benefits and costs, they often produce harmful side effects and not enough of the desired effect. The solution is invariably a substitution, either of nature or other artifact, that all too often results in unpredicted and deleterious effects in other domains of human activity, and other natural ecologies.

So, at least from Ellul's perspective, technical solutions are very much the essence of the problem facing humankind. We are stuck in a rut, in a particular way of thinking about problems that inevitably leads to new but still imperfect solutions. The essence of this, the technics-out-of-control thesis (Winner: 1997), is that the extraordinary scale of technicization we see nowadays threatens to destroy Nature's dynamic equilibrium, heralding dire consequences for humankind.[2] It is thus imperative to break the circle and find an effective point of intervention in this process from which to lever change. Finding the source of suitable tools to act as levers is no less a challenge. Thus far, neither has been met adequately. In the author's opinion, to create both the desire and appropriate tools for the task will require the concept of "technology" to be understood more widely, not in terms of new and innovative products, but as a human phenomenon. That there is evident a lack of agreement on what technology is, is another substantial obstacle to meeting these challenges. And one must not forget that capitalism, acting as an institutional structure in the sense that Giddens means, constrains future action as well as it enables present action. What is needed, then, is a new value system, a new paradigmatic framework in which the natural and the technical are reconciled.

The Emergence of a Deep Ecology Paradigm and the Case for a Biology of Technology

Although prosaic concerns often arise when discussing the need for a better theory of technology, such as how to gain competitive edge, how current levels of industrial and economic growth can be sustained, and so on, the need for a specifically biological theory of technology derives from deeply seated concerns about humankind's longer term relationship to the earth.

The idea of a deep ecology paradigm was put forward by physicist Fritjof Capra (1997) to encapsulate a more holistic and systemic way of understanding the world and as a reminder of the looming ecological crisis. A crisis, he says, that is born of a series of misperceptions, one of which is the belief that unlimited material progress could be achieved through economic and technological growth. Likewise, natural scientist Edward Wilson says, in his book *Consilience*, there is already a crisis of the environment, one he believes has been brought about by a lack of understanding of nature (Wilson 1998). Responding to the crisis in an effective way, indeed even recognizing its existence, is made more difficult by the lack of a common reference point for scholars. What is missing Wilson refers to as a "unifying theory of humanity," at the heart of which is natural science.[3] The key to the necessary unification is "consilience," defined as a "'jumping together' of knowledge to create a common groundwork of explanation" (Wilson: 1998). Edward Wilson's major contribution to the process of unification is as co-developer, with Charles Lumsden, of a mathematical socio-biology of gene-culture coevolution (Lumsden & Wilson: 1981 and 1983). See also Durham (1991). Gene-culture co-evolutionary theory, is one of the new tools from complexity science; it addresses the question of *dual-inheritance*, the interaction between genetic inheritance and cultural inheritance, of which tools and tool-using is clearly the predominant feature. However, the issue of economic growth and technology *per se* is not pursued in any practical manner and its highly mathematical approach makes it unlikely as a candidate for achieving even some limited form of consilience in the shorter term.

On the other hand, Capra's *deep ecology* provides a welcome emphasis on life and nature while acting as an umbrella for the new sciences. The fact that various of these new sciences are also finding application in organization and management theory would seem to open a path to a biology of technology. They include: dissipative-systems theories derived from Prigogine (1985), see also Bergquist (1993); chaos theory models (Priesmeyer 1992; Stacey 1993), and a variety of complex systems perspectives (Kelly and Allinson 1999; Lissack and Roos 1999; Stacey 2000; Lewin and Regine 1999; Mitleton-Kelly 1997). Their application inaugurates what some see as a paradigm shift in management and organization theory. The inference, of course, is that current theories are underpinned by the equivalent of a Newtonian physics perspective with which we are *unable* to engage with the complexity of the real world.

Out of the crop of new science approaches come two possible candidates for a potential intellectual framework for a biology of technology. The first espouses similar assumptions to gene-culture co-evolution theory and is known as biogenetic structural theory. The principles of this approach were originally outlined by Laughlin and d'Aquili (1974) in a book of the same name. Although without a profile in the managerial literature, biogenetic structuralism eschews all the characteristics of new science, being a body of theory that integrates anthropology, human evolution, phenomenology, and neuroscience.[4] Mindful of the complementarity of the two approaches, the favored candidate is the biology of cognition developed by the biologists Humberto Maturana and Francisco Varela (1980 and 1992), and is most widely known as autopoiesis or autopoietic theory. There have been a number of attempts to apply its principles to social systems, by the originators themselves, Maturana (1980) and Varela (1981a and 1981b) and also social scientists, including, Hejl (1984), and Mingers (1995 and 1996). Mingers makes a useful comparison between aspects of autopoiesis and Anthony Giddens' structuration theory, which will also be drawn upon presently. The intellectual approach developed by Maturana and Varela has been categorized by Whitaker (1998) as a "radical constructivist" epistemology. Not surprisingly, there is thus some complementarity to be found with other constructivist explanations of cognition and social phenomena, especially of Watzlawick (1984) and von Glasersfeld (1995), who coined the term radical constructivism. Crucially, one is able to connect with social constructivist approaches to technology (Bijker 1997; Bijker, Pinch, and Hughes 1987; and Brey 1999), and, arguably a constructivist approach, actor-network theory, of which the work of John Law (2000) is most interesting, both from the standpoint of a biology of cognition and complexity thinking.

There are a number of aspects of autopoietic theory that lend themselves to the development of a biology of technology. First is that the character of the social systems we create are inextricably linked to the biology of cognition— the way we think. Second is the emphasis that is placed on the significance of the object, in both cognitive and social processes. The term "object" referring to concepts *for* artifacts, concepts *of* artifacts, and natural objects. The third is the approach adopted by Maturana and Varela's, known as "mechanicism." The choice of the third aspect is only tentative at this stage since it is unclear from the original literature whether a mechanicism is synonymous with the usual meaning of mechanism, (Whitaker: 1998). From a "mechanicismic" stance, it appears that the operation of a living machine would be explained in the same way as a non-living machine, as the behavior of both is structure-determined (more of this presently). With the growth in bio-technology and the increase of hybrid organic-inorganic devices, mechanicism may be a useful stance to adopt. As such, the whole of the approach outlined in this paper may be considered an extension and deepening of the organic metaphors of organization e.g. the enterprise as organism and brain, even psychological prison (see Morgan: 1985).

While Maturana and Varela's theory can provide both structure and process to a theory of technology, Feenberg's metatheory of technology has been found to be a useful means of bridging the gap between autopoiesis and more mainstream studies of technology and human (social) systems. The metatheory, therefore, will be introduced following an introduction to the ideas of Maturana and Varela and significant others.

Autopoietic Theory and the Radical Constructivist Perspective

Constructivism is the general label for an epistemological position that (a) denies that what we come to know through experience unequivocally mirrors an objective reality and (b) claims that individual knowledge is instead constructed in response to the medium in which one operates, through one's own constitutive features. That is to say, the sensory apparatus available to us as homo sapiens, and what we already know. Radical constructivism is primarily associated with the work of Ernst von Glasersfeld, although the formative concepts of constructivism can be traced back to philosophers such as Berkeley, Kant, and Vico. Although Von Glasersfeld makes brief reference to the ideas of Maturana and Varela, the principles of his approach to learning and education are primarily based on his revised account of Jean Piaget's theory of cognitive development in children. He says: *"[R]adical constructivism...is radical because it breaks with convention and develops a theory of knowledge in which knowledge does not reflect an 'objective' ontological reality, but exclusively an ordering and organization of a world constituted by our experience"* (von Glasersfeld 1995: 25). Whitaker (2) also categorizes Maturana & Varela's theory of autopoiesis as radical constructivist. The common ground of the two approaches is the idea that: *"knowledge, no matter how it be defined, is in the heads of persons, and that the thinking subject has no alternative but to construct what he or she knows on the basis of his or her own experience"* (ibid: p.25).

The consequences of adopting this closed system view of the cognizant human being are profound. What we sense as reality is merely a cognitive construction and, moreover, what we can know is limited by the physical nature of our sensory apparatus, including the brain itself. We cannot know the world in the way of a dolphin, a whale, or a bat.

Cognition and Maturanian Objects

According to autopoietic theory, the fundamental operation of cognition is bringing forth entities, or unities, by drawing distinctions between them and the mediums in which they operate. A unity is *"That which is distinguishable from a background the sole condition necessary for existence in a given domain. The nature of a unity and the domain in which the unity exists are specified by the process of its distinction and determination, this is so regardless of whether this process is conceptual or physical"* (Maturana & Varela 1980: 138). An object is thus: *"[A]n entity, concrete or conceptual dynamic or static, specified by operations of distinction that delimit it from a background and characterized by the properties that the operations of distinction assign to it"* (Maturana 1978: 31–32). This is the general case, the primary operation underpinning Piaget's explanation of cognitive development who has described how a basic cognitive scaffolding is built from concepts of objects, that is the physical objects we carve from our physical environment, along with concepts such as space, time, and causality (cause and effect). Such a construct serves as a framework for creating a coherent experiential reality— our world. From concepts of object, space, and time descriptions of systems can be built; and with concepts of causality explanations of systems behavior can be devised. Given the operationally closed nature of cognition, the objects we "see" are cognitive constructs that we treat as if they existed in a concrete real world. This is not a denial of reality but acceptance of the principle that reality can only be known through the apparatus we have to know it with.

When necessary to aid clarity of communication, the term "Maturanian object" will be used to distinguish it, a conceptual object, from a real object (a machine, a tool, and so on). Maturana and Varela distinguish two types of Maturanian objects (also referred to as a unity or entity), simple and composite. A composite unity is brought forth by a cognitive process of deconstructing an otherwise simple unity, an operation of making distinctions to create both the components and the relationships between them. This cognitive act of deconstruction co-creates a notion of the unity's structure. A simple unity is one that has not been so deconstructed. In more conventional systems analysis, the simple unity is the component we choose not to resolve into its constituent parts, thereby excluding its parts from any analysis. The behavior of composite unities, and the properties revealed by such behavior, can only be explained with reference to the structure revealed by deconstruction. What we think of as science, therefore, can only be practiced with respect to composite unities (Maturana 1988). Given the nature of cognition, we can only know that actual structure indirectly. We can only create concepts, models, or cognitive constructs of the actual structure of the real object.

Scientific Explanation and Structure-Determined Systems

In everyday English the word "structure" normally denotes something solid and unchanging. To give structure to something is to organize it, to give distinctive form to a set of components belonging to a whole, to establish relations. Within the framework of autopoietic theory, description and classification of objects is made with reference to their *organization* and to their *structure*. These have quite specific meanings within the theory. Both of the words refer to both the components from which a composite unity is constructed, and the relations between those components. *Organization,* however, refers to the relations between components that must always be present so that the composite unity will be a unity of a particular type. Structure on the other hand refers to the *actual* components plus the actual relations that take place between them. It is through its structure that a particular type of organization is realized and is maintained. To quote Maturana: *"the structure of a particular composite unity is the manner in which it is actually made by actual static or dynamic components and relations in a particular space, and a particular composite unity conserves its class identity only as long as its structure realises in it the organization that defines its class identity."*

Structure, so defined, is not quite the same as the one offered at the beginning of this section, it also has a much more dynamic aspect. In autopoietic theory, the concept of structure is an indispensable element of explaining how entities interact with each other and with the medium in which they operate. It is thus an indispensable aspect of the practice of science, the intention of which is to explain (Maturana, 1988). Significantly, the structure of a composite unity determines the manner in which it interacts with other unities. It is important to grasp the idea that the structure of a composite unity can change without the loss of class identity so long as the relations that constitute its organization are conserved. Structural change takes place leading *to* the conservation of organization. If the organization of a living entity is not conserved through its structure it disintegrates. A structure determined system is also a mechanism, or mechanicism. Machines may be autopoietic, a self-producing living system, or allopoietic, a machine that produces something other than itself. The latter applying to machines we design and also to techniques (technical systems) and wider social systems that involve an autopoietic machine, such as ourselves.

As a structure-determined system everything that happens in a composite unity is determined by its structure. Any change that takes place within a composite unity is a structural change. It follows that no changes can take place in the structure that are not permitted by it, and the actions of external agencies *do not* determine the changes that take place. That is, interaction with other unities triggers only changes that a specific structure allows. Furthermore, it is clear that only certain structural states, to use Maturana's terminology, will be "admitted" by the composite unity. Moreover, it also follows, that the concept of cause-and-effect, the mainstay of conventional scientific explanation, is somewhat displaced by the structure-determined explanation of interaction (ibid). Restructuring takes place when a state is reached between two or more entities that is conducive to spontaneous and structure determined interaction. Interaction is deemed to have taken place when a change in structure can be observed and there is a rearrangement of components such that they define a new space. Although difficult to articulate without using the explanatory device of cause and effect, structure-determined interaction might be likened to a continuous unfolding rather than a process punctuated by the creation of outputs that then become inputs, a process that only proceeds under the right conditions. Rather than cause-and-effect, perhaps effect-and effect-is more accurate.

Maturanian Objects and Language

According to Maturana, it is only through language that objects exist, before language there were no objects. Clearly, he is not claiming there weren't any objects before language, rather that we could not articulate their nature, nor communicate their presence. Maturana's explanation as to how Maturanian objects arise in language derives from his explanation of cognition, hence:

[W]e bring forth a world of distinctions through the changes of state that we undergo as we conserve our structural coupling in the different media in which we become immersed along our lives, and then, using our changes of state as recurrent distinctions in a social domain of co-ordination of actions (language), we bring forth a world of objects as coordinations of actions with which we describe our coordinations of action.....[W]e give the object an external preeminence and validate it in our descriptions as if it had an existence independent from us as observers. (Maturana, 1983, Section H) (cited by Whitaker 1998).

Objects that we may once have thought of as a simple, straightforward and 'just there,' suddenly, through the insights of autopoietic theory, become a complex and highly significant cognitive phenomenon, and as the quote below suggests, the basis of social coordination.

"Maturana characterizes natural language as 'the system of co-operative consensual interaction between organisms.' (Maturana & Varela, 1980: 31) As such, language is reconsidered as connotative (as opposed to denotative), meaning that 'its function is to orient the orientee within his cognitive domain without regard for the cognitive domain of orienter.' (Maturana & Varela 1980: 32) The functional role of

language, then, is '... the creation of a co-operative domain of interactions between speakers through the development of a common frame of reference, although each speaker acts exclusively within his cognitive domain....' (Maturana & Varela, 1980, p. 57)" *Extracted from Randall Whitaker's Encyclopaedia Autopoetica* (Whitaker: 1998).

This is the only explanation possible when two cognitive entities are operationally closed structure-determined systems—the basis of radical constructivism. There are no inputs to our minds, no connections to the outside world. Therefore, *"The primary function of linguistic interaction is [..] not conveyance of 'information quanta', but the mutual orientation of the conversants within the consensual domain realized by their interactivity. 'Communication' becomes a matter of mutual orientation.....*" Whitaker (ibid.) on language and languaging.

Maturana has said of conversations that: *"In daily life we call conversation a flow of coordinations of actions and emotions that we observers distinguish as taking place between human beings that interact recurrently in language...the different systems of co-existence, or kinds of human communities that we integrate, differ in the networks of conversations (consensual coordinations of actions and emotions) that constitute them, and therefore, in the domains of reality in which they take place."* Maturana (1988: 53).

The style and content of conversations in each of the networks of conversations serve to maintain those networks and our identities within them. We appear to be maintaining multi-verses as opposed to a universe. Conversing, and other practices, serve to maintain what is, in effect, the virtual structure of the social groupings, While the concrete artifacts (about which we may also have conversation) act as constant reminders of the concept of their structures, so confirming them as a conceptual objects. In this way, concepts of organizational structure, in the Maturanian sense of the word, appear concrete and real.

Maturana, linking conversation with emotions, as he does in the above quote, is emphasizing that conversations are a whole body experience, an emotioning experience, practices that give rise to biological changes of state. Maturana has said that: *"The western culture to which we modern scientists belong depreciates emotions, or at least considers them a source of arbitrary actions that are unreliable because they do not arise from reason. This attitude blinds us about the participation of our emotions in all that we do as the background of bodyhood that makes possible all our actions and specifies the domain in which they take place. This blindness, I claim, limits us in our understanding of social phenomena."*

Towards a Framework for a Biology of Technology

The author and main proponent of biogenetic structuralism, Charles Laughlin, understands technology as a natural phenomenon. Writing with reference to philosopher Martin Heidegger, Laughlin (1996) suggests that it is naive to think of technology as *things* that are independent of human *con-sciousness* and experience, or as either good or bad, or that human "techno-logical culture" is distinct from nature. He says that to do so is to fail to understand technology phenomenologically, and thus to be constantly trapped in our culture's bias toward mind vs. body dualism and its corollaries: mental vs. physical, technical vs. natural. As previously suggested, herein lies the fundamental problem of technology-determinism (technics-out-of-control the-sis) and the major obstacle to understanding technology or, what it is in effect, an *ecology* of ideas-made-concrete. Laughlin says tools should be understood as extensions of body-mind (not simply of the body), as a means of harnessing the energies available in the world-as-resource to fulfill desires. It is the body-mind that is the essence of the phenomenon of technology. Perfectly consis-tent with the body-mind view is philosopher of technology Andrew Feenberg's metatheory of technology, which will be outlined next.

It is taken for granted that the first tools were natural objects, including rocks and pieces of wood. However, the real significance of the act of tool creation is rarely spoken of, it is the cognitive act of recognizing functionality within the many attributes a natural object may present to its beholder. At-tributes such as sharpness, weight, or transparency,[5] have to be captured by the mind before they can be embodied in a tool.

Andrew Feenberg has devised a generic model, not only highlighting this link between cognition and the production of material artifacts, but also the emergence of specialization within a community of practice (Feenberg: un-dated). The crux of his thesis is that the fundamental nature of technology is social and that, historically, the processes by which it emerges have not changed, even over millennia.

The meta-theory is explained in terms of two levels or processes that appear to operate concurrently. These are described as Primary and Secondary Instrumentalization; they each contain 4 steps, which Feenberg refers to as *moments*. Briefly, Primary Instrumentalization begins with a de-worlding of the desirable property of a natural object. This is essentially a cognitive act that must take place before the extracted property of nature can be (re) incor-porated into a new concrete device or mechanism. Secondary Instrumentalization is the process by which the new device becomes a true social object by becoming embedded in social practice. The phenomenon of tool-using or technical action begins thus: early hominids created the flint tool by "taking" sharpness or heaviness from a stone, in effect, releasing them from nature as a technical property. These "fragments of nature" are recon-structed and appear in a concrete and technically useful form as part of a tool, which is understood to be so within the context of a technical action. In other words, an object gains meaning as a tool, only in the context of technical action or a technique, being a particular and characteristic way of achieving a desired result (see also Rammert: 1999). Primary Instrumentalization involves the establishment of relations between technical objects (tools) and subjects (tool users) and through action to an object of action. Secondary Instrumentalization is the *realization* of the relations between, the newly constituted tools, the tool-user, and the object of action in an actual socio-technical network. Secondary Instrumentalization operates *concurrently* as a process of recontextualizing the functionality found in Nature into a socio-technical-cultural space (as opposed to a natural space or simply a technical system). This principle would apply even if it were magnetism, electromagnetism, or some other field force that was being captured from nature, hence the metatheoretical nature of Feenberg's model. Despite the absolute artificiality of many devices, none can contradict the laws of nature. Space limitations prevent a full description of the meta-theory, but within the process of Secondary Instrumentalization two moments take on particular significance in the development of a biology of technology. The first is that a tool can seem to "take on" new dimensions of value. Through an evolution in the way it is utilized, an artifact can have conferred upon it, by the community in which it is used, new or extended meaning, perhaps becoming more symbolic within a ritual or as part of a story or legend (e.g. the Christian crucifix or the holy grail). The second is that users, and developers of new tools, take on the mantle of specialists. The former moment is known as the moment of mediation; the latter as the moment of "vocationalization."

The result of instrumentalization (primary and secondary) is a technique embedded in a socio-technical-cultural network, a seamless web of relations that may be said, by an observer of this process, to have precipitated from the appearance of the tool. However, it must not be forgotten that the concept for the tool, or more accurately the technique for achieving some goal within which an object gains this meaning, itself emerges from the activity and collective desires of the social group. If this were not so, the technique would fail to become embedded. Interestingly, Feenberg's metatheory would appear to provide an explanation of technology push and market pull, as concurrently operating processes.

Objects Performing Relations

In the words of actor-network theorist John Law, objects perform relations. In the preceding section it was suggested that an observer of the instrumentalization process might venture to say that as a new tool is created relations appear to form around it. First a relation is created between the tool-user and the tool, and in use a relation is formed between the tool and the object of action. The technical action itself then becomes an embedded social practice, becoming part of how the community sees itself, part of its identity. John Law contends that objects perform relations to create a syntactic space. He applies the conventional meaning of the word *object,* and, since he is primarily concerned to understand the nature of technology, he applies it exclusively to artifacts like ships (Law: 1987), even the textbook that becomes the "bible" of a profession (Law and Singleton: 2000). Syntactic space is a notion Law introduces in a paper on objects, spaces, and others, and is taken to mean a description, written or spoken, an attempt to articulate the structure of a system by specifying the functional components, their functions, and their relationships. Syntactic space might be interpreted as the description of a functionally decomposed composite unity. In the light of Laughlin's notion of the function of the brain, namely, to provide meaning to objects, it seems a reasonable step to extend Law's idea to objects in the Maturanian sense. Such a step serves to tie together autopoiesis, actor-network theory, and biogenetic structuralism around the nature of the object. With this in mind, it is suggested that the environment of the artificial has the potential of providing a constant reminder of who we are and what we do, of what is desirable and what is not, of what is good and what is bad, and so on. It is an idea material to Andrew Feenberg's metatheory of technology, in the sense that once a tool is made concrete a set of relations appears to precipitate from it to form, what we tend to call, a technological society. Alternatively, a human system could be described as a polytechnical community (of practice). Human systems have ever been thus, and the mechanisms whereby they become so have not changed over millennia, in fact they are genetically programmed and based on a particular biology of cognition, the way we come to know.

Human Solution-Making and Amplification of the Technical

Why do we seek to know? The answer to this question is fundamental to understanding the human being as a natural phenomenon. Like the shark that swims or dies, it appears that we cannot stop learning, cannot stop creating new knowledge. As cognitive entities we are drawn and driven, guided and persuaded, into situations in which we can, at best, only anticipate what might happen. By coping with what arises from the unknown, we learn and come to value successful strategies and successful solutions. To quote Piaget: *"Human beings never remain passive but constantly pursue some aim or react to perturbations by active compensation consisting in regulations. It follows from this that every action proceeds from a need which is concerned with the system as a whole and that values, likewise dependent on the system as a whole, are attached to every action and every situation if favorable or unfavorable to its executor"* (von Glasersfeld 1995: 114).

The emphasis here is on the experience of the individual, the knowing person. Raul Espejo also sees such disturbances in terms of problems. He sees experience not as a smooth process but one that is constantly punctuated by the need to address problems. He says: *"[P]roblem solving is a daily concern in organizations. Problematic interruptions in the flow of our interactions are all too natural. They come in varied forms sometimes as threats, sometimes as major concerns, some others as almost imperceptible disturbances, sometimes as well defined demands, some others as ill-defined feelings. In all cases we feel the need to produce responses of one kind or another"* (Espejo 1992: 8).

Due to the nature of our cognitive apparatus, we are able to reflect upon our actions and, to a degree, we can anticipate problems and rehearse what might be successful. In other words, we can experiment reactions to them in what has been called the space of possibilities, or our imaginations. Such capability is due to species specific genetic makeup from which also arises three invariant characteristics of humanity, wherever it is found. These are: tool using, languaging, and social coordination, a co-evolution of which has produced the unique phenomenon of the technological human society. There is, however, one other characteristic that emerges from, and co-evolves with them, a significant variable of any explanation of human success, namely, the effect of the development and persistence of a multiplicity of means of dealing with that relentless and largely unpredictable flow of environmental disturbances that punctuate, what would otherwise be, an unvarying existence. The factor was referred to earlier as polytechnicity.

Being human, our natural tendency is to embody solutions in the use of tools. Human systems have thus evolved through the creation and application of a multiplicity of tool based techniques, in pursuit of a multiplicity of objectives, so producing a complex network of socio-technical relations embedded in Nature's own web of relations. Polytechnicity is the resultant phenomenon, not so much a theory as an expression of an essential characteristic of human organization, a constant feature over millennia that has been synonymous with the very notion of human society and what it is to be human. Polytechnicity is, arguably, the original subject of archaeology and anthropology, and is most vividly reflected in the history of the arts and crafts and more recently in the co-dependent factors of technology and the enhanced scientific method of advanced industrial societies. Polytechnicity has enabled what, in the first instance, might be described as flexibility, which entails a combination of agility and responsiveness. In short, and as embodied in Ross Ashby's famous law of requisite variety, this means being able to respond to a variety of events with an equal variety of counter actions. Polytechnicity is also a manifestation of the systems principle of equifinality, that more than one means might be devised in pursuit of an end.

Hand in hand with polytechnicization goes complexification, driven by our demand for improvement, for efficiency, effectiveness, and economy of effort and energy that can only be satisfied by greater and more detailed *know how* and *know why*—technics and explanation—technology and science. But, apart from the names, things have not changed for humanity in thousand of years, complexification has obscured the simpler relationships that are best revealed by taking the long view of technical, *ergo,* human evolution.

The Implications of Adopting a Biological Perspective of Technology

The major implication of adopting a radical constructivist approach to organization and related science and technology studies is that, because of the operationally closed nature of cognition, we can only know the world indirectly. Whatever conceptualization we, as individuals, have of our society and our organizations, can only be, at the very most, taken-to-be-shared. Our worlds are cognitive constructs that, according to Francisco Varela, are enacted. Enaction is, *"the term for the reciprocal process by which; (i) an observer educes unities from her medium within the limits of her phenomenology* (i.e., as constrained by the embodiment of her knowing the equivalent of Piaget's cognitive framework) and (ii) *the ontogenic coupling results in incremental regularisation in the structure of the observer* (i.e. literally the physical/biological embodiment of knowing). It describes *"a history of structural coupling that brings forth a world"* (Varela et al.: 1991: 206). Our conception of organizations thus emerges from our flow of individual experience within them. It follows that individuals will act, uniquely, to maintain the structure they conceive of as enabling. An essential element of that activity is conversation, which may underline or undermine the taken-to-be-shared structure. Just as every individual evolves along a path that no other treads, the same is true of organizations. Every organization has a different starting structure, which becomes a variable in determining its future state, and through the collective experiences of the people within it, will evolve along a path different to every other. Since structure is enacted by individuals, it is unevenly distributed, multiple and emotioning conversations ensue in a way that reinforces or undermines existing structures and hence collective behaviors. Understanding of objects, again in the autopoietic sense, devices used to orientate the behavior of others, that becomes central to understanding organization behavior. From an observer's point of view, real world objects, as artifacts and natural objects, continuously impress themselves on our experiences, acting as reminders of roles, as extensions to biological memory and as manifestations of technological nature.

We observe, and describe in our conversations with others, a multiplicity of objectives (objects of activity) being pursued and realized with a multiplicity of techniques, with an equal number of specialists to match. Also part of our world is the construct of self that emerges from experience to be validated and confirmed by the coherence of the world we have constructed (Damasio 2000 for a readable neuroscientific description of how a conception of *self* arises). That coherence is constantly being challenged and constantly being changed, constantly being enlarged through a process of equilibration (von Glasersfeld:

1995), essentially a process of maintaining one's equilibrium with the world by accommodating and assimilating new experiences. Learning to solve problems adds to our experience and our knowing. The constant challenge to the coherence of the structure of our world Von Glasersfeld refers to as perturbations, and conversation is one of the main sources of structural evolution.

Summary: A Biology of Socio-Technical Systems

Having introduced a perspective of technical progress, the concept of structure-determination was outlined with respect to the nature of Maturanian and real objects. Objects, cognitive and real, are central to any discussion of the nature of technology. How they are brought into existence, first through language, then through a process of making them concrete or real will be pivotal to the development of any "theory of technology." Feenberg provides the metaprocessual explanation, and autopoietic theory would appear to provide the deeply underlying cognitive mechanisms. Cognitive anthropologists, such as Laughlin and Donald, provide the context for cognitive development while Laughlin, Wilson and Lumsden emphasize the influence of genetic structure on subsequent cultural developments. Objects, as well as being concepts of "captured" functionality, become technical objects and subsequently conversational devices for achieving social coordination. Objects may be treated as simple unities but science can only be practised on composite unities. The result is a technical perspective of community development, characteristics of which are derived from many the techniques involving symbolic and more physical tools.

The technology of the community (like any other "ology") is defined as the *knowledge* of the totality of the means by which it attempts to achieve the ends that are collectively deemed to be desirable. Depending on the evolutionary stage a community has reached, especially with respect to "symbolic techniques," knowledge will be more or less shared, more or less tacit, more or less explicit (see Edward Bohn 1994 on the nature of what he calls "technological knowledge"). Given that an object can also be dynamic i.e. a behavior or an act that has been distinguished from a background, a technology might be considered as an ecology of intertwining ideas of means, ways or methods of doing tasks. Such an ecology develops in response to problems, and in the case of human communities, has led to their elaboration and complexification.

In ecological terms the development of many techniques, enables a social group to respond to more problems. If, as new techniques are added, a knowledge of older techniques is retained, greater and greater flexibility and responsiveness—in other words—greater agility, would be expected. This is an advantage of a polytechnic system.

With mechanism and biologics in mind, one might also find it easier to approach the invention and innovation of new tools, that is, new techniques (even new objects), from an ecological perspective, saying that in order to become embedded and appear as persistent characteristics they must "fit." That is, they must fit into an existing web of socio-technical-natural relationships, the existing structure of the organization-community within the context of a natural ecological system.

This chapter was written with the intention of exploring the possibilities and potential of developing a biological perspective of the technological phenomenon. Only the reader can say whether or not it has succeeded in stimulating new ideas.

Notes

1. This chapter is based on an earlier and more extensive exposition of the biology of technology, including the description of new conceptual tools, in a paper entitled: "The Biology of the Technology of Magic Bullets: From BPR to Objects of Art." Presented at the Standing Conference on Organizational Symbolism (SCOS). Cambridge University, July 2003.
2. The technology-out-of-control thesis was, and still is, contended, sometimes with a lack of grace, even in the pages of philosophical journals and books. For example, see Joseph Pitt's book entitled *Thinking about Technology* (see below for reference) and the subsequent (mostly unsupportive) reviews by his colleagues who seem to be more in-tune with the arguments of Ellul and his notable supporter, Langdon Winner.
    Recent theoretical developments arising from complexity science lend themselves to a reappraisal of Ellul's original work that should confirm the correctness of his arguments. In particular the economic models developed by Brian Arthur <*www.santafe.edu/arthur*>.
3. Lumsden and Wilson are not the first to put forward the idea of a unifying framework for the sciences. Bertalanffy, also a biologist, developed a "general systems theory" that was meant to unify the sciences but, despite the wide use of terms such as system, process, inputs and outputs, it failed to live up to expectations.
4. An on-line course in the principles of biogenetic structuralism can be seen at: <*www.carleton.ca/%7Eclaughli/tutindex.htm*>.
5. For a fascinating insight into the (pre)history of the "capture" and use of transparency and shape from natural minerals see The Crystal Sun by Robert Temple (Random House Books 1999).

References

Bergquist, W. (1993) *The Postmodern Organization*, Jossey-Bass, San Francisco, CA.

Bijker, W. E. (1997) *Of Bicycles, Bakelite, and Bulbs, Toward a Theory of Sociotechnical Change*, MIT Press, Cambridge, MA.

Bijker, W., Pinch, T., and Hughes, T. (eds.) (1987) *The Social Construction of Technological Systems: New Directions in the Sociology and History of Technology*, MIT Press, Cambridge, MA.

Bohn, R. E. (1994) "Measuring and Managing Technological Knowledge." *Sloane Management Review*, Fall 61–73.

Boisot, M. (1995). *Information Space*, Routledge, London.

Brey, P. (1999) "Philosophy of Technology Meets Social Constructivism." *Techne*. Volume 2, No 3–4.

Capra, F. (1997) *The Web of Life*, HarperCollins, London.

Damasio, A. (2000) *A Feeling of What Happens*, Random House, London.

Dipert, R. (1993) *Artifacts, Art Works, and Agency*, Temple University Press, Philadelphia.

Donald, M. (1991) *Origins of the Modern Mind*. Harvard University Press.

Donald, M. (1997) "Précis of Origins of the Modern Mind: Three stages in the evolution of culture and cognition." *Behavioral and Brain Sciences* 16 (4): 737–91.

Donald, M. (1999) "Preconditions for the Evolution of Protolanguages", in: M. C. Corballis & I.Lea (Eds) (1999) *The Descent of Mind*, Oxford University Press, pp. 355–65.

Durham, W. H. (1991) *Co-evolution: Genes Culture and Human Diversity*, Stanford University Press: New York, NY.

Ellul, J. (1964) John Wilkinson (Trans.) *The Technological Society*, Knopf: New York, NY.

Espejo, R. (1992) "Management of Complexity in Problem Solving." *Trans Inst*. MC, 14(1)

Feenberg, A. (undated) *From Essentialism to Constructivism: Philosophy of Technology at the Crossroads*. Posted on the Internet at Feenberg's homepage <www-rohan.sdsu.edu/faculty/feenberg>.

Giddens, A. (1984) *The Constitution of Society: Outline of the Theory of Structuration*. Cambridge: Polity Press.

Gille, B. (1986) *The History of Techniques—vol. 2*. Gordon and Breach, Montreux.

Glasersfeld, E. (1995) *Radical Consructivism, A Way of Knowing and Learning*, Falmer Press, London.

Hejl, P. (1984) "Towards a Theory of Social Systems: Self-Organization and Self-Maintenance, Self-Reference and Syn-Reference." in Ulrich, H., and G. Probst (eds.), *Self-Organization and Management of Social Systems: Insights, Promises Doubts, and Questions*, Berlin: Springer-Verlag, 1984, 60–78.

Kelly, S. and M. A. Allinson (1999) *The Complexity Advantage: How the Science of Complexity Can Help your Business Achieve Peak Performance*, McGraw-Hill, New York and London.

Law, J. (1987), "Technology and Heterogeneous Engineering: the Case of the Portuguese Expansion", pages 111–34 in Wiebe Bijker, T. Hughes, and T. Pinch (eds), *The Social Construction of Technical Systems: New Directions in the Sociology and History of Technology*, MIT Press, Cambridge, MA.

Law, J. (2000) "Objects, Spaces, Others" (draft) published by the Centre for Science Studies and the Department of Sociology, Lancaster University, UK at: <www.comp.lancaster.ac.uk/sociology/soc027jl.html>.

Law, J. and V. Singleton (2000) "This is not an object." Published by the Centre for Science Studies and the Department of Sociology, Lancaster University at <www.comp.lancs.ac.uk/sociology/soc032jl.html>.

Laughlin, C. and E. G. d'Aquili (1974) *Biogenetic Structuralism*, Columbia University Press: New York, NY.

Lissack, M., and J. Roos (1999) *The Next Common Sense: Mastering Corporate Complexity through Coherence*, Nicholas Brealey, London.

Lewin, R. and B. Regine (1999) *The Soul at Work: Unleashing the Power of Complexity Science for Business Success*, London: Orion.

Lumsden, C. J. and E. O. Wilson (1981). *Genes, Mind, and Culture: The Coevolutionary Process*, Cambridge, MA: Harvard University Press.

Lumsden, C. and E. Wilson (1983). *Promethean Fire: Reflections on the Origin of Mind*. Cambridge, MA: Harvard University Press.

Malinowski, B. (1944). *A Scientific Theory of Culture and Other Essays*, Chapel Hill: University of North Carolina.

Maturana, H. (1978) "Biology of language: The epistemology of reality." in Miller, G., and E. Lenneberg (eds.), *Psychology and Biology of Language and Thought: Essays in Honor of Eric Lenneberg*, New York: Academic Press, 1978, 27–64.

Maturana, H. (1983) "What is it to see? ¿Qué es ver?" *Arch. Biol. Med. Exp.*, Vol. 16 (1983), pp. 255–269.

Maturana, H. and F. Varela (1980). *Autopoiesis and Cognition*, Reidal Publishing, Dordrecht, Holland.

Maturana, H. and F. Varela (1992) *The Tree of Knowledge: The Biological Roots of Human Understanding*, Shambhala, Boston.

Maturana, H. (1980) "Man and Society." in Benseler, F., P. Hejl, and W. Köck (eds.), *Autopoiesis, Communication, and Society: The Theory of Autopoietic System in the Social Sciences*, Frankfurt: Campus Verlag. pp. 11–32.

Maturana, H. (1988). "Ontology of observing: The biological foundations of self consciousness and the physical domain of existence." in Donaldson, R. (Ed.), *Texts in Cybernetic Theory: An In-Depth Exploration of the Thought of Humberto Maturana, William Powers, and Ernst von Glasersfeld*, Felton CA: American Society for Cybernetics.

Mingers, J. (1995) *Self-Producing Systems: Implications and Applications of Autopoiesis*, Plenum Press, New York.

Mingers, J. (1996) "A Comparison of Maturana's Autopioetic Social Theory and Giddens' Theory of Structuration." *Systems Research* 13 (4): 469–82. John Wiley and Sons, Chichester.

Mitleton-Kelly, E. (1997) 'Organizations as Co-evolving Complex Adaptive Systems.' *Proceedings of British Academy of Management Conference 1997*. Also posted on the Internet at <www.lse.ac.uk/complex>.

Morgan, Gareth (1995) *Images of Organization*, Sage, London.

Priesmeyer, H. R. (1992) *Organizations and Chaos*, Quorum Books, London.

Prigogine, I. and I. Stengers (1985) *Order out of Chaos*, London: Flamingo, HarperCollins

Rammert, W. (1999) "Relations that Constitute Technology and Media that Make a Difference: Toward a Social Pragmatic Theory of Technicization." *Techne Journal of Philosophy and Technology*, 4–3 Spring.

Stacey, R. (1993) *Strategic Management and Organizational Dynamics*, Pitman, London.

Varela, F. (1981a) "Autonomy and Autopoiesis." in Roth, G., and H. Schwegler (eds.), *Self-organizing Systems*, Frankfurt: Campus Verlag, 1981, 14–23.

Varela, F. (1981b) "Describing the Logic of the Living." in Zeleny, M. (ed.), *Autopoiesis: A Theory of Living Organization*, New York: Elsevier, 1981, 36–48.

Whitaker, R. (1998) *Encyclopaedia Autopoietica: An annotated lexical compendium on autopiesis and enaction*. Posted on the Internet at <www.informatik.umu.se/%7Erwhit/EA.html>.

Winner, L. (1977) *Autonomous Technology: Technics-out-of-Control as a Theme in Political Thought*, MIT Press, Cambridge, MA.

Wilson, E. O. (1998) *Consilience: The Unity of Knowledge*, Knopf, New York, NY.

9

Technological Semantics and Technological Practice: Lessons from an Enigmatic Episode in Twentieth-Century Technology Studies

Kelvin Willoughby

The core thesis of this chapter is that, in the sphere of technology, good semantics can lead to good practice and, conversely, poor semantics can lead to poor practice. This claim will be supported by some analysis of the semantics of an international technology-related social movement that rose to prominence in the 1970s and 1980s. Before addressing my thesis and its supporting evidence directly, however, it will be helpful to reflect briefly about the prominence of technology and technological semantics in contemporary industrialized societies.

The Ubiquity of Technology

Technology has become the *leitmotif* of the modern world and a linchpin of the international economy. Businesses, governments, community organiza-

Kelvin W. Willoughby is the W. R. Sweatt Chair in Technological Leadership and Management of Technology Program Director at the Center for the Development of Technological Leadership, Institute of Technology, University of Minnesota. His research, teaching, and consulting concentrate on strategic technology management, intellectual property management, technology-based entrepreneurship, technology-based industry development, and regional economic development planning. He holds doctoral degrees in both technology studies and strategic management. Kelvin has conducted research or directed programs in technology management at the State University of New York at Stony Brook, the University of Utah, and the University of California at Berkeley. He is also an active participant in the Entrepreneurial Technology Apprenticeship Program of the U.S. Minority Business Development Administration and the National Technology Transfer Center. He can be reached at <kelvin@umn.edu>.

tions, and individuals, seemingly everywhere, look to technology as a key to attaining their goals. In opposition, there are those who are reluctant to adulate technology, and who point to the technological causes of human and environmental problems. Even these unbelievers, however, seem unable to avoid becoming embroiled in the new polemics of technology and to escape the technological milieu against which they protest. In short, during the twentieth century technology has become ubiquitous.

The ubiquity of technology has at least two important dimensions: the rise of technology itself as a part of society and the rise of human concern about technology.

The first dimension, the rise of technology itself, means that the practical functions of society and the economy (such as agriculture, transportation, building construction, manufacturing, the fighting of wars, communication, health care, and even analysis of problems) are increasingly carried out in a technological manner. Whereas these functions used to be carried out *directly* by people, sometimes aided by technological artifacts, they now tend to be *mediated* by technologies or technological systems.

For example, whereas most people used to have a *direct* role in the cultivation and preparation of food, in urban-industrial societies this relationship is now *mediated* by household appliances for reheating factory-processed foods, bought from supermarkets that have technologically sophisticated food storage and distribution systems; and the raw food itself is normally produced in technologically complex ways, such as by mechanized farms producing genetically-engineered crops. Even functions that used to be thought of as intimate and personal activities between individual people, such as producing children, may now be conducted artificially, by the application of techniques such as in vitro fertilization, embryo transplants, artificial insemination, and embryo storage.

Of course, technology has probably always been present in human society, perhaps in the form of simple hunting, farming, cooking, food preservation, or fire-making implements. Its pervasiveness appears to have increased so much, however, that it may no longer be thought of only as a collection of "things" to help people do a better job of whatever they want to do. Rather, technology has become an integral part of the environment in which people live, form their values, and make decisions.

For example, while the automobile may still be quite legitimately described as "a machine to get me from *point A* to *point B*," it is more than that. The shape of the landscape in modern cities, such as Los Angeles, is molded by the requirements of car travel: new technologies such as cellular phones have emerged as a means of coping with time spent in automobiles; "drive-in" convenience outlets now exist for almost any service such as banking, takeout food, and consumer goods sales; and businesses restructure their organizational form to take advantage of the opportunities for decentralizing certain activities to "back offices" in the suburbs, to which employees may travel by car. The automobile becomes part of the *context* that determines where *point A* and *point B* are, and how frequently the driver needs to travel between them; it is no longer simply a means for connecting *point A* and *point B*.

The general point here is that the ubiquity of technology in society transforms technology from simply being a collection of *means* for making human actions easier into a force for framing the *ends* that human actions serve. It is this phenomenon that was popularized through Jacques Ellul's writings during the 1960s and that helped make the phrase "the technological society" (Ellul, 1964) common.

The second dimension of the ubiquity of technology, the rise of human concern about technology, has no doubt been fed by popular perceptions of the emergence of the technological society. Until recently the general public in the now industrialized societies tended to relegate technology to the professional domain of the engineer or technologist, or take it for granted as the benevolent provider of material wealth. While turbulent responses to the introduction of new technology did occur during earlier periods, it would appear that popular attitudes towards technology per se are now more intense and deeply rooted. This insight is probably readily apparent to the casual observer, but a number of serious studies have now been published that confirm such observations about public attitudes to technology (and science) (Pecotich & Willoughby, 1989; Beveridge & Rudell, 1988; Postman, 1988; Kuhlman, 1987; Williams, 1986; Miller, 1983; Yankelovitch, 1982; Pion & Lipsey, 1981; Maderthaner et al., 1976; Mazur, 1975).

The normative status of technology is now contentious. Some view it as a savior, capable of solving most of the perennial problems of human existence; others view it as a demon that threatens the health of human society and the environment. Some argue that a felicitous future will only be possible with continually increasing technological growth; others plead for the rejection of technology, arguing that it is intrinsically destructive. It is not the purpose of this paper to explain the details of public disagreements over the normative status of technology, as this has been explored elsewhere (e.g.: Willoughby, 1990; Yearly, 1988; Frankel, 1987; Borgman, 1984; Braun, 1984; Mazur, 1981; Nelkin, 1981; Gendron, 1977; Schuurman, 1977; Ferkiss, 1969; Marcuse, 1964; Mumford, 1963; Jünger, 1956). Rather, my purpose is to recognize the contentious role of technology in society and to explore some of the implications this has for semantics in the field of technology studies.

The ubiquity of technology in contemporary society means that most social, political, economic, and environmental problems have a technological dimension to them. This means that most political, administrative, or judiciary functions of society that at one time might have been relatively free of technological considerations must now carefully incorporate such considerations. Thus, political debates about whether a country's energy policy ought to emphasize nuclear energy, energy conservation, fossil fuels, or renewable energy sources revolve around highly *technical* disputes over the relative safety of alternative waste disposal technologies. Likewise, debates about the ethical legitimacy of military action may hinge on *technical* disputes about the ability of the attacker to deploy the latest military technology to win a strategic target without hurting civilians. Or, debates on whether to introduce a national identity card may hinge on the possibility of providing technological assurance of confidentiality of information about citizens.

In summary, the ubiquity of technology *within* society has meant that human society *itself* has become more technological in character.

The Importance of Technology-Practice

A consequence of society becoming more technological is that a particular sphere of human endeavor—what will be labeled here as "technology-practice"—has become more important. The meaning of "technology-practice" will be explained later (see Glossary at end) in more detail, as will be the meaning of "technology." Basically, however, what this means is that technological competence has become a prerequisite for competence in other spheres of human endeavor.

It is now commonplace for relative technological prowess to be seen as a measure of relative economic competitiveness between nations, or relative commercial strength between business enterprises. Competency in the sphere of technology-practice is important not only to economic competitiveness, however, but also to a community's capacity to solve problems in spheres of human endeavor such as political conflict resolution, human resources development, health care, environmental management and remediation, social service delivery, household management, or interpersonal communication. Two examples will illustrate this.

First, the importance of competence in technology-practice vis-à-vis political conflict resolution may be illustrated by the role of technological change in the timber milling industry. As logging and timber milling have become more capital intensive, small towns throughout the world with economies based around these industries have experienced economic problems connected with rising unemployment among timber workers. This creates political pressures to intensify logging as a means of maintaining employment levels. At the same time, the growth of environmentalism means that logging companies also experience political pressures from the opposite extreme, aimed at reducing the intensity of logging operations. This may lead to political conflict between families and sympathizers of loggers and those people in the community who have a strong concern for environmental preservation.

Viewed from one perspective, technological change may be legitimately described as a source of such political conflict. From another perspective, however, it may be viewed as a potential source of rapprochement. The application of micro-computer control systems to a small-scale sawmill can make it possible to increase the efficiency of finished-timber output from a given log input, and improve the commercial competitiveness of these normally labor-intensive operations. By such means it is possible to both reduce the amount of logging required for a given level of timber production, and increase or maintain local employment levels. Thus technological competence (of a more sophisticated kind than that which is aimed simply at the automation of large-scale mills) may help appease the fears of both environmentalists and timber workers. This, in turn, may assist resolution of conflict between social groups in timber towns.

A second example may be drawn from the spheres of interpersonal communication and household management. A person who travels frequently in his or her profession, or who operates a business in more than one location, may have troubles maintaining contact with family, friends, and colleagues, and may have trouble managing household practicalities such as paying bills on time, ensuring bank accounts are balanced, or ordering household services efficiently.

There are many electronic systems now available to help solve these kinds of problems, e.g.: facsimile machines, touchtone telephone services, electronic funds-transfer networks, computerized electronic mail systems, modems to connect personal computers with telephone systems, cellular telephones, voicemail services, telephone answering machines, and digital paging services (you know…the kind designed to sound-off during a performance!). Anyone with the above kind of lifestyle, and who has tried to use such technological aids seriously can readily relate anecdotes of frustrating experiences where "the system was down," "the software had a bug," "the networks were not compatible," "the computer malfunctioned," "the instruction manual was ambiguous," "the file was corrupted with a virus," "I eventually got through, but it took me until 1:00 a.m.," "I forgot the commands," "Somebody else got credited with my payment," "I gave up after the voicemail computer asked me to press '9' if I wanted to leave a message for the operator," or "the computer system's firewall wouldn't allow a file of that format to enter the network."

The point here is not that all of these communication and computing technologies are not useful (to the contrary), but rather that their usefulness depends upon a certain degree of *mastery of the technology-practice*, even by "dumb users." For such technologies to actually help an "average" business person or householder, that person must expend a considerable amount of effort both to evaluate options in the technology before buying or subscribing, and to become proficient in the practical operations of the technology. This level of competence in technology-practice is normally not as high as the level of competence required of engineers, technicians, and systems managers, but it is still technological in nature. Thus, in the technological society, lay people (i.e., non-technicians) need to develop a degree of comfort in technology-practice in order to cope with the practicalities of modern life. Technology can no longer be left only to the experts...well, not unless you don't care if it doesn't work properly.

Human competence in technology-practice is not just a matter of technical experts designing a more powerful machine than their competitors. Rather it involves at least two other important processes. First, it is important that *technologies* and technological systems be designed and constructed so that their use is convenient and efficient for non-experts. An example of this phenomenon in the computing market would be the emergence of the Apple Macintosh group of personal computers and software.

Second, *institutions* need to emerge which make it easier for non-experts to manage technology "as it is." Once again, in the computing market, an example of this would be the emergence of organizations such as the Berkeley Macintosh Users' Group (an independent community organization that runs meetings, newsletters, magazines, and advisory services for users of Macintosh computers). The various consumers' organizations that publish magazines that evaluate alternative brands of consumer products, or even the companies that publish automobile magazines that may be found in newsagents' stands, may also be examples of the phenomenon.

To summarize thus far, the ubiquity of technology in society, which has given more importance to technology-practice as a sphere of human practice, indirectly creates the need for both more sophisticated approaches to technological design and new types of technology-related institutions. This is partly expressed in the growth of technical training institutes and technical universities, but also in the growth of special technology-related organizations and services for lay people, as well as academic programs in technology management at universities.

The Problem of Technological Semantics

As the practicalities of human society and governance become increasingly entwined with technology, human language increasingly contains references to matters technological. Whereas the work of a scholar at a desk might once have been described as "writing a paper," the activity might now be described as "working at a computer" or "editing some files on disk." In the area of banking, "I wonder whether the teller will recognize me well enough to give me the money?" might be replaced by a phrase such as "Will the Automatic Teller Machine accept this card if I type that PIN?" Put simply, "tech talk" has become an important part of everyday language.

An essential dimension of technology-practice is the development and use of technology-related language. Developing competence in technology, and in solving practical human problems linked with the application of technology, requires the assignment of words to technological objects and processes, and to concepts about the human use of technology. Without such language, problem solving in technological-practice becomes difficult because problems become hard to define, clarify, and communicate. With new technology, however, new phenomena in technology-practice emerge. These require new terms. Human language must therefore adapt, and this process is necessarily experimental, complicated, ambiguous, messy, and problematical. Nevertheless, the process is inevitable.

Words carry meanings, and the meanings associated with a set of words may be quite different for one person compared with another. Semantic problems are therefore a normal part of human society. When technological language becomes prominent in a society, concomitant with a rise in the importance of technology-practice, technological semantics become more significant. Thus, the ubiquity of technology in society raises the importance of technology-practice as a sphere of human competence, and raises technological semantics as an element of human practice. This leads towards the main concern of this chapter: What is the relationship between technological semantics and the familiar stuff of contemporary human life?

The core argument of this chapter, as mentioned earlier, is that in the sphere of technology, good semantics can lead to good practice, and, conversely, poor semantics can lead to poor practice.

A corollary of this argument is that because technology-practice has become a prominent part of human affairs, good technological semantics is becoming a prerequisite of effective performance in many fields of human endeavor. Another way of putting this is to say that technological semantics have become a problem for society.

Before the above argument is presented in detail, the meaning of "good semantics" and "good practice" should be explained. Here, "good semantics" means language that involves richly textured nomenclature with internally consistent definitions; it also refers to a system of words that is not only capable of neatly and consistently describing phenomena but that is capable of helpfully elucidating critical contemporary issues. "Good practice," in the sphere of technology, refers here to technology-practice in which technology effectively meets the primary objectives which it is intended to serve without creating significant negative side effects, or without negating secondary objectives intended for the technology.

Identifying, as abstract principles, some of the general parameters of good practice in technology is one of the central challenges of technology studies as an academic field. This challenge will only be met if an orthodox language of discourse is established, at the center of which is a lucid concept of technology. Presently, however, the field of technology studies appears to be stuck in a semantic quagmire.

The trend in the literature and in the conference circuit to describe almost anything as "technology" (it seems easier to get a paper published that way) means that, because technology is everything, it is also, in effect, nothing. Consequently, the word "technology" is used by commentators with such a wide variety of meanings that it is exceedingly difficult to know whether two people saying ostensibly similar things about "technology" have even remotely similar meanings in mind. The word "technology" can mean anything from "organization" (Hibbard & Hosticka, 1982, p. 4), "a human activity" (Goldhaber, 1986, p. 4) or "routineness" (Miller, Glick, Wang & Huber, 1991) to a "form of life" (Winner, 1986); and for some (e.g., Reinecke, 1982) it means little more than "computers!"

One reason to be concerned about this trend is that it degrades language and makes it difficult to talk coherently about matters technological. For example, at an international meeting on large-scale technical systems attended by the author of this chapter a whole session was devoted to discussing cities as large-scale technical systems because they are large and may be construed as systems. A debate about whether or not they are really "technical" systems could not be resolved because of lack of agreement about the meaning of "technical." The inability of the meeting to agree on the meaning of technological nomenclature meant treating a city as a similar system to a telecommunications network.

This kind of situation, while probably quite familiar to scholars, may be passed off as of no real importance because it is only of relevance to academic pedants. Confusion about the nature of technology, however, has very practical ramifications for governments (who may allocate funds to technology programs in the belief that economic benefits will ensue) or businesses (who may invest in the stocks of "high technology" companies in the belief that they will yield high returns on investments). Does investment in technology mean investment in people, education, science, skills training, the purchase of machines, the purchase of intellectual property, the reform of organizations, or the provision of higher salaries for engineers? It is difficult to make informed decisions about such matters without a clear idea of what we have in mind by the word "technology."

A case study of one episode in the history of technology studies may be instructive here. An example of where poor technological semantics has led to inadequacies in technological practice may be found in the "appropriate technology" movement that emerged in the mid-1970s. This movement, popularized through the use of E. F. Schumacher's emblematic phrase, "small is beautiful" (Schumacher, 1973), provided a lively stimulus to the emergence of technology studies as a field, yet the sloppy use of language, apparent in the movement's literature, meant that people with opposite views frequently appeared to be saying the same thing. One result of this sort of confusion was that many of the important policy insights of this movement were overlooked in mainstream technology policy debates that took place during the closing two decades of the twentieth century.

While a certain fluidity in the use of language is probably an essential part of a living academic discipline, some kind of semantic orthodoxy at the core of a field is nevertheless necessary to facilitate orderly policy analysis and debate. In this chapter I therefore hope to assist the emerging formation of a core nomenclature to unify discourse in the general field of technology studies. My intention is not be to set definitions in concrete but rather to outline a workable nomenclature that will, no doubt, evolve over time.

By reviewing the semantic dimensions of the appropriate technology social movement I hope to elucidate a general approach to semantics for the broader field of technology studies. Before outlining suggestions for a preferred approach to technological semantics, a range of existing approaches to defining technology will be examined.

The Semantic Problems of Appropriate Technology

By drawing upon a particular sub-field within the technology studies literature—the debate over the appropriateness of technology—the following analysis illustrates how a more coherent approach to semantic conventions might enhance scholarship and policy analysis in technology studies.

Comprehensive Definition

The concept of Appropriate Technology was first synthesized by the British economist E. F. Schumacher, drawing upon important foundations laid by Gandhi and others (Schumacher, 1962a; Schumacher, 1965; cf., Hoda, 1976). Drawing upon the ideas of that pioneering literature, an appropriate technology is defined here as a *technology tailored to fit the psychosocial and biophysical context prevailing in a particular location and period* (cf., Willoughby, 1990, p. 37). This definition does not completely embrace all the viewpoints that have emerged under the rubric of "appropriate technology," but is comprehensive enough to incorporate most of the credible definitions in the literature, and it accords closely with the original ideas of Schumacher. Nevertheless, as the following discussion shows, despite the fact that the primary progenitor of the appropriate technology literature commenced with a coherent set of ideas, and despite the fact that a simple and cogent expression of those core idea can be articulated, the pertinent literature has been plagued by inconsistency in the application of the "appropriate technology" concept and rubric.

Definitional Problems

During the 1970s and 1980s the rubric of "appropriate technology" was taken up by a plethora of organizations, interest groups, individuals and schools of thought, and its usage consequently became loose and confusing. It was used variously to refer to particular philosophical approaches to technology (Drengson, 1982), to ideologies (Morrison, 1978), to a political-economic critique (Lodwick and Morrison, 1982), to social movements (Winner, 1979), to economic development strategies (Robinson, 1979; Diwan, 1979), to particular types of technical hardware (Canadian Hunger Foundation, 1976; Darrow, 1976; Magee, 1978), or even to anti-technology activities (Office of Technology Assessment, 1981, p. 18). The diffuse nature of the Appropriate Technology movement during that period was illustrated by the comments of one of its veteran practitioners and critics who described Appropriate Technology (dubbed "AT" by many of its proponents) as being part lay religion, part protest movement, and part economic theory, and who censured it for the "bandwagon" effect that it produced. He wrote as follows (Rybczynski, 1980, p. 28-29):

> AT was a protest movement and for many it also became a True Belief. But it was more than that; AT developed into a bandwagon of Pullman-car proportions. And what a strange set of travelling companions one found: well dressed World Bank economists rubbing shoulders with Gandhians in metaphorical, if not actual *dhotis*; environmentalists, Utopians, and bricoleurs; conventional politicians like President Jimmy Carter and less conventional politicians like Governor Jerry Brown of California who had both met E. F. Schumacher (himself recently made a Companion of the British Empire by Queen Elizabeth II).

In practice the term "appropriate technology" was used to describe far more than just technology and, as Rybczynski's comments indicate, it was a symbol for a heterogeneous social movement that had not itself reached universal agreement on what the notion meant. Any concise definition (such as the one I have provided above) must therefore be stipulative and not merely descriptive.

After Appropriate Technology was first publicly promoted by Schumacher and colleagues at a conference at Oxford University in 1968, and following its subsequent popularization through the publication of Schumacher's seminal book, *Small is Beautiful: A Study of Economics as if People Mattered* (Schumacher, 1973), many related terms came into widespread use. Examples include: "alternative technology" (Undercurrents, 1972-1985), "appropriable technology" (de Pury, 1983), "community technology" (Hess, 1979; Wade, 1975), "convivial tools" (Illich, 1973), "eco-technology" (Bookchin, 1977; Boyle, 1984), "humanized technology" (Fromm, 1968), "intermediate technology" (Schumacher, 1962), "liberatory technology" (Bookchin, 1971), "light-capital technology" (Long, 1977), "modest technology" (Vacca, 1980), "participatory technology" (Carrol, 1971), "progressive technology" (Marsden, 1970), "radical technology" (Boyle, 1976), "soft technology" (Clarke, 1972), "technology with a human face" (Dunn, 1978), "utopian technology" (Dickson,

1974), "vernacular technology" (Illich, 1980), or "village-level technology" (Lutheran World Service, 1977). Each of these terms reflected their author's particular viewpoint, and consequently exhibited considerable diversity in the meanings attached to them. This led to some confusion and unproductive polemic. The definition stipulated in this chapter, in contrast, is intended to be consistent with the original ideas of Schumacher, to be comprehensive enough to embrace the majority of the credible ideas implied by the terms just listed, but yet specific enough to be of practical use.

In addition to the diversity of ideas associated with Appropriate Technology and the diversity of terms related to the concept, a variety of definitions of the term itself also appeared. Considerable discussion of the definitional problems appeared in the technology studies literature, and two contrasting approaches emerged: these may be labeled here as the *specific-characteristics* approach and the *general-principles* approach. The stipulative definition proposed in this paper is of the latter type, the *general-principles* approach. Both approaches to defining Appropriate Technology have their own advantages and disadvantages, as discussed below. Definitions of the former type tended to predominate within the Appropriate Technology movement itself; and among those people outside the movement who were familiar with its main ideas, a concept of Appropriate Technology in keeping with the specific-characteristics approach also appeared to predominate (e.g.: Cooper, 1979; Stewart, 1983; Reddy, 1979; Thomas, 1979; Jéquier, 1976; Jéquier, 1979; Miles, 1982).

General-Principles Approach

The general-principles approach has the advantage that it abides by the normal conventions of language by keeping to the commonly accepted meaning of words. The word "appropriate," employed as an adjective, conventionally means that something (technology, in this case) is specially fitting, suitable, proper, or applicable for or to some special purpose or use (Murray, 1933; Skeat, 1910; Sykes, 1976). Used in this way, the adjective places emphasis on technology as a means to certain ends and on the importance of articulating the ends in each case. It raises the question, "Appropriate to what?" The general-principles approach to defining Appropriate Technology contains no specific and tangible content. Rather, it emphasizes the universal importance of examining the appropriateness of technology in each set of circumstances.

A difficulty with this type of definition is that it is very formal. While this fact gives it validity, its all-embracing nature makes it somewhat vague and amorphous. Consequently, it is possible for opposing interest groups in a community to adopt the rhetoric of Appropriate Technology while in practice promoting radically different types of technology. This was demonstrated, for example, by the difference of approach between Roby and Swinkels, who both participated in a session of an international conference of the Australian and

New Zealand Association for the Advancement of Science on "appropriate levels of technology for Western Australia." Roby (1979) argued the case for low-cost, small-scale technology, while Swinkels (1979) argued the case for costly, large-scale technology—both speakers employing the same rubric. A further example was Robertson's use of the term "appropriate technology" as part of his advocacy of the CANDU nuclear reactor system (Robertson, 1978; cf., Institute for Local Self Reliance, 1981), in stark contrast to the pronounced anti-nuclear stance of the Appropriate Technology movement in general (Bender, 1975; Lovins, 1975; Merrill, 1977; Schumacher, 1973, pp. 24-135).

The lack of specific criteria and parameters leaves the abstract type of definition open to diverging interpretations at the practical level. This is because all technology must be "appropriate" for something—irrespective of the possible absurdity of that "something." A further problem with the general-principles type of definition is that the widespread usage of the term "appropriate technology" during the 1970s and 1980s in fact invoked connotations of specific characteristics, even when it was defined in general terms—this led towards trivial and sometimes fatuous usage of the term, as illustrated by the article entitled "Pen registers: The 'appropriate technology' approach to bugging," which appeared in the journal of the American Association for the Advancement of Science (Shapley, 1978).

Specific-Characteristics Approach

The specific-characteristics approach avoids the above difficulties by assigning specific and tangible operational criteria to the definition. In this way the specific-characteristics definition is more than a concept about the nature of technology and the way it relates to ends. It is simultaneously a normative statement (because it assumes priority for certain ends rather than others) and an empirical statement (because the practical criteria of appropriateness must be based upon some assessment of which technical means generally best serve the ends in question). Whereas the general-principles approach tends to leave the evaluation of ends and means relatively open, the specific-characteristics approach embodies the results of previous efforts to evaluate both of these factors. The specific-characteristics type of definition is therefore of more immediate practical use because it contains various signposts for planning and decision making. It contains substantive judgments about the real nature of particular technologies in particular contexts.

Despite these advantages, the rhetoric of the specific-characteristics approach has been employed for trivial and misleading purposes as much as that of the general-principles approach. For example, in deference to the reputed advantages of small-scale and low-cost technology, Schumacher's phrase "small is beautiful" has become something of a symbol of the Appropriate Technology movement; the phrase has now been used with reference to the possible emergence of smaller and cheaper fusion reactor technology—despite its un-proven nature and its high cost relative to other forms of energy technology and its inability to measure up easily against most of the commonly accepted criteria of Appropriate Technology (Waldrop, 1983).

Comparison of Definitions

Some examples from the literature will illustrate these two approaches. The following three quotes from an analyst of Third World affairs (Harrison, 1980, p. 40), a report from a United Nations Industrial Development Organization con-ference (United Nations Industrial Development Organization, 1979, p. 4), and a philosopher of technology (Drengson, 1982, p. 103), respectively, are examples of the general-principles approach to defining appropriate technology:

"Appropriate technology" means simply any technology that makes the most eco-nomical use of a country's natural resources and its relative proportions of capital, labour and skills, and that furthers national and social goals. Fostering AT means consciously encouraging the right choice of technology, not simply letting business men make the decision for you.

The concept of appropriate technology was viewed as being the technology mix contributing most to economic, social and environmental objectives, in relation to resource endowments and conditions of application in each country. Appropriate technology was stressed as being a dynamic and flexible concept which must be responsive to varying conditions and changing situations in different countries.

"Appropriate (technology)" here refers to the right and artful fit between technique, tool and human and environmental limits.

The next three quotes, from an O.E.C.D. economist (Jéquier, 1983, p. 1), a brochure from an American Appropriate Technology organization (National Cen-ter for Appropriate Technology, 1981, p. 1), and from a science journalist (Wade, 1980, p. 40), respectively, illustrate the specific-characteristics approach:

Appropriate technology (AT) is now recognized as the generic term for a wide range of technologies characterized by any one or several of the following characteristics: low investment cost per workplace, low capital investment per unit of output, organi-zational simplicity, high adaptability to a peculiar social or cultural environment, spar-ing use of natural resources, low cost of final product or high potential for employment.

An appropriate technology is relatively inexpensive and simple to build, maintain and operate; uses renewable resources rather than fossil fuels, and does not require high energy concentrations; relies primarily on people's skills, not on automated machin-ery; encourages human scale operations, small businesses and community cohesion; is protective of human health, and is ecologically sound.

Appropriate technology differs from the other kind in being labour-intensive, acces-sible to its users, frugal of scarce resources, unintrusive on the natural ambience, and manageable by the individual or small groups.

The first three definitions were generalized formulations emphasizing the achievement of a good fit between technology and its context, and they avoided explicit normative assertions. The latter three clearly exhibited elements of advocacy and stipulation and they also gave the reader a better comprehension of the actual type of technologies that were typically associated with the Appropriate Technology movement.

In some cases, as illustrated by the following quote from a study of the commercial prospects of "AT" in the United States (Magee, 1978, pp. 2-3), the specific-characteristics approach was taken to extremes by defining appropriate technology in terms of specific tangible features of the hardware involved:

> In order to concentrate on specific aspects of small AT businesses, the author is defining appropriate technology in terms of products and technical systems—solar collectors, composting toilets, recycling, organic agriculture, wood stove manufacturing, small-scale hydropower, energy conservation, methane, greenhouses, adobe, and so on.

While the author of the study just mentioned provided reasons for taking such an approach in that particular case, the definition exemplified a fundamental problem with the specific-characteristics definitions. They broke the conventions of normal language by giving the word "appropriate" a substantive meaning it did not have in general usage. The phrase "appropriate technology," a noun preceded by a qualifying adjective, became a compound word "appropriate-technology," which amounted to being just a noun but with the adjectival connotations associated with the word "appropriate." The semantic confusion resulting from widespread adoption of the specific-characteristics approach was significant for at least two reasons.

Firstly, it resulted in a lack of rigor in the analyses and action programs of people within the Appropriate Technology movement, leading to considerable waste of scarce resources. Secondly, it did damage to the way in which the general-principles approach to Appropriate Technology was received by policy makers and the broader public—who may have ignored its value as a policymaking tool because of its association with some community activities and technical experiments with very limited applicability or isolated relevance.

In addition to the above problems, the adoption by a country or political group of policies for the promotion of Appropriate Technology, where such policies were based upon a specific-characteristics definition, could lead to the adoption of technology that was in fact inferior or did not best serve stated social, economic, or environmental objectives. The more specific the characteristics in the definition became, the more static the definition became, with the result that the responsiveness of the associated policies to the dynamic environment (both natural and human) may also have been reduced. When discussing this problem, a scholar of technology and development economics demonstrated the semantic dilemma that had been created by the wide usage of the specific-characteristics approach within the Appropriate Technology movement. By adopting the terminology of this approach in her analysis she was forced to state that, in effect, "inappropriate" technology might sometimes be the most "appropriate!" (Stewart, 1983, p. 280, emphasis added):

> This (i.e., the adoption of so-called "appropriate technology" which does not serve a region's actual needs) might arise because the technology with appropriate characteristics was very inefficient in a technical sense (of low productivity) compared with one with inappropriate characteristics. In some cases, the technology with appropriate characteristics might still be the best choice if its effects on some objectives...outweighed its low productivity. But in others this might not be so, and therefore the technology with inappropriate characteristics should be preferred.

Despite its attractiveness to engineers and practitioners who may have desired straightforward technical design criteria, the specific-characteristics approach to defining Appropriate Technology exhibited severe shortcomings. The semantic difficulties, which created problems in themselves, illustrated that the specific-characteristics definition was only valid when applied to specific circumstances. The general-principles approach, in contrast, was suitable for universal application; it provided a basis for the development of a specific-characteristics definition within specified circumstances.

Preferred Type of Definition

As has been argued elsewhere (Willoughby, 1990), the substantive ideas of the Appropriate Technology movement, of both the normative and empirical kind, may make a valuable contribution to policy formulation and action. As the foregoing discussion reveals, however, the lack of consistency in the literature of the movement created obstacles to the achievement of this goal. Consequently, the general-principles approach to defining Appropriate Technology therefore appears preferable over the specific-characteristics approach. Nevertheless, the insights and practical ideas that emanated from the specific-characteristics approach still represented some important insights and principles.

The theory, policy and implementation of Appropriate Technology during the last few decades of the twentieth century would have been enhanced by employing only the general-principles approach for general definitions and by restricting the use of a specific-characteristics approach to specific contexts for which the circumstances had been clearly defined.

If more attention had been paid by participants in the Appropriate Technology movement to technology-related lexicography and formal technological semantics, could such problems have been avoided, or at least significantly mitigated? Let us now review some of the formal literature about technological semantics in an attempt to cast light on this matter.

Existing Approaches to Defining Technology

Dictionary Definitions

Providing a consistent and workable definition of technology is fraught with difficulties. The *Concise Oxford Dictionary* (Sykes, 1976, p. 1188), in a similar manner to other dictionaries, defines technology as the "(science of) practical or industrial art(s); (the) ethnological study of the development of such arts; (the) application of science." Definitions of this type are of limited value, however, because the meaning and use of the word "technology" has changed over time, it is used differently by different schools of thought and between different languages, its common use is haphazard, and the definition does not convey much of the complexity of meaning attributed to the term in the literature. A number of different approaches to defining "technology" should therefore be examined.

Historical Approach

Technology evolves historically and may therefore only be fully understood from an historical viewpoint. Technology is not static and many different technologies have been developed and superseded in a variety of times and places. This has led many scholars (e.g., Landes, 1969) to adopt an historical approach to the study of technology and has encouraged others to speak only of technologies and groups of technologies in the conviction that it is not possible to discern such a thing as technology itself (Bresson, 1987; Rapp, 1981, pp. 24-25). This view has received considerable criticism in the literature (Ellul, 1980, pp. 23-33). It reflects the eighteenth- and nineteenth-century perspectives, as embodied in the dictionary definitions. Referring to this period Winner (1977, p. 8) has written:

> Technology, in fact, was not an important term in descriptions of that part of the world we now call technological. Most people spoke directly of machines, tools, factories, industry, crafts, and engineering and did not worry about "technology" as a distinctive phenomenon.

Despite the criticisms it has received, the perspective of those in the historical school lends itself to an approach that gives preference to the historiography of tangible technological change, and that avoids the awkward task of defining technology in systematic or philosophically precise terms. This approach also has a certain attraction to contemporary technologists and business people who are disinclined to "waste" time on abstract academic discussions of technological theory.

While it is true that an historical study of technology would be required to do justice to its diversity and complexity, it does not follow that some common elements may not be observed throughout that diversity, thereby justifying the place of a systematic analysis of technology in addition to an historical analysis (Rapp, 1981, pp. 24-25). Evidence for the continuity of technological phenomena throughout history has been surveyed elsewhere (David, 1975; Mumford, 1963; Pacey, 1975; Singer, 1954-1958; Schuurman, 1977) and need not be duplicated here. It should be stressed, however, that the validity of Appropriate Technology as a theoretical category depends itself upon the validity of *technology* as a theoretical category. In short, if taken to extremes and embraced in isolation, the historical approach to defining technology militates against effective treatment of the Appropriate Technology idea.

Ambiguity of English Terminology

"Technology" is employed in the English language to denote and connote a mixture of phenomena and concepts. It is therefore impossible to provide a precise and universal definition of the term without it becoming specialized jargon. Some other languages, in contrast, are less ambiguous. French, for example, distinguishes between *"technologie"* and *"technique"* (Ellul, 1980, pp. 23-33); *technologie* is the science of analyzing and describing *technique* or *techniques*, whereas the latter are the object of study of the former. A similar distinction is made in German (Ströker, 1983) between *"technologie"* (technological science) and *"Technik"* (technology, or technical things). Thus, *"technologie"* (French) conforms to the dictionary definitions of "technology" (English) but not the common English-language usage of the term.

Techniques (French) are the individual technical means, either processes or objects, and *technique* (French) is the general phenomenon of which *techniques* (French) are particular examples. English, in contrast, uses the word "technology" to denote both the science and its object of study. This lack of discrimination in the English language usage of "technology" may partly explain why technology is so frequently defined as applied science—rather than as technology *sui generis*. It may also explain why "technics" has become popular among some sophisticated American commentators (e.g., Winner, 1977) as a general term for all things technological.

The rapid expansion of the role of technology in modern society, both in the level and scope of its deployment, has led to a closer integration of technological phenomena with other factors and to the spread of new phrases such as "the technological order" (Ellul, 1963), "the technological society" (Ellul, 1964), "the technocratic society" (Roszak, 1969), "technological man" (Ferkiss, 1969), "the technostructure" (Galbraith, 1972), or "the technetronic age" (Brzezinski, 1970). In the rhetoric of the counterculture of the 1960s and early 1970s the ubiquitous influence of technology was symbolized in an extreme form simply as "the system" (Guiness, 1973). One scholar has observed that there is a tendency among those who write or talk about technology in our time to conclude that "technology is everything and everything is technology" (Winner, 1977, pp. 9-10). It appears that during the previous century the term "technology" grew from something with a quite limited meaning to become an all-embracing symbol. For the purpose of analysis a more discrete definition of technology is required; but such a definition must of necessity be stipulative rather than merely descriptive, due to the lack of uniformity in general usage.

Broad Scope of "Technology"

A selection of definitions will now be considered so as to establish consistent terminology for analyzing the Appropriate Technology movement. One important observation that may be made of the definitions that are propounded in most studies is that they tend to portray technology as something much more than the hardware, machines, or individual apparatus normally associated with "technology" in popular thinking.

The dictionary definitions refer to technology as a group of arts or as the science of such arts—in other words, as a form of human skill or activity. This concurs with the main etymological root of the term, the Greek *techné*, which denotes art, craft, skill, or practical knowledge (Burnet, 1930; Heidegger, 1977; Koenker, 1980; Runes, 1962, pp. 93, 183-184, 314). *Techné* was used by the Pre-Socratics to denote a process, rather than a set of objects, and in such a way as to emphasize the unity of action and knowledge (*epistémé*, Greek). The other main etymological root of "technology" is the Greek word *logos*, which denotes the ideas of word, reason, or principle.

The modern usage of the term "technology" normally embraces some reference to social or cultural institutions. This is illustrated by the term "technological society," a phrase first coined in France (*societé technicienne*) in 1938 by Georges Friedman (Friedman, 1956; Friedman, 1961).[1] There is a growing trend in the serious literature for technology and society not to be viewed as discrete phenomena that interact, but rather as overlapping and mutually determining phenomena: society becomes technologized and technology reflects the structures and interests of society. The debate over this issue is complex and a thorough discussion may not be properly conducted here, but we may concur with Johnston and Gummett (1979, p. 9) who have concluded: "Technology is not merely a matter of physical and social hardware, but a force which permeates our political, economic and social systems." Recognizing the broad scope and influence of technology does not, however, guarantee us a clear grasp of its distinguishing characteristics. Further discussion is required.

Technique and Structure

Galtung (1979, p. 15) has produced a formula that echoes some of the above observations and draws upon the distinction, as stressed in French, between *technologie* and *technique*: technology = technique + structure. He describes *technique* as the "visible tip of the iceberg": the tools and the know-how (or, skills and knowledge). The structure is defined as the social relations or "mode of production" within which the tools become operational, and the cognitive structure within which the knowledge becomes meaningful. Galtung's notion of *structure*, while narrower and differing from it in a number of ways, corresponds to the notion of *psychosocial and biophysical context* in the comprehensive definition of appropriate technology that I proposed earlier. While it usefully emphasizes the social context of *techniques*, Galtung's formula uses the English "technology" with a broader and more equivocal meaning than the French *technologie*. The term *technique* is given a broader meaning than is normal in English by including technical apparatus as part of the concept; it thus accords closely with the French usage of the term.

Galtung's approach helpfully stresses how the social relations surrounding the application of technical knowledge substantially determine the nature of the resulting technology. Nevertheless, the formula does not provide us with an actual definition of technology.

Humanity, Nature, and Economics

In addition to the foregoing formula Galtung provides a functional definition of technology as the modification of natural or ecological cycles into economic cycles (Galtung, 1979, pp. 5, 29). In this way he appears to define technology as a *process* (for modifying cycles) rather than as *apparatus*; he also portrays technology as a form of mediation between people and non-human reality, drawing upon a conception of people as primarily economic beings. This theme of the modification of nature by people is also emphasized in the following paraphrase[2] of Rapp's definition of technology:

> Technology is the refined totality of procedures and instruments which aims at the domination of nature through transformation of the outside material world, and which is based on action according to the engineering science and on scientific knowledge.

While Rapp chooses to limit the definition of technology to those things that affect "the outside material world," he does this simply out of a desire to limit the scope of his analysis and to approximate certain popular viewpoints, rather than on etymological or logical grounds (Rapp, 1981, pp. 35-36). There appears to be no reason for not applying his notion of "procedures and instruments for the domination of nature" to the transformation of the "inner world" of human experience.

For Karl Marx also, technology concerns the interaction of people with nature. In *Capital* (Marx, 1954, p. 352) Marx writes:

Technology discloses man's mode of dealing with nature, the processes of production by which he sustains his life, and thereby also lays bare the mode of formation of his social relations, and of the mental conceptions that flow from them.

Marx relates technology here to what he viewed as a definitive characteristic of human existence, *production*. This perspective appears to undergird Galtung's emphasis on economic cycles vis-à-vis technology. A striking feature of Marx's conception is his idea that technology *reveals* things.

The German metaphysician Martin Heidegger, along with Marx, has also emphasized technology's capacity for revealing things—nature in particular. In fact, he describes technology as *a mode of revealing*. By taking this approach Heidegger contrasts certain modern technologythat, in revealing nature, works *against* it by dominating it and transforming it (to echo Rapp's terminology) and certain pre-modern technology that tends to reveal nature by working *with* nature's inner principles and by cultivating it. An example of such pre-modern technology would be a windmill that causes very little apparent disruption to nature, while an example of the other type would be a nuclear fission reactor that, according to Heidegger, works by "extracting from" nature. Heidegger's perspective is important to note here because it illustrates how domination is not the only mode of relationship between people and nature that may be invoked by the term "technology" (Heidegger, 1977, pp. 12, 15-16).

Despite their differences, the thinkers just considered each emphasize the role of technology in *mediating* human relationships and activities, both in relation to nature and as part of economic life. It is still necessary to inquire, however, what special characteristics technology gives to this mediating role.

Efficient Means

The reference to "the engineering sciences and scientific knowledge" in Rapp's definition is meant by him to indicate that technology always involves efficient goal-oriented activity (Rapp, 1981, p. 32). Accordingly, Skolimowski (1966) has noted how an increase in the efficiency of technological procedures has been a defining characteristic of technological progress since the industrial revolution. The French sociologist Jacques Ellul has been among the strongest proponents of the view that efficiency has been the overriding feature of technology (*La Technique*, French) since its origins, viz. (Ellul, 1980, p. 26):

[Technology is] the ensemble of the absolutely most efficient means at a given moment... Wherever there is research and application of new means as a criterion of efficiency, one can say that there is a technology.

This emphasis on *efficient means* as the distinctive feature of technology accords with Habermas' view of technology as purposive-rational action

(Habermas, 1971), accords with theoretical conceptions of technology that emphasize technology's mediating role, and either amplifies, or is consistent with, the other definitions and formulae outlined above. It therefore appears that such an emphasis should be used to provide substantive content to the definition of technology adopted earlier.

Knowledge

Other scholars choose to emphasize knowledge as the defining characteristic of technology—an emphasis that, as previously indicated, is consistent with its etymology. MacDonald (1983, p. 27), for example, writes:

> Technology is really the sum of knowledge—of received information—which allows things to be done, a role which frequently requires the use of machines, and the information they incorporate, but conceivably may not.

He argues against those who treat technology's characteristics as no more than those of the machine. He employs the term "techniques" to denote what he refers to as the tools of technology (e.g., machines). This emphasis on technology as knowledge has grown with the widespread deployment of technologies for processing and transmitting information (cf., Stonier, 1983); the term "technology" has even come to be used as a synonym for "information technology" (e.g., in Reinecke, 1982). The literature on the "sociology of knowledge" (e.g., Jagtenberg, 1983; Knorr-Cetina, 1981) also tends to view technology as a special form of knowledge.

While knowledge is, with some justification, recognized by this school of thought as an essential aspect of technology, the tendency by MacDonald and others to define technology as a particular category of knowledge *per se* may be questioned. Firstly, popular English language usage of "technology" normally refers to tangible manifestations of technology—machines, apparatus, tools, and technical artifacts, etc. Secondly, MacDonald's definition does not fit easily with the dictionary portrayals of technology as a category of human activity; the "sum of knowledge" is surely a product of human activity rather than human activity as such.[3] Thirdly, by limiting "technology" to mean knowledge, we are forced to use the English term "technique" to denote artifacts as well as human skill and method—which sits rather awkwardly with common English parlance. Fourthly, any approach that separates the knowledge aspects of technology too rigidly from its operational and tangible aspects runs the risk of over-emphasizing the role of explicit knowledge as opposed to implicit knowledge in the historical development of technology. The development of technology from predominantly explicit, scientific knowledge (e.g., the nuclear fission bomb) is historically far less common than the development of technologies from the gradual accretion of practical experience (e.g., indigenously developed efficient agricultural implements such as the Mexican *sembradora* [Walt, 1978]) and from the practical innovativeness of technology-users and engineers (Ihde, 1979; Ihde, 1983; White, 1962; McClellan & Dorn, 1999). Fifthly, as I will subsequently attempt to demonstrate, it becomes difficult to discuss the problems of "appropriate" versus "inappropriate" technology in a given context if technology is viewed simply as knowledge to the exclusion of artifacts or to the exclusion of the tangible embodiment of knowledge.

In conclusion, there are some etymological reasons and some indications from other languages besides English that may provide a *prima facie* case for defining technology as a particular form of knowledge; and, it appears possible, in principle, to construct an internally consistent taxonomy based upon such an approach. This approach will not be adopted in this chapter, however, because to do so would *inter alia* break with certain entrenched conventions of the English language, and would also depart from the common use of "technology" in English-language literature on technology. In raising a definition of technology it is nevertheless still important to incorporate the useful insights of the "technology-as-knowledge" school of thought, but with a different semantic convention.

Artifacts

Some commentators avoid the difficulties of the "technology as knowledge" precept by emphasizing *artifacts* as characteristic of technology. Scriven (1985, p. 25), for example, defines technology as "the systematic process, and the product, of designing, developing, maintaining and producing artifacts." Artifacts, according to the *Concise Oxford Dictionary* (Sykes, 1976, p. 52), are the products of human art and workmanship.

This approach avoids the semantic problems cited above; it includes much of the meaning attributed to *technique* (French), *technik* (German) or "technique" (English,[4] as per Galtung, MacDonald, etc.) under the rubric of "technology." Scriven (1985, p. 40) qualifies his definition with the comment that "technology is artifacts *and* knowledge [implicit or explicit] in the service of artifact production," and makes the distinction between the *application skills of technology* (meaning roughly equivalent to "technique" [English, as per the *Oxford English Dictionary*]), the *embodiment of technology* (artifacts), and *technological theory* (either explicit or implicit) (1985, p. 27). He avers (1985, p. 39) that techniques (English) may be thought of as technology when they are employed in using or creating artifacts.

Scriven's definition is a useful advance on some of the artifact-free definitions of technology within the English language, but it exhibits a weakness. The part of his definition that refers to technology as the *product* of producing artifacts in effect makes "technology" equivalent to "artifacts." This gives technology the ubiquitous status of being all things produced by human art and workmanship. Given the meaning of the term "artifacts," the other part of his definition (i.e., the *process* of "designing, developing, maintaining and producing artifacts") may be logically reduced to mean, roughly, "systematic human art and workmanship." Such a formula would include crop rotation and modern managerial practice, but Scriven (p. 26) explicitly rules these out as examples of technology (interestingly, MacDonald [1983, pp. 26-27] includes these activities as part of technology). Scriven's definition does not provide a sufficiently clear indication of the distinguishing features of technology, in addition to those of artifacts. His emphasis on the *process of producing* artifacts does however imply concurrence with the Marxist economic depiction of technology as the means of production.

Technology-practice

Most discussions of technology in the English language technology studies literature are consistent with Galtung's formula of technology as technique plus structure, in that they consider other factors in addition to specific technical means themselves. Some scholars have attempted to maintain this syncretic approach and strengthen it with more precise definitions, thereby incorporating both the knowledge emphasis and the artifacts emphasis while hopefully avoiding semantic ambiguity. For example, Winner (1977, p. 12) includes the following under the rubric of "technology": *apparatus* (the physical devices of technical performance); *technique* (human activities characterized by their purposive, rational, step-by-step manner); and, *organization* (social arrangements of a technical form).

The Dutch engineer and philosopher, Schuurman (1977, p. 377), makes a broad distinction between *practical activity* (*techniek*, translated from Dutch as *technology*) and *theoretical activity* (*technische wetenschap*, translated from Dutch as "technological science" or "technicology").[5] He also (1977, pp. 8-50) divides *technology* (i.e., *techniek*) up into three categories: *technological objects* (things or processes that are put to use in technology); *technological form-giving* (the execution and operation of technology); and *technological designing* (the preparation for technological objects and form-giving). Schuurman's taxonomy brings helpful precision and semantic consistency to the task of explicating the scope of technology. It does so, however, at the price of introducing new jargon that may be cumbersome and have difficulty becoming adopted beyond the confines of specialized scholarship.

Pacey has coined the compound word *technology-practice*, and in doing so he has managed to synthesize the various perspectives on technology illustrated by the above examples. He defines technology-practice as "the application of scientific *and other knowledge* to practical tasks by ordered systems that involve people and organizations, living things and machines" (Pacey,

1983, p. 6, emphasis added). In doing so he has managed, we might add, to achieve semantic consistency without giving the word "technology" a meaning it does not possess in popular usage. Pacey outlines three aspects of technology-practice: the technical aspect (equivalent to technique in Galtung's formula), the cultural aspect, and the organizational aspect (which together correspond to structure in Galtung's formula) (1983, pp. 4-7). The concept of technology-practice covers all the content normally indicated by "technological" in both popular and specialist discourse. While technology-practice corresponds closely to some usages of "technology" it should nevertheless be viewed as possessing a broader meaning than is normally given to "technology" in the English language.

Pacey's schema is not very precise for analytical purposes and it contains a number of problematical elements but it illustrates the diversity of factors associated with technology-practice and provides a convenient starting point for the development of a more effective nomenclature. It may act as a kind of map for locating technology-related concepts. For example, *Appropriate Technology* (as generally understood throughout the literature) may be viewed as a particular type of technology-practice, while a particular *appropriate technology* would be included as part of the Pacey's technical aspect; Schuurman's *technological objects* would fall within the technical aspect of technology-practice, while his *technological form-giving, technological designing* and *technicology* (or technological science) would embrace the organizational and cultural aspects as well; Winner's notions of *apparatus* and *technique* would fall within the technical aspect of technology-practice, while his notion of *organization* corresponds to the organizational aspect of technology-practice; and, the definitions of both Heidegger and MacDonald, different though they are, embrace all three aspects of technology-practice.

Pacey's notion points clearly to the cultural and organizational context that always surrounds the technical aspects of technology. By including the cultural aspect as a fundamental component of technology-practice Pacey focuses attention on the normative dimension of technology. While normative factors may have been implicit in the other definitions considered here, his concept encourages explicit examination of such factors.

Pacey's concept of technology-practice accords with the reference by European critics to the notion of *technical praxis* (favored by European scholars [e.g., Ströker, 1983, pp. 323-331]) and to the use by American writers of the term "technics" (Ihde, 1979; Winner, 1977) in discussing the general subject of technology. His emphasis on "the application of scientific and other knowledge," however, while not strictly at odds with it, does not appear to adequately address the growing emphasis among theorists of technology on the distinction between science and technology (see, e.g.: Agassi, 1966; McLellan & Dorn, 1999). Despite the usefulness of "technology-practice" for discussing technological matters in general, Pacey's notion does not provide substantive content to the term "technology" itself. An informative and reliable *definition* of technology (in addition to *statements* about technology) is still needed here.

Preferred Nomenclature

Need for a Stipulative Definition of Technology

There is no universally agreed upon definition of technology in the technology studies literature, although, as the foregoing discussion indicates, there is much overlap in the definitions raised and there is a general consensus that a field of study may be identified under the rubric of "technology." It is therefore necessary in this chapter to stipulate a definition, rather than adopt a single definition from elsewhere that is widely in use. The semantic rules outlined below could be debated at some length, but an exhaustive analysis of all relevant issues is beyond the scope of this chapter. The conventions advocated below, although based upon an extensive survey of the literature extant during the period when the Appropriate Technology movement was at its peak, ought to therefore be viewed as stipulative.

Technology has relevance to most fields of human endeavor and appears to be deeply enmeshed in most aspects of modern society. It is important that this be recognized; but, at the same time, it is important to avoid adopting a definition that is so general as to render the concept indistinguishable from other concepts. A spectrum exists in schools of thought vis-à-vis technology between those who adopt a broad, all-inclusive definition and those who adopt a narrower, more discriminating definition. The narrower approach is adopted here. The main reasons are that this sits more easily with popular English usage, it assists in resolving some of the confusion in the technology studies literature, it allows a more lucid discussion of the relationship between technology and other factors, and it is to some extent a necessary condition for a fruitful analysis of problems that have plagued some of the policy literature on technology.

"Technology"

Technology is defined here as the *ensemble of artifacts intended to function as relatively efficient means.*[6]

This definition has the advantage of resolving the difficulties that result from reducing technology to a category of knowledge alone and it also goes beyond the limitations of the artifact-based definition discussed earlier. By including "the function of being relatively efficient means" it is possible to distinguish between artifacts-*qua*-technology and artifacts-*qua*-artifacts. The word "artifacts" denotes the products of human art and workmanship, and hence does not necessarily refer only to physical apparatus and machines; my stipulative definition is therefore capable of embracing such less tangible technologies as computer software or cybernetic control systems. My emphasis on artifacts incorporates the knowledge aspects of technology but stresses that such knowledge needs to be realized, incarnated, embodied, or objectified if it is to be deemed "technology." The inclusion of "artifacts" in the definition also indicates the human or social element of technology, but without reducing technology to being simply an aspect of society.[7] In this way it is possible to avoid treating technology as being either entirely discrete or autonomous, at one extreme, or as lacking endogenous characteristics and a dynamism of its own, at the other extreme.

The use of the term "means" as part of the definition emphasizes technology's instrumental function, and the inclusion of efficiency as part of the definition makes possible a distinction between means-*qua*-technology and means-*qua*-means. The term *"relatively* efficient means" is used in preference to "efficient means" only in acknowledgement that: the efficiency of technology may vary geographically and over time, due to innovation and other factors; perfect efficiency may in fact never be attainable[8]; and, the degree of efficiency also relates to such things as the degree of specialization of the technology's function, the nature of the task for which it is in fact used, and the manner in which it is used. It also reflects the recognition that although technical efficiency may be an important factor for technologists and others it is not the only factor influencing the adoption of technology. In accordance with the above definition, individual technologies, in contrast to technology in general, may be defined as *artifacts intended to function as relatively efficient means.*

There are other characteristics of technology that deserve attention, such as its systemic tendencies, but the restriction of space means that a discussion of these will have to be left for further writings.

"Technological" and "Technology-practice"

"Technological" may be used to qualify all operations, activities, situations, or phenomena that involve technology. "Technological" should be distinguished from "technical," which has a more specific and concise content. "Technology-practice" is the noun equivalent of "technological," and covers the scope of meanings expressed by Pacey; i.e., "technology-practice" denotes all things technological, and possesses a scope of meaning similar to that associated with Galtung's use of "technology." It may be used on occasions when, as in many (if not most) popular discussions of technology, an all-inclusive meaning is intended and semantic precision is not considered to be a top priority.

"Technical" and "Technicity"

"Technical" may be used as the adjective or adverb to qualify phenomena (either human or non-human) dedicated to efficient, rational, instrumental, specific, precise, and goal-oriented operations. Unfortunately there appears to be no commonly used English word suitable to be employed unequivocally as the noun corresponding to "technical"—i.e., to denote the factor or quality itself which makes something technical. I therefore propose the term "technicity" for this purpose.

"Technicity" exudes specialized jargon but, unfortunately, for the purposes of scholarly rigor and to enable adequate differentiation of technology-related concepts, there appears to be no alternative here to the introduction of a rarely used word.[9]

Technicity is thus a defining feature of technology; but technology, as I have defined it, and as generally understood, may involve features other than technicity (in the same way, for example, that "humanity" is not an exact substitute for the noun "human"). Accordingly, some technologies may be more technical than others—i.e., the degree of technicity may vary between different technologies.

The crucial importance of this observation becomes more apparent following detailed analysis of the topic of technology choice (Willoughby, 1990), but an example here may help. Horticulture may be considered to be a technological activity because it involves the use of technology (e.g., drip-trickle irrigation systems or rotary hoes) but it might not always generally be conducted in a highly technical manner. Some aspects of modern horticulture (e.g., cloning of hybrid plants, or automated computer control of temperature and fertilizer levels in hydroponic systems) may, however, be highly technical. Nevertheless, just because some horticulturalists do not employ highly technical procedures or highly technical apparatus—preferring instead to work with so-called "low" or less complicated technologies—it does not follow that their operation is therefore not technological.

"Technique"

"Technique" may denote *human skill* that involves a significant technical element. Used in this way the term therefore corresponds closely to the meaning of Scriven's term "application skills of technology." It should be realized, however, that not all skills in *using* technology involve a significant degree of technicity (e.g., storing food in a refrigerator). The normal English meaning of the word "technique" may therefore be adopted here, and other terms such as "technology," "technicity," or other phrases, may be used when appropriate to denote the meaning given to *technique* in French (or to equivalents from other languages). In contrast to the tendency of some thinkers who employ "techniques" to denote particular examples of technological artifacts, I propose the use of "technologies" for this purpose. As implied above, and in parallel to the situation of "technology," some techniques may be more technical than others.

"Technological Science"

As discussed earlier, *technologie* is used in continental European languages (e.g., in French, German, and Dutch) to denote an essentially scientific or theoretical activity, but in such a manner as to avoid confusion between the science itself and its object (i.e., *technique* [French], *technik* [German], or *techniek* [Dutch]). English language theorists should therefore avoid using the term "technology" in this sense, and instead consistently employ "technological science" as the English equivalent of *technologie*. The term may denote either the scientific study of technological matters or scientific practice that involves a significant amount of technology.

"Mode of Technology-practice"

By defining technology as the ensemble of artifacts intended to function as relatively efficient means, I have adopted a narrower and more precise formula than is often found in the technology studies literature. For example, Hibbard and Hosticka (1982, p. 4) write:

> Technologies are thus not only objects and material processes, but also organizational forms, methods of knowledge production, decision-making techniques and so on. For example, the common organizational form of the pyramidal bureaucracy is as much a technology as the word-processors, microcomputers, filing systems and calculators which facilitate the work of the organization. One only has to consider the current search for more effective and efficient organizational forms to appreciate this.

To help them address broad issues of technology and society, the authors of this statement have defined technology to incorporate factors normally considered to be part of the environment of the technology, rather than technology itself. In other words, they have fallen into the logical trap of including something other than the thing being defined in the definition of that thing.[10]

The intellectual and practical issues addressed by the field technology studies are quite eclectic. Questions of organizational form, social relations, political bias, and human experience, amongst others, are integral to the field. It does not follow, however, that in order for these factors to be adequately addressed they must be included by definition as part of technology. It also does not follow that because, logically, they ought not to be included as part of technology, they do not exhibit some intrinsic relationship to technology. I therefore suggest that technology should be construed within the academic field of technology studies as technology *sui generis*. A corollary of this principle is that factors or phenomena related to technology should be referred to in their own right and not as part of technology. For example, organizational structure should be denoted by the term "organizational structure" (or something similar) rather than by the term "technology."

So that we will be able to simultaneously account for both the "narrow" aspects of technology, as implied by the definition stipulated in this chapter, and the "broad" aspects, as referred to in quotes such as the one by Hibbard and Hosticka above, I suggest that we adopt the term "mode of technology practice." This term embodies the recognition that specific technologies may be employed as part of technology-practice in a wide variety of ways, and that technology-practice itself may take a variety of forms. Recognizing the possibility of a variety of modes of technology-practice will enable us to break away from the absurd impasse of the "pro-technology" versus "anti-technology" debate that has dominated much of the technology studies literature. Much of the public debate in western industrialized countries about technology has centered on whether or not technology as a whole is "good" or "bad," or on whether or not technology ought to be "accepted" or "rejected." The nomenclature I have proposed above allows careful discussion of the types of social, cultural, political, and environmental issues that motivate critics of technology, in such a manner that the normative concerns of the critics may be embraced, but without the necessity of thereby also embracing an anti-technology attitude. Thus, the important issues in contemporary policy debates over public acceptance of new technology may be approached as problems of choosing between alternative modes of technology-practice, rather than being about rejecting or accepting new technology.

Conclusions

While much of the above discussion may appear somewhat pedantic when compared with seemingly more practical analysis of technology-studies topics, such as technology and employment, computers and productivity, biotechnology and environmental safety, etcetera, I would argue that poor use of language has led to many of the more "practical" debates in technology studies having less policy impact than they might otherwise have had. The apparent failure of the Appropriate Technology movement—that flourished worldwide during the 1970s and 1980s—to exert significant influence on mainstream debates in technology policy, illustrates this theme. Poor technological semantics can lead to poor technology-practice. Hopefully, however, the converse is also true. The definitions I have stipulated above (and as are summarized in the Glossary) are proposed at this stage as starters for an ongoing debate about semantics in technology studies. I welcome criticisms and suggestions for improvements.

Table 1
Technology-related nomenclature

Term	Definition/Explanation
technology	The ensemble of artifacts intended to function as relatively efficient means.
technology-practice	The ensemble of operations, activities, situations, or phenomena that involve technology to a significant extent.
technological	A term used to qualify operations, activities, situations, or phenomena that involve technology to a significant extent (i.e., the adjectival form of "technology-practice").
technical	The adjective or adverb used to qualify phenomena (either human or non-human) dedicated to efficient, rational, instrumental, specific, precise, and goal-oriented operations.
technicity	The distinguishing factor or quality that makes a phenomenon technical (i.e., the noun equivalent of "technical").
technique	Human skill that involves a significant technical element.
technological science	The scientific study of technological matters, or scientific practice that involves a significant amount of technology (i.e., the English language equivalent of the European word *technologie*).
appropriate technology	Artifacts that have been tailored to function as relatively efficient means and to fit the psychosocial and biophysical context prevailing in a particular location and period (i.e., technology that is compatible with its context).
Appropriate Technology	A mode of technology-practice aimed at ensuring that technology is compatible with its psychosocial and biophysical context. The term may also be used to denote the general concept, social movement, or innovation strategy associated with this mode of technology-practice.

Source: The author.

Notes

1. Jacques Ellul (1980, p.12) acknowledges Friedman as the progenitor of the term *societé technicienne*.
2. This paraphrase is the present author's and draws upon several partial definitions provided by Rapp (e.g., Rapp, 1981, pp. 33-36) See also (Tondl, 1974).
3. Some commentators resolve this particular difficulty by referring to technology as the *application* of knowledge rather just as knowledge. Schaiberg (1980, p. 278), for example, drawing on the work of Schooler (1971), defines technology as the "application of knowledge in the processes of social production," and in doing so he links the knowledge aspect of technology with the economic and political aspects emphasized by Galtung (1979), drawing on Marx (1954).
4. When used in this sense "technique" ought perhaps to be labeled as pseudo-English rather than English in the strict sense.
5. These notions correspond to the notions of *technique* and *technologie*, respectively, in French.
6. This definition of technology belongs to the author of this chapter.
7. Many writers in the political-economy tradition (e.g.: Bresson, 1987; Levidow, 1983; Thompson, 1980) strongly resist discussing technology *sui generis* because of a fear that this would amount to reifying or "fetishing" particular technologies.
8. An amusing survey by Papanek and Hennessey (1977), entitled *How Things Don't Work*, of technologies that are poorly designed and ineffective, illustrates how in the "real world"—as opposed to the "drawing board"—efficiency in technology-practice is elusive.
9. "Technicity" has been used elsewhere in an attempt to translate some of Heidegger's ideas into the English idiom (see Schuurman, 1977, pp. 87-95).
10. Jacques Ellul (1964, p. xxv) has coined the term *La Technique* to denote "the totality of methods rationally arrived at and having absolute efficiency [for a given stage of development] in every field of human activity." This is a much broader concept than that of technology, as defined in this chapter, and it does incorporate such human products as organizational forms; however, *La Technique* (as per Ellul), although related to it, is different in meaning than *technique* as normally used in French. Ellul thereby accomplishes what Hibbard and Hosticka appear to be seeking but without falling in to the logical trap into which they fell.

References

Agassi, J. (1966). The confusion between science and technology in the standard philosophies of science. *Technology and Culture*, 7(3), 348-367.

Autrement. (1980). Technologies douces. *Autrement*, Special Edition, 27.

Bender, T. (1975). *Sharing Smaller Pies*. Portland: RAIN.

Beveridge, A. A. & Rudell, F. (1988). An Evaluation of "Public Attitudes Toward Science and Technology" in Science Indicators; The 1985 Report. *Public Opinion Quarterly*, 52(3), 374-385.

Bookchin, M. (1971). Toward a liberatory technology. In *Post-Scarcity Anarchism*, pp. 83-139. San Francisco: Ramparts Press.

Bookchin, M. (1977). The concept of ecotechnologies and ecocommunities. *Habitat*, 2(1/2), 73-85.

Borgman, A. (1984). *Technology and the Character of Contemporary Life: A Philosophical Inquiry*. Chicago & London: The University of Chicago Press.

Boyle, G. (1978). *Community Technology*. Milton Keynes: Open University Press.
Boyle, G. (1984). A.T. is Dead—Long Live E.T.! Paper presented to "A.T. in the Eighties," Conference. London, June 16, 1984.
Boyle, G. & Harper, P. (Eds.). (1976). *Radical Technology*. Ringwood, Aust.: Penguin.
Braun, E. (1984). *Wayward Technology*. London: Frances Pinter.
Brzezinski, Z. (1970). *Between Two Ages: America's Role in the Technetronic Era*. New York: Viking Press.
Burnet, J. (1930). *Early Greek Philosophy*. London: Adam and Charles Black.
Canadian Hunger Foundation & Brace Research Institute (1976). *A Handbook on Appropriate Technology*. Ottawa: Canadian Hunger Foundation.
Carrol, J. D. (1971). Participatory technology. *Science*, 171, 647-653.
Clarke, R. & Clarke, D. (1972). Soft technology: Blueprint for a research community. *Undercurrents* (2).
Coe, G. (1979). *Present Value: Constructing a Sustainable Future*. San Francisco: Friends of the Earth.
Cooper, C. (1979). A summing up of the conference. In A. Robinson (Ed.), *Appropriate Technologies for Third World Development*, pp. 403-409. London: MacMillan.
Darrow, K., Keller, K., & Pam, R. (1976). *Appropriate Technology Sourcebook*. Stanford, Cal.: Volunteers in Asia.
de Pury, P. (1983). *People's Technologies and People's Participation*. Geneva: World Council of Churches.
Dickson, D. (1974). *Alternative Technology and the Politics of Technical Change*. London: Fontana/Collins.
Diwan, R. K. & Livingstone, D. (1979). *Alternative Development Strategies and Appropriate Technology: Science Policy for an Equitable World Order*. New York: Pergamon.
Drengson, A. R. (1982). Four philosophies of technology. *Philosophy Today*, 26(2/4), 103-117.
Dunn, P. D. (1978). *Appropriate Technology: Technology with a Human Face*. New York: Schocken.
Ellul, J. (1963). The technological order. Paper presented to the Encyclopaedia Britannica conference on the technological order, March 1962, Santa Barbara, California. In C. F. Stover (Ed.), *The Technological Order*, pp. 10-37. Detroit: Wayne State University Press.
Ellul, J. (1964). *The Technological Society* (J. Wilkinson, Trans.). New York: Alfred A. Knopf.
Ellul, J. (1980). *The Technological System*. New York: Continuum.
Ferkiss, V. (1969). *Technological Man: The Myth and the Reality*. London: Heinemann.
Frankel, B. (1987). *The Post-Industrial Utopians*. Cambridge and Oxford: Polity Press in association with Basil Blackwell.
Friedman, G. (1956). *Probléms humains du machinisme industriel*. Paris: Gallimard.
Friedman, G. (1961). *The Anatomy of Work: The Implications of Specialization* (W. Rawson, Trans.). London: Heinemann.
Fromm, E. (1968). *The Revolution of Hope: Toward a Humanized Technology*. New York: Harper and Row.
Galbraith, J. K. (1972). *The New Industrial State* (2nd ed.). Harmondsworth: Penguin.
Galtung, J. (1979). *Development, Environment and Technology: Towards a Technology for Self-Reliance*. New York: United Nations.
Gendron, B. (1977). *Technology and the Human Condition*. New York: St. Martin's Press.
Goldhaber, M. (1986). *Reinventing Technology: Policies for Democratic Values*. New York and London: Routledge & Kegan Paul.

Guiness, O. (1973). *The Dust of Death: A Critique of the Counterculture*. Downer's Grove, Ill.: Inter Varsity Press.

Habermas, J. (1971). Technology and science as "ideology." In *Toward a Rational Society*, pp. 81-122. London: Heinemann.

Harrison, P. (1980). *The Third World Tomorrow*. Harmondsworth: Penguin.

Heidegger, M. (1977). The question concerning technology, translated from the text of a lecture delivered before the Bavarian Academy of Fine Arts, June 6th, 1950, entitled "Die frage nach der technik." In W. Lovitt (Ed.), *The Question Concerning Technology—And Other Essays*, pp. 1-35. New York: Harper Colophon.

Hess, K. (1979). *Community Technology*. New York: Harper and Row.

Hibbard, M. & Hosticka, C. J. (1982). Socially appropriate technology: Philosophy in action. *Humboldt Journal of Social Relations*, 9(2), 1-10.

Hoda, M. M. (1976). India's experience and the Gandhian tradition. In N. Jéquier (Ed.), *Appropriate technology: Problems and promises*, pp. 144-155. Paris: Organization for Economic Cooperation and Development.

Ihde, D. (1979). *Technics and Praxis*. Dordrecht: D. Reidel.

Ihde, D. (1983). The historical-ontological priority of technology over science. In P. T. Durban & F. Rapp (Eds.), *Philosophy and Technology*, pp. 235-252. Dordrecht: D. Reidel.

Illich, I. (1973). *Tools for Conviviality*. London: Calder and Boyars.

Illich, I. (1980). Vernacular values. In S. Kumar (Ed.), *The Schumacher lectures*. London: Blond and Briggs.

Institute for Local Self Reliance (1981). Appropriate nukes? *Self Reliance*, (25), 2.

Jagtenberg, T. (1983). *The Social Construction of Science*. Dordrecht: D. Reidel.

Jéquier, N. (1976). The major policy issues. In N. Jéquier (Ed.), *Appropriate Technology: Problems and Promises*. Paris: Organization for Economic Cooperation and Development.

Jéquier, N. (1979). Appropriate technology: Some criteria. In A. S. Bhalla (Ed.), *Towards Global Action for Appropriate Technology*, pp. 1-22. Oxford: Pergamon.

Jéquier, N. & Blanc, G. (1983). *The World of Appropriate Technology*. Paris: Organization for Economic Cooperation and Development.

Johnston, R. & Gummett, P. (Eds.). (1979). *Directing Technology*. London: Croom Helm.

Jünger, G. F. (1956). *The Failure of Technology*. Chicago: Regnery.

Knorr-Cetina, K. D. (1981). *The Manufacture of Knowledge*. Oxford: Pergamon.

Koenker, E. B. (1980). The being of the material and the immaterial in Heidegger's thought. *Philosophy Today* (Spring), 54-61.

Kuhlman, A. (1987). Problems associated with the acceptance of new technologies in industrialized societies. *International Journal of Technology Management*, 2(2), 209-217.

Landes, D. (1969). *The Unbound Prometheus*. Cambridge: Cambridge University Press.

Levidow, L. (1983). We won't be fooled again? Economic planning and left strategies. *Radical Science Journal*, 13, 28-38.

Lodwick, D. G. & Morrison, D. E. (1982). Research issues in appropriate technology. Paper presented to the Rural Sociological Society, Cornell University, Ithaca, New York, August 20-23, 1980 (Michigan Agricultural Experiment Station Journal #9649). In D. A. Dillman & D. J. Hobbs (Eds.), *Rural Society: Issues for the Nineteen Eighties*. Boulder, Col.: Westview Press.

Long, C. D. (1977). *Congressional Record*, February 8th. Washington, D.C.: U.S. Congress.

Lovins, A. (1978). Soft energy technologies. *Annual Review of Energy*, (3), 477-517.

Lovins, A. & Price, J. H. (1975). *Non-Nuclear Futures: The Case for an Ethical Energy Strategy*. San Francisco and Cambridge, Mass.: Friends of the Earth International and Ballinger.

Lutheran World Service (1977). *Village Technology Handbook*. Geneva: Lutheran World Service.

MacDonald, S. (1983). Technology beyond machines. In S. MacDonald et al. (Eds.), *The Trouble with Technology*. London: Frances Pinter.

Maderthaner, R. et al. (1976). *Perception of Technological Risks: The Effect of Confrontation*. Laxenburg, Austria: International Institute for Applied Systems Analysis.

Magee, J. (1978). *Down to Business: An Analysis of Small Scale Enterprise and Appropriate Technology*. Butte, Montana: National Center for Appropriate Technology.

Marcuse, H. (1964). *One Dimensional Man*. Boston: Beacon Press.

Marsden, K. (1970). Progressive technologies for developing countries. *International Labour Review*, 101(5), 475-502.

Marx, K. (1954). *Capital* (first published in English in 1887). London: Lawrence and Wishart.

Mazur, A. (1975). Opposition to technical ionnovations. *Minerva*, 13, 58-81.

Mazur, A. (1981). *The Dynamics of Technical Controversy*. Washington, D.C.: Communications Press.

McLellan, J. E. & Dorn, H. (1999). *Science and Technology in World History: An Introduction*. Baltimore and London: The Johns Hopkins University Press.

Merrill, R. & Gage, T. (1977). *Energy Primer* (updated and revised from 1974 ed.). Sydney: Second Back Row Press.

Miles, D.W.J. (1982). *Appropriate Technology for Rural Development: The I.TD.G. Experience*. London: Intermediate Technology Publications Ltd.

Miller, C. C., Glick, W. H., Wang, Y., & Huber, G. P. (1991). Understanding technology-structure relationships: Theory development and meta-analytic theory testing. *Academy of Management Journal*, 34(2), 370-399.

Miller, J. D. (1983). *The American People and Science Policy: The Role of Public Attitudes in the Policy Process*. New York: Pergamon Press.

Morrison, D. E. (1978). Energy, appropriate technology and international interdependence. Paper presented to the annual conference of the Society for the Study of Social Problems. San Francisco, September 1978.

Mumford, L. (1963). *Technics and Civilization* (first published in 1934). New York: Harcourt Brace Jovanovich.

Murray, J.A.H. et al. (Ed.). (1933). *The Oxford English Dictionary*. Oxford: Oxford University Press.

National Center for Appropriate Technology. (1981). *Information Brochure*. Butte, Montana: National Center for Appropriate Technology.

Nelkin, D. (Ed.). (1984). *Controversy: Politics of Technical Decisions*, 2nd ed. Beverly Hills: Sage.

Norman, C. (1978). *Soft Technologies, Hard Choices*. Washington, D.C.: Worldwatch Institute.

Office of Technology Assessment. (1981). *An Assessment of Technology for Local Development*. Washington, D.C.: U.S. Government Printing Office.

Pacey, A. (1975). *The Maze of Ingenuity*. New York: Holmes and Meier.

Pacey, A. (1983). *The Culture of Technology*. Oxford: Basil Blackwell.

Papanek, V. & Hennessey, J. (1977). *How Things Don't Work*. New York: Pantheon.

Pecotich, A. & Willoughby, K. W. (1989). *The Ambiguous Status of Science and Technology: A Study of Management Attitudes and Public Policy in Australia*. Berkeley: Institute of Governmental Studies, University of California at Berkeley. IGS Working Paper 89-9.

Pion, G. & Lipsey, M. (1981). Public attitudes towards science and technology. *Public Opinion Quarterly*, 45, 303-316.

Postman, N. (1988). *Conscientious Objections: Stirring Up Trouble about Language, Technology and Education*. New York: Knopf.

Rapp, F. (1981). *Analytical Philosophy of Technology*. Dordrecht: D. Reidel.

Reddy, A.K.N. (1979). *Technology, Development and the Environment: A Re-appraisal*. Nairobi: United Nations Environment Programme.

Reinecke, I. (1982). *Micro Invaders: How the New World of Technology Works*. Ringwood, Aust.: Penguin.

Robertson, J.A.L. (1978). The CANDU reactor system: An appropriate technology. *Science*, 199(4329), 657-664.

Robinson, A. (Ed.). (1979). *Appropriate Technologies for Third World Development*. London: MacMillan.

Roby, K. R. (1979). The appropriate levels of technology for Western Australia. In ANZAAS, *Prospect 2000*. Perth, Australia: Australian and New Zealand Association for the Advancement of Science.

Roszak, T. (1969). *The Making of a Counter Culture: Reflections on the Technocratic Society and its Youthful Opposition*. London: Faber and Faber.

Runes, D. D. et al. (1962). *Dictionary of Philosophy*. Totowa, N.J.: Littlefield Adams.

Rybczynski, W. (1980). *Paper Heroes: A Review of Appropriate Technology*. Dorchester: Prism.

Schnaiberg, A. (1980). Responses to Devall. *Humboldt Journal of Social Relations*, 7(2), 278.

Schooler, D. (1971). *Science, Scientists and Public Policy*. New York: Free Press.

Schumacher, E. F. (1962a). Help to those who need it most. Paper presented to the International Seminar, Paths to Economic Growth, January 21-28, 1961, Poona, India. In *Roots of Economic Growth*, pp. 29-42. Varanasi: Gandhian Institute of Studies.

Schumacher, E. F. (1962b). *Roots of Economic Growth*. Varanasi: Gandhian Institute of Studies.

Schumacher, E. F. (1965). How to help them help themselves. *Observer*, Weekend Review (London), August 29, 1965.

Schumacher, E. F. (1973). *Small is Beautiful: A Study of Economics as if People Mattered*. London: Blond and Briggs.

Schuurman, E. (1977). *Technology and the Future: A Philosophical Challenge* (H. D. Morton, Trans.). Toronto: Wedge.

Scriven, M. et al. (1985). *Education and Technology in Western Australia*. Report of the Working Party on Education and Technology. Perth, Australia: Western Australian Science, Industry and Technology Council.

Shapley, D. (1978). Pen registers: The "appropriate technology" approach to bugging. *Science*, 199, 749-751.

Singer, C. et al. (Eds.). (1954-1958). *History of Technology*. Oxford: Oxford University Press.

Skeat, W. W. (Ed.). (1910). *An Etymological Dictionary of the English Language* (4th ed. [originally published in 1879-1882]). Oxford: Oxford University Press.

Skolimowski, H. (1966). The structure of thinking in technology. *Technology and Culture*, 7(3), 371-383.

Stewart, F. (1983). Macro-policies for appropriate technology: An introductory classification. *International Labour Review*, 122(3), 279-293.

Stonier, T. (1983). *The Wealth of Information: A Profile of the Post-Industrial Economy*. London: Thames Methuen.

Ströker, E. (1983). Philosophy of technology: Problems of a philosophical discipline. In P. T. Durbin & F. Rapp (Eds.), *Philosophy and Technology*, pp. 323-336. Dordrecht: D. Reidel.

Swinkels, D. (1979). The appropriate levels of technology for Western Australia. In ANZAAS, *Prospect 2000*. Perth, Australia: Australian and New Zealand Association for the Advancement of Science.

Sykes, J. B. (Ed.). (1976). *The Concise Oxford Dictionary of Current English* (6th ed.). Oxford: Oxford University Press.

Thomas, A. & Lockett, M. (1979). *Choosing Appropriate Technology*. Milton Keynes: Open University Press.

Thompson, H. (1980). The social significance of technological change. *The Journal of Australian Political Economy*, 8(July), 57-58.

Tondl, L. (1974). On the concept of "technology" and "technological sciences." In F. Rapp (Ed.), *Contributions to a Philosophy of Technology*. Dordrecht: D. Reidel.

Undercurrents. (1972-1985).

United Nations Industrial Development Organization. (1979). *Conceptual and Policy Framework for Appropriate Industrial Technology*. New York: United Nations.

Vacca, R. (1980). *Modest Technologies for a Complicated World*. Oxford: Pergamon.

Wade, N. (1975). Karl Hess: Technology with a human face. *Science*, 187, 332-334.

Wade, N. (1980). Appropriate technology and the too high outhouse. *Science*, 207, 40.

Waldrop, M. M. (1983). Compact fusion: Small is beautiful. *Science*, 219, 154.

Walt, B. D. (1978). Appropriate technology in rural Mexico: Antecedents and consequences of an indigenous peasant innovation. *Technology and Culture*, 19, 32-52.

White, L. J. (1962). *Medieval Technology and Social Change*. Oxford: Oxford University Press.

Williams, R. & Mills, S. (Eds.). (1986). *Public Acceptance of New Technologies: An International Review*. London: Croom Helm.

Willoughby, K. W. (1990). *Technology Choice: A Critique of the Appropriate Technology Movement*. Boulder and San Francisco: Westview Press.

Winner, L. (1977). *Autonomous Technology: Technics-out-of-Control as a Theme in Political Thought*. Cambridge, Mass.: Massachusetts Institute of Technology Press.

Winner, L. (1979). The political philosophy of alternative technology: Historical roots and present prospects. *Technology in Society*, 1(1), 75-86.

Winner, L. (1986). Technologies as forms of life. In *The Whale and the Reactor: A Search for Limits in an Age of High Technology*. Chicago and London: The University of Chicago Press, 3-18.

Yankelovitch, D. (1982). Changing public attitudes to science and the quality of life. *Science, Technology and Human Values*, 7(39), 123-129.

Yearly, S. (1988). *Science, Technology and Social Change*. London: Unwin Hyman.

Index